LEEDS COLLEGE OF BUILDING LIBRARY
CLASS NO. 690 vos
BARCODE

Vocational A-level Construction and the Built Environment

Third Edition

Des Millward
Kemal Ahmet
Clara Greed
John Hassall
Chris Heuvel
Chris Longhorn
Keith Roberts

LEEDS COLLEGE OF BUILDING
WITHDRAWN FROM STOCK

Longman

Pearson Education Limited
Edinburgh Gate
Harlow
Essex CM20 2JE
England

and Associated Companies throughout the world

Visit us on the World Wide Web at:
www.pearsoned.co.uk

© Longman Group Limited 1995
© Addison Wesley Longman 1998
© Pearson Education 2000

All rights reserved; no part of this publication may be reproduced,
stored in any retrieval system, or transmitted in any form or by any
means, electronic, mechanical, photocopying, recording, or otherwise
without either the prior written permission of the Publishers or a
licence permitting restricted copying in the United Kingdom issued by
the Copyright Licensing Agency Ltd., 90 Tottenham Court Road,
London W1T 4LP.

First published 1995
Second edition 1998
Third edition 2000

British Library Cataloguing-in-Publication Data
A catalogue record for this book is available from the British Library.

ISBN 0-582-41883-6

10 9 8 7 6 5 4
07 06 05 04

Set by 32 in $9\frac{1}{2}$/11 Sabon and News Gothic
Printed in Malaysia, KVP

Contents

Preface

Qualifications for technician occupations associated with construction are undergoing development by the National Council for Vocational Qualifications. This has resulted in a qualification known as the General National Vocational Qualification: Construction and the Built Environment. The General National Vocational Qualification (GNVQ) replaces the former BTEC First Diploma and National Diploma awards, and is available at Foundation, Intermediate and Advanced levels.

The GNVQ qualifications are awarded by the City & Guilds of London Institute, the Royal Society of Arts (RSA) and EdExcel (formerly the Business and Technology Education Council). GNVQs consist of mandatory, key skills, optional and additional units; the syllabi for the mandatory and key skill units are common to all three awarding bodies. This textbook has been designed to meet the revised requirements of the three bodies for the eight mandatory units of the Advanced award.

While the text has been primarily designed to satisfy the requirements of the Advanced GNVQ, it will also be useful reference for the Foundation and Intermediate awards, plus the relevant optional and additional units, and National Vocational Qualifications (NVQs).

The book has been written in units which follow the order and titles of the eight mandatory units of the Advanced award. These are:

- The Built Environment and its Development
- Design for Construction and the Built Environment
- Science and Materials
- Structures, Construction Technology and Services
- Town Planning and Development
- Surveying Processes
- Resource Management
- Financing and the Built Environment

Each **unit** is divided into sections which reflect the unit's learning requirements; key words and phrases related to these are highlighted throughout the book. Students should be encouraged by their tutors to recognise the inter-relationship of the units in order to develop an integrated understanding of all aspects of the built environment.

Spread throughout each unit are **self-assessment tasks** designed to encourage the reader to reinforce their learning, some of which integrate the key skills of Communication, Application of Number and Information Technology.

The presentation of the information in the individual units has not always followed the exact order of the unit specifications. This has been done to allow the text to be presented within a more logical structure and allow relevant and complementing issues to be placed together for the reader's benefit. It is hoped, however, that the careful organisation and sign-posting of information, together with the comprehensive index, will allow students to easily satisfy the requirements of each unit.

The text will be useful if not essential reading for those who are intending to pursue careers in building management, building surveying, architectural design, planning, civil engineering and building services engineering. It may also prove to be a source of reference to current practitioners.

The book is not meant to be an exemplar of construction and associated information, but rather to indicate the basic approaches which may be adopted to fulfil the various requirements. Where dimensions are stated with construction details, they are intended to give an idea of scale rather than be prescriptive in meeting particular requirements.

The authors, in writing this book, have been conscious of the need to reflect the philosophy of the GNVQ awards and realise that there will be important omissions apparent to the informed reader. These omissions have been made in order to reduce any possible confusion in the student due to the inclusion of material not required by the various syllabi. The authors and publishers, however, would be pleased to receive any constructive comments or suggestions that may be incorporated into future revisions.

Des Millward
2000

Acknowledgements

Kemal Ahmet would like to thank Turhan Ahmet, Tarkan Ahmet, Martyn Baker and Richard Tomlin for their help in the preparation of Unit 3.

The authors and publishers are grateful to the following for permission to reproduce copyright material:

The Controller of the Stationery Office for our Fig. 6.54, Crown copyright; University of the West of England for our Fig. 5.45 from Burton, in Scrace T. & Chick M. (eds) *Agricultural Diversification and the Planning System*. Our Fig. 5.27 is reproduced from Harris and Ullman *The Nature of Cities*, published in the Annals of the American Academy of Political and Social Science.

Addison Wesley Longman for our Fig. 3.11 from Smith *et al*. *Environmental Science*; our Figs 3.30 and 3.34 from Taylor *Materials in Construction* (2nd edition); our Figs 3.43 and 3.44 from Reid *Understanding Buildings*; our Fig. 3.49 from Lucas *et al*. *Making Sense of Science*; our Figs 4.3, 4.69 and 4.70 from Foster & Harington *Structure and Fabric Part 2* (5th edition); our Figs 4.38, 4.65 and 4.66 from Osbourn *Introduction to Building* (2nd edition); our Figs 4.57 and 4.58 from Ashcroft *Construction for Interior Designers* (2nd edition); our Figs 4.87 and 4.100 from Burberry *Environment and Services* (8th edition); our Figs 4.89 and 4.90 from Hall *Building Services and Equipment Volume 2* (2nd edition); our Figs 5.12 and 5.15 from Morris *History of Urban Form*; our Fig. 5.10 from Roberts *The Making of an English Village*; our Figs 6.28, 6.30, 6.33, 6.35, 6.37, 6.39–6.42, 6.45, 6.47, 6.49–6.51, 6.57, 6.59, 6.60, 6.66–6.68, 6.74, 6.77, 6.79, 6.80, 6.118, 6.121, 6.123–6.125 from Bannister, Raymond & Baker *Surveying* (6th edition); our Table 3.8 from Smith, Phillips and Sweeney *Environmental Science*; our Tables 3.9, 3.10, 3.11 and 3.16 from Everett *Materials* (5th edition); our Table 3.12 from Smith & Taylor *Construction Science Level 2*; our Tables 3.15 and 3.17 from Taylor *Materials in Construction* (2nd edition); our Table 4.4 from Ashcroft *Construction for Interior Designers* (2nd edition).

Extracts from British Standards are reproduced with the permission of BSI (our Table 4.5 from BS 8004: 1986; our Table 4.17 from BS 6700: our Table 6.21 from BS 5606: 1990). Complete copies can be obtained by post from BSI Customer Services, 389 Chiswick High Road, London W4 4AL; Telephone: 0208 996 9001.

The Built Environment and its Development

Chris Heuvel

For most of us, the built environment that surrounds us and shapes our lives was constructed before we were born, and will continue to stand perhaps long after we die. The built environment is an evolving **heritage** – something we inherit from previous generations, something we may improve and expand in our own time (according to our needs and wishes), and something we must eventually pass on to others. Each generation changes the environment it inherits, in order to make it safer, more comfortable and more convenient for itself.

If we in our turn are planning a **career** in construction and the built environment, we must recognise that we are not dealing simply with certain kinds of objects and technologies. Rather, we are participating in certain processes that are changing our world in different ways and at different speeds:

- extending from the past, with all its associations and remembered history
- continuing into the present, with our own economic conditions and aspirations
- affecting the quality (and perhaps even the possibility) of life on earth in the future.

Time is a 'continuum' in which past, present and future are intermingled, constituting a basic condition of life on earth – as important to the built environment as the effects of gravity or of solar radiation. This chapter is concerned, accordingly, with the interaction between social development, economic development, and environmental protection (Fig. 1.1). At the intersection of these spheres lies the all-important consideration of **sustainability** – the sole criterion by which we can judge the real value of all operations in the built environment.

The main learning activities covered by this chapter are:

- the development of settlements
- historical features of settlements and buildings
- environmental conservation and protection
- the construction and built environment sector of the economy.

The purpose of this chapter is to support the preparation of

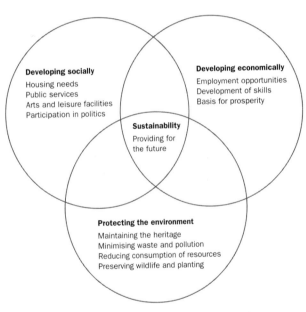

Figure 1.1 Agenda for the built environment and its future

reports on each of the above kinds of investigation. Firstly, in exploring the historical evolution of a chosen settlement, the aim is to help you to:

- explain how **climate and topography** may have influenced the variety of forms of building and infrastructure found in a particular locality
- describe how **developmental factors** (including **population trends**) may have affected the way in which the buildings and infrastructure of a settlement have changed over time
- compare buildings in terms of their **functional purpose, architectural style** and **construction features**.

Secondly, in investigating the predictable environmental effects of activities in construction and the built environment, the aim is to help you to:

- assess the **environmental impact** of construction projects in terms of potential types and sources of **pollution**
- suggest **techniques for conserving the use of resources** and **methods of protecting the environment** in relation to construction projects.

Finally, in investigating present-day activities in construction and the built environment (in order to develop personal **career plans**), the aim is to help you to:

- describe the **job types** available in different sectors of construction and the built environment and the **qualifications** associated with them
- identify the activities associated with different **sectors of the built environment**

- identify the contribution of construction industry activities in the UK to the **local economy**, to the **national economy**, and to the economy of the **European Union**.

Fundamentally, the aim of **construction and the built environment** is to make our planet more habitable for ourselves. Studying the built environment and its development is not simply a matter of learning a few 'facts' about something external to ourselves. Our purpose is to understand how construction activities help sustain human existence. Our own learning activities form part of 'the built environment and its development', and must therefore incorporate the same values.

This unit will be assessed by an External Assessment in which you will be asked to compile a report of an investigation into a local settlement.

1.1 Development of settlements

Our purpose in investigating the evolution of a particular settlement is to raise awareness of the relationship between social context and construction. The more confident we feel in discussing the relationship between building and other social activities, the sounder will be our own decisions in helping to shape an appropriate built environment. What factors influence, or ought to influence, our decisions about the built environment? Why is it built the way it is? We can develop instructive answers by considering the circumstances surrounding other people's decisions in the past. Through an awareness of how settlements have changed over time, and of the effects of historical decisions about buildings and infrastructure, we enable ourselves to determine how best to meet our own construction objectives.

The topics covered in this section are:

- Prehistory: motives for development
- Ancient history: the origins of architectural style
- Recent history: features of settlements and buildings in Britain

Motives for development

For a sound understanding of how settlements evolve, it is instructive to begin by considering *why* people ever engage in construction activity at all. We quickly discover that the development of the built environment reflects our own **evolution** in terms of social cooperation – the process we term 'civilisation'. By examining our prehistory, when (in the absence of writing) social expectations of the environment were still relatively uncomplicated, we perceive how technological development is not an irresistible force that shapes society, but something that occurs in response to the changing demands we make in terms of the **functional purposes** served by buildings and structures.

The planet **Earth** is the only place in the universe that currently provides the miraculous combination of conditions required for our existence. Upon its **land** surfaces, and in conjunction with its **atmosphere**, we have learnt to feed and breed. This learning process has involved both actively adapting, and passively adapting to, the **natural environment**. From the Earth's crust (defined in terms of **geology**) must come all the **materials** we use, while the **climate** (driven by the Sun) provides the warmth and fresh **water** we require for survival. The natural interaction of geology and climate produces the landscapes (or **topography**) we inhabit and fertile conditions for the foodstuffs we eat. We only begin to construct **built environments** where we recognise opportunities to make the natural environment more comfortable and convenient for ourselves.

For over 90 per cent of the time that our particular species has evolved on Earth, and to this day still in certain remote corners, people have led a **Stone Age** lifestyle. Our oldest and most deeply rooted habits, inherited from animal ancestors over 2.5 million years ago, involve living in close conjunction with the **natural environment**:

- hunting and gathering in order to obtain **food** and **water** (and later, **fuel**)
- using natural **caves** for shelter (not merely as **climate barriers**, but for protection also against other animals)
- planning and **manufacturing** first basic tools and then clothing and other objects out of the **materials** immediately at hand – initially stone, wood, and animal skins and bones

Our ability to construct **built environments** for ourselves has developed as a branch of our manufacturing skills. Food, water and fuel are now delivered through the physical **infrastructures** we create, while the **buildings** we inhabit are increasingly located within **settlements**. The **natural environment** is still relevant; however – as the closing part of this chapter will show – we ignore it at our peril.

As the human body is almost defenceless against extremes of heat and cold, we need to explore the world around us for sheltered places in which to eat and rest safely. We find it most convenient to live in areas where the **climate** is 'temperate' – where we find it neither too hot in summer, nor too cold in winter. When we encounter uncomfortable weather conditions, and when we can find no natural **shelter** in the landscape around us, we have learnt to survive by modifying its shape through the formation of **buildings**. Having created buildings and structures for ourselves, they begin to affect the way we operate in the world, and to influence the demands we make of our surroundings. Before all else however, **climate** and **topography** represent the two main influences over building form and settlement pattern.

Self-assessment tasks

Our instincts with regard to building seem to have developed very little since we first began to make things out of stone, wood, and animal skins and bones: our choice of structural techniques today remains limited to load-bearing, framed, and stretched membrane construction.

1. Identify three famous buildings that clearly demonstrate each of these forms of structure, and draw sketches of them to illustrate this.
2. Note the name of the designers, the date, and the location of each of these buildings.

Climate and energy

Although the human race now occupies almost every kind of habitat the Earth can offer, our animal ancestors are thought to have originated in the temperate conditions that used to prevail in East Africa. The **climate**, and the resulting **fertility** of the land, relieved the early 'hominids' of the need to spend all their time hunting and gathering. Because of their diet, they developed larger brains and better memories, enabling them gradually to learn the advantages of thinking and planning in advance of acting. Rather than immediately gratifying their every instinct, they developed skills in **manufacturing** and in **communicating** with one another – and so improved their ability to survive in less favourable climates.

As their **population** grew, our ancestors began to spread

over the Europe/Asia land mass after 1 000 000 BC – advancing around sea-shores and up river valleys as the ice retreated. Where they encountered less hospitable conditions, they were obliged to extend their tool-making skills to the manufacture of spears, clothes and containers – and to the erection of **shelters**. The first built enclosures (low stone **walls** or primitive timber **huts**) were constructed simply in order to provide **barriers** against excessive heat, cold, wind or rain.

By about 300 000 BC, our ancestors were also making use of **fire** (initially as part of their technique for hunting in groups and to improve defence against wild animals and enemies). Being a distinctively human characteristic, the development of control over **energy** had (and continues to have) an enormous impact upon our **social evolution**. In addition to beginning to reduce their dependence upon **topography** and **materials** for the provision of comfortable accommodation, our ancestors gradually recognised other benefits of fire:

- for warmth and **light** – providing a focus for social interaction (the electric light bulb was only invented in 1878)
- for cooking – making more kinds of **food** edible, leading to greater **population growth** and making more **time** available for the development and communication of ideas and skills
- for **manufacturing** – initially simply for hardening wooden spear-tips, but later for baking pottery and eventually (after about 6500 BC around the Mediterranean) for melting softer kinds of **metal** like gold and copper

As a result of the thaw that followed Britain's last major ice age (resulting in the growth of dense forests), the English Channel, separating the British Isles from mainland Europe, reappeared in about 6500 BC. While western Europe is generally located within the Earth's current 'temperate zone', it enjoys several different types of climate – each associated with distinctive **construction features** in its inhabitants' simpler dwellings:

- The Atlantic climate dominates **Britain** and the western shores of the continent, with relatively mild winters, cool summers and constant humidity – favouring the growth of deciduous and coniferous **forests**, **grasslands** and **moorlands** (producing **timber**, **thatch** and **peat** as **building materials** or as **fuels**). Domestic buildings are characterised by steeply pitched roofs with chimneys, reflecting the need to shed **rainwater** quickly and to provide effective means of heating and ventilation (Fig. 1.2).
- The Mediterranean climate, with mild wet winters, hot dry summers and infrequent but heavy rainfall, produces scrubby or steppe vegetation consisting mainly of shrubs able to withstand the summer drought. Domestic buildings are typically constructed around open courtyards, with shuttered openings in **stone** walls and with overhanging balconies and flat roofs, in order to provide plenty of shade from the **Sun** (Fig. 1.3).
- The mountain climate – varying in weather conditions and vegetation with region, altitude, and aspect. Buildings need to be low and heavy in order to avoid wind damage, to be well insulated against the cold, and to have wide overhanging eaves in order to protect supplies of wood (for **fuel**) and to prevent the blockage of pathways by drifting **snow** (Fig. 1.4).

Population movement, the precursor to **settlement**, invariably results from perceptions that there is insufficient

Figure 1.2 Atlantic climate

Figure 1.3 Mediterranean climate

Figure 1.4 Mountain climate

land area to sustain the number of people who wish to occupy it. All construction activity, and much of our other 'work' also, involves some form of rearrangement of the **materials** (animal, vegetable and mineral) immediately available through the land around us. The construction of public structures in prehistoric times, required the unpaid efforts of thousands of unskilled **labourers**, moving massive quantities of earth or rock. The evolution of **craft skills** is associated with a gradual reduction in the amount of material required – with knowledge developed (until about 1800) on a trial and error basis. Experience was passed down from parents to children over many generations, largely unquestioned, resulting in the establishment of a few, fixed construction techniques and principles.

Over the last century, with the required technical knowledge becoming more widely dispersed, we have sought to use **materials** more efficiently by calculating quantities required on the basis of their scientific properties. At the same time, we have significantly increased our consumption of **energy** in the construction industry:

- in converting the Earth's **raw materials** into the more complex **components** of which our buildings today are formed – requiring us to re-use components wherever possible in the future in order to use **energy** more efficiently also
- in manufacturing new construction materials out of organic matter previously used mainly as **fuels** – based upon tar and pitch (derived from **coal**), upon cellulose and natural resins (derived from **plants**), and upon polymers (derived from **oil and petroleum** deposits)
- in transporting materials and components to site at higher speeds and over greater distances, overcoming obstructions in the **topography** through the creation of **infrastructure**

Topography and infrastructure

As land-based animals, our lives are shaped physically and psychologically by the **topography** we occupy. The landscape, and the various forms of infrastructure through which we modify its form, determine our ease of **access** to the primary resources required for survival:

- fresh **water** – for drinking and washing
- fertile **land** – to support edible plants and wild life
- **materials** with which to fashion means of protecting, asserting and developing ourselves

Our social infrastructure – the way we organise ourselves as a society – is simply an extension of our physical infrastructure, and determines our access to resources less directly linked to mere survival – above all, our relationship with other people, their ideas, skills and attitudes. We have learnt therefore to use the development of technology (especially – because of their size relative to our own bodies – physical infrastructure and 'significant' buildings) as a means of extending our political influence.

The earliest 'civilisations' developed in the 'fertile crescent' stretching between the Nile delta and the flood plains of Mesopotamia (Fig. 1.5). The first fixed or 'built' environments were constructed with the coming of **agriculture** after about 10 000 BC, when people (probably women) began to plant cereal crops as an alternative to gathering seeds. **Building** emerged as one of many practices associated with the development of a more settled way of life that agriculture made possible:

- walled **enclosures** for herds of livestock (domesticated between 8500 and 6500 BC)
- **granaries** with roofs for storing dried grain (after 7000 BC)

The most readily available **building materials** were the mud or clay washed over the land by the rivers, dried or baked into **bricks**, with **timber** and bundled **reeds** used to form roofs. To guard the stores of grain against theft or destruction by enemies, a defensive function (using military technology) was gradually developed for some of these buildings.

Crop-growing was significantly expanded after about 5000 BC by developing **drainage systems** in marshy areas (in Mesopotamia), and **irrigation systems** in drier areas (in Egypt). The original need to produce a food surplus sufficient to feed the population arose in particular in areas where annual **flooding** made agriculture impossible – freeing people for less directly productive activities:

- participation in religious rituals (burial of the dead – implying belief in some form of afterlife – was practised about 60 000 BC)
- the production of 'symbolic' or ornamental objects (including buildings) – not distinguished from 'functional' objects as today, but reflecting the attachment of higher 'value' to particular products (equivalent to our use of money today)
- experimentation with **materials** (leading to the development of scientific or philosophical ideas)
- exploration through military expeditions (leading eventually to the development of **trading** – first in goods, and later in services)

Water-borne **transportation systems** (requiring the least consumption of **energy**) were among the first forms of long-distance travel to be developed. In ancient Egypt, the larger irrigation channels were used as **canals**, and developments in spinning and weaving led eventually to the use of sail-boats after 4000 BC. With the movement of livestock and grain, agricultural principles spread first around the Mediterranean, and then north and west into Europe – reaching the British Isles (with a population of about 20 000) by about 3000 BC.

Population movement in search of suitably fertile sites for **settlement** was always found easy in Europe because it has such a variety of topographical features relative to its area (3.7 million km^2). As Europe in general, and Britain in particular, has a long coastline and numerous navigable rivers relative to its area, our predecessors made extensive use of boats to move between **harbours**, across **lakes** and along **rivers**. These were later supplemented with **canal systems** (including **weirs** and **locks**), allowing produce and materials to be moved even further upstream. Britain was populated by successive waves of settlers from across the sea, gradually making inroads into a heavily wooded landscape by using rivers for water transport, and bringing with them from the south skills and beliefs which were already well developed.

Along Europe's numerous river and rift valleys, and especially across great plain that occupies two-thirds of the continent's area, it was easy to establish a network of **trackways** linking fertile areas and their associated **settlements** to one another. The development of overland **transport**

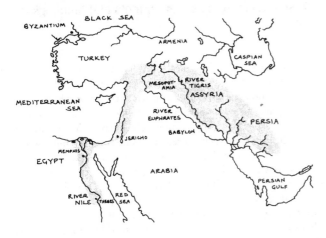

Figure 1.5

systems consisted originally of modifications to the topography:

- **cuttings** and **embankments** – ideally, the surplus material from the former being used as the raw material for the latter
- **causeways** and **paved surfaces** to ease movement over swampy or loose terrain (especially after the invention of wheeled vehicles in about 3000 BC)
- **bridges** and **tunnels** (as shorter-distance, energy-reduced alternatives to natural fords and mountain passes)

Because of their interrelationship, both topographical and infrastructure features provide effective points from which to control **access** to a land's resources, and are therefore commonly chosen as locations for **fortresses, castles** or even whole **walled towns**, because of their strength in terms of defence and security:

- relatively safe points from which to observe and guard against the approach of enemies
- long-term reminders of political superiority over people in the surrounding area

In peacetime conditions, the same locations served well for trading through **markets**, later supplemented with **inns** and **entertainment facilities**. Settlements (and **shops** in particular) always thrive best if located at **cross-roads**, where different routes or forms of transport connect with one other, allowing different groups of people to exchange not only goods and services, but also ideas and skills.

The evolution of **infrastructure**, like that of buildings, has been influenced strongly by the growing availability of man-made **energy** – especially following the industrial revolution. Since the **Victorian period**, for example, we also learnt the importance of separating waste water from drinking water – we no longer draw our **water supply** directly from rivers, but pump it mechanically through networks of **reservoirs** (with **dams** and **water-towers**) and underground **pipelines**. Waste water is intercepted by **public sewers**, which carry it to **sewage works** for treatment before being discharged into rivers.

The mechanisation of **transport systems**, allowing continuous and faster travel, has made it more practicable to move food and materials over longer distances. With the development from **rail** to **road** to **air** travel over the last 150 years, the focus of technology has shifted from construction (involving modifications of the land surface) to engineering (centred around the power available as a product of **fuel** combustion). For the movement of ideas and knowledge, we have developed increasingly sophisticated **communication systems**.

Other forms of infrastructure are specifically associated with the distribution of **energy** for consumption within buildings and settlements – which are now themselves becoming increasingly mechanised. In Britain, **electricity** from **power stations** is supplied through the **national grid** – a network of high-voltage **cables** and **wires**, mostly carried through the air on enormous **pylons**, but located underground in towns and cities. **Substations** containing **transformers** are used intermittently in order to 'step' the power up or down according to the demands of different end-users.

Town gas was first manufactured from **coal** in the **Victorian period**, and was stored in **gasometers**. Since the 1970s, a network of **pipelines** has also been constructed across Britain for supplying **natural gas** from the North Sea – both to private consumers and for gas-fired **power stations**.

As petroleum gas can also be liquefied (LPG) for transportation and storage in cylinders, consumers living in remote areas use '**bottled gas**' (usually brought to them by road).

Control over the way we use **energy** has always been associated with revolutions in both technological and social development. In prehistoric times, the advent of fire-making (after about 30 000 BC) marked a critical point in the evolution from animal to human existence. It was our ancestors' use of **fire** that originally enabled their activities to become less centred around mere survival, so that 'special' significance was attached to the individuals who possessed the technology that appeared to have the power to influence the mysterious forces inhabiting the world around them. The effect was to increase social cohesion, leading to the formation of 'tribes' dominated by a ruling class of priests and priestesses, armed guards and courtiers grouped around hereditary god-kings.

To demonstrate (and so to reinforce) the superior social importance of these individuals and their activities, 'special' kinds of built environment were provided for them. As they make **significant use** of particular **construction features**, communicating ideas rather than simply performing technical functions such as defence against climate or enemies, these structures have served ever since as models for 'important' buildings (described next). The kinds of buildings that we regard as 'significant,' however, have changed in parallel with the evolution of society's values (described in the last section of this part of Unit 1).

Self-assessment tasks

The people who have control over energy and information continue to exercise the most powerful influences in the world today.

1. Look up the financial statistics showing the five wealthiest companies in
   (a) the United Kingdom
   (b) Europe
   (c) the world.
2. Identify what business each of these companies is in. Compare their financial value (termed 'market capitalisation') with that of the largest firms operating in the property or construction sectors of the economy. With colleagues or friends, discuss the significance of your findings.

Historical features of settlements and buildings in Britain

By considering the historical development of the United Kingdom's built environment in the context of social history, we may demonstrate the kinds of evidence that might be used in explaining how one particular settlement has changed over time. As historical 'facts' in themselves have no meaning, it would be futile to seek merely to establish who built what, where and when. Instead, we have to 'construct' this explanation in much the same way as we construct the built environment itself. Our social development has determined different forms adopted for settlements and buildings in different **historical periods**. For this reason, we can often identify the age of a building or structure by considering its **construction features**.

Self-assessment tasks

1. Find out whose wealth or political power has exercised the strongest influences over the pattern of your chosen settlement's development. Identify the origins of this wealth – through particular estates, industries, families or other sources.
2. Identify what other events or personalities (present or past) have had particular influence over the layout and construction of the place you are studying.
3. What evidence (either existing physically or recorded in documents) of this influence remains? What other conclusions might you have drawn from this evidence? List in detail the sources of your information.

The medieval period (1066–1485)

The era 1066–1485 is commonly called the Middle Ages, or the **medieval period**. The architectural styles chiefly associated with significant buildings at this time are:

- **Norman** – named after the part of France from which William the Conqueror came
- **Gothic** – named after one of the tribes that overran the Roman empire, in order to indicate the extent to which the conventions of 'classical' architecture had been left behind

Just as the Romans had done when they ruled Britain as a colony, the Norman conquerors engaged in a large-scale building programme, using forms of technology that ignored local traditions and effectively demonstrated their superiority. The Normans constructed massive **castles** and **cathedrals**, characterised by rounded **arches** like those developed by the **Romans** (a style of architecture which is therefore sometimes termed 'Romanesque').

Medieval **castles** were initially built on the 'motte and bailey' principle (Fig. 1.6):

- centred on a mound (the '**motte**') – based either on a naturally hilly feature or on earth thrown up by digging a circular ditch
- encased by two or three high walls – the land between them being called '**baileys**'

Later castles were made more imposing by the construction of stone towers and **keeps**, and later still water defences were developed by filling the ditches with water (forming **moats**). Inside, the centre of the castle usually consisted of a single large space with a huge fireplace, the great hall, in which people ate, slept and lived. Behind the fireplace were kitchens, pantries and butteries, and the lord of the castle used a suite of private rooms called the solar. The same layout was adopted for the larger timber-framed houses of medieval times, which were divided into separate bays by **crucks** or various forms of **truss** (Fig. 1.7).

The building form associated with the development of Christianity in Europe was not the pagan temple but the Roman **basilica** – originally a kind of court, with a long nave leading to a raised dais. In the East, a separate branch of the Christian church centred on Byzantium (renamed Constantinople by the Romans) adopted the centralised **dome** as its characteristic building form, which was then developed by the Moslems for their **mosques**. In the medieval period, this technique was gradually reintroduced to Europe as a result of Arab influence in the south and knowledge of

Figure 1.6

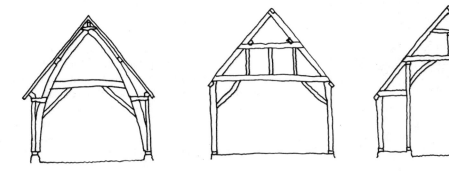

Figure 1.7

Eastern architecture brought back (along with many ideas relating to mathematics and science) by men returning from the crusades.

In contrast to their Eastern counterparts, the Christian churches of Europe became increasingly directional in design, emphasising the vertical through single or double towers, sometimes topped with spires, and through the decorative fluting of columns. The building element that, more than any other, characterises what we now identify as the Gothic style, was the **pointed arch** – stronger than the rounded arch (as it exerts less lateral thrust) and useful as a means of spanning openings of different sizes while preserving uniformity of height (Fig. 1.8).

The development of a structural function for the ribs that divided up wall and ceiling areas (reflecting medieval awareness of the principles of framed structures, stemming from extensive practice with timber construction) enabled the builders of the middle ages gradually to increase the provision of windows, and to reduce the thickness and weight of walls and columns. Ultimately, with the invention of the **flying buttress** (transferring a building's load to an external framework – Fig. 1.9), it was made impossible to understand a building's structural principles from its interior.

Britain's **population** during the medieval period rose from between one and three million (living mainly in the east of the country) to over 4.5 million by 1348. Only ten towns had more than 2000 residents, and 90% of the people lived in completely rural communities. London was by far the biggest and wealthiest town, with its buildings jammed tightly against one another, accommodating about 2% of the population. A series of disasters in the fourteenth century reduced the population to about two million:

- what has been called a 'little ice age', followed by great floods
- sheep and cattle plagues in 1313 and 1319, reducing the food supply
- several plagues carried by black rats from central Europe – notably the Black Death of 1348–9, and then others in 1361 and 1368–9

The resulting labour shortage enabled working people to demand better living conditions, and wages in the construction industry doubled between 1348 and 1415. Considerable social disorder, with peasant protests and considerable feuding between different groups of nobles, accompanied the enormous shift of power that marked the end of the medieval period.

Figure 1.8

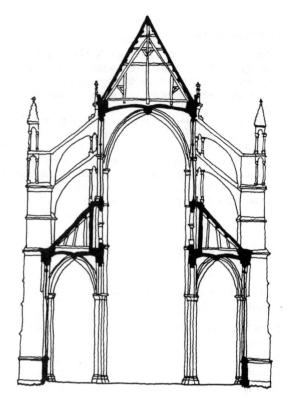

Figure 1.9

The Tudor/Elizabethan period (1485–1603)

The accession to the throne of Henry Tudor in 1485 marked the beginning of a period of uneasy peace and prosperity which gradually strengthened during the sixteenth century. As merchants and craftspeople began to move about more freely, money gradually became more important as the medium of exchange. With money, people had a broader choice of opportunities, allowing some to move into the more 'comfortable' social circumstances that were previously available only to the nobility. Ceremonial display began to matter more than armed conflict, and construction features in the **Gothic** style were increasingly applied to non-religious buildings:

- walls with buttresses, plinths and parapets
- small window openings with iron casements and stone surrounds, with hood mouldings over them
- flattened pointed arches with straight sloping members, or four-centred arches

The church had become extremely unpopular, and Henry VIII's dissolution of the monasteries (1536–40) suddenly released large areas of good farmland and sites for new mansions and cottages. The overthrow of the church cut Britain off from the rest of Europe, where the Renaissance style of architecture was developed (literally, a 'rebirth' of the Classical tradition, originating in Italy early in the fifteenth century) that flourished on the continent. Britain's resources were poured instead (through cutting down acres and acres of woodland) into the creation of a strong navy, on the basis of which the colonies abroad were founded. The same technology was utilised for construction, as the use of timber allowed buildings to be shaped freely around their new peacetime **function** – providing space for a gracious lifestyle.

Tudor and Elizabethan architecture is associated above all with a few 'great houses' built by courtiers as places for entertaining their monarch (Elizabeth built no palaces of her own). Most working people's houses, by contrast, were dark, squalid and cramped, consisting of two rooms – a hall (heated by an open fire placed in the middle of the floor) and a bower, open to the rafters and thatch above. They were timber-framed (even in stone areas) on rubble foundations, with infilling panels of reinforced mud.

For wealthier people, buildings were increasingly regarded as opportunities to show how witty and fashionable their owners were. Larger houses no longer needed to be built in stone to withstand attack, so it became feasible to increase the sizes of window openings (with large bay and oriel windows – Fig. 1.10), and to experiment with new forms of applied decoration:

- imposing gatehouses with mock fortifications (including flooded moats with bridges) and coats of arms carved over the entrance
- complicated, irregular skylines with numerous twisted brickwork chimneys projecting through steep tiled roofs (rather than being located against gable walls)
- interiors lined with oak panels, often with linen-fold carving

With rents replacing direct 'service' as the basis of wealth, larger houses could be located on sites chosen for their convenience and beauty rather than in the centre of their estates. As it was no longer necessary to accommodate large numbers of attendants and servants, new forms of planning could be tried, aiming to provide better comfort, lighting, privacy and sanitation. In particular, the growing use of **coal** as fuel led to the development of better designed, internal flues to carry smoke away. This allowed the introduction of multiple fireplaces and more complicated floor plans on two storeys, rather than centring the activities of a house around a single high-ceilinged hall.

The most notable Tudor buildings are located in the east of England, being at that time the wealthiest and most populous part of the country. In the absence of stone, they are characterised by their extensive use of brickwork, popularised through contact with the Low Countries (where the wool exported from England was woven into cloth).

In other parts of the country, the tradition of timber construction persisted. In the fifteenth century, the skeleton structure usually involved floor and roof joists projecting

Figure 1.10 Tudor building

slightly beyond their supporting walls, overhanging and therefore protecting doors and windows from the rain. Curved timber struts were introduced to provide lateral stability. With open halls going out of fashion in the second half of the sixteenth century, the timbering itself (particularly in the arrangement of bracing members) was increasingly used for decorative effect rather than for structural stability. Houses framed in timber display a variety of façade patterns (Fig. 1.10):

- framing determined by the sizes and shapes of timber available, or by the habits developed by craftsmen in a particular locality
- panels filled with brick (which might be painted or plastered), or with plaster on a timber lath backing
- freedom in the positioning of doors and windows – the latter being located wherever required in relation to the building's **function**

Due to the increasing influence of Renaissance ideas, and reflecting people's desire for social order, important buildings of the Elizabethan age (1560–1603) are characterised by an increasing regularity, rather than informally organising construction features for their picturesque value:

- buildings were deliberately constructed with symmetrical plans, often shaped like the letters **E** or **H**, often at the expense of internal functional convenience
- Classical ornamentation such as pilasters, cornices and broken pediments (often constructed by imported Italian craftsmen) was introduced as a fashionable novelty – especially around the entrance or fireplace
- windows were large and rectangular, consisting of a simple grid of vertical mullions and horizontal transoms with diamond-shaped or square leaded panes between, topped with a Gothic hood mould or Classical detailing

The hall began to serve merely as an entrance feature (with open-well rectangular staircases, often with elaborate balustrades and newel posts). Social gatherings were held instead in the connecting 'long gallery' on the first floor – often stretching the whole length of the building. Displays of virtuosity in craftsmanship appeared in the details (Fig. 1.11):

- Flemish 'strapwork' patterns
- ogee-roofed turrets (extending the principle of the Gothic pointed arch)
- stepped and curved parapet gables (in the Dutch tradition)

Analysis of parish registers (records of births, deaths and marriages, ordered to be kept by priests after 1538) gives a more accurate picture of the structure of the **population** than for any previous period. By the 1470s, the population was rising again, for the first time since the Black Death, and this growth continued through the sixteenth and early seventeenth centuries. Despite further epidemics following poor harvests in 1557–9 (when there were more than twice the annual average number of burials), by the end of Elizabeth's reign the population of England had risen to over four million again.

The Jacobean/Classical period (1603–1714)

National **population growth** levelled out in the seventeenth century, but more and more people sought to live in towns and villages. By 1700, seven provincial towns had populations of over 10 000 inhabitants, and twenty-three of over 5000. Despite major epidemics in 1603, 1625, 1636 and (most

Figure 1.11 Elizabethan style

famously) 1665, London grew from 200 000 (5% of England's population) to 400 000 between 1600 and 1650, and by 1700 accommodated 11% of the country's population.

In the Jacobean period (1603–25), the influence of the Renaissance (particularly through the way it was interpreted in France and in Flanders) became more pronounced. In a form of exuberant experimentation termed 'Mannerism', **Classical** design features such as columns, pediments and porticoes were outrageously reinterpreted, broken apart and reassembled in more complex forms. The finest examples of the Jacobean style are found in a few large but increasingly compact country houses, associated with particular courtiers and their surveyors. Like the furniture inside them, these houses contained a mixture of grotesquely ornate decoration (Fig. 1.12):

* dubiously 'Classical' columns – often with strange foliage carvings around their bases, and sometimes topped with heavy-busted caryatids
* bulbous balusters, carved tassels, arabesques, masks and erotic statues
* Gothic-style heraldry, lattices and strapwork incorporating geometrical ornamentation

In terms of innumerable smaller houses and farmsteads, there was a wave of rebuilding across all of England (except in the most northerly counties) between 1570 and 1640. This was made possible because of the increasing availability of money, as rents and costs were fixed but higher and higher prices could be obtained for food, leather and wool. Whole villages were rebuilt – in stone wherever the material was available, and elsewhere (such as in the Midlands) in efficiently constructed 'black and white' timber framing. Merchants and farmers began to demand the same privacy and comfort in their own homes as had previously been enjoyed only by the nobility:

* first floors, ceilings and staircases were introduced
* through the construction of partitions, more rooms with distinct functions were provided (in particular, bedrooms were located upstairs)

Figure 1.12 Jacobean interior

- additional fireplaces were provided, requiring the construction of multiple chimneys
- more windows were inserted, now mostly glazed

Among the fashion-conscious nobility, the rising demand for particular individuals as designers of important buildings, rather than for anonymous or imported craftspeople skilled in particular materials or styles, led to the late development in Britain of Classical architecture. In Italy, surrounded by the ruins of Roman monuments, the Classical style had never been completely displaced by the Gothic of northern Europe. It became customary for wealthy people to visit Italy and to study Classical antiquity as part of their education. When they returned home, in order to display the learning they had been able to afford, they demanded that buildings constructed for them adopted Classical principles:

- simplicity of form – with a strong preference for squares, cubes and spheres (manifested in plans for ideal towns)
- clarity of organisation – with the laws of perspective providing a rational basis for the arrangement of shapes in space
- balance of proportions – with emphasis upon symmetry and repetition at different scales

Although not influential in his own lifetime, Inigo Jones (1573–1652) was chiefly responsible for introducing authentic Italian Renaissance design to Britain. As 'Surveyor of the King's Works' between 1615 and the outbreak of civil war in 1642, Inigo Jones insisted on the 'correct' shaping and detailing of buildings in accordance with Classical design principles described by Andrea Palladio (1518–80), whose work he had studied in Italy. In particular, the Queen's House at Greenwich (Fig. 1.13) – with its high principal rooms and a loggia at first-floor level over a solid-looking 'rusticated' base – set a design precedent that was followed (especially in urban situations) until the beginning of the twentieth century.

Inigo Jones made little attempt to adapt the Italian villa style to English materials, techniques and functions, and his 'Palladianism' became discredited with the breach between court and parliament that led eventually to the beheading of Charles I. Classical architecture returned in a new form with the Restoration of the monarchy in 1660, when Christopher Wren (1632–1723) began to demonstrate how Roman design principles could be satisfactorily integrated with construction features such as steeply pitched plain tile roofs, multiple chimney stacks, and large window areas set in brickwork.

Wren never visited Italy, but learnt instead from Dutch and French Renaissance models (inevitably, the son of Charles I looked to his powerful and unpopular neighbour, Louis XIV of France, rather than to parliament, for support). In Paris, Wren met Bernini – architect of the Piazza of St Peter's in Rome, grandly linking together open space and sculptured architecture in a single curving sweep (the style termed Baroque). Louis had found the principles of Baroque planning ideal for expressing the immensity of his state power (later embodied in his vast palace of Versailles). Wren developed a more restrained form of Baroque, using straightforward (rather than undulating) Classical elements to unify the variety of construction features developed in response to the English climate. Wren's simple, graceful designs were widely copied both in Britain and in North America.

Following his appointment as 'Surveyor General and principal Architect for rebuilding the whole City' following the extensive destruction caused by the great fire of London in 1666 (13 200 houses over 450 acres, but – miraculously – not a single life), Wren's output was prolific:

- Within six days of the fire, a monumental plan for replacing London's tortuous street pattern with a logical hierarchy of avenues (90 feet wide), streets (60 feet wide) and lanes (30 feet wide) – impractical and never adopted.
- The reconstruction of 51 of the 86 churches that had been burnt – with spacious, light-filled interiors (despite cramped and awkward sites), centred around a preaching space rather than stretched along a nave, and crowned with spires formed of ingenious combinations of Classical elements.
- The construction of St Paul's, with its great dome (a symbolic rival to St Peter's in Rome) an engineering feat equivalent to anything that had been achieved in Italy – especially as operations on site took only 35 years.
- The introduction of regulations restricting the use of timber in buildings, controlling floor heights and wall thicknesses, and demanding simplification of shape and detail in order to improve fire-resistance – marking the death of the timber-framed house.
- Groups of buildings designed and constructed together, and therefore sharing the same materials, proportions, and details – hipped roofs with dormers, balustrading and cupolas, regular and relaxed façades with openings spaced apart precisely, framed with tall pilasters, cornices, and segmental and triangular pediments.

Wren was consulted on a wide variety of projects for town halls, hospitals, schools, almshouses, market halls and custom houses throughout the country. His most widespread influence may be seen in the smaller 'Queen Anne' style houses (so called after the short reign (1702–14) of the last Stuart monarch that encompassed the closing years of Wren's long life) that are now familiar features of both town and countryside:

- simple rectangular plans, with projecting quoins at the angles, and hipped roofs with small dormers (with curved or triangular pediments over)
- symmetrical façades in brick or stone with evenly spaced sash windows (with thick glazing bars) with flat arches over, the keystone projecting
- central door-cases with a canopy consisting either of a straight or curved pediment, or of a deep rounded hood shaped like a shell
- well-proportioned rooms (the principal ones on the ground floor) with panelled walls, decorative plaster ceilings, and doorways and fireplaces surrounded by Classical motifs

In the eighteenth century, the grand Baroque style was adopted throughout Europe for palaces and chateaux and

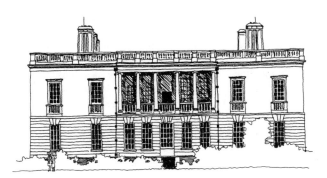

Figure 1.13

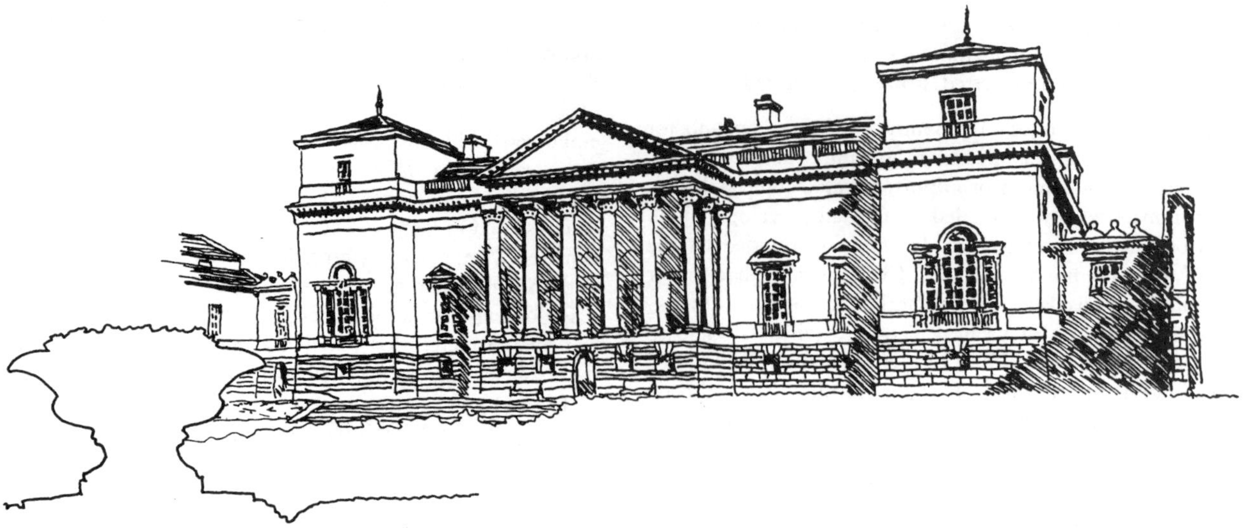

Figure 1.14

their surrounding landscaped gardens or even for the layout of cities around them. The desire to unify apparently endless sequences of space through merging painting, architecture and sculpture in a single fantastic vision (sometimes using theatrical trickery), held little appeal in Protestant Britain and northern Europe, however. In a few larger houses, Baroque principles were used simply to exaggerate the impression of size. This was usually done by organising the buildings in the form of a central block (usually with a pediment and portico – Fig. 1.14) with distant wings connected by curving colonnades, and by planning the landscape around them with radiating avenues.

The Georgian period (1714–1837)

Reflecting a preference for political toleration rather than the kinds of despotism that prevailed elsewhere in Europe, the built environment of eighteenth-century Britain blended the 'rational' with the 'natural.' Returning to the ideas of Inigo Jones and Palladio about the design ideals of ancient Greece and Rome, country houses were designed in a serene and sober neo-classical style. In contrast, the parklands surrounding them were laid out as 'picturesque' landscapes with glimpses of lakes, ornamental classical temples, grottoes or imitation ruins – all carefully designed to look natural and timeless. As the period corresponds approximately to the reigns of Georges I–IV and William IV, buildings dating from this time are generally described as Georgian.

The Georgian period has been called 'the age of elegance,' as comfortable homes and noble public spaces became available to more and more people. Following a century of political and religious upheaval, the Georgian period was a time of relative stability, security and accelerating population (from about six million in 1700 to nearly nine million in 1800, and doubling in size between 1780 and 1840). Although Britain was involved in a succession of expensive wars, they were fought on foreign soil by a professional army, and were consistently followed by improvements in foreign trade (which nearly doubled between 1700 and 1780).

Land values almost doubled between 1700 and 1790, and about four million additional acres were brought into cultivation in Britain. This process occurred mainly through parliamentary Acts permitting the 'enclosure' of ancient open fields, commons, and heath land – converting a complex pattern of narrow strips of farmland into the now familiar chequer-board of small, almost square fields surrounded by hawthorn hedges or dry stone walls. The effect was to drive whole villages of smallholders either into work as labourers for major landowners, or into towns – which therefore began to grow rapidly as centres of commercial (and construction) activity.

Land ownership, increasingly concentrated in the hands of the aristocracy, remained the main source of wealth throughout the eighteenth century:

- due mainly to improvements in **agriculture** (generating a 47% increase in productivity)
- from land holdings in colonies abroad (particularly the Caribbean), where vast fortunes were made through the exploitation of slave labour
- through royalties on the production of **coal** and **iron** ore (coal production doubled between 1750 and 1800, between 1800 and 1830, and again between 1830 and 1845, while pig-iron production rose fourfold between 1740 and 1788, and fourfold again between 1788 and 1808)
- by developing **canals** (42 new canals were projected in the 1790s), ports (such as Liverpool and Bristol) and – perhaps the most distinctive feature of the Georgian built environment – urban residential accommodation

As marriage remained the main way to wealth, social activities became enormously important in Georgian times, expanding demand for residential accommodation within prosperous towns and fashionable resorts such as spas. The Georgian period is associated above all with the development of the urban terrace as a building type, enabling the same architectural treatment to be applied to whole streets of houses (even to the extent of constructing new frontages to medieval buildings). In all parts of the country – both in small towns and villages and on whole estates in London, Bristol, Bath, Dublin and Edinburgh – similar 'rules' of good taste were accepted. Façades and plans with elegant proportions and dignified scale were described and illustrated in widely available 'copy books'. The same principles were applied to a variety of building types (including churches, assembly rooms and warehouses), often using local building materials and techniques:

Figure 1.15

- all decorative features Classical in origin, and often painted white (whether constructed of stone, brick or timber) in order to show off their shapes
- principal rooms with tall sash windows (with slim wooden glazing bars) located at first floor level, with a 'rusticated' storey beneath accommodating kitchen and storage facilities
- parapets with stone copings concealing sloping slate roofs, and thick walls between each dwelling supporting unobtrusive chimney stacks
- steps up to the panelled front door, with semicircular fanlight over, and fine wrought iron railings in front

Larger residential areas were developed as 'speculative' projects, undertaken in conjunction with major urban landlords seeking to attract tenants able to afford high rents. For this reason, more attention was paid to the design and construction of the street facade than to the rear. Layouts initially adopted the grand Roman manner, with simple straight streets and crescents, linked to one another through large squares or circuses with gardens in the middle. Pediments were provided for the central properties, and roofs were set back behind parapets, so that terraces looked more like palaces than mass-produced accommodation for the growing middle classes.

In the middle of the eighteenth century, a lighter, more delicate form of design called the Rococo style was developed in Europe, characterised by free-flowing, partly asymmetrical ornamentation. The parallel in Britain was an interest in oriental and other exotic styles of decoration (including some whimsical forms of Gothic), but Classical interiors also became increasingly graceful and playful in their decoration, based on ancient Greek rather than Roman models.

Being associated with a decadent aristocracy, frivolity no longer seemed appropriate following the French Revolution (1789), and there was a 'romantic' revival of interest in the architecture of ancient Greece, identified as the seat of democratic ideals. Individuals' taste and learning, gradually supplemented by archaeological accuracy, became the basis for judging 'beautiful' architecture. The Regency period (1811–30) – named after the Prince Regent (who became king in 1820) – is therefore associated with the extensive use of 'neo-Greek' design features, both in terraces and in small detached houses (Fig. 1.15):

- thin and intricate wrought iron railings, gates, verandas and balconies (sometimes roofed in curving metal)
- lightweight mouldings such as slender or fluted columns, complicated cornices, and swatches of folded drapery
- semicircular headed ground-floor windows in addition to doorway fanlights, and gently curved bow windows, all with tiny glazing bars, and sometimes painted shutters also
- elegant interiors, with domed ceilings, large halls and decorative friezes
- excessively low-pitched slate roofs and wide projecting eaves
- brickwork covered with stucco (moulded and painted sand/lime plaster rendering) rather than carved stonework – making houses affordable for middle-class inhabitants

The Victorian period (1837–1901)

During Queen Victoria's reign, Britain rose to a position of unparalleled global influence through its leadership of the **industrial revolution** – in which machines come to replace or to supplement human and animal labour. As people's activities change from agricultural to factory-based production, there is a general **population movement** from the countryside into towns (already happening in Britain as a consequence of the enclosure movement, which continued until the 1850s). More significantly, however, the national population rose from 16.9 million in 1851 to 30.8 million in 1901 – due less to migration than to natural increase within Britain's towns and cities. London grew from one million inhabitants in 1801 to two million in 1841, to three million in 1861, to four and a half million by 1901 – the largest city in the world at that time (and therefore the most concentrated market), reaching six and half million in 1911 and eight and a half million in 1939. Elsewhere in England and Wales, the number of **cities** with populations of over 100 000 grew from five in 1837 to 23 by 1891 (there were none in 1800).

In the initial absence of efficient transport systems, minor villages developed rapidly into large industrial towns, with residential development concentrated densely around the factories. Where linked to ports and navigable waterways however, towns developed into prosperous **cities**, attracting immigrants both from rural areas and from foreign countries. Terraced accommodation – typically with overhanging eaves and bay windows after the lifting of a tax on windows in 1851 – was provided for increasingly wider groups within the population, sharpening the segregation of areas inhabited by rich and poor citizens. Those who could afford to move tended to demand larger, detached or semi-detached houses with gardens, located further away from the urban centre – preferably to the west (usually the upwind side) of the city's noise, smoke and smells.

On the other hand, when Victorian citizens or their elected councils wished to express pride in their commercial success, they punctuated their cities with grand public buildings, often with landscaped parks and gardens around them. In a nostalgic reaction to the general squalor of the urban environment, and to the size and speed of social and economic change, significant buildings were designed to look as if they belonged to distant foreign lands or to past historical periods (interest in all things medieval was particularly strong). A serious 'battle of the styles' developed between the Classical and the Gothic Revival – the former associated with high social status, continuity and taste, but the latter being said to carry stronger associations with Christianity and the traditions of northern Europe. Not only churches therefore, but also many town halls, police stations, law courts, hospitals and museums, in addition to numerous houses, were built with Gothic construction features – often with considerable inconvenience to their internal layout. Towards the end of the century, it became more usual to reserve the Gothic style for the façades of schools and churches, and to use heavy Classical detailing for civic and commercial buildings.

The development of a comprehensive **railway** infrastructure provided industry and people with new choices of **location** in relation to one another, resulting in a rapid geographical expansion of the country's main industrial centres (in place of further increase in density). The construction of railways required a large labour force, and attracted significant **population movement** from Ireland in 1845–6 (when the country was devastated by famine). Around many stations, it is still possible to identify terraces originally constructed for railway workers. The general availability of steam trains in the 1860s enabled middle-class people to live in spacious **suburbs** several miles from their city-centre workplaces.

The Victorians enjoyed displaying their wealth, and lavished extravagant ornamentation on the products upon which they chose to spend their money. Not only buildings, but textiles, furniture and household objects of all kinds were made available in a wide variety of decorative 'styles', applied with little consideration for their actual use. The Victorians disliked being reminded of the industrialisation that represented the source of their wealth – the machinery, the workers, and the squalor of rapid urbanisation. While

they admired feats of engineering and enjoyed the economic benefits of an infrastructure no longer restricted by boggy roads and uncontrolled rivers, the Victorians were reluctant to accept the use of **iron** within the 'significant' buildings associated with the word Architecture. Iron was associated with machinery and engineering, and its use in the built environment (discounting glass-houses) was initially limited to infrastructure, mills and factories which they found distasteful and therefore unworthy of ornamentation in any style.

It was nevertheless the Victorians' pioneering development of techniques for making different forms of iron available in large quantities, rather than their 'revivals' of previous architectural styles, that had the larger influence on the design of buildings in the twentieth century. Mass-produced **cast iron** was first used in construction in 1777 for the prefabricated sections of a 100-foot arched bridge over the river Severn at Coalbrookdale, near the factory where the process (involving smelting the material with coke rather than with charcoal) had been pioneered at the beginning of the century. Because of its good fire resistance, cast iron was subsequently used in mills for columns, floor beams and window frames. The use of cast iron reached a climax in the 1840s and 1850s, when used in new kinds of structures such as glass-houses, railway stations, and – most famously – the gigantic Crystal Palace of 1851 (Fig. 1.16).

The mass production of **wrought iron** was originally developed in 1781, and became famous when used for the girders of spectacular structures such as Stephenson's tubular rail bridge over the Menai Straits (1845), the nave of Crystal Palace (Fig. 1.16), the roof of St Pancras Station (1863), and – at 320 m, the **tallest structure** in the world for over thirty years – the Eiffel Tower in Paris (1889). Being less brittle than cast iron, and therefore more suitable for beams, wrought iron was commonly used in combination with cast iron until about 1890.

The use of modern **steel** dates from the invention of the Bessemer converter in 1856 (in which hot air is blown through the molten metal in order to burn impurities away). Although a spectacular precedent was set by its use in the Firth of Forth rail bridge (1882–90), the development of steel-framed buildings was subsequently led by Chicago in the United States, following the wood-built city's destruction by fire in 1871. Being stronger, more durable and 30% cheaper to produce than wrought iron, I-sections of steel became commercially available in Britain in the 1880s, although the country's first significant steel-framed building, the Ritz Hotel in London, was not constructed until 1905.

In addition to developing the use of iron and steel for columns and beams, Victorian engineers also began to exploit the tensile strength of these materials in new forms of 'suspension' structure. Borrowing an idea patented in the United States, the first significant **suspension structure** in Britain was **Telford**'s 140 m span road bridge over the Menai Straits (1815), using wrought-iron chains and a cast-iron deck. **Brunel** later used the same principle for his 200 m Clifton Suspension Bridge in Bristol (1829–63), in which the chains are suspended from massive Egyptian-style 'pylons' of stone (Fig. 1.17). In 1844, **Roebling** introduced the use of **high-tensile steel cables** for suspension bridges in the United States, although it was found that the material's flexibility made it more appropriate for roads than railways. Roebling's finest creation was the 1596-foot Brooklyn Bridge in New York (1867–83), the **tallest structure** in the city on completion and carrying two roadways, two railways and a path for pedestrians.

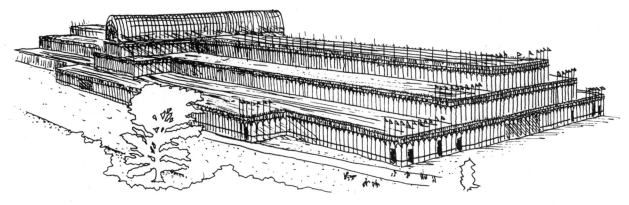

Figure 1.16

These kinds of technological achievement were made possible because they were calculated as efficient solutions to engineering 'problems', rather than as opportunities to display architectural 'good taste' (through the provision of stylistic construction features). Central to the Victorian age was the loss of relationship between makers and their finished products caused by mechanisation. Reacting against this effect, William Morris proposed a 'romantic' revival of medieval traditions involving skilled craftsmanship and ideals of social cooperation, not merely the superficial details of **Gothic Revival** ornamentation. The design and furnishings for his own Red House (1859) laid the foundations for the emergence, towards the end of the century, of an internationally influential attitude to designing (rather than a style) known as the **Arts and Crafts** movement:

- external elevations shaped informally by the internal layout, rather than applied independently, and methods of construction revealed both internally and externally
- simple, careful forms constructed of hand-shaped rather than machine-produced materials

Two connected ideas, fundamental to the development of building design in the twentieth century, may be traced to the **Arts and Crafts** approach. On the one hand, the precedent of drawing inspiration from nature and raw materials for the forms of designed objects led to the asymmetrical free-flowing, organic shapes characteristic of the **Art Nouveau** movement – developed in Belgium and France in the 1880s and spreading with industrialisation through other countries of Europe, reaching its high point in Britain in the work of Charles Rennie Mackintosh around the turn of the century (Fig. 1.18). On the other hand, the 'rationalist' idea of basing the design of buildings upon considerations such as function and material (returning to basic principles rather than simply imitating particular traditions) lies at the very core of the **Modern Movement** that has sought, through most of the twentieth century, to close the gap that opened up between engineering and architecture in the Victorian period.

The twentieth century (1901–present day)

The 'Revival' styles of building developed in Victorian times continued to be used for major public buildings and for hotels, theatres, department stores and office blocks until the 1920s, many in a sub-Baroque style now usually described as 'Edwardian'. Gothic was used only for church buildings. In the new residential districts growing rapidly around **public transport** systems, small middle-class houses and terraces were

Figure 1.17

Figure 1.18

mostly constructed in either a neo-Georgian or various forms of 'Old English Revival' style (characterised by extensive use of pebbledash, tile-hanging or half-timbering on gables over two-storey bay windows).

In the boom years leading up to the First World War, Britain grew economically complacent, living off trade and finance rather than manufacturing, and therefore requiring office blocks rather than factories. First in Germany and the United States (which had overtaken Britain in terms of production and productivity), but later in other second-generation industrialised countries also – such as France and Austria (where there was less anxiety about the new technology) – new approaches to design were developed with closer links to the objectives of mechanised production than to historical precedents.

In Germany, in a burst of optimism and idealism following the First World War, through a highly influential technical school called the Bauhaus, students were encouraged to explore how furniture, typography, a wide range of household objects, and later buildings also, could be designed around shapes and techniques that were related visually to mechanised production. Design became linked with the work of painters, sculptors, writers and composers who were exploring the possibilities of 'abstract' art elsewhere in Europe and Russia – shaped by internal processes rather than by external factors (such as site, history or cultural references). Bauhaus designs are usually described as 'functionalist', reconciling art with technology, and architects with engineers:

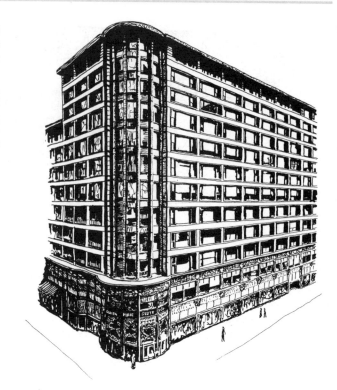

Figure 1.19

- effectiveness – the forms of objects (including buildings) determined by the logic of their function, involving the abundant use of 'pure' geometric shapes
- efficiency – all ornamentation and non-essential matter stripped away, in order to reveal the use of materials in accordance with their inherent properties

The Bauhaus was closed down by the Nazis in 1933 and its members of staff fled to other parts of the world (including Britain), justifying the identification of Modernist architecture as 'the International style'. In the United States, steel-framed buildings had been developed and were being built increasingly higher following the advent of the electric passenger lift (used in conjunction with revolving doors), architects had begun to expose rather than to disguise the structural framework, allowing the façade to 'express' its construction (Fig. 1.19). Under the influence of Bauhaus ideas, the rectangular framed building clad with glazed **curtain walls** became the standard form for office buildings throughout the developed world (especially when speculatively built) in the second half of the twentieth century.

Figure 1.20

The same principle of a rectangular grid of standardised columns and beams was adopted initially in the use of reinforced concrete for buildings, as it permitted the economical re-use of formwork. Portland cement – so called because of its resemblance to Portland stone – had been invented in Britain in the 1820s, but was of limited use as a structural material until reinforced with steel (in order to provide the tensile strength required in beams) – a technique which was developed half a century later in France. At the beginning of the twentieth century, engineers began to base the design of reinforced concrete structures not on the discipline of repetitive formwork but on calculations of ways in which forces were transferred internally, resulting in the development of forms such as rigid curved slabs (Fig. 1.20)

Figure 1.21

Figure 1.22

and 'mushroom' structural systems for buildings (in which columns widened at the top and became integral with the floor slabs they supported).

In the United States, reinforced concrete was exploited first for cantilevered floor, balcony and flat roof slabs in private houses around Chicago, designed by Frank Lloyd Wright in the first decade of the twentieth century – described as 'prairie houses' because of their close, organic relationship to the landscape around them (Fig. 1.21). In 1936, Wright developed the concrete core-and-cantilever principle for tall buildings – a construction technique that was later widely used for skyscrapers.

In Europe, by contrast, the characteristic 'Modern Movement' dwelling of the 1930s was typically designed as a free-standing, sculptural object bearing little relationship to its surroundings – usually in white-painted reinforced concrete (Fig. 1.22):

- lifted off the ground on concrete columns (called '*piloti*')
- walls separated from structure
- large openings provided – especially in the form of long horizontal strips
- flat roofs used as gardens or sun decks

With a few isolated exceptions (being used mainly for individually designed private houses, though also adopted by London Transport in the 1930s), 'Modern Movement' architecture came only very gradually to Britain, and is still widely resisted – usually on the grounds that it does not 'fit in' with its surroundings. In the decade preceding the Second World War, the largest areas of construction activity were in the low-density suburbs to nearly every city – especially in the form of speculative 'ribbon development' alongside arterial roads in response to the increasing use of private motor cars. Five million new houses were built between 1911 and 1939 (and 350 000 slum properties demolished). To give glamour to non-domestic buildings such as factories, cinemas, swimming pools and hotels, the escapist 'Art Deco' style was applied (the American form of Art Nouveau, associated especially with Hollywood):

- setbacks in imitation of **ziggurats**, and numerous elements based upon ancient Egyptian architecture
- curved corners, setbacks and an emphasis on horizontal elements (especially implying 'streamline' motion – Fig. 1.23)
- jagged zigzag decoration, brightly coloured tiling and use of the sunburst motif in glazing and garden gates

In Britain, most of the buildings we now associate with the term 'Modern Architecture' have been built in the wake of the social and political upheaval of the Second World War (in

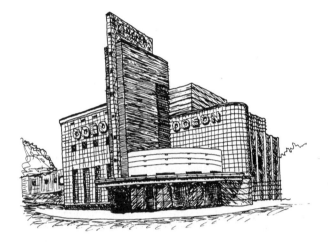

Figure 1.23

conjunction with the package of social reforms known as 'the welfare state'). Due to shortages of materials and labour, the great surge of building activity only began in the 1950s, when about four million people were still living in unmodernised nineteenth-century houses. The total population of England rose slowly from 41 million in 1951 to 46 million in 1971, and then grew by only 0.2 million over the next decade. The birth rate rose to a peak in 1966, but then fell to a low in 1977.

With faith in the establishment of the town and country planning system as a means of ensuring that different types of building were only undertaken in appropriate locations, vast numbers of dwellings, schools and colleges, hospitals, libraries, and whole new towns were built – typically with exposed brickwork and precast concrete or stone surrounds to openings (Fig. 1.24). Architects and planners were publicly respected for their commitment to achieving social ideals with efficiency and effectiveness, and 'modern architecture' was widely believed to provide exactly the kind of environment that people desired and deserved. Since the 1970s, however, many people have lost faith in the ability of 'professionals' to deliver a pleasant built environment, and the design of buildings has reverted to the Victorian approach – in which 'style' is applied merely as a system of decoration, and history is regarded as a catalogue of options.

'Modernist' buildings have come to be characterised by their distinctly non-traditional appearance, involving the exploitation of new materials such as aluminium and plastics, increasingly in the form of prefabricated components, for their new structural and technical possibilities. More and more components are now being

Figure 1.24

manufactured off-site (for closer control over quality and accuracy), transported over long distances (facilitated by infrastructure) and simply (and therefore rapidly) assembled – resulting in reduced demand for expensive craft skills. A large part of the design process today consists of selecting items from manufacturers' catalogues. To increase choice or where components are not readily available, designers simply specify the standards of performance expected of various elements of the construction, and leave the complexities of their design to specialist manufacturers or consultants. This has led to an increasing diversity of options for people embarking upon a **career** in the construction industry.

Self-assessment tasks

1. Compile a comprehensive list of all the different types of buildings we now commonly construct in our settlements.
2. Group these building types according to the main kinds of activity that take place within them.
3. Compare the range of activities you have identified with the main headings listed in CI/SfB Table 0. Add any omitted building types.
4. On a plan of the settlement you have chosen to investigate, identify the functions of areas or buildings by reference to a colour coding system based upon the headings listed in task 3 above.

1.2 Environmental conservation and protection

Most of us live in built-up surroundings and tend to make sharp distinctions between 'town' and 'country' or between 'buildings' and 'landscape'. There are few sites in Britain, however, that have not been physically changed many times by human hands, using tools and machinery. Nearly all of our landscape has already been shaped irreversibly by our activities. Because of its scale in time and space, construction has a greater **impact** on the environment than perhaps any other industry. We must take care that our own construction activities do not leave the world a poorer place for our descendants.

Topics covered in this section are:

- Reasons for protecting the environment
- Pollution and conservation issues
- Methods of protecting the environment

Reasons for protecting the environment

As the environment is our only resource for living, we face choices in the use we make of it. We make these choices in accordance with our values and attitudes. The easiest, unthinking approach is simply to regard the external environment as a threat – presenting us with no choice but to use the built environment as a means of overcoming its various hostile features. If we ignore social values, technology begins to play the dominant role in our lives, and we speak of unstoppable 'progress'.

It comes as a shock to discover that, in many respects, technology is making conditions worse for ourselves rather than better. We find that many of the familiar conditions of our existence on Earth are being spoilt:

- **water** – the source of all life – is being permanently **contaminated**
- **wildlife** – other parts of our own 'biosphere' – is being extinguished rapidly
- **residents** – our own neighbours – seem to be behaving antisocially
- **aesthetics** – the sensations that are supposed to give us pleasure – often reveal ugliness, odour, noise and change for the worse

By facing up to these issues socially, rather than depending solely upon further technological 'fixes' for the environment, we realise that the world around us is available not merely as a supply of 'dead' resources, but as a living fellow-traveller. Being attached to the environment, we must take and contribute in equal proportions in order to 'sustain' the relationship. By looking after our world, we are in fact looking after ourselves.

Self-assessment tasks

1. Identify the various effects of construction-related activities on the natural environment. Which of these effects do you consider the most serious, and why?
2. Discuss what can be done to reduce these effects. How can you personally contribute towards the alleviation of these effects?

The water table

Most of the **rain** which delivers freshwater to the land infiltrates the soil and rock, and becomes groundwater – sinking down until it reaches impermeable rock **strata**. It collects here and spreads as a **zone of saturation**, the top level of which is termed the **water table**. The depth of the water table varies from a few centimetres to many metres below ground level, according to:

- the porosity of the soil
- the angle of its slope
- the amount of vegetation

The level of the water table can also fluctuate over time because of variations in rainfall. When the **topography** of the land dips below the water table, the groundwater seeps out as **springs** that feed the streams or lakes forming the run-off from the local **catchment area** (Fig. 1.25).

Both **quarrying** and deep **excavation** for buildings can easily intercept the water table, causing new streams or lakes or emptying old ones. Excavation may also interfere with the boundaries of the catchment area (termed the **watershed**), changing the groundwater's drainage patterns. The construction of whole **towns** and **cities** usually changes the local groundwater conditions completely (Fig. 1.26):

- Impervious asphalt and concrete replaces the porous soil, preventing infiltration and increasing surface-water run-off to as much as 85% of total rainfall.
- Surface-water sewers replace the streams, ponds and marshes of the natural watershed, increasing the chances of **flooding** caused by sudden storms (with the associated hazards of washing toxic waste into areas where it can cause permanent damage).
- Buildings replace vegetation, which both reduces run-off (and **erosion**) and extracts moisture from the ground and passes it back into the atmosphere (a process known as **transpiration**).

Wildlife

The impact of our activities upon the other living things with which we share our planet has, in many instances, only been recognised too late. Many species of animals and plants have been lost altogether as a result of industrialisation and urbanisation. This is described as **loss of biodiversity**, and often reflects a failure to deal with the 'spillover' effects of our activities – either through ignorance or stupidity. We now understand life on Earth as a chaotically complex **ecosystem** in which every part draws inputs from and produces outputs affecting every other part. We therefore carry responsibility for **sustaining the environment** in all its rich complexity. If any one organism is removed, the whole ecosystem is changed irreversibly and (we now recognise) unpredictably. When we allow whole species of plants and animals to disappear, we deny ourselves the opportunity of ever understanding what roles they might have played in sustaining our own existence on the planet.

Loss of biodiversity (often associated with **desertification**) is usually the result of numerous small-scale developments

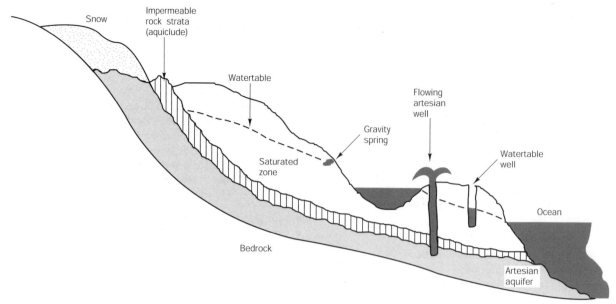

Figure 1.25 Groundwater formation

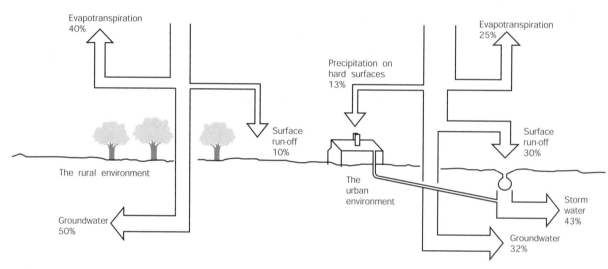

Figure 1.26 Modification of the hydrological cycle arising from urbanisation

in widely dispersed locations. Removal of hedgerows, for example, causes loss of the topsoil required for **agriculture**, and the silting up of **drainage** ditches. Whenever we engage in construction activities on new 'green field' sites, in forests or even in water, we cause **destruction of habitat** – disrupting a local ecosystem, displacing animals and killing plants. The **re-use of land** which has been previously built on is clearly a primary strategy for conserving the natural environment.

Residents

The **residents** of an area can also find their lives disrupted by nearby construction activities. If they have lived there for some time, they will have established themselves as a **community**, sustained through a network of friendships. As large construction projects are often undertaken for the benefit of powerful interest groups far removed from the local community, it is important for planners and developers to be sensitive to the 'social fabric' of the neighbourhood – not merely the physically measurable features of the terrain.

There are many ways in which developers can make themselves aware of local residents' views:

- conducting private interviews based upon **questionnaires**
- holding **public meetings** to explain proposals and to listen to responses
- inviting community **representatives** to participate in the decision-taking processes

To ensure that new development is properly integrated with existing communities, the most successful strategy of all is to involve local residents in the construction of their new environment, especially if they have also contributed to the design process. When people feel they have played a part in forming their built environment, they tend to take greater responsibility for its maintenance – redecorating when required, planting and helping each other gain access to local amenities.

Aesthetics

As we build in order to accommodate social requirements, we must make allowances for other people's tastes, beliefs and opinions. If we deny other people's values, we immediately negate our own viewpoint also. A degree of social **consensus** is needed in order to underpin our individual freedoms to choose the way we live. The built environment inevitably reflects the extent of this consensus. To support and perpetuate 'civic' attitudes, our finished buildings must interact with one another in a similarly respectful and supportive way, their appearance and functions complementing the existing environment.

The design of many of today's buildings, by contrast, is determined by narrow, short-term constraints such as function, technological convenience and budget – at the expense of regard for context and social responsibility. In urban situations especially, where new buildings can affect many people, there is a temptation to design them primarily as oppressive 'expressions' of individuals' political beliefs, commercial interests or imagined social status. Buildings can easily influence people's feelings, attitudes or behaviour:

- through their 'superhuman' scale (in height, span or length)
- through their technical sophistication and complexity of servicing
- through extensive repetition of, or even absence of, construction features

The 'civilised' alternative is to design buildings that appear deliberately to accommodate people's feelings, making them feel comfortable or even welcome in its presence:

- humanity of scale – with small parts to which people can relate closely (in terms of proportion, for example) to larger parts that hold the building's overall composition together
- 'honesty' in terms of construction materials and structural principles – including 'transparency' in the relationship of inside to outside
- ease of external access and internal direction-finding – assisted in particular by the provision of distinctive 'places' within the built environment

Different environments each possess their own characteristics, determined largely by the historic use of locally available resources:

- open spaces and wildlife, landscaped parks and wilderness areas
- people and their skills, interests and demands
- the fabric of buildings, infrastructure and other forms of land development (including agriculture and mining)

In order to maintain a sense of continuity with our past, to remind ourselves of who we are, we must identify what physical features give our communities their visual quality, and construct the built environment in ways that 'conserve' this character.

New construction undertaken in the midst of an environment we wish to sustain is therefore required to 'fit in' with its surroundings – blending with them in visual terms, in addition to supporting them functionally. Typical **construction features** need to be perceived as parts of an integrating whole – distinct as subcomponents, but at the same time merging quietly with a greater totality (Fig. 1.27), so that the whole becomes 'greater than the sum of its parts'. Throughout the arts in the western world (since Classical times), the adoption of this principle is recognised as a primary component of aesthetic pleasure. ✎

Figure 1.27 'Greater than the sum of its parts'; Royal Crescent, Bath (1767)

Pollution and conservation issues

Because construction activities involve modifications to **topography**, consuming **energy** in the process and therefore also modifying the **climate**, the choice of **materials** for building raises many questions about the 'appropriateness' of technology in sustaining our natural environment:

- **Extracting** the material requires specialised energy-consuming **plant**, producing **noise, dust, fumes** and **waste** – some of which may be **hazardous to health**.
- **Moving** the material may require the construction of additional **infrastructure** and other energy-consuming **plant** to carry it, with possibilities of **spillage** and **ground contamination**, and further **waste** associated with **storage**.
- **Processing** the material may require further fuel-consuming **plant**, often with **noise** and useless or **hazardous waste** products which then become a **disposal** problem.

It is not only in obtaining and processing materials that the construction industry makes an impact upon the environment. Activities on site can also be **sources of pollution**:

- The **transportation of materials** to site may disturb local **residents**, due to the **noise, fumes** and **dust** produced.
- The **storage of materials** on site may cause **ground contamination**, so that when it rains there is also **groundwater** contamination.
- The **use of plant** on site may not only disturb local residents, but may present **health hazards** for the operatives themselves.
- **Demolition activities** are not only hazardous for **operatives**, but expose the whole problem of failing to perceive continuity between the natural and the built environment.

Closer consideration of the various **types of pollution**, and of their **sources** in various kinds of construction activity, allows us to understand better how human development feeds into the Earth's ecosystem, with consequences in the form of particular kinds of change in our resource – some permanent, some reversible, but all part of the legacy we leave our descendants:

- the **contamination** of land, air and water (including global warming)
- the depletion of the Earth's **finite resources** (including tropical rain-forests)
- **waste disposal** difficulties (including nuclear waste)
- **hazards** to human safety and health (including the stress associated with new working conditions)

As most materials used for construction originate from below the land surface, they need to be excavated – leaving holes in the ground that make a significant long-term impact upon the **aesthetics** of the landscape. It is usually most appropriate to obtain materials from as near as possible to the sites where construction is to be carried out:

- reducing the area likely to be affected by any forms of pollution caused by extraction, transportation or processing
- reducing energy-consumption (in designing roads and railways, the aim is to balance the volume of material extracted from cuttings against the amount required for the construction of embankments)
- making it more likely that **reinstatement** of the landscape will be included as part of the construction project

Noise

Noise may be defined as unwanted sound. In relation to construction work, noise may originate from a variety of **sources:**

- the **transportation of materials** – including traffic along roads and railways, deliveries to site, reversing signals, unloading and carrying away demolition waste
- the **use of plant** on site – including **cutting** and mixing materials, **moving** them from storage areas to their location in the final construction, fixing components, or even listening to radio-cassette players
- **demolition** work – including 'peak' explosions of sound, and vibrations

The sound of these activities becomes a nuisance if it interferes with **safety and health**, communications, or progress on site, or if it disturbs local **residents**.

Levels of noise on site are controlled under the **Noise at Work Regulations 1989**, which require employers to provide hearing defenders for their workers where noise levels rise above 85 dB(A). If subjected for more than half a minute to noise such as a 115 dB(A) pneumatic breaker at a distance of less than 1 metre, hearing may be damaged temporarily or sounds may appear muffled for several hours. If the exposure is repeated, the damage may be irreversible and socially disabling.

Noise is largely subjective and different people react to it in different ways. What may irritate some people (causing stress and ill health) may be hardly noticed at all by others. There is therefore no measurable level of noise that can be defined legally as a 'nuisance'. Judgement must be based upon the particular circumstances of each case:

- the likely reaction of the average, reasonable person in this situation

- when, how often and for how long the noise occurs
- the pitch and volume of the noise

Noise from **road traffic** (which is generally the responsibility of the Department of Transport) is the most widespread source of noise nuisance in the whole built environment. The problem can be tackled in a number of ways:

- reducing the noise at source, by using quieter vehicles
- routeing vehicles away from sensitive areas by traffic management schemes or even by constructing new roads
- protecting nearby residents by sound-insulation measures (such as double-glazing), sound absorption, and reflective noise barriers

Properties adjacent to new roads may be eligible for grants towards the cost of sound-insulation measures.

In residential areas, it is quite usual for the **local planning authority** to impose noise conditions on the **planning permission** granted for development:

- restricting deliveries and work on site to 'normal' business hours
- regulating the use of power tools
- insisting on the provision of noise barriers

Even after construction operations have commenced, local authorities and magistrates' courts also have powers (under the **Environmental Protection Act 1990** in England and Wales) to deal with noise that is judged to be a 'statutory nuisance'. The building contractor needs to be able to show that the best practicable means have been taken to prevent or limit the noise. Disturbing the neighbours near a construction site causes ill-will, and possibly leads to legal action being taken, doing nothing but harm for the contractors involved.

Contaminated air

Air can be contaminated by particles of **dust** or by gases, some taking the form of obnoxious or even poisonous **fumes**. Dust particles come in a range of sizes:

- **grit** – originating from materials stored on site, the surface of the site itself, **demolition** activities, or the process of grit-blasting
- **dirt** – produced when dust settles on or sticks to surfaces which are intended to be kept clean
- **fine particles** – originating from powdery materials used on site (such as **cement** and gypsum **plaster**), from **ash** left by combustion processes, or as the by-products of **cutting**, grinding or rubbing processes. When suspended in the air, fine particles (especially wood-flour produced by joinery activities) are highly explosive

Grit settles quickly, but is raised by the movement of vehicles or wind in dry conditions. It can cause a number of problems:

- irritation to the eyes (goggles may be required in certain situations)
- wear, excessive **noise** and reduced efficiency in uncovered engines
- interference with good finishes in painting, varnishing or sealing
- blockage of drains or ditches

Part of the solution may involve spraying water over the surface of an exposed site in dry conditions, especially road surfaces (roadways should, in any case, be kept away from site huts). Vegetation may form a useful screen against flying particles of grit.

Dirt may quickly become a serious problem for **neighbours** to a construction site. In some situations, a policy of washing the wheels of all vehicles leaving the site may be demanded by local authorities in order to keep adjoining highways clean. Window-cleaning services may be offered to local **residents** as part of a contractor's 'good neighbour' policy. Keeping building interiors and windows clean becomes a problem for contractors themselves as they approach practical completion.

Fine particles from any source are the most serious kind of health hazard of all, as they can escape the body's respiratory filters and enter the lungs, causing breathing and chest problems, headaches, or even cancer (from asbestos fibres):

- **Organic particles** carried in dust include mould spore, pollen, mites, bacteria and viruses, causing allergic reactions, asthma, and illnesses such as influenza, tuberculosis, or (fatally) Legionnaire's disease.
- **Toxic particles** are associated with irritants such as smoke, pesticides (such as preservatives for timber) and **plastic** dusts. Glass fibres (from insulation, for example) are also irritants, though non-toxic.
- **Metal particles** which are toxic include lead, cadmium, mercury and copper. The titanium oxide which has now replaced lead in white paint is only slightly less harmful – particularly to children. The absorption of aluminium into the body has been linked to Alzheimer's disease.

Fumes – both unpleasant to smell or even toxic to inhale, may arise from **hazardous chemicals** stored or in use, or from **combustion** processes such as burning waste materials on site (especially during **demolition** work), producing CO_2 – the main **greenhouse gas** associated with **global warming**.

A number of liquids and solids used in the construction process release toxic or irritant vapours at room temperature or below. These are known as **volatile organic compounds** (VOCs), being extracted or synthesised from petrochemicals:

- **Formaldehydes** – used in the manufacture of electrical switches and sockets, plastic laminates, as cavity foam insulation, and as the adhesive in plywood and chipboard, but known to be an irritant, lowering the threshold of allergic reactions, and suspected of being carcinogenic.
- **Organochlorines** – used in many pesticides, solvents and cleaning fluids, but mostly toxic, reacting with and accumulating in live tissue (the very worst type being **polychlorinated biphenyls** – PCBs).
- **Phenols** – used in disinfectants, cleaners, polishes, varnish, paints and fabric coatings, but known also as irritants, causing skin rashes, nausea and breathing difficulties.

While the soft plastics now widely used in construction (especially **polyvinyl chloride** – PVC) appear generally to be associated with exposure to potentially harmful VOCs, the main hazard is their combustibility. Plastics will suddenly burst into flames at a lower 'flashover' than other materials, and then burn twice as fast and hot. Enormous quantities of thick, black, smoke and highly toxic fumes and gas are produced rapidly, preventing people from escaping.

The main problems with **combustion gases** arise in still conditions or in unventilated spaces. Fine particles of **soot** and deadly **carbon monoxide** fumes are produced as the by-products of combustion in bonfires, fireplaces, solid fuel boilers and furnaces. The smoke from timber contains carcinogens, while the burning of plastic or rubber is thought

to produce deadly **dioxins**, in addition to **hydrochloric acid** and **hydrogen cyanide**. Normally, chimneys are used to conduct the byproducts of combustion to a position where they can escape without prejudice to health or being a nuisance. Under the **Clean Air Acts 1956/1968**, local authorities are empowered to declare 'smokeless zones' in parts of their area, in which only fuels authorised by the Secretary of State are permitted to be burnt. In most construction projects however (especially where local **residents** may be affected), the burning of **waste** on site is expressly forbidden in the **contract documents**.

Hazardous gases are usually localised problems, but no less serious as threats to health:

- **Radon** – odourless and colourless but radioactive, accounting for 50% of all the natural background radiation and now thought to be the second biggest cause of lung cancer after smoking. High concentrations of radon are found in the ground in particular parts of Britain (Cornwall, Devon and Derbyshire), where ground floors need to be sealed and ventilated beneath in order to prevent the gas seeping into buildings. Construction materials such as **granite** and **bricks**, **concrete**, and **plaster** made from radon-rich sources are also sources of this form of pollution, often long after operations on site are finished.
- **Ozone** – an unstable toxic gas present in small quantities in the air, generated by the action of sunshine on hydrocarbons and nitrogen oxides (from vehicle exhausts). This reaction produces **photochemical smog**, reducing visibility, and causing eye irritation and chest problems. Ozone is also generated by electrical discharges from brush-type motors and photocopiers.

While excess ozone at ground level poses local environmental issues, it is the depletion of ozone high in the Earth's atmosphere that presents a global problem. The 'ozone layer' shields the planet from excess **ultra-violet radiation**, which can cause skin cancer, crop failure and enhanced **global warming**. Large 'holes' have been discovered in the ozone layer, and attributed to a group of pollutants known as **chlorofluorocarbons** (CFCs), widely used as aerosol propellants, refrigerants, and in the manufacture of foamed plastics and halon fire extinguishers.

Contaminated ground and water

The **spillage** of materials on construction sites generates several kinds of pollution:

- **fumes** passing into the air, mainly from **hazardous chemicals** used in the processing of materials (see above), but also from damage to **gas supply** pipes, or from **diesel engines** used in plant and equipment on site
- **contamination of the ground** due to the spillage of **plant fuel** or other chemicals, damage to an existing **foul drainage** system, or overflow from temporary site drainage installations
- **contamination of watercourses** by surface-water run-off from construction sites, quarries, or gravel and sand pits
- **wastage of building materials** in transportation, storage and handling on site

The main reason for concern about **contamination of the ground** is that toxic substances may enter the **groundwater system** or neighbouring **watercourses** and pass into the ecological life-chain of an area. Even a minor discharge of certain metals or organic substances to watercourses can be toxic to fish or wildlife, and may contaminate water abstracted for drinking or agricultural use many miles downstream of the pollution outfall.

Pollution of watercourses is generally measured in terms of **biological oxygen demand** (BOD) – caused by an increase in the presence of bacteria, removing oxygen from the water and threatening the survival of many species of fish and insects. Cloudy surface run-off from **construction works**, **quarries** and **pits** begins by reducing the light penetration required for plant growth, and this leads to the smothering of fish, insects and microbiological organisms. Watercourses can silt up in consequence, causing further flooding and unsightly land contamination. Rubbish and grit carried into the drainage systems cause blockages and excessive wear on pumps and machinery.

The potential for liquid spillages on site, and the routes likely to be followed by the contaminant, should be assessed as part of the **safety planning** process. It is usual to allow about 5% in pricing construction work for **wastage of materials** on site – usually due to careless off-loading between **transportation** and **storage**, and avoidable through proper planning for deliveries. **Storage** areas for **plant fuel** should be concrete lined and surrounded by low embankments or walls called **bunds** to prevent the escape of accidental spillages (which are, in any case, an expensive waste of product). The presence of an oily sheen or discoloration of water, even when classified as a minor environmental threat, may still be regarded by local **residents** as a nuisance in terms of **aesthetics**.

Demolition waste

The main **hazard** associated with **demolition** activities is to the **operatives** involved, as the process of dismantling a building means causing it to become structurally unstable, which makes the site an extremely dangerous place to work – especially if the task is being carried out in a hurry. More **time** also needs to be allowed for the demolition in order to provide more opportunity for salvaging materials for **recycling**, in addition to reducing the nuisance caused by **noise**, **fumes** and **dust**.

The first consideration has to be whether it is really necessary to undertake demolition work at all. If an existing building can be retained, at least in part, there will be less impact on the environment from all the processes related to reconstruction – above all, in terms of total energy consumption and the associated depletion of **fuel** reserves and production of CO_2 **emissions**. There will be less disturbance to local **residents**, who often regard the **aesthetics** of the existing built environment as preferable to any new alternative.

As the principle of **waste minimisation** applies through the whole life cycle of the built environment, not merely at the end of it, buildings need to be designed so that they can be easily dismantled and their components re-used as **salvage** or recycled – an approach called **low- and non-waste technology** (LNWT). This is becoming especially important with the growing shortage of **landfill** sites for the disposal of solid waste, as household refuse now accounts for around 80% of municipal waste. The growing use of LNWT also reduces problems of **groundwater** contamination associated with landfill disposal.

Even the 'minimisation' of waste implies a negative view, suggesting acceptance of some loss or disruption to the environment. A more positive approach is to seek solutions that creatively integrate human development with environmental considerations. Demolition activities need to be regarded as an opportunity to enhance the whole ecosystem, so that the residues from one part of our habitat life cycle become the resource for another. Demolition waste provides the materials we require for replacement buildings and infrastructure.

Replacing **gravel and sand**, for example, **clay** products and broken concrete can be used as aggregate in new concrete. Clay products can also be ground to a powder and used as a binder in the manufacture of blocks, as burnt clay powder reacts with lime. **Timber** can be re-processed for the manufacture of chipboard, waferboard, blockboard, or fibreboard (although the **formaldehyde** glues commonly used to bond them together may be regarded as environmentally unacceptable). Even **contaminated soil** and sludge can be re-processed as a concrete for foundations that 'lock up' the **hazardous chemicals** instead of allowing them to pollute the groundwater system. In general, **demolition** can provide the opportunity to obtain a wide variety of building components and services equipment without depleting any resources at all – simply demanding human imagination and ingenuity. The materials which are easiest to re-use, however, are those associated with the least processing – those closest to the state in which they are found in the **natural environment**.

Stone

The extraction of rock for building is undertaken by **quarrying**, with methods varying considerably depending upon:

- the type of stone being quarried (above all, in relation to its hardness)
- the depth of the stone below the land surface

Most stone is obtained from open quarries, but where the stone beds lie very deep underground, mining is also used. Open quarries for the more popular types of stone may also be extremely deep (over 25 m), having been worked for centuries. The impact of open quarries on the landscape is significant and permanent, though often regarded as attractive **landmarks** after quarrying operations have ceased.

For most kinds of stone, **quarrying** simply leaves neat holes in the landscape, as loose material can be used leaving no **wastage** at all. The mining of **slate** is particularly untidy however, with over 90% of material excavated being discarded as 'useless'. Several ways of reducing the impact of quarrying upon the environment may be suggested:

- taking advantage of the durability of stone by using stone widely as a construction material and by **recycling** it whenever possible
- using only **locally available** stone where new material is required in construction
- using stone particles or **dust** to manufacture **reconstructed stone** or as an ingredient in mortar or concrete

Stone is often used 'as found' and much of its processing is labour-intensive rather than energy-intensive. Most of the energy embodied in its preparation arises from the cranes and trucks required for lifting and **moving** the material – often in blocks as large as 1 m^3 initially. The loosening of rock is often undertaken by hand, inserting metal wedges at intervals along 'fissures' or between distinct layers, gradually and uniformly hammering them in until whole slabs become detached. Hard sandstone usually requires **blasting** to loosen the stone, and then pneumatic **drilling** is used to provide holes for wedges. Each slab obtained is roughly squared up with a large hammer before **moving** it out of the quarry.

Further energy may be consumed in 'dressing' the stone to the precise shapes required. Mechanical saws perform the initial **cutting** operations, with **water** used to keep the blades cool. To hide the machine marks, the surface of the stone may then be **rubbed**, using sand, carborundum and water as abrasive agents. Pneumatic hammers are used to produce particular mouldings if required, and a wide variety of surface finishes may be applied by hand on the 'true face' of the stone (visible in the final construction). Water is essential throughout these processes in controlling the production of silica-rich dust, which is known to be a significant health hazard for **stonemasons**.

Because of the noise associated with them (produced above all in **blasting**), stone quarries are usually located far away from built settlements. Their very remoteness sometimes leads to major environmental conflicts of interest however, as rock is found predominantly in sparsely inhabited hilly areas – often formally designated as National Parks in Britain, cherished for their value as recreational facilities for the country's largely urbanised population. The activity of heavy lorries **moving** large quantities of stone to distant construction sites is highly disruptive to the amenity of a National Park, in addition to being extra energy-intensive because of the **topography**.

Timber

In comparison with other structural building materials, the use of **timber** can have a minimal environmental impact, associated with relatively low-energy consumption and leaving no major holes in the Earth's crust. **Trees** perform an important function in the environment, each consuming on average 9.1 kg of carbon dioxide per year, and producing about 7 kg of oxygen – or even more in the case of young growing trees (suggesting that timber extraction and replacement may actually be beneficial to the atmosphere, 'locking up' the carbon taken from it).

Timber is obtained by **logging** in forests – a process of felling the trees, removing their branches, cross-cutting them into logs, and removing their bark:

- **Clear-cutting** involves the total clearance of whole blocks of forest, which is highly damaging to the local ecosystems.
- **Selective felling** involves **cutting** down only those trees which are identified as commercially useful, with less disturbance to the local ecosystem.

An **infrastructure** of roads (or occasionally railways) is created through the forest (serving also as fire-breaks), in order for lorries or tractors – equipped with special lifting-gear – to move the timber to a permanently sited sawmill. To reduce the environmental impact of these operations, **rivers** are used wherever possible to float the timber downstream.

Timber is often treated with **preservatives** in order to make it more resistant to attack by fungi and insects, but with harmful environmental side-effects:

- **Tar-oil preservatives** – such as creosote, highly effective and relatively inexpensive but only suitable for external use, as the **fumes** are intrusive (especially near foodstuffs).

- **Water-borne preservatives** – using pressurising equipment to force salts dissolved in water into the timber, therefore requiring further **seasoning** (an energy-intensive process involving **kiln-drying** if low moisture-content is required).
- **Organic solvent preservatives** – using the superior penetrating power of petroleum spirits to carry **toxic chemicals** deep into the material, usually based upon vacuum-impregnation equipment. The use of the insecticide **lindane** in this type of preservative has been found to have particularly harmful environmental effects, endangering certain species of bats.

Britain's geographical position enables us to grow timber suitable for construction, but not on a scale equal to demand. Most **hardwoods** grown in temperate climates such as ours are not sufficiently durable to be used other than for decorative purposes (unless treated with preservative) – oak and sweet chestnut are the exceptions, and may be **recycled** many times. For commercial reasons, as they have a growing cycle twice as rapid (about 40 years), we prefer to grow **softwoods** in Britain. Some of the plantations created in Britain have been criticised for their adverse environmental impact, however – seedlings of the same species being planted in narrow straight rows for many miles across former moorlands or natural mixed woodlands, reducing **wildlife** diversity and **aesthetic** or recreational amenity.

Its potential as an indefinitely renewable resource is the chief environmental advantage of timber, making it possible to specify timber obtained only from **managed forests**, where more trees are planted than felled. Over 60% of the hardwood imported by Britain comes from tropical rainforest sources, having fallen from 75% ten years ago. Much of this decline may be attributed to environmental alarm about the destruction of rainforests, which is feared to be having a measurable global impact. Taken together, the Earth's forests play a significant role in maintaining the quantities of oxygen and water vapour in the atmosphere, and counteracting the effect of CO_2 emissions. Brazil alone contains over one-third of the Earth's forested land (about 5 million km^2 – larger than the whole of Europe). This area is being reduced by over 40 000 km^2 per year – mostly being burnt (unlocking further CO_2) in order to clear space temporarily for cattle ranching, iron mining, and the associated road and rail construction.

Around the world, 60% of timber used for construction is **hardwood**, of which 45% comes from tropical rainforests. Only a tiny proportion of tropical hardwood is used for construction purposes, however. Across South America, Asia and Africa generally, 78% of growing trees removed from rainforests are used for fuel and charcoal in the country of origin, and only 3% of the timber cut for lumber is exported (two-thirds as dimensioned stock, the remainder as logs). By insisting on tropical hardwoods only from properly managed sources, the construction industry may in a small way be contributing to better forestry practices.

Clay bricks and tiles

Clay – the raw material for bricks and tiles – is only a slightly more durable version of mud, usually lying very near the surface of the ground. Its extraction (called '**winning**' the raw material) is therefore very simple and relatively low in energy consumption. On the other hand, large land surface areas may be affected, making a significant (if temporary) impact upon the visual quality of the landscape.

Following the removal of topsoil, clay may be extracted from the ground to depths of up to 2 m by simple hand-digging from a **clay pit**, or deeper by **quarrying** with mechanical excavators. In some clay pits, the material quarried takes the form of hard shale, which has to be loosened by **blasting** before it is loaded into trucks.

The trucks used for **moving** the clay or shale out of the pit are either lorries or wagons called bogies, running on rails and pulled either by tractor or on an endless wire rope (which returns empty wagons to the pit). When lorries are used, low-gradient ramps need to be constructed to form a strong roadway, consuming larger areas of land. Bogies on rails have a smaller environmental impact – especially as the rails can usually be **recycled**.

The clay or shale extracted from pits is usually transported directly to a grinding or crushing mill, where its **preparation** may include washing, drying or blending:

- with other clays (mixing different strata in order to produce particular colours)
- with fuel materials (to ensure uniform burning)
- with stabilisers (to reduce shrinkage during the later baking process), such as **sand**, **limestone** or 'grog' (produced by **recycling** waste bricks or burnt clay ground to a powder)

Following its preparation, the clay is moulded into the required shape and stacked in kilns for **firing** at temperatures up to $1000\,°C$. The external energy consumed at this stage may be reduced by using clays with a high fuel content (such as found in the manufacture of Fletton bricks).

As clay deposits are usually found in **valleys**, there are often conflicts of interest between the use of land for agriculture and for quarrying. So long as the **winning** of clay occurs at a small scale, it is always possible to return the land afterwards to agricultural use. Modern methods of winning the raw material using drag-lines and multi-bucket excavators require less excavating area than before, but are associated with deeper **cutting** into the landscape, with longer term effects upon local **drainage** patterns.

Concrete

Our industrialised processes of manufacturing and transportation have a significant impact upon the global environment due to the CO_2 emissions (usually measured in kg/m^3) associated with the extraction and processing of the common construction materials. Energy use in buildings accounts for almost 50% of Britain's CO_2 emissions, with a further 8% attributed to the production and transportation of building materials. Over 1% of our emissions arise simply from the calcination of Portland Cement – the key ingredient of **concrete**.

On the other hand, **gravel** and **sand** (the usual aggregates in concrete) require less energy in processing than almost any other construction material:

- **washing** may be required in order to remove dirt particles which reduce adhesion in an aggregate
- **grading** (through sieves) may be required in order to provide the industry with a range of different sized particles

Well-graded aggregates are demanded for the production of concrete with fewer voids in it, reducing the need for expensive (and energy-intensive) cement.

On the other hand, there is little cause for environmental concern about the extensive use of **gravel and sand** as these minerals are the commonest (and therefore cheapest) ingredients in the Earth's crust, and may be obtained in a variety of ways:

- as **crushed rock** produced as **waste** from stone quarries (ideal as an aggregate because of the increased friction caused by its angularity)
- by **quarrying** from dry pits, usually without having to excavate very deeply below the land surface
- by **dredging** from river beds, wet pits or at sea (the latter being less useful as aggregate because of its salt content and lack of angularity)

The main environmental impact associated with the extraction of aggregates from the ground arises from the vast quantities of material involved – the construction industry uses more **gravel and sand** than any other material. There is considerable scope, therefore, for the **recycling** of aggregate-based products. 'Secondary aggregates' such as **crushed concrete** are widely used in Europe for road construction, and may also be used in concrete production.

When gravel and sand extraction is undertaken close to built-up areas, however, local **residents** often object to the **aesthetic impact** of quarrying activities on the landscape. Even where dredging is undertaken at sea, the adjacent coastline is often affected by subsidence and the gradual replacement of beaches by salt marshes. Quarrying contractors are therefore required (as a 'condition' attached to the planning permission granted for their operations – even if looking some twenty-five years into the future) to leave a pleasantly landscaped environment behind them.

Landscape reclamation schemes usually centre around the use of water as recreational amenities or new habitats for **wildlife**. Being commonly located on river flood plains and on low-lying ground, pumping of water is required in order to lower the **water table**, temporarily affecting vegetation and wildlife in the surrounding area. When quarrying ceases, the pumping also stops, and gravel and sand pits tend to fill with water. Demand for facilities for water sports is especially strong in south-east and midland Britain, where the population is relatively concentrated but lacks large bodies of inland water.

Former gravel pits are also useful for **landfill** – the tipping of household or industrial refuse:

- **Hazardous chemicals** require elaborate precautions to prevent toxic substances entering the subsoil drainage system.
- **Organic refuse** produces **methane** (CH_4 – another 'greenhouse gas') as it decomposes anaerobically, providing a possible alternative fuel source but also presenting an explosion hazard.
- Non-biodegradable waste (including builders' rubble from **demolition**) is more stable for future built development.

Where extraction is not deep, it is easier to reclaim the land for agricultural use, and the natural drainage patterns of the landscape are almost unaffected.

Self-assessment tasks

1. Describe the various kinds of machinery associated with obtaining clay, stone, gravel and sand, and timber from the natural environment. Rank these materials in order of the energy consumption generally associated with their extraction.
2. Identify the possibilities for recycling each of these materials in order to reduce the need to extract them from the natural environment.

Methods of protecting the environment

Our responsibilities in relation to the environment may be understood in several ways:

- Through **technology** (including **construction**), we began by taking responsibility for making modifications to the environment, in order to make the world more comfortable for ourselves.
- Through **pollution** – the side-effects of technology, we recognise that we bear the main responsibility for having caused many other, undesirable modifications to the environment.
- Through our **community**, we must now take responsibility for restricting undesired modifications to the environment, exercising some social control over technology rather than submitting to its abstract logic (based solely upon measurable quantities, scientific principles and efficiency-oriented economics).

Our decisions and actions as a community may be taken at three distinct 'levels':

- **legislation** and **local policy** – in the name of society in general
- **organisations** – in the name of groups to which we attach ourselves
- **personal** – in our own right as individuals

To sustain the kind of environment we wish to enjoy in the future, we need to operate on all these levels at the same time.

Legislation

As **legislation** changes rapidly in order to reflect social values, a number of important Acts of Parliament have been passed within the last decade that reflect our concern for **protecting the environment**. In particular, legislation has been passed in respect of land use, water services and pollution control.

The **Town and Country Planning Acts 1990** are not really new, but simply update a system of controls over land use in England and Wales that has been in place since the end of the Second World War. One of the Acts describes local authority control over certain **hazardous substances**, the storage of which requires special consent to be granted, which will only be given in the context of consideration for adjoining land uses. Another of the Acts describes **Listed Buildings and Conservation Areas**, requiring 'Listed Building Consent' (in addition to the usual planning permission) for demolition or construction works affecting buildings or areas considered to be of special architectural or historic interest:

- 'Listed Buildings' – identified by statutory bodies such as **English Heritage** as Grade I (nearly 10 000 entries), Grade II* (about 19 000 entries) and Grade II (about 446 000 entries). The grades relate partly to possibilities of grant aid for repair work.
- 'Conservation Areas' are identified by **local planning authorities** where they wish to preserve or enhance the 'character' of parts of their area. Specific consent is also required for cutting down or lopping trees in these areas (while trees elsewhere may be similarly protected by **Tree Preservation Orders**).

The main planning legislation is supplemented by government advice in the form of occasional **Planning Policy Guidance** and **Mineral Planning Guidance** notes – the latter dealing specifically with issues related to mineral extraction.

The basis for control over **water** and **drainage** management in England and Wales is the **Water Act 1989**, which established the **National Rivers Authority (NRA)** and cleared the path for privatisation of the water industry (dealing with water supply and distribution, the sewerage system and sewage treatment). The **Water Resources Act 1991** covers water resources and the functions of the NRA:

- land drainage and water pollution control
- flood defence, including sea defences
- fisheries, navigation, recreation and conservation along rivers

The **Control of Pollution Act 1974** has long given local authorities (through their **environmental health** departments) the power to issue notices specifying how construction, demolition and similar works must be carried out so as to minimise noise:

- the type of plant or machinery which is or is not to be used
- the hours of operation
- permitted noise levels from particular types of machinery

Under the same legislation, local authorities are entitled to declare a 'noise abatement zone', specifying the particular premises to which their orders apply. The authority then has to keep public records of the noise emanating from the premises, and it becomes an offence to exceed the registered noise level without written consent.

The main legislation now controlling pollution in England and Wales is the **Environmental Protection Act 1990 (EPA)**. This introduces a system of 'integrated pollution control' involving the services of a number of agencies:

- **Her Majesty's Inspectorate of Pollution** (set up in 1987 to deal with industrial air pollution, radioactive substances and hazardous wastes) monitors and controls the more hazardous contaminants of air, land and water.
- **Local authority environmental health** departments control the emission of less hazardous pollutants in the atmosphere and waste disposal.
- The **NRA** monitors discharges into watercourses and sewers.

The EPA lists over 100 'prescribed processes' for which authorisation is required (even for Crown departments) from the appropriate agency, which then rigorously monitors the activities of the applicant in order to ensure they comply with conditions imposed. EPA powers are implemented through the service of certain Notices:

- Enforcement Notices – issued even in anticipation of contravention of conditions
- Prohibition Notices – issued whenever the controlling authority believes there is imminent risk of pollution, regardless of any authorisation

Organisations

The main statutory authorities responsible for protecting the environment have been identified above in relation to the legislation defining their powers:

- local authority environmental health departments
- local planning authorities
- the National Rivers Authority and the Water Authorities
- Her Majesty's Inspectorate of Pollution

In general terms, the Secretary of State in the Department of the Environment holds central government responsibility for environmental protection, administering the town planning and building control systems, managing inner city policy and controlling the spending and activities of local government. A separate Department of National Heritage carries responsibility for the care of ancient monuments and environments of architectural value.

From time to time, central government has established advisory groups in respect of particular environmental issues, some of whom carry significant influence as QuANGOs – quasi-autonomous non-governmental organisations (for the sake of conciseness, only English bodies are listed):

- the British Waterways Board
- the Council for British Archaeology
- the Countryside Commission
- English Heritage (the Historic Buildings and Monuments Commission for England)
- English Nature
- the National Heritage Memorial Fund
- the Royal Commission on Environmental Pollution
- the Royal Commission on Historic Monuments in England
- the Rural Development Commission

Legally imposed measures for environmental protection are ineffective unless underpinned by public awareness and concern for the same issues. Much of the thinking behind the development of legislation came originally from pressure groups focused around particular issues, and these pressure groups continue to exist, monitoring the implementation of the legislation and developing wider public concern. Some of the voluntary bodies find a function for themselves as 'statutory consultees' with whom authorities taking decisions about the environment are required to consult.

In most of the legislative processes associated with environmental controls, there are rights of participation and appeal, which conservation pressure groups usually exercise in performance of their functions. These include a wide range of private-sector initiatives and voluntary societies, charities and trusts – often with members paying subscriptions, holding meetings and publishing literature. Again, for the sake of conciseness, only a few English bodies are listed as examples:

- the Ancient Monuments Society
- the Architectural Heritage Fund
- the Civic Trust
- the Commons, Open Spaces and Footpaths Preservation Society
- the Council for the Protection of Rural England
- the Friends of the Earth
- the Georgian Society
- the Historic Churches Preservation Trust
- the Historic Houses Association
- the National Trust

- the Redundant Churches Fund
- Rescue: the British Archaeological Trust
- the Royal Fine Art Commission
- SAVE (Save Britain's Heritage)
- the Society for the Preservation of Ancient Buildings
- the Twentieth Century Society
- the Victorian Society

Personal

Ultimately, it is as individuals that we contribute to the environment around us. In attempting to make our buildings more habitable and comfortable for ourselves, we have a fundamental choice, although we usually follow unthinkingly the precedents set within our own particular culture:

- We could incorporate 'active' systems and mechanisms within buildings specifically designed to produce particular kinds of comfort (requiring the consumption of fuels in order to provide power and energy).
- We could meet comfort (and health) requirements through 'passive' features of a building's construction – taking advantage of a site's aspect and location, and harnessing the energy flows freely available from the Sun, wind, water and even the Earth itself.

It has been the purpose of this chapter to demonstrate that we do have this choice – that the technology associated with the formation of our built environment needs to be harnessed to broader concerns for the quality of our surroundings. To a considerable extent, our industrialised culture encourages us to rely upon energy-intensive and polluting technologies to provide 'solutions' to our needs. Over the last quarter century in particular, we have been alarmed by many of the 'spillover' effects of industrialisation.

By joining pressure groups and lobbying for stricter legislation, and by taking direct action to protect the environment, people have raised a 'post-industrial' consciousness of 'green issues', and have succeeded in influencing government policy in consequence. Individuals acting alone may feel powerless, small groups protesting on their own may feel weak, but the fact is we are not alone. We are part of a whole – called society, humankind, the Earth. Everything we do has environmental consequences for everyone else. It is not impossible to bring change about – in fact, it is impossible not to cause change. We must therefore consider design for construction and the built environment carefully, as our technological choice begins here.

Self-assessment tasks

1. Identify the different kinds of environmental policy influencing activities in the built environment. Describe how individuals and organisations can play a part in influencing environmental policy.
2. Explain who is responsible for determining this policy, who is responsible for implementing it, and who is responsible for monitoring its effects. Explain why the word 'responsibility' is used so much in this context.

1.3 Structure and economic contribution of the construction and built environment sector

Construction finds its customers widely dispersed geographically and involved in nearly every other industry in the country, in private households, and in both private and public organisations. It is distinctive in that most of its products are custom-built to unique specifications. The number, physical scale and variety, and often complexity, of construction components, and their enormous **transportation** and **handling** requirements, all combine to give a distinctive character to the industry. It therefore involves a wide range of interesting kinds of work – located on site and in workshops and offices, using both sophisticated equipment and hand-tools, and requiring different levels of specialist knowledge and skills.

The topics covered in this section are:

- Job types and qualifications in construction
- Activities in the construction industry
- The economic significance of construction

Job types and qualifications in construction

Employers traditionally recruit candidates to the construction industry by first carefully defining the tasks to be performed, and then matching them against the **abilities** of candidates presenting themselves for the appointment. These abilities may be indicated in a variety of ways:

- **qualifications** – derived through specific training programmes or educational courses (such as the Vocational A-level in Construction and the Built Environment)
- **evidence** – contained in a portfolio (which needs to be tidily organised) of illustrated reports, technical drawings, photographs and annotated sketches
- **experience** – with written 'references' provided by previous employers or teachers, describing their impressions of the candidate's performance at work, and suitability for employment

According to the kind of qualification achieved, employees have traditionally remained 'stuck' in distinct roles within the construction industry:

- as **operatives** – involved in the physical formation of the built environment on site
- as **technicians** – communicating information about the construction of the built environment
- as **practitioners** – organising activities and leading decision-taking processes in the construction industry

Our employability would be severely limited if we could offer only manual labour, although demand for this kind of work is unlikely to disappear completely in the foreseeable future. As we progress in terms of skills and experience from hand-tools to sophisticated machinery, we improve the quality and speed of our output, so that we become more valuable to our firms and possibly better paid. We can only begin to speak of a 'career', however, in connection with the development of an ability to move – in accordance with our plans or wishes – into other sectors of activity. This development depends largely upon our

creation of opportunities to learn from our work experience.

We can no longer hope for life-long job security if our abilities remain narrowly tied to particular kinds of task, nor even if relevant only within the construction industry:

- The quality and speed of output is being increased more through the introduction of new **technology** than through the gradual improvement of craft, communication, or management skills.
- In order to survive large swings of **demand**, firms are now finding it necessary to become much more 'flexible' in the goods and services they offer their customers.
- With their staff **costs** continually rising, construction firms are employing fewer people, and are therefore being more careful in choosing new recruits.

As our technical knowledge grows in depth and breadth, and particularly as we begin to make greater use of **information technology**, we open up a wider range of employment possibilities for ourselves, enabling us to choose those which offer greater rewards in terms of pay, status and personal fulfilment. Job satisfaction is considerably enhanced if we feel we have the freedom to organise our time independently (often balanced by the assumption of increased responsibility for other people's work), or to select tasks that challenge our abilities and extend our usefulness still further.

The idea of a career must now be associated less with the development of industry-specific skills and knowledge (as the nature of technology is constantly changing), but more with a demonstration of the kinds of **personal** qualities that clients, colleagues and employers will always find relevant:

- the desire to learn, especially in relation to developments in information technology
- the ability to work in groups, especially in contributing original ideas for discussion
- communication, problem solving, and mathematical skills

These qualities all contribute to the overall **effectiveness** of the employee. It is effectiveness, rather than productivity, that enlightened employers now seek in their staff. This suggests removing the barriers between operative, technician and professional functions, so that the idea of a **career** may include a learning-based **progression** through all three 'levels' of activity.

Self-assessment tasks

1. Make a rough list of all the office-based jobs you would associate with the construction industry. Consider how you might group these roles and responsibilities under distinct headings.
2. Construct a diagram linking your proposed headings together in a way that illustrates the main interrelationships between them. Group together those who work as smaller 'teams' within the construction process.
3. Identify the order in which people with different jobs normally become involved in the construction process, and then when they become no longer involved. Which jobs appear to be the most significant?

Operatives

Operatives traditionally distinguish themselves as skilled and unskilled workers, employed either on construction sites or in workshops and factories (manufacturing materials and components):

- **craftspeople** have expertise (based upon years of practice) in specific **trade** areas related to the material or technical system in which they have developed skills
- **labourers** generally assist the crafts-based operatives by mixing and transporting components, materials and accessories as required, and by cleaning and clearing premises ready for occupation on completion

Traditional construction **crafts** include:

- **bricklayers** – bedding both bricks and concrete blocks in courses of mortar
- **carpenters** – working on site with timber components – making, cutting and fixing both structural and non-structural elements, permanent and temporary (called **formwork**), concealed and decorative
- **concretors and floor layers** – spreading ground slabs to the correct thickness and levelling floor screeds
- **demolition specialists** – taking down existing construction safely, retaining materials for salvage as required
- **joiners/woodworking machinists** – in workshops producing timber components such as doors, windows, staircases and panelling
- **painters and decorators** – preparing surfaces and applying paint, varnish, wallpaper, fabrics, or ceramic tiles, sometimes also glazing and sign-writing
- **plasterers** – mixing and applying gypsum plaster or cement rendering, achieving decorative effects (including on both plasterboard and expanded metal lath)
- **plumbers** – traditionally specialising in leadwork for roof coverings and pipes, but now working also with other metals and plastics, installing rainwater goods and flashings, boilers and heating systems, gas appliances, hot and cold water systems, and sanitaryware
- **slaters/tilers** – using their products both for roof coverings and for wall claddings
- **stonemasons** – with 'bankers' cutting and smoothing the stones, while 'fixers' erect them prepared
- **wall and floor tilers** – cutting and laying ceramic tiles of different kinds to particular patterns

On the basis of their development of distinct crafts skills, operatives may obtain 'occupational' qualifications such as National Vocational Qualifications (**NVQs**) – now replacing certificates such as those issued by the 'City and Guilds of London'. In the construction industry, NVQs are readily available in most of the skill areas listed. To obtain NVQs, operatives have to be observed performing specified items of work to carefully defined standards, in addition to being able to answer questions about the technical background to their activities.

The advent of technically sophisticated building components has drastically reduced the need for crafts-based operatives in the construction process (except for the repair of existing work). Where **suppliers** are required to take responsibility for the fixing of their own products, new kinds of **semi-skilled** operatives are emerging, specialising in the installation of particular manufacturers' systems:

- fencing and paving systems
- steeplejacks and scaffolding systems
- plant mechanics/operators
- steel erectors/fixers
- metalworkers and cladding/glazing systems
- foam cavity-fill and dry-lining systems
- suspended-ceiling and raised-flooring systems
- floor finishes and roof-covering systems (felt, asphalt, metal sheeting)
- shop-fitting and furniture systems
- heating and ventilating and air-conditioning (HVAC) systems
- electrical, communications and security systems

For these kinds of installations, the operatives require only a limited amount of training, usually related to health and safety procedures and often provided by the manufacturers anxious to maintain a good reputation for the performance of their products.

Technicians

Technicians undertake mental rather than physical work, applying knowledge and skills in the use of established techniques:

- to communicate clearly
- to calculate accurately
- to solve problems efficiently

Much of their activity is therefore located within offices – both on construction sites and away from them, and operating both in the private and public sectors.

On site, technicians may be employed to assist in the planning and monitoring of construction activity:

- **site surveying** – making and recording measurements of distance and height (related to a 'datum' level fixed with reference to a specific topographical feature on site or nearby)
- **programming** – working out and demonstrating how to complete construction operations as efficiently as possible in terms of the time, materials, people and plant available
- **safety planning** – assisting in the preparation of a plan specifically describing safety precautions and procedures to be followed during site operations
- **controlling quality** – inspecting and reporting on materials delivered and standards of workmanship in the completed construction
- **assessing progress** – measuring and reporting on the amount of construction work completed, often in relation to expectations (following **work study**) about amounts of work that might be reasonably expected and therefore determining the payment of a **bonus** for additional efforts made

Technicians may also be employed in the offices of public-sector **authorities** or private-sector **consultants** offering various kinds of advice to clients about the building work they want:

- **administrative work** – for local authorities in particular, checking applications for **planning permission** or **building regulations consent,** and inspecting sites to report on work required or completed
- **measurement** – working out the quantities of materials, components and equipment required for a construction project

- **estimating** – calculating the costs of a construction project, based upon its material and labour requirements
- **buying** – identifying the best prices for materials and plant hire, placing orders for them and checking the associated invoices
- **technical drawing** – working out and illustrating the layout and construction details of a building or engineering project
- **specification** – describing the standards of materials, workmanship or performance required in particular projects

Technician training involves the achievement of '**vocational**' qualifications such as Vocational A-levels (GNVQs) certificates and diplomas:

- at part-time First Certificate (FC) or full-time First Diploma (FD) level – usually involving a one-year course of study
- at part-time National Certificate (NC) or full-time National Diploma (ND) level – usually involving two years of study, with three **GCSEs** (grade C or higher) the normal admission requirement
- at part-time Higher National Certificate (HNC) level or full-time Higher National Diploma (HND) level – also involving two years of study, following completion either of the NC or ND programme, or (rarely) two or more successes at A-level or AS-level

GCSEs and A-levels usually involve written examinations which are set and marked by certain examination boards (**Edexcel** has taken over the former London Examination Board). Examinations in certificate and diploma courses, as in degree programmes, are set and assessed by the colleges who run them.

Programmes involving part-time study are supposed to be supplemented with knowledge and skills developed through experience in the workplace. Work at HND level is usually equivalent to the first year of a **degree** course, and is described as Higher Education (HE) rather than Further Education (FE). The various subjects studied on these kinds of programme are often packaged as 'modules' so that the award is gained when a suitable number of modules have been satisfactorily completed. In some colleges, the same modules form part of several HNC/HND and degree programmes.

A-levels and **AS-levels** are more usually regarded as the entry requirement for '**academic**' qualifications such as a Bachelor of Arts (BA) or Bachelor of Science (BSc) degree – sometimes awarded 'with Honours' (which are graded 1, a First; 2.1, an Upper Second; and 2.2, a Lower Second). Completion of a degree programme usually requires three years of full-time study, or four years of part-time study, undertaken at a university or polytechnic. A further 'post-graduate' programme of studies is the standard route for subsequent qualification as a professional **practitioner**, capable of carrying responsibility for decisions involving change in the built environment.

Practitioners

Practitioners act as the organisers and leaders of activity in the construction industry. Separate 'professions' have emerged in association with the disciplines and values that underpin their distinctive approaches:

- **planning** – coordinating land-use in order to provide a sustainable balance between built and natural environments
- **surveying** – applying physical and financial measurement in order to understand, plan and monitor activity in both the urban and the rural environment
- **architecture** – designing built environments that integrate technical soundness, functional efficiency and attractive appearance
- **engineering** – taking technological design decisions in accordance with calculated scientific principles
- **management** – planning and controlling activities in order to ensure that organisational objectives are met

The development process is too complex to have all aspects of its planning and design, and its production and maintenance handled entirely by any single profession. Practitioners therefore work in **teams** as 'consultants' to a team leader. It is traditionally the **architect** who acts as team leader, reflecting the client's concern that design considerations should form the basis of decisions.

In identifying **practitioners** as '**professionals**', we indicate recognition that they possess specialist knowledge and skills which they have undertaken to exercise in the best interest of the public. Because the built environment is such a significant investment for most people, they need to be reassured that they are being given good, unbiased advice. Professionals claim to give such advice – not taking commercial advantage of their clients' relative ignorance about construction. Two features are therefore common to professional practitioners:

- **competence** – a background of proper training, demonstrated by having passed certain **tests** (usually written examinations and interviews) before qualifying for admission as a member of a professional **institution**, and then by maintaining a programme of **Continuing Professional Development (CPD)** in order to keep up-to-date in terms of knowledge and skills
- **ethics** – characteristics of good behaviour and honesty, based upon promises to abide by the **code of conduct** laid down by the institution

What distinguishes professional from commercial activities is said to lie in the **attitude** with which tasks are approached. Professionals are expected to take decisions and to give advice that best matches their client's needs (while respecting the interests of the community), rather than operating in ways that merely benefit themselves.

By joining a **professional institution**, practitioners enable themselves to maintain contact with colleagues engaged in similar work elsewhere. The usual channel of communication is a regularly published journal, supplemented by meetings and activities organised by local branches of the institution. In order to give their members higher status (enabling them to command higher fees from their clients), admission to a professional institution is often made difficult and expensive. Most institutions set and assess their own examination papers for entrants studying on a part-time basis, including final 'Professional Practice' examinations and interviews that test candidates' practical ability and judgement.

Some institutions carry the prefix 'royal' in their name, indicating the monarchy's recognition of their value and importance to society, and entitling their members to call themselves 'chartered' practitioners. Practitioners may also seek to indicate their competence and values to the public by attaching after their name the initials of the professional Institute to which they have been elected:

- RTPI – the Royal Town Planning Institute
- RICS – the Royal Institution of Chartered Surveyors
- RIBA – the Royal Institute of British Architects
- ICE – the Institution of Civil Engineers
- CIOB – the Chartered Institute of Building
- BIFM – the British Institute of Facilities Management

In order to understand the kinds of activities associated with each of these professions, usually undertaken in offices in which technicians work alongside practitioners, we must consider how the role played by each 'sector' of the industry within the development process.

Activities in the construction industry

The built environment requires continuous renewal as people's requirements change and grow and as infrastructure and buildings themselves wear out and decay. Development activities undertaken to renew the built environment may be understood as a sequence of operations carried out by different specialists, overlapping with one another in terms of function in order to ensure continuity:

- **planning** – determining patterns of development in both urban and rural areas, and assessing the suitability of particular sites for particular forms of development
- **designing** – working out ways of organising sites and buildings in conjunction with one another, so that they meet their owners' requirements effectively and inoffensively
- **constructing** – purchasing materials, components and equipment, and assembling them on site within specified constraints of time and money, and all in accordance with design proposals and contract conditions
- **maintaining** – looking after completed projects, in order to ensure that they continue to serve their purpose efficiently, adapting them or changing their use when necessary

By performing each of these functions with an understanding of its relationship to others in the sequence, we enable ourselves to develop environments that properly integrate natural and social processes. With the increasing complexity of the construction industry, a number of subsidiary professions (each with its own specialist organisations) have developed around these main disciplines.

Self-assessment tasks

1. List the different kinds of knowledge and skills required for careers in the construction industry. Give **six** examples of typical activities undertaken by
   (a) operatives
   (b) technicians
   (c) professionals
   and identify the features common to each category of activity.
2. Explain why the distinction between operatives, technicians and professionals in the construction industry is gradually becoming less significant.

Planning

Before the design details of a development project are worked out, it is essential to explore its likely impact both upon the natural environment and upon the lives of everyone living in the surrounding built environment – especially in such a densely inhabited country as Britain. For this reason, we have established a **town and country planning** system – a democratic process through which the local community participates in the decision about whether or not to permit particular forms of 'development' (a word which therefore has a carefully defined meaning within the associated parliamentary legislation).

Professional **planners** are therefore appointed to frame and lead discussions about the long-term interests of the community, covering all aspects of the environmental and social impact of development. This requires a great breadth of understanding, coupled with an ability to listen sensitively and to communicate clearly. Planners tend to come from an 'arts' background – with interests in geography, environmental science, urban design, sociology, law, politics and economics. The 'plans' they propose usually take the form of generalised statements of land use policy, rather than precisely detailed maps or layouts.

Any plans for the future, even if indicative only, need to be rooted in the existing situation and evidence of current development trends, such as **population growth and movement**. Plans are therefore based upon various kinds of survey, designed to produce factual information about the present circumstances. Planners therefore work in close cooperation with **surveyors**, who specialise in gathering and interpreting measurable data – both physical dimensions and the business and financial implications of alternative forms of development.

Planners and **planning** surveyors work either in the **private sector** (within practices offering services to developers or aggrieved members of the public, or within specific departments of large commercial organisations), or in the **public sector**, where decisions taken as part of the **development control** process are linked to the formulation and adoption of **planning policies** for different areas of the country.

Planning involves a wide variety of **research** exercises, many of which require the assistance of **technicians**. The more that is known and understood about the present circumstances of an area, it is said, the more relevant will be any plans for its future. Before developing it, therefore, we need to understand the area from as many different kinds of evidence as can be gathered within the constraints of time and funding available:

- physical evidence such as existing buildings, maps, and written records
- verbal evidence such as people's stories and opinions
- observation and measurement of different forms of activity pattern along particular routes (for example, counting pedestrians, timing traffic of different kinds, measuring noise or light levels)

The survey of an area, and an analysis of its findings, forms the basis of the **development brief** for a site, suggesting appropriate kinds of environment to be constructed and its layout in relationship to landscaping and infrastructure. This sort of activity is often termed **master planning**, and is usually led by professional **surveyors** or **planners**. Technicians assisting them become involved in gathering and sorting out survey data, and in preparing maps and diagrams to illustrate the context of land use proposals. The **Society of Surveying**

Technicians (SST) exists to support and to represent the interests of these technicians.

The **Royal Institution of Chartered Surveyors (RICS)** has combined the various disciplines of its members under the umbrella of a single organisation with seven distinct 'divisions':

- **planning and development surveyors** – advising developers on property strategy, negotiating with local authorities in respect of planning applications, preparing design briefs, and marketing completed projects
- **land and hydrographic surveyors** – measuring the earth's surface, both over land and under water surfaces, and presenting the information in the form of maps and profiles
- **minerals surveyors** – handling quarrying and associated land management issues
- **rural practice surveyors** – advising farmers and landowners on the management, development, marketing and valuation of property, including livestock
- **general practice surveyors** – specialising in residential and commercial property valuation and management (extending even to the contents of buildings, such as works of art, furniture and machinery), and negotiating sales, leases and purchases
- **building surveyors** – advising owners on the economic, technical, and functional aspects of their buildings, and on their cost-effective maintenance
- **quantity surveyors** – providing expert guidance on the costing and financial management of buildings, of civil engineering projects and even of heavy industry investments

Design

The process of designing buildings and their surroundings involves the integration of a wide variety of considerations about the future:

- **durability** – the soundness of a building's construction, based upon the performance of its fabric in changing conditions of loading, temperature, and humidity, both externally and internally
- **usefulness** – the convenience of a building's internal and external layout in relation to the purposes for which it is to be used, changing over time
- **attractiveness** – the continuing pleasure given by a building to people in and around it

For the design of a built environment to be judged 'successful', it must take account of technical principles, functional requirements and human values all at the same time. If any one of these dimensions of the task is neglected, the built environment fails to provide the full range of benefits demanded by society.

Speculative developers motivated by a desire for financial **profitability**, and **engineers** interested mainly in technical **efficiency**, usually regard design simply as a matter of producing plans, sections and elevations of development proposals, supplemented with the technological information required for their construction. Building **surveyors** and **technologists** are often highly competent in meeting such requirements, combining their technical knowledge of construction with skills in drawing and rational thinking – enabling them to demonstrate that the accommodation provided in their buildings corresponds to specific functional requirements. Disregard for the human dimension, however (embracing people's history and culture, for example), invariably results in the kind of built environment that most of us find alienating, hostile and psychologically uncomfortable.

The activity of designing a built environment needs to involve as broad a range of considerations as possible. Where we judge the resulting construction to have succeeded in reconciling the different constraints affecting its design, so that its whole seems 'greater than the sum of its individual parts', we describe it as '**Architecture**' in order to distinguish it from 'mere building'. The 'added value' that characterises Architecture is said to lie in its conscious attempt to contribute to the development of people's aesthetic, social and cultural awareness, in addition to providing them with a technically efficient and functionally appropriate built environment. Only **architects** are specifically trained to incorporate these kinds of consideration into their work, and only a few of them succeed in meeting such lofty objectives.

Through a long programme of studio-based activity, architects are nevertheless taught to approach the design task as a distinctive kind of intellectual activity – combining technical knowledge with artistic skills, and quite different as a decision-taking process. The key to this difference is a focus on the generation of ideas rather than on a logical analysis of constraints (which is how engineers generally work). As their designs vary according to the ideas being integrated, it is only through suggesting 'solutions' that architects begin to understand the nature of their problems. This approach makes design an open-ended artistic endeavour rather than a methodical scientific activity, which is difficult to encompass within a business operation.

Architectural design is therefore not a purely logical process of working out an optimal response to a brief, but is usually presented to clients as a series of 'Work Stages' in order to identify points at which payment should be made. In practice, design is a cyclical process, involving the testing and refinement of **models** of proposed environments, using different media for communication:

- sketches and drawings
- three-dimensional mock-ups in various materials and sizes
- mathematical calculations
- verbal presentations

Modelling represents the way designers search for answers, progressing from the rough to the sophisticated and gradually narrowing the scope of their trial and error experimentation. By working from 'soft' or vague possibilities towards 'hard' actual products, architects enable themselves to enrich their work with layer upon layer of interest, so that it will continue to give pleasure to the community long after the original clients have finished using the premises in the way originally intended.

As the design process involves the integration of numerous ideas, principles and constraints (scientific, artistic and managerial), designers need above all to be able to communicate effectively with other practitioners offering particular skills and knowledge. They also need access to a vast range of information sources – usually taking advantage of **Information Technology** systems to identify up-to-date data with a minimum of delay. As each design project has its own resource and information requirements, architects commonly organise their consultants as **design teams**, in which each member is required to coordinate his own professional contributions with the overall project objectives.

The **Architects and Surveyors Institute** (ASI) has been established as an organisation dedicated to the encouragement of closer cooperation between the numerous professions associated with the built environment.

The **design team** for a typical low-rise development project might consist of about half a dozen practitioners from other professions, acting as consultants to the architect (best suited to lead and coordinate the team's activities, being the only practitioner whose whole formal training is centred around the activity of designing):

- **architectural technologists** or **building engineers** (to advise on the buildability and performance of different methods of construction, and to assist in communicating project information accurately)
- **structural engineers** (to advise on appropriate dimensions and locations of load-bearing elements in the construction)
- **quantity surveyors** (to advise on building costs, related to the selection of components and amounts of material required for construction)
- **building services engineers** (to advise on appropriate systems for heating and ventilation, the electrical and gas installations, plumbing and drainage, communications, security, fire detection etc.)

Others drawn into the team may include other **surveyors** (to provide information about the site), **facilities managers** (to represent the clients' interests more directly), or even the **builders** if it is known in advance who will be awarded the contract for construction. Local authority **planning officers** and **building control officers** may also be drawn into team discussions when negotiations are required for statutory permissions.

Technicians are commonly required as assistants to all members of the design team, and are therefore located in most kinds of practitioners' offices:

- helping to ensure that all the appropriate information passes quickly and accurately both between design team members and to other parties who become involved in the design process
- working on drawings showing proposed construction details, or on schedules providing other technical information

With experience, architects' technicians may develop skills as professional **architectural technologists**, with the ability to work out construction details and to prepare written specifications describing standards of materials and workmanship, or defining performance requirements for building components, services and equipment. Since 1994, the **British Institute of Architectural Technologists** (BIAT) has identified a separate role for professionals engaged in turning architectural vision into buildable reality – as if located midway between architects and builders.

Where specialist design work is required, consultants may also be appointed from other design-based professions. **Urban design**, concerned with large-scale development projects demanding the integration of infrastructure and buildings, has emerged similarly as a distinct profession located midway between architecture and town planning. For the planning both of 'green-field' sites and of the spaces around buildings, the equivalent profession is **landscape architecture** – in greater demand as increasing importance is attached to environmental considerations in the design process. For the internal colours and textures of buildings, including the choice of fabrics, furniture and fittings, architects often delegate decision taking to specialist **interior design** consultants.

In Britain, the **Engineering Council** exists to provide a degree of compatibility between the numerous divisions that have emerged within the general discipline of engineering. In general, 'consulting engineers' may be called upon to carry out feasibility studies, project design and contract administration. Larger construction projects are more likely to be led by **civil engineers** than architects, as they specialise in larger projects involving substantial earth-moving and water-retention:

- all forms of **infrastructure** – including roads, railways, canals, docks, tunnels, bridges, dams and offshore installations
- **tall** ('high-rise') **buildings**, wide-span buildings, deep basements, and other deep excavations

In addition to the **Institution of Civil Engineers** (ICE) and the **Institution of Civil Engineering Surveyors** (ICES) – for land and quantity surveying associated with civil engineering projects, a number of other specialist institutes and associations are affiliated to the Engineering Council:

- The **Institution of Highway Incorporated Engineers** (IHIE) – supporting professionals and technicians involved in highway design and in traffic and transportation planning.
- The **Chartered Institution of Building Services Engineers** (CIBSE) – covering the design, manufacture and installation of systems for heating and ventilation, air-conditioning, lighting, electricity, fire safety, lifts and escalators, and communications.
- The **Institution of Structural Engineers** (IStructE) – for engineers specialising in the design and analysis of load-bearing structures of all kinds.
- The **Association of Building Engineers** (ABE) – a general term for professionals specialising in building technology and management, introduced in 1992 for the sake of compatibility with other countries in the European Union.

Construction

The production of a built environment requires the coordination of a wide range of resources:

- appropriately timed deliveries of materials and components, and planned space in which to store or move them
- supplies of the right kinds of skilled and unskilled labour, at the times when required on site
- availability of the appropriate tools and equipment, together with the relevant power and water supplies
- sufficient flows of money to pay for all the above when requested
- managerial enterprise to win profitable projects and to organise them efficiently

Only for very small-scale construction projects is it possible for one person to perform all these functions, with distinct advantages in terms of clarity of communications (providing the builder is careful to maintain a notebook). More usually, building work requires contributions from a number of parties, with the consequence that the primary objective of many activities within the construction process is to ensure that smooth, rapid, and accurate communications are maintained. For this reason, there is a persistently strong demand for well-organised **technicians** in the construction industry.

The first requirement of a 'standard' one-off construction project is to **estimate** the cost of the resources required, based on **production information** provided by the **designers** on behalf of their client:

- location, assembly and component **drawings** and schedules (lists of items of a similar nature)
- written **specifications** of standards of materials and workmanship or of the performance of components
- summaries of the resources required provided in **Bills of Quantities**
- descriptions of the terms and conditions under which they will be required to work, to be described in a formal **Contract**

In competition with others, the builders accordingly submit a price for the work, known as the **tender**, and the successful firm is invited to sign a **contract** with the client for the building. At this point in the **procurement** process, the builders become **main contractors** and are legally obliged to complete the building by a defined date in accordance with the information provided in what become designated as the **contract documents**. In return, the client is legally obliged to pay in accordance with certified **valuations** of work completed, within the overall framework of a defined **contract sum**.

Because of their intimate links with the activities of operatives, most **small building contractors** and many **subcontractors** work almost independently of one another, often attached only to organisations that enable them (in return for payment of a subscription) to indicate 'guaranteed' standards of craftsmanship. They are sometimes assisted by trainees or labourers, though these – historically – have often been self-employed also. Sometimes, there is no 'office' beyond the home of one individual, equipped with a desk, a calculator and possibly a filing cabinet. Communications are maintained through the use of mobile telephones and answerphones, but paperwork is usually poorly managed.

As the firm grows, the administrative part of the business usually expands first as additional staff are employed to handle the required office-work. Functions relating to the construction process are then split up as specialisms are developed within the organisation:

- On the **procurement** side (based in the contractor's office), **project planners** decide on the method and sequence of construction operations while **buyers** order the materials and plant required. Contractors also employ their own **quantity surveyors** to provide cost control throughout the project.
- On the **production** side (based on site), **site engineers** are employed first to set out the exact location for the works, and then – throughout the progress of the building or engineering operations – to ensure they proceed in accordance with the design information.

We may define 'large' building contractors as those who are able to have several different projects running at the same time. Separate groups of staff operate out of a head office (possibly located many miles from the nearest construction site), undertaking activities relating to the firm's principal business functions:

- procurement
- marketing management
- personnel management
- financial management

At the core of the large organisation (Fig. 1.28), the **managing director** is under constant pressure from the firm's owners or

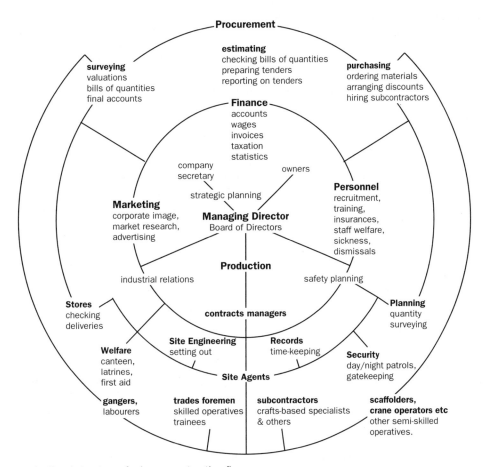

Figure 1.28 The organisational structure of a large construction firm

shareholders to produce returns upon the money they have invested in it. Large contractors therefore seek recruits who will enjoy the 'cut and thrust' of a competitive atmosphere, who are prepared to move with the work, and who are ambitious for high responsibility. Ultimately, in order to retain their key staff, it becomes necessary for large contractors to reward their high performers with some share in the ownership of the firm.

Each site has a production organisation of its own, coordinated by a **contracts manager** (who may be responsible for several sites at once) and supervised on a daily basis by a **site agent** (traditionally called the 'general foreman', but now also known as 'site manager'). The production operations coordinated by the **site agent** may involve several distinct groups of workers:

- skilled and semi-skilled **operatives** – tradespeople employed by the main contractor, working in groups under separate '**trades foremen**'
- **domestic subcontractors** – operatives hired rather than employed by the main contractor to provide specific services, including plant operators
- **nominated subcontractors** – operatives appointed by the client to work in conjunction with the main contractor
- **labourers** – employed by the main contractor, working in groups (called 'gangs') under separate 'gangers'

The site agent is also responsible for coordinating deliveries, welfare facilities, time-keeping, and security.

Building contractors have traditionally organised themselves to provide all the functions associated with construction activity, with the consequence that their firms have grown into vast organisations, making them extremely difficult to manage. In order to simplify their structure (in the interests of improved communications), many construction firms have – until new tax legislation introduced in 1997 – sought to replace their outer layers of **operatives** by increasing the numbers of self-employed labourers and **subcontractors** they engage.

The effect of this kind of 'downsizing' has been to narrow the work of main contractors to a **project management** function. The **Association of Project Managers** (APM) acts as the professional institution for practitioners specialising in this kind of work. Some building firms now consist simply of a core of professional managers, and exist by hiring plant and workers for specific tasks, 'contracting out' most of their surveying and technician functions. The role of the project manager consists largely of planning, monitoring and (as necessary) replanning operations on site within the contractual constraints of time and money.

Both contractors and project managers require **technicians** to assist them:

- by preparing programmes and reports on progress
- by establishing, calculating and summarising costs
- by requesting and coordinating the distribution of up-to-date information

Numeracy and communications skills, linked through the extensive use of information technology, are therefore essential for the technician's function. Being more closely linked to managers than to construction operatives, technicians are increasingly compelled to work as if they too are 'professionals', taking responsibility for their own quality and productivity.

The **Chartered Institute of Building** (CIOB) has defined four distinct 'functions' for candidates seeking membership through its final 'professional studies' examinations:

- **facilities management** – with a strong bias towards building maintenance and property strategy
- **commercial management** – related to the operation of a building firm as a business
- **project management** – concerned with the planning and implementation of specific construction programmes
- **construction management** – covering the control and coordination of production activities on site

Management

Having planned, designed and constructed a building, it needs to be looked after in order to remain useful and to hold its market value. This function is traditionally performed by a **building manager**, who may be charged with responsibility for supervising the work of **operatives** such as cleaners, caretakers, car-park attendants, or boiler-room engineers. In many situations, all these roles (including the management of them) are performed by a single person – usually a craftsperson or labourer formerly employed in the construction industry.

The care of a completed building is primarily in the hands of its **cleaners**, who come into closer, regular contact with the wear and tear on its surfaces than any other occupants. The cleaners' role is often overlooked, being a low-status unskilled manual job, usually performed during unsociable hours, and only becoming noticeable when not performed. Building managers often entrust their cleaners with responsibility for reporting minor defects as soon as they appear, in order that they can be dealt with before growing into significant problems. It is usually more economical to take numerous preventive actions than to wait until larger **repairs** are required.

In situations where a building or item of infrastructure is surrounded by extensive landscaping, the supervision of maintenance staff may be entrusted to someone with the title **estate manager**. This is commonly someone who has followed a 'career path' from labourer to gardener (sometimes called 'groundsman') to head gardener – all on the same site. With the constant pressure to make landscaping steadily less labour-intensive, through the introduction of native planting regimes (that require less maintenance) and of more sophisticated machinery, the number of staff employed in maintaining the grounds of a property is constantly being reduced. For this reason, the 'rise' of estate operatives to positions of apparent managerial responsibility sometimes consists of little more than a change of title.

Where the 'estate' consists of a number of properties (sometimes spread over several sites), its owners may employ an estate manager with professional qualifications (typically, membership of **RICS**) to look after them. This arrangement is commonly found in a variety of organisations:

- central and local government departments and statutory undertakings
- major landlords, housing associations and privatised infrastructure operators
- hotel, shop or restaurant chains
- hospitals, schools, colleges and military establishments

Each building may have its own building manager, who reports to and takes instructions from the estate manager, whose office may therefore include **technician** and secretarial staff. This kind of estate manager is likely to be responsible for **property strategy** – ensuring that the organisation's staff occupy premises which are appropriate for them in terms of location, size, design and environmental standards, and costs.

As the organisation changes, so its property needs change. The **estate manager** therefore needs to work closely with the organisation's other managers in planning for this change, which may result in construction activities being commissioned (in which case the estate manager may become involved in preparing a **brief** for the design work required). Some of the most critical decisions concerning a building's use relate to the choice between adaptation (possibly involving an extension), or – in extreme cases – demolition and the commissioning of new premises or occupation of an alternative existing property (possibly involving its conversion from a different use).

The new profession of **facilities management** is based upon a similarly expanded view of the kind of after-care service that building contractors are increasingly offering their clients (especially since the recession of the early 1990s, when little new construction work was available). Traditionally, after a building or structure was completed, the planners, designers and builders lost all involvement with the project except for the **making good of defects** or (sometimes) alterations and adaptations. The **British Institute of Facilities Management** (BIFM) is now promoting the idea of locating the management of buildings and infrastructure alongside all the other 'support' activities required in conjunction with a business or industry.

In many company budgets, premises costs have been found to lie second only to staff costs. Facilities managers argue that the running and maintenance of people's work environments needs to be coordinated and monitored as a single, major function. The **facilities manager** is required to take integrated responsibility for all the activities that do not form part of an organisation's 'core business':

- negotiating the terms of building and property contracts
- maintaining buildings, services and equipment (including the communications and IT systems)
- planning the use of space and the movement of people, furniture and equipment
- organising the provision of services such as catering, security, cleaning, reprographics, stationery supplies and vehicles

Most of these functions (including the facilities management operation itself) may be 'outsourced' or 'contracted out' (that is, performed by suppliers and subcontractors from outside the organisation). The facilities manager is therefore involved mostly in setting performance standards, negotiating their inclusion in contracts, and monitoring the work of contractors accordingly.

Building managers and facilities managers rarely require the assistance of **technicians** as – if their premises are large and complex – they can install computerised monitoring devices to detect anomalies in the building's performance:

- building management systems (BMS) can detect doors or windows left open or unlocked, and lights or other equipment left on, and even occupancy
- energy management systems (EMS) can chart the consumption of fuel and power, room temperatures and humidity levels, and ventilation rates

Buildings with these kinds of equipment installed (alongside the conventional fire-detection and security systems) are often described as 'intelligent buildings', and are increasingly demanded for highly serviced premises such as offices, hotels, hospitals, theatres, computing centres and – increasingly – people's own homes.

The development of **facilities management** as a profession has demonstrated to the construction industry how its activities need to be integrated seamlessly with its clients' values and objectives. Rather than being identified as work done 'for' people, construction projects may come gradually to be understood as work done 'with' people. This will not only ensure continuity of work opportunities, but may help bring about a long-overdue change of image for the industry. Above all, the construction industry has become aware that it is not a self-contained, self-serving activity, but is undertaken in a larger economic context.

The economic significance of construction

One of the best ways of understanding the wider context in which construction activities are performed is to consider their economic significance. Economics is concerned with how we make the best use of resources (all of which are in limited supply):

- **land** – everything provided in the natural environment, including both the ground on which we build and all the **materials** available over and under it
- **labour** – not only people's physical skills and strength, but also their knowledge and their capacity for ideas
- **capital** – products which are not directly consumed but which are available for creating further products and for use in the future (for example – tools, machinery, factories and money itself)

These resources make **production** possible, although **capital** is special in that it can itself be created through production processes.

Buildings and infrastructure may therefore be identified as a fixed part of the **capital** in which we have invested – as individuals, communities and whole countries. We have devoted time, energy and imagination (bought with considerable sums of money) into the construction of a built environment which now serves us both collectively and individually:

- making it easier for ourselves to move from one place to another
- providing ourselves with more comfortable living conditions
- enabling us to spend further time, energy and imagination on enriching our lives in other ways

The use of **money** allows us to exchange our resources more freely. We sell our labour (or other people's) in return for income, and produce goods and services for each other to buy with their income. Economic activity may be understood as a continuous flow of goods and services, which produces a counter-flow of money (described by economists as the **circular flow of income** – Fig. 1.29). If an economy was as simple as this, with no other factors interrupting the flow, total income would be exactly matched by total expenditure, which would also be the same as the value of total production. A country's **national accounts** therefore measure its level of economic activity in three separate ways (which should result in similar final values):

gross domestic income = gross domestic expenditure
= **gross domestic product** (GDP)

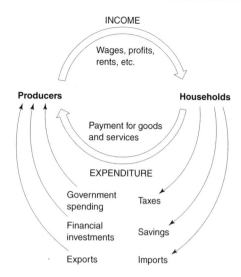

Figure 1.29 The circular flow of income

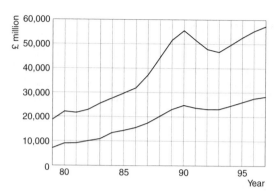

Figure 1.31 The contribution of repair and maintenance within the output of Britain's construction industry. (*Source*: Office for National Statistics)

The term 'domestic' is used to indicate that the total (or 'gross') comprises the value of all the goods and services produced within a country, but excludes net income from abroad. If property income from abroad is included, the figures are described as **gross 'national' product** (GNP). Statistical data describing levels of economic activity in these kinds of terms are readily available through the government's Central Statistical Office (CSO). The statistics for particular parts of a country are usually available through local planning authorities or Chambers of Commerce, while data relating to the wider European context are published by Eurostat – the Statistical Office of the European Communities (based in Luxembourg). Within the statistics, we may observe how economic activities have varied – from one place to another, over different points in time, and within distinct 'sectors' of activity.

The construction industry represents about 6% of the value of all productive activity in the United Kingdom, and contributes over three times as much as agriculture, forestry and fishing to Britain's **gross domestic product** (GDP). The total output of the industry in 1991, for example, was £43 709m (Fig. 1.30), although this figure does not include:

- the extraction of the vast quantities of raw materials required for building

- the production by other manufacturing industries of all products and components used in construction
- the costs of advertising and transporting these materials to their different destinations throughout the land (and abroad)
- the fees of the different kinds of professional and technical consultant involved in taking decisions about what should be built where, and how

Residential construction represents over one-third of Britain's construction output, and is particularly sensitive to changes in government policy. On the grounds that people like to live together and share facilities, **households** are counted as basic economic units, and in the twentieth century the government began to identify the provision of an adequate amount of accommodation for them as one of its functions. With social expectations of ever-improving standards of living however, and a constantly rising number of households, there is a permanent shortage in relation to demand.

Measured in terms of output value, the **repair and maintenance** of the country's stock of existing buildings is the largest sector of activity in the whole construction industry. In Britain, this type of work has increased in proportion to the industry's total workload from about 25% in the 1950s to nearly 50% through the 1980s (Fig. 1.31). The figures are almost certainly an underestimate, as much of the work is undertaken by small-time jobbing builders from whom data about earnings are unreliable, while the activities of **do-it-yourself** occupiers are excluded from the industry statistics altogether.

About 1.5m people are directly employed in construction, with perhaps a further 0.7m self-employed. In total, this represents about 8% of the total employed labour force, indicating – when compared with the 6% contribution to gross domestic product described above – that construction remains a relatively 'labour-intensive' industry.

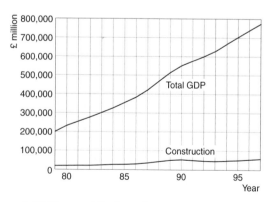

Figure 1.30 The contribution of construction within Britain's GDP. (*Source*: Office for National Statistics)

Self-assessment tasks

1. Visit a major city and identify the sites where major construction activities are being undertaken. Identify the firms involved and the kinds of building they are constructing (described in terms of structure, function and appearance).
2. Identify any common features of these projects that help explain why they are being constructed in these locations, by these firms, in these ways, and at this time.

Design for Construction and the Built Environment

Keith Roberts

The role of the designer and the contribution of the design team are vital to the success of built environment projects. This unit explores the framework of design, from inception to the production drawings. Effective drawing methods communicate the design intention to the builder and the results of the project are available for all to see: success or failure. The result is the final assessment of the design team's skills and innovations.

The key areas covered by this unit are:

- Spatial organisation of the built environment
- Development and appraisal of design brief solutions
- Drawing techniques for communicating design and technical solutions
- Evaluation of design solutions

After reading this unit you will be able to:

- describe types of space utilisation in the built environment
- recognise and describe elements of a design specification
- explain the needs of different construction clients
- describe key features of the design specification
- recognise and describe design constraints and their impact on the cost and buildability of the project

- describe information to be communicated for construction projects and methods for communicating that information
- identify recommended conventions and symbols which help the communication of information on drawings
- describe the use of information on drawings and schedules
- describe applications of computer aided design (CAD) within the construction industry
- identify the function of the main hardware components of a CAD system
- identify key design features of a completed design and describe the main aspects of legislation which apply
- assess the impact of key construction constraints on a completed design
- identify design and performance standards
- assess completed designs against elements of the client's design specification

There is ample opportunity to use evidence gathered from other units to indicate mastery of skills and knowledge in this unit. For example, Unit 1 (development of settlements), Unit 3 (the science of human comfort; production and supply of electricity; water supply), and Unit 4 (performance of building structure), can be usefully deployed in this unit.

2.1 Spatial organisation of the built environment

Topics covered in this section are:

- Types of space in the built environment
- Recording space utilisation
- Design guides on space allocation

Types of space in the built environment

Space is often used to describe land. This is a narrow definition but we will use this to illustrate the types of space required in a building. Land is a resource and is expensive, so we must maximise the use of land. That causes problems since the use of buildings may change:

- The building owner may require a different function to be performed within the building.
- New technologies may make the building redundant.
- Social pressure groups may restrict the use of land or legislation may create new demands on the building owner.

All this will affect the use of space within the built environment. To meet these new demands within the existing built environment will call for creativity and flair, but that is all part of the designer's role, whether the designer is an architect, town planner or building services engineer. There will be design constraints to work within as the building user becomes more sophisticated.

Just think of the requirement for electrical appliances. Over the years people have acquired more electrical appliances. Some very misguided people have used adaptors to allow the use of several appliances from one power point. Why endanger life just because the designer did not include sufficient power points?

In most towns and cities there is insufficient off-street parking for residents. Why? Because the developer did not foresee the rise in car ownership.

Shrewd businesspeople purchased prime agricultural land to meet the housing demand on the outskirts of towns. People moved away from the city centres to pleasant residential areas. Inner cities decayed; commuters demanded better roads. Residential front gardens were compulsorily purchased by the local authority for road-widening schemes.

Industrial decline left large areas of land polluted and unfit for development until land prices forced house builders to look at these **brownfield sites**. The extra cost of cleaning up these brownfield sites was borne by the house purchaser, who was balancing the cost of commuting with living and working in the city centre.

Over several decades the size of speculative houses has been reduced to maximise company profits. Garden areas have been reduced to a minimum with little open spaces between houses. The quality of life has been reduced due to different demands on the designers. Large housing developments in the 1960s won architectural awards, only later to become out of fashion and demolished to allow **low-density housing** with open spaces. Now can you see why we have to analyse the use of space within the built environment?

Space can be analysed into different categories according to its function. Take, for example, the building development shown in Fig. 2.1.

The **block plan** records several different uses of space. The natural environment determines to some extent the use of land. For example, the river will become a feature of the development. Views out of the windows will be a selling point, especially if the area has outstanding natural beauty. Some of the space or land has been used for the infrastructure, that is the road network. The volume of traffic and the economic value of the road will determine the road width. Take a closer look at the proposed site (Fig. 2.2).

The developer has to obtain planning permission from the local planning authority. The role of the local planning authority is discussed in more detail in Unit 5. Central government demand that the local authority, called a unitary authority, produce a development plan for their area. The **unitary development plan** was called the **structure plan**. The developer's business acumen suggests that three houses could be a profitable activity.

- How big will each house be?
- How much garden and open space will be required?
- Will the location of each plot have kerb appeal?
- Who will be the prospective purchasers?
- What will be the size of the families?
- What will be the selling price for each house?

Most of the answers to those questions will be assumptions, involving an element of risk which the developer must take. Go back to Fig. 2.2 and look at the **road access** to plot 2 and the third house. This road cost will be shared by two **house**

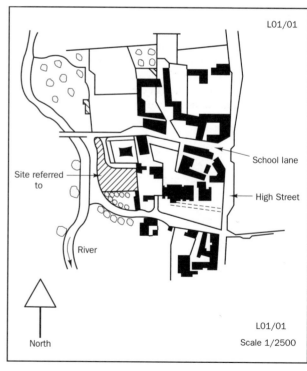

Figure 2.1 Block plan

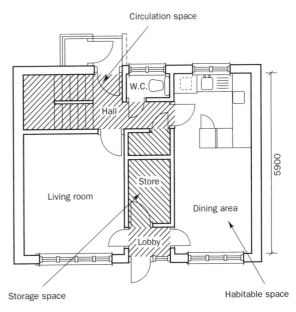

Figure 2.4 Floor plan showing residential space

- kitchen and dining room for eating
- living room for leisure activities, possibly with some occasional eating
- WC or toilet for personal needs
- hall and stair as circulation space

The main question: How much room or space is required for each different activity?

There are several design guides available which suggest acceptable **spatial requirements** for different functions. The **National House Building Council** publish the *NHBC Standards The Home – Its Accommodation & Services*. One of its rules states that the minimum size of a single bedroom should be at least 4.5 square metres. The **Chartered Institute Building Services** also publish design guides on the location of building services. Even legislation stipulates the minimum area allowed in an office as 4.5 square metres per person. These guides are only a minimum but are a useful starting point for spatial analysis and building design.

To analyse the **space utilisation** we need to define the space usage and consistently measure similar building types. The larger the sample analysed the more accurate the results will be. The type of space in residential developments can be categorised (as shown in Fig. 2.4):

- habitable space
- circulation space
- storage space

To be of value in design the different types of space need to be quantified.

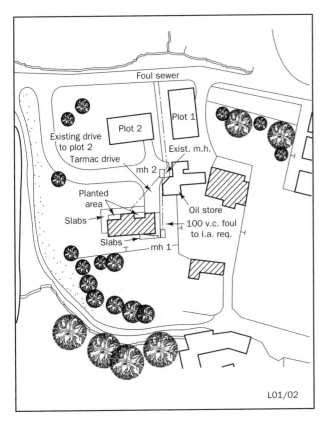

Figure 2.2 Site plan

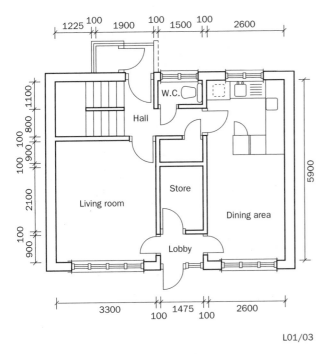

Figure 2.3 Floor plan showing layout of rooms

buyers, whereas plot 1 must pay for that single road access. But all three house buyers will share the cost of the foul drainage.

Now you have some idea about the use of external space. This type of space is called **locality**. The space utilisation is often determined by local and central government, but the internal space utilisation is often determined by the developer.

The ground floor plan (Fig. 2.3) shows several types of space usage:

Recording space utilisation

An **accommodation schedule** (Fig. 2.5) is one method of recording room size and type.

If we are to analyse data we must have in mind a use for this data. The acid test is when the building is in use and the end user can comment on the design. This is called **user requirement studies**. If under analysis the building functions

Accommodation schedule

House type: 3 bedroom/5 person   Project no. 123

Room title	Type of space			Room size (m)	Room area
	Habitable	Circulation	Storage		
Hall		✓		3.225 × 1.900	6.1275
		✓		1.600 × 0.800	1.2800
					7.4075
WC	✓			1.500 × 1.000	**1.5000**
Dining/kitchen	✓			2.600 × 5.900	**15.3400**
Lobby		✓		1.475 × 0.900	**1.3275**
Living room	✓			3.300 × 4.100	**13.5300**
Store			✓	1.475 × 0.900	1.3275
			✓	1.475 × 2.100	3.0975
					4.4250

Figure 2.5

Spatial balance

Accommodation	Room dimension (m)	Room area (m²)	Percentage of net floor area (%)
Hall	3.225 × 1.900		
	1.600 × 0.800		
		7.4075	17
WC	1.500 × 1.000	1.5000	4
Dining/kitchen	2.600 × 5.900	15.3400	35
Lobby	1.475 × 0.900	1.3275	3
Living room	3.300 × 4.100	13.5300	31
Store	1.475 × 0.900		
	1.475 × 2.100		
		4.4250	10
Total floor area		**43.5300m²**	**100**

Figure 2.6

well, then replicate the good **spatial balance**. The raw data collected in Fig. 2.5 needs to be reworked as a percentage for each spatial category, as shown in Fig. 2.6.

Since this real building functioned well according to the end user we can use this information in the **design specification** for a new house, reasonably confident that the spatial balance will be acceptable. This idea will be explored in the next section called Elements of design.

There are other elements requiring space. The small, low-density housing development does not have a gas supply so space is required for fuel storage. The developer has chosen to use oil as the heating fuel (see Fig. 2.2).

However, the amount of space required for the oil store depends on the number of occupants, the building volume and the design temperatures for each room. This is developed in Unit 3, Science and materials, in which the **heat loss** for a building is calculated. Based on the heat loss and the heat load the building services engineer will calculate the fuel consumption for the dwelling. The ability of the supplier to maintain adequate deliveries must be considered when sizing the oil storage tank. The weekly fuel at peak load requirement may be 300 litres, and with a delivery period of two weeks the design storage load will be

weekly consumption × delivery period = storage requirement
300 litres × 2 weeks = 600 litres

The shape of the oil storage depends on the availability from manufacturers. Most components are manufactured in standard sizes and to either a **British Standard Specification** or **European Building Code**. The capacity required was 600 litres, but unfortunately the standard size is 750 litres. Most

designers will choose the standard range of products or components to keep within the cost parameters established by the client.

Legislation will also influence the space requirements of the oil store. To avoid **ground contamination** a bundwall must be constructed, capable of holding the oil tank capacity plus an additional 10%. Even when the fuel oil is in the building space is required for the boiler. The Building Regulations stipulate that there must be a certain size of hearth, as well as space to protect combustible materials against heat. These requirements use **internal space** and must be accommodated.

The inclusion of services such as electricity, water, gas and telephones will use space. These **utility supplies** can be accommodated within the building structure or fabric. The incoming electrical supply is often incorporated into the wall, as shown in Fig. 2.7.

Similarly the cable routes are incorporated into the **building fabric**. The wiring routes are often **not visible**, whereas the water pipes are surface fixed and the location of the services routes is described as **visible**. Under current **Construction Design and Management Regulations** the planning supervisor must deposit with the client a health and safety file. A record drawing showing the location of all services, both visible and not visible, is a necessity. This final location of all services runs, capacities and depth below surfaces will be a **measured drawing**.

Can you see the benefit of this type of record drawing? Can you see the benefit of **standardisation of services location** with the highways? That is one of the advantages of complying with design guides; at least you have a rough idea where the buried electricity cable lies in the path! Before we trace the utility supplies back to the source, we must consider other design guides and the effect on the internal use of space.

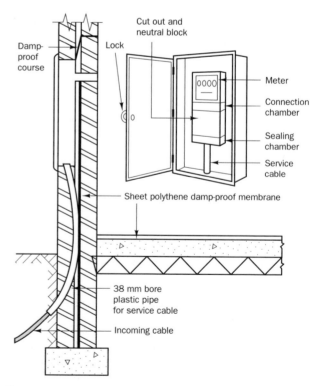

Figure 2.7 Electrical supplies to a property. (*after Hall 1994 Building services and Equipment* Volume 2, Addison Wesley Longman)

Design guides on space allocation

If the building is to function well it must take into account the safety of the occupants, whether these are workers, residents or visitors. The owner has a duty of care to all these users and, by implication, the designer also has a duty of care. This applies to the people employed in the construction of the building, users of the building and maintainance operatives such as the window cleaner.

The Building Regulations offer guidance on the space requirements to ensure public safety and health. The house design could be checked for compliance with the Building Regulations by the Building Control Office at the local authority. Plan approval and site inspections carried out by the Building Control Officer guarantee compliance and safeguard the building user.

The space requirements for circulation are indicated above in the house plan shown in Fig. 2.3.

The Building Regulations Approved Document K (Stairs, ramps and guards) stipulates the minimum width of a **private stair**. A private stair is defined by the Building Regulations and, according to Table 2 of that document, stairways must have an unobstructed width of 800 mm. This can be reduced to a minimum of 600 mm when the private stair provides access to one room only. The staircase illustrated in Fig. 2.8 is a half-turn staircase. The landing which allows the staircase to change direction must have a minimum width at least equal to the stair width, that is 800 mm.

This **circulation space** is necessary but also non-usable. Often this is called **sterile space** as opposed to usable space such as the kitchen.

Circulation space is also determined by the volume of movement. The Building Regulations make a distinction between private dwellings, commercial and industrial buildings because of the volume of pedestrian traffic and safety requirements. An assembly building must have a staircase of at least 1000 mm unobstructed width. Space requirements is not just two dimensional; according to the Building Regulations there must be a minimum headroom of 2000 mm in a private stair, as shown in Fig. 2.9.

A ventilated lobby is a further requirement regarding public health (Fig. 2.10).

According to Building Regulations Approved Document G (Hygiene), the location of a space containing a toilet must not open directly into a space used for food preparation, and this necessitates another little space that must be paid for by the house buyer. How, though, can ventilation be achieved?

Mechanical ventilation such as an extract fan automatically operated by the light must have a certain capacity. The Building Regulations insist on a fan with a capacity of 15

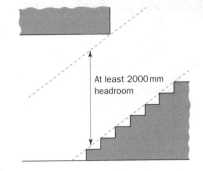

Figure 2.9

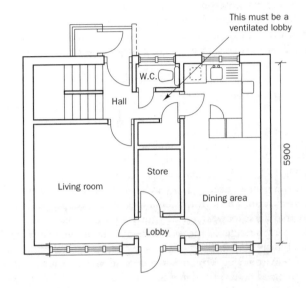

Figure 2.10

litres per second, or three air changes per hour. There are, of course, other design guides such as the Chartered Institute of Building Services design guides or British Standard Specification 5720, 'Code of practice for mechanical ventilation and air conditioning in buildings'. Whichever design guide is selected it will need space allocation for compliance. Alternatively, there is the low-technology solution – the good old window – provided there is one ventilation opening equivalent to 1/20th of the floor area.

The toilet accommodation was 1.500 m × 1.000 m. If natural ventilation was used to comply with the Building Regulations the opening window area must be

$$\frac{1.500 \times 1.000}{20} = 0.075 \, \text{m}^2 \text{ minimum opening window}$$

It cannot be that simple. There has got to be something else. Unfortunately, you are right. **Fire safety** dictates that buildings be a certain distance apart. A brick wall is non-combustible until you include a window. **Passive fire safety** requires a notional distance between buildings regardless of fire load. Approved Document B (Fire safety) in the Building Regulations states that there must be a certain **space separation** between different buildings. Different types of building are classified as **purpose groups**. For example:

- a private dwelling is classified as a **dwellinghouse**
- a public building, not an office, is classified as an **assembly**
- a retailing outlet is classified as a **shop**

For each purpose group there is a specific space separation based on the **unprotected area** and **enclosing rectangle**. An

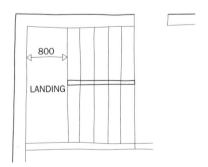

Figure 2.8

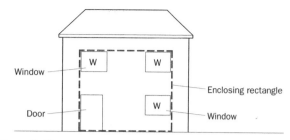

Figure 2.11

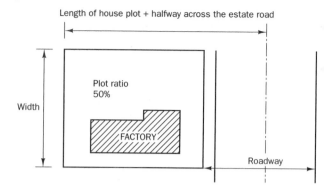

Figure 2.13 Floor space index

unprotected area in an elevation is a window, door or any area of combustible material (Fig. 2.11).

There are tables in Approved Document B (Fire safety) which determine the **distance from the relevant boundary**. In Fig. 2.11 the percentage enclosing rectangle was

$$\text{percentage unprotected area} = \frac{\text{enclosing rectangle}}{\text{wall area}}$$

$$= \frac{3 \times 5}{5 \times 10} = \frac{15}{50} = 30\%$$

The minimum distance from the boundary has to be 1.5 metres, which involves more use of external space.

The planning authority has considerable powers on environmental issues, such as the creating of laws on **conservation areas, listed buildings** and **tree preservation orders**. These powers are to ensure an acceptable quality of life, but the role of the architect must be to maximise the natural environment and minimise the intrusion caused by the built environment. With this aim in mind, the intrusion of the building should not diminish the quality of life or the landscape, townscape or industrial scape. These built environments are a necessary part of our life so the work of an architect should be seen as a contribution to society.

The actual shape of the site and the building size, known as the density of the development, can be constrained by the local planning authority. **Residential densities** are usually measured in habitable units, not just the number of buildings per hectare. There are two types of residential densities: **net** and **gross**.

A net density is shown in Fig. 2.12.

Gross density is a measure of the number of housing plots plus the space for amenities, shops, distributor roads, pedestrian areas and open spaces required by the planning authority. A gross density has therefore a lower ratio per hectare than a net density and is often called a **neighbourhood density**. The quantity surveyor will prepare the financial appraisal based on cost-modelling techniques.

Plot coverage for commercial developments is stipulated by a floor space index (Fig. 2.13), which gives the relationship between the size of the plot and the total floor space.

The combinations for building shape and mass are endless if all the solutions comply with the plot density.

Sometimes the planning authority may stipulate the density of development as 10 dwellings per hectare, and this type of density would allow for large executive style dwellings. The style and social mix of the development would also come under the control of the planning authority.

The Highways Act 1980 requires the developer to enter into an agreement under section 38 to construct the roadway to the highways authority's specification. On completion of the development the highways authority would 'adopt the roadway'. The maintenance and upkeep of the road would then pass to the local authority, rather than the private individual. Sometimes advance payment was made by the developer to the local authority under sections 219 and 228 of the Highways Act. This guaranteed that access onto a highway would be constructed to the local authority's specification. Section 38 agreements are modified slightly by the New Roads and Street Works Act 1991. Other negotiations are entered in with the utility services for infrastructure connections and permanent supplies, such as water and electricity. Drainage is covered by the building control permission.

Any development that requires access onto a classified road requires permission from the highways authority. Permission for a **drop access** is acceptable provided the contractor is approved by the highways authority and carries the minimum public liability insurance cover. Otherwise the highways authority will carry out the drop access work and charge the client.

The highways authority has the power to designate **improvement lines** for road widening and classified road widths. This information is available in the local planning authority and indicated on **structure** or **local plans**. The local highways authority should be consulted on road widths, provision of paths, street furniture and road signs. The local distributor roads and residential spine roads should have an overall width of 5.5 m. The road curves should be designed for a maximum intended speed of 50 kph, but smaller access roads and cul-de-sacs may be reduced in width. Private driveway widths are nominally 2.3 m. Some highways authorities classify the roads into types; for example, a type 6 road is an internal estate road (Fig. 2.14).

There are also requirements for street furniture, set back distances for lighting columns, and positions of utility services under the footways (Fig. 2.15).

Off-street parking is often required and the provision of **1 off-street parking space per dwelling** should be allowed on

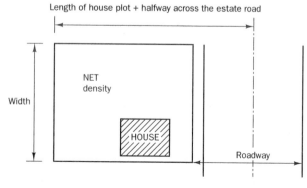

Figure 2.12 Net density

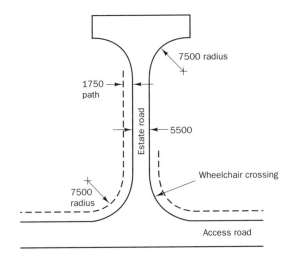

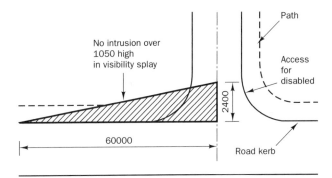

Figure 2.16 Visibility splays

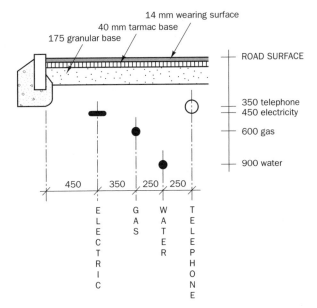

Figure 2.14 An example of an internal estate road (type 6)

Figure 2.15 Positions of utility services beneath footway

Visibility splays for minor junctions are specified according to traffic design speed. The **sight lines** for all visibility splays are measured at 1.05 m above the road line. This unobstructed view is based on the traffic design speed and stopping distance. No obstruction including hard or soft landscaping, is allowed to form an obstacle in the sight lines.

the planning application. Further off-street parking depends on the size of the development but, as a guide, there should be 1 additional off-street parking space for each additional 2 dwellings. The normal car parking space is 2.40 m × 4.80 m. Other classes of buildings have different ratios.

Access to a highway requires visibility splays and sight lines in accordance with the highways department. The **visibility splays** depend on the type of junction and classification of the road (Fig. 2.16).

Self-assessment tasks

There are opportunities in this section to gather evidence for key skills, especially communication and application of number.

1. Measure and record the dimensions of two rooms in your own home. Make sure you measure the length, width and height to the nearest whole number of millimetres:

    • measure the size and location of furniture
    • measure the door sizes and locations
    • measure windows sizes and locations, the window sill heights above the floor and the window heights
    • sketch the room floor plans showing position and sizes of furniture, direction of access and movement around the room

2. Interview users of the rooms to establish the function and usage of the rooms throughout the day and week:

    • record the number and frequency of users
    • record the usage of the rooms by the users
    • tabulate the results of the survey as a histogram
    • plot the results on a time interval against the number of users

3. Obtain the users' opinions on the use of space within the two rooms. Obtain their opinions by one-to-one interview technique:

    • produce a questionnaire for use with the interviewees
    • accurately record the interviewees' responses to the questionnaire
    • tabulate as a pie chart the interviewees' responses to the questionnaire

2.2 Development and appraisal of design brief solutions

Topics covered in this section are:

- construction clients and their needs
- development of the design specification
- design features and constraints

Construction clients and their needs

We are all likely to become clients of the construction industry. The mere redecoration of the living room makes you a customer, or a client, of the construction industry. However, in this section we are looking at a client who requires the skills of an architect to design and supervise construction.

Our clients may vary from the **individual**, such as the house owner who wishes to have an extension built, to the **institutional** client who requires a prestigious office block. The client could also be a private company wanting its existing office block renovated to accommodate new technologies. This wide variety of clients will make demands on the designer's abilities to communicate the client's needs to the design and construction team. Technical skills are required to solve the constraints of the site and the client's financial limitations.

The different clients will also vary in their knowledge of the construction industry. The private individual may not understand the role of the architect or the quantity surveyor. The institutional client may have its own design team and a very knowledgeable understanding of the people involved in the construction industry. Whether the client is a private individual or an institution such as a bank, the architect will have to determine carefully the client's needs.

Client needs

What do we mean by client needs? Remember that the private client may have little knowledge of the construction industry and may find it difficult to state requirements. The client may want an extension to a house but is not certain about the use or function of the extension; possibly a bedroom is needed, but should this be a single bedroom or a double bedroom with ensuite facilities? The architect must obtain this information if a design is to be successful. If the architect misunderstands the client's real needs then the end result will be a badly designed project.

There must be some structure or logic to the design process. The Royal Institute of British Architects (RIBA) have developed a '**Plan of Work**' which reduces the possibility of errors and lessens the amount of abortive work by the design team. At the start of the design process the architect must carefully define the client's needs. This is sometimes called the **client brief**.

A useful technique is called the **briefing chart** (Fig. 2.17). In our example of a private individual requiring a small

extension to the house, the family will already have discussed their needs and arrived at a solution to their problem. They require a small extension with two rooms, a dining room and an extra bedroom. In this simple case, all our client needs is a technical draughtsperson to produce the builder's plans. There is no need to seek the services of an architect. Often the builder will prepare the plans, submit them for Planning and Building Control approval, then build the extension.

The briefing chart will encourage the client, whether a private individual or an institution, to think in **activities**, not solutions. The architect's role is to find **solutions** to the problems. When the activities are classified, this will lead to other relationships which the briefing chart will highlight. For example, in the small extension required by the family, leisure and sleeping are the **activities** and the briefing chart will focus on three key considerations: firstly, the location or arrangement of rooms; secondly, the shape and orientation; and thirdly, the features, such as heating and finishes.

With the briefing chart the **circulation diagram** (Fig. 2.18) will aid the design team to produce solutions that are acceptable to the client. The circulation diagram will show in graphic form much of the information on the briefing chart, thereby assisting the designers in the arrangement of activities. All of this architectural work is called **inception**. The architect prepares the general outline of requirements and presents a strategy for future action.

So far we have tried to define as carefully as possible the client's needs. We have not yet considered solutions as this could lead to abortive work; our primary consideration is to

BRIEFING CHART

Room Title _____ Job No. _____
Activity _____ Prepared by _____
Occupancy rates _____

Arrangement
    Shared with
    Next to
    Near to
    Floor

Shape
    Aspect
    Size
    Equipment
    Plant

Features
    Temperature
    Humidity
    Light
    Power
    Floor finish
    Wall finish
    Ceiling finish

Remarks

Figure 2.17

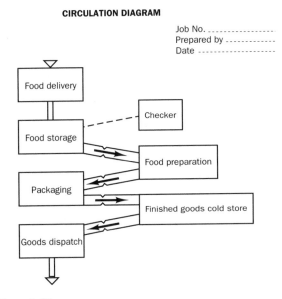

CIRCULATION DIAGRAM

Job No. _____
Prepared by _____
Date _____

Figure 2.18

- durability of the project
- form of the building
- structure of the building
- environment
- water exclusion
- ventilation and air movement
- heat
- lighting
- sound
- privacy and security

ascertain the facts and make sure that all the client's needs, and constraints, are logically listed. The architect also requires other information, some of which will be easily obtained, but for further details it may be necessary to resort to **user requirement studies**. The amount of additional information required will depend on the type of client.

Basically the two types of client – the private individual or the institutional client – can be classified broadly by their motives for building: i.e. clients who built for their own use or clients who build for profit. The latter are often called **speculative developers**. The different clients will exercise different constraints on the design of the building. The speculative developer must have carried out a considerable amount of market research, since a profit must be made from the sale of the building.

A user requirement study is the process of identifying the purpose of the building, in relation to activities and human needs, and the important words of the study are: **fitness for purpose**. This means that the building allows the occupants to carry out their activities conveniently, economically and under a suitable environment. This is a simple statement, but is difficult to do, and the user requirements will assist the design process in three ways:

- by clarifying the brief
- by establishing performance standards for activities, area, environment and cost
- by comparing design alternatives with the client brief

Functional requirements

There are three aspects to any design process which must be considered.

1. What are the **functional demands** of the problem?
2. What are the **technical constraints**?
3. What are the **aesthetic considerations**?

Satisfying these three aspects will ensure a functional building, which is fit for purpose. For the design process to succeed, the architect must have detailed information on the following areas, which is obtained from the client or the site investigation:

Durability of the project

During the inception stage of the RIBA Plan of Work the architect must ask the question: 'What is the required building life?' Most clients would have no idea, but the question is crucial to the design process. It could determine the structural form and type, material selection, orientation of the building and the building cost.

The architect must explain these reasons to the client and jointly decide on the **building life expectancy**. Take, for example, a refurbishment of the office block for a private client.

- Must the design solution allow for changes in information technologies?
- Product life expectancies are five years, yet the building refurbishment life expectancy is 15 years. The architect must allow for three changes in information technology systems.
- How will this flexibility be built into the design solution?

Once the building life expectancy is established the degree of durability of each element can be calculated.

Durability then becomes a **design requirement**. As well as determining the material selection, the decision on durability may affect the building form or shape.

Form of the building

For the design solution to work well the architect must analyse the activities and the working environment specified in the client brief. To a certain extent this will depend on occupancy rates and spatial requirements. This **anthropometric data** – i.e. the space required to perform human activities – will allow the definition of space. The client brief will have this information in outline.

For example, the small extension required by our private client included an extra bedroom. The occupancy rate would probably be one person, but there must be circulation space, furniture and fitting space and, if the activity was to allow for studying, then there would need to be space for study.

The total activity space, circulation space and open spaces will determine the building size on plan. Room proportion will also affect the height of the room. The space requirement, the circulation diagram and the overall building height will determine the overall building mass. Up to this point there has been no allowance for aesthetic considerations, such as proportion or symmetry.

Further constraints to the building form would become apparent from the site investigation. Unity of form, and architectural style could be determined by the planning authority. A compromise must be made between the functional dimensions based on the client's needs and the planning authority's legal constraints. At least the outline shape and size of the building, the building form, is established. From this design data the type of structure can be considered.

Structure of the building

Remember that these decisions are not final, but are only outline solutions that will be evaluated during the **feasibility** stage of the Plan of Work. The purpose of the preliminary investigations by the architect is to collect data that will allow **viable designs** to be evaluated. The architect should allow the structural materials self-expression and determine the structural form. Basically the structural form can be classified into **rectilinear forms** or **curvilinear forms** (Fig. 2.19).

Rectilinear forms are generated by beam, post and lintel structures, cross-wall or framed beams and columns. Apart from the cross-wall and framed structures, traditional materials impose a severe limitation on the structural form. Where aesthetic considerations such as proportion, dynamics and unity are used a very pleasing building form can be obtained. To use trabeated construction, that is beam and post, would impose limitations on the span due to material availability.

Curvilinear forms are generated by domes, arches or geodesic domes. The dome form demands a plan based on the square and will affect the building shape. Arched construction, often named **arcuated construction**, allows the mass of the building to be exploited. A distinctive character to the building form is achieved.

The choice of structure will be affected by buildability and cost, and the cost will also affect the required environment.

Environment

The briefing chart identified several features which will **modulate** the building environment. The building enclosure will modify the macro climate – that is, the outside environment, such as rain and wind, and the built environment, such as noise. At this preliminary stage the architect must have details of the expected internal environment and micro climate. These can be obtained through detailed user requirement studies or published environmental data. Even with published environmental data the site will be unique and the design requirement will need to be interpreted to ensure that the design solution will satisfy the user requirements. Since comfort levels vary according to individual taste, the design solution has to accommodate a range of demands.

Water exclusion

This is a function of the building enclosure. The prevention of rain penetration as a **design requirement** is categorised by degree of exposure. Water exclusion also includes groundwater and condensation control, created by the client's activities.

Ventilation and air movement

Trying to create a building environment which allows the client to use the building economically and comfortably, means that the architect has to analyse the design working environment. Decision making is made easier by a systematic approach to design requirements and constraints. Accurate filing of information will allow alternative solutions to be checked and the optimum solution chosen. Special attention may be vital to remove unpleasant fumes, bacteria or to ensure that the macro climate is not polluted by the building activity. With such exact criteria the architect would be advised to use a specialist services consultant.

Heat

The thermal capacity of the building enclosure is an important aspect of the heat characteristics of a building. Legal constraints imposed by the Building Regulations, often defined by heat loss, are a design requirement. The architect has to create an ambient working environment. Published design data will help the architect to standardise solutions, but these need to be interpreted to satisfy the individual client's need. The site orientation and views out of the building will also affect the solar gain or glare (Fig. 2.20).

Lighting

The client's view of **natural daylight** or **artificial light** needs to be known by the architect. As the design solution must satisfy the client's demands, the architect has to consider the building use and type of activities. The lumens for each activity has to be analysed and the level of lighting for each space identified. This design data should be available from the architect's personal library.

Site orientation and contour will affect the natural daylight and glare within the structure, as well as the colour and texture of the internal decoration. If the client's design criteria are critical, the services of a specialist would assist the architect to produce a successful design solution.

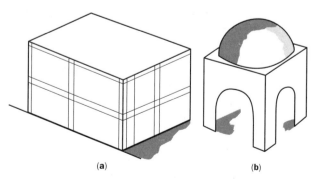

Figure 2.19 Structural forms: (a) rectilinear; (b) curvilinear

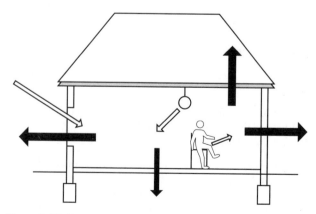

Figure 2.20 Heat paths showing gains and losses

Sound

Legal constraints control the noise levels allowed and the architect must quantify the noise levels created and the need for sound exclusion from the macro climate. Noise pollution can have a serious effect on employee efficiency and morale. If the architect's commission was to design a theatre, then acoustics will become a priority design requirement in the auditorium.

Privacy and security

The amount of privacy depends on personal preference and the type of activity carried out. The need for privacy and security can affect other design requirements. For example, the views out of the building, which may be desirable for employee motivation, could conflict with the need for **security** from intruders, or privacy of activity. During briefing, the architect will try to elicit this information from the client, and the site investigation will also aid the decision on privacy and security. The priority of employee safety may affect the general arrangement of rooms and the type of structure.

Economic use of resources

All of the above client requirements cost money, and the architect must estimate the overall cost. As there will also be a great deal of information gathering and filing, it is essential that the architect has a good library system. Information is the architect's stock in trade and knowing where the information is stored can be crucial to the success of the commission. **Information gathering** and **retrieval** are vital at this stage for the assessment of building costs.

Nothing is definite, yet the architect's commission depends on the ability of the client to pay for the design and building costs.

The role of the **quantity surveyor** is helpful in calculating the **projected building costs**. If again we consider the extension required by our private client, there must have been thousands of similar extensions made to houses, and the quantity surveyor will almost certainly have recorded the final building cost of those similar projects. Information about the floor area will also be available, so the quantity surveyor will calculate the **building cost per square metre of floor area**. This **historical data** could be used to predict the building cost for the new project.

The **accommodation schedule** (Fig. 2.21) lists the rooms required and the floor area is used as a basis for calculating the building cost.

Figure 2.21 shows that the proposed floor area was 27 metres square, and the historical building cost was £450.00 per square metre. It is very likely that the predicted cost will be about the same.

$$\text{predicted building cost} = 27\,\text{m}^2 \times £450.00\,\text{m}^{-2}$$
$$= £12\,150.00$$

However, this was based on *historical costs*, so an allowance must be made for design changes and price variations. This at least gives an indication of the possible costs. It is now necessary to discover if the client can afford this and, if not, to either abort the project or redesign it within the client's financial constraints.

Having established the types of client and the suitability of the commission to the architect, we then proceed with the design process according to the RIBA Plan of Work.

ACCOMMODATION SCHEDULE			
House extension ... traditional build			Project 123/1
Room title	Size		Floor area
	length	width	m²
Dining room	4.00	4.50	18.00
Bedroom 2	3.00	3.00	9.00

	Total floor area		27.00 =======

Figure 2.21

Development of the design specification

Content

Basically the **design specification** sets out the functional specification for the project. The client brief needs to be translated into a written list of tasks to be achieved. The client brief should not state how the design is to be achieved but should give the end result. It is the architect's role to solve the technical and functional requirements of the client. Other consultants will be involved in the design process, so the design specification becomes an important document for **communicating** the client's needs, **monitoring** progress during the design stage and **evaluating** the success of the design solution. Defining the client brief will allow prioritisation of requirements. For example, the client design requirement for privacy and security may conflict with the design requirement for views out to enhance employee motivation. The design specification allows the design team to produce an excellent design **solution** in terms of **function, aesthetics** and **technology**.

Design methodology may be divided into four phases:

- **assimilation**, where the gathering and filing of information is done
- **study**, where investigation about the nature of the problem is isolated and refined
- **development**, where tentative solutions are isolated and refined
- **communication** of the preferred solution to the design team and the client

This takes a lot of time, and a well-prepared design specification will save valuable design time.

The client brief was defined by two documents, the briefing chart and the circulation diagram. These two documents are used to define the design aims into **function** and **performance** specifications (Fig. 2.22).

At the moment we are treating all the performance and functional requirements as equal. In reality we cannot, and the functional requirements such as '4 person eating' and the performance requirements need to be **ranked**. The weighting column allows the priorities to be identified. The architect needs to be paid for all this work, and the client must be

DESIGN SPECIFICATION	
House extension ... traditional build	Project 123/1 Date 1/4/1994
Function requirement	Weighting factor

Dining room
Functional requirements:
    4 person eating
    views of garden
Performance requirements:
    lighting: natural supplemented with
    artificial
        2% sky factor
        200 lumen
    heating: extension of wet system
        19° C
    ventilation: natural
        2 air changes per hour	

Total weighting	

Figure 2.22

made aware of the design costs. The RIBA recommends that a contract should be signed between the architect and the client during the inception stage of the Plan of Work.

Contract signing

The RIBA **Condition of Engagement** should form the basis of any agreement with the client. This standard contract covers the following points:

- the type of architect's services
  - design only
  - design and supervision of building
  - hourly rates
  - payment details
  - limits of responsibility for partial services
  - settlement of accounts
- expenses and additional disbursements
- copyright conditions
- appointment of other consultants
- procedure if work aborted
- possible building contract arrangements

This formalised and legal document is signed by both parties, with specific performance required by the two contracting parties. The architect now acts as an agent for the client, but the architect's power to act as the employer's agent is severely limited in the Contract of Engagement. Under **contract law** the architect could be sued for **negligence**. The **period of liability** depends on the type of contract used. If the contract is **under hand**, then the period of liability for negligence is 6 years. If the contract is **under seal** then the period of liability for negligence is 12 years.

The architect acts as an agent for the client or employer, and should exercise **reasonable care** in carrying out the design function. The architect is subject to the **law of agency**, which is part of contract law. **Professional indemnity insurance** is carried by the architect to cover the situation if things go seriously wrong and the architect is sued for negligence. The scope of a claim for alleged negligence can include the cost of the mistake as well as the cost of remedying the defect. This can be very expensive, and architects must always keep up to date with published information, whether technical or legal research.

ARCHITECTURAL PARTNERS

Aesthetic View
Function Lane
Technical Park
New Town

page 17

Mr P Kliant   1st April 1994
Knead House   Ref. 123/1
Borrowby
Nr Broke.

Dear Mr P Kliant,

re: Extension to house

May I confirm the details of our meeting dated 1st April 1994. We are pleased to accept your invitation to act as architects for the above project. I have included 2 copies of the Contract of Engagement, and the briefing checklist which we completed during our initial meeting.
Our services will consist of the following:

- design of the building but not any external work
- preparation of production information
- obtaining planning and building control approval
- advice on the appointment of a contractor
- inspection and supervision of the construction work

Our fee for these services is 10% of the final contract sum payable in instalments. VAT will be charged at the rate ruling on the date of supply.
Confirmation of your agreement to the appointment of the following consultants:

Quantity surveyors: Takeoff, Abstract & Bill
Their work will be cost planning and advice, bills of quantity and tender adjudication, supervision of interim and final account

Structural engineer: Bending & Shear
To prepare the design of structural elements

Services engineer: Plumb, Heat & Vent
To produce the design, production information and site inspection of the plumbing, heating and ventilation, electrical and alarm systems

The consultants' fees should not exceed 5% of the final contract sum. On 4 April 1994, we will begin the site survey and investigation.

Yours sincerely

A Drawer, RIBA
Chartered Architect.

Enclo: Contract of engagement
       Briefing checklist

Figure 2.23 A letter of appointment

Directives from the European Parliament will also affect the contract and legal status of the architect and client, making it more onerous for the architect. In all instances the client must be made aware of the services the architect is prepared to offer. An example of a letter of appointment is shown in Fig. 2.23.

A strategy must now be prepared to enable the architect to deliver his or her contractual duty, namely a design solution. We shall therefore return to the design brief.

Design brief

The RIBA **Architect's Jobbook** should now be prepared. This contains the Plan of Work scheme and acts as a job diary. To reduce the possibility of errors, a **checklist** should be used during the design process (Fig 2.24). At the inception stage, a large amount of information must be gathered, and checklists are a vital source of information gathering and dissemination.

The checklist cannot be exhaustive but should cover all **keypoints**. The briefing chart, the circulation diagram, the

```
                    BRIEFING CHECKLIST
Job architect: A. Drawer            Project 123
                                    Date: 4th April 1994
PERSONNEL
1.01   Client's name
            P Kliant
            Knead House
            Borrowby
            New Town
            Telephone .............. Fax .............

1.02   Briefing meeting
            date ................
            time ................
            venue

1.03   People in attendance

1.04   Type of project

1.05   Other architects/consultants involved
            Contact name:
            Address
            Telephone .............. Fax .............

1.06   Target dates

1.07   Target cost          \

APPROVALS
2.01   Planning authority
            Outline planning permission         Yes/No
            Detailed planning permission        Yes/No
            Planning reference .......................................

2.02   Building control
            Local authority
            Private certifier

2.03   Fire certificate                         Yes/No
            Fire authority

2.04   Licences
            Public                              Yes/No
            Music                               Yes/No
            Drinks                              Yes/No

SITE
3.01   Site survey
            Location
            Boundaries

3.02   Buildings
            No. and types
            Listed building                     Yes/No

3.03   Services
            Water                               Yes/No
            Electric                            Yes/No
            Gas                                 Yes/No
            Drains
                        Public    Foul          Yes/No
                        Private                 Yes/No
                        Public    Storm         Yes/No
                        Private                 Yes/No
            Telephone                           Yes/No

LEGAL
4.01   Ownership
            Freehold
            Leasehold
            Solicitor

4.02   Easements
            Easements (specify)
            Respective covenants
```

Figure 2.24

design specification and the briefing checklist form the **design brief** and arrangements can then be made to brief the remainder of the design team.

Consultants

Architects should be aware of the strengths and weaknesses of their practice. Certain commissions will require the help of other professionals to ensure that the employer or the client obtains a quality service and product. This means that the architect should be in communication with a network of consultants who are familiar with the practice's working methods and ethos. The client, who now is known as the *employer*, should already have been alerted to the need for certain **consultants**, such as

- a quantity surveyor
- a structural engineer
- or a building services engineer

Dependent on the complexity of the brief and the client's needs, the architect should analyse the relevant experience available in the practice to highlight where further assistance is necessary.

For example, the user requirement studies may highlight the critical performance standard of factory planning, the skills of which are not usually available in the architectural practice. The use of the design methodology will give the architect the chance to identify those tasks for which consultants will be required. The assimilation stage in the design methodology, where the architect accumulates and prioritises information, will assist. The next stage in the design methodolgy, study, is where the problems are isolated. If doubts exist about the practice's ability to solve these design problems, the architect will then search through the network for additional assistance.

Even with this careful planning, problems may suddenly occur, such as a difficult planning application, involving an appeal against the decision of the local planning authority. In such instances there are **town planning consultants** who can provide valuable assistance in the appeal procedure. Certain commissions will necessitate the use of a **fire safety consultant** or the user requirement studies may include original research and investigation by the Building Research Establishment. A trade organisation such as the Brick Development Association or the Cement and Concrete Association may also be approached for advice and suggestions. All this valuable information and advice needs to be analysed, and development, the third stage of the design methodology, draws the information together to enable tentative solutions to be produced.

The consultants will probably belong to independent concerns and the need to coordinate their activities is part of the architect's role.

Design team coordination

Most of the coordination will be carried out at **design meetings** chaired by the architect. As each participant will want to know the purpose of the meeting, an agenda should be prepared beforehand and circulated. Some meetings will simply be for briefing purposes, while others will be for brainstorming or decision making. Each different meeting will require a different approach by the chairperson to achieve the required result.

The first design meeting with the consultants must be a briefing meeting. An example of an agenda is shown in Fig. 2.25.

The meeting is chaired by the project architect and minutes are taken and circulated to each design team member. It is important that any tasks assigned and release dates for the work are accurately recorded in the minutes of the meeting (Fig. 2.26) to enable progress to be monitored.

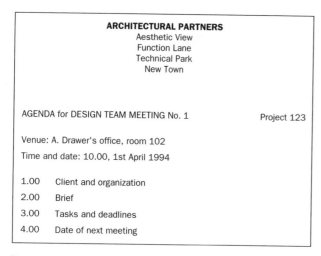

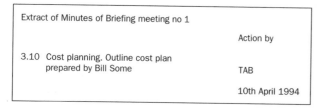

Figure 2.25 A meeting agenda

Figure 2.26

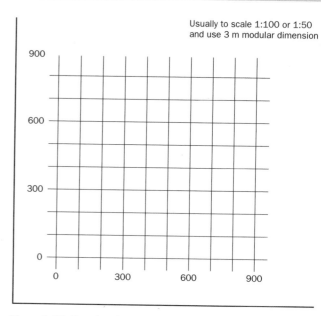

Usually to scale 1:100 or 1:50
and use 3 m modular dimension

Figure 2.27 Preprinted modular grid on detail paper

At the next meeting the minutes of the previous meeting are read and agreed as a true record. **Matters arising** from the meeting are then discussed before the meeting agenda moves ahead.

All this information must be filed and the use of a computer will allow the architect to interrogate the database. Irrespective of how the information is stored, it needs to be accessible and the filing system must allow for updating and ease of retrieval.

Design features and constraints

Dimensional coordination

As the building will be constructed from **standard** components, it would seem logical to make the overall dimensions compatible. The use of materials to the relevant British Standard (BS) Specification allows accuracy in component sizes, such as bricks manufactured within acceptable tolerances of size. The standard sizes of wash-hand basins, or standard range of drainage goods, limits the architect's design flair, but makes economical sense. The basic **modular dimension** is **300 mm**, often described as 3M.

As the private client or the institutional client sometimes has difficulty in visualising the finished design the architect may have to produce **sketch plans** and **perspectives** during the **conceptualisation** of the design solution. Grid detail paper allows the architect to sketch the layout arrangements quickly, using a grid to show size and proportion (Fig. 2.27).

Even perspectives can be drawn quickly using perspective grid detail paper (Fig. 2.28).

The sketch drawing is one of the most difficult skills to acquire, but at the inception of the **detail design** stage the

architect will use this drawing skill to good effect. **Modular grid detail paper** is an ideal medium for this type of communication. The detail paper, sometimes called *layout* paper, is used chiefly for preliminary sketch drawings. Conceptualisation of design solutions for the institutional client may involve colour rendered perspectives, models and a presentation to committees. This is sometimes a large investment of the architect's time and money to secure a commission. Computer-aided design will also allow further options, owing to the graphic abilities of 3D modelling.

It is essential to remember that the purpose of the drawing is simply to convey the overall mass of the building or the general arrangement of rooms, so the sketch should be basic and should never be too elaborate (Fig. 2.29).

Each consultant will use the general arrangement prepared by the architect, so the use of a coordinated modular dimension will aid the coordination of the design process.

Anthropometric data will help the general arrangement of room sizes. The proportion of space must be allocated according to intended activities, and suitable shapes and sizes must therefore be determined. **Dynamic anthropometrics** considers the size and the **envelope of space** occupied by the activity – for example, a group of spectators occupies less space than the same number of people participating in the sport. Design for the disabled or elderly will require different space requirements and a study of ergonomics will help in the general arrangement.

The design specification will be used to consider any alternative solutions. Room proportion is difficult to resolve, because it requires a **holistic** rather than an **elemental** approach. The proportion of length to width can be considered as an *element*, but when considered in proportion to the height the whole room may be unbalanced. The *holistic* approach takes into account not just the room measurements and their relation to each other, but also door openings and window sizes in an effort to achieve a well-proportioned or balanced room.

The overall proportion or **mass** of the building is important in relation to the site situation. The rules of aesthetics will help the architect produce a visually pleasing, functional building for the client's use.

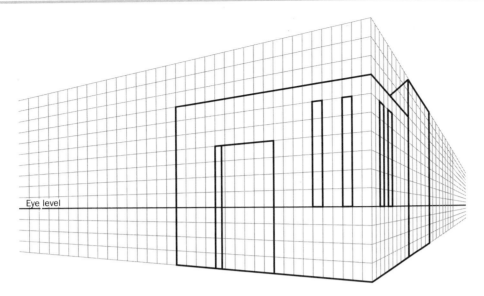

Figure 2.28 Preprinted perspective modular grid on detail paper

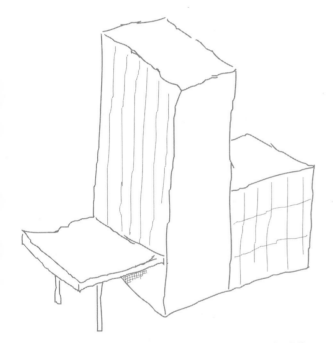

Figure 2.29 Thumbnail sketch showing form and mass of building

Aesthetics

Proportion is an integral part of good design, but there are other aesthetic principles which help the architect, such as

- unity
- balance and symmetry
- duality

These factors affect the mass of the building or its apparent mass.

Unity

Where the individual parts of the building contribute to the building mass then we have a sense of *unity*. This belonging together is important, even though different shapes and sizes add up to the total building mass.

Unity of *shape* does not necessarily mean monotony; the repetition of form has a powerful effect on a person's perception and acceptance of the building. Consistency of shape or form reinforces the sensation of completeness.

Unity of *scale* would be important to the planning authority and they may insist on this through the structure plan of similarly sized buildings. Dominance of one element or an oversized building can destroy the unity of scale.

Balance and symmetry

A building design needs a *focal point* – i.e. a particular point to which the eye is naturally drawn – and this visual position can be the entrance or any other part of the building. The focal point also acts as the pivot for balance, and it should be noted that *visual* balance can be achieved in similar ways to *physical* balance.

Duality

This equilibrium of design must not be confused with duality. In visual balance the basic arrangement of volumes and space around the central focus creates balance. Other factors add to the visual balance such as *detail*, *colour*, *texture* or *finish*. If the mass of the building is wrong, then no amount of detail will rectify the situation. At the earliest possible time the correct mass must be decided, then the additional items such as details will fit in and the overall design will be visually acceptable. Applied decoration should not scatter the visual impact of the building composition or mass, but should emphasise the design concept.

Colour

Colour is known to be a mood changer. If the building is to receive critical acclaim, then the way the eye receives and interprets colour images must be considered. For instance, the very soothing effect of green, contrasting with the vibrance of yellow, can create discord. The psychological effect of colour is well documented – think of the dramatic effect of a red/purple colour scheme in the hospital waiting room or the works canteen. These colours are aggressive, not restful or soothing.

The **Munsell colour chart** is used to convey to the paint manufacturer the dimension of colour required. The Munsell diagram shows three dimensions of colour – **hue**, **chroma** and **value**. British Standard Specification 4800 uses the Munsell notation, and colour designated 10.0YR8/4, follows this notation

10.0YR   represents the hue (yellow/red)
8   represents the value
4   represents the chroma

Dull colours have a low chroma while bright colours have a high chroma. The chroma is the characteristic of the colour, whereas the value indicates lightness or darkness. White has the top value, that is 10, but black has a darkness value of 1.

To ensure the correct external rendering and images it may be necessary to include a colour consultant in the design team. The need for this will be reflected in the design specification, where priorities are established for the client's needs. Colour and image are also affected by the texture and materials used.

Texture

Texture is the **surface appearance** and finish of the materials. A masonry wall texture will be influenced by the light reflection from the individual brick, wall size and shape, and shadow lines created by the joint profile. Care over such small items can make a big difference to the aesthetic impact of the building. The materials selected will be either naturally occurring, processed or manufactured. The textural surface could therefore be natural or dressed, open or closed, which allows the architect considerable freedom to design a building with pleasing visual tones and shades. Hard textures can be reduced by the use of soft landscaping such as trees and shrubs. Initially the building texture and colour may be acceptable, but how will the façade treatment endure the ravages of the weather? What will the building elevations look like in ten years' time? Will they still be pleasing or will they be unattractive due to rain stains and discoloration? To a certain extent that depends on the design life and the durability of the selected materials.

Design life

Imagine the effect on a bank customer who spots a bank branch in the distance. As the customer draws closer it appears to be a grubby timber shack, with paint peeling off the entrance door. What impression has this created in the customer's mind?

The **corporate image** the bank wanted to give has been erroded by the appearance and upkeep of the branch. It is important at the inception stage of design to know precisely what image the client wishes to create. The composition of the building, the mass of the building and its unity all give impressions to the outsider. Take, for example, a bank, which needs to create an atmosphere of trust, security and long standing. The size of the building does not necessarily indicate this but the materials selected and the proportion certainly convey ideas of stability and long standing.

During the inception stage of design the architect will differentiate **real** design requirements from **perceived** requirements. Even the institutional client will not be able to articulate all of its needs to the architect; some will be written 'between the lines', i.e. not directly stated, but nevertheless inferred. The design life has a strong correlation with costs. Some clients may be concerned about the initial cost of the building, often referred to as the **capital cost**; others are more concerned about life cycle costs, which take into account the capital cost, and the cost of repairs and maintenance over the life of the building.

The design life for wooden window frames with preservatives is estimated to be 10 years, but the expected life of the building is 100 years, so the window frames will have to be replaced several times. Although the initial cost will be lower with wooden frames, the **life cycle** cost will be greater than if aluminium frames were used. Major components such as windows, doors, and fabric elements can have different product design life periods and the architect must assess the effect of juxtapositioning materials. An example could be an oak front door with steel screws to hang the door to the frame. Staining will soon occur and the steel will corrode, leading to the door element failure. This would be an example of two incompatible materials next to each other, or in juxtaposition. The design specification will outline the functional and performance standards required for the project. There must be some **tolerance** because of the uniqueness of the site, and the fact that the product design life expectancy has been assessed in a laboratory by a standardized **accelerated weathering test**.

The architect will make some well-founded design assumptions regarding the site conditions. The degree of exposure will be based on historical data and used to predict the required durability. The roof construction will be designed to withstand wind damage that is likely to occur, statistically, once every 50 years. In other words, the **design life** will influence the selection of materials and method of construction.

Materials

Materials are available in a wide variety. For example, the architectural brick, better known as the facing brick, is manufactured in many different forms, and which form should the architect select?

The design methodology with its functional and performance standards will focus attention on key elements and aid the selection of suitable materials. Information gathering should be screened by the design life requirement and performance specification. During the study and development stages of the design methodology viable alternatives are prepared. This does not consider only the material and form of the building, but also the ease with which the building should be constructed. **Buildability** is about the construction methods involved in translating the architect's design solution into reality. Leading edge technology and materials have high risk labels, and as the architect will still be liable for design mistakes due to negligence, great care must be exercised when selecting materials and construction methods. The use of consultants has brought experience into the architectural practice, and similarly the use of a building contractor at the design stage may allow the design solution to be influenced by buildability, or construction needs.

Materials must meet strict **quality standards**, so the use of tested materials is imperative. Specifying materials to British Standard Specification will guarantee a **minimum** standard of quality and performance. Using suppliers who are accredited to BS 5750, 'Quality assurance', will minimize the risk of substandard materials. New materials that have not yet been listed by a British Standard may be used if the **Agrément certificate** indicates their suitability. The Agrément certificate is restricted, and the application must comply with the certificate if product life and function are to be guaranteed.

Trade Associations and independent testing laboratories can be used to assess the suitability of chosen materials and methods of construction. The Fire Research Station could be used to assess materials for compliance with the client's need for safety under fire loads. Compliance with the Building Regulations also ensures that the design is safe, both structurally and under fire conditions.

This care during the design stage to ensure that the finished building functions correctly can be undermined during the construction stage by substandard workmanship. To avoid this the architect and the quantity surveyor, who prepares the tender documents, make sure that the **minimum acceptable workmanship** is concisely described in the **specification** section of the **Bill of Quantity**. The collaboration by the design team to reference materials and specification in the production information – namely, drawings, bills of quantities and specification – is enhanced by the use of **Coordinated Project Information** techniques.

The buildability of the project may also be affected by physical constraints such as site orientation and ground conditions.

Physical constraints

One of the earliest tasks for the architect is to carry out the **site investigation** to identify key construction and design constraints. These constraints may be physical, financial or legal.

A checklist (Fig. 2.30) is always valuable in reducing the chance of incomplete data. A checklist does not diminish the architect's intuition since each site is unique. This work has moved the architect from stage A of the RIBA Plan of Work, *inception*, to stage B, *feasibility*.

This graphical and written report will become a source of reference when compiling the **feasibility report** for the client. Hard data about the site is essential: this involves a site survey showing boundaries, areas, and dimensions to enable a site plot to be drawn to scale. This will also allow the size of the site to be calculated. Any other necessary details will be collected from the site.

- The architect must specify the position of utility services, whether overhead or underground, and their size and

depth. Letters should also be written to the utility suppliers asking for ground clearance. The positioning of the services their size and location is called **marking and ascertaining services**.

- Existing buildings need to be measured on the site: the surrounding built environment, any adjoining buildings, the streetscape, the roofscape and the natural environment must be recorded.
- Ground levels must be obtained and bench mark location recorded. **Soil investigation** may take the form of a field survey or a desktop survey using geological maps.
- Infrastructure details, road and rail links, access points and egress to site must be considered and a survey of the natural habitat carried out.

The collected information and plans will form the basis for the feasibility report. Ideas about the viability of the project will often depend on the predicted costs.

Cost and budgets

The role of the **quantity surveyor** is vital to assess the possible building costs. Using cost planning techniques based on historical data, the quantity surveyor can use these building costs to predict **outline cost limits**. If this type of costing is to be reasonably accurate, the buildings must be similar; for instance, the cost of building an office block cannot be used to predict the building cost of a detached house.

Our private client wanted an extension built, but needs to know relatively soon how much will it cost. The quantity surveyor will use the accommodation schedule and the briefing chart to calculate the outline building costs.

The quantity surveyor will analyse the final accounts for completed buildings into the **cost per floor area** and the percentage cost per element. The **primary elements**, substructure, superstructure, internal finishes, services and external works are further subdivided to allow the design to be monitored and the result will be a well-balanced building design, built within budget

Similar extensions are analysed for this purpose. A two-storey extension to a traditionally built house cost £9 000. The floor area of the extension was 20 m^2.

$$\text{building cost} = \frac{\text{final account}}{\text{floor area}}$$

$$= \frac{£9000}{20\,\text{m}^2} = £450/\text{m}^2 \text{ of floor area}$$

The quantity surveyor uses the **accommodation schedule** to establish the cost limit (Fig. 2.31).

This will establish the predicted cost outlay for the client, known as the **cost limit**. It may be that the client had a cost limit before commissioning the architect, in which case the architect should be told at the briefing that a cost limit applies, which becomes a design constraint. The architect will then inform the quantity surveyor of this cost limit and the maximum floor area will be calculated to keep costs within this limit.

$$\text{maximum floor area} = \frac{\text{cost limit}}{\text{floor area}}$$

$$= \frac{£7500}{£450} + 20\% \frac{\text{(design and price}}{\text{risk percentage)}}$$

$$= 13.08\,\text{m}^2 \text{ maximum floor area}$$

SITE CHECKLIST

Prepared by: A. Drawer   Job 123
Date of survey: 11th April 1994

Initial site inspection

1.01	Existing buildings
1.02	Built environment
1.03	Natural environment
1.04	Adjoining buildings
1.05	Surrounding built environment and activities
1.06	Surrounding natural environment
1.07	Photographs and sketches
1.08	Initial impression of commission

Figure 2.30

TAKEOFF, ABSTRACT & BILL
Quantity Surveyors

OUTLINE COST PLAN

2 Storey extension
brick built
Date: 14th April 1994

Room title	Floor area (m²)	Building cost (£/m²)	Cost (£)
Dining room	10.50		
Bedroom	10.50		
	21.00	450.00	9450
Add design risk	10%		945
price risk	10%		945
			11340

Figure 2.31

Once the cost limit is agreed, the design team must monitor the design against this constraint. **Elemental cost** is used to ensure that the design is within the cost limit and that the client receives a well-balanced design. The elemental cost percentages (Fig. 2.32) are based on similar suitable buildings.

The quantity surveyor will monitor the design proposals to ensure that the design solutions are within the budget. Considerable amounts of published cost data are available to the architect and the quantity surveyor, such as the RICS Cost Information Service. The storage of this cost information is based on the CI/SfB system or the CAWS, as defined by the Coordinated Project Information. The Common Arrangement of Work Section (CAWS) is based on the reference system used in the Standard Method of Measurement 7, which the quantity surveyor uses in preparing the Bill of Quantities.

There are several other methods of analysing building costs for cost planning purposes, two of which are:

- *Cost per unit of accommodation*, often used for cost planning hospitals, or schools. The unit of measurement

TAKEOFF, ABSTRACT & BILL
Quantity Surveyors

ELEMENTAL COST PLAN
Cost limit: £11 340

2 Storey extension
brick built
Date: 14th April 1994

Element	%	Elemental cost (£)	Designed cost	Within budget	Outside cost
Substructure	20	2268			
Superstructure	30	3402			
Internal finishes	15	1701			
Services	30	3402			
External works	5	567			
	100	11340			

Figure 2.32

for the building cost is the person using the facility. A design brief for a 600 pupil school enhances the need to analyse data in this way.

- *Cost per cubic metre of building*. The building costs are analysed into cost per cubic metre. Instead of using the floor area the volume of the building is taken. The design brief for a warehouse, for example, may be defined in metres cubed, therefore the cost needs to be calculated in a compatible unit of measurement.

Apart from the cost acting as building constraint, there are also legal constraints to be considered.

Legal constraints

There are two main groups of laws: **common law**, which follows custom and precedent, and **legislative law**, which is made by Parliament.

The **law of property** and land may influence the building design. Boundaries and **easement** may seriously restrict development; for instance, the local council may have **right of access** to lay drains under the land, and this easement can be used by the council to restrict the siting of any building. The restriction may be that a building cannot be erected within three metres of the public sewer.

Adjoining owners have a **right of support** from the client's land. Or the adjoining owner may have acquired a **right of light**, which could restrict the siting and height of the proposed building. Easements may be granted by deed or over a period of time, usually 20 years. **Right of way** may be limited to a particular user or the general public and **wayleaves** are often obtained by utility companies for cable or pipe routes.

There may also be **restrictive covenants** attached to the site. In the sale of the freehold building land the owner may include a restrictive covenant, limiting development to a particular size or type of building. However, the solicitor should have obtained all this information from the searches carried out at the time of purchase.

The **Defective Premises Act** relates to dwellings. This, in addition to any contractual obligation, requires that the architect carries out the design in a workmanlike manner, to ensure that the dwelling or conversion work is fit for habitation. The **Health and Safety at Work, etc.** Act places a duty of care on employers or their agents to provide a safe system of work. This is in addition to other legislation such as the **Control of Pollution** and the **Control of Substances Hazardous to Health**. It is imperative, therefore, that the architect has an up-to-date library on legislation. Other legislation may apply to certain types of development; for example, the **Fire Precaution Act** and the various **Highways Acts** will restrict the size, siting and provisions included in the proposed development.

Town and country planning

The Town and Country Planning Acts have given the local authorities considerable powers to regulate the development of the built environment within the council boundaries. A **structure plan**, prepared by the county council, is available for developers, explaining the county council's strategy for development, and zoning of different areas for different purposes, which will include Green Belt land.

These development plans are produced after consultation with interested parties. The district council, on the basis of the larger structure plan, will prepare the **local plan**. Development control may introduce further constraints regarding the density of activity permitted in the zoned area; for example, the density of housing development could be stipulated as a maximum number of dwellings per hectare. Other constraints limit the size of a building or the number of storeys.

Areas of outstanding beauty or special scientific interest can be designated **conservation areas**. If development is allowed in a conservation area there will be stringent rules limiting the type, mass and the use of materials. It is not only the built environment that is subject to planning controls, but also the natural environment. Planning authorities have the power to designate **tree preservation orders**, affectionately known as TPOs. Listed buildings form another group that preserve the character of the planning area. When a building is **listed** permission is required to alter the building in any shape or form.

Delegated powers allow the planning authority to request an **Environmental Impact Analysis**. By this requirement, the developer or agent (the architect) must submit to the planning authority an assessment showing the effect that the proposed new development might have on the natural habitat, both flora and fauna.

Planning controls require that the majority of developments have **planning permission**. There are few exemptions and a development can be a **permitted development** if it complies with the structure or local plan. This reduces the need to obtain outline planning permission, and is a useful procedure to reduce the risk of planning refusal. At an early stage the planning authority can be asked to consider the proposal in outline, rather than in detail. If **outline planning permission** is obtained, full planning permission must also be obtained at a later date. This is known as **reserved matters**.

Submission for full or reserved matters must be accompanied by various certificates, together with the planning fee, and a written acknowledgement is returned to the architect. Four copies of the plans, and an application form, must be submitted to the planning authority. From the date of receipt the planning authority has eight weeks in which to render a decision. Some applications will require consultation with interested parties and the local residents can register their objections. All correspondence relating to public consultation is available for inspection.

The planning committee's decision will take one of the following forms:

- granted
- granted with conditions
- refused, stating the reasons

Where the planning application is refused, the applicant can appeal against the planning authority's decision. This appeal must be lodged within six months of the refusal and on special forms. Appeals are often best dealt with by a town planning consultant.

For a more detailed discussion, see Unit 5, section 5.2 (Town plan features), p. 223.

Self-assessment task

Produce a design specification to satisfy the client's requirements for a 3-bedroomed, 5-person, two-storey brick-built house on an infill plot within the village boundary.

The evidence gathered for this task can be obtained from:

- Unit 6 (Surveying Processes): the site to be developed is to be measured and plotted.
- Unit 5 (Town planning and Development): evidence for the locality of the site.
- Unit 8 (Financing and the Built Environment): basis for the design specification, using current building costs per square metre.

Site survey: The site has all the utility supplies available in the highway. North and west aspects overlook open undulating countryside. The east boundary is bounded by the local highway, and access onto the site is by this busy road.

The accommodation schedule is shown in Fig. 2.33.

Accommodation schedule	
House type: 3 bedroom /5 person	Project no. 2/2
Room title	Size: minimum net floor area
Living room	17.5 m²
Dining room	13.5 m²
Kitchen	13.5 m²
Bedroom 1	13.0 m²
Bedroom 2	10.5 m²
Bedroom 3	10.5 m²
Bathroom	7.0 m²

Figure 2.33

Write a letter to the client accepting the commission and detailing the design services offered.

1. Prepare **two** scheme layouts based on the accommodation schedule.
2. Select **one** preferred layout for a presentation to the client.
3. Based on the preferred layout, produce a circulation diagram.
4. Produce a perspective sketch of the house.
5. Produce a briefing chart for each room.
6. Prepare the outline cost plan.
7. Record and confirm details of the presentation to the client.

2.3 Drawing techniques for communicating design and technical solutions

Topics covered in this section are:

- Drawing techniques and media
- RIBA Plan of Work
- Types of drawings
- Schedules
- Drawing management
- Architectural library
- Computer-aided design

Drawing techniques and media

The drawing is a piece of communication, therefore the architect must have in mind the user and the purpose of the drawing. This will affect the drawing technique and the media used to transmit that information.

The types of drawings can be classified according to purpose.

Production drawings

These are used basically by the builder and are the final instruction to the builder from the design team. The production drawing is the last in a series of drawings communicating the design team's ideas and requirements. As such the quality and accuracy should be very high. Before the production drawings are completed, the design team will have analysed several design alternatives.

Freehand drawings

Sketch drawings are a means of determining alternative design solutions and, as such, are only for circulation among the design team. Some sketch drawings will become **conceptualisation drawings**, well presented to influence the client, whether single or institutional, to make a design choice. Whatever type of drawing is produced, certain basic drawing skills are used.

Sketch drawings are sometimes called preliminary drawings. This type of drawing includes

- site layouts
- site conditions
- outline proposals – plans, elevations and perspectives
- design solutions – plans, elevations and perspectives
- thinking drawings – architect's brainstorming ideas

Often the drawings will be soft pencil sketches, but crayon, charcoal or pastel sketches would sometimes be more appropriate if the client is to be influenced. The **drawing medium** is usually **detail paper**, supplied in rolls or pads up to A2 in size. The detail paper or layout paper is sufficiently transparent to allow for tracing, yet opaque enough to show original work clearly, taking crayons, pastels or felt/fibre pens.

The sketch drawings will be photocopied for circulation among the design team. Acceptable dyeline prints can be obtained from detail paper.

The end user determines the content and size of the sketch drawings. This type of drawing is short lived, often being converted into formal design proposals, yet the drawings need filing and recording. Usually sketch drawings are numbered with the prefix 'P', denoting **preliminary work**.

The use of grid ruled paper will aid the accurate proportion of length to width, or component size to element size. The modular dimension of 300 mm is used with a subgrid of 100 mm. Preprint sheets are recommended with a standard titleblock based on British Standard 1192. Although a tedious task, it is absolutely necessary that each drawing should be numbered and recorded in the job logbook. Design periods are sometimes very long and the original decisions become blurred in time. Even work that has been superseded needs to be filed away from the working file. Alterations, additions and amendments to the concept of the drawing should be noted and dated. This avoids the use of outdated details.

Scale drawings

Once decisions have been made on the design, scale drawings can be prepared. These are not 'short-lived' drawings like sketches but will be drawn to scale on tracing paper or film. Pencil scale drawings are acceptable, but for clarity of copying and durability ink scale drawings are preferred.

Drawing paper

There are two main groups of drawing paper:

- **Machine-made** drawing paper, like **cartridge paper**, is satisfactory for most pencil drawings. Unmounted cartridge paper has a right and wrong side. Cartridge paper is made in three thickness: thin, medium and stout. Medium cartridge paper is used for pencil drawings and stout cartridge paper will take ink drawing moderately well. If durability and copying of the drawing are essential requirements then ink drawings must be used.
- **Hand-made** and **mould-made** papers are obtained in standard sheet sizes and have three surface finishes. Hot pressed, which is smooth and known as HP paper, can be used for most kinds of pencil or ink renderings and wash work. The other surfaces are NOT (medium) and R (rough).

Standard sizes of drawing paper sheets are given in Table 2.1.

Table 2.1 Standard drawing paper sizes

Size of sheet	Dimensions (mm)
A0	1189 × 1682
A1	841 × 1189
A2	594 × 841
A3	297 × 594
A4	210 × 297

Tracing paper, cloth and film

Tracing paper is the most economical and is classified into three grades: thin, medium and stout. All tracing paper will accept pencil or ink. The thin tracing paper is not very durable and although it will be good enough for preliminary sketches it is not suitable for final negatives. Smooth surface is better than rough surface for pencil drawings. The tracing paper is usually described by the weight per square metre (Table 2.2).

Table 2.2 Qualities of tracing papers

Material	Weight (g/m^2)	Grade
Natural tracing:		
Smooth or matt	63	Thin
	90	Medium
	112	Thick
Prepared tracing:		
Smooth or semi-matt or matt	50/55	Thin
	70/75	Medium
	85/90	Thick

Where humidity rapidly changes, the tracing paper may buckle, and if dried out too quickly it becomes brittle. **Record drawings** should not be stored on tracing paper. This causes problems for archiving plans, where accuracy and definition of drawing are important.

Tracing cloth is more expensive than tracing paper and is often used for master negatives. Unlike tracing paper, it does not age or crease in storage.

Tracing film is better than either tracing paper or cloth. Film has superior transparency and is both stretch proof and waterproof. The ink-based **master negatives** should be drawn on tracing film.

Basically there are two types of drafting film: (1) the surface is roughened by chemical or mechanical abrasion; or (2) the surface is applied by lacquers. On both types of drafting film, one side has been prepared for drafting. Lacquered drafting film gives a finer tooth (roughness), a more consistent surface and better resistance to eraser wear. A special ink and pencil – polymer resin-based pencils rather than the traditional graphite pencil – should be used on drafting film. The choice of drafting medium depends on the type of drawing (Table 2.3).

Table 2.3 Choice of drafting medium

Drawing medium	Type of drawing
Measured drawings or surveys	Ink on tracing paper. If dimensional stability important use drafting film
Preliminary sketches	Pencil or felt-tip pen on detail or tracing paper
Scheme details	Pencil on detail paper or tracing paper
Working drawings	Ink on tracing or drafting film, good line permanence with ink, but polymer resin pencil on drafting film

Drawing equipment

Drawing board and tee square

Drawing boards (Fig. 2.34) and drafting machines are produced to suit the standard drawing sizes A1, A2 or A3. The

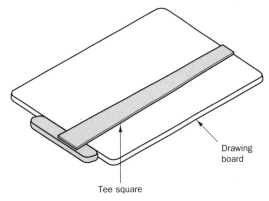

Figure 2.34 Drawing board and tee square

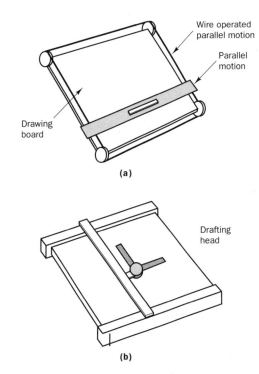

Figure 2.35 Drafting machines: (a) parallel motion unit; (b) track or trolley type

A3 drafting machine is portable and has a drafting head which acts as a tee square and set square.

Drafting machines may have a **parallel motion unit** (Fig. 2.35a) – this type of machine may have a drafting head – or may be of the **track** or **trolley** type (Fig. 2.35b).

Set squares are used for vertical or inclined lines. There are three types of set square, but the adjustable set square is the more useful (Fig. 2.36).

Drawing instruments

The standard instruments are dividers and compasses, which may be of spring bow (Fig. 2.37a) or beam type (Fig. 2.37b).

Drawing pens

These are used for ink drawing and allow for variable line thickness to prioritise drawn information (Fig. 2.38). The drawing is a communication between the producer and the user and the information requires to be graded to help the user identify important items.

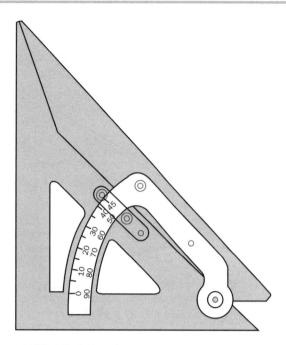

Figure 2.36 Adjustable set square

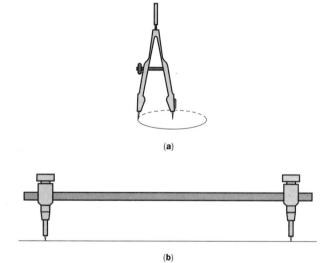

Figure 2.37 Compasses: (a) spring bow; (b) beam

Figure 2.38 Line thicknesses

Primary information should be represented by thick intense lines, while lower order information will be represented by thin, less intense, lines.

Drawing pencils

Graphite pencils are in general use, with grades ranging from 6B (very soft) to 9H (very hard). The choice of graphite pencil will depend on:

- the effect required (e.g. outline thumbnail sketch)
- the drawing medium (e.g. smooth detail or cartridge paper)
- the nature of the drawing (e.g. preliminary, sketch, outline)

High polymer leads which are very thin and do not require to be sharpened, are used in clutch pencils. The leads are very fine, with diameters of 0.2–0.9 mm, and are used where line thickness and consistency are important criteria for the drawing:

- **Smearproof plastic** This type of drafting pencil should be used on drafting film.
- **Smearproof and waterproof plastic** This type of pencil should be used for permanent drafting on drafting film.

Scale rule

All drawings are generally produced to a scale, and a **scale rule** (Fig. 2.39) is useful when producing scale drawings; BS 1192 recommends certain scales for different types of drawing. For instance, the floor plan is drawn to a scale of 1 : 50, the actual room dimension may be 5000 mm, but on the scaled plan the drawn length would be 100 mm:

$$\text{drawn length (scaled length)} = \frac{\text{actual length}}{\text{scale ratio}}$$

Templates and curves

These – for example, the French curve shown in Fig. 2.40 – are very useful efficiency aids to the architect.

Erasers

Alterations, corrections and removal of constructions lines to improve the general appearance of the drawing are carried out by **erasing**. Pencil lines are erased with a **gum** or **vinyl** eraser. The removal of pastel, charcoal or soft pencil shading will occasionally need the use of a special **putty** eraser.

Ink lines on tracing paper are removed with an **ink** eraser, and an **eraser shield** would assist in targeting the correction. Ink lines (etching or non-etching ink) on film are erased with a vinyl eraser.

Presentation drawings

We have concentrated on architectural plans, but sometimes the architect will have to produce **presentation** drawings, such as

- planning drawings
- landscape drawings
- measured drawings

Figure 2.39 Scale rule

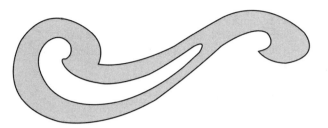

Figure 2.40 French curves

Stage D   Scheme design
Stage E   Detail design
Stage F   Production information
Stage G   Bills of quantities
Stage H   Tender action
Stage J   Project planning
Stage K   Operations on site
Stage L   Completion
Stage M   Feedback

These drawings will be rendered, that is coloured or shaded, to show the proposed building in its final setting, with people, cars, trees, etc., superimposed on the line perspective. Dry transfers are often used to add subjects and details. The presentation drawing may be rendered in a 'dry' media, for example pastel or crayon. The main media used for rendering drawings are ink washes, water colours, poster colours, pastel, coloured pencils, dry transfer tones and colour, pencil or ink only.

Planning drawings

These are survey maps and diagrams used to depict the existing infrastructure and buildings. A structure plan or local plan prepared by the planning authority is a typical example of this type of drawing.

Landscape drawings

This type of drawing can be a site analysis and preliminary, main report or working drawing. If the planning authority require an environmental impact analysis, this type of drawing would be submitted.

Measured drawings

These are scale drawings accurately detailing the actual buildings or services. Listed buildings may be accurately measured and drawn to scale as a measured drawing for archive purposes. Displays by the planning authority during structure plan consultation may utilise measured and rendered drawings. A record of the location of building services after commissioning would be given to the client as an accurate record of service layouts. This measured drawing is also known as **services as installed**.

RIBA Plan of Work

There are several reasons why drawings should be presented in accordance with agreed conventions and scales. Consistency of presentation aids the end user, who becomes familiar with standard symbols and conventions, to interpret the information accurately. The Royal Institute of British Architects have developed a sequence, similar to a checklist that the architect should follow. The stages may not have clear boundaries but the sequence will avoid the possibility of abortive work and aid coordination of the design team.

The stages of the RIBA Plan of Work are:

Stage A   Inception
Stage B   Feasibility
Stage C   Outline proposals

Inception

The purpose of inception is to agree the general outline of client's needs and a strategy for developing the scheme. The work at this stage will include:

- the client brief – an initial statement of the client's needs, including the time scale and finance
- the appointment of the architect – a letter of confirmation, a contract of engagement, the use of consultants
- site details – the initial site visit and obtaining the site plan

Feasibility

This is to provide the client with an **assessment** of the scheme in outline. The appraisal and recommendation should show the project to be **technically**, **functionally** and **financially** viable.

The work will involve the various members of the project.

- Design team:
  - initial briefing meeting
  - allocation of tasks and time periods
- Architect:
  - site survey
  - boundaries, rights of ways, easements
  - structure plan for permitted development
  - obtain outline planning consent
  - utility services and letters for ascertaining and marking services
- Quantity surveyor:
  - user studies on cost implications, access, local building economy
  - prepare outline cost plan
- Structural engineer:
  - investigation of soil, including site borings and geological maps
  - investigating site exposure to wind damage and rainfall
  - checking at local authority to ascertain ground conditions and workings or highway access and development
- Services consultant:
  - user studies for services loading
  - preliminary views of utility suppliers
  - establish environmental and services requirement

Outline proposals

To obtain the client's approval on the general approach to layout, design and construction.
- Architect:
  - study circulation and space requirements
  - analyse design solution and identify design requirements and constraints, such as planning controls
  - prepare key plans indicating critical dimensions, main space location and uses

- collate design dossier, sketches, notes and design assumptions
- collate the design specification into function and performance requirements
- Quantity surveyor:
  - identify key cost elements in the design specification
  - prepare costs for alternative design solution
- Structural engineer:
  - advise the design team on: types of structure, methods of construction, types of foundation
  - identify key constraints in the design specification
- Services consultant:
  - evaluate service requirements based on design specification
  - identify key constraints in the design specification

Scheme design

The various design solutions are analysed and an agreed design solution is prepared and presented to the client. After this stage the **brief should not be modified.**

The scheme design should now be presented to the client and approval obtained.

- Architect:
  - develop detailed design solutions
  - negotiate and consult on the final scheme design
  - produce the full scheme design
  - prepare presentation drawings for client approval
- Quantity surveyor:
  - prepare comparative cost studies on design alternatives
  - finalise the cost plan and prepare elemental cost plans
- Structural engineer:
  - based on the scheme design, prepare design sketches, calculations and structural material
  - assist in the preparation of cost plans
  - select building form and type
- Service engineer:
  - based on the scheme design, prepare design sketches, calculations and service equipment and material
  - assist in the preparation of cost plans

Detailed design

The purpose of the detailed design is to finalise and coordinate the design solutions into a coherent project. The fine detail of the scheme design is resolved. There should be no further changes in location, mass or cost after this stage, or the design work will be abortive.

- Architect:
  - design the component and assembly details
  - check with the quantity surveyor about the detailed costings
  - check the scheme and detailed design for compliance with planning, building control and legal requirements
  - review the scheme and detailed design with design specification
- Quantity surveyor:
  - cost check the design details with the elemental cost plans
- Structural engineer:
  - carry out detailed design of structural elements
  - confirm loadings and structural behaviour
  - interpret services layout requirements and builder's work requirements

- Services engineer:
  - carry out detailed design of services elements
  - confirm environmental loadings and macro climate influences
  - produce services layout requirements and builder's work requirements

Production information

The design team will now produce the working drawings for the builder to use on site. Drawings, specifications and schedules will be prepared, explaining all the design team's requirements. The bill of quantities is also prepared. All statutory approvals, such as planning and building control approvals, should now be obtained.

- Architect:
  - draw to scale all the necessary plans, sections and elevations
  - annotate the production drawings with specifications and material conventions
  - prepare schedules
  - submit the production drawings for planning and building control approval
- Quantity surveyor:
  - agree contract procurement method and contract conditions
- Structural engineer:
  - draw to scale all the necessary structural plans, sections and elevations
  - annotate the production drawings with specifications and material conventions
  - prepare schedules, such as foundation schedule, bending schedule, etc.
  - submit the production drawings to enable the architect to obtain planning and building control
  - advise the quantity surveyor on nominations
- Service engineer:
  - draw to scale all the necessary mechanical and electrical plans, sections, elevations and diagrammatical layouts
  - annotate the production drawings with specifications and material conventions
  - prepare schedules for plumbing fittings, lighting, etc.
  - submit the production drawings to enable the architect to prepare builder's work drawings and obtain planning and building control
  - advise the quantity surveyor on nominations

Bills of quantities

The purpose of the bill of quantities is to **describe accurately** and **quantify** the building project. The quantities and specification should be based on the full production drawings, schedules and specification.

The bill of quantities has four sections, or bills:

- contract particulars
- specification, sometimes called 'preambles to trade'
- measured section
- appendix

The bill of quantities will allow all the tenderers to submit their estimates on a common basis. This will ease the tender adjudication process, by which the builder is selected.

The bill of quantities is prepared according to the rules of measurement and classification found in *Standard Method of Measurement for Building Work 7th edition*; affectionately called SMM7.

Tender action

Based on the production information and the bill of quantities, building contractors are invited to **submit a price** for building the project. **Tender documents** are sent to building contractors; that is:

- tender drawings
- tender bill of quantities
- tender contract conditions

The **JCT Standard Form of Building Contract 1980** is often used by the architect to describe the obligations of the client, the design team and the contractor during the construction stage.

The JCT Form has four editions:

- Private edition without quantities
- Private edition with quantities
- Local authority edition without quantities
- Local authority edition with quantities

The quantity surveyor will advise on the type of building contract to use and the method of procurement.

There are several ways to obtain tenderers. The **open tender** method allows anyone to submit a bid or offer to carry out the work. There is no selection or screening of suitable tenderers. **Selective tendering** reduces the number of tenderers, and local authorities often use this method, inviting only the listed contractors to price the tender documents.

The building contractor is not involved in the design process and therefore is limited in the advice that can be offered on construction methods until the design is firmly completed. Buildability has been considered by the design team during the development of the scheme design, but the specialist in construction methods cannot enter any discussions on the project unless a negotiated tender process is used.

Once tenders have been received by the submission date, the architect and the quantity surveyor will open the bids. For security the bids are sent in a special envelope and opened at a predetermined, and publicised, time.

The procedure for tendering should follow the recommendations outlined in the **NJCC Code of procedure for tendering** (Fig. 2.41).

FORM of TENDER

Dear sirs:
  TENDER for PROJECT at . . . .   Project No. . . . . . .

  We agree to execute and complete the works as described and in accordance with the tender drawings, bill of quantities and contract conditions supplied to us for the sum of . . . .
  . . . . £ . . . .

  The construction programme will take . . . . . . weeks from the date of possession.
  The tender will remain open for a period of . . . . . . weeks.

Yours faithfully

Name of Contractor . . . .
Address   . . . .
                  . . . .

Date . . . .

Figure 2.41

Dear Sirs:
  TENDER for PROJECT at . . . .   Project No. . . . . .

  The tenders for this project were opened on 30th June 1994 at 10.00, in the offices of A. Drawer, Architects.
  Your tender was priced lowest, and subject to checking your bid, we will be recommending acceptance of your tender to our client.
  Please submit the priced bill of quantities to this office, so that it may be checked.

Yours sincerely

Figure 2.42 Letter of acceptance of tender

Once the tenders have been opened and a contractor has been selected, all those who submitted tenders should be notified of the architect's decision (Fig. 2.42).

Contract signing

The builder has been appointed and the contract must be signed by both parties. The **client** and the **builder** are the two parties to the **contract**. The builder offers to carry out the work described in the tender documents for a tender sum. The client accepts this offer and the consideration to the two contracting parties will be:

- client's consideration is the building
- builder's consideration is the tender sum.

The tender documents now become the contract documents:

tender drawings	contract drawings
tender bill	contract bill
tender conditions	contract conditions
tender documents =	**contract documents**

The construction stage now commences. A peculiarity of the construction industry is that there are at least two names for everything, and in this respect even the RIBA Plan of Work has other names which relate to the various stages:

- Inception and feasibility (stages A and B) = Briefing
- Outline proposals and scheme design (stages C and D) = Sketch plans
- Detail design, production information, bills of quantities and tender action (stages E, F, G and H) = Working drawings
- Project planning, operations on site, completion and feedback (stages H, J, K and L) = Site operations

The builder will be the end user for the contract documents and all information will be available on the **contract drawings** and in the **contract bill**. There should be a concerted effort to reference information to minimise search time and reduce errors. In this respect, **coordinated project information** techniques are of great assistance to the architect.

This will structure the type of drawings, annotation and referencing across drawings showing plans, elevations, sections, schedules and specifications.

Drawings

The structure and issue of drawings should follow this method.

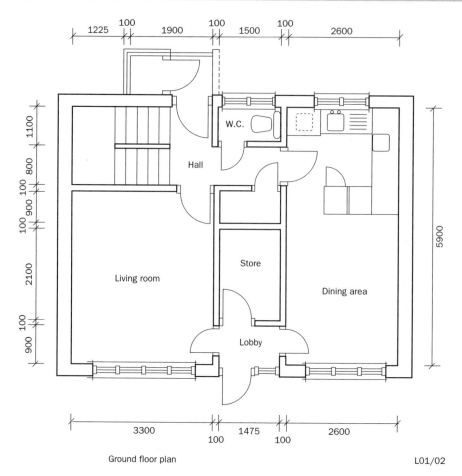

Ground floor plan

L01/02

Figure 2.43 Location drawing (all dimensions in mm)

Types of drawings

Location drawings

The information shown on the location drawing will be overall sizes, levels and references to assembly drawings. The plans are intended to show the location of the work, not detail.

The location drawings, which can be plans, elevations or sections, are numbered consecutively with the prefix L (Fig. 2.43). Typical location drawings will be

- block plans
- site plans
- floor plans
- foundations plans
- roof plans
- section through the building
- elevations

Assembly drawings

The purpose of assembly drawings is to show how the building is erected on site. Information will include component identification and reference, assembly dimensions and tolerances, with reference to component drawings.

The assembly drawings can be

- plans
- elevations
- section

The assembly drawing number is prefixed by the letter A (Fig. 2.44). Standard details are often produced, thus, instead of redrawing, a standard detail drawing is reproduced. **Standard details** need an efficient library coding system to aid retrieval and sorting, and the Common Arrangement of Work Section (CAWS) reference system is considered to be ideal since this is based on the coding system found in the Standard Method of Measurement (SMM7). Some assembly drawings will show:

- substructure section
- external wall details

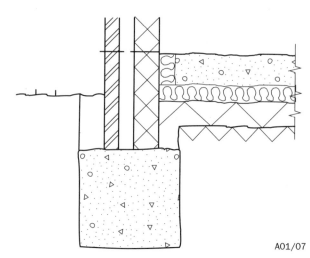

A01/07

Figure 2.44 Substructure detail assembly drawing

- wall openings such as head, sill and jamb sections, plans
- eaves details
- internal walls
- stair details

Component drawings

This type of drawing shows individual components in the unfixed state. Information will include component sizes, tolerance and specification with reference to the bill of quantity.

The component drawing number is prefixed by the letter C (Fig. 2.45), and typical component details are:

- wood window head detail
- special door construction
- sill
- coping stone

Projections

Orthographic projection is a way of illustrating three-dimensional objects in a two-dimensional drawing. The basic drawing layout for a location drawing of a house is shown in Fig. 2.46.

Drawing projections must comply with the relevant British Standard to prevent misunderstanding and avoid errors in interpreting the drawing.

The orthographic projection commonly used in Britain is called the **first angle projection**, but there are other less common projections that can be used to illustrate a three-dimensional object.

Axonometric projection

The advantage of an axonometric projection (Fig. 2.47) is the true plan set at 45°. It is suitable for **interior** and **kitchen** layouts. Planning drawings are effective as axonometric projections to show the relationship of existing buildings, topography and the proposed building.

Isometric projection

Unlike the axonometric projection, the **isometric** plan view is slightly distorted (Fig. 2.48) and can be used to show the nature of the design more clearly than an orthographic projection. It is sometimes used during the conceptualisation of the design to help the client grasp the mass of the proposal.

Oblique projection

When primary information is drawn in elevation, the interpretation can be enhanced by an oblique projection (Fig. 2.49).

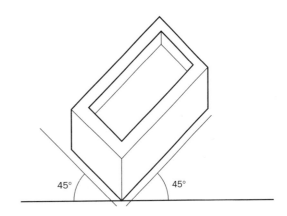

Figure 2.47 Axonometric projection

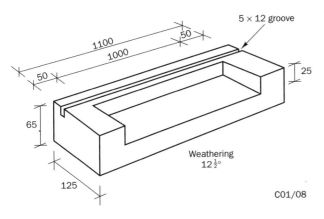

Figure 2.45 Sill detail component drawing

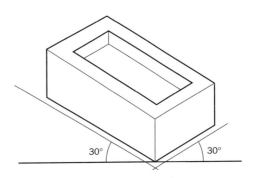

Figure 2.48 Isometric projection

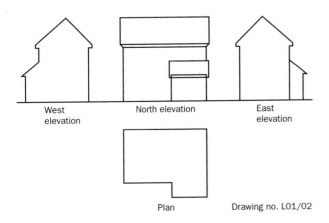

Figure 2.46 Orthographic projection

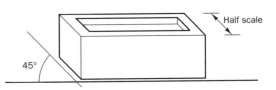

Figure 2.49 Oblique projection

Preliminary drawings

These drawings are often referred to as **thinking** drawings, where the architect illustrates elements of the design. The freehand sketches are broad strokes with little detail and illustrate either mass, proportion or other aesthetic principles. Soft pencil or felt tip on detail paper is the preferred medium. To avoid deception the detail paper is often grid paper to ensure a correct proportion of images. The focal point of the building can be quickly illustrated by a preliminary sketch. Simplicity and avoidance of detail are the main aspects of a good preliminary drawing.

Sketch drawings

The entire range of drawings can be illustrated as sketch drawings. A location drawing can be used as a 'key' or control drawing, showing control dimensions or levels. A sketched assembly drawing (Fig. 2.50) can be used by the architect to instruct the technician preparing the ink negative. To avoid misinterpretation of size, it is advantageous to use a modular, grid ruled plan, in which the main grid is 300 mm, with a secondary grid of 100 mm.

Working drawings

These are the **final drawn instructions** which the builder will use on site to convert the design ideas into a real building, and care must be taken to ensure accuracy of dimensions and specification. In preparing the location plan it is best to use a **control box** – that is, the maximum design length and width are drawn on the tracing film in pencil (Fig. 2.51). All details should fit within this control box, and if you find you are drawing outside the control box you should stop immediately as this indicates an error in the detailed measurements. Once the drawing has been completed in ink, clean up the drawing and erase the control box.

When a drawing is being produced, thought must be given to the **structuring** of information. A drawing contains certain information that must be observed. This is **primary** information, shown by thicker lines and/or high intensity. **Secondary** information will be shown by lines of medium thickness, while **tertiary** information will be indicated by thin

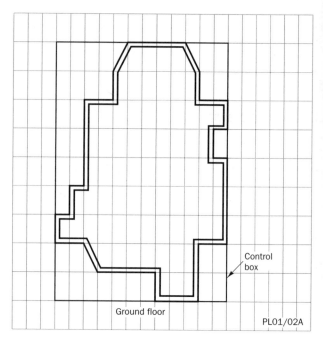

Figure 2.51 Working drawing control box

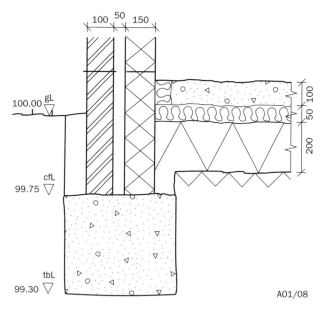

Figure 2.52 Assembly drawing showing an information hierarchy

lines (Fig. 2.52). With ink drawings on film or tracing paper, different pen thickness will achieve the necessary **information hierarchy**.

Specification

All drawings require **annotation**, i.e. letters describing the elements or identifying the components (Fig. 2.53). As these descriptive notes and words must be clearly understood, it is essential to aim for legibility, which means taking time to

- form and shape each individual letter
- space letters and words correctly
- arrange the text to help the end user
- arrange the text in hierarchical context

To help achieve clarity of specification, stencils and dry letter transfers are available.

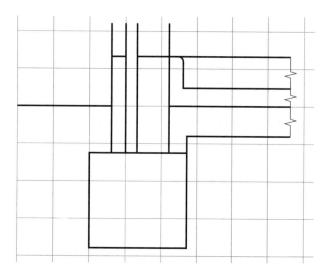

Figure 2.50 Sketch assembly drawing on grid plan

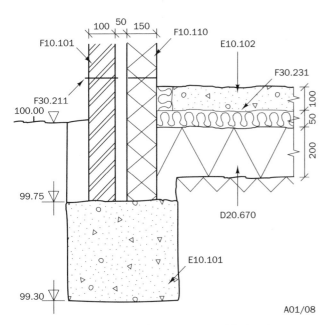

Figure 2.53 An annotated substructure assembly drawing

Bill of quantities

The bill of quantities – which is, first, a vital tender document, then a contract document – should be an accurate description and quantification of the project. There should therefore be a cross-reference to the tender drawing and architect's notes or specifications. To achieve this the CAWS is used (see Figs 2.54 and 2.55).

Coordinated project references

Based on the SMM7, some of the main cross-references are:

- Concrete work:
  - Concrete foundation — E10.1
  - Concrete bed (floor) — E10.4
  - Concrete cavity filling — E30.8
- Masonry:
  - Clay brickwork in walls — F10.1
  - Cavities — F30.1.1
  - Damp-proof course, vertical — F30.2.1
  - Damp-proof course, horizontal — F30.2.3

F10.101 Brickwork above d.p.c. level			
Bricks: Clay to BS 3921			
Special shapes: None			
Manufacturer and reference: LBC			
dapple white			
Mortar: see Z21, 1:6			
Joint: 10 mm bucket handle			

Figure 2.54 Extract from bill of quantities – specification

F10 Brick/block walling			
facing brickwork to spec. 101			
Walls			
Half brick thick, pointed on side	100	m²	

Figure 2.55 Extract from bill of quantities – measurement

- Carcass timber:
  - Rafter — G20.9.2
  - Floor joist — G20.6
  - Floor boarding — K20.2
  - Trussed rafter — G20.2
- Finishing joinery:
  - Wood window — L20.1
  - Double glazing — L40.2
  - Wood door frame — L20.7
  - Wood door — L20.1
  - Architrave — P20.1
- Roofing:
  - Concrete roof tiles — H60.1
- Plastering
  - Plasterboard and skim — M20.2
  - Plaster to walls — M20.1
  - Floor screed — M10.5

This information and cross-referencing should be applied to the architect's drawings.

Location drawing

British Standard Specification 1192 has recommended or preferred scales for location drawings.

- **Block plans** These usually show the siting of the project, in relation to Ordnance Survey Maps. Conventions are used to depict boundaries, roads and other details (Fig. 2.56). Recommended scales are: 1:2500; 1:1250; 1:500. Conventions used on a survey or block plan are shown in Fig. 2.57.
- **Site plans** These usually show the extent of the site but no surrounding detail (Fig. 2.58). Recommended scales are: 1:500 and 1:200.
- **Floor plans** These usually show layout of rooms (Fig. 2.59), key dimensions and levels, and may also use

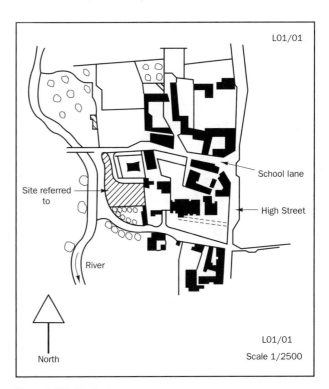

Figure 2.56 Block plan

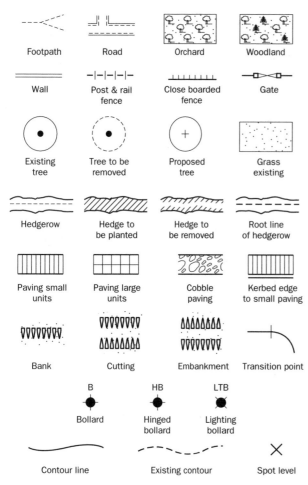

Figure 2.57 Conventions used on a survey or block plan

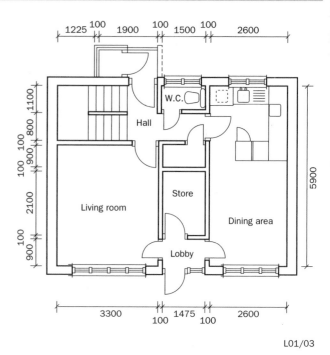

Figure 2.59 Floor plan showing layout of rooms

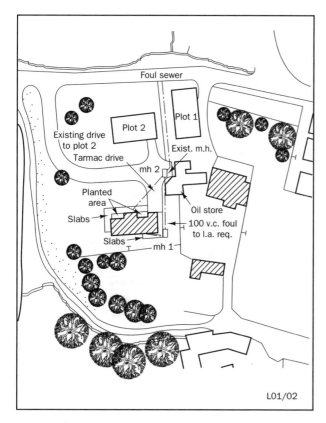

Figure 2.58 Site plan

conventions and symbols to show materials and location of fittings and appliances. Recommended scales are: 1:200; 1:100; 1:50.

– **Line types** (Fig. 2.60) are used to differentiate information.
– **Hatching** or conventions are used to illustrate materials (Fig. 2.61).
– **Symbols** are used to show fittings and appliances often with standard abbreviations (Fig. 2.62).

● **Elevations**   These usually show the outline of the building, opening details and sizes, level datums and floor positions (Fig. 2.63).

● **Estate road layout**   Recommended scales: 1:1250 and 1:500. Line types will fulfil an important role in this type of location drawing. The identity of buried items and various services will be indicated by different line types. Conventions and symbols will indicate hard and soft landscape details and street furniture will be indicated by symbols.

Assembly drawings

The structuring of drawn information into specific sheets helps the search patterns of the end user. Some unenlightened architects would fill the drawing sheet with a mixture of plans, elevations and, if there was room, a detailed section. The title chosen for the drawing sheet is the first indication of the content of the sheet. Search procedures by the end users follow a pattern and the drawings should be structured and titled to maximise this procedure. Recommended scales are: 1:50; 1:20; 1:10.

The drawings will comprise plan views and sections, and the thickness of lines will depend on the information hierarchy. Outlines and different components drawn with thicker lines alert the user to key information as the eye scans the entire drawing. The placing of sections on the drawing sheet should be carefully laid out to minimise search time for the end user.

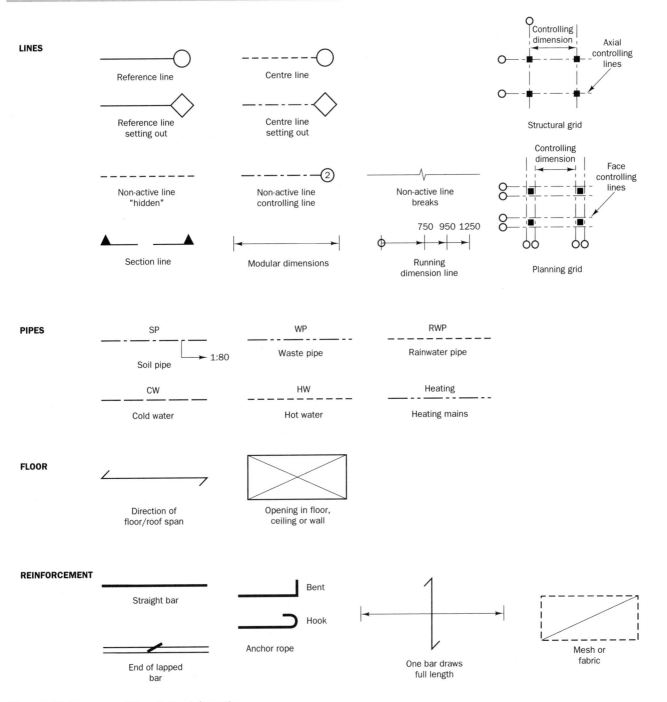

Figure 2.60 Line types: differentiating information

Identification of materials using standard conventions will complement the annotation and convey the extent of the material used in the assembly detail.

The amount of text and dimensions included on the sheet should be just enough to achieve the purpose of the drawing. As the drawing in this instance is a *substructure* detail, text or specification relating to the roof should not be included. When placing text or dimensions on the sheet try to assist the end user by leaving the drawing area uncluttered. The focal point is the **drawn detail**. Once the diagram has been assimilated, further information is sought, with the eye radiating out from the focus diagram. The diagram should therefore be encircled with dimensions and text, and the text should be **legible, concise** and **accurate**.

Code references direct the user to other further drawn information such as component drawings or to the bill of quantities. The **specification** or the **measured section** of the bill of quantities will explain the quality of the materials or workmanship. This will avoid expensive duplication of specifications on the drawings, reducing the possibility of discrepancies between tender and ultimate contract documents.

Component drawings

These will be large-scale, sometimes full-sized drawings showing individual components (Fig. 2.64). The assembly

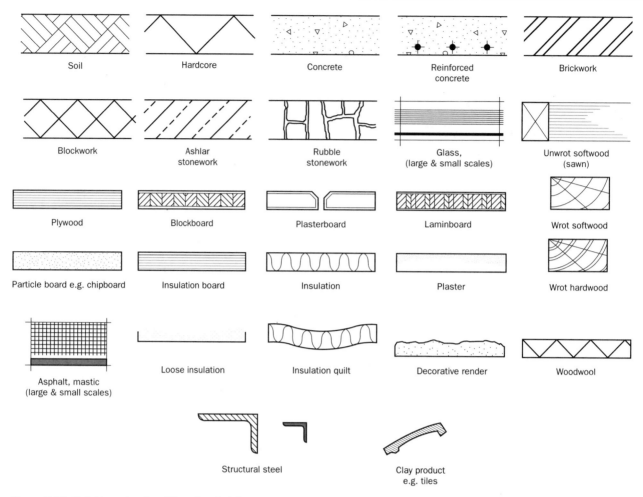

Figure 2.61 Hatching: showing different materials

drawing will contain several components, showing how the individual components fit together to make a building element. Recommended scales are: 1:10; 1:5; 1:2; 1:1.

The component drawing will contain dimensions and some text, but the material specification and the minimum acceptable quality will be defined in the specification section of the bill of quantities. The CAWS reference code will direct the end user to the correct part of the bill of quantities.

Schedules

Drawn or graphic information is a major communication medium in the construction industry, but there are occasions when drawn information needs to be supplemented by schedules.

A schedule presents design information in a tabulated form for **repetitive elements** and **components**. Typical components will be:

- windows
- doors
- ironmongery
- manholes
- finishes
- bending schedules

Location drawings, such as a reinforced steel layout (Fig. 2.65) are always prepared with a bending schedule (Fig. 2.66). The bending schedule explains the shape and number of identical reinforcement bars (often called rebars). The structural engineer will produce the steel layout drawing and bending schedule, linked by the number of the drawing.

Window and door components are ideal subjects for schedules, collecting together similar types of windows and, finally, totals of similar window types. On the location plan (Fig. 2.67) the windows should be numbered consecutively as this is the cross-reference to the window, lintel or opening schedule (Fig. 2.68).

A similar arrangement can be used for

- doors
- door frames
- door ironmongery
- sanitaryware
- kitchen units
- electrical fittings
- foundations

The list is endless. A schedule is a very effective way of transmitting information, but its use should not be abused. Before deciding on the communication method, it is prudent to ask certain questions:

- What is the purpose of the communication?
- Which communication method will best achieve this purpose?
- How will the end user benefit?

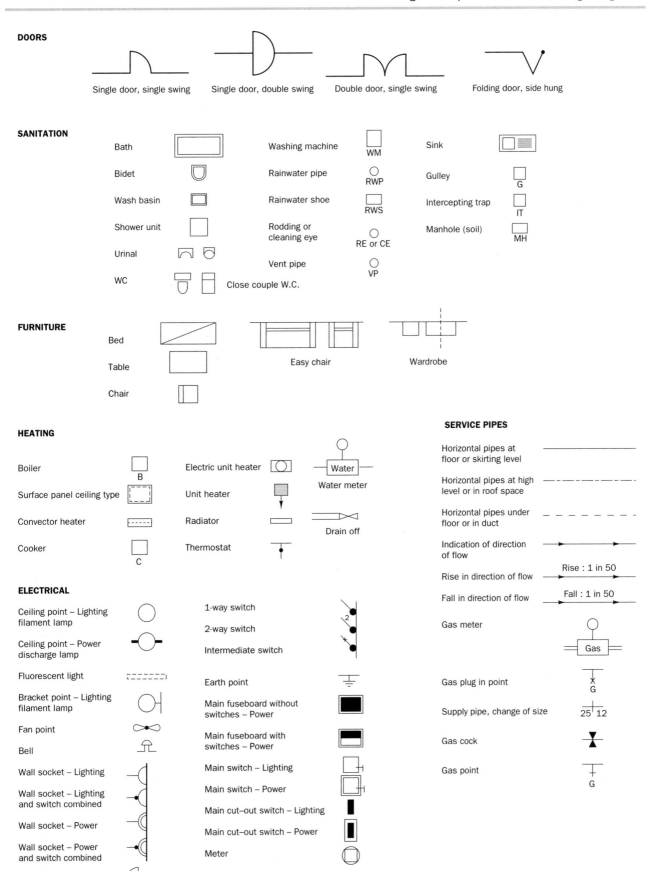

Figure 2.62 Symbols: identifying appliances and services

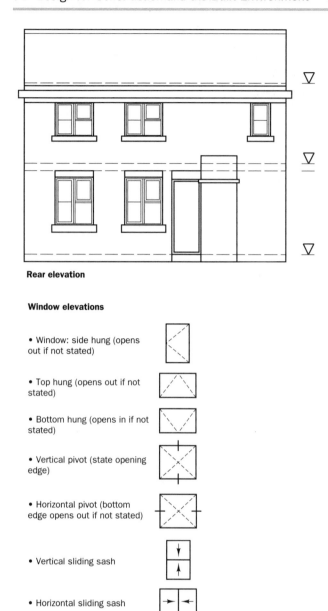

Rear elevation

Window elevations

- Window: side hung (opens out if not stated)
- Top hung (opens out if not stated)
- Bottom hung (opens in if not stated)
- Vertical pivot (state opening edge)
- Horizontal pivot (bottom edge opens out if not stated)
- Vertical sliding sash
- Horizontal sliding sash

Figure 2.63 Rear elevation diagram

By considering these questions each item of communication will be effective. There are also other types of schedules that are effective methods of communicating design information; for example:

- finishes schedules (Fig. 2.69)
- builder's work schedules.

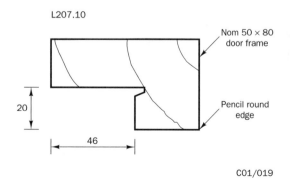

Figure 2.64 Component drawing

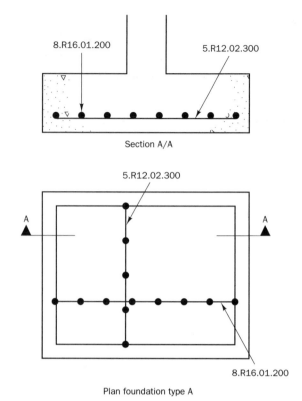

Figure 2.65 Reinforced steel layout drawing

The services consultant will prepare location drawings showing pipe runs, service ducts and cable runs. The final location of all service runs will be recorded in a **measured drawing**. The client often calls this type of drawing **services as installed**. This measured drawing is usually prepared after commissioning of the plant.

Builder's work drawings

These are an overlay of the services location plan onto the structural location plan and will indicate the location and size of holes. Holes through walls, chases, and ducting in concrete for the plumber, heating engineer or electrician are all described as builder's work. Because of the risk of fire, and for public safety, the Building Regulations will insist on compartmentalisation for certain types of buildings. Holes for services in compartment walls and floors will require **fire protection**. Identification of the type of hole, the need for fire stopping, and the location suggest that a builder's work schedule would be ideal. This schedule is also of benefit during the construction stage as it can be used as an **inspection checklist** by the architect or the **clerk of works**.

Drawing management

Decoration schemes are best conveyed through schedules, and with such an amount of information being generated there must be a system by which it can be accessed. Drawing management allows for information to be accurately filed, archived and retrieved.

Each commission should be given a **unique job number**,

Member	Bar mark	Type & size	No. of memb.	No. of bars in each	Total no.	Length of each bar	Shape code	A* mm	B* mm	C* mm	D* mm	E/r* mm
	01	R16	10	8	80	2250	35	2050				
	02	R12	10	5	50	1700	20	1700				

Site Reference   Foundation type A

Drawing: L01/27

Schedule No. L01/27.01

Figure 2.66 Bending schedule for reinforced steel

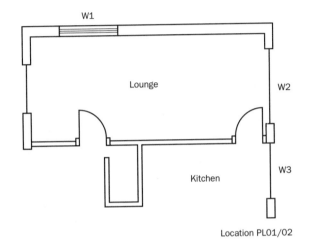

Figure 2.67 Location plan for windows and doors

The drawing sheet will generate the main volume for filing and each drawing sheet should be given a unique number and title (Fig. 2.70). BS 1192 recommends certain title blocks, and the architectural practice will often have its drafting film and detail paper preprinted with a title block and border.

FINISHES SCHEDULE

Job no. 123
Schedule no: IF/1
Prepared by: A.D.
Date: 7th April 1994

Room reference	Room title	Ceilings plastbd & skim	Floors		Walls 2ct plast
			Tiles	Screed	
				35	50	
R1	Kitchen	✓	✓	✓	✓
R2	Dining	✓		✓	✓
R3	Lounge	✓		✓	✓

Figure 2.69

WINDOW SCHEDULE

Job no. 123
Schedule no. W/1
Date: 8th April 1994

Window catalogue: Boulton and Paul
Window type: Sovereign

Window reference	Location	Window type		Remarks
		210C	310C	
W1	Lounge	1		
W2	Lounge		1	
W3	Kitchen		1	
	Totals	1	2	

Figure 2.68

which will occur on all drawn information as a drawing number and on all correspondence as a letter reference. All information should be filed in the job file until the commission is completed and the building handed over to the client. Stage M of the RIBA Plan of Work is titled 'Feedback'. After the defects liability period and the final account is agreed, the job file should be archived for at least six years.

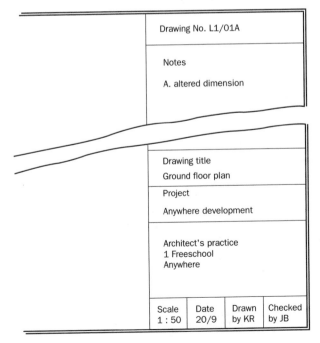

Figure 2.70 An example of a drawing – numbered and titled

All the information on the production drawings should be checked for accuracy. This is part of the **quality assurance** procedure by the practice. The architect or a member of the design team may produce the ink negatives, but another person should check and verify the data and sign the title block.

Structuring drawn information into **location, assembly** or **component** drawings suggests the use of a checklist and predetermined numbers for a sheet title.

The drawing sheet checklist in Fig. 2.71 is not comprehensive and each commission will require a separate drawing. However, the **ink negatives** are not produced directly from outline proposals, but from the design solutions prepared in the scheme design, which are often carried out on detail paper as sketches for the draughtsperson to draw to scale.

The ink negatives, from which **prints** will be taken, may require minor alterations and changes. These changes are called *amendments* and must be identified on title block of the ink negatives. For example, if the drawing number L1 is amended, an alphabetic suffix 'A' will be added and the amended drawing number will then become L1A. If further amendments or revisions are necessary the suffix will be changed to 'B', 'C', etc. and the amendments indicated in the title block. The issue of drawings should be recorded in the drawing register (Fig. 2.72).

Where the drawing sheet has to be redrawn, a new drawing number should be allocated and the old drawing should be withdrawn and clearly marked 'superseded'. During the design coordination meeting an agenda item titled 'Drawings issued/withdrawn' will ensure all the design team are aware of current and superseded drawings. During the construction period a similar procedure is followed at the monthly **Architect's site meeting**.

Circulation and copying

In the design process all design team members will need to be informed of progress and kept up to date, but they will not all

DRAWING SHEET CHECKLIST				
Job no. 123				
Job architect. A.Drawer				
Design team _ _ _ _ _ _				
Drawing number	Sheet title	Scale	Drawn by	Date completed
Location Drawings =============				
L1	Block plan	1 : 500		
L2	Site plan	1 : 100		
L3	Ground floor	1 : 50		
L4	First floor	1 : 50		
L5	Elevations	1 : 50		
L6	Foundation plan	1 : 50		
L7	First floor joist	1 : 50		
L8	Roof plan	1 : 50		
L9	Section building AA	1 : 50		
L10	Services ground floor	1 : 50		
L11	Services first floor	1 : 50		

Figure 2.71

DRAWING REGISTER													
										Job no. 123			
Drawing no.	Drawing Title	Date issued	Amendments							Circulation			
			A	B	C	D	E	F	G	qs	se	bse	cont
L1	Block plan	24/4								✓	✓	✓	2
L2	Site plan	25/4	✓							✓	✓	✓	2
L3	Ground floor	25/4	✓	✓						✓	✓	✓	2

Figure 2.72

require *every* piece of information. The architect may 'blanket' issue drawings to everyone, but this can create a communication overload and negate efficient coordination.

Copies of drawings are also called **prints**. A common system of obtaining prints is the **dyeline** method, which is a semi-dry process requiring an **ink negative** or **tracing**. The dyeline process must have **light-sensitive paper** such as diazo paper. Ultra-violet light burns off the clear part of the ink negative, leaving the lines showing on the diazo paper. As the diazo paper is passed through the ammonia box the lines are developed into black/blue lines. Different grades of diazo paper are available for use, depending on the reason for copying. On presentation or display drawings the ink negatives can be copied onto display sheets with different line colour. The copy – black or blue print – will tend to fade on long exposure to daylight, but the copies are relatively cheap and can be easily produced.

Working drawings, from which multiple copies will be made, have **intermediates** created to protect the tracing paper negative. A diazo copy of the negative will be made on special paper, while the intermediate is more durable and capable of withstanding repeated handling.

Photostats, thermographic, electrostatic and diffusion transfer copiers are excellent for rapid copying of drawings. These do not require an ink negative, and pencil preliminary sketches and perspectives can be quickly and cheaply obtained. It should be noted, however, that both dyeline prints and photocopies slightly distort scaled work.

True to scale copies are expensive, but if it is essential to retain the drawn accuracy, allowing dimensions to be scaled off, then TTS (true to scale) prints must be used. Having copied and circulated all the prints, the drawings must now be filed.

Filing systems

Drawings contain important information and should be filed. **Dyeline prints** can deteriorate under exposure to **sunlight** and would best be filed in a **drawing chest** with drawers for location, assembly, components and schedule sketches. **Ink tracings** or **negatives** can be stored by the same method, but tracing paper, unlike tracing film, will deteriorate with age, and can be easily damaged. A drawing filing cabinet will add security to the ink negatives, which should be stored vertically in plastic wallets.

Preliminary drawings, sketch plans and 'thinking' drawings should be filed for later reference, and not discarded. During the feedback stage of the design process, all **design** assumptions will be appraised. The volume of **archived** drawings can be reduced by a **microfiche** information system, in which photographs are taken of the ink negatives and reduced to a slide, possibly A5 size. The slide can hold approximately eight A1 drawing sheets and by this method the archived volume is considerably reduced. To access the microfiche, a reader is necessary.

Architectural library

Apart from *producing* information the architect will *receive* large volumes of information:

- **trade literature** must be obtained and should be filed and updated
- **material samples** pose a problem for storage and filing
- **textbooks, design guides** issued by the planning authority, British Standard Specifications and Codes of Practice
- **design notes** from trade associations, the Building Research Establishment, the Chartered Institute of Building Services (CIBSE) and the Department of the Environment

With government publications the architect must distinguish between mandatory requirements and advisory guidelines.

Textbooks and guidelines can be classified by the Dewey decimal system. This is a library classification system which uses a numerical reference under topic areas. For example, building subjects are referenced under 690, whereas the subject architecture is coded under 720. There is a cross-referencing system within the Dewey classification which helps information retrieval. When looking for a book on architectural history, the books referenced 720.9 would be searched, with the suffix '9' indicating histories.

Trade literature can be filed under the CAWS reference or the CI/SfB classification system. The Swedish classification system provides a framework for retrieving information. Each item of trade literature is coded as detailed below. The appropriate code can be seen at the top right corner of the literature.

- Table 0: *Built environment* (numbers without brackets). This indicates the type of building for which the product is suitable. If no code is used then the material or product is intended for general use.
- Table 1: *Elements* (numbers in brackets). This indicates part of a building or components of a building.
- Table 2/3 (letter without brackets). This indicates the construction type by a capital letter; a lower-case letter denotes the material.
- Table 4: *Activities and requirements* (letters in brackets). This indicates the type of activity for which the material or product is suitable.

To find a suitable trade product for a domestic wood window frame using the CI/SfB library system, look for trade literature with the coding 81(31)Xi.

- 81 = domestic building (Table 0)
- (31) = window frames (Table 1)
- Xi = wood (Table 2/3)

Any trade literature with this code on the top right corner (as shown in Fig. 2.73) should be selected.

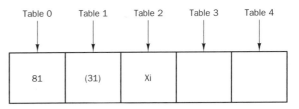

Figure 2.73 The CI/SfB classification system for a domestic wood window frame

There are commercial building product files which are trade literature based, such as the RIBA Product Library. Some commercially available trade libraries use both trade literature and microfiche.

Design guides published by professional institutes and government agencies are best filed under the building group based on Table 0 of the CI/SfB classification in date of issue order, which is shown at the front of the file.

Keeping up to date with legislation and legal issues means that the practice must subscribe to commercial organisations specialising in an updating service. The professional journals of the RIBA and BIAT publish articles on current legislation and practice, and it is imperative that the architect keeps abreast of developments, both technical and legislative. As an agent for the client, the architect has a duty to exercise professional judgement. Failure to do so could lead to the client suing the architect for negligence.

Computer-aided design

Computer systems and hardware

Basic hardware

Hardware is defined as the equipment that makes up a computer system, such as the monitor, keyboard, central processor unit and mouse.

Central processor unit

The central processing unit or **CPU** is the microprocessor (Fig. 2.74). It controls all the computer functions, makes all

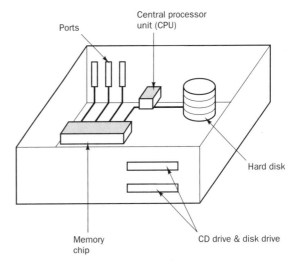

Figure 2.74 Diagrammatic view of a computer box

the calculations and processes all the data. The microprocessor is an integrated circuit, that contains transistors, wires and other electronic devices on a **silicon chip**. Microprocessors from different manufacturers are often **non-compatible**. The internal design of the computer is called **architecture**. Where programs are written on chips or microprocessors such as the Intel Pentium, additional software or hardware may be necessary to network the different computers.

Microprocessors are available as 8-bit, 16-bit, or 32-bit chips. The larger the chip the faster the **processing time** will be and the microcomputer will run more powerful programs. Software manufacturers often state the minimum size of computer to run their software programs. The microprocessor has various instructions etched onto the silicon chip. These instruction sets are now **reduced instruction set chips** (RISC) and the processing time is faster than the traditional chip called **complex instruction set chip** (CISC). The use of a **coprocessor** also speeds up the processing time.

Data entry from the keyboard is stored in the computer's internal memory (Fig. 2.75). **Read only memory** (ROM) chips cannot be altered and the ROM is often called the **non-volatile** memory. Plug in ROM chips are called **programmable ROMS** (PROMS). Loaded programs from a disk are stored in the **random access memory** (RAM). As the computer processes the data, the location of the data in the RAM chip can be short-lived memory. A static RAM can store data for longer periods of time. A battery in the computer allows data to be retained in the RAM memory. The most common memory chip is the **dynamic RAM** (DRAM), which retains memory for a short period of time. The memory chip must update the stored data over 300 times per second. **Bubble memory** chips are non-volatile memory storage.

Matching the input speed to the processing speed is difficult and several techniques are used to allow a constant input. **Virtual memory** is used on larger programs and data files to relieve computer capacity. The virtual memory uses the **hard disk** to help processing time and memory overload. **Buffers**, which are allocated small memory areas in the RAM, are also used to ease processing time. Keyboard buffers store input while the CPU is processing data, and when the buffer is full a warning 'bleep' is sounded. All inputs after the bleep are lost and must be re-entered. A print buffer stores data while a **hard copy** is being obtained, freeing the microcomputer for additional tasks.

Data is frequently transferred between the CPU, the disk and the memory. Processing data is first transported to the

CPU from a store. The stored data is held in an area of the RAM designated a **cache**, and disks known as **disk caches** can be used in this way to increase the computer capacity. A complex processing calculation could be repeated later in the program sequence. To save processing time this processed data can be stored in the disk caches until required. The storage of processed data can also be stored in a **memory cache**, which is a high-speed chip. The CPU searches the memory caches to see if the data is stored there, and if not found, it will search the main memory to process the data.

Peripherals to the computer are connected by cables to **ports**. The connection of the right cable to the right port is called **plug compatibility**. There are two types of port:

- serial port
- parallel port

The data sent down a serial port is sent one **bit** at a time. The parallel port sends data one **byte** at a time (1 byte = 8 bits). The hardware design and layout is known as **architecture**, and the communication path is called a **bus**. The **data bus** is used to transport data from the CPU to the memory chips and external components, such as plotters. The **address bus** is similar to the data bus but is used to transport data and communicate within special areas of the memory and components in the system. All the communication and transporting of data are determined by the **clock rate**. The clock rate controls the frequency of the computer's operation and keeps everything in order. Clock rates are expressed in megahertz (MHz).

Further expansion boards and slots can be added. The computers that have expansion slots are called **open architecture**, but if the computer *cannot* be expanded this is known as **closed architecture**.

Care for the computer is essential.

- If the display screen is not in use, turn the screen intensity down. Do not constantly switch the computer on and off.
- Use a **surge protector** on the electricity supply to reduce the damage to data from surges or spikes on the power supply.
- Do not smoke. The smoke and grit will penetrate into the drives and corrupt the data held on the disks.
- Do not leave the display screen exposed to direct sunlight.
- Use a screen filter to avoid damage to the operator's eyes.
- Do not position computers back to back. This will avoid excessive radiation to the operators.

Peripherals: inputing devices

Keyboards The computer keyboard may have a **keyboard lock**. The keyboard lock in the off position will disable the keyboard from the CPU. **Auto-repeat feature** is the term given to the function by which the character continues to repeat until the character key is released.

Text-scanning devices Optical Character Recognition (OCR) devices will convert texts, but not graphic images or illustrations, into computer files.

Graphic scanners These are sometimes called **image digitisers**. Graphic images are not converted to ASCII codes, but the scanner divides the printed image into a grid of small dots called **picture elements** or **pixels**. Graphic scanners are available in 1-bit, 8-bit or 16-bit ranges. The 1-bit scanner can only convert images or drawn pictures into black and white images.

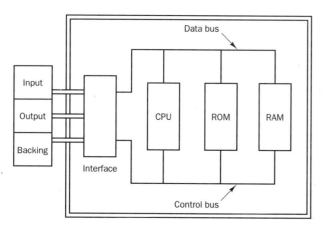

Figure 2.75 The routeing of information

Graphic scanners checklist:

- resolution
- conversion
- software compatibility
- interfaces
- down-loading time

Graphics tablet This is sometimes called a digitiser, a digitising tablet or a graphics pad. The pad area is divided into a grid or individual pixel to enable drawings to be converted into computer drawings. Other input devices are used with the tablet. A mouse is used especially for **pull-down menu-driven software** and **third-party software.**

A **puck** is used or a **stylus** to select the icons from the graphic tablet. The puck is like a mouse but has a cross-hair for accurate selection of the icon and digitising an existing drawing. A **light pen** enables the operator to draw directly on to the display screen. The disadvantage of the light pen is inaccuracy in line definition.

- Digitiser checklist:
  - size of stylus
  - number of cursor buttons
  - resolution
- Mouse checklist:
  - number of buttons
  - serial or bus fitting
  - emulation

Peripherals: outputing devices

Display screen This is sometimes called the display monitor. The display screen gives you instant feedback while operating the computer. The text is inputted through the keyboard into the RAM and **echoed** to the screen. Cathode ray tube (CRT), flat panel display, liquid crystal display (LCD) and electroluminescent displays are different types of display screens, and images are displayed on the screen as a series of dots or pixels (Table 2.4).

Table 2.4 Pixels and colours available for various display screens

Type of screen	Pixels	Colour
Monochrome	320 × 200	1
Colour graphics card	320 × 200	4
Enhance graphics adaptor	320 × 200	4
	640 × 350	16

The display screen will be either **high resolution** or **low resolution.**

Some programs display images on the screen as a **bitmap.** All the pixels or points are **addressable.** To use a program that utilises bitmapping you must have a **graphics display screen.** Additional graphics cards may be inserted into one of the expansion slots if the computer does not have graphic capabilities. There are two types of graphics board:

- CGA colour graphic adaptor
- EGA enhanced colour graphics

Different **fonts** – that is, additional characters – can also be added using **add on boards.** The fonts can be down-loaded into the computer memory by an additional ROM chip.

Graphics cards and display resolution levels are normally 1024 × 768, but 1280 × 1024 and 1680 × 1280, which will be needed for highly detailed drawings, are also available. These high-level resolutions are necessary for software programs with zoom and pan facilities.

- Graphics card checklist:
  - resolution
  - number of colours
  - size of display
  - single or dual screen
  - split screen
  - multi-viewport display
- Monitors checklist:
  - screen size
  - resolution
  - type of connections
  - dot pitch

Printers and plotters

Printers Fully formed character printers work like a typewriter, using a **daisy wheel** or a **thimble. Dot matrix** printers form the characters using an array of dots, and the resolution and density of the dots can approach near letter quality (NLQ). The print quality is determined by the number of dots per inch.

Impact printers are daisy wheel, thimble or dot matrix types, whereas **non-impact printers** are **inkjet, thermal, laser LED** and **electrostatic.** The printers are rated according to the printer speed, which is given in **characters per second** (CPS). Printers are used for graphics software rather than computer-aided design, and printers are now available that are suitable for CAD, with near photographic quality in rendering. Dye-sublimation printers can produce quality prints, while thermal, laser and inkjet printers are often used for preliminary drawings.

- Printer checklist:
  - size of paper
  - speed
  - noise
  - emulation
  - colours

Plotters Pen plotters (often called Vector plotters) have a physical speed limit and have the disadvantage that the pen may dry out during plot runs, although ink technology has now produced a **smart pen plotter.** The plots in a pen plotter have a finite life span so important presentation drawings and quality plots require to be constantly monitored. Good line quality is a characteristic of a pen plot, and the pen distance is monitored to prevent the pen drying out. At predetermined intervals an optical sensor checks the line thickness and the print contrast specification. If no pen replacement is available the smart pen plotter will stop the plot. A customary bleep alerts the operator. The types of plotter pens are:

- ink, re-fillable
- ink, disposable
- roller ball
- fibre tip
- ceramic tip

Penless plotters, often called **raster plotters,** are also available. Penless plotters draw the graphic image according to dots (raster dots). This allows extra speed on plotting, shading or rendering drawings. Data for the plot is stored in the internal memory and is converted by a vector-to-raster converter. Penless plots are available as

- electrostatic
- thermal
- laser
- inkjet

Penless plotters are used where a high-quality dense plot is needed. In CAD applications, monochrome thermal plotters are preferred because of their lower cost.

- Plotter checklist:
  - maximum, minimum plot speed
  - colour
  - sheet or roller feed
  - type of media
  - noise
  - pen/ink type
  - pen speed

Storage devices

External storage is another form of permanent storage of data. **Floppy disks, CD ROM** and **hard disks** are described as external storage or secondary storage. Floppy disks are either single sided or double sided, with the data stored on tracks. The spacing of the tracks is measured in tracks per inch (TPI):

- single density disk (24 TPI; 360 kb)
- double density disk (48 TPI; 720 kb)
- high-density (quad-density) disks (96 TPI 1.44 Mb)

Before use the disks must be formatted. This is often called **high-level format**. The disks are split into sectors.

The hard disk is sometimes called the fixed disk. The hard disk drive uses a rigid metal platter to store the data. The rigidity allows for a higher density of data. Hard disks generally provide a storage capacity of 2 Gb or more, whereas the most commonly used floppy disk can store 360 kb, 720 kb or 1.44 Mb. The time the computer takes to locate the stored data is called **access time**. Modern PCs also have the facility to use a CD or Zip drive for storage of data, allowing more data to be stored.

Protecting disks or making disks secure is difficult with the use of a hard disk, and for this reason a floppy disk is used to store the data using an **encryption program**. The encrypted file can only be accessed by a password, which provides added security to the files. **Backup** copies are another form of securing the data and **archived disks** should always be kept in a safe place.

Software

Operating system

The microcomputer may need to have its software installed. The operating system is usually Microsoft Windows. The use of MS-DOS allows multi-tasking by splitting the screen into windows, called **windows environment**. The heart of the computer is the operating system. The **input/output** (I/O) manager coordinates the computer's communication with all the peripherals. The **command processor** interprets the input demands, while the **utilities program** manages the filing of data.

The computer also needs to know which drives to **address**. The **default drive** is usually set at drive A. After a command the computer will first search the default drive. If no program is found, the computer will move to drive B, repeating the

search until the program is located. Drive C is reserved for the hard disk, which can also be **partitioned** to create a disk drive D. The operating system is installed in drive C.

CAD configuration program

Computer-aided drawing software programs will be held on floppy disks and must be transferred to the computer hard disk. The software manufacturer will issue instructions on how to install the program. This action is often called **configuration**. The files on the disk will be labelled with a file extension and the configuration files will be designated in one of two ways:

- filename.sys
- filename.cfg

These disks should first be copied and archived, and the copy disk loaded into the computer hard disk drive C.

There are operating programs that will check the disk and give the following information:

- total disk space
- number of bytes in the file
- number of files on the disk
- hidden files
- space available on the disk
- memory of the computer
- memory free to use

To prevent unauthorised copying of the software disk some software manufacturers build into the operating system an **electronic hardware lock** called a **dongle** which prevents pirate copying of the operating system. The dongle is attached to one of the ports in the CPU. The software program may require drivers to operate various peripherals. Once the software is installed, the CAD work can then begin.

There are many software manufacturers producing numerous CAD programs:

- AUTOCAD
- ROBOCAD
- CADVANCE
- VERSACAD
- FASTCAD
- MICROCAD
- MICROSTATION

The product manufacturers are producing software programs that work in unison with the CAD programs. This type of software is called **third-party software** and is usually held on a floppy disk in drive A and is mouse driven. The third-party software must be compatible with the main CAD software.

The software CAD program can be either 2D or 3D, but most programs now offer the three-dimensional facility. The program should be capable of carrying out the following functions:

- drawing: lines, circles, arcs, variable line thickness, variable line types
- edit commands: erase, undo, move, copy, extend, trim, rotate, array, fillet, endpoint, midpoint, centre location, and edit by single, window or last command
- zoom and pan: dynamic by selection, window and all multi-viewport
- layer: number of layers, suppression, status indication
- dimensioning: vertical, horizontal, angular, customise
- attributes and blocks: customise, explode edit, scheduling

- hatching and symbols
- annotation: customise
- 3D: multi-viewpoints, perspectives (one point, two point, three point, variable view, variable height, zoom, suppression of lines), axonometric, isometric
- scheduling
- third-party software
- input devices: mouse, tablet, scanner, keyboard

Typical CAD hardware installation

- Computer:
  - minimum 640 kb memory
  - hard disk 1 Gb
  - floppy disk drives and CD drive
  - cache memory
  - Pentium processor chip
  - maths coprocessor to reduce regeneration times
- Monitor:
  - VGA
  - colour for layers and attributes
  - screen resolution to enable **visibility accuracy** (when operating zoom commands
- Tablet and digitiser:
  - size 280 × 280; this will allow the input of data from the tablet and digitising of existing plans and images; the keyboard can be used for help commands, toggles and other inquiry commands
  - puck or stylus operated
- Plotter:
  - A0 size
  - 8 pen
  - smart buffer, to aid in reducing computer down-load time, thereby releasing the computer for drafting operations
  - drawing media, by which the plotter accepts cartridge, tracing film and paper
  - roller feed, which reduces the floor space compared with a flat-bed plotter
- Dot matrix printer:
  - A3 flat or roller; this is required for conceptualisation and preliminary ideas
  - NLQ (near letter quality) for draft reports
- Laser printer:
  - for schedules and report production

CAD drafting

The formatted floppy disk or CD will be the data disk containing the drawing. The file must have a filename and this is often the job number followed by the drawing number, e.g. 123L001; where '123' is the number and 'L001' indicates location drawing number 1. The drawing management is important in CAD, so the project architect should allocate to the drawings a number based on

- location (prefixed L)
- assembly (prefixed A)
- component (prefixed C)

The drawing scale should be the preferred scales according to BS 1192. Since the display screen is addressable the draftsperson should reference the control box by the screen coordinates (Fig. 2.76).

The absolute coordinates are referenced to the fixed Cartesian coordinates system. Some software programs will

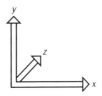

Figure 2.76 Cartesian coordinates

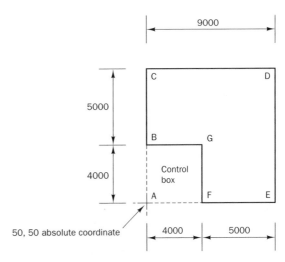

Figure 2.77 The control box, ensuring accuracy of the drawn shape

show the coordinate reference on the status bar. The absolute coordinates should be noted for the control box, as this ensures accuracy whether using computer drawings or manual drawings. The control box is the smallest rectangle that can enclose the whole of the planned shape (Fig. 2.77). The absolute coordinates for the corners are shown in Table 2.5.

The endpoint of lines can also be calculated by the use of polar coordinates (Fig. 2.78). The polar coordinate reference to draw a line from corner B to corner C is @(distance) 5000<(angle)90. The polar reference from corner C to corner D is @9000<0.

Table 2.5 Absolute coordinates for Fig. 2.77 (Control box: 50, 50)

Corner	Distance	Absolute coordinate	
		X	Y
A	—	50	50
B	4000 (4.00)	50	54 (50 + 4)
C	5000 (5.00)	50	59 (54 + 5)
D	9000 (9.00)	(50 + 9) 59	59
E	9000 (9.00)	59	50 (59 − 9)
F	5000 (5.00)	(59 − 5) 54	50
G	4000 (4.00)	54	54 (50 + 4)

Once the **model** shape has been defined, the draftsperson can select the internal partitions. When the walls have been positioned, the various symbols can be inserted to indicate doors and windows. The pixels can be addressed to position the door and window openings accurately. The door openings and window openings may be selected from the tablet using the puck or the mouse and the screen pull-down menus. The edit commands will allow accurate positioning of these entities. Symbols for the kitchen units and sanitaryware will be selected from the tablet or the screen pull-down menus. Location can be effected through the edit commands such as midpoint, centre or through absolute coordinates.

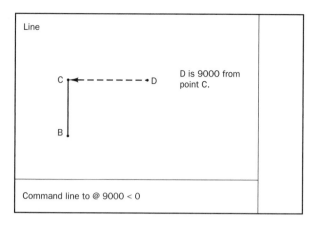

Figure 2.78 Calculating the endpoint of lines by use of polar coordinates

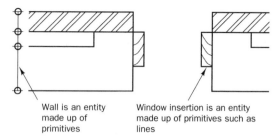

Figure 2.79 Using primitives to compile entities

Most programs have the facility to measure lines and entities, enabling the plan to be fully dimensioned. Textual data can be inputted and items annotated and hatched in accordance with the current BS 1192.

Once the drawing is complete the file should be saved to the floppy disk. The file name will be **123L001.dwg**. Some computer CAD programs will make a backup file after the use of the **end command**. The backup file name is 123L001.bak; where '123' is the job number, 'L001' is the location drawing number, and 'bak' indicates a backup file. Periodically the drawing should be saved to the floppy disk in case that fatal error message 'disk full' arrives. The completed drawing held on the floppy disk should then be archived. The archived disk copy should be stored securely and away from any magnetic fields to avoid corruption of data.

Using the plot or print command, a **hard copy** of the drawings should then be obtained for distribution to the design team. Software manufacturers have varying commands for the print and plot option. The drawing size is selected with the preferred scale and various options are available in the plot.

- A prototype drawing may be obtained. The standard block titles for the architectural practice are held by a drawing file called 'prototype drawing'. All the text except the job title and the drawing number and title are written onto this drawing.
- Dimensions can be inserted in metric or imperial form.
- Measurements can be given to the nearest whole number. One software program will accurately dimension to 10 decimal places.
- The whole drawing or part, called a window display, may be plotted.
- It is possible to rotate the model (that is the name given to the CAD drawing).
- Different pen thicknesses can be used for hierarchical information.

Drawing management through the use of drawing registers is available, but there are software programs, known as **Document management**, that will record all drawings produced and issued. Where the architectural practice operates quality assurance to BS 5750, then a computer document management system is essential.

The CAD software program will allow the production of schedules with the use of a database. Certain entities, such as windows, are a series of **primitives**. The primitives are fundamental units of the computer, like lines, circles,

hatching, rectangles and text. The window insertion is made up of a number of primitives (Fig. 2.79).

The window insertion and other entities should be **layered** to allow the annotation to be **free** or **coupled**. The free annotation will be data such as levels on plans, room and area labels or titles, and general dimensions. The coupled annotation is always with an entity, such as the window reference.

The coupled annotation will be used to produce the window schedules. Other schedules such as doors, kitchen units or sanitaryware can be produced by this method using a database. This added facility will allow the interrogation of the database. Additional fields to the database could involve the cost of the element and the CAWS or Ci/Sfb classification for bill of quantities production.

Within the model, layering is available, which is similar to using a film overlay of another drawing and superimposing the building services layout. The layering is part of the **data structure** of the CAD model. Careful thought should be given to the layering of drawings and information within the model. The layer attribute assigned could be

- conceptual design, including the use of space diagrams and three-dimensional wire or solid modelling
- outline scheme design, preliminary proposals
- scheme design
- production information
- record drawings, as measured drawings

The structuring of information in layers will need file information and retrieval systems using a computer-based drawing management system. When using various layers the software program should allow for **layer visibility** or **layer suppression**, which means that the layer would not appear on the display screen.

Data exchange, using third-party software, aids the drafting efficiency by introducing manufacturer's details into the model. The use of a neutral format for graphics exchange (Product Data Exchange Specification – PDES) will ease the availability of data not only from the material and component manufacturer, but also from different design consultants using the Initial Graphics Exchange Specification (IGES).

The software program will log all the commands used, and there is also a facility for 'undo' commands. This is very useful but also creates a problem with the disk space. For example, if a line command is wrongly positioned and is deleted, the sequence of commands is still stored and saved to the disk even though the command was 'deleted' from the drawing. It has taken up space on the floppy disk. This erroneous activity causes files to be **fragmented**. A file is stored on a sector and track somewhere on the disk, and any deletions leave gaps, producing a **non-contiguous file** rather than a contiguous file. Using the save command on some computer applications will not create a backup file like the end command. Left on the file will be all the good commands and the fragments caused by deletions. At the commencement of the working period it is good practice to clean the file of these fragments by using the **purge** command.

Drawing time can also be logged by the computer, enabling the costings to each job to be more accurate and allowing the practice to be more competitive over the scale of fees charged to the client.

Networking

Up to this point we have concentrated on **stand-alone** computer application, but with the high initial cost of plotters and peripherals it would be more sensible to **network** the system.

Stand-alone and **dedicated** computers – i.e. working to one application – leave the workstation with some idle time called downtime. Multi-tasking the computer with various **application programs** will allow an efficient computer operation. The cost of the software and licensing agreement with the software manufacturer may lead to the networking of the computer suite. There are several types of network available.

- **WAN** (wide area networks). Owing to the distance between the users on the network, data is transferred through a modem or floppy disk.
- **LAN** (local area network). In this network the computers are wired together by coaxial cable and a **server** downloads the programs and organises the data storage.
- **Ring** networks. These have a dedicated microcomputer as the **server** and the PC users **log** on to the network through a **password** and **identity** system. The PC user can interrogate and use certain programs and data but, because of password protection, some **sensitive** data cannot be used. Read/write access may be obtained by the system's **protocol**, and the data will be stored at the file server. The file server is often a dedicated microprocessor and controls the use of the peripherals for input and output of data. The plotter may have a dedicated computer which will allow plots to be obtained, but releases the user to continue designing through the network. Accurate time recording of computers will allow a high degree of job costing. The use of peripherals will also be maximised.
- Internet In industry it is increasingly common for drawings to be placed on the internet or a company intranet, where they can be viewed or manipulated by colleagues or clients in remote locations.

Different design consultants on the network can interrogate and work on the design, the server controlling the use and data storage. Logging on and off will cause the server to update the files and create backup files on the hard disk. At a later date the operator may make an archived floppy disk of the job files. The file is updated by the use of the **end** command where a backup copy is made on the hard disk. The new user who logs on to the network and uses the drawing file will work on the drawing file, designated filename.dwg not the backup file. Each software and computer has its own protocol to follow but the sequence of using backup and archived files is essential to all CAD systems.

Applications of CAD

Drawing and drafting

Computer-aided design and drafting ensures an accuracy that is greatly superior to manual drafting. The use of primitives such as lines, circles, grids and line types can all be accurately positioned through coordinates and such edit commands as endpoint, midpoint, tangent, centre. The dynamic screen positioning of entities such as sinks and toilets should be avoided. The zoom command will allow accurate positioning along with edit commands. Three-dimensional modelling allows the visualisation of the mass of the building and virtual reality modelling gives street views and inside walk throughs, at any stage of design. Different line thicknesses and line types will allow information to be displayed on the screen to indicate hierarchical information and location of services.

Standardised libraries of hatching and symbols will reduce the design time by using icons to select and dynamically position on the screen. Ease of change, through such edit commands as move and rotate, allows the designer to analyse layouts and locations to maximise space and usage. Layering of data will allow services, roof joist layouts and other overlay plans to be easily developed. The suppression or visibility of the layer is quickly secured by the pull-down menus.

Since the screen pixels are addressable, the grid can be displayed on the screen. The use of modular dimensions with the grid set at 300 mm will aid the architect in space layout decisions. Some software programs use a snap command which sets the computer to measure only in set increments, which is ideal for modular dimensions where the snap is set at 300 mm. Any line distance recorded at non-modular distances is not drawn on the screen. An additional benefit is the ability of the software program to produce **space layouts** from areas or an area and one distance. This is ideal for preliminary space decisions and massing if the program has 3D facilities.

Common libraries of wall types can be produced and these entities may be selected by the tablet icons or pull-down menus. The wall status – such as inner and outer skin thicknesses, cavity thickness, wall height, measurement from the centre line outside or inside the wall – can all be changed, allowing the designer maximum choice. The entity attributes are often displayed on the screen by a dialog box.

Floor plans can be assigned levels so that elevations can be displayed on the screen, and window frames and door types can be added to the elevations with dimensioning and annotations. Multi-viewports allow orthographic views, or any viewing port, to be selected. The suppression of hidden lines allows the composition of the elevations to be considered.

Detailing and modelling Once the model has been drawn the user can search into the rooms by means of the **zoom commands**. The scale of the drawing plot can be selected, but the dynamic zoom commands allows a small component to be designed in detail. Once the detailed design is completed the screen is regenerated. With complex models this regeneration takes a lot of computer processing time. The use of a mathematical coprocessor will reduce the **redraw** time considerably. Since the location plans may be used by more than one consultant in the design team, the use of layers would be an advantage in detailing the services and the builder's work such as holes and chases. The ground floor plan contains setting-out information, levels and references to other drawings. The general arrangement of rooms and space layout will be required by

- the structural engineer
- the services engineer
- the interior designer
- the landscape architect

The work of each consultant will be layered. All the layers can be visible and display the complexity of the design. The layers are coloured and different services or components can be traced by the colour of the layer, which will reduce the possibility of service ducting passing through a beam and fouling the reinforcement. The structural engineer on a reinforced concrete framed building will produce from the general arrangement layer the following details:

- steel layout drawings showing positions of rebars
- beam reinforcement and sections
- column reinforcement and sections
- wind wall reinforcement and sections
- lift shaft wall reinforcement and sections
- foundation types, details and sections

In addition to these location and assembly drawings there will be the corresponding bending schedules. Layering with the ability to suppress or show the layer will allow these disparate design decisions to be coordinated.

Some architectural practices have standard details, for example an eaves detail. The standard details will be built up from primitives into entities in the CAD system. Data structuring will allow the entities to be **instanced** on the drawing from the tablet or pull-down menu. These details are called **sub-models** and will represent building products or components. Libraries will be

- selected entities, e.g. roof verge details
- building products, e.g. kitchen floor unit or wash-hand basin with taps
- project specific entities, e.g. reinforced concrete infill beam due to building shape

Referencing of the standard details will give the architect time to evaluate the component assembly rather than spend time redrawing the details.

Attributes can be added to the entity for schedule production, and both numerical and textual information may also be assigned to the entity. The coordinated project information could also be assigned to the attribute – for example, the textual data could be the National Building Specification (NBS) or the National Engineering Specification (NES) clauses. To ease the reading of the screen and the drawings the attribute may be suppressed or frozen from specific plans.

The details can be plotted and printed using the zoom command to isolate the detail from the background model. A scaled hard copy of the detail may be made at any time during the design process, and this will allow critical evaluation by other team members, resulting in a design solution that is not only buildable but also satisfies the client brief.

Visualisation

In the feasibility stage and outline proposals ideas are being generated and discarded. The computer, with its 3D modelling facility, will allow the spatial requirements to be generated as floor areas; the insertion of windows and doors will complete the floor arrangement; and multi-viewports will allow the architect and client to visualise the building. One-, two- or three-point perspectives can be generated within the specified viewing position, and variable height and line of sight adds realism to the visualisation of the building composition. Faster processing time and 3D libraries of components allow a high degree of interaction that borders

on virtual reality. **Wire modelling** or **solid modelling**, with the views rendered on the screen, will give the client an unprecedented idea of the finished building.

Building products and components will be modelled in detail as **object-oriented software**. The designer selects the component and its position in the building. From a 3D internal view the design team can see the reality of the suggestion, can introduce colour rendering to the 3D model and **walk through techniques** and can give the client the opportunity to see the internal views of the proposed design.

The building position and orientation will be considered at the outline proposals stage. The details of the ground contours, natural environment, background and foreground need to be identified to present the client and the design team with the maximum information to assess the design options. Computer 3D modelling will enable the architect to generate external views with background and foreground details. Virtual reality and colour rendering of the built environment will give the design team and the client a step-by-step view along the street. These perceived views can be a screen display, or hard copies can be produced for presentation purposes. **Rendering technology** helps users to set up rendered scenes which are photo-realistic. The user establishes the viewport and target, then selects the materials and lighting conditions. A virtual reality 3D view is generated. Interaction by the user can create an image of the building in the natural and built environment, showing different shading as the Earth rotates around the Sun. Flora and fauna are added to complete the 3D visualisation using **photo-realistic rendering software**.

Production of schedules

Schedules form an important method of communication for the design team. The generation of space accommodation, window, door, and lintel schedules are obtained by the use of a database. Third-party software, which the product manufacturers produce, will be incorporated into the CAD model. These entities and the specification clauses in NBS or NES will produce the required schedules for use by the

- quantity surveyor for cost planning and bill of quantities production
- structural engineer for reinforcement bending schedules, beam, column and foundation schedules
- services engineer for builder's work details, fire stopping, sanitaryware and luminaires
- builder as part of the production information used for tendering and contract control

During design the solutions may be fluid and require the design to have major or minor modifications, but any update in the design will have an effect on the schedules. Amended schedules and information must be processed quickly to the design team to reduce abortive work. The data exchange of CAD models and schedules will be affected by

- coordination by the design team and a two-way transfer
- 'read only' data transfer – often on a network the end user will be debarred from altering the background model by limiting access to the file to 'read only'
- a permanent record of the design decisions

Location drawings, with the attributes layered to the entities, will need to be altered. To ease the accessing time by the CAD technician the entities and attributes are kept on the same layer, such as reinforced concrete bar details and shapes. Coupled annotations such as

- symbol and component labels
- service pipe identification
- textual information

should be kept on a separate layer. This will allow maximum flexibility in amending the plans. Product changes and updates can be effected through layer control and the screen display of the model is uncluttered by suppression of the layer.

DXF files are the external format for data exchanges into the database. The data can be interrogated, selectively sorted, totalled and page layout selected prior to the production of a hard copy. Schedules should be produced in accordance with SMM7 and CAWS. This will reduce the workload of all the end users and eliminate duplication. The data exchange files will be formatted to allow for individual use without corrupting the design solution.

Trade literature and third-party software

Product data is available that can be incorporated into the CAD model through floppy disk and third-party commands. The windows environment allows the user to select the product and its position on the CAD model. Coupled annotations are fixed on a layer for ease of scheduling. Some product manufacturers have listed their product range on floppy disks, or offer CAD design using their products;

- Bricks. Special shapes and predefined patterns are introduced into the drawings and schedules of shapes produced

- Lintels. Standard sections are available on floppy disk. CAD programs should include the use of third-party software. The product entities are attributed to enable schedules to be produced stating type, length and total numbers
- Drainage goods
- Windows and doors
- Radiators and convectors
- Air-conditioning units
- Roof coverings
- Roof sheeting

The RIBA offers RIBACAD with installation details on a range of products. RIBACAD is a floppy disk system. With the current development into CAD the user will be in a position to simulate the construction process, which will be just one advantage of CAD.

Self-assessment tasks

Based on the design specification and approved layout for the self-assessment tasks on p. 57:

1. Produce an annotated scaled drawing for a ground floor and first floor layout.
2. Draw a scaled section through the building showing all critical details.
3. Draw the elevations to a suitable scale.
4. Draw the following component drawings to a suitable scale:
   - substructure
   - window head showing lintel
   - door jamb detail

2.4 Evaluation of design solution

Topics covered in this section are:

- design constraints
- key construction constraints
- legal constraints
- quality control

Design constraints

The **briefing chart** and **circulation diagram** are working practices that help the architect to satisfy the client's needs. During the design stage the architect will monitor progress and evaluate design solutions against the design specification. Compiling the client brief into functional and performance requirements will make evaluation objective, leading to an unbiased decision.

A building is a three-dimensional object, and that is how the architect will view it. Hence many of the 'thinking' drawings will be thumbnail perspectives. The architect must be aware of the massing likely to be generated by the accommodation arrangement. **Site constraints** will determine the building spread with the room locations mapped out from the circulation diagram. **User requirements studies** are used to monitor the space needs for each activity, along with published design guides. These design guides will indicate the acceptable space norms. The National House Building Council (usually abbreviated to NHBC) supplies anthropometric data for domestic projects, whereas the Department of the Environment and the RIBA publish design guides for most types of building.

This data is used to develop the preliminary space arrangement. Design solution and critical evaluation of alternatives must be consistent. Time to produce the completed design often means that quality control and critical evaluation are minimised, but these design assumptions are validated by operational appraisal during the feedback stage of the RIBA Plan of Work. The checking of design before issue takes place in two stages: the first at the scheme design and the second at the production information stage. The latter is to verify content and accuracy of data, not the design assumption.

The users of the building must be quantified into numbers, age, sex and other special characteristics that affect the spatial requirements of the building, such as disabilities, clothing, work patterns and degree of occupancy. All this data is collected at outline proposals and is used as the basis for decisions on the structural enclosure. The completed designs will have to go through a series of evaluation techniques before the optium design solution is finalised. **Flow diagrams** and **travel diagrams** will highlight the suitability of workplace location and circulation routes.

This type of analysis is only in one plane; space envelopment also relies on **psycho-physical** conditions, such as the floor to ceiling heights, or the heights of worktops or work planes above the finished floor levels. Partition spacing and the division of the internal environment are also considered. Statistically determined space norms can be verified by the information gathered from **operational appraisal** and used to give a balanced design layout between activity space, storage and circulation areas. The use of building classes, as coded by the town planners, will allow design anthropometric data and ratios to monitor the suitability of space management. These design ratios are very useful at outline proposals to obtain a well-balanced layout. By aiming to have a compact layout the architect will avoid the introduction of **sterile** areas, i.e. 'wasted' space.

The overall allocation of space in Fig. 2.80 is about right, but the mixture of room space to each activity is unbalanced compared to successful existing buildings. Using this sort of analysis will reduce the ever-present risk that the design will not be functional, due to space inequalities.

Some basic decision on building shape, layout positions and size of openings must also be considered, such as access and egress, daylighting and sunlight, orientation and views. When these decisions have been made, there is a final check to bring the design solution 'to life', but only on paper. The **user functional requirements** are now used to assess the design. What are the sunlight requirements for the user? Does the design satisfy this functional requirement? In this respect, CAD's facility for perceiving views out and virtual reality views are an obvious bonus when debriefing the client at the outline proposal stage.

Aesthetics

There are other questions that should be asked under a review of the building's aesthetic qualities:

- How will the building feel in the built environment?
- Are the mass and proportion right and does it have kerb appeal?
- Are the proposed façade treatments sympathetic?
- Does the building treatment jar on the landscape?

A building that is attractive, well proportioned and visually pleasing has an aesthetic design. Architects may know that a structure has visual appeal, but do they understand *why* it has

SPACE BALANCE			
			Job no. 125
Accommodation	Room dimensions (m)	Room area (m²)	Percentage of gross area (%)
Kitchen	3.00 × 4.00	12.00	12
Dining	4.00 × 4.00	16.00	16
Lounge	5.00 × 4.00	20.00	20
Hall	3.00 × 2.00	6.00	6
Passage	2.00 × 4.00	8.00	8
Bedroom 1	5.00 × 4.00	20.00	20
Bedroom 2	4.00 × 2.00	10.00	10
Bathroom	2.00 × 4.00	8.00	8
		-----	---
		100.00	100

Figure 2.80 Designing a compact layout

visual appeal? The use of aesthetic principles will allow the designer to be correct rather than simply have some intuition that 'it looks nice'.

Does the building have a sense of unity? **Unity** signifies a sensation of completeness, and the building composition should have unity of **colour, texture** and **shape**. Colour allows for variation and avoids monotony, but there should still be a sense of belonging about the building. Colour will also create zoning, and promote personal and corporate behaviour. Does the building composition create the desired ambience? Perspective drawings will indicate to some extent the building composition, but are usually drawn from only one viewpoint, probably due to the time required to develop the perspective. The architect may feel that the best view is created from a particular vantage point, and this will help to sell the design to the client. The client, on the other hand, may have difficulty in perceiving the completed design from a two-dimensional drawing. Semi-pictorial drawings, where the background is omitted, but shadow is indicated to show texture and vertical plane alignment, are very often used.

Pictorial drawings put the building into its surrounding. The drawing will be rendered; that is, coloured with **shadow projections** (sciography). Surroundings of the building if added to the rendered drawing add realism and give 'scale' to the composition. Background and foreground details can also be added, such as sky and clouds, trees, people, vehicles, roads and paths. All these techniques can be used to help to decide the aesthetic appeal of the building form, colour, texture and detail.

These pictorial drawings will aid an analysis of the building composition, which should have a unity of **shape**. If the architect does not achieve a unity of shape, then discord and visual rejection will occur. The layout plan of activities or ease of construction should generate the outline shapes and fits. Unity of **scale** is also an important factor in the production of an effective design, and the use of CAD will facilitate large numbers of 3D wire or solid modelling views to obtain the necessary unity. While considering the unity of scale the architect should ask:

- Are the building elements in proportion?
- Is there a focal point?
- Does the composition have symmetry?

If symmetry is an important design requirement, the building elements should lead the eye to the building *focus*; and to resolve this conflict the architect should ask these questions:

- Is the point of focus sufficiently strong to negate these divisive elements?
- Does the design of the elements need to be changed to allow priority to the focus?

While concentrating on resolving the focus of the composition, the architect will also want to review the **character** of the composition to ensure that massing of the building is correct from different viewpoints. **Style** is defined as the adoption of decorative or structural features to develop a character. Do the building views create style or discord? **Rhythm**, the repetition of openings, projections, panels, dimensional control, has an important effect on character, and will be enhanced by punctuation or emphasis of the façade details. In reviewing the aesthetic context of the building composition, the architect will hope that he or she has achieved an excellent design and not simply a fashionable design.

Design life

At the outset, certain parameters will have been agreed with the client. The design specification will have been prepared stating **functional** and **performance** requirements. Working rigidly to these criteria may result in a 'tight fit' design, so some flexibility has to be allowed. Design life is an assumption that the product will function for a period of time, before becoming useless – that is, **life expired**. Product manufacturers predict the product life in accelerated weathering test. The standard test procedures are outlined in the relevant British Standard. A carefully assembled building solution may have a design life, but the vagaries of the marketplace may determine an entirely different building life. Look around most cities and you will find redundant buildings, their usefulness has ceased for a particular activity, but the building enclosures are still functioning, showing that they are not 'life expired'.

The completed design needs to be assessed against the criteria in the design specification. Key design assumptions will need to be analysed in use and will form part of the feedback. This costing will be prepared by the quantity surveyor. The outline cost planning has already been carried out, but **cost in use** studies need to be prepared. The initial cost should not always be the deciding factor; the building will incur costs during operation, and different design solutions will have a serious effect on these operating or running costs. 'Cost in use' studies take into account the initial cost and operating costs, giving a more accurate indication of the financial involvement to the client. At an early stage in design the effect of alternative building shapes, wall to floor ratios, and building form will have been considered for initial cost, and the operating cost will include maintenance, heating, lighting and cleaning. **Life cycle costing** is another name given to 'cost in use' studies.

The **building maintenance manual** is another reason for considering the design life of the building, components and elements. The building maintenance manual will help the client to operate and maintain the building and equipment to achieve optimum efficiency.

The gathering of data for the **technical appraisal** will be vital for updating the product file and especially the design life predictions. If the technical appraisal data is stored on a computer database, updating of the product list becomes a simple task.

Materials

The material selection will have been analysed against the functional specification, performance specification and aesthetic consideration. At this review stage the design team are concentrating on **buildability** and making decisions regarding nominations.

Buildability is about the ease of constructing the project and decisions have been taken without the advice of the specialist – that is, the builder. Sound reasons have been considered on the type of procurement method for the project and open tendering has been selected. This prevents the builder from offering advice on construction techniques and methods. In the JCT Standard Form of Contract, 1980 edition, with quantities, clause 8 deals with materials. If the contract was placed under this form of contract, the contractual obligation on the builder is to obtain materials as **specified in the contract documents**. The specification in the bill of quantities describes the materials and quality to be used in the project.

F10.1.101 Brickwork below d.p.c. level Bricks: Clay to BS 3921 Special shapes: Manufacturer and reference: Commons Mortar: see section Z21, 1:6 Bond: stretcher Joints: 10 mm					

Figure 2.81 Extract from a bill of quantities – materials

Allow the following prime cost sum of £9000.00 for the erection of the structural frame by E Wreck Ltd, Steel Forge, Sheffield Add for cash discount			2½%	9000	00

Figure 2.84 Extract from a bill of quantities – prime cost sum for nominated subcontractors

For example, Fig. 2.81 shows an extract from the materials section of the bill of quantities.

The specification requires the contractor to purchase clay bricks to BS 3921. The minimum quality and dimensions have been clearly defined and the contractor is free to choose the supplier, as long as the bricks meet the specification.

An extract from the masonry section of the bill of quantities is shown in Fig. 2.82.

Now the contractor must purchase only London Brick Co. Dapple White facings. If an alternative is substituted, the contractor is in breach of contract and the architect can demand the removal of the substandard work and reinstatement of the work with contractual materials.

No consideration has been given by the design team to the delivery problems or availability of materials. The contractor has accepted that risk, with only the proviso in the contract that the materials are **so far as procurable**. When preparing the specification and contract documents the architect must decide which materials will be obtained from a **nominated** supplier. The contractor will be told where to purchase the materials. The instruction is included in the **prime cost sum** section of the contract bill of quantities (Fig. 2.83). According to the JCT Standard Form of Contract, the contractor is then entitled to 5% cash discount, and the prices are adjusted by the quantity surveyor at the final account stage.

Another decision the architect must make at the bill of quantities stage of the RIBA Plan of Work is whether to nominate a specialist subcontractor to carry out a certain part of the work under the main contractor. This specialist becomes a **nominated subcontractor**. Often the structural frame, services are sublet to a nominated subcontractor. In the tender bill of quantities this instruction would occur as a prime cost sum. The cash discount in this instance is only $2\frac{1}{2}$% of the nominated subcontractor's final account (Fig. 2.84).

Where there is no current British Standard to specify minimum quality and coordinate size, an **Agrément certificate**

F10.1.111 Brickwork above d.p.c. level Bricks: Clay to BS 3921 Special shapes: Manufacturer and reference: LBC dapple white Mortar: see section Z21, 1:6 Bond: stretcher Joints: 10 mm bucket handle					

Figure 2.82 Extract from a bill of quantities – masonry

Allow the following prime cost sum of £1000.00 for door ironmongery to be obtained from AJ Supplies Ltd, Knobs and Knockers House. Add for cash discount		5%	1000	00

Figure 2.83 Extract from a bill of quantities – prime cost sum

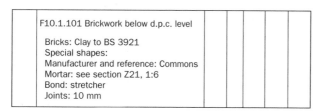

MATERIAL CHECKLIST				
				Job no. 125
Element	Quality definition	Workmanship definition	Site inspection	

Masonry Brick/blockwork F10
  Common bricks
  Facing bricks
    Joint profile
    Modular coordination
    Sample panel
    Expansion joints
	BS 3921
	BS 3921
		BS 8000
		BS 8000		

Figure 2.85

can be used. Alternatively, the architect can instruct the builder to accept the manufacturer's own specification. To minimise the risk of interpretation errors and aid efficiency, the National Building Specification contains thousands of material specifications. The NBS, as it is known, uses the CI/SfB classification system. It is also being updated to use CAWS (Common Arrangement of Work Sections). This will aid all involved in the design and construction team through **coordinated project information** (often abbreviated to CPI).

The specification is a statement of requirement and should give clear requirements on minimum quality and performance. The specification should also describe

- appearance requirements
- composition of materials/components
- quality
- test or sample approval
- acceptable tolerances

A material checklist (Fig. 2.85) will be useful as a site inspection list for the architect or, in a large project, the clerk of works. The **Clerk of Works** (COW) acts as an inspector on site for the architect but has to rely on the architect's contractual authority for enforcement. Often for building services requirements the specification is written in functional and performance terms.

Environmental

In reviewing the completed design the architect must be satisfied that the design solution will function as a whole building. Since all the elements and components will interact to produce the micro-climate, operational appraisal will be carried out to match the actual building environment with the designed environment. Technical appraisal of individual elements, dealing with responsiveness of controls, location and ease of use, will be used to check design assumptions, often based on statistical data and ergonomic techniques. Some of these design assumptions were:

- rates of occupancy of the building
- users' preferences (often the design user is different to the actual user)
- daylight requirements
- sunlight, solar gain and glare
- views out and views in
- privacy and security
- air quality
- noise, internal or external sources
- heat, design temperature ranges

There are also other assumptions regarding the effect of the site and orientation of the layout:

- site contour and proximity of buildings
- climate and natural environment, such as the intensity of the sun, cloud cover, tree cover, effect of artificial shading
- rainfall intensity and direction as determined by the degree of exposure, air infiltration or the effect of local pollution

These factors are summarised as **design context**.

The user requirements will help to reduce the incidence of a design failure, but these are only statistical averages and tolerance and range need to be built into the building environment. The **design appraisal** will highlight successes and failures in location, position and numbers of fittings; the **technical appraisal** will show the durability and tolerance of individual fittings to abuse and overload; and the **operational appraisal** will show how the building is functioning under working conditions. All this feedback data has a cost implication, and the cost of gathering, analysing and storing this information is called the **utility cost**. Not everything needs to be appraised and monitored, but sampling techniques will reduce the utility costs and targeting 'key' functions will also reduce the information load.

The aim of the design was to produce a suitable micro-climate for the occupants to enjoy their activities in the building and **key design features** were identified, based on user requirements. However, the whole building must also function in the macro-climate, without destroying the natural balance of life-sustaining cycles. Building emissions should not pollute the atmosphere, and conservation of fossil fuels will determine the size and type of heating and ventilation system. This **greening policy** should be consistently applied throughout the design process. The selection of materials should be from non-environment threatening, non-polluting or sustainable sources.

The building maintenance manual will be supplemented by the measured services drawing. The services runs and fittings are accurately recorded as finally installed. Sometimes the measured services drawings are called **services as installed**. The building maintenance manual is part of the facilities management packages available through computer technology.

The use of intelligent buildings and facilities management has created problems for other consultants over service accommodation and flexibility of activities. The Building Research Establishment has produced several digests on the conflict of design decisions and the performance of individual elements. It was, in the past, traditional practice to lay cables in the roof space of domestic buildings and to overlay the thermal insulating blanket or quilt, thus insulating the roof. This is now considered to be a fire hazard as the heat that is generated by the cabling cannot dissipate, the insulation rapidly deteriorates around the wiring, and there is a possibility of combustion. In service ducting the position and spacing of the services are critical, and design data is available to reduce the problems caused by incorrectly spaced services.

The flexibility of layout has forced the designer to consider **cable management**, and the compromises can have a serious effect on the layout on shape of the building.

Key construction constraints

Physical

When we discuss physical construction constraints, we are looking at the site, building type, and the surrounding built and natural environment.

Site survey

The architect or a land surveyor will physically measure the site. A site reconnaissance will allow familiarity with the site and its potential. **Site topography** and size will determine the mass and building form, and as the completed design is being evaluated the following questions should be considered:

- Does the building make full use of the site's natural potential?
- Does the building enhance the built environment?
- Does the building minimise the effect on the local flora and fauna?
- What effect does the building create at the kerb?
- Has the building got kerb appeal?

Since the work of the architect is very visible, these questions must be answered and analysed.

Access road levels and the site level will determine the position of the site entrance and internal road layouts. The soil investigation and orientation of the site will also affect the site access and the mass of the building.

Building type

One of the reasons for cost planning was to ensure a 'balanced' building. Successful buildings are analysed and the resultant elemental cost plans are used to ensure both value for money and that the elements are balanced. For example, let us assume that the soil investigation borehole logs recorded poor soil until 6.00 m depth and that undisturbed soil samples were used to determine the safe bearing capacity of the soils under laboratory conditions. The architect's **initial design concept** specified a low spread building with shallow foundations, within the floor space index criterion, but the cost of substructure in this instance will distort the element balance, while the cost limit imposed by the client will remain the same. Some element must pay for the extra cost of foundations if the design is to keep within the cost limits.

Certain building forms are economical and the shape generates consistent value for money. Below are some guidelines to value-for-money building forms.

- Keep the building envelope to floor ratio as low as possible. A compact site layout will be more economical to build.

- Do not enclose unnecessary space.
- Keep the roof scape simple by avoiding hips, valleys, etc.
- Match the site contour with the floors. This reduces foundation costs.
- Use structural form at the maximum span, not the minimum.

Of course, there will be other key construction constraints and conflicting design requirements. After all a building is a set of compromises and often cost is the overarching criterion.

Existing natural habitat

One maxim is 'if it's working well don't alter it', and that is very true for the architect. Already there will be established natural and wildlife patterns. If you are extremely lucky you may be commissioned to develop a **greenfield** site. The site is often described as a **brownfield** site due to previous land use and contamination.

The creativity lies in blending the design solution into the existing natural and built environment. In the design methodology, open spaces can be established where the natural habitat can be protected and used to create harmony and balance. **Hard landscaping** was a feature of the natural landscape, and hard and **soft landscaping** can be mixed together to good effect. The help of a landscape architect may assist the design to blend with the natural habitat. Observe how buildings relate to their surroundings, analyse their strengths and weaknesses, copy their good points, and with the current concern for the natural environment, legislation may well make this a high priority.

The cost of this abuse of the natural environment will have to be borne by the developer, although political correctness may eventually introduce government directives for brownfield sites.

Financial

The completed scheme has been carefully monitored by the quantity surveyor throughout the design process and the data used was based on similar historical buildings. From the **outline cost plan** the chosen design solution went through a process of refinement and development during the scheme design stage and firm design decisions were taken based on functional and performance specifications. The **comparative costing** of viable alternatives that enables the design team to select the optimum method is the role of

ELEMENTAL COST PLAN				
				Job no. 125
Element	Budget (£)	Actual (£)	Saving (£)	Loss (£)
Substructure	2340	1889	451	–

Figure 2.87

the quantity surveyor. The structural engineer has designed two suitable foundation methods – the traditional strip foundation or the deep narrow strip foundation – and both methods are functional (Fig. 2.86). How will the choice be made?

Rather than using historical data for the comparative costs, the quantity surveyor will use real time data from a builder's current price book. Maintaining consistency of pricing is important to enable results to be compared, and the use of **partial costing** can reduce the workload of the quantity surveyor. The comparative study indicated that the deep narrow strip foundation was 15 per cent cheaper. This saving can be calculated and summarised in the elemental cost plan (Fig. 2.87) and can be used to offset overspends in other elements.

All the data used has been historical or in current price books, but the acid test is the receipt of the tender bids. The data used so far has not included the element of competition. The builder's bids are all based on the **tender documents**: the builder offers to carry out the described project, and the client accepts. The consideration to the builder is the tender sum, and the client receives the building. A legal contract depends on an offer being made, acceptance of the offer, consideration, intention to enter into a contract and the legality of the contract. Therefore, a legally binding contract can be signed by the two parties – that is, the client (known as the **employer**) and the builder (known as the **main contractor**).

In the construction stage, certain decisions will be made by the architect which will modify or alter the contract documents. The architect is allowed to do this under the JCT Standard Form of Building Contract, 1980 edition with quantities. Clause 13, 'Variations and provisional sum', is the contractual authority for the architect. A variation is defined as a change in design, quantity or quality. The expenditure of prime cost sums or provisional sums is also a variation. The architect then issues to the builder, or more correctly to the main contractor, a **variation order** or an **architect's instruction** (Fig. 2.88). As this will affect the final cost of the building, the contract sum will be adjusted to take into account variation orders. The quantity surveyor, acting for the architect, then measures and agrees with the main contractor the **final account**.

Often the excavating work is provisional and subject to remeasurement on site. The contract conditions set down four methods of calculating the price for a variation:

- bill rates
- pro rata to bill rates
- fair valuation
- daywork rates

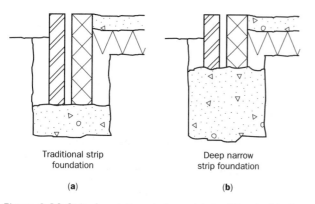

Traditional strip foundation

Deep narrow strip foundation

(a)

(b)

Figure 2.86 Strip foundation designs: (a) traditional; (b) deep narrow

ARCHITECT'S INSTRUCTION

Issued by: A. Drawer

Address ....
Employer ....
Address ....

Serial no. ....
Job no. ....
Issue date ....
Contract dated

Contractor

....

Address ....
Works ....
Situated at

....

Under the terms of the above contract (Clause 13) I/we issue the following instruction

	Cost	
	(£ omit)	(£ add)
Omit Bill ref. 21/a D20.2 Excavating 0.5 Trenches > 300 mm wide not exceeding 1.00 deep		
20 m³		
Add Bill ref. 21/a D20.2 Excavating 0.5 Trenches > 300 mm wide not exceeding 1.00 deep		
40 m³		
Signed by		

Figure 2.88 Architect's instruction concerning changes to the contract document

Once the contract is completed and the architect has issued the **Certificate of Practical Completion** the period of final measurement starts. This period runs for six months and is concurrent with the **defects liability period**. The quantity surveyor prepares the final account and adjusts the contract sum.

$$\frac{\begin{array}{l} \textbf{contract sum} \\ + \text{ variation orders} \\ - \text{ contingency sum} \\ - \text{ adjusted contract sum interim payments} \end{array}}{\textbf{final sum}}$$

The architect now issues the **Final Certificate** to the builder. The final certificate is presented to the employer (client) for payment. At last we have arrived at the total building cost.

The **building costs** are analysed into building cost per square metre of floor area. The **primary elements** and **secondary elemental** breakdown of cost is prepared and the data filed in the building cost file, usually under the planning classes. A new commission and this historical cost data are used to predict the outline cost. Do not forget to add a price risk percentage and a design risk percentage. A good guide towards the percentage addition for design risk is the cost of variations on previous similar projects.

$$\frac{\text{Percentage addition}}{\text{for design}} = \frac{\text{variation order costs}}{\text{adjusted contract sum} \times 100}$$

The other item that must be checked in the completed design is **compliance with the law**.

Legal constraints

Common law follows custom and legal precedent. Certain **easements** will be obtained by adjoining owners, but the **right of support** is an easement with which the architect must comply. During the excavating operation next to the boundary, the adjoining property must be supported until the ground support is permanently restored. Easements may be granted or secured over time.

Statute or legislative law

The architect has a duty of care on health and safety legislation. The onus is on the main contractor on site to maintain safe working methods, but the architect can help by considering building methods at the design stage. Certain legislation from the European Commission will make both the architect and the client responsible for site health and safety methods. The European Commission require **environmental impact assessment** on larger schemes to be submitted with planning applications. **Green belt** development is restricted and the planning authority is unwilling to allow development on high-grade agricultural land. On Ministry of Agriculture, Fisheries and Food (MAFF) maps, this high-grade agricultural land is coloured blue. There are five grades of agricultural land of which grades I and II are high-grade farming land.

Special classes of building might have specific legislation with which the architect must comply, such as:

- Chronically Sick and Disabled Persons Act 1970–1976
- Control of Pollution Act 1974
- Countryside Act 1968
- Civic Amenities Act 1967
- Civil Aviation Act 1971
- Clean Air Acts 1956 and 1968
- Control of Pollution Act 1992
- Control of Substances Hazardous for Health Act 1992
- Defective Premises Act 1972
- Disabled Persons Act 1981
- Environmental Protection Act 1990
- Fire Precautions Act 1971
- Highways Act 1971 and 1980
- Historic Buildings and Ancient Monuments Act 1953
- Housing Act 1985
- Mines and Quarries Act 1954
- Mineral Workings Act 1971
- Minerals Act 1981
- Noise Abatement Act 1960
- Offices, Shops and Railway Premises Act 1990

Other legislation is embedded in the Building Regulations and Planning Law.

Quality control

British Standards

British standards assist the architect in several ways, such as design codes, material specifications, building codes and standardised testing methods. Some design codes are:

- BS 6399: Loading for buildings
- BS 6399, Part 1: Code of practice for dead and imposed loads

- BS 8110: Structural use of concrete
- BS 8110, Part 1: Code of practice for design and construction
- BS 8301: Code of practice for building drainage

There are also material specifications, which specify the minimum quality and methods of assessing quality. This guarantees an acceptable quality and places limitations on material selection. For example, BS 3921, Clay bricks, defines standardised testing for frost-resistant bricks and the designation to be used by the brick manufacturers. The dimensional tolerances are also defined, together with the sample size.

Building codes

British Standards use codes of practice to define good site practice. The workmanship specifications in the contract bill will use a code of practice, as will drawing annotations where working methods are being described. For example:

- BS 5628: Code of practice for the use of masonry
- BS 6232: Thermal installation of cavity walls by filling with blown man-made fibre; Part 2, 1982: Code of practice for the installation of blown man-made mineral fibres in cavity walls with masonry and/or concrete leaves
- BS 5262: Code of practice for external rendering

Standardised testing procedures

Another important use of British Standards is in the standardisations of testing procedures and the designation of products. For example, the designation of surface spread of flame is defined in BS 476.

The British Standards Institution will issue **Draft for development** (DD) notes. After a period of consultation the development notes are written into standards. For example, DD 93: Method of assessing exposure to wind-driven rain. Compliance with British Standards is an integral part of compliance with the Building Regulations.

Building Regulations

The enabling act for the Building Regulations was the Building Act 1984. Based on the legal framework outlined in the Building Act 1984, the Building Regulations 1985 became law. The Building Regulations were contained in **Approved Documents**:

- A: Structure
- B: Fire safety
- C: Site preparation and resistance to moisture
- D: Toxic substances, 1985 edition
- E: Resistance to passage of sound
- F: Ventilation, 1990 edition
- G: Hygiene
- H: Drainage and waste disposal, 1990 edition
- J: Heat-producing appliances, 1990 edition
- K: Stairs, ramps and guards
- L: Conservation of fuel and power, 1990 edition
- M: Access and facilities for disabled people
- N: Glazing – materials and protection
- Regulation 7: Materials and workmanship

Application

The Building Regulations are concerned with the health and safety of the public. Building work consists of the erection, re-erection or extension of buildings, and material change of use of a building. Certain developments are **exempt**. Greenhouses, carports under 30 m² and open on two sides, builder's temporary site accommodation, porches under 30 m² and conservatories under 30 m² with a translucent roof are exempt developments. Basically any other building work must comply with the Building Regulations.

When a **full plans notice** is made the plans are deposited with the local authority building control. The local authority checks the deposited plans for compliance with Building Regulations and either **approves** or **rejects** the plans for non-compliance. During the construction stage the building control office will inspect and approve the construction at specific stages. These **Building Notice Cards** are sent to the architect with the Building Control Approval Notice. Once the builder has been selected, the Building Notice Cards are handed over to the builder. The builder must then notify the building control office at the prescribed stages.

Commencement	7 days' notice
Excavation	24 hours' notice
Concrete foundations	24 hours' notice
Damp-proof course	24 hours' notice
Oversite preparation	24 hours' notice
Drains, stage 1	24 hours' notice
Drains, stage 2	24 hours' notice
Completion of the work.	

The local authority is empowered to **relax** or **dispense with** most of the requirements of the regulations. Since the Building Regulations are described as **functional performance** statements, the relaxation is only allowed for unreasonableness.

Each local authority has regulations for the depositing of plans and calculations.

Two copies of the drawing must be submitted. The drawing should be a block plan to a scale of 1 : 1250, showing the size and position of the building in relation to adjoining property, the curtilage of the building, the width and position of any street within the boundaries of the curtilage of the building, drainage details and access for the removal of refuse.

Plans and sections to the proposed building should be submitted at a scale of 1 : 100. There should also be a key plan, to a scale of 1 : 2500, showing the position of the site. (If the block plan shows sufficient detail to locate the proposed building, the key plan can be omitted.)

One copy of the full plans must also be submitted, together with all payable fees.

The local authority is required to give a decision within five weeks from the date of submission. Structural calculations in connection with structural stability must be submitted unless the architect has used the design tables and guides within the Building Regulations, Approved Document A: Structure. Since the regulations are described in functional requirements the architect is allowed to trade off certain details, such as thermal transmission. The calculations and the loadings of the building service engineer will have to be submitted, although the design codes of the British Standards Institution for drainage would be an acceptable method. CIBSE (Chartered Institute of Building Service Engineers) 'Design notes and methodology' is also acceptable for the heating calculations.

Approval procedure

Acknowledgement of the application is made to the agent (architect). The building control officer will check the plans and calculations for compliance, often using a checklist for each approved document. Other local authority officers are involved in checking the drawings:

- environmental health officer
- drainage engineer
- fire officer
- public health officer
- highways engineer

After the checking is completed the agent is notified of the building control decision. If the decision is to reject the deposited plans, then the agent can appeal to the Secretary of State for the Environment, but this must be done within one month of the date of refusal. Unauthorised building work can be removed by the local authority building control with a court order. The period of approval is usually three years. If work has not commenced within that period the building control approval is not valid. The agent may choose not to use the local authority to check and inspect the work.

An approved inspector

An **initial notice** is sent to the local authority giving notice of the use of a **private certifier**. The initial notice is served jointly by the architect and the approved inspector. This must be accompanied by the revelant plans and a declaration of insurance, showing that the policy applies to the building work. The building control has 10 days to reject the initial notice. The plan is then examined by the private certifier, and a notice is sent to the local authority. The **plan certificate** which shows that the plans comply with the Building Regulations, is sent to the developer or agent. If the developer so requests, the plan certificate can be sent to the local authority.

On completion of the work the approved inspector or private certifier issues a **final certificate** to the developer and the local authority. Certain corporate bodies are available as approved inspectors, such as the National House Building Council. The NHBC building control will issue the initial notice and plan certificate, inspect the work during construction and issue the final certificate. The final certificate issued by the NHBC forms part of the 10-year insurance warranty under the NHBC Buildmark scheme.

Either method of building control will still have to comply with other legislation, when applicable.

Planning control

Application

Nearly all developments require planning permission. There are, however, some **permitted developments**, such as house extensions not exceeding 15% of the original volume, and if the house is a terrace this is reduced to 10%. Other permitted developments are a small porch or hedge below 2.0 m high.

A development is defined under planning law as 'the carrying out of building, engineering, mining or other operations in, on, over or under land, the making of material

change in use of any building or other land'. Under planning law, uses of buildings are classified under the **Use Classes Order**.

- Class A1: Shops, including superstores and retail warehouses
- Class A2: Financial and professional services, such as banks and building societies
- Class A3: Food and drink; for example restaurants
- Class B1: Business use, such as offices
- Class B2: General industrial use
- Class B3–7: Special industrial use
- Class B8: Storage and distribution
- Class C1: Hotels and hostels
- Class C2: Residential homes and institutions used as hospitals
- Class C3: Dwelling homes for family use with a maximum of 6 persons in the household
- Class D1: Non-residential institutions, such as public halls and religious buildings
- Class D2: Assembly and leisure facilities, such as cinemas

The class definition is important since certain planning orders will be applicable to one class of building. The classes of use are also important for **Change of Use** permission. Each building has an established use according to the planning authority, and another use of the designated building would require planning permission for 'change of use'.

Under planning legislation a planning authority has to produce **structure plans**. The structure plans provide the overall policy for the county-wide economic and social development. The district council, based on the overall county strategic development plan, produce a **local plan**. The local plan outlines the next five years' development in a particular village or district. Originally there were three types of local plans for larger areas: a **district plan** for a whole village; an **area action plan**, which comprehensively outlined the planning strategy for a particular subzone; and a **subject plan**, such as a country parks development within the county boundaries.

With the reorganisation of the district and local councils, the new unitary system will change the structure and local plans. The unitary councils will be required to produce a **Unitary Development Plan** (UDP). Part I of the UDP is devoted to strategic policy statements, while Part II covers detailed land use issues and planning in specific areas. Unitary development plans and the older structure plans indicate permitted developments within the planning district. The need for outline planning permission has been simplified by checking the structure or local plan, although it may still be advisable to obtain outline planning permission. This establishes the broad principles for the development, but **full planning permission** is still required prior to commencing building operations. The submission for full planning permission is called **reserved matters**, when outline permission has been granted.

Approval

Submission for planning permission must comply with the planning authority's procedures. Certain developments are 'permitted developments' and do not need planning permission. For example, a porch can be built as a permitted development if the size does not exceed 3 m^2, is less than 3.00 m high and at least 2.00 m from the boundary of the road. A loft extension could be a permitted development, as could house extensions up to 15% of the original cubic capacity and where the extension is not more than $70\,m^3$. Rules are complicated, and if there is a doubt contact the local planning authority for advice.

Full planning application

Forms

Planning application forms must be completed and four copies submitted. Any fees payable should also be submitted.

Plans

Four copies of plans and elevations must be submitted.

- A site plan at a scale of 1 : 2500, with the application land shown in red, and adjoining land in the control of the applicant marked in blue.
- A layout plan at a scale of 1 : 1250 but preferably at a scale of 1 : 500. The layout plan should show boundaries and positions of existing buildings, roads and utility services. The layout plan is used for large developments.
- A block plan at a scale of 1 : 500, showing the following details: boundaries; existing buildings with dimensions from the site; lines and details of foul and surface water; and access to the highway. The block plan will usually contain all the necessary detail.
- Building plans. This will include plans and elevations at a scale of 1 : 100, showing the following details: a plan of every floor with details of construction; all elevations of the building showing materials selected.

Certificates

Certificate of lawful ownership (or section 66 certificates) must be completed with the planning application:

- Part A is completed by a sole owner.
- Part B is completed if the ownership is shared and Notice 1 sent to each owner.
- Part C is used where the applicant cannot discover all the names of the land owners.
- Part D is used where the applicant cannot discover any of the names of the land owners.

With the application forms and a minimum of four copies of plans, the application may be sent to the planning authority.

Acknowledgement

The planning authority will acknowledge receipt of the application, and record the planning application in the *Register of Planning Applications*. The list of new planning applications will be published in the local newspaper and the neighbours informed of the application. On-site notices will alert the public to the proposals and 21 days are allowed to enable the public to inspect deposited plans and make **written representations**. All the representations are available for public scrutiny. From the date of entering the application on the register the planning authority has eight weeks to determine the application. The applicant may be asked for an extension to determine the application beyond the statutory eight-week period.

Consultation period

Several interested parties will be consulted over the planning application, some with a view of compliance to other pieces of legislation. The various local authority departments such as the highways, environmental health, drainage will inspect and report on the proposals. Other interested parties such as the electricity or water boards will be notified and comments discussed at the planning meeting.

After the consultation period the planning officer will prepare a report and submit the authority's recommendation to the local planning committee. The local planning committee meets at publicised times and the public can be present during the planning meeting. Often the local councillor on the planning committee will be lobbied by individuals to influence the decision. The applicant will be notified of the planning committee's decision, which may be rendered as:

- approved
- approved subject to planning conditions
- rejected

The very political nature of the planning committee means that **planning gains** and **highway gains** are often discussed to secure planning approval. A planning gain is a concession that the local authority derives from the developer. Planning approval lasts for a period of five years. Appeals are allowed against the conditional approval or rejection of planning permission, but the Secretary of State for the Environment must be notified of the appeal within six months of the rendered decision.

Conservation areas

One of the aims of the planning authority is to maintain the fabric and quality of the built environment. Various powers are delegated to the local authority to designate conservation areas and listed buildings. The Civic Amenities Act 1967 established conservation areas, which gave the planning authority more powers to protect historical areas as a whole, the surrounding townscape, street appearance, trees and other non-listed buildings. The aim of conservation areas is to maintain the overall visual quality and character of the area. Further powers were given to the planning authority under the Town and Country Amenities Act 1974. The planning authority can prevent the demolition of a building to further protect trees, plants, streetscape and furniture. Under the Town and Country Planning Act 1990 it is illegal to prune certain trees without planning permission, so it is advisable to check whether the tree carries a preservation order.

All conservation legislation was combined under the Planning (Listed Building and Conservation Areas) Act 1990. **English Heritage** advises the Department of the Environment on listing buildings, designating conservation areas and town schemes. A Grade I listed building must not be removed in any circumstances. There are two types of Grade II listed building, dependent on the building's historical importance. A Grade II* (starred) building cannot be altered or demolished without good reason. Often buildings of regional importance and heritage are listed as Grade II*, whereas nationally important buildings would be Grade I. A Grade II (unstarred) listed building is described as a 'more ordinary structure'.

The local planning authority must maintain a list of all listed buildings and their grading. As a rule, all buildings built before 1700 will be listed. Buildings between 1700 and 1840 are also most likely to be listed.

The effect of conservation areas, the demands made on the architect by the planning authority and the listed buildings must be researched at the feasibility and outline proposal stage of the RIBA Plan of Work.

Self-assessment tasks

In relation to the self-assessment tasks on pp. 57 and 83:

1. Prepare an exhibition of your final design solution depicting the evolution of the design.
2. Give an oral presentation to the Local Planning Committee on the impact of the development on the locality.
3. Deposit your design portfolio with the client for final approval. Include a written explanation on the final design criteria and reasons for material selection.

Further reading

Barritt C M H 1995 *The Building Acts and Regulations Applied: Houses and Flats*, (2nd edition) Longman

Dean Y 1995 *Mitchell's Materials Technology* Longman

Ezeji S 1992 *Technical Drawing 3: Building Drawing* Longman International

Fane W 1996 *Autocad Essentials*. Addison Wesley

Greed C 1996 *Introducing Town Planning*, (2nd edition) Longman

Macpherson G 1993 *Highway and Transportation Engineering and Planning* Longman

NHBC 1996 *NHBC Standard: The Home, Its Accommodation and Services* National House Building Council

Science and Materials

Kemal Ahmet

Science means knowledge. More accurately, science means an organised body of knowledge that has been accumulated from both theory and experimentation.

This unit helps to develop the understanding of scientific principles and knowledge of the properties of materials necessary to appreciate how buildings work. First, Section 3.1 discusses measurement in relation to the correct use of units. All the base quantities required throughout this unit are explained, and presented in detail in Table 3.1. The essential use of a calculator is also discussed.

In Section 3.2, the science of human comfort, the following scientific areas are discussed:

- temperature and heat
- ventilation
- relative humidity
- sound
- lighting

A large part of this unit is dedicated to building materials (Section 3.3), and their properties and uses. Areas discussed include:

- durability and resistance to degradation
- thermal insulation
- thermal movement
- moisture content and water absorption
- elasticity
- electrical insulation
- strength
- chemical properties

This section also describes the various types of equipment used to measure these environmental factors.

A large variety of materials is used in construction. A good knowledge and understanding of the science of materials leads to the construction of safe, reliable and predictable buildings. It enables the professionals to select the most appropriate materials for the job. Ignorance of the scientific knowledge often results in major problems and may lead to the catastrophic failure of a structure.

The most important and versatile type of energy used in the built environment is electricity. The section on electrical energy (Section 3.4) includes:

- the physics of electricity
- electromagnetic induction
- generators
- transformers
- the distribution of electricity

Water is vital for survival. The final section of this unit (Section 3.5) is about water supplies and includes:

- sources of water supply
- properties of 'natural' water
- water treatment

Finally, the answers to selected self-assessment tasks are given at the end of the book. Students should not look at the answers until they have attempted the questions.

3.1 Introduction

Units

When a measurement is made the resulting number needs to be followed by the correct **unit**. Here is an example: 'The temperature of the water was 30.' This, of course, is meaningless. The sentence makes sense when the unit is included: 'The temperature of the water was 30 °C.' The same is true in shopping: not only do you ask for a certain amount of something, you must also say what it is you want!

In science the unit must always be included in the answer. The main units are known as **SI units** (Système International units). These units are standard throughout the world. All the base quantities required in this chapter and the SI unit for each are presented in Table 3.1. *All* other standard units are obtained from those in Table 3.1. These are called **derived units**. Sometimes it is convenient to use other metric units. The more important of these are shown below under the relevant headings.

Table 3.1 The seven base quantities and their SI units

Physical quantity	Name of unit	Symbol for unit
length	metre	m
mass	kilogram	kg
time	second	s
electric current	ampere	A
temperature	kelvin	K
luminous intensity	candela	cd
amount of substance	mole	mol

Mass

The gram (g) is a popular unit; so is the kilogram (kg). The conversion is

$$1000\,g = 1\,kg$$

Also, for large masses the tonne is used:

$$1000\,kg = 1\,tonne$$

Length

Apart from the metre (m), the millimetre (mm), centimetre (cm) and kilometre (km) are also commonly used:

$$1000\,mm = 1\,m$$
$$100\,cm = 1\,m$$
$$1000\,m = 1\,km$$

(N.B. The cm is not an SI unit.)

Time

In addition to the second, minutes and hours can be used although these are not SI units:

$$60\,s = 1\,min$$
$$60\,min = 1\,h$$

Temperature

As shown in Table 3.1, the SI unit for temperature is the kelvin (K). Frequently, however, the degree celsius (°C) is used. Conversions from one scale to the other are as follows:

$$\text{temperature in }°C = \text{temperature in K} - 273$$

or

$$\text{temperature in K} = \text{temperature in }°C + 273$$

For example, room temperature, which is around 20 °C, can also be written as 293 K. It is important to remember that a *change* in temperature of 1 K is equal to a change in temperature of 1 °C.

Self-assessment tasks 3.1

1. Show that, as there are 1000 mm in 1 m, there must be 10^9 mm^3 in a volume of 1 m^3.
2. A volume of 1000 mm^3 of water has a mass of 1 gram. Show that 1 m^3 has a mass of 1 tonne.

Another commonly used unit worth mentioning is the litre. The litre is a measure of volume:

$$1000\text{ litres} = 1\,m^3$$

Before going onto the next section it is important to emphasise again that all other units used in the rest of Unit 3 are derived from those quoted in this section.

Using a calculator

Throughout this unit, a calculator will be needed for doing calculations. It is essential that the reader has a *scientific* calculator available while studying this unit. In fact, professional scientists always carry calculators and they do their calculations everywhere! Calculators are very inexpensive to purchase.

Most calculators are very easy to use, but it is always worth reading the manufacturer's instructions. The following quiz should be tried before going on to study the rest of this unit. The reader should ensure that he or she can use a calculator to obtain the correct answer to all the calculations below.

Quiz

Try all the calculations with a calculator and make sure that your answers match those given below.

1. 8.9×7.6
2. $0.000\,32 \times 28.3$
3. $(45.1 + 50.8 + 47.3 + 49.0) \div 4$
4. $10.1 \div (0.06 \times 0.000\,85)$
5. $48\,830 \div 61.6$
6. $\pi \times 12^2 \times 108$
7. $(250 \times \cos 40°) \div 3.6^2$

8. $1.7 \times 10^8 \div 4.4 \times 10^5$
9. $10^{-5} \div 10^{-12}$
10. $10 \times \log ((1 \times 10^{-3}) \div (1 \times 10^{-12}))$

Answers: 1. 67.64; 2. 0.009 056; 3. 48.05; 4. 198 039 (to the nearest integer); 5. 792.7 (to one decimal place); 6. 48 858 (to the nearest integer); 7. 14.78; 8. 386.4; 9. 10^7; 10. 90.

Checking by making estimates

Although using a calculator is very important, the reader should be able to check that the answer obtained is sensible. There have been some major disasters where engineers have not bothered to check the calculations.

Checks are easy to carry out. The rule is to 'round off' numbers so they are easy to manage. So, checking question 1, the figures become $9 \times 8 = 72$. This check tells us that the answer is going to be very roughly 72 when the full calculation is carried out.

Checking question 3, we can round off the numbers as follows: $(50 + 50 + 50 + 50) \div 4 = 200 \div 4 = 50$. The answer, then, is expected to be about 50.

Question 5 can be rounded as follows: $48\,000 \div 60 = 4800 \div 6 = 800$. This gives us a rough 'feel' for the correct answer and forms a check. Checks like these help to avoid ridiculous numbers being accepted as the correct answers. Whenever possible, the student should make checks by estimating the answers.

3.2 The science of human comfort

What makes people feel comfortable inside buildings? There are many factors but the following are the most important:

- **Temperature** – for thermal comfort the temperature must be neither too cool nor too warm. In the UK, the climate is such that we require to heat buildings for many months of the year.
- **Humidity** – the moisture in the atmosphere closely controls how we feel. For example, when it is too hot and too humid, it feels very 'sticky' and uncomfortable. When the humidity is too low, people can suffer from sore throats and the skin tends to dry up.
- **Ventilation** – the air smells 'fresh' if there is adequate ventilation. We are all aware of how unpleasant it can smell if there is too little ventilation. Ventilation also ensures that the level of oxygen remains adequate; where the oxygen level falls appreciably, people feel tired and drowsy.
- **Noise** – high noise levels are most irritating and can cause much distress. There are few people who have never been annoyed by noisy neighbours! Very high noise levels cause distress and permanent damage to hearing.
- **Lighting** – lighting must be appropriate for people to feel comfortable. Too much light can be off-putting in a leisure environment, such as a restaurant. Insufficient light can cause much discomfort, and can easily cause accidents and mistakes to occur in the workplace.

It must be stressed that the desirable conditions for comfort vary slightly from person to person. Where many people occupy a given internal environment, it is most sensible that the conditions for comfort are chosen to satisfy the majority.

The physical processes for achieving comfort levels were previously mentioned in Unit 2 (Section 2.2) and are discussed in detail below.

Thermal comfort

Buildings need to be kept at reasonable temperatures so that the occupants feel comfortable. The necessary temperature depends on the use of the building. The typical internal temperature needs to be around 20 °C. The recommended values for internal temperatures for a number of situations are given in Table 3.2.

Table 3.2 Recommended values for internal temperatures

Indoor environment	Temperature (°C)
Dwellings	
Living rooms	21
Bedroom	18
Offices	20
Factories	
Light work	16
Heavy work	13

(From Smith, Phillips and Sweeney 1982 *Environmental Science* Longman)

In many countries such as the British Isles, the external temperature is below comfort levels for much of the year. To maintain appropriate temperatures for comfort, buildings must be heated for a large proportion of the year. Heat flows out of a building whenever the external temperature is below the internal temperature. By choosing appropriate materials for the skin of a building the heat losses can be reduced to very low values. The Building Regulations stipulate the minimum level of thermal insulation necessary for the various parts of all types of buildings (see p. 100).

It is essential to remember that if heat is being lost, the building will cool down unless more heat is being generated inside. If the heat supplied is equal to the heat losses, the temperature always remains constant. Figure 3.1 shows heat losses from an existing, uninsulated house.

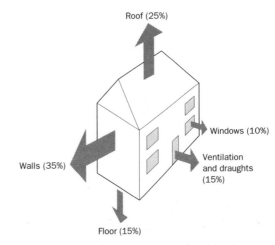

Figure 3.1 Typical heat losses from an uninsulated house

Temperature, heat and thermal power

Temperature, heat and thermal power are all related, but they must *not* be confused with each other:

- Temperature is a measure of the hotness of substances and is measured in °C or K.
- Heat measures the thermal **energy** which flows *into* or *out of* (for example) buildings. Heat is measured in joules (J).
- Power is the rate at which heat flows, or the **heat flow per second**. Power is measured in joules per second (J/s) or watts (W). We often say *thermal* power to emphasise that we are referring to heat.

Measuring temperature

Temperature is measured using thermometers. In buildings, electronic thermocouple thermometers are often used for measuring the temperature. The thermocouple sensor is made from two different metals joined together. (This produces a tiny voltage that varies with temperature.) Unlike mercury thermometers, thermocouples are not easily broken. Figure 3.2 shows a thermometer being used to measure the difference between the inside and outside air temperatures. The two thermocouple probes can be seen to the left of the instrument.

Figure 3.2 Thermometer with two thermocouple sensors

Heat losses from surfaces

When the surrounding air temperature is lower than that of the building, the surfaces of the building can lose heat by the following processes:

- **Conduction** – this is where heat is passed directly from the surface to the surrounding air. This process is also responsible for carrying heat *through* the building fabric and is described in the next section.
- **Radiation** – all surfaces give off infra-red radiation or 'heat waves'. This process is most important when the surface temperature is very hot. Dull or dark surfaces are good radiators while white or shiny surfaces are relatively poor at radiating heat.
- **Convection** – air currents carry away heat efficiently. Clearly, surfaces exposed to high winds lose heat fast.
- **Evaporation** – water absorbs much heat during evaporation and cools down a surface. (This is why people sweat, in order to cool down.) For this reason, damp surfaces lose heat quicker than dry surfaces.

Heat losses through the fabric

Thermal conduction

Heat flows through solid materials only by **thermal conduction**. The thermal conductivity is a measure of how good the material is at conducting heat. Table 3.9 shows the values of thermal conductivity for a range of common materials. As copper has a high value of thermal conductivity (see Table 3.9), it is termed a good **thermal conductor**. On the other hand, expanded polystyrene and glass fibre quilt have low values. These materials are called **thermal insulators**. Thermal conductivity is often abbreviated to k. The unit for k is W/m °C. This is because thermal conductivity is defined from the equation used to calculate the thermal power (P) which flows through a material:

$$P = \frac{kA(T_1 - T_2)}{x}$$

In this equation, A is the area and x is the thickness measured in m² and m respectively. ($T_1 - T_2$) is the temperature difference (in °C or K) between the two parallel surfaces which are 90° to the direction of heat flow. Figure 3.3 shows this pictorially. If the above equation is written in terms of units:

$$W = [k] \times m^2 \times \frac{°C}{m}$$

This can be rearranged to find $[k]$, that is the unit for thermal conductivity:

$$[k] = W \times \frac{m}{(m^2 \times °C)} = W/m\,°C$$

This is read as watts per metre per degree Celsius.

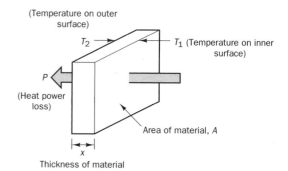

Figure 3.3 Heat flow through a material. The thermal conductivity is defined from the quantities shown

---

Self-assessment task 3.2

*For the question below, the student is advised to **prepare the information** before doing the calculations. All data should be written using the correct units.*

Thermocouples (which measure temperature) were placed in contact with both the inner and outer surfaces of the glass in a window pane of length 2 m and width 1 m. The temperatures recorded were 15 °C and 12 °C. Taking the glass to be 6 mm thick and its thermal conductivity to be 1 W/m °C, find the power loss through the window.

Thermal resistivity

The thermal properties of materials are sometimes compared by using thermal **resistivity**. This quantity is the 'opposite' of thermal conductivity and is calculated by

$$\text{thermal resistivity} = \frac{1}{\text{thermal conductivity}}$$

The unit for thermal resistivity is m°C/W. (The reader should check this.) For example, from Table 3.9 the thermal resistivity of granite is $1/2.93 = 0.34$ m °C/W. A greater thermal resistivity means a better insulator of heat.

Thermal resistance

It is well known that the thicker a material is made the better are the insulating characteristics. For example, loft insulation (e.g. glass fibre quilt) can be fitted at thicknesses of 100 mm or 150 mm. The thicker one is clearly a more effective insulator. The **thermal resistance** takes into account the thickness of the material. To calculate the thermal resistance:

$$\text{thermal resistance} = \frac{\text{thickness}}{\text{thermal conductivity}}$$

This formula immediately tells us that the best thermal insulation is achieved by

- using a material with the lowest possible thermal conductivity
- making the material as thick as possible

The unit for thermal resistance is $m^2\,°C/W$ and is easy to show from the formula above.

Example

(i) Find the thermal resistance of expanded polystyrene of thickness 50 mm.
(ii) What thickness should (dense) concrete be in order to achieve the same thermal resistance?
Comment on this value.

Answer

(i) Thermal resistance = thickness/thermal conductivity = $0.05/0.034 = 1.47\,m^2\,°C/W$.
(ii) The formula must be rearranged to obtain the thickness: thickness = thermal resistance × thermal conductivity = $1.47 \times 1.44 = 2.12\,m$.
This is very thick! It is best to use another material for insulation purposes.

Finally, and most importantly, the thermal transmittance coefficient (U-value) is now defined and discussed.

U-values

For a given building component, the U-value is a measure of the overall rate of loss of heat. The exact definition of U-value is the power loss per square metre of surface when the temperature difference between the inside and outside air is 1 °C (or 1 K).

For standard single-glazed windows, typically, $U = 5.6\,W/m^2\,°C$ (or $W/m^2\,K$). This means that 5.6 W of power flows through each square metre of surface when the inside air temperature is 1 °C greater than the outside air temperature.

The formula for calculating the total thermal power transfer through any component is:

$$P = U \times A \times (T_i - T_o)$$

Example

A small flat within a multi-storey block has one wall measuring 4 m by 2.5 m, exposed to the external environment. The wall includes a double-glazed window of sides 1.5 m by 1 m. Calculate the total power loss in equilibrium given the following information:

U-value of wall = $0.4\,W/m^2\,K$
U-value of window = $2.8\,W/m^2\,K$
Internal air temperature = 20 °C
External air temperature = 5 °C

Answer

It is best to organise the information into a table:

Component	U-value (W/m² K)	Area (m²)	$T_i - T_o$ (°C or K)	Power (W)
Wall	0.4	8.5	15	51
Window	2.8	1.5	15	63

So, the total power loss is $51 + 63 = 114\,W$.

N.B. This does not take into account ventilation power requirements (see page 101). Also, it has been assumed that the flat is neither gaining nor losing heat to the other apartments within the block. This is valid when the internal temperatures are the same in all flats.

---

where P = power (W)
U = U-value (W/m² °C)
A = surface area (m²)
T_i = inside air temperature (°C)
T_o = outside or external air temperature (°C)

When the U-value of a partition is unknown, it can be calculated using

$$U = \frac{1}{R_{total}}$$

where R_{total} is the total thermal resistance of the partition. R_{total} is calculated by adding together the resistances of all the components of the partition. The calculation must *always* include the resistances of the external surface and internal surface air layers, i.e. R_{so} and R_{si} respectively. The reason for this is that air very close to the surface on both the external and internal sides of the partition always helps to reduce the overall heat losses. The values of R_{so} and R_{si} are typically taken to be 0.055 and $0.123\,m^2\,K/W$ respectively. At this stage, it is best to give some examples, see below.

Example

The walls of a domestic garage are constructed from brick, thickness 103 mm, see Fig. 3.4. Calculate the U-value of the walls, assuming that the thermal conductivity of the bricks used is 0.9 W/m K.

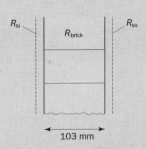

103 mm

Figure 3.4 Sketch of section of garage wall

From Fig. 3.4, it can be seen that

$$R_{total} = R_{brick} + R_{si} + R_{so}$$

The value of R_{brick} needs to be calculated:

R_{brick} = thickness ÷ thermal conductivity (this formula is from page 98)

thickness = 0.103 m and $k = 0.9\,W/m\,K$,

therefore

$$R_{brick} = \frac{0.103}{0.9}\,m^2\,K/W$$

Substituting the three resistance values into the formula for U-value gives

$$U = \frac{1}{0.114 + 0.123 + 0.055} = \frac{1}{0.292} = 3.43\,W/m^2\,K$$

Self-assessment task 3.3

This problem should be completed by using a computer, by entering the data into the appropriate software.

The exposed components of an existing small building have the following *U*-values and areas:

	U-value (W/m² K)	Area (m²)
Walls	0.8	104
Flat roof	2.5	80
Floor	0.6	80
Doors	2.0	3
Windows	5.6	4

Using a computer *spreadsheet*, calculate the power loss from the building under steady conditions. Take the internal temperature for comfort to be 21 °C; the external temperature is 3 °C (this includes the underfloor temperature). The completed spreadsheet, is shown in Fig. 3.5. It is essential that the calculations are carried out by using formulae such as the one shown in the figure. (Values of power shown in Fig. 3.5 may also be checked using a calculator.)

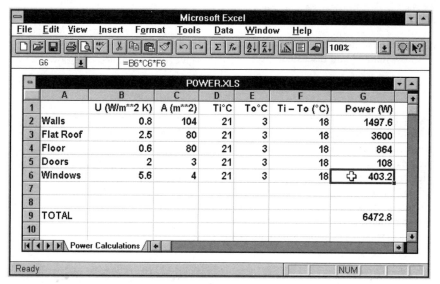

Figure 3.5 Spreadsheet to calculate *U*-values

Building Regulations

Part L of the Building Regulations is concerned with the conservation of fuel and power. Thermally insulated buildings require less power to maintain thermal comfort levels. There are a number of ways in which the insulation of the building fabric can meet the required standards. In the *elemental method*, the maximum value is stipulated for the *U*-value for each of the various elements of the building. Table 3.3 lists the standard *U*-values for domestic buildings.

Table 3.3 Standard *U*-values for dwellings (based on the government's Standard Assessment Procedure energy ratings of over 60*)

Element	*U*-value (W/m² K)
Roofs	0.25
Exposed walls	0.45
Exposed floors and ground floors	0.45
Semi-exposed walls and floors	0.6
Windows, doors and rooflights	3.3

*The Building Regulations should be consulted for further details.

Example

A certain external wall consists of the following components: external brickwork, 50 mm cavity and internal lightweight blockwork. Resistances (in m² K/W) are as follows:

$R_{brick} = 0.12$
$R_{block} = 0.50$
$R_{cavity} = 0.18$
$R_{si} = 0.123$
$R_{so} = 0.055$

Calculate the *U*-value and comment on the answer obtained.

Answer

First, calculate the total resistance:

$$R_{total} = 0.12 + 0.50 + 0.18 + 0.123 + 0.055 = 0.978 \, m^2 \, K/W$$

therefore,

$$U = \frac{1}{R_{total}} = \frac{1}{0.978} = 1.02 \, W/m^2 \, K$$

This is much greater than that permitted by the Building Regulations for new constructions (see Table 3.3).

Self-assessment task 3.4

Calculate the *U*-value for the cavity wall in the previous example, assuming that the cavity is completely filled with foamed polyurethane (thermal conductivity = 0.024 W/m K). Comment on this value. (*N.B.* All data must be recorded using the appropriate units.)

So far, power losses through the fabric of the building have been considered. The power requirements for **ventilation** are now discussed.

Ventilation power losses

Fresh, clean air consists of a mixture of gases of the following composition: nitrogen (78%), oxygen (21%), inert gases including mainly argon and neon (1%), and carbon dioxide (0.03%). Small amounts of water vapour are also present. Breathing, cooking and smoking are a few examples where the composition of the air becomes affected. Fresh air intake into the internal environment is vital to remove smells, excess carbon dioxide and so on.

Ventilation means bringing in fresh air from outside to replace the stale/moist air from within the internal environment. Ventilation should not be confused with draughts. Ventilation is a *controlled* intake of air; it can be varied as desired, for example, by opening and closing windows. Draughts are *unwanted* and occur because a building is not adequately sealed. Draughts are a nuisance and necessitate having to provide extra heat.

When the outside temperature is below inside temperature, the air needed for ventilation is usually heated. The air leaving the building is warm. (The process which carries away the heat is **convection**.) This means that heat is lost. The rate of loss for ventilation can be calculated using the following formula:

$$P = \frac{N c_v V (T_i - T_o)}{3600}$$

This is a long, but easy to use formula provided the meaning of all the terms are understood:

P = power loss resulting from ventilation (W)
N = the number of air changes per hour (/h)
c_v = the heat capacity of the air per unit volume (J/m^3 °C)
V = volume of the room (m^3)
T_i = internal air temperature (°C)
T_o = external air temperature (°C)

Note that N is the number of air changes *per hour*. This is not an SI unit. This is the reason why the formula for the power loss includes the figure of 3600. This converts the 'per hour' to 'per second'. The quantity c_v is a constant and has the value $c_v = 1300$ J/m^3 °C. This means that 1300 J is required to heat every cubic metre of air to raise the temperature by 1 °C. (There is no need to remember this figure as it is always provided when required.)

For maintaining reasonable levels of comfort, one air change per hour is recommended for most internal environments such as domestic living rooms and offices. For comfort, air speeds should be neither too high nor too low. Less than 0.01 m/s leads to stagnant conditions. More than about 0.2 m/s causes draught effects unless the internal temperature is raised suitably.

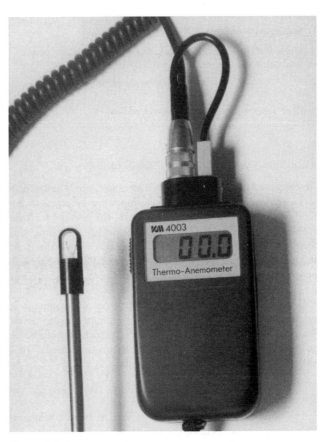

Figure 3.6 An anemometer

Air speeds can be measured using an anemometer. Figure 3.6 shows an anemometer suitable for use in buildings. The sensor, seen on the left, is a heated wire. The faster the air flows, the cooler the temperature becomes. The instrument therefore gives readings by correlating the temperature with the air speed.

Example

Calculate the ventilation power loss given that a room measuring 10 m × 6 m × 3 m requires a ventilation rate of 1 air change per hour. Assume that the internal environment needs to be maintained at 25 °C while the external air temperature is −5 °C. (In what type of establishment might this room be situated?)

Answer

First, the volume of the room needs to be calculated:

$$V = 10 \times 6 \times 3 = 180 \, \text{m}^3$$

Now summarise all the known quantities:

N = 1/h
c_v = 1300 J/m^3 °C
V = 180 m^3
T_i = 25 °C
T_o = −5 °C

Substitute all figures into the formula for ventilation loss:

$P = N c_v V (T_i - T_o) \div 3600$
$\quad = 1 \times 1300 \times 180 \times (25 - (-5)) \div 3600$
$\quad = 1300 \times 180 \times 30 \div 3600 = 1950 \, \text{W} = 1.95 \, \text{kW}$

(This room is probably in a hospital or nursing home as the temperature required is quite high.)

LEEDS COLLEGE OF BUILDING
LIBRARY

Self-assessment task 3.5

Show that the formula for calculating the ventilation power loss can instead be written as:

$$P = 0.36NV(T_i - T_o)$$

(Hint: replace c_v with the value given earlier.)

Total energy loss and the cost of energy

As explained above, to maintain a constant temperature in a given environment, the total power loss must be equal to the total power gain. As we have seen above, the power loss from a building is due to heat losses both through the fabric and through ventilation requirements. Heat gains are usually from the heaters. (There can be significant heat gains from the sun, people at work, and many other sources, also. These are not further discussed here.)

If the total power loss from an internal environment is calculated, then the total energy can be found for any given length of time. Total energy is very important because it enables the cost of the energy used to be calculated. Total energy is given by the following formula:

total energy loss (J) = total power loss (W) × time (s)

The units have been written in brackets to avoid confusion. This formula arises because the unit W is equal to J/s:

$$J = \frac{J}{s} \times s$$

As can be seen, the seconds cancel out to leave joules on both sides.

Example

The average power losses from a small flat were as follows over a one-week period during winter:

fabric power loss = 2.4 kW
ventilation power loss = 0.6 kW

Calculate the total energy (in MJ) required to heat the flat for one day and one week.

Answer

Total power loss = 2.4 + 0.6 = 3.0 kW = 3000 W
Time = 1 day = 24 × 3600 = 86 400 s

Therefore:

Total energy loss = 3000 × 86 400 = 259 200 000 J ≈ 259 MJ

So, the total energy needed to heat the flat is about 259.2 million joules per day. In one week this is 259.2 × 7 = 1814.4 MJ.

At the present time one million joules of electrical energy (peak rate) costs around 2p for domestic consumers. The cost of one million joules of gas is currently about 0.5p.

To avoid dealing with very large numbers, the total energy consumed is calculated in units of **kilowatt hours** (kWh) by the people who supply us with energy. This is further discussed on page 137.

Example

To maintain a comfortable temperature and adequate ventilation during a one-week period in winter, an industrial workshop required the following average powers delivered:

fabric power loss = 18.4 kW
ventilation power loss = 5.6 kW

Calculate the total energy supplied (in MJ).

Answer

Total power supplied = 18.4 + 5.6 = 24 kW = 24 000 W
Total time = 1 week = 7 days = 7 × 24 hours = 168 hours
$\quad\quad$ = 168 × 60 × 60 seconds = 604 800 s

Therefore, total energy supplied is

$$24\,000 \times 604\,800 = 14\,515\,200\,000 \text{ J}$$

To obtain the answer in megajoules (i.e. millions of joules) we need to divide by 1 00 000. Therefore, the total energy is

$$14\,515\,200\,000 \div 1\,000\,000 = 14\,515.2 \text{ MJ}$$

As the numbers in this problem are very large, it is much neater to use index notation. Here is the solution using index notation:

Total power supplied = 18.4 + 5.6 = 24 kW = 2.4×10^4 W
Total time = 1 week = 7 days = 7 × 24 hours
$\quad\quad$ = 7 × 24 × 60 × 60 seconds = 6.048×10^5 s

Therefore, total energy supplied is

$$2.4 \times 10^4 \times 6.048 \times 10^5 = 1.452 \times 10^{10} \text{ J}$$

To obtain the answer in megajoules (i.e. millions of joules) we need to divide by 10^6. So the total energy is

$$1.452 \times 10^{10} \div 10^6 = 1.452 \times 10^4 \text{ MJ}$$

(to four significant figures)

Self-assessment task 3.6

For the last example above, calculate the energy supplied (in kWh) to the workshop in one week.
(Answer: 4032 kWh)

Relative humidity

Humidity refers to the moisture in the air. The moisture in the air is caused by the presence of water vapour. Water vapour is water in the form of a gas and it is invisible. Water may also be present in the air in the form of very tiny droplets. These droplets of water can form mist, fog, steam or clouds. In these cases, the moisture is visible and appears white or greyish.

Relative humidity is a convenient measure of the amount of water vapour in the air. In fact, relative humidity is a measure of the amount of moisture in the air *relative* to the maximum water vapour the air can support at that temperature. It is expressed as a percentage and defined as follows:

$$\text{relative humidity} = \frac{M_v}{M_{sv}} \times 100$$

where M_v = mass of water vapour per m^3 of air, and
$\quad\quad M_{sv}$ = mass of water vapour per m^3 of saturated air at the same temperature.

Saturated air is air which contains the maximum amount of water vapour possible at that temperature. The air in Turkish baths is saturated: as more water vapour is produced from the heated water, more of the vapour immediately condenses back into water and 'falls out' of the air. This makes the surfaces including the bathers feel very damp!

From the definition of relative humidity, the smallest relative humidity possible is 0% (air completely dry) and the greatest value is 100% (air saturated). At 20 °C, each kilogram of saturated air (relative humidity = 100%) holds about 15 grams of water.

For human comfort, the relative humidity must neither be too high nor too low. When the relative humidity is above about 70%, people tend to feel uncomfortable. 'Sticky' and 'muggy' are terms often used to describe high relative humidity at higher temperatures. High relative humidity at low temperatures makes people feel chilly.

When the relative humidity is below about 40%, the air becomes too dry for human comfort. Skin tends to dry out and people's throats become dry. Another problem with low humidity is that static electric charges can build up on surfaces. This is a common problem where carpets are made from synthetic materials such as nylon. Friction between the shoes and the carpet causes a person to become electrically charged in dry conditions. Subsequent contact with a metallic object such as railings in a shop, often causes very uncomfortable electric shocks.

Measuring relative humidity

Various types of instrument can be used to measure relative humidity. The whirling hygrometer is commonly used (Fig. 3.7) and consists of two mercury thermometers mounted in a frame, together with a handle for rotating the apparatus. As can be seen from Fig. 3.7, one thermometer has muslin material surrounding the bulb (producing a wet bulb) while the other thermometer remains dry (dry bulb). The material surrounding the wet bulb remains damp because one end of the muslin is inserted into a small water reservoir, seen on the left hand side of Fig. 3.7.

To measure the relative humidity the whirling hygrometer is held at arm's length and rotated at high speed. Following the whirling, both thermometer readings are immediately recorded. Note that the wet bulb temperature is always lower than the dry bulb temperature unless the air is saturated. This

is because evaporation causes cooling; the drier the air, the faster the evaporation and the lower the final temperature of the wet bulb becomes.

With the temperatures measured, a chart such as that shown in Fig. 3.8 can be used to work out the relative humidity. Such graphs are called **psychrometric** charts.

It is easiest to learn how to use the chart with an example. Let:

Wet bulb temperature = 14 °C
Dry bulb temperature = 21 °C

To work out the relative humidity using Fig. 3.8, go vertically upwards from the line labelled '21' on the dry bulb temperature axis. Go diagonally downwards from the line labelled '14' on the wet bulb temperature axis. The relative humidity is now read using the curved lines at the point where the two straight lines cut each other. In this case, the relative humidity is 45%.

Self-assessment task 3.7

1. A student used a whirling hygrometer in a sauna. After whirling the instrument, she recorded the following temperatures:

   Wet bulb temperature = 25 °C
   Dry bulb temperature = 25 °C

   What is the relative humidity? Are you surprised?

2. Find the relative humidity given the following information:

   Wet bulb temperature = 18 °C
   Dry bulb temperature = 22 °C

Specific heat capacity

The author recently visited a newly built energy efficient home. Figure 3.9 shows part of what he observed under the floorboards, many bottles filled with water. In fact, the house contains 1600 bottles, each one with 5 litres of water. This means there is 8000 kg or 8 tonnes of water in the voids of this house! (The reader should verify that this mass is correct. The density of water is 1000 kg/m^3 and 1 litre of water has a mass of 1 kilogram.) What is the purpose of this water? This question will be answered at the end of this section.

To raise the temperature of a substance, energy in the form of heat must be provided. The heat (energy) necessary to raise the temperature of a material is known as the **heat capacity** (or thermal capacity). This quantity is measured in J/°C. The heat capacity of a small room is much smaller than that of a large hall. This means that far more heat is required to raise the temperature of a large hall by 1 °C compared with the room. The higher the thermal capacity, the 'harder' it is to heat up a material.

The **specific heat capacity** is the heat necessary to increase the temperature of 1 kg of material by 1 °C. Various values of specific heat capacity are given in Table 3.4. As can be seen, 376 J is required to heat 1 kg of copper in order to increase its temperature by 1 °C. On the other hand, 1 kg of polyethylene needs about six times as much heat as copper to raise the temperature by 1 °C.

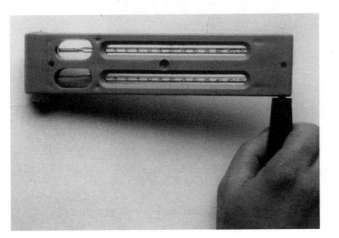

Figure 3.7 Whirling hygrometer

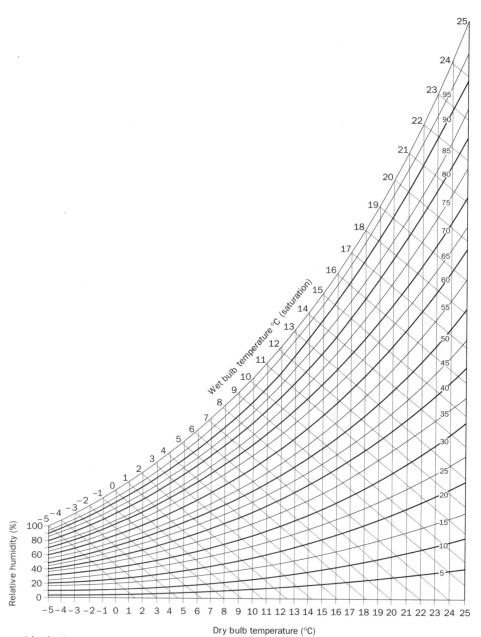

Figure 3.8 Psychrometric chart

Figure 3.9 Bottles of water used to store heat

Table *3.4* Specific heat capacity for a range of materials

Material	Specific heat capacity (J/kg °C)
Granite	330
Copper	376
Mild steel	502
Glass	830
Concrete	880–1040
Aluminium	920
PVC	1040
Polystyrene	1250
Standard hardboard	1250
Insulating fibreboard	1400
Perspex	1460
Timber	1500
Polyethylene	2300
Water	4187

It is important not to forget that specific heat capacity is defined *per unit mass*. Suppose it is required to find the best type of brick to use in electric storage heaters. Here, 'best' means the one which absorbs the greatest amount of heat. This depends on the total mass of material which can be packed into the heater and also the specific heat capacity. The best material, then, has the highest value of (density × specific heat capacity). In terms of units we are looking for the highest value of (kg/m^3 × J/kg °C) = J/m^3 °C. In other words, we need to maximise the heat which can be absorbed per cubic metre per °C.

Back to the question asked above, what is the purpose of the large amounts of water in Fig. 3.9? The house is partly heated by solar gain, where infra-red radiation from the sun is captured through large south-facing windows. The scientist who designed the house wanted to store as much of this 'free' heat as possible, which could then be recovered when no solar heating is available. Table 3.4 shows that the water has a very high specific heat capacity. The water is able to store about 4000 J of heat per kg for every °C rise in temperature. Eight tonnes of water stores around 8000 × 4000 = 32 MJ for an increase in temperature of just 1 °C. This is equivalent to the heat produced by a 1 kW heater in about nine hours. As the temperature of the house starts to fall the water gradually releases the heat. The water, then, forms a cheap effective store for the heat.

In summary, materials with higher specific heat capacity require more thermal energy to heat them up. However, upon cooling the temperature falls more slowly and more heat is released.

Self-assessment task 3.8

A large open plan office is to have various shoulder height partitions installed to improve privacy. As extra heating will not be provided it is intended to use materials which minimise the increase in the time needed to heat the office at the beginning of each working week. List the factors which ought to be considered.

Sound

Sound is produced and carried by vibrations of particles. Sound in air is transmitted by oscillations of the air molecules. As the molecules sway backwards and forwards, the air pressure continuously increases and decreases. Energy is passed from one molecule to the next by collisions. The speed at which sound travels through the air is around 330 m/s.

When the sound energy reaches the ear, the energy of the vibrating particles makes the ear drum vibrate. This results in the sensation which the brain interprets as sound. The sensitivity of the ear depends on the number of vibrations per second or the **frequency** of the sound. Frequency is measured in hertz (Hz). So, 1 Hz is 1 vibration per second. Young people can hear sounds between about 20 Hz (very low pitch) and about 20 000 Hz (very high pitch). Older people have hearing over a smaller range of frequencies.

The sensitivity of the ear varies with frequency. For example, sounds with the same energy appear to be louder at 1000 Hz compared to 60 Hz.

Sound is one of the most important methods of communication. Unfortunately, undesirable sounds, or **noise**, can also be a nuisance. Worse still, noise is a well-known health hazard.

We need to understand how sound is measured so that noise levels can be measured and assessed.

Speed of sound

The speed of sound can be calculated using the following formula:

$$\text{speed} = \text{frequency} \times \text{wavelength}$$

The wavelength is the distance between one pressure maximum (compression) and the next compression produced, as the sound travels through the material. Wavelength is measured in metres. With the frequency measured in hertz (Hz), the speed is calculated in metres per second or m/s. As already stated, the speed of sound in air is around 330 m/s; this is about 1 km every 3 s. Sound travels much faster in building materials than in air. (The reader should try to think why this is the case. Hint: sound energy is transmitted by vibrating molecules.)

Self-assessment task 3.9

Given that the speed of sound in air is 330 m/s, which one of the following is correct?

A If the frequency = 330 Hz, then the wavelength = 1 cm
B If the frequency = 33 Hz, then the wavelength = 10 mm
C If the frequency = 330 kHz, then the wavelength = 1 m
D If the frequency = 330 Hz, then the wavelength = 1 m

Sound intensity

As already mentioned, there is an energy flow as sound travels through the air. The sound intensity is defined as the sound power passing at right angles through 1 m^2 of surface. The unit is W/m^2. The quietest sound which can *just* be heard by a person is defined as 1×10^{-12} W/m^2 or 0.000 000 000 001 W/m^2. This intensity is known as the **threshold of hearing**. The human ear is an extremely sensitive (and delicate) instrument to be able to detect such a small intensity.

At the other end of the scale, the human ear is capable of detecting sounds which are extremely energetic, having intensities more than a million million times greater than the threshold value. Because the human ear has such a vast response range, the **sound intensity level** is defined for convenience as follows:

$$\text{sound intensity level} = 10 \times \log\left(\frac{I}{I_0}\right)$$

where I = intensity in W/m^2 and I_0 = threshold intensity = 1×10^{-12} W/m^2. The sound intensity level is measured in **decibel** or dB. To use this formula, a calculator is essential as the 'log' function must be used.

The sound level can alternatively be defined using sound pressure measurements. This is discussed next.

Sound pressure

As already mentioned, as sound travels, the air pressure increases and decreases. This change in sound pressure is often used to measure the level of the sound. Changes in air pressure (p) are measured in pascal (Pa or N/m^2). In terms of sound pressure, the threshold of hearing (p_0) is 2×10^{-5} Pa. The **sound pressure level** (in dB) is defined as

$$\text{sound pressure level} = 20 \times \log\left(\frac{p}{p_0}\right)$$

For any given sound, this formula gives the same value of decibels as the previous formula for sound intensity level.

The decibel scale is very convenient for measuring sound levels. On the decibel scale, 0 dB corresponds to the smallest sound which can just be detected by the ear; 140 dB is the **threshold of pain**. Most sounds lie between these two values. An increase of 10 dB roughly corresponds to a doubling of the loudness perceived. Thus, a noise at 90 dB sounds about twice as loud as a sound at 80 dB.

Figure 3.10 lists the range of the decibel scale, up to very loud sounds. Various examples are given. The values shown in Fig. 3.10 should be studied carefully and 'digested' so that the reader has a feel for the decibel scale.

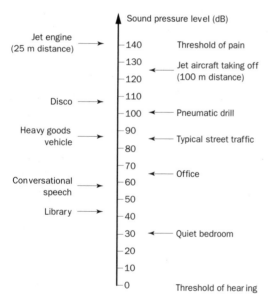

Figure 3.10 Sound pressure levels up to 140 dB

Example 1

Calculate the sound pressure level given that $p = 0.02$ Pa and $P_o = 2 \times 10^{-5}$ Pa = 0.00000 Pa.

Answer

Formula:

$$\text{sound pressure level} = 20 \times \log(p \div p_0)$$

Substitute values:

$$\text{sound pressure level} = 20 \times \log(0.02 \div 0.00002)$$
$$= 20 \times \log 1000 = 20 \times 3 = 60\,\text{dB}$$

Example 2

The mean sound pressure at a certain student disco was measured to be 7.8 Pa. Calculate the sound pressure levels in decibels. Comment on this value.

Answer

The formula required is:

$$\text{sound pressure level} = 20 \times \log(p \div p_0)$$

Substitute the given values:

$$\text{sound pressure level} = 20 \times \log(7.8 \div 0.00002)$$
$$= 20 \times \log 390\,000$$
$$= 20 \times 5.59 = 111.8\,\text{dB} \approx 112\,\text{dB}$$

Comment: this is very loud and continuous exposure can cause damage to hearing. As this is an average value it is likely that some of the sound is actually causing pain (remember that 140 dB is the threshold of pain).

Self-assessment task 3.10

The average sound pressure in a certain library was 0.06 Pa. Calculate the sound level in dB. State whether you think this is acceptable for a library.

Damage to hearing

People can become annoyed and irritated by very low levels of sound (e.g. even the ticking of a clock annoys some people when they are trying to sleep). However, actual damage to our ears occurs when the sound level is too high. For this reason, noise can be a health hazard. It is now known that possible damage to the ear depends not only on the level of the sound but on the duration also. Here are some facts:

- A single, short burst of sound above 140 dB can produce permanent damage to hearing.
- It is generally accepted that no harm occurs below 75 dB.
- Temporary loss of hearing can result from short exposures to high noise levels.
- Between 75 and 140 dB, permanent damage is possible, depending on the length of the exposure. (This also depends on the individual.)

Table 3.5 shows various levels of noise and maximum times of exposure above which ear protection should be used.

Table 3.5 Maximum exposure for various levels of sound

Continuous sound level (dB(A))*	Maximum exposure time per day (hours)
90	8
93	4
96	2
99	1
102	0.5
105	0.25

(Adapted from Smith, Phillips and Sweeney 1982 *Environmental Science* Longman)
*The meaning of dB(A) is explained on page 108.

The subject of noise is also described in Unit 1 (Section 1.3). You may wish to go back and read that section again.

Noise criteria

It is well known that, in addition to the irritation, background noise can cause difficulties in communication. Have you ever tried having a conversation with someone at a disco or at a noisy party? Background noise can be produced by many types of sources including fans, heaters, refrigeration equipment, etc.

To be acceptable, how low must the level of background noise be? This is a difficult question to answer. Various methods have been developed to assess the level of noise to decide whether it is low enough. One method is by use of **noise criteria** (NC) curves. Such a set of curves is shown in Fig. 3.11. The reason why the NC curves shown in the figure vary with frequency is because the sensitivity of the human ear depends on frequency, as explained previously.

To understand the NC curves in Fig. 3.11, the line labelled NC50 will be used as an example. At a frequency of 2000 Hz, this curve corresponds to a sound power level of 50 dB. At 250 Hz, the corresponding value is 60 dB, and so on. (The reader should check these values.) Now, suppose that NC50 is stipulated for a certain environment. This means background noise level should not go above this line at *any* frequency. In this example, it would not be acceptable to install (say) a ventilation system producing a noise level of 65 dB at 250 Hz (even if the noise level was below the NC50 line at other frequencies). To conform to any given NC criterion, then, the noise level must not exceed the corresponding sound pressure levels at any frequency.

Some suggested noise criteria are given in Table 3.6. Note that higher values are suggested for noisier environments. Why?

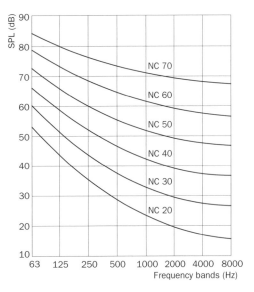

Figure 3.11 Noise criteria curves. (*after* Smith *et al.* 1982 *Environmental Science* Addison Wesley Longman)

Measuring sound levels

A sound level meter can be conveniently used to measure sound levels. Figure 3.12 shows one of these instruments being used to assess the noise level in a house. Note that because of the enormous range of hearing of the ear, this instrument has three ranges: for low, medium and high intensity sounds.

Table 3.6 Noise criteria for various examples

Location	NC (dB)
Concert halls	< 20
Meetings rooms	20–25
Classrooms	25
Private offices	25–40
Restaurants	35–45
Hospital kitchens	40
Workshops	55–75

(Adapted from Smith, Phillips and Sweeney 1982 *Environmental Science* Longman)

Self-assessment task 3.11

The measured background sound pressure levels (SPL) were measured in a hospital kitchen at various frequencies. The findings were as follows:

Frequency (Hz)	63	125	250	500	1000	2000	4000	8000
SPL (dB)	44	41	40	38	36	32	31	30

1. Plot a graph of SPL against frequency. Ensure that the *x*-axis is on a logarithmic scale (as in Fig. 3.11).
2. Compare the results with the appropriate value in Table 3.6 and the required curve in Fig. 3.11.

Figure 3.12 A sound level meter being used to assess the noise level in a room

It was explained earlier that sounds are produced over a very wide range of frequencies. The sensitivity of the ear is also dependent on frequency. For this reason, sound level meters usually employ the so-called 'A' frequency weighting. When a sound level meter is used in the 'A' mode, its frequency response is similar to that of the ear. Measurements carried out on this setting are usually referred to as dB(A) or just dBA. For example, a pneumatic drill at a distance of 5 m produces noise at a level of around 100 dB(A). This explains the unit used in Table 3.5.

Lighting

There are three quantities used to measure light:

- **Luminous intensity** – This is a measure of the 'concentration' of light in a cone radiating from the source. A laser beam is concentrated into a very narrow cone. Consequently, the intensity is extremely high. Luminous intensity is measured in **candela** (cd) which is one of the most important units in physics (see Table 3.1).
- **Luminous flux** – Flux measures the rate at which light falls onto a given surface. It is measured in **lumen** (lm).
- **Illuminance** – The illuminance is the amount of luminous flux which falls on 1 m^2 of surface. It is measured in **lux** (lx).

Illuminance is the most important measurement when designing lighting for buildings. The outdoor illuminance on a sunny day can be as high as 100 000 lux. Typically, a bedroom may be illuminated to 100 lux. The sensitivity of the human eye is variable, so it can adjust to very high and very low levels of light. The human eye is able to 'see' light levels much less than 1 lx. Nevertheless, there are recommended levels of lighting for internal situations. These are defined under the heading 'Artificial lighting', below.

Lighting in the indoor environment

Light within buildings can be either **natural** or **artificial** or a combination of both.

Natural lighting

All natural light on Earth comes from the Sun. Even moonlight is actually sunlight which is reflected from the Moon. (Starlight is too faint to provide any significant illumination.) Daylight reaches us either directly from the Sun, or from the sky. The Earth's atmosphere and the clouds scatter light from the Sun, so that daylight can reach us from all parts of the sky.

Buildings should be designed to utilise as much daylight as possible. Daylight enters a building mainly through the windows. Sometimes, 'optical pipes', which are really just thick optical fibres, are used to carry natural light into buildings. These can be very useful where windows are not possible. Figure 3.13 shows how daylight can reach a given point in a room through a window. As can be seen from this figure, the light is usually a combination of the following components:

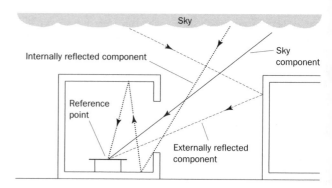

Figure 3.13 Daylight can reach a given point in a room either direct from the sky or by reflection

- direct sky
- externally reflected
- internally reflected

The **daylight factor** measures the extent of daylight at a given position within a room. It is defined as follows:

$$\text{daylight factor} = 100 \times \frac{E_i}{E_o}$$

where E_i is the illuminance provided from daylight and E_o is the outdoor illuminance. More precisely, E_o is the illuminance at the same point if the sky is unobstructed by the fabric of the building. Note that daylight factor has no unit: it is just a percentage. The average daylight factor for many interior environments, such as classrooms and libraries, is recommended to be 5%. Obviously, greenhouses require much greater daylight factors, while photographic darkrooms should have a daylight factor of zero!

Example 1

Calculate the daylight factor if the internal illuminance at the point of measurement is 200 lx and the unobstructed sky illuminance is 10 000 lx.

Answer

$$\text{daylight factor} = 100 \times \frac{E_i}{E_o} = 100 \times \frac{200}{10\,000} = 2\%$$

Example 2

The daylight factor on a table in a room was measured to be 4%. Calculate the (natural) illuminance at that point if the external illuminance is 15 000 lx.

Answer

First, rearrange the formula for daylight factor, so that E_i is the subject:

$$E_i = \frac{\text{daylight factor} \times E_o}{100}$$

Now, substitute the values into the formula and do the calculations:

$$E_i = \frac{\text{daylight factor} \times E_o}{100} = \frac{4 \times 15\,000}{100} = 600 \text{ lx}$$

There are recommended values of daylight factors for all internal environments. For example, for domestic situations, the recommendations are 2%, 1% and 0.5% for the kitchen, living room and bedroom respectively. Other recommendations are provided in Table 3.7.

Table 3.7 Various recommendations of daylight factors (%)

Environment	Average d.f.	Minimum d.f.	Position
General offices	5	2	Desks
Bank-counters	5	2	Desks
Library, reading rooms	5	1.5	Tables
College classrooms	5	2	Desks

Artificial lighting

Artificial lighting is required in all buildings because daylight may be insufficient and in any case occurs for only part of the day. Various types of electric lamp are used for illumination when there is insufficient or zero daylight. Common types include:

- **Tungsten filament lamps** – These are low-cost lamps and produce very good quality light. Unfortunately, the lifetimes of these lamps are relatively short and they are very inefficient, producing large amounts of heat as well as light.
- **Fluorescent lamps** – These produce a reasonable quality light and are suitable for kitchens, offices, workshops, etc. They are more expensive than tungsten lamps. However, they are much more efficient than tungsten lamps. Compact fluorescent lamps are becoming very popular because they fit directly into ordinary bayonet lamp fittings.
- **Sodium lamps** – These produce a yellow-orange light and are extremely efficient. They are rarely used indoors because of the unacceptable colour appearance. Most street lighting consists of sodium lamps.

Spectra

The range of colours produced by a source of light is called a **spectrum**. The Sun's spectrum includes the colours spanning *all* shades of red, orange, yellow, green, blue and violet. As there are no missing colours, this is said to be a **continuous** spectrum and the combination gives us the sensation of daylight. The rainbow is a natural (and beautiful) display of the Sun's spectrum.

The quality of the light produced from an artificial source of light depends on how well the spectrum compares to that of the Sun.

Like the Sun, tungsten lamps have a continuous spectrum. Their spectrum is very similar to daylight but with less shades at the violet end of the spectrum. Tungsten filament lamps are said to have excellent colour rendering ability.

Fluorescent lamps produce **band** spectra. These lamps give bands of colours but with noticeable gaps, with various missing shades of colour. The quality of the light, or colour rendering, in this case is reasonable.

Sodium lamps produce a **line** spectrum, with just a few lines or colours. It should come as no surprise that the main colour output is yellow-orange (just look at a street lamp at night!). The colour rendering is poor.

Table 3.8 lists the recommended illuminances for a range of internal environments. It is important that these values are used when designing lighting for internal conditions. The reader should browse through the list. Generally, the higher the illuminance, the clearer the detail becomes. For this reason, it should be clear why certain light levels in Table 3.8 are much greater than others. For example, the illuminance on the table in an operating theatre should be at least 10 000 lux. This is many times brighter than the lighting needed for most other situations. The high illuminance ensures that the fine details are visible and helps surgeons to do a good job!

Table 3.8 Examples of standard service illuminance

	Standard service illuminance (lux)
Offices	
General offices	500
Deep-plan general offices	750
Drawing offices	750 (on boards)
Shops	
Conventional shops	500
Supermarkets	500
Industrial	
Assembly shops	
casual work	200
rough work	300
medium work	500
fine work	1000
very fine work	1500
Structural steel fabrication plants	
general	300
marking off	500
Woodwork shops	
rough sawing	300
fine bench work	750
Warehouse	
racks	200
Hospitals	
Wards	100 (floor)
	30–50 (bedhead)
	150 (reading)
Operating theatres	400–500 (general)
	10 000–50 000 (on table)
Further education establishments	
Teaching spaces	500
Laboratories	500
Homes	
Kitchen	300
Reading areas	300

(*Source:* Smith, Phillips and Sweeney 1982 *Environmental Science* Addison Wesley Longman)

Calculating illuminance

Many factors affect the illuminance in the indoor environment. These include:

- the colour of the surfaces and their ability to reflect
- the number, the type and the position of lamps used
- the type of lamp fitting used (luminaire)

Where there is natural lighting, the sizes and positions of the windows also strongly affect the illuminance.

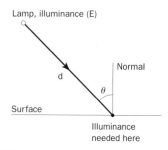

Figure 3.14 Definition of terms used to calculate the illuminance

There are various formulae for calculating the illuminance provided in internal conditions. The simplest, but most important, formula is the cosine law of illuminance. This formula applies for a single, small source of light. The cosine law of illuminance enables the illuminance (E) to be calculated at any given distance (d) from a light source having intensity I:

$$E = \frac{I \cos \theta}{d^2}$$

The angle θ and the other terms used are defined in Fig. 3.14.

Example

A small lamp having luminous intensity 50 cd is fitted at ceiling level and is used to illuminate a photographic darkroom.

(i) Calculate the illuminance at point X on a work surface 2 m directly below the lamp.
(ii) Determine the illuminance on the work surface at point Y, where Y is a horizontal distance of 1.5 m from point Y.
(iii) What assumptions have been made in carrying out the calculations above?

Answers

(i) Write down all known information:
$I = 50$ cd; $d = 2$ m; $\theta = 0°$ (as there is no angle between the light and the normal to the surface)
Now write the formula and substitute the values from above:

$$E = I \cos \theta / d^2$$
$$= 50 \times \cos 0° / 2^2 = 50 \times 1/4 = 12.5 \, \text{lx}$$

(ii) It is best to draw a diagram for this part, see Fig. 3.15.

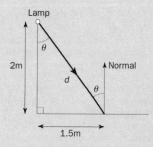

Figure 3.15 Diagram for part (ii) of example

The required distance d can be calculated using Pythagoras' theorem:

$$d^2 = 2^2 + 1.5^2 = 6.25, \text{ so}$$
$$d = \sqrt{6.25} = 2.5 \, \text{m}$$

In this example, there is no need to calculate θ as we can easily calculate $\cos \theta$, which is what is needed in the formula.

$$\cos \theta = \text{adjacent/hypotenuse} = 2/2.5 = 0.8$$

Substitution of these values into the formula gives:

$$E = I \cos \theta / d^2 = (50 \times 0.8)/2.5^2 = 6.4 \, \text{lx}$$

(iii) Assumptions: (a) no other sources of light; (b) any reflected light has been ignored.

Self-assessment task 3.12

Predict the direct illuminance on the floor 2 m directly below a single 100 cd tungsten lamp.

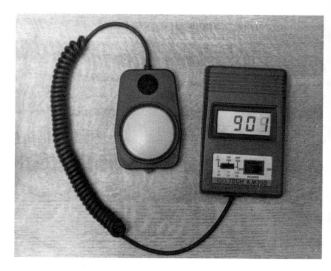

Figure 3.16 A lux meter is used to measure the light level in lux

Measuring illuminance

A lux meter can be used to measure the level of light in a given environment, see Fig. 3.16. Measurements are normally made at the **working plane**. This is the normal height at which work is carried out in a given environment (e.g. desk height).

An interesting exercise is to measure the illuminance (provided by artificial lighting) in various locations and then compare the measurements with the recommended levels given in Table 3.8.

Self-assessment tasks 3.13

Figure 3.17 shows how the lighting, sound level and temperature varied at a certain point in a college laboratory over a period of 24 hours. No artificial lighting, nor any heaters were used in the room over this period.

The following questions should be answered, making sensible assumptions where necessary:

1. Identify and explain the main features of each set of data presented in Fig. 3.17.
2. At what time of the year were these measurements taken?
3. Was the level of light adequate for working in between 16 and 24 hours? Why?
4. What was the *background* sound level (in dB) in the laboratory?

5. What is the probable cause of the relatively high sound level between about $t = 19$ hours and 21 hours?
6. Was the noise level unacceptably high at any time?
7. Write down values for the maximum and minimum temperatures over this period of time.

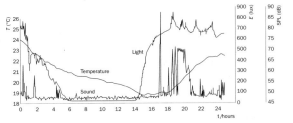

Figure 3.17 The graphs show the variations in the lighting level, sound level and the temperature of a college classroom over a period of 24 hours. A three-channel datalogger was used for the data collection. Note that the times shown on the *x*-axis are not the times of the day. This is the time in hours after the start of the experiment

3.3 Materials

Following brief notes on durability, the properties and performance of materials used in buildings are then investigated in this section. Also included in this section are the outline procedures for several relevant experiments.

Durability and resistance to degradation

After completion, a building is expected to remain in good condition for many years, with the minimum of maintenance. The correct choice of materials for the intended usage is the most important factor to minimise defects and failures.

Durability is a general term describing the resistance of a material against

- decay
- wear
- the action of the atmosphere

The slower the deterioration process, the greater is the durability. The durability, then, depends on factors such as exposure to the weather, especially the rain, frost and the Sun's radiation. Chemicals in the air and soil can also strongly affect the durability of materials. The degradation process in building materials can also be caused biologically. These physical, chemical or biological processes which degrade materials are called **degradation mechanisms**.

Water often has an important part to play in the failure of building materials. In fact, problems associated with water include:

- corrosion of metals
- decay of organic materials
- reduction of strength

Moisture in materials is further discussed later in this section.

A material which may be durable under certain conditions may become perishable in different usage. Ordinary chipboard flooring will last for many years in the interior of a building but will deteriorate rapidly (by the action of moisture) if used in the external environment. The conditions of use clearly affect the durability of materials. In order to minimise maintenance costs, the materials used should have durability consistent with the expected lifetime of a building.

The choice of materials for use depends on other factors as well as the durability and the resistance to degradation. These include:

Properties

As already explained, certain properties of materials affect the resistance to degradation. Other properties also decide whether the material is suitable for the intended use. The important properties for materials in construction are discussed in the sections which follow. Clearly, a good knowledge of the properties is important in deciding the fitness for purpose. Other essential considerations are described below.

Cost

The cost is always of primary consideration. Not only must the chosen materials have the required properties, they must be affordable. (Refer to Unit 1, Section 1.2, for economic considerations.)

Availability

This is a major consideration when choosing materials for construction. Availability can be a problem when there is a local, national or worldwide shortage. When the shortage is local, goods can be transported by various means to almost any destination. However, the increase in cost usually does not justify using materials in short supply.

Environmental considerations

There is much evidence suggesting that we have been damaging the atmosphere of our 'fragile' planet. Huge increases in the burning of fossil fuels continue to increase the carbon dioxide level in the atmosphere. This is enhancing the greenhouse effect. For this reason, it is clearly better to use materials which require less energy to produce. Another problem is the use of certain gases to manufacture various materials. This has resulted in damage to the ozone layer in the upper atmosphere. This means that more ultra-violet radiation reaches ground level. There is now a widespread ban on such gases.

Ease of working

Ease of working is another consideration when selecting materials. Some materials are easy to prepare on site (e.g. cutting and shaping of timber for joinery). Others have to be prepared just before using (e.g. concrete for foundations). Yet other materials are prepared at the factory (prefabricated) and delivered after manufacture (e.g. aluminium window frames). While preparation on site has obvious advantages, the attraction of prefabricated materials is that the quality and uniformity are much easier to control.

Appearance

Aesthetics is subjective. This means that not every person will agree that a given building is attractive. Nevertheless, the external materials should be chosen with care so that the finished product appears pleasing and looks good in its surroundings.

Thermal insulation

Thermal conductivity was also discussed previously on page 98. Values of thermal conductivity for common building materials are tabulated in Table 3.9.

The smaller the thermal conductivity, the better is the thermal insulation. Table 3.9 shows that expanded polystyrene and foamed polyurethane are good materials for thermal insulation. Indeed, these two materials are widely

Table 3.9 Thermal conductivity of various materials. Density is also given for comparison purposes

Material	Bulk density (kg/m^3)	Thermal conductivity k (W/m °C)
Expanded ebonite	64	0.029
Expanded polystyrene	16; 24	0.035; 0.033
Foamed polyurethane	24; 40	0.024; 0.039
Glass fibre quilt	16–48	0.032–0.04
Mineral and slag wools	48	0.03–0.04
Wool, hair and jute fibre felts	120	0.036
Corkboard (baked)	128	0.040
Balsa	160	0.045
Sprayed insulating coatings	80–240	0.043–0.058
Insulating fibre building boards	240–350	0.053–0.058
Exfoliated vermiculite (loose)	80–144	0.047–0.058
Rigid foamed glass slabs	128–136	0.050–0.052
Medium fibre building boards	350–800	0.072–0.101
Aerated concrete (low density)	320–700	0.084–0.18
Compressed straw slabs	365	0.101
Wood–wool slabs	450	0.093
Exfoliated vermiculite concrete	400–800	0.094–0.260
Expanded clay – loose	320–1040	0.12
Standard and tempered hardboards	800 and 961 (min)	0.125 and 0.180
Softwoods and plywoods	513	0.124
Diatomaceous earth brick	721	0.141
Asbestos-silica-lime insulating board (BS 3536)	881 (max)	0.144 (max)
Particle boards	449–800	0.101–0.158
Plasterboard	961	0.16
Hardwoods	769	0.16
Exfoliated vermiculite plaster	641	0.19
Perspex	1190	0.21
Foamed blastfurnace slag concrete	960–2000	0.24–0.93
Expanded clay and sintered PFA concretes	720–1760	0.24–0.91
Polyester glass fibre laminate (GRP)	1620	0.35
Asbestos cement (semi-compressed) (BS 690))	1200	0.37
Clinker concrete	1041–1522	0.37–0.58
Plaster (dense)	1442	0.48
No-fines concrete	1142–1842	0.562–0.75
Asbestos cement (fully compressed) (BS 4036))	1600 (minimum)	0.65
Aerated concrete (high density)	1602	0.65
Brickwork	1700	1.45–0.73
Mastic asphalt	2100	0.60
Cement:sand	2306	0.53
Glass	2520	1.05
Rendering	1778	1.15–1.21
Sandstone	2500	1.29
Concrete 1 cement: 2 coarse aggregate: 4 sand	2260	1.44
Limestone	2310	1.53
Slate	2590	1.88
Granite	2662	2.93
Zinc	7140	117.64
Steel	7850	57
Aluminium and alloys	2700	214
Copper	9000	400
Lead	11340	35.71

(*Source*: Everett *Materials* Addison Wesley Longman)

used in building for thermal insulation purposes. Table 3.9 shows that, in comparison, glass is quite a poor thermal insulator. Even with double-glazed windows, the heat loss through glass (per square metre) is much greater than through most other components of buildings.

The reader is advised to spend some time studying Table 3.9 to get a 'feel' for thermal insulation. Remember, the smaller the value of k, the better the insulation.

Thermal movement

The thermal properties previously discussed were in connection with heat transfer and heat loss. **Thermal movement** is caused by the **expansion** or **contraction** of materials. Materials generally expand when heated and contract when cooled. The forces involved in expansion or contraction are extremely large.

Self-assessment task 3.14

You have been asked to select a particular type of cladding for a given building from a range of materials. What questions would you ask before making up your mind?

In buildings, thermal movement must be taken into account otherwise problems can arise: large walls and glass in windows may crack due to this process if they are restrained. Another example is roofing felt which expands and buckles irreversibly under the influence of heat. For this reason this material is usually covered with some sort of heat reflecting surface layer. This can be a layer of white coloured stones or a metallic (aluminium) reflecting surface.

Figure 3.18 shows a gap provided inside a large building to allow for expansion and contraction. By allowing free expansion/contraction the problems of damage caused by cracks developing and growing is avoided.

Long pipes carrying hot water or steam (for example, for the central heating in a hospital) expand and contract

Figure 3.18 Expansion gap in a large building (indoor shopping centre)

Figure 3.19 Pipe with expansion bend

substantially. Unless provision is made for the expansion and contraction the pipe would soon fracture because of the thermal movement. Figure 3.19 shows a way of overcoming the problem. Thermal movements resulting from heating and cooling are absorbed by slight movements in the region of the bend. This ensures that cracks or fractures do not occur.

The actual amount of thermal movement depends on the type of material used. In order to compare various materials the coefficient of linear (thermal) expansion needs first to be defined:

$$\frac{\text{coefficient of}}{\text{linear expansion}} = \frac{\text{change in length}}{\text{original length} \times \text{change in temperature}}$$

The **coefficient of linear expansion** is also known as the **linear expansivity** and is a measure of the thermal movement for a given change in temperature. The unit is per °C or per degree Celsius. This is easy to see from the formula above as the units of length cancel out when change in length and original length are both measured metres. As the *change* in length is usually small, sometimes this is measured in mm, while the original length is measured in m, the unit for the coefficient of linear expansion then becomes mm/m °C.

Table 3.10 lists the coefficient of thermal expansion for various materials used in building. These are classed low, medium and high, depending on the degree of movement. Take aluminium as an example. It is labelled 'medium' and has an expansion coefficient of 2.4×10^{-5}/°C. This means that a 1 m length of aluminium will expand by 2.4×10^{-5} m ($= 0.024$ mm) per °C rise in temperature. This may not seem very much but buildings are subject to large changes in temperature, especially on their external surfaces. Also, the lengths involved in buildings are frequently many metres or even hundreds of metres long. This makes thermal movement quite substantial.

Example

The total length of aluminium used for a gutter outside a building was 50 m. Estimate the maximum thermal movement of the gutter assuming no gaps were provided between the sections.

Answer

In England the winter temperature can easily drop to -10 °C. Let the maximum temperature be 30 °C (in fact, due to solar heating the temperature can go to much higher values). Now the formula for the coefficient of thermal expansion can easily be rearranged:

change in length = coefficient × initial length
   × change in temperature
   = $2.4 \times 10^{-5} \times 50 \times (30 - (-10))$
   = 0.048 m $= 48$ mm

This distance is quite substantial. If the material is not free to move it will become damaged by buckling as a result of thermal movement.

Table 3.10 Coefficients of thermal expansion for a range of building materials

	Material	Coefficient of thermal expansion ($\times 10^{-6}$/°C)
High 26–200×10^{-6}/°C	Polythene, HD/LD	144/198
	Acrylics	72–90
	PVC	70
	Timber: across fibres	30–70
	Phenolics	15.3–45
	Zinc	31
	Lead	29
Medium 15–25×10^{-6}/°C	Aluminium	24
	Polyesters	18–25
	Brass	18
	Copper	17.3
	Stainless steel	17.3
	Gypsum plaster	16.6
	GRC	13–20
Low 1–14×10^{-6}/°C	Sandstones	7–16
	Concretes: various aggregates	10–14
	Mild steel	11–13
	Glass	6–9
	Granite	8–10
	Slates	6–10
	Marbles	1.4–11
	Limestones	2.4–9
	Aerated concretes	8
	Plywood	4–16
	Fired clay bricks: length	4–8
	Fired clay bricks: width and height	8–12
	Mortars	11–13
	Asbestos-cement BS 690	12
	Asbestos-silica-lime insulating board	5
	Timber: longitudinal	3–6

(*Source*: Everett *Materials* Addison Wesley Longman)

Self-assessment tasks 3.15

1. A certain brick wall has length 100 m. By selecting the relevant information from Table 3.10, estimate the decrease in its length when the wall temperature falls from 25 °C to 0 °C. What measures should be taken during construction to avoid cracking?
   (After doing this problem the reader should find a large brick wall and observe the gaps provided at regular intervals for expansion.)
2. Referring to Table 3.10, which lists values of the coefficient of thermal expansion, should any precautions be taken when manufacturing windows with aluminium frames?

Measuring the coefficient of linear expansion

Warning: *In this experiment great care must be taken as the steam and very hot equipment can cause severe scalding and burns.*

Figure 3.20 shows one type of apparatus suitable for measuring the coefficient of linear expansion for a metal. The metal rod under test should first have its length (L) measured to the nearest mm with a ruler. The temperature of the rod should also be obtained.

To follow, the rod is placed into the apparatus, as shown in Fig. 3.20. The rod is pushed as far as possible to the left to

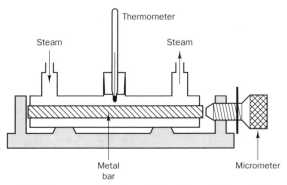

Figure 3.20 Apparatus for determining the coefficient of thermal expansion

ensure contact is made with the frame. The micrometer (which reads to an accuracy of 0.01 mm) is now read to obtain the initial position of the right-hand side of the rod (call this reading l_i). The initial temperature (T_i) is recorded using the thermometer. With the micrometer fully unscrewed to allow for free expansion, the rod is heated using steam from a steam generator.

After several minutes of heating the new micrometer reading is obtained. The micrometer should be unscrewed again in case expansion is not complete. Further readings should be taken regularly until no further changes are observed. The final micrometer reading, l_f, and the final temperature, T_f, are both recorded.

The coefficient of linear expansion can now be calculated using the data as follows:

$$\text{coefficient of linear expansion} = \frac{l_f - l_i}{L \times (T_f - T_i)}$$

Note that if the change in length and original length are both entered in metres and the change in temperature is in °C, then the unit for the coefficient of linear expansion is m/(m °C) = /°C. If the change in length is in mm with the other quantities unchanged, then the final unit becomes mm/m °C.

Values obtained from the experiment should be compared with those given in Table 3.10.

Self-assessment task 3.16

The student will have noticed from previous pages that experimental data is normally tabulated. This means that a clear table should be drawn with a number of headed columns, together with units, in order to record the results.

Produce a table to present the data effectively. Assume that there are five different metals to be tested.

Moisture content and water absorption

Many building materials contain water or moisture to a greater or lesser extent. The moisture may be the remainder after the material was prepared and used (e.g. plaster), or it can occur within the substance naturally (e.g. timber). In any case, it is important to know how to measure the moisture content in the materials used.

Inappropriate moisture content causes many problems. For example, if timber is put into an internal environment with an 'incorrect' moisture content, shrinkage and warping may

occur as the moisture levels change. It is not uncommon to see effects which arise from changes in the moisture content, for example, see Fig. 3.21. Further, untreated timber which has a high moisture content (usually on the exterior of a building) is prone to decay.

The moisture content of a sample of a material is usually defined as follows:

Figure 3.21 One type of problem associated with variations in the moisture content of timber: moisture movement

$$\text{moisture content} = \frac{\begin{array}{c}\text{mass of sample} \\ \text{with water}\end{array} - \begin{array}{c}\text{mass of sample} \\ \text{oven dried}\end{array}}{\text{mass of oven-dried sample}}$$

The moisture content can be written as a percentage by multiplying the right-hand side by 100.

Example

A small sample of wood was extracted from a timber beam in order to determine the moisture content by oven-drying. Using the results shown below, determine the moisture content of the material:

Original mass of specimen $= 21.5\,g$
Mass after oven-drying $= 17.8\,g$

Answer

Moisture content $= (M_{wet} - M_{dry})/M_{dry} = (21.5 - 17.8)/17.8$
$\qquad\qquad\quad = 3.7/17.8 \approx 21\%$

Note that, if plaster on a wall was at 5% moisture content it would be considered to be very wet. On the other hand, timber at 5% moisture content is very dry!

Some materials do not absorb or give out any moisture. Examples are bituminous materials, metals and most plastics. These materials are frequently used for water-proofing (e.g. mastic asphalt), as vapour barriers to stop the penetration of water vapour (e.g. aluminium foil) and for damp-proof courses (e.g. polyvinylchloride sheeting) respectively.

As already observed, substantial movement can occur when the moisture level changes in many materials. Table 3.11 shows the percentage movement caused by a dry material tending to moisture saturation. Note that in certain materials a portion of the movement is *irreversible*.

Water is absorbed by a vast range of materials which are **porous** and/or have voids. The physical process which allows this to happen is **capillary action**. The water molecules are attracted to the particles of the material and are 'sucked' into the gaps. This same process allows paint to be drawn into a brush or ink into blotting paper. Bricks, blocks and timber are examples of porous materials.

The actual level of moisture within a given material depends also on the temperature and relative humidity of the surrounding air. In damper environments moisture levels in materials are higher than in drier environments. Obviously a material will absorb more moisture if it is exposed to rain. The moisture content can also be greatly modified depending on what the material is in contact with. If a brick wall is constructed without a damp-proof course then moisture from the ground is absorbed by the brick by capillary action. Likewise, moisture can be absorbed by bricks if moist earth is in contact with the wall. Both these effects lead to rising damp. Note that as the moisture content of the bricks increases, the thermal resistance decreases and so the thermal insulating characteristics are reduced.

Another problem with high moisture levels in bricks is that if the temperature drops below the freezing point of water frost damage is likely to occur. Basically, as water freezes it expands (this is opposite to most materials). This expansion can force apart the material in the brick, which damages the brick and eventually causes it to crumble

Table 3.11 Percentage moisture movement which results from dry to saturated conditions

Material	Movement (%)	
	Irreversible	Reversible
Metal, glass	–	–
Limestone: Portland	–	0.01
Clay brick (typical good facing)	0.10–0.20 (expansion)	–
Calcium silicate bricks	0.001–0.05	0.001–0.05
Glass fibre polyester	–	0.02
Lightweight aggregate concretes	–	0.03–0.35
Dense concrete and mortars	0.02–0.08 drying (shrinkage)	0.01–0.06
Aerated concrete (autoclaved)	–	0.06–0.07
GRC	–	0.07
Timber: longitudinal	–	0.10
Hardboards	slight	0.11–0.32
Sandstoned Darley Dale	–	0.15
Perspex	–	0.35
Insulating fibreboard	–	0.20–0.37
Laminated plastics	0.10–0.50	–
Aerated concrete (air-cured)	–	0.17–0.22
Plywoods	–	0.15–0.30
Softwoods: radial	–	0.45–2.0
tangential	–	0.6–2.6
Hardwoods: radial	–	0.5–2.5
tangential	–	0.8–4.0
Chipboard	large	0.1–12.0

(*Source*: Everett *Materials* Addison Wesley Longman)

Figure 3.22 Frost damage in bricks

away. Figure 3.22 shows obvious frost damage to bricks in a wall.

For clay bricks there are three categories for frost resistance: frost resistant (class F), moderately frost resistant (class M) and not frost resistant (class O). Bricks in the latter category should not be used externally unless protected adequately from moisture in the external environment.

For the reasons already mentioned, it is important to measure the amount of water bricks can absorb. The **water absorption** is given as a percentage as follows:

$$\text{water absorption} = \frac{\text{mass of water absorbed}}{\text{mass of oven-dried brick}} \times 100$$

Porosity

As already explained, as the void content of a material increases so does the ability to absorb water by capillary action. The ability, however, to absorb moisture depends on the size of the voids and how accessible the voids are to the water at the surface. Timber, for example, has a large void content but surface water is absorbed quite slowly.

In general, there is no direct correlation between porosity and other properties such as durability. Nevertheless, it is a useful quantity to calculate. For a given material:

$$\text{porosity} = \frac{\text{volume of pores}}{\text{bulk volume}} \times 100$$

Alternatively, if the bulk density and solid density of the material are known:

$$\text{porosity} = \frac{\text{solid density} - \text{bulk density}}{\text{solid density}} \times 100$$

Example

Calculate the porosity of a lightweight concrete block given the following data:

bulk density $= 800\,\text{kg/m}^3$

solid density $= 2400\,\text{kg/m}^3$

Using the second formula from above:

$$\text{porosity} = \frac{2400 - 800}{2400} \times 100$$

$$= \frac{1600}{2400} = 66.7\% \approx 67\%$$

Self-assessment task 3.17

A standard brick has a volume $1.4 \times 10^{-3}\,\text{m}^3$. The volume of pores in the material is $5.6 \times 10^{-4}\,\text{m}^3$. Calculate the porosity of the brick.

Common bricks can absorb large amounts of water (they have water absorption up to around 20%) and many types are susceptible to frost damage. On the other hand, engineering bricks absorb only about 6% and are frost resistant. Although certain bricks are frost resistant even when they have high moisture levels it is best to try to keep bricks as dry as possible before, during and after construction of a building.

Experiment to find the water absorption of bricks

Warning:

- *Ensure all electrical apparatus has overload cutout facilities. Equipment must be plugged into a circuit with a residual current detector (RCD).*
- *Care should be taken to avoid burns when using the drying-oven.*
- *Appropriate handling aids should be used and care must be taken when immersing materials into the boiling water as severe scalding may otherwise result.*

The experiment should be carried out for a number of bricks of the same type. The average water absorption can then be calculated.

Bricks should first be oven-dried for 2 days at $100\,°\text{C}$. After cooling, they should then be weighed on an electronic balance. This gives the oven-dried mass of each brick.

The bricks are then placed in a tank of boiling water for 5 hours. After this process the bricks should be left in the tank to cool down for 16 to 19 hours.

To follow, excess moisture is removed from each brick after removal from the water tank. The mass of each one is then determined again. (Alternatively the brick can be immersed in cold water for 24 hours, but in this case the results usually give a lower water absorption value than the previous method.) The mass of the water absorbed is obtained by using:

$$\begin{array}{c}\text{mass of water}\\\text{absorbed}\end{array} = \begin{array}{c}\text{mass of brick}\\\text{with water}\end{array} - \begin{array}{c}\text{mass of oven-dried}\\\text{brick}\end{array}$$

The water absorption can now be calculated from:

$$\text{water absorption} = \frac{\text{mass of water absorbed}}{\text{mass of oven-dried brick}} \times 100$$

Moisture meters for general moisture measurements

Electronic instruments called moisture meters are often used by building surveyors and other building professionals to check for damp and to measure the moisture content of materials in buildings. Figure 3.23(a) shows a non-intrusive device placed against the plaster of a wall. Figure 3.23(b) clearly shows two electrodes inserted into a timber skirting board to measure the moisture content. This type of instrument measures the electrical resistance of the material. Basically, as the moisture content increases, the resistance decreases. As the resistance varies with the amount of moisture, the meter is calibrated in percentage moisture content. In this technique small marks are left on the timber after measurements have been made. Although these devices are extensively used, the accuracy is limited as there are many variables which can affect the readings.

Self-assessment task 3.18

(i) Explain in a few sentences the physical process which causes water to be absorbed into materials.
(ii) Make a list of problems that are associated with moisture in building materials.

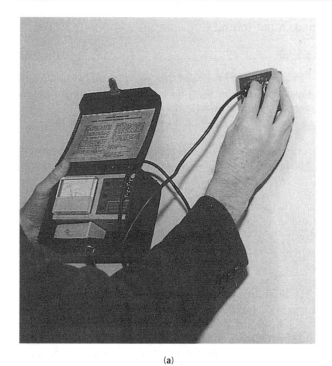

(a)

(b)

Figure 3.23 Use of electronic meters to measure the water content of materials: (a) non-intrusive device; (b) electrode insertion type

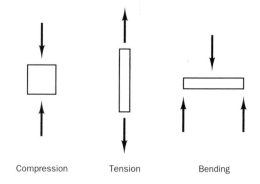

Figure 3.24 Various loading configurations

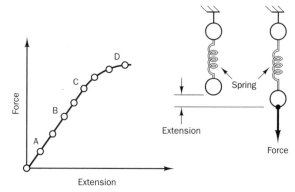

Figure 3.25 The behaviour of a spring when a force is applied

are partly in compression and partly in tension. It will be seen later that some materials behave well in tension while others perform better in compression.

We are mainly concerned with the **elastic** properties of materials. (Elastic properties are also described later, in Unit 4.) The word elastic is easy to understand using the example of a spring. Figure 3.25 shows how the extension varies with the force applied. If the force is removed at point A or B or C the spring goes back to its original size. This is said to be elastic behaviour. However, at point D, the spring has gone considerably beyond the **elastic limit**. In this region of the graph, if the force is removed the spring does not go back to its original size.

Most materials have elastic behaviour up to a certain level of applied force. Glass, steel, iron, timber are examples of materials which exhibit elastic behaviour to a greater or lesser extent. Fresh putty and frame sealants do not have any elastic properties. Elastic behaviour is important because it is predictable. This means we can accurately forecast how the material is going to behave. To do this some new quantities need to be defined.

Elasticity

Elastic properties

Forces cause the materials in a building to squash, stretch and bend. See Fig. 3.24. The forces are frequently (but not always) caused by gravity. Squashing forces are termed **compressive** and stretching forces are called **tensile**. The columns or walls or foundations holding a building up are in **compression** while the wires holding up a suspended walkway are in **tension**. Beams have bending forces acting on them and

Strain

The **strain** measures the change in length of a material compared with the original length. In other words, strain is a measure of the deformation of a material. It is calculated using:

$$\text{strain} = \frac{\text{change in length}}{\text{original length}}$$

As length is divided by length, strain has *no* unit. It should be ensured that the top and bottom of this formula are measured using the same unit of length. A material in tension has **tensile**

strain and in compression it has **compressive strain**. (Strain is also described in Unit 4.)

Large strains can easily be produced in some materials. For example, it is quite easy to stretch a rubber band to strain = 1. This means that the rubber band has been doubled in length. Other materials, say a piece of mild-steel wire, may fracture (break) at a very small strain, around 0.02 or 2%.

Force

The force applied is measured in newtons (N). A force can be applied in any direction. For example, by applying a horizontal force, a bulldozer can be used to push a pile of rubble.

Gravity causes vertical forces to act. The force of gravity acts on all objects. The size of the gravitational force can be calculated using

$$force = mass \times g$$

where g is called the acceleration of gravity. In Britain, $g = 9.8 \text{ m/s}^2$ is used, but its value varies slightly from place to place. For many calculations it is good enough to use $g = 10 \text{ m/s}^2$. So, the force of gravity acting on a 1 kg object is $1 \times 10 = 10 \text{ N}$. The force of gravity is often called **weight**. The term **load** is also used to mean the force applied. As an example, if a bucket of sand hanging from a rope has a mass of 30 kg, then its weight is 300 N. The force stretching the rope (or the *tension* in the rope) is also 300 N. Alternatively, the load on the rope is 300 N.

Stress

Stress is a measure of the force causing deformation. Alternatively, stress is the 'concentration' of the applied force. It can be tensile or compressive and is calculated using:

$$stress = \frac{force}{cross\text{-}sectional\ area}$$

(This important quantity is defined again in Unit 4.) As force is measured in newton (N) and area is measured in m^2 or mm^2, stress is measured in N/m^2 or N/mm^2. The unit N/m^2 is also known as pascal (Pa). To convert between these units:

$$1\,000\,000 \text{ (or } 10^6) \text{ N/m}^2 = 1 \text{ N/mm}^2$$

In engineering, the unit kN/mm^2 is also frequently used:

$$1 \text{ kN/mm}^2 = 1000 \text{ N/mm}^2$$

Stress is a very important concept. Suppose a given load-bearing column is at the maximum allowed stress. If the load on the column needs to be increased this can only be done by increasing the area of cross-section. So, for a given material the permitted load can be doubled if the area of cross-section is doubled. Expressing this another way, for a given stress the load is directly proportional to its cross-sectional area.

Self-assessment tasks 3.19

1. A rod of diameter 10 mm had an initial length of 1000.0 mm. After a tensile force of 500 N was applied to the rod its length increased to 1001.5 mm. Calculate (a) the strain and (b) the stress in N/mm^2.
2. Another rod of the same material as in (1) above also has the same stress. However, this one has diameter 20 mm. Find the new tensile force.

Young's modulus

If a force is applied to a given sample of material the strain can be measured as the stress is increased. If the results are plotted out as a graph some interesting features can be seen. Figure 3.26 shows the stress plotted against strain for two different materials using the same scales. Note that both the graphs start with a straight line. This was mentioned previously: this is the elastic region. (**Hooke's law** is said to be obeyed where the line is straight.) In building engineering the straight line is the important part, it is the predictable region. In this region, if the stress is doubled then the strain is doubled also. When the stress is reduced to zero, the strain also goes to zero. This makes sense: with no applied force, the material has no extension.

In the *elastic* region of behaviour, **Young's modulus** is defined as follows:

$$Young's\ modulus = \frac{stress}{strain}$$

Young's modulus is also known as the **elastic modulus**. This quantity is a measure of the stiffness of the material or its resistance to squashing or stretching. The unit for the elastic constant is N/mm^2 (or N/mm^2). The reader should check this. Table 3.12 gives values of the elastic constant for various common materials. Mild steel, for example, is more than ten times stiffer than certain types of concrete. Mild steel is about 400 times stiffer than rubber.

Young's modulus is mentioned again in Unit 4.

Table 3.12 Values of the Young's modulus for various materials

Material	Young's modulus E (kN/mm^2)
Cast iron	250
Wrought iron	200
Mild steel	200
Copper (rolled)	95
Aluminium (rolled)	62
Brass	90
Gunmetal	78
Phosphor-bronze	93
Timber	11
India rubber	0.5
Crown glass	70
Flint glass	55
Concrete	14 to 70

(*Source*: Smith & Taylor *Construction Science Level 2* Addison Wesley Longman)

Example

Using Fig. 3.26, a value for Young's modulus can be calculated for each of the two materials. To do this, a value of stress and the corresponding strain must be chosen in the elastic region:

Material 1: stress = 0.32 N/mm^2
strain = 1.6×10^{-3}

therefore, Young's modulus = $0.32/1.6 \times 10^{-3}$
= 200 kN/mm^2

Material 2: stress = 0.16 N/mm^2
strain = 3.2×10^{-3}

therefore, Young's modulus = $0.16/3.2 \times 10^{-3}$
= 50 kN/mm^2

The reader should confirm using the graph that these are appropriate values for calculating the elastic constant.

(The curved parts of the graphs in Fig. 3.26 will be described later.)

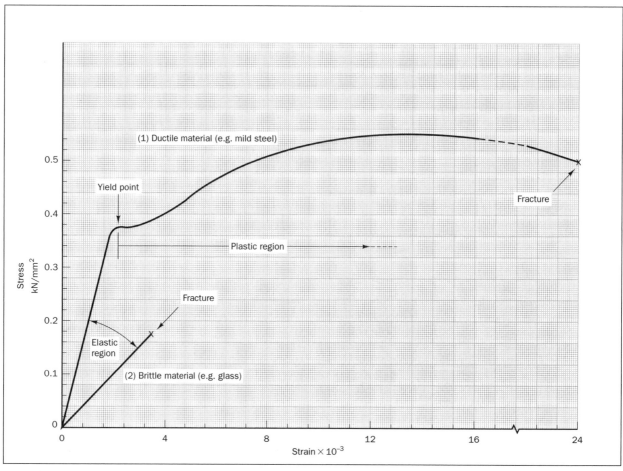

Figure 3.26 The behaviour of two different materials under the application of tensile forces.

Self-assessment task 3.20

Calculate Young's modulus for the material in the previous self-assessment task.

Testing materials using a tensometer

Safety warning:

- *When using the tensometer the safety shield must ALWAYS be used.*
- *Impact type safety goggles must be worn.*
- *Manufacturer's instructions should be followed throughout the experiment.*

A **tensometer** is often used to perform mechanical tests on samples of materials. This apparatus may be used to apply either tensile or compressive forces. Figure 3.27 shows a tensometer.

Before mounting the sample, the cross-sectional area (A) is measured in mm^2. For cylindrical specimens, $A = \pi r^2$. The radius (r) is obtained from the diameter, where the diameter is measured with Vernier callipers or a micrometer screw gauge.

Once the sample has been mounted, rotation of the handle enables an increasingly large force to be applied to the specimen. By means of gears, the drum turns as the specimen is extended (or compressed). The position of the mercury in the tube gives the force applied to the specimen (in kilonewtons). The marker is used to prick holes into a paper chart which is mounted on the surface of the drum. Thus the series of small holes in the paper records the behaviour of the sample.

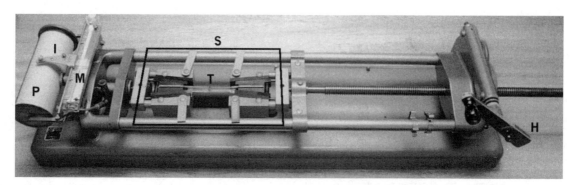

Figure 3.27 Tensometer: H = rotation of handle causes force to be applied; T = material being tested; S = safety shield; P = paper on drum to record results; M = mercury level in tube gives applied force in kN; I = pointer to indent the paper

Figure 3.28 shows typical results for a mild steel specimen. Note that the *y*-axis has been calibrated in units of force, kilonewtons. This was done by making a mark on the paper at 0 kN, 1 kN, 2 kN, 3 kN, . . .

Figure 3.29(a) shows a small mild steel specimen in the tensometer just before **fracture** (breaking). Note that this material undergoes 'necking' before catastrophic failure occurs. At this point the material is well into the plastic region of behaviour (p. 124).

Figure 3.29(b) shows a sample of timber (beech) after compressive failure. Failure in this case occurred as a result of buckling of the fibres in the material.

Defining the strength of materials

Using the results, such as those shown in Fig. 3.28, some important quantities for measuring the **strength** can be worked out. **Yield stress** is the stress at which the material starts to change from elastic to plastic behaviour. There is a sudden change in the slope of the graph. To calculate the yield stress, which is a very important quantity for engineering purposes:

$$\text{yield stress} = \frac{\text{force at yield point}}{\text{original area}}$$

Breaking stress is the stress at fracture, that is at the point the material breaks. It is calculated using

$$\text{breaking stress} = \frac{\text{force at fracture}}{\text{original area}}$$

Ultimate stress is the greatest value of stress the material can withstand before failure. It is defined as follows:

$$\text{ultimate stress} = \frac{\text{maximum force}}{\text{original area}}$$

Yield stress, breaking stress and ultimate stress are all measured in N/mm^2 or N/m^2. These are very important quantities for building engineers. As already explained, these are all measures of the tensile **strength** of materials.

When materials are tested in compression, the **compressive strength** is defined thus:

$$\text{compressive strength} = \frac{\text{force applied at failure}}{\text{area of specimen}}$$

Care must be taken when a material is tested in compression. Under certain conditions the specimen may fail by shearing. Also, the sample may buckle if the material is slender.

As already observed, Fig. 3.29(b) shows the non-catastrophic failure of a timber sample after testing in a tensometer. Figure 3.30 shows the various failure modes of concrete cubes after compression tests. The concrete cube test is discussed on page 122.

Self-assessment task 3.21

Working to an appropriate level of accuracy, find the ultimate tensile force and breaking force for the results in Fig. 3.28. Work out the ultimate stress and also the breaking stress. (Take the initial diameter of the sample to be 4.5 mm.)

(a)

(b)

Figure 3.29 Specimen testing: (a) mild steel undergoing tensile testing in a tensometer; (b) timber specimen after failing in compression test

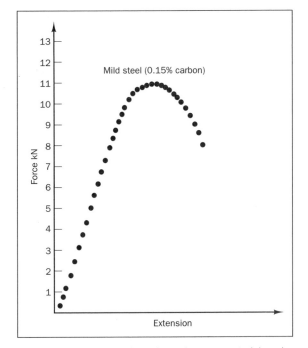

Figure 3.28 Typical results of testing a material using a tensometer

Measuring Young's modulus

Warning: *Observe safety precautions as described previously under tensometer tests.*

1. The initial cross-sectional area (A) of the specimen is carefully measured and recorded in mm^2.
2. The specimen is mounted into the tensometer (the use of this apparatus was discussed above).
3. A dial gauge or extensometer (see Fig. 3.31) is fixed to the specimen over a length of 50 mm. (As extensions are very small, these instruments accurately measure changes in length over this distance.)
4. The dial gauge reading is recorded when the force is zero.
5. An increasing tensile force is now applied to the specimen. Both the force and the dial reading are recorded at various points in the elastic region of behaviour. For example, readings may be taken at 1 kN, 2 kN, 3 kN, ...
6. Results should be recorded into a table such as:
   Material tested:
   Gauge length, $l =$
   Cross-sectional area, $A =$

Force (kN)	Gauge reading (mm)	Extension (mm)

7. Results are plotted with force (y-axis) against extension (x-axis). This should produce a straight line (see the self-assessment task below). The gradient (slope) is calculated from the line in units of kN/mm.
8. Young's modulus can now be determined using

$$\text{Young's modulus (kN/mm}^2) = \frac{\text{gradient (kN/mm)} \times l\,(\text{mm})}{A\,(\text{mm}^2)}$$

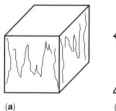  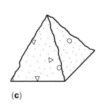

(a) **(b)** **(c)**

Figure 3.30 Concrete cubes after failure in compression tests: (a) and (b) non-explosive; (c) explosive. (*After* Taylor *Materials in Construction* Addison Wesley Longman)

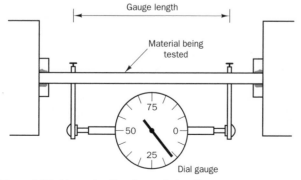

Figure 3.31 Measuring the change in length

(The student should check and confirm that this formula follows directly from the definition of Young's modulus. Also, the units shown in brackets should be checked.)

Self-assessment task 3.22

The graph and results summarised in Fig. 3.32 are for a certain steel specimen. Record the data given in appropriate units. Hence, determine Young's modulus. Check the answer from an appropriate source.

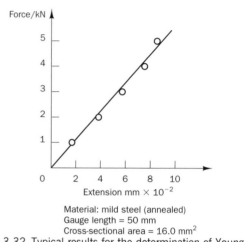

Material: mild steel (annealed)
Gauge length = 50 mm
Cross-sectional area = 16.0 mm^2

Figure 3.32 Typical results for the determination of Young's modulus

---

Measuring the compressive strength of concrete

The commonest method of testing concrete is by means of the **cube test**. In this experiment a compression testing machine such as the one shown in Fig. 3.33 is used. As with all experimental work safety procedures should be observed and safety spectacles must be worn. Note that compression testing machines are normally equipped with an overload cut-out. This prevents excessive forces from being applied which may otherwise cause damage to the machine.

Concrete cubes of side either 100 mm or 150 mm should be produced using special moulds. The concrete is compacted either by means of a vibrator or a tamping rod. For each trial mix, a number of cubes should be made. After typically 24 hours in the mould, the concrete cubes must be removed and immersed in water for the required period of curing (e.g. 28 days). After this time the cubes are placed individually into the testing machine and tested to destruction. The compressive load is increased at the required rate until the cube fails. The failed specimen should appear as previously shown in Fig. 3.30. It should be noted that the results from certain modes of failure are unacceptable.

As usual, the compressive strength is given by

$$\text{compressive strength} = \frac{\text{load at failure}}{\text{area of cross-section}}$$

Remember that if the load is measured in kN and the area in mm^2, then the strength is given in units of kN/mm^2.

Where a large number of results are obtained from a given type of mix, the data can be analysed statistically.

Figure 3.33 Compression testing machine with concrete cube shown. (*Note*: Safety guards were removed for the photograph)

Self-assessment task 3.23

The following results were obtained for the maximum load (in kN) when 20 concrete cubes of sides 100 mm were tested (at 28 days):

| 251 | 255 | 375 | 243 | 289 | 248 | 325 | 297 | 331 | 290 |
| 291 | 300 | 251 | 315 | 314 | 279 | 345 | 282 | 341 | 262 |

Use these results to determine the mean compressive strength of the concrete samples in N/mm^2 and MN/m^2. Use checking procedures to verify your answers. (N.B. 1 MN/m^2 = 10^6 N/m^2.)

Bricks are frequently used in compression in load-bearing walls, particularly for domestic buildings. It is important, therefore, to measure the strength of bricks in compression.

Determining the compressive strength of bricks

Warning:

- *Safety (impact type) spectacles must be worn during the compression test.*
- *The safety screen must be present and all persons must stand clear of the machine during testing.*
- *Emergency stop buttons should be present and must be used to cut the electrical power in case of emergency.*

The strength of bricks is quite variable even when they are the same type and from the same batch. For this reason it is suggested that the experiment is performed for 10 representative bricks in order to even out statistical variations. From this, both the mean compressive strength and the range of strength can be calculated.

The bricks to be tested are numbered and then immersed in a tank of water for 24 hours. They are then removed and excess water is wiped off. For each brick the dimensions of the two largest faces are measured and the area of each is calculated (in mm^2). If the areas of the two faces are not the same, the smaller area is recorded and used in the later calculations.

For the compression test, the brick is mounted centrally into the compression machine (e.g. see Fig. 3.33). Plywood sheets are used to sandwich the brick in position. The compression load is applied at a rate of 15 N/mm^2 per minute until failure occurs. The compressive force at failure is recorded. The compressive strength is calculated using:

$$\text{compressive strength (N/mm}^2) = \frac{\text{maximum load (N)}}{\text{area (mm}^2)}$$

If the test is performed for ten samples, both the average strength and the range of strength can be calculated. Results should be recorded as follows:

Sample number	Maximum load (N)	Area of smaller face (mm^2)	Compressive strength (N/mm^2)

Average compressive strength = _____ N/mm^2

Range of strengths = _____ N/mm^2 to _____ N/mm^2

Additional important points:

1. Bricks should be inserted into the machine in the same orientation as intended for use.
2. If bricks have frogs then the frogs must be filled with the appropriate mortar a number of days before the tests. Mortar is not necessary if the bricks are laid frog-down.

Factors of safety

Table 3.13 shows values of ultimate stress for a number of materials. These figures are extremely important as they

Table 3.13 Values of ultimate stress (strength) for several materials in tension and compression

Material	Ultimate stress (N/mm^2)	
	Tension	**Compression**
Steel (mild)	500	500
Concrete (1:2:4 at 28 days)	1.5–3	15–40
Bricks: common	–	7–40
engineering	–	45–110
Brickwork in cement mortar:		
common	–	7–15
engineering	–	15–20
Timber: softwood	30–60	30–40
hardwood	50–90	45–60
Stone: granite	–	90–140
sandstone	–	20–90
limestone	–	7–20

indicate the ability of materials to withstand loads. Values of ultimate tensile stress are not given for some materials as they have little or no strength in tension. As an example, concrete in compression is about 10 times stronger than in tension. If concrete is to be used in tension it must be reinforced. This is usually achieved by use of steel bars embedded within the concrete. This is because steel is very strong in tension.

A range of values is given for most of the materials in Table 3.13. This is because materials are quite variable: for example, no two pieces of timber are identical even if samples are taken from the same tree. Likewise, bricks and most other materials too have a range of behaviour. For this reason, construction materials employed for load-bearing purposes are used with the maximum stress values well below the ultimate stress. The criterion used to obtain the **working stress** (or permissible stress) varies from material to material. For example, for mild steel the working stress is chosen to be one-third of the ultimate stress. We say that the **factor of safety** is 3. For natural building stones the safety factor is 10 because these materials are far more variable than steel. (Factor of safety is also mentioned in Unit 4, Section 4.1.)

Other relevant mechanical properties

Materials which have substantial plastic phase when tensile forces are applied (such as shown for example graph 1 in Fig. 3.26) are said to be **ductile**. Ductility is also the ability of a material to be drawn into wires. At the other extreme, some materials under tension fracture without any plastic deformation whatsoever. A good example is glass where the stress–strain relationship is shown in Fig. 3.26. Note that there is no curved region for this material. This material is said to be **brittle**.

For engineering purposes ductility is an important consideration. The property of ductility (e.g. in certain types of steel) allows loaded materials to redistribute localised stresses which may build up at the positions of notches. On the other hand, this does not happen with brittle materials. Localised stresses may build up as there is no yielding and continue to do so until failure suddenly occurs.

Hardness is the resistance of a material to becoming indented. Hardness is an important factor to consider for the construction of floors and walls. By definition, a material X is harder than another material Y if X is able to scratch Y. For metals, hardness is determined by measuring the resistance offered by the material to the penetration of either a hardened steel ball or a diamond into its surface under standard loading conditions. For a given load, the harder the material being tested, the smaller is the area and depth of penetration.

The term 'toughness' should not be confused with strength. **Tough** materials can easily absorb energy by impact. For example, ceramic materials tend to be very strong in compression but they are not tough. They are easy to break by sudden blows. Timber is generally a tough material. Tempered glass is much tougher than normal glass and has many uses including the back walls in some squash courts.

Self-assessment task 3.24

In your own words, briefly explain the meaning of:

(i) elastic behaviour
(ii) Young's modulus
(iii) compressive strength

Electrical insulation

Materials which are good electrical conductors can pass large electric currents. A very good electrical conductor is copper. Copper wires have very low electrical resistance and are frequently used in power cables, telephone wires, etc. Aluminium, too, has long been in use for electrical conductors, e.g. in the grid system. At the other extreme, plastics (for example) are very poor conductors; they are said to be **electrical insulators** and have very high resistances. Plastics are used to electrically insulate conducting wires and electrical fittings inside buildings. The ability of a given type of material to oppose the flow of an electric current is called the **electrical resistivity**.

Table 3.14 compares the resistivity of a few different materials. As can be seen, metals have very low resistivities. Most non-metals have very high resistivities. Metals are very good **conductors** while non-metals are very good **insulators** of electricity.

Table 3.14 Comparison of the electrical resistivity of a number of different materials

Material	Electrical resistivity (Ω m)
Polyethylene	10^{13}–10^{16}
Polystyrene	$>10^{14}$
Polytetrafluoroethylene	$>10^{16}$
Polyvinylchloride	$>10^{14}$
Aluminium	2.7×10^{-8}
Copper	1.7×10^{-8}
Iron	9.1×10^{-8}
Silver	1.6×10^{-8}

The electrical resistivity of a material can be calculated using the formula:

$$\text{electrical resistivity} = \frac{\text{area of cross-section} \times \text{resistance}}{\text{length}}$$

In this formula, the electrical resistance must be known before the resistivity can be calculated. The resistance of many materials can be measured using an ohmmeter. The unit for resistance is the ohm (Ω) and this is explained on page 136.

It is easy to see from the above formula why resistivity has the unit Ω m (or ohm metre). Readers should check this for themselves.

Example

Samples of two different metals were obtained, and measurements were made as follows:

Metal A: diameter = 0.9 mm, length = 1.9 m, resistance = 0.08 Ω

Metal B: diameter = 1.2 mm, length = 0.8 m, resistance = 0.05 Ω

Which **one** would be better for use as the conductor in electric cables?

Answer

The electrical resistivity needs to be calculated for each one before a decision can be made:

Metal A:

$$\text{electrical resistivity} = \frac{\text{area of cross-section} \times \text{resistance}}{\text{length}}$$

$$= \frac{6.36 \times 10^{-7} \times 0.08}{1.9}$$

$$= 2.68 \times 10^{-8}\,\Omega\,\text{m}$$

Metal B:

$$\text{electrical resistivity} = \frac{\text{area of cross-section} \times \text{resistance}}{\text{length}}$$

$$= \frac{1.13 \times 10^{-6} \times 0.05}{0.8}$$

$$= 7.06 \times 10^{-8}\,\Omega\,\text{m}$$

Therefore, metal A appears to be the better material to use because it has the smaller resistivity.

In general, other factors need to be taken into account also. For example, the relative cost of the materials is important as well as the ductility of these metals. It would be no good using a material which would be difficult to manufacture in wire form!

Self-assessment tasks 3.25

1. Explain, using the term electrical resistivity, the required condition for (a) power cables and (b) insulation material.
2. (a) What does the presence of moisture do to electrical resistance? (b) Why are mains electrical sockets not fitted into bathrooms?

Chemical properties

The properties discussed so far have been **physical** properties. However, some important properties are of a **chemical** nature. In a chemical reaction the atoms or molecules of two or more substances combine irreversibly to form a new material. Metals suffer from various chemical reactions which cause corrosion. These reactions result in degradation of the material. These mechanisms for degradation are now briefly discussed.

Oxidation

Oxidation is a common chemical reaction between oxygen and many metals. This reaction often causes damage to the building material. Here are two examples of the oxidation process.

Unprotected iron and steel will react with oxygen in air only in the presence of water:

$$\text{iron} + \text{oxygen} \rightarrow \text{iron oxide (rust)}$$

The chemical reaction is complex. However, it can be summarised as follows:

$$4\text{Fe (solid)} + 3\text{O}_2 \text{ (gas)} \rightarrow 2\text{Fe}_2\text{O}_3 \text{ (solid)}$$

(In words: four iron atoms plus three oxygen molecules react to give two molecules of iron oxide, or rust.)

Remember that water is *essential* for this reaction to take place. The reaction is speeded up when salts are present (e.g. in sea water). The rust formed flakes away from the remaining metal and not only spoils the appearance but more importantly reduces the strength of the structure. Where moisture is present, it is most important to protect steel from rusting. Several important methods for protecting steel are discussed later.

Aluminium is very reactive in air:

$$\text{aluminium} + \text{oxygen} \rightarrow \text{aluminium oxide}$$

This can be written as a chemical reaction:

$$4\text{Al} + 3\text{O}_2 \rightarrow 2\text{Al}_2\text{O}_3$$

Unlike rust, aluminium oxide sticks to the surface of the metal and protects the material from further oxidation. Nevertheless, aluminium is usually anodised. In this process the natural oxide film is thickened. This increases the resistance to degradation. The process of anodising also improves the appearance of the surface.

Being very reactive, aluminium reacts with both acids and alkalis. Cleaning with washing soda, for example, will damage the surface of this metal.

Electrolytic corrosion

If two different metals are joined together, for example in plumbing, **electrolytic corrosion** may occur if precautions are not taken. In this electrical and chemical process one of the two metals is gradually 'eaten away' by corrosion.

Figure 3.34 shows zinc and copper rods inserted into an aqueous solution and joined together by a wire. Electricity flows from one rod to the other. In fact electrons flow from the zinc to the copper, forming a simple cell (battery). As electrons flow, the effect causes the zinc immersed in the liquid to dissolve or corrode away. This is an example of electrolytic corrosion.

For any two metals joined together it is easy to find out which of them will corrode. Table 3.15 compares the **electrode potentials** of a number of metals. When two different metals are connected together, the one having the more negative electrode potential has an increased willingness to supply electrons. This partner dissolves or corrodes away (it is said to be *sacrificial*). The more positive metal – the protected partner – is more willing to accept electrons.

A greater *difference* in the electrode potentials of a pair of

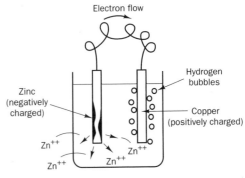

Figure 3.34 When two metals are joined together in the presence of moisture, electrolytic corrosion occurs; in the example shown here, zinc is corroded but the copper is protected. (*After* Taylor *Materials in Construction* Addison Wesley Longman)

Table 3.15 The standard electrode potentials for various pure metals (hydrogen is included for reference

Metal	Electrode potential (V)
Magnesium	-2.4
Aluminium	-1.76
Zinc	-0.76
Chromium	-0.65
Iron (ferrous)	-0.44
Nickel	-0.23
Tin	-0.14
Lead	-0.12
Hydrogen (reference)	0.00
Copper (cupric)	+0.34
Silver	+0.80
Gold	+1.4

(*Source*: Taylor *Materials in Construction* Addison Wesley Longman)

metals joined together results in an increased voltage and hence current. This means that the more negative partner (anode) will dissolve away more rapidly. Remember that the more positive partner (cathode) is protected and does not corrode.

Example

A strip of magnesium is often connected to galvanised steel cisterns and immersed under the water. Why?

Answer

As the magnesium is more negative (reactive) it becomes the sacrificial electrode and protects the zinc coating.

The corrosion process can be accelerated further

- as the salt or acid concentration in the solution is increased
- if the area of the anode is small compared with the cathode
- if there is an increase in temperature of the solution

Self-assessment task 3.26

Steel is frequently protected from corrosion by using a thin coat of zinc (galvanising). Explain why the steel (which is mainly iron) is still protected against corrosion if small areas of the zinc coating becomes damaged. (Hint: select and use information from Table 3.15.)

Sulphate attack on mortar

Chemicals known as **sulphates** are present in clay, clay-based materials and also in sea water, certain groundwaters and sometimes rainwater. These chemicals react slowly with tricalcium aluminate (a component of Portland cement) which is present in mortars and the chemical reaction produces calcium sulphoaluminate. This causes the mortar to expand and soften and then disintegrate. Structural failure can eventually result. The reaction takes place in very wet conditions. This is yet another good reason for the need to keep brickwork dry.

Self-assessment task 3.27

Make a list of the various problems which can arise when moisture is present on building materials.

Fire

Fire is basically a chemical reaction requiring **fuel, oxygen** and **heat** as the ingredients. Many solids and liquids emit vapour in the presence of heat; it is this which burns as a flame. The heat produced in the exothermic reaction is able to produce further combustible vapours, and so sustains the fire. A large range of materials burn if sufficient oxygen can reach the material. Petrol readily evaporates at room temperature and so burns violently as oxygen is easily able to reach the fuel vapour. It is easy to see why open-textured materials burn easily. Wood shavings or sawdust will ignite and burn far more rapidly than large blocks of timber as copious oxygen is able to reach the fuel. Some materials, especially plastics, release toxic gases such as carbon monoxide and cyanide when they burn. Frequently victims are killed from smoke inhalation rather than directly from the fire itself.

Common materials are categorised according to whether or not they are combustible in Table 3.16. It is important to realise that although a material may not be combustible it can still undergo failure in the conditions present in the fire. Unprotected structural steel is a good example of this. As it becomes heated, the yield stress of steel first increases until it reaches about 250 °C. Beyond this temperature the strength is gradually reduced. At around 550 °C, despite the factors of safety used at the design stage, the material is usually weak enough to fail. This is not the only problem! As steel has a high thermal conductivity (see Table 3.9) it is able to carry heat rapidly to areas remote from the fire. If the temperatures at these places reach ignition point, then the fire spreads by this process. Further, thermal expansion is quite substantial and causes distortion.

Although Table 3.16 shows timber to be a combustible material, its behaviour is very predictable in a fire.

The reader should do the next self-assessment task to calculate the increase in the length of a steel beam in a fire.

Table 3.16 Materials categorised as combustible or non-combustible

Combustible	Non-combustible
Timber (even if impregnated with flame retardant)	Asbestos-cement products
Fibre building boards (even if impregnated with flame retardant)	Asbestos insulation board
Cork	Gypsum plaster
Wood-wool slabs	Glass
Compressed straw slabs	Glass wool (containing not more than 4–5 per cent bonding agent)
Gypsum plasterboard (rendered combustible by the paper liner)	
Bitumen felts (including asbestos fibre-based felt)	Bricks
Glass wool or mineral wool with combustible bonding agent or covering	Stones
	Concretes
All plastics and rubbers	Metals
Wood-cement chipboards	Vermiculite
	Mineral wool

(*Source*: Everett *Materials* Addison Wesley Longman)

Self-assessment task 3.28

Estimate the thermal expansion (in mm) of an exposed 10 m steel beam in a substantial fire. What happens to the steel as a result of the expansion?

Summary of the important materials used in building

In studying the properties above, the reader will already have observed that a large range of materials exist for use in the construction industry. It should be clear that various considerations have to be made regarding the suitability for given applications. In summary these are:

- **General properties** – The general properties and experiments to understand the behaviour of materials have been discussed extensively. Ultimately, it is these properties which determine the suitability.
- **Health and safety** – Safety depends on using appropriate materials under the right conditions. Materials used must not be hazardous to health. For example, certain types of asbestos have been banned because of the carcinogenic effects of this material.
- **Resistance to degradation and durability** – The material should not deteriorate substantially in the expected lifetime of a building.
- **Cost** – As in all industries, construction is dominated by economics. Consideration of the cost of materials is vital.
- **Availability** – The required quantities of materials must be obtained with ease to meet building schedules.
- **Environmental friendliness** – It is extremely important to ask whether the material is from a renewable source and how much energy is required in the manufacture of that material. An increase in energy means that more fossil fuels are burned, resulting in increased global warming.
- **Fire resistance** – The materials used must have an acceptable level of fire resistance.
- **Aesthetics** – The appearance of the buildings is extremely important. Architects are blamed for distasteful designs. However, the materials of the external fabric of the building must look good and continue to look good. As an example, concrete buildings erected in the 1960s were often left bare. These can appear to be very unsightly. Many of these are now being refurbished with cladding of a more attractive appearance.

Many materials were mentioned and discussed earlier in the chapter. The various groups of materials frequently used in building are now briefly discussed in turn, concentrating on the main aspects.

The various self-assessment tasks in the sections to follow may involve using material from previous sections. The reader should not hesitate to refer back to earlier sections as and when necessary.

Concrete

Although concrete is widely regarded as a modern building material it has been in use since the times of the Roman Empire and the ancient Egyptian civilisation. Concrete has become popular in modern times as it is low cost and is a strong material in compression. It is, however, a brittle material and the *tensile* strength of non-reinforced concrete is low (about 10% of the compressive strength). This is because there are many imperfections in concrete, namely cracks and voids. When a tensile load is applied, these positions become highly stressed resulting in the growth of cracks.

Concrete is manufactured using **cement, aggregate** and **water**. The aggregate usually contains a range of particle sizes, from fine to coarse. Fine aggregate is referred to as sand.

Mortars are produced using cement, fine aggregate (sand) and water.

Various types of concrete exist. Some are high density (roughly 2500 kg/m^3) and others are low density (between roughly 400 and 2000 kg/m^3). They have reasonably high values of stiffness or Young's modulus.

Plain (non-reinforced) concrete may be used for foundations in buildings where the forces are mainly compressive. Where there are bending forces (e.g. beams) the concrete is usually reinforced with steel bars and mesh. This ensures that the parts of the concrete in tension are strengthened by the steel. Some cracking of the concrete may occur on the face in tension. However, the steel reinforcement is strong in tension and does not allow the cracks to spread.

Figure 3.35 shows a certain building under construction. It is made almost entirely from concrete. The reinforced concrete foundations and walls are cast in situ. The roof consists of precast reinforced concrete beams spanning 17 m, supported only at the two ends.

What factors determine the compressive strength of concrete? The answer is

- the type of aggregate used
- the free water/cement ratio

The second reason is more important. The *free water/cement ratio* is just the mass of water added to the concrete mixture divided by the mass of cement used. As an example, let the mass of water in a certain mixture be 40 kg and the mass of cement 80 kg. The free water/cement ratio is 40/80 = 0.5.

The smaller the value of the free water/cement ratio, the greater is the strength of the concrete produced. Figure 3.36 shows this clearly. The problem is that if the water content is too low, it becomes very difficult to compact the fresh concrete, which means that some of the air gaps remain. If the

Figure 3.35 Building with concrete foundations, walls and roof

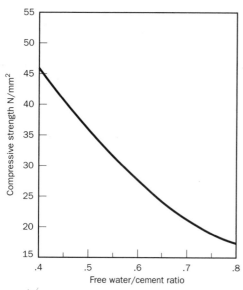

Figure 3.36 Compressive strength plotted against free water/cement ratio for test cubes at 28 days

fresh concrete is not fully compacted, these air voids reduce the final strength. For this reason there must be sufficient water to ensure that the *workability* of the fresh mixture is adequate. Figure 3.36 assumes that the fresh concrete has been fully compacted.

At the other extreme, if the free water/cement ratio is too high, air voids are formed when the excess water eventually dries out; the material is now more porous. This effect clearly reduces the strength of the concrete. So, all other factors being the same, a mixture with a free water/cement ratio of 0.5 will produce stronger concrete than one with ratio of 0.8. Figure 3.37 shows how the strength of concrete is reduced as the air voids increase. Concrete which contains just 5% by volume of air has about 70% of the strength of the same concrete which contains no voids.

In summary, the lower the free water/cement ratio the greater the strength of the concrete. However, if the free water/cement ratio is too low, the material cannot be fully compacted and air voids remain. The presence of voids (pores) reduces the strength because they create high stress regions. Cracks are produced when the stresses become extremely large. (Concrete is briefly discussed in Unit 1 also.)

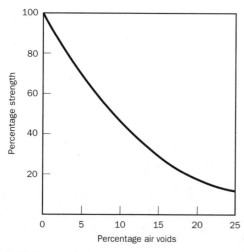

Figure 3.37 The graph shows how the strength of concrete varies as the percentage of air voids increases

Self-assessment tasks 3.29

1. Identify and explain the main features of the graph in Fig. 3.37.
2. By approximately what percentage does the strength of concrete *decrease* when the percentage of air voids is increased from 5% to 15%? (Use Fig. 3.37 to obtain the answer.)
   A 70%
   B 60%
   C 50%
   D 40%
   E 30%
3. Although reducing the water/cement ratio increases the strength of concrete, why should very low values of the water/cement ratio not be used?

Timber

Timber is a natural, fascinating material. Although it has been in use since prehistoric times it is still a very valuable material in building. The great advantage of timber over almost all other materials is that as trees are living, they provide a renewable source of building material.

Historically, timber was classed into hardwoods and softwoods. Today, there is little correlation between the hardness or softness of the timber and the classification. Softwoods are produced from coniferous trees which have cones and needle-like leaves. Hardwoods are produced from deciduous trees having broad leaves. Their seeds are enclosed in some sort of shell.

Most materials have non-directional characteristics. Metals, for example, have the same behaviour irrespective of direction. Timber is different. Along the axis of the grain, timber is much stronger both in tension and compression than the two other perpendicular axes.

Timber is composed of fibrous materials (made of cellulose) which occupy about two-thirds of the total space. These materials are held together by lignin which serves as a bonding and stiffening agent. As can be seen in Fig. 3.38, the vertical elements in softwoods are called tracheids which are arranged fairly regularly. In hardwoods, the majority of the fibres are thick walled, having a range of sizes.

If a section of a tree trunk is observed, the wood nearer the centre is often darker and is known as heartwood. External to this region the wood is called sapwood. Generally sapwood is regarded as having low resistance to fungal and insect attack. The resistance to degradation of heartwood depends very much on the species. Beech is classed as perishable and is used internally for joinery and furniture. On the other hand, greenheart is very resistant to degradation and is used for making bridges and constructing piers.

Variations in moisture content affects the movement of timber. As the moisture content is gradually reduced during the seasoning process the shrinkage is not significant until around 30%. Below this value movement is substantial, except along the grain. Figure 3.39 shows typical distortions which result from movement in drying. An inappropriate moisture level for timber used in internal joinery can result in severe shrinkage and warping after installation.

Timber has a high strength/mass ratio both in tension and compression. This is because timber is considerably less dense (lighter) than most other building materials. Timber-framed buildings are relatively lightweight, strong structures having

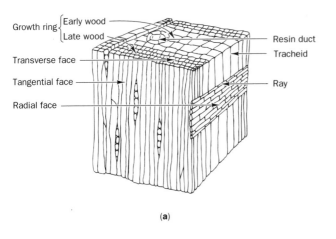

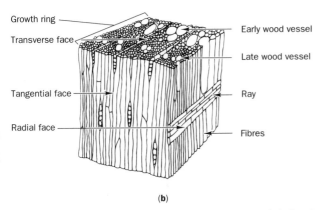

Figure 3.38 The diagrams show why the behaviour of timber is highly directional: (a) the structure of softwood; (b) the structure of hardwood

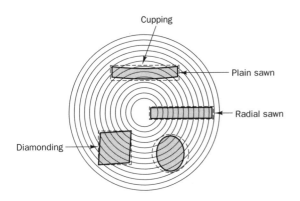

Figure 3.39 Drying shrinkages in timber

the added advantage of fast erection. Dense timber is usually stronger than light timber. On the other hand, as the moisture content increases the strength is reduced. The strength of timber at roughly 30% moisture content is only about two-thirds the strength at 12% moisture content.

Although timber burns (see Table 3.16), the speed of charring is predictable. This is important because it means that timber structures can be designed with a known time period for fire resistance. The thermal conductivity of timber is low (see Table 3.9). This implies that if the outer layers of the timber are on fire, the temperature within is quite low. This is important because the strength of unburnt timber is fully retained.

Unfortunately, timber can suffer from a number of degradation mechanisms. At high moisture contents, i.e. more than about 20%, timber can suffer fungal attack. Decay may result from either **wet rot** or **dry rot**. Timber suffering from decay loses its strength, leaving a structure unsound. Wet rot occurs where there are varying dry and wet conditions (e.g. in window joinery). The dry rot fungus thrives in timber in continuously damp environments without satisfactory ventilation (e.g. cavities in floors where there may be a damp problem).

Various insects attack timber, namely certain types of beetles. The common furniture beetle is responsible for most of the damage caused to structural timber and joinery in this country. Other pests include wood wasps.

Insect damage is favoured in wood with a high moisture content, and damage is more likely to be in sapwood rather than heartwood (see also page 128).

You may now wish to go back and read the section on timber in Unit 1.

Materials manufactured from timber

Products manufactured from more than one material are known as **composite materials**. What are the advantages of manufactured products made from timber compared with solid timber? Generally, the cost is well below that of solid timber. Also, manufactured boards overcome directional weaknesses associated with the grain direction of solid timber. These materials can be manufactured in a wide range of sizes.

There are various types of timber products on the market. Some of these are briefly described:

- **Fibre boards** – These are produced from compressed wood fibres. Although some types can be used externally, most types of fibre board (e.g. hardboard) are damaged by exposure to moisture and should only be used inside buildings.
- **Particle boards** – Chipboards are made from particles of wood and are usually bonded with synthetic resins. Various types exist: (a) standard, (b) suitable for flooring and (c) improved moisture resistance grade.
- **Plywoods** – Plywoods are made from a number of thin sheets of timber. Each successive layer has the grain at 90° to the previous layer. For this reason plywood is much stronger than solid timber. It has various uses such as flooring and soffit boards.

Self-assessment task 3.30

Give at least two good reasons why the majority of homes in the Scandanavian countries are timber frame buildings.

Stone

Natural stones used in building include granites, sandstones, limestones, slates and marbles. They are generally extremely resistant to degradation, but certain chemicals, e.g. acid rain, may attack and damage the surface of certain types. The cost of these materials is relatively high because of wastages which occur in quarrying. Cutting and polishing add to the final cost. The cleaning of stone buildings is also very expensive.

Stones are strong in compression (see Table 3.13) and the strength generally increases as the density increases. The movement which results from moisture content change is only very slight. Thermal movement is fairly low. Expansion joints must nevertheless be included when using certain types of stone, e.g. granite.

Stone is more extensively discussed in Unit 1.

Glass

Glass is used in buildings mainly for glazing in windows. Because of the low cost and ease of availability of raw materials, glass is unlikely to be superseded as a glazing material for the foreseeable future.

In the basic form, glass consists mainly of silicon dioxide, the main ingredient of sand. Glass is very unusual in that it is neither a true solid nor a liquid. Heating gradually softens the material and it becomes increasingly runny. (In a solid, the material changes from solid to liquid at a given temperature.) As already observed, glass is a brittle material at room temperature. Under sufficient stress it does not yield, but fractures.

Allowances should be made for the different thermal movements of the glass and frame in the design of windows. It should also be clear that if certain parts of the glass are heated substantially more than other parts, large stresses can build up. This may result in the glass undergoing fracture. (This sometimes happens when hot water is poured into a glass container – for example, when making jelly. Expansion causes the glass to fracture.) A ventilated cavity behind the glass can help cooling and reduce the chances of breaking.

Unlike most building materials glass is transparent to light (a maximum of about 90% of the incident light is transmitted). Although it transmits short-wavelength radiation (e.g. heat rays from the Sun) it does not allow long-wavelength infra-red radiation to pass through it. This means that heat is trapped by this method, commonly known as the greenhouse effect. (In houses, south-facing windows are usually favoured because of this heating effect.)

Regarding thermal insulation, glass is actually a reasonably good conductor of heat, in other words it is a poor insulator (see Table 3.9). On page 98 it was stated that the thermal resistance of a material is given by $R = \text{thickness}/k$. So, for standard 4 mm thick glass, $R \approx 0.004/1 = 0.004\,\text{m}^2\,^\circ\text{C/W}$. By doubling the thickness of glass its resistance is doubled to $R = 0.008\,\text{m}^2\,^\circ\text{C/W}$. However, the rate of heat flow through the thicker glass hardly decreases in reality! Why? The reason is that the heat flow through a window (or any other partition) depends on the *total* thermal resistance as previously explained. As with all materials glass has both an internal and an external surface layer of air which contributes to the total thermal resistance (where $R_{si} + R_{so} \approx 0.178\,\text{m}^2\,^\circ\text{C/W}$). So the total thermal resistance for 4 mm glass is

$$0.178 + 0.004 = 0.182\,\text{m}^2\,^\circ\text{C/W}$$

For 8 mm glass the total resistance is about

$$0.178 + 0.008 = 0.186\,\text{m}^2\,^\circ\text{C/W}$$

As can be seen, the total resistance has hardly gone up. The reader should now do the next self-assessment task.

Self-assessment task 3.31

It was shown above that the total resistance of a 4 mm single-glazed window is about $0.18\,\text{m}^2\,^\circ\text{C/W}$. Show that in order to double the total thermal resistance of a *single-glazed* window the thickness of glass should be about 190 mm.

This self-assessment task shows that it is not realistic to improve the insulation properties of glass by making it thicker. For this reason double-glazing is used. Two 4 mm panes separated by an air gap of 12 mm effectively doubles the total thermal resistance (or halves the U-value), because the trapped air is a very good thermal insulator.

Bricks

Bricks are made essentially from clay (mainly silica and alumina). Water and certain other chemicals may also be added during manufacture. After removal of impurities such as stone the material is then ground. To follow, the material is pressed into moulds. The bricks are then fired at temperatures up to 1000 °C.

Bricks are used in conjunction with mortar to make walls. Exposed brickwork is very durable, generally attractive and is used widely inside as well as outside buildings. Little maintenance is required.

The majority of bricks are rectangular. They exist in various sizes but all types can be picked up easily using one hand. The most common size has dimensions $215 \times 102.5 \times 65$ mm.

Structurally, bricks are used in compression. The compressive strength depends very much on the type of brick and the void content of the material. There are also variations between different samples of the same type of brick. Very roughly, the range of compressive strength is 4 to 180 N/mm². It should be noted that the strength of a wall can be quite different to that of the individual bricks. The overall strength depends on the strength of the mortar used and the size and shape of the wall as well as the strength of the bricks.

Increasing the water content of bricks reduces both the compressive strength and the thermal resistance. Roughly speaking, the likelihood of frost damage also increases as the water content rises (see page 116). Engineering bricks are an excellent example of low-porosity, high-density bricks. These are used where high compressive strengths and high resistance to degradation are demanded.

Building blocks are substantially larger than bricks and may be made of clay or concrete. The main advantage is that structures can be built more quickly with blocks. The fact that clay bricks are usually hollow gives them increased thermal resistance (why?). Likewise, high thermal insulation is also achieved using low-density concrete blocks.

Self-assessment task 3.32

Figure 3.40 shows white powdery deposits on the surface of a brick building, caused by *efflorescence*. The student should investigate the cause of this effect and find out whether or not efflorescence has any harmful effect on the bricks.

Figure 3.40 Efflorescence on brickwork

Metals

Although some metals can be mined uncombined (e.g. copper), most metals in the Earth's crust exist as compounds. For this reason metals have to be produced using chemical methods in industrial processes. Iron is obtained from various ores including haematite, while aluminium is extracted from the mineral bauxite.

Alloys are mixtures of metals, containing two or more different components. Metals can be used in pure form but are stronger as alloys. The reason for this is now briefly explained.

Metals are *crystalline* materials. This means that the atoms are stacked in regular patterns. The presence of defects (dislocations) within the crystals means that *pure* metals are generally not strong enough to be used structurally. Metals are made stronger and stiffer by introducing 'alien' atoms into their crystals. This presence of impurities obstructs the movement of dislocations, making the material much stiffer and stronger. To produce **steel**, a small, controlled, amount of carbon is introduced into iron for this reason. (**Ferrous** metals are those which contain iron.) Steel is a very important building material. The exact percentage of carbon can be varied to alter the properties of the steel.

As another example, pure aluminium has low strength. However, various alloys are produced (e.g. Duralumin) by adding impurities such as manganese and copper. This makes the material much stronger. Aluminium alloys are important engineering materials.

Metals have a wide range of uses in building. Some of these include

- structural uses
- roofing
- cladding
- pipes and radiators
- window frames
- electrical (cables)

Figure 3.41 shows an extension being built onto a certain commercial type of building. The frame can be seen clearly in Fig. 3.41(a) and is made from steel. Figure 3.41(b) shows the new part nearing completion. The light-coloured cladding consists of panels made from steel sheeting filled with polyurethane foam, which is an excellent thermal insulator. The external surface of the steel is coated with a thin layer of plastic to prevent corrosion. A section through one of the cladding panels can be seen in Fig. 3.42.

In summary, the advantages in using metals in construction are as follows:

- very high stiffness (large Young's modulus)
- many types are strong (generally high tensile and compressive strength)
- they are non-porous
- the joining together of metals results in strong bonds (depending on the metal this can be soldering, brazing or welding)
- their electrical and thermal conductivities far exceed most other material types and so are exclusively used where these properties are demanded

The disadvantages are that

- they are expensive
- many types corrode under normal conditions
- they are considerably denser than most other building materials

(a)

(b)

Figure 3.41 Steel frame extension to an existing building: (a) the frame; (b) near completion

Table 3.17 summarises the major metals used in building together with the typical applications and other relevant comments.

Self-assessment tasks 3.33

1. Explain why zinc or aluminium used for roofing should not contain impurities of other metals. (Hint: read the section on electrolytic corrosion.)
2. From Table 3.9 it can be observed that aluminium is a very good conductor of heat. Why, then, is aluminium foil used on the surface of *insulating* plasterboard?
3. A vapour barrier is used to stop moisture entering a partition. Explain why aluminium foil is a very effective vapour barrier.

Bituminous materials

Bitumen is a black material which can occur naturally but the majority is produced from petroleum. Because of its low stiffness (small Young's modulus) it is rarely used on its own but is combined with other materials depending on the specific use.

Table 3.17 Various metals and their uses

Metal	Uses	Comments
Aluminium	Gutters, flashings, foil used to reduce heat loss by radiation	Low-density, corrosion resistant in clean atmosphere
Aluminium alloys	Lightweight frames, roofing, cladding	Stronger than pure aluminium
Copper	Roofing, flashings, pipes	Good corrosion resistance
Iron	Boilers, radiators; historically much used structurally	Hard, brittle and dense
Lead	Roofing, flashing	Very dense, ductile, extremely durable
Steel	Used structurally for steel sections, used widely for reinforcing concrete; plastic coated steel used for cladding	Various types of steel exist, depending on carbon content and composition of alloy; many types rust in presence of moisture
Zinc	Roofing, flashing, frequently used to protect steel	Quite ductile, fairly durable

(*Source*: Taylor *Materials in Construction* Addison Wesley Longman)

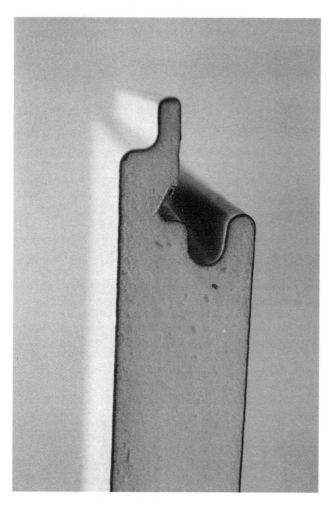

Figure 3.42 Section through cladding for the building in Fig. 3.41. This is plastic-coated steel, encasing foamed polyurethane insulation

Some of the other important properties are as follows:

- It is brittle at low temperatures. (Bitumen softens as the temperature is increased but as bitumen is composed from a variety of molecules there is no definite melting point.)
- It is waterproof.
- It has good adhesion properties.

Bitumen is used to manufacture various kinds of asphalt. The type known as mastic asphalt is frequently used in building. Mastic asphalt contains bitumen and filler, which is usually powdered limestone. It needs to be heated to temperatures around 200 °C before application. This material is used for

- flat roofing
- damp-proof courses
- road surfaces

Plastics

Plastics are mainly organic materials. Their molecules consist of long chains formed from carbon atoms. For this reason they are also known as **polymers**. Plastics are usually manufactured from petroleum.

The density of most plastics is comparable with water, making plastics very light building materials. Their low stiffness means that they are not used structurally.

There are two types of plastics: **thermoplastics** and **thermosetting** plastics. Thermoplastics become soft as they are heated. Cooling makes them harden. Thermosetting plastics do not become soft when heated. Instead, charring may occur if these are excessively heated. Many plastics do not absorb water and are unaffected by frost. Their resistance to degradation enables them to have a wide range of uses in building. These include pipes, damp-proof courses, window frames, floor coverings, fillers and sealants. As an example, pipes made from unplasticised polyvinylchloride (uPVC) are extremely resistant to chemicals and are suitable for use below ground level. Because they are very good electrical insulators, plastics are used for plugs, sockets, light fittings and cable insulation. In the form of foam (for example, expanded polystyrene) these materials are excellent thermal insulators and are used widely.

Table 3.18 summarises the main properties of some of the main plastics. Note that one of the disadvantages of plastics is that they have high coefficients of linear expansion, i.e. they suffer from large thermal movement.

Although plastics are generally quite durable and unaffected

Table 3.18 Some thermoplastics and their important properties

Polymer	Density (kg/m^3)	Coefficient of thermal expansion ($\times 10^{-6}$/°C)	Short-term tensile strength (N/mm^2)	Tensile elastic modulus (kN/mm^2)
LD Polyethylene	920	220	8	0.5
PTFE	2100	110	20	0.5
HD Polyethylene	950	130	27	0.9
Polypropylene	900	110	30	1.3
Nylon 66	1140	90	70	2.6
Polycarbonate	1220	55	60	2.7
Polymethylmethacrylate	1180	65	70	2.9
Polystyrene	1050	70	50	3.0
Polyvinylchloride	1400	70	50	3.2

by various chemicals, many types are degraded by ultra-violet radiation from the Sun. For this reason, certain plastics are used in internal environments only.

Self-assessment tasks 3.34

1. Why is polyvinylchloride (PVC) used in damp-proof courses and damp-proof membranes?
   (*N.B.* A short answer is required with several key words.)
2. Using Table 3.18, give two possible reasons why (unplasticised) PVC is used for window frames in preference to other plastics.
3. Which **one** of the following is the most suitable material for waste pipes placed below ground level?
   A brass
   B uPVC
   C steel
   D glass

Buildings and materials

A building basically consists of the following components:

- **Foundations** – This is the base of a building and it sits on the subsoil. Its purpose is to withstand the loading produced by the materials of the building such that subsidence does not occur.
- **Superstructure** – This basically consists of walls, floors and the roof and cladding. The purpose is to provide shelter and security and it is designed to minimise the loss of heat. It also keeps out the rain, wind and noise. The load-bearing components ensure that the building stays erect and is stable against the various forces which act on it.
- **Fittings** – This includes doors which provide access. Windows admit daylight and ventilation. Other fittings include stairs, partitions, and so on.
- **Services** – Services include water supply and drainage, electricity and gas.

The materials for the major components of several types of buildings are now discussed in outline. The reader should think and list the various reasons for the use of the chosen materials.

Typical domestic dwelling

Figure 3.43 shows a traditional or brick-joisted house. Starting from the bottom, the property usually has strip foundations made of non-reinforced concrete. Reinforcement is not normally necessary as the material is employed exclusively in compression.

The ground floor may be composed from a layer of concrete (around 100 mm deep) which sits on hardcore (broken stone). For large areas the concrete slab is reinforced with a steel mesh. A damp-proof membrane (bituminous felt or plastic (PVC)) must be included to exclude ground moisture. A large number of older houses have a suspended timber ground floor above the concrete.

The walls of the building consists of two leaves with an air gap between them. To reduce heat losses and *U*-values to acceptable levels, insulating foam (e.g. expanded polystyrene)

is inserted into the cavity. A damp-proof course near to the ground, but not at ground level, excludes rising damp. (What physical process causes rising damp?) External leaves are normally brick and the internal layer is blockwork. Metal or plastic ties are used at about 1 m intervals to fasten the inner and outer leaves to improve the stability of the structure.

Note that houses can also be timber-framed. These are very common in certain countries, e.g. USA. In the UK, most timber-framed houses are made from factory assembled open-framed sheathed panels. Stability and rigidity are obtained when the panels are bolted to the foundations and also joined to each other. Such houses frequently have brickwork as the external cladding.

The first floor is supported using timber joists. Although tongue-and-groove boarding was used for floors in the past, chipboard (e.g. BS 5669, type II) is employed almost exclusively at present.

Glass is almost universally used in windows but the frames may be made from various durable materials:

- **Timber** – both softwoods and hardwoods are used provided they are preservative treated against decay. The great advantage of timber is that it is readily cut and easy to shape on site.
- **Metal** – frames can be galvanised steel but lightweight aluminium frames are widely used at present. These usually sit inside hardwood frames.
- **Plastic** – window frames made from uPVC need very little maintenance (e.g. no painting) and are frequently used in domestic buildings at the present time. In fact uPVC is at present being extensively used as cladding over timber surfaces, for example, on fascia boards. Unlike many plastic materials, uPVC is not degraded by ultra-violet radiation from the Sun.

The roof is pitched and consists of triangular trusses made from timber, making the structure both light and strong. Concrete or clay tiles are fixed to battens and give the building primary defence against rain. Sarking felt is present below the tiles as a secondary defence against rain. Insulating material (e.g. 150 mm glass-fibre wool or exfoliated vermiculite) is placed into the loft for insulation purposes.

Finishes refers to plastering, rendering, floor covering, tiling and decoration. The following are brief notes on the various finishes:

- **Plaster and plasterboard** – Plaster consists mainly of calcium sulphate (gypsum). Application of the prepared material must be made on to dry, clean surfaces. As it is a 'wet' material adequate time must be allowed (typically four to six weeks) for the moisture to dry out before the application of paint or wallpaper. Plasterboard consists of gypsum sandwiched between strong paper liners. It can be cut or sawn. Plasterboard can be used effectively, for example, for internal partitions. Certain types have aluminium foil, and others have expanded polystyrene fixed to one face. Can you think of reasons for these different types?
- **Paints** – Paints are used to provide protection to surfaces and to improve the appearance. There are many types including those for 'specialist' purposes, such as heat reflection. The wide range includes many types such as emulsion, gloss and masonry paints. Surfaces to which paint is to be applied must be sound and dry. For many applications, a primer is necessary to protect the surface from deteriorating (e.g. by corrosion). The purpose of the

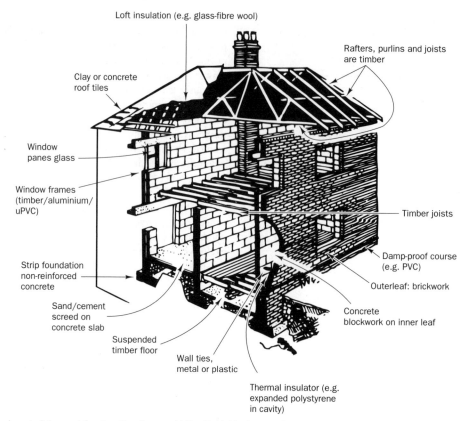

Loft insulation (e.g. glass-fibre wool)

Rafters, purlins and joists are timber

Clay or concrete roof tiles

Window panes glass

Window frames (timber/aluminium/ uPVC)

Timber joists

Strip foundation non-reinforced concrete

Damp-proof course (e.g. PVC)

Outerleaf: brickwork

Sand/cement screed on concrete slab

Concrete blockwork on inner leaf

Suspended timber floor

Wall ties, metal or plastic

Thermal insulator (e.g. expanded polystyrene in cavity)

Figure 3.43 Typical materials used for dwelling house. (*After* Reid *Understanding Buildings* Addison Wesley Longman)

undercoat is to provide cover and a good base for the final coat. The finishing coat provides a decorative and durable finish.

- **Tiling** – For internal walls, ceramic tiles may be fitted to bathrooms, toilets and kitchens to provide a waterproof, easy to clean, durable finish. The adhesive used must be compatible with the final usage. For less damp conditions polyvinyl acetate adhesives are adequate. For very damp conditions such as shower units, acrylic based adhesives are required.

Finally, let us take a brief look at the materials for services. For the water supply, a service pipe brings water to the house. The service pipe can be made from copper, galvanised steel or plastic (uPVC or polythene). Metal pipes have to be protected against corrosion by, for example, encasing them inside a plastic covering. Soil pipes that carry away waste water and waste solids, are made from galvanised steel, cast iron or uPVC. Service pipes for the delivery of gas are normally made from galvanised steel. Inside the house, the pipework is either mild steel or copper.

Electricity arrives by means of underground cables. Copper is the usual material used to carry the electric current (copper being an excellent conductor of electricity.) The copper conductors are contained inside plastic materials which are excellent electrical insulators. Likewise, the cables inside the house use copper cables with PVC as the insulating material.

Example of industrial buildings

Factories and warehouses and other industrial buildings often need wide spans, without columns in the middle. This

can be achieved by a (rigid) portal structure as shown in Fig. 3.44. Note that the structure (usually made of steel) is strengthened at the three corners above ground. This ensures that these parts are rigid so that some of the bending forces caused by the upper part of the structure are transmitted to the legs. The vertical supports are bolted to the reinforced concrete slab floor to prevent horizontal motion.

Externally, these types of buildings usually have metal cladding. For example, Colourcoat® HP200, which is produced by British Steel, is widely used in the UK. It has a 0.2 mm high performance plastic coating on galvanised sheet steel and comes in a wide range of colours. As this material is a poor insulator of heat it is usually used in conjunction with insulating materials (e.g. mineral wool, glass fibre, polyurethane, insulating board, etc.).

Another type of portal structure, called hinged portal, is

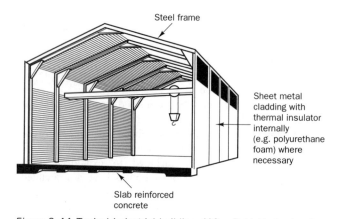

Steel frame

Sheet metal cladding with thermal insulator internally (e.g. polyurethane foam) where necessary

Slab reinforced concrete

Figure 3.44 Typical industrial building. (*After* Reid *Understanding Buildings* Addison Wesley Longman)

strengthened by deepening the section at only two corners and not at the centre of the top member. These buildings may be constructed from reinforced concrete or laminated timber (Glulam).

Example of commercial building

A modern commercial type of building has already been shown in Fig. 3.41. The building shown is steel framed and has reinforced concrete pile foundations. All floors and the roof are constructed from reinforced concrete. The flat roof is waterproofed using felt and mastic asphalt. The cladding is plastic-covered steel, encasing foamed polyurethane insulation. All windows have aluminium frames and double-glazed sealed units.

Self-assessment task 3.35

Cladding can be used for decorative purposes. Give four other important purposes of cladding.

3.4 Production and supply of electricity

The physics of electricity

It is hard to imagine our world without electricity, electrical equipment and the vast range of electronics we use today, in everyday life. In fact, almost every aspect of the built environment is dependent on the use of electricity.

Electricity is a fascinating subject. In this section, the basic ideas of electricity are first introduced, and the production and distribution of electric power to the built environment are then discussed.

What is electricity?

Gases, liquids and all solid materials are *all* made from incredibly small particles. The three commonest particles are the proton, the electron and the neutron. These particles make atoms, which are the building blocks of matter.

Protons and electrons have a property called electric charge. Protons each have $+1$ unit of charge while electrons have -1 unit of charge. Generally, there are equal numbers of electrons and protons in materials so that the overall electric charge is usually zero. This means that although our bodies are made from electric particles, we are usually electrically neutral! There are occasions, however, where there is a surplus or deficiency of electrons. This makes substances electrically charged. An example is thunderclouds which in various parts contain enormous surplus of either positive or negative charge. We have all experienced thunderstorms. The lightning produced is caused by the charge flowing either towards the Earth or towards the cloud. Tall buildings such as churches are equipped with lightning conductors which safely carry the electric charge into the ground.

In summary, electricity is a physical property possessed by some of the particles of nature.

Current

An electric **current** is simply the *movement of electric charge*. When charge is transferred from a thundercloud to the ground, an electric current is said to flow. Electric current can result from the flow of negative or positive particles.

In metals, the charge carriers are electrons. When a battery is connected to a personal stereo (say), electrons flow from the negative to the positive terminal. Whenever the flow of current is resisted, some heat is always produced.

Electric current is measured in amperes (A). A current of 1 A is flowing when about 6.25 million million million electrons pass any point in a circuit every second! (Physicists have defined the charge on 6.25 million million million electrons to be 1 coulomb. The reader will be happy to know that there is no need to remember this huge number.)

Mains power sockets in our homes can deliver up to 13 A. A home computer may require about 2 A to operate, while an electric kettle needs about 10 A. High voltages can cause dangerously large electric currents to flow through the human body. A current of just 0.001 A passing through a person can be lethal. All electric power supplies must always be treated with the utmost care.

Voltage

The term **voltage** (or potential difference) is a measure of the electric energy difference *across* two points. A 9 V battery *gives* 9 joules of energy to every 1 coulomb of charge it delivers. A mains lamp connected to a 240 V supply *uses* 240 joules of electric energy for every 1 coulomb of charge which passes through it.

It should be noted that as the voltage (energy) is increased, the current usually increases also. For many materials such as metals, the voltage is directly proportional to the current (Ohm's law). This means that doubling the voltage also doubles the current.

Resistance

Electric resistance is the opposition to the flow of current. Resistance is closely related to resistivity, which was introduced on page 124. Resistance is measured in ohms or Ω. Good conductors of electricity have low resistances. For example, a piece of copper wire may have a resistance of just $0.00001\,\Omega$ (or $10^{-5}\,\Omega$). On the other hand, a length of plastic (e.g. PTFE) may have a resistance of well in excess of $1\,000\,000\,000\,000\,000\,\Omega$ (or $10^{15}\,\Omega$). Clearly, very low resistance materials are necessary for power cables while very high resistance materials are used as electric insulators.

Resistance is easy to calculate. The formula is

$$\text{resistance} = \frac{\text{voltage}}{\text{current}}$$

Example

A low-voltage shop display lamp operates at 12 V and passes 2 A in normal use. Calculate the resistance of the filament.

Answer

$$\text{resistance} = \frac{\text{voltage}}{\text{current}} = \frac{12}{2} = 6\,\Omega$$

Self-assessment tasks 3.36

1. Which one of the following indicates the best conductor of electricity (i.e. has the smallest resistance)?
   A 12 V; 10 A
   B 20 V; 2 A
   C 6 V; 3 A
   D 15 V; 1 A
2. Which unit is identical to the ohm (Ω)?
   (Hint: check the definition of resistance from above.)
   A V A
   B A/V
   C V/A
   D /(V A)

Electric power

Power was previously discussed in relation to heat transfer. Electric power is simply the electric energy produced or converted per second into other forms. The unit is joules per second or watts (W). Examples: A 60 W bedroom lamp converts 60 joules of electric energy into 60 joules of heat and light every second. A 100 MW generator produces 100 million joules of electric energy per second.

The reader should know that

- 1 kW = 1000 W
- 1 MW = 1 000 000 W
- 1 GW = 1 000 000 000 W

Electric power can be calculated using the following formula:

$$\text{power} = \text{current} \times \text{voltage}$$

Another useful formula for power, which will be used later, is

$$\text{power} = (\text{current})^2 \times \text{resistance}$$

This formula is very easy to derive from the definition of resistance earlier, and the previous formula for power. (See the next self-assessment task.)

Self-assessment task 3.37

Using

$$\text{power} = \text{current} \times \text{voltage}$$

and

$$\text{resistance} = \text{voltage} \div \text{current}$$

show that an alternative expression for power is

$$\text{power} = (\text{current})^2 \times \text{resistance}$$

Example

An immersion heater of resistance 24 Ω is used to provide hot water in a tank. Calculate the power of the heater if the current rating is 10 A.

Answer

The values given can be substituted directly into the formula:

power = (current)^2 × resistance
$= 10^2 \times 24 = 100 \times 24 = 2400\,\text{W} = 2.4\,\text{kW}$

This is a typical power rating for an immersion heater for heating water.

Self-assessment task 3.38

Calculate the power loss in a long cable of resistance 2 Ω when a current of 8 A is flowing through. What happens to this power?

Energy

People often say that they 'pay for the electricity used'. In fact, we buy electric *energy*. The particles carrying the energy (electrons) remain in the wires. We merely use the energy of the electrons. The energy used is often calculated in the unit known as the kilowatt-hour (kWh). This is simply the energy which is converted by a 1 kW heater (or any other appliance) when it is switched on for 1 hour. At present, the day-time charge for 1 kWh of electric energy is around 7p. To calculate the energy used in kWh, the following formula is used:

$$\text{energy (kWh)} = \text{power (kW)} \times \text{time (h)}$$

Self-assessment tasks 3.39

1. Show that an energy of 1 kWh is the same as 3 600 000 J. (Hint: 1 W is 1 J/s.)
2. In a certain household, a 3 kW immersion heater is used to heat water for an average of 4 hours per day. Calculate the energy used by the heater over a period of 13 weeks (one quarter). Calculate also the cost of heating the water assuming that 1 kWh costs 7p. Ignore standing charge and VAT.
3. Electricity is much cheaper if off-peak tariffs are used. Find out the cost of 1 kWh of off-peak electricity.
4. Find out the cost of 1 kWh of gas.
5. Figure 3.45 shows a domestic electricity meter. State which **one** of the following the meter measures.
   A the energy
   B the current
   C the power
   D the voltage

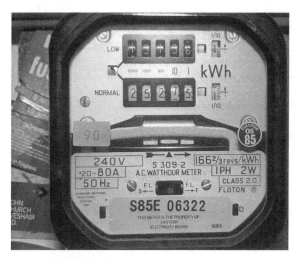

Figure 3.45 Electricity meter

Electromagnetic induction

So far, we have been learning about electricity without being concerned about the sources of electric energy. As we have seen, electricity is all around us; we are all made from electric particles! But *how* do we obtain electric power?

Batteries are a familiar source of electricity. Batteries produce electricity by using chemicals. There are many types of batteries: zinc-carbon, alkaline, lead-acid accumulators, and so on. A huge range of applications make batteries invaluable in everyday life. The problem with batteries is that the power supplied is quite limited and the actual energy provided by them is very expensive. This makes them useless for large-scale applications such as heating, lighting, powering machinery, etc. (Note that batteries are used in buildings for emergency lighting.)

Large-scale electric power for the built environment is derived from **electromagnetic induction**. It was the genius of Michael Faraday, who is on the back of a £20 note, that led to the discovery of electromagnetic induction. Previously, the Danish scientist Oersted in 1820 discovered that an electric current *always* produces a magnetic field. He had discovered that electricity and magnetism are closely related. The natural question which followed from Oersted's discovery was: 'Can magnetism be used to produce electricity?'

In 1831 Michael Faraday made the discovery which has since revolutionised our world. He discovered that if the magnetic field inside a loop of wire *changes*, an electric current always flows. This was done by simply inserting and removing a magnet from a coil, as shown in Fig. 3.46. Provided that the magnet is moving relative to the coil, electricity is *always* produced. This process is called electromagnetic induction (inducing electricity by the use of magnetism).

Another way of explaining electromagnetic induction is as follows. Electrons (which are electric particles) experience a force inside a changing magnetic field. This force pushes them along, making an electric current. An interesting demonstration is shown in Fig. 3.47. It is quite obvious that the electrons which produce the picture on a TV screen are greatly influenced by the presence of the magnet. (This experiment is quite safe to carry out at home using a black and white monitor. A colour monitor must **not** be used.)

Before going on to the next stage, it is important to state Faraday's law of electromagnetic induction. The most precise statement is that the voltage is directly proportional to the rate of change of the magnetic field through a coil of wire. In other words, the faster the magnetic field is changing, the greater is the electric energy produced. In the case of Fig. 3.41, the voltage (and current) produced depend on

- the **speed** of movement of the magnet
- the **strength** of the magnet
- the **number of turns** of wire on the coil

Figure 3.47 A simple experiment showing that moving electrons (inside the black and white television) are affected by a magnetic field. Upper picture: without magnet; lower picture: with magnet. Warning: this experiment must NOT be tried out using a colour TV

Generators

Generators work by utilising Faraday's law of electromagnetic induction, as explained above. Figure 3.48 shows a very simple

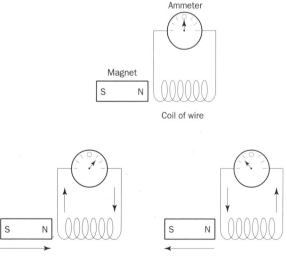

Figure 3.46 A simple experiment to show electromagnetic induction

generator or dynamo. (Dynamos are sold in bike shops for powering lamps on cycles. See Fig. 3.49.) The principle of operation is as described previously. As the coil is made to rotate, the magnetic field through the coil changes continuously. This results in electricity being produced by induction.

Commercial generators for producing large amounts of power do not have permanent magnets. Their magnetic fields are produced by large coils powered by a d.c. supply (also produced by the generator). These are known as field coils and are wound on the **rotor** of the generator. The coils into which electricity is induced are called **stator** coils. Stator coils remain stationary. The rotor (producing the magnetic field) turns inside the stator coils, thus producing electricity by electromagnetic induction.

The rotor is turned by turbines which are usually powered by high-pressure steam. The steam is produced by heating water from gas, coal, oil or nuclear energy. In hydroelectric power stations, the turbines are turned by the force of water as it flows downwards (from high to low potential energy).

Increasingly in the UK, wind turbines are being used to produce electricity. Can you see the advantage in using wind power?

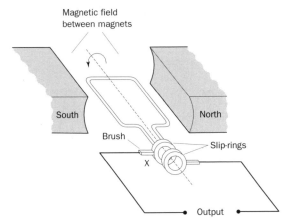

Figure 3.48 A simple generator of electricity

The generators in power stations have **three** stator coils placed symmetrically around the rotor. This provides three power outputs. Each output is called **single-phase**. Low-power equipment such as that used domestically operates on single-phase power. For industrial applications, all three phases may be used. An example is for the operation of very powerful motors. The advantage in using **three-phase** supplies is that much more power is available. Can you see why there are *three* sets of powerlines on each side of the transmission tower in Fig. 3.58?

Self-assessment tasks 3.40

1. Figure 3.49 shows a bicycle dynamo which works by using the same physical principles as a large commercial generator. With reference to this figure, explain carefully how the dynamo works.

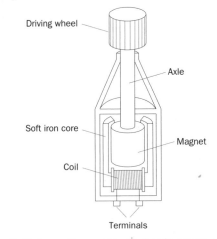

Figure 3.49 A small generator of electric power: a bicycle dynamo. (*After* Lucas *et al.* 1986 *Making Sense of Science: Physics* Addison Wesley Longman)

2. A student set up apparatus similar to that shown in Fig. 3.48. He decided to keep the magnet stationary, but to move the coil backwards and forwards instead. Did he succeed in producing electricity?

The nature of alternating current

There are two types of current (and voltage):

- direct
- alternating

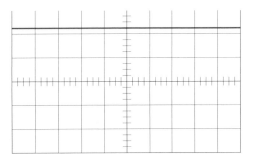

Figure 3.50 Direct current displayed on an oscilloscope

Direct current (d.c.) is produced from sources such as batteries. Here, the current is steady: it does not change with time. Figure 3.50 shows a d.c. being displayed on an oscilloscope. (An oscilloscope can be used to display waveforms.) It should be clear from this figure why the current is said to be *direct*: the current always flows in the same direction.

Direct currents and direct voltages are easy to measure because they do not change with time.

Alternating currents (a.c.) are produced by generators. As the rotor turns, the current induced into the coils flows one way for half a revolution. The current is then reversed for the next half of a revolution. For this reason, the current continuously *alternates* in direction.

Alternating currents change continuously and predictably. Figure 3.51 shows several cycles of a.c. The current alternates, or flips, from positive to negative, then back to positive and so on. The waveform is repetitive. The repeat time is called the periodic time, as shown in Fig. 3.52.

In the UK and the rest of Europe, the periodic time is 0.02 s or 1/50th of a second. This means that there are 50 repetitions or cycles every second. We say that the mains frequency is 50 hertz or 50 Hz. In the USA the frequency is 60 Hz.

Self-assessment tasks 3.41

1. Why is the mains frequency 50 Hz?
   (Hint: the rotor in the generator turns at the rate of 3000 revolutions per minute.)
2. Figure 3.51 shows single-phase. Sketch a diagram showing three-phase power.
   (Hint: read pages 138 and 139 again, if necessary, and remember that three waveforms should be suitably drawn, each displaced one-third of a cycle from the others.)

We shall now discuss how (single-phase) alternating current and alternating voltage are *measured*.

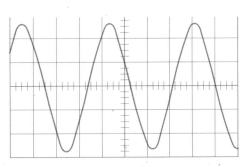

Figure 3.51 Alternating current displayed on an oscilloscope

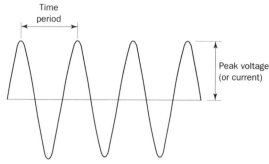

Figure 3.52 Definition of time period and peak voltage (or peak current)

Peak and r.m.s. values

The **peak** value is defined to be half the full height of the waveform, as indicated in Fig. 3.52. A more important definition is the **root-mean-square** value. The root-mean-square, or r.m.s., value is found by dividing the peak by $\sqrt{2}$. The relationship can be written for current as:

$$I_{\text{r.m.s.}} = \frac{I_{\text{peak}}}{\sqrt{2}}$$

Likewise for voltage:

$$V_{\text{r.m.s.}} = \frac{V_{\text{peak}}}{\sqrt{2}}$$

The reader may be wondering what r.m.s. *actually* means. The r.m.s. current is that value of a.c. which gives the same heating effect as the same value d.c. The definition is similar for r.m.s. voltage. Thus, if a certain alternating current is 5 A (r.m.s.), then this provides the same heating effect as a 5 A d.c. source. Note that in the equations for power used earlier, r.m.s. values of current and voltage should normally be used.

The domestic mains power supply in the UK has an r.m.s. value of 240 V. The peak voltage is in fact 339 V. The maximum r.m.s. current supplied by domestic sockets is 13 A. The peak current is in fact 18.4 A. The reader should check these figures.

Example

A 110 V (r.m.s.) supply used for powering equipment on a building site delivers an average of 20 A (r.m.s.).
  (i) Calculate the peak value for both the voltage and the current.
  (ii) Calculate the mean power delivered.

Answer

(i) From above:

$$V_{\text{r.m.s.}} = V_{\text{peak}} \div \sqrt{2}$$

Rearranging:

$$V_{\text{peak}} = V_{\text{r.m.s.}} \times \sqrt{2} = 110 \times \sqrt{2} = 110 \times 1.414$$
$$= 155.5\,\text{V}$$

Likewise:

$$I_{\text{peak}} = I_{\text{r.m.s.}} \times \sqrt{2} = 20 \times \sqrt{2} = 20 \times 1.414 = 28.8\,\text{A}$$

(ii) The formula for power is:

$$\text{power} = \text{current} \times \text{voltage}$$

As already explained, r.m.s. values should be substituted into the formula:

$$\text{power} = 20 \times 110 = 2200\,\text{W} = 2.2\,\text{kW}$$

(iii) Show that the average power used by an electric by an electric appliance is always one-half the peak power.

Self-assessment tasks 3.42

Figure 3.53 shows a certain alternating voltage.

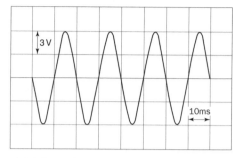

Figure 3.53 A certain a.c. waveform

1. Find the peak voltage.
2. Calculate the r.m.s. voltage.
3. Work out the periodic time and show that the frequency is 50 Hz.

Transformers

A **transformer** is used to increase or decrease the size of *alternating* voltages. (They do not work with *direct* voltages.) Transformers used to increase voltages are called **step-up** transformers. Those which reduce voltages are called **step-down** transformers. Transformers are essential for the distribution of electricity.

Figure 3.54 shows the parts of a simple transformer. The core is made from a material which is easily magnetised and demagnetised, such as 'soft' iron. The core is laminated, i.e. made from thin strips of iron which are electrically insulated from each other. This is essential as the core would otherwise get extremely hot and melt during operation. Two coils surround the core, as can be observed from Fig. 3.54. The input voltage is connected across the primary coil. The output voltage is produced across the terminals of the secondary coil.

Like a generator, a transformer works by electromagnetic induction. The current flowing through the primary coil creates a magnetic field. This magnetic field is contained within the iron core and passes through the secondary coil. As the current in the primary coil is continuously changing (because it is *alternating*), the magnetic field generated is also continuously changing. It was explained earlier that a changing magnetic field through a coil induces electricity. This is precisely what happens in the secondary coil: electricity is produced by induction.

The secondary or output voltage of a transformer depends on the number of turns on the secondary coil (N_s) as well as

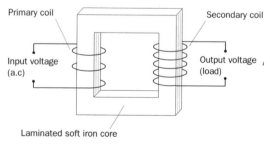

Figure 3.54 Structure of a transformer

the number on the primary coil (N_p). The equation to calculate the output voltage (V_s) is given by

$$V_s = \frac{N_s}{N_p} \times V_p$$

where V_p is the primary (input) voltage. This equation applies for a perfect transformer, i.e. a transformer which is 100% efficient. In real transformers some energy is always lost as heat. Nevertheless, well-designed transformers can be almost 98% efficient. Sometimes, the transformer equation is written as ratios:

$$\frac{V_s}{V_p} = \frac{N_s}{N_p}$$

In words, the ratio of the voltages is equal to the ratio of the number of turns on the respective coils.

These equations show that if the number of turns on both the primary and secondary coils is the same, then the output voltage is equal to the input voltage. It is easy to see that

- for step-up transformers, $N_s > N_p$
- for step-down transformers, $N_s < N_p$

(The symbols '>' and '<' mean greater than and less than, respectively.) Note that the voltages referred to in this equation are r.m.s. values.

Self-assessment tasks 3.43

A student constructed a small transformer as shown in Fig. 3.55. The primary coil consisted of 20 turns of insulated wire. The a.c. voltage applied to the primary coil was 2 V (r.m.s.) and was kept constant throughout the experiment. The output voltage, V_s, was measured each time the number of turns on the secondary coil was varied. The results are shown below:

N_s	10	20	30	40	50	60	70	80
V_s (volts)	0.8	1.9	2.9	3.8	4.8	5.9	6.7	7.8

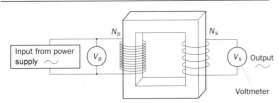

Figure 3.55 Transformer used in experiment

1. Plot a graph of N_s against V_s. Label the axes and record the units where appropriate.
2. Explain the relationship observed.
3. Is this a perfect transformer? Why?
4. The student noticed that the transformer was making a slight humming noise similar to that from a substation. What is the cause of the noise?

Example 1

A certain step-up transformer was designed with 500 turns on the primary coil and 2500 turns on the secondary coil. Calculate the output voltage, taking the input voltage to be 40 kV.

Answer

Assuming that the transformer is 100% efficient:

$$V_s = \frac{N_s}{N_p} \times V_p$$

Substitute given figures:

$$V_s = \frac{2500}{500} \times 40 = 200 \,\text{kV}$$

Example 2

A certain transformer is used to power low-voltage (12 V) display lamps from a 240 V mains supply. If the number of turns on the primary coil is 400, how many windings does the secondary coil have?

Answer

Rearranging either formula for N_s gives

$$N_s = \frac{V_s}{V_p} \times N_p$$

Substitute the given values:

$$N_s = \frac{12}{240} \times 400 = 20 \text{ turns}$$

Self-assessment tasks 3.44

1. A student tested a small transformer where $N_s = 200$ and $N_p = 40$ turns. The input voltage was provided using a 9 V battery (note that this is d.c.). What was the output voltage? Why?
2. Having realised that he had made a 'silly' mistake, the student then proceeded to use a 6 V (r.m.s.) a.c. supply. Calculate the output voltage in this case. What assumption has been made in carrying out the calculation?

The distribution of electricity

There are around 70 large generators that produce electric power for the UK. How is this electric energy delivered to the built environment? A **national electricity grid** which uses transformers, cables and pylons is used to distribute the electricity to every locality. Figure 3.56 shows the extent of the grid system in England and Wales. There are even power lines under the English Channel which enable us to export or import electric energy depending on the demand.

International links
Power lines with a capacity of 2000 MW run beneath the bed of the channel to connect our national grid to the French grid. Other connections link the mainland countries of Europe.

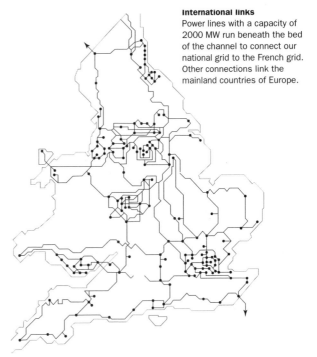

Figure 3.56 Schematic map of England and Wales showing the national electricity grid

Figure 3.57 is a sketch showing, in simplified form, the production and distribution of electricity. The process can be summarised as follows:

- Power from the generator is produced at a voltage of (typically) 25 kV.
- A step-up transformer is used to increase the voltage to 400 kV (maximum for the UK).
- The output of the transformer is fed into power cables and the electricity is then carried across the country using pylons such as those shown in Fig. 3.58. In the UK, there are over 7000 km of overhead transmission lines.
- At locations where heavy industry requires large amounts of electricity, the voltage is reduced to 33 kV by a step-down transformer. Another transformer is used to provide 11 kV supplies to light industry. Centres where the voltage is reduced and redistributed are called substations.
- Yet another transformer is used to reduce the voltage for domestic and commercial customers. Homes require a 240 V supply. In built-up areas power cables are placed underground.

Self-assessment task 3.45

Power lines are made from aluminium with a steel core. Can you think of any reasons for including steel as well as aluminium?

At this stage the reader may be asking questions like:

- *Why* is electricity transmitted at very high voltages?
- *Why* is the voltage increased and decreased at various places during the distribution of electricity?

The simple answer to these questions is *to reduce energy losses to a minimum*. Another way of saying this is *to increase the efficiency to a maximum*. Because of their importance, these fundamental questions require more detailed answers.

The first equation needed to answer the question is:

$$\text{power} = (\text{current})^2 \times \text{resistance}$$

This equation was investigated previously and the reader should refer to page 137 if unsure of its usage. This equation tells us that the power loss in a given transmission line depends on both the current and the resistance of the cable. The greater the power loss, the more energy that is lost. Ideally, the power loss should be zero, which would make the energy transmission 100% efficient. But this can only happen if the resistance of the wire is zero and, at the present time, wires with zero resistance are only possible at very low temperatures. These metals are known as superconductors and may become commercially possible in the future. At the present time, however, all transmission lines have some resistance, which is unavoidable.

Our equation shows that the power loss is also affected by the current which runs through the cable. More precisely, the power loss is proportional to the current *squared*. This means that a reduction in the current in a cable by a factor of 2 reduces the power loss by a factor of 4. Likewise, a reduction in the current by a factor of 10 reduces the power wasted by a factor of 100.

Clearly, the way to reduce power losses in transmission lines is by **minimising** the current flowing through them.

The power output from a power station can be calculated by the other equation for power (from page 137):

$$\text{power} = \text{current} \times \text{voltage}$$

This equation shows that, if the current is to be as small as possible, then the voltage *must* be maximum. There is no way

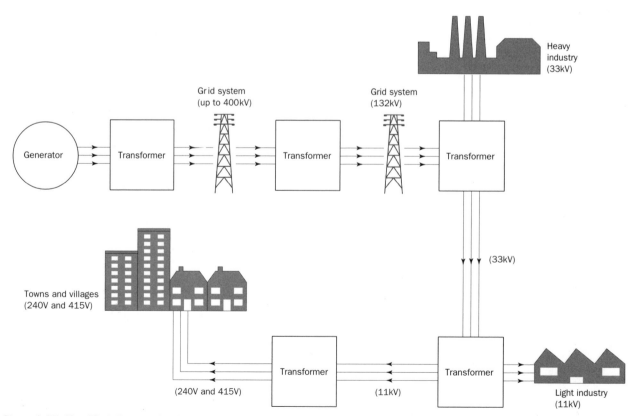

Figure 3.57 Simplified diagram showing how electricity is distributed nationally

Figure 3.58 400 kV power lines and transmission towers

to avoid this fact. As energy must be conserved, the only way to transmit a certain amount of electric power is by satisfying this equation.

The questions from above can now be answered. In order to reduce power losses in the transmission lines, the current must be as small as possible. This implies that the voltage must be extremely large. Transformers must be used to increase the voltage. For use in the built environment, voltages must then be reduced down to much lower voltages. Transformers are used for this purpose also.

In conclusion, the efficiency of transmission is high when the power lines are at many kilovolts. As explained earlier, the national grid operates at voltages up to 400 kV. Over long distances, transmitting power at a mere few hundred volts would be foolish as most of the power would be lost in heating the cables.

Summary

- Electricity is the most important type of energy used in the built environment.
- The electricity supply is produced by electromagnetic induction.
- Electromagnetic induction occurs whenever there is a change in the magnetic field through conducting coils.

- Generators and transformers work on the principle of electromagnetic induction.
- The mains electricity supply is alternating current which means that the live cables continuously change between positive and negative voltages at a frequency of 50 Hz.
- Electricity is distributed nationwide by means of a network of power lines.
- To minimise energy losses very high voltages are used to carry the electricity.

Example

The power input from a certain generator to a power line of resistance $1\,\Omega$ is 1 MW.
(i) Determine the current if the power is supplied at
   (a) 25 kV
   (b) 200 kV.
(ii) Find also the power lost (to heat) in the cable in each of the cases above.
(iii) What can be learned from these calculations?

Answers

(i) (a) power = current × voltage

   Rearranging:

   $$\text{current} = \frac{\text{power}}{\text{voltage}}$$

   Now convert units as appropriate and substitute into the formula:

   $$\text{current} = \frac{1\,000\,000}{25\,000} = 40\,\text{A}$$

   (b) $\text{current} = \dfrac{1\,000\,000}{200\,000} = 5\,\text{A}$

(ii) The formula here is

   $$\text{power} = (\text{current})^2 \times \text{resistance}$$

   Substitute values:

   (a) power = $40^2 \times 1 = 1600\,\text{W}$
   (b) power = $5^2 \times 1 = 25\,\text{W}$

(iii) Much less power is wasted as heat in power lines if the transmission voltage is extremely high.

Self-assessment tasks 3.46

1. Explain the importance of using transformers in power transmission.
2. (a) Calculate the power input into a transmission line if the current is to be 50 A at 400 kV.
   (b) Taking the resistance of the line to be $2\,\Omega$, determine the power loss within the cable.
   (c) What has happened to the power 'lost'?

3.5 Water supply

Water, or H_2O, is by far the most important chemical for the survival of life. It can exist as solid (ice), liquid or gas (water vapour). Earlier in this unit, the effects of water vapour on human comfort were described. We have also seen that the solid form of water, frost and ice, can cause damage to various building materials.

In the liquid form, water is important for a huge range of reasons. Drinking, cleaning and industrial processes are just a few of the vital uses of water. Typical consumption rates in this country are around $0.5\,m^3$ (0.5 tonnes) of water per household per day.

Sources of water supply

Approximately two-thirds of the surface of the Earth is covered with water. The present estimate is that the total volume of water on our planet is 1400 million cubic kilometres. The majority consists of seas and oceans. Sea water contains huge amounts of impurities much of which is salt (sodium chloride). It is often uneconomical to purify sea water for human consumption. Only about 3% of the total water content of our planet is freshwater. Of this amount, about 80% is frozen.

Most of the water we use has its origins as rain. But where does rain come from? Figure 3.59 shows the hydrological cycle which occurs throughout the world. This is the continuous exchange of moisture and heat between the land, the sea and the atmosphere.

Water evaporates from lakes, seas and oceans especially when there is wind and direct heating from the Sun. This water vapour (which is a gas) then rises into the atmosphere by the process of **convection**. As the temperature falls, the vapour eventually condenses; clouds start to form. Clouds are made from very tiny water droplets and ice crystals. (The process is similar to breathing on a cold day. As you breathe out the water vapour cools and turns to tiny drops of water.) A large rain cloud can easily contain 100 000 tonnes of water!

Eventually, the water returns to the earth, usually, as rain, sleet, snow or hail stones. This is called **precipitation**. Some of the precipitation falls onto the sea directly. Where the rain falls onto land, it eventually finds its way back into the sea by first flowing into rivers, or by **percolation**, as can be seen in Fig. 3.59. Percolation occurs because the rocks are porous and the water is able to seep through.

The process is then repeated and the water is continuously recycled. It is quite likely that the water you have been drinking today has been consumed previously by other people!

In recent years there have been an increasing number of droughts in this country. Various smaller rivers throughout the country have dried up. We are gradually accepting that water is a precious commodity, not to be wasted. We are fortunate in having good quality water. It is worth mentioning at this point that, world wide, 25 000 people die *every day* from the use of bad water.

We shall now turn to the sources of water supply in the UK.

Surface water

A large proportion of the water supply in this country is obtained from **surface** water. Natural examples of surface water include lakes and rivers. There are many rivers throughout the British Isles. Lakes are numerous in certain parts of the UK, notably Scotland.

The problem with abstracting (extracting) water from rivers is that the quality progressively deteriorates as the water flows downstream. This is caused by both natural and man-made pollution. In the past, waste products from industry were poured away without thought and the resulting contamination 'killed' many of Britain's rivers. Today, the situation has greatly improved. Strict controls have meant that the pollution levels have been lowered. Many rivers, such as the Thames, are much cleaner and contain fish.

Reservoirs, which are constructed for large towns and cities, are artificial lakes used for the collection and storage of water. A quick look at a map of London will show that there are many large reservoirs, especially to the west and the north-east of the city. London's reservoirs are supplied mainly from the River Thames and River Lee. London's reservoirs are known as pumped storage reservoirs because most of the water contained results from pumping. Figure 3.60 shows one of the reservoirs which supplies water to the north of London.

Groundwater

About one-third of the water supplied in England is derived from underground sources. Such water is known as **groundwater**. Most people are unaware of the importance of

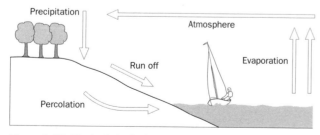

Figure 3.59 The hydrological cycle

Figure 3.60 Large reservoir near the River Lee in London

groundwater as the sources are hidden from view, well beneath the surface.

Rocks which are sufficiently porous to store water and are permeable enough to allow large amounts of water to flow through them, are called aquifers (see Fig. 3.61). In England, the most important aquifer is **chalk**, followed by **sandstone**.

At greater depths, below the aquifer, the rocks are impermeable, which means that they do not allow the water to penetrate through them. Rainwater gradually fills aquifers by means of percolation. The water table is the natural level of the water. Below this plane, the material is saturated. In recent years, the rainfall in various parts of the UK has been low, which means that the water table has been falling, and droughts in recent years have caused some of the wells used to extract the water to dry up. (The water table is also described in Unit 1.)

Figure 3.62 shows how water from these underground rocks is extracted and delivered to the consumer.

Electric pumps are used to lift the water against gravity, up to ground level. The pumping station then directs the water to either a service (or distribution) reservoir or a water tower. Service reservoirs and water towers are located on the highest land in the area to provide the greatest possible pressure head for the water. (The water tank in a house is located high up in the loft for the same reason.) The use of a distribution reservoir ensures that there is always some water available, even when pumps may not be operating. Figure 3.63 shows a large water tower. A service reservoir is present to the left of the picture, hidden under grass.

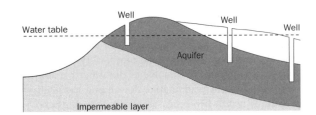

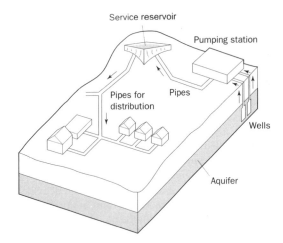

Figure 3.61 Simplified diagram showing groundwater supplies

Figure 3.62 Areas which are supplied from underground water sources have water distribution systems similar to that shown here

Properties of 'natural' water

Pure water is also known as distilled water and contains no impurities, just the chemical H_2O. On the other hand, water occurring naturally contains various dissolved 'impurities'. Water for consumption, such as bottled spring water, is often labelled as being *pure*, even though many substances are dissolved in the water. 'Pure' in this context is taken to mean free from foul or polluting ingredients.

The amount and types of impurities in water vary enormously. These affect the colour, taste and odour of the water. Some of the impurities enter the water by natural means, e.g. various salts become dissolved as water seeps through rocks. Salts such as calcium carbonate, calcium sulphate and magnesium sulphate are **inorganic** impurities. These impurities are the cause of **hardness** in water (see page 147).

Organic matter in water comes from a range of sources, including plants and animal life, partially treated domestic effluent and industrial waste. Much of the organic matter in water eventually undergoes biodegradation, resulting in relatively harmless materials.

Water-borne bacteria are very harmful and can cause terrible diseases, such as cholera, typhoid and dysentery. Fortunately, such diseases have been eliminated in the UK as a result of very strict controls and disinfection of water supplies (see page 149). Unfortunately, in some underdeveloped countries, many people are dying from these diseases every day. Water-related diseases are also caused by the presence of viruses, worms and protozoa in contaminated supplies.

Other impurities enter the water artificially, e.g. pesticides used on farms may dissolve into rainwater.

Figure 3.63 Large water tower

Pollutants in water

The definition of 'pollutant' is something that causes contamination, especially with man-made waste. It is unfortunate that increasing industry throughout the world has led to greater pollution of natural sources of water. Today, there is great attention on waste water produced by industry because many of the poisonous materials cannot be removed by normal purification processes. Depending on location, the law requires industry to clean its waste water sufficiently before discharging into drainage systems.

Some pollutants in water which affect health include:

- **Lead** – Historically, lead was used for water pipes and there are still houses with lead pipes. Very small quantities of lead can dissolve as the water passes through. Lead is a cumulative poison and has been linked to health problems, especially in youngsters. Kidney failure and brain damage can be caused by excess lead absorption.
- **Aluminium** – There is growing evidence that aluminium compounds in water form a serious health hazard as aluminium has been connected with premature senility. In 1988, a large amount of aluminium sulphate (20 tonnes!) accidently entered the water supply in one part of Cornwall. Many people became very sick as a result of consuming this contaminated water. Note that aluminium sulphate is actually used in the treatment of water, but in *very low* concentrations.
- **Nitrates** – Artificial fertilisers used in farming consist of chemicals called **nitrates** (and to a lesser extent, phosphates). Inevitably, these chemicals end up in streams, rivers and underground water. Agricultural chemicals percolating into water kill fish and degrade the water quality. Nitrates are said to cause stomach problems, and problems with the blood.
- **Pesticides** – These chemicals are used to control pests which damage crops. Pesticides are sprayed onto plants to kill various insects and other pests, but widespread application means that the chemicals invariably end up in streams, rivers, lakes and underground water. Even in small concentrations, pesticides are toxic materials. The pesticide content in water in some areas in the UK is at present unacceptably high.

Figure 3.64 A pH meter being used to measure the acidity of contaminated water. Do you think that the pH of this water is acceptable?

Acidity

Pure water is chemically **neutral**. It is neither acidic or alkaline. Certain chemicals can become dissolved which make the water acidic. Carbon dioxide reacts with rainwater to produce carbonic acid, making 'natural' rainwater slightly acidic. Sulphur dioxide gas, which is often produced from burning fossil fuels, dissolves in water to produce sulphurous acid:

$$SO_2 + H_2O \rightarrow H_2SO_3$$

This reaction can occur with water in the atmosphere, to produce 'acid rain', which can not only be dangerous to health but is also said to cause decline in fish populations and damage to forests. Acid rain causes increased weathering of building stones. (What might acidic water do to metals? If you don't know, read the section on electrolytic corrosion.) There are many other reactions between atmospheric pollutants and moisture in the air giving rise to acidic water.

The effects of acidic water are not always direct. The combination with other chemicals often results in the release of toxic materials into the water in rivers and lakes.

Water can also become acidic when it passes through peat and other vegetation. On the other hand, certain rocks such as calcium carbonate (chalk) tend to make the water alkalinic.

The extent of the acidity is measured using the **pH scale**:

- pH = 7 means that the water is neutral
- pH < 7 indicates that the water is acidic
- pH > 7 shows that the water is alkalinic

As the pH falls further and further below 7, the acidity becomes stronger. It should be emphasised that when the pH decreases by 1, the acidity becomes 10 times stronger. Thus, water with a pH of 4 is 100 times more acidic than water with a pH of 6. Very strong acid rain was once recorded at Pitlochry, Scotland, where the pH was measured to be as low as 2.4!

Water supplies should be neither too acidic nor too alkalinic. The range of pH considered to be acceptable is typically 6 to 8.

The acidity or alkalinity of water can be checked with litmus paper. The final colour indicates the type of water. For example, if blue litmus paper turns from blue to red, the water is acidic. Electronic sensors can be used to measure pH. Figure 3.64 shows an instrument being used to measure the pH of contaminated water. As can be observed, this water has been polluted to a very high acidity level.

Self-assessment task 3.47

Water which was originally neutral has percolated through chalky soil. What is its pH now most likely to be?
A 2 (very acidic)
B 5 (acidic)
C 7 (neutral)
D 9 (alkaline)

Hardness

Hard water does not easily form a lather. The opposite is true for **soft** water.

Various impurities cause hardness in water. These are primarily the sulphates and bicarbonates of magnesium and calcium. These impurities either dissolve into the water directly or are formed by chemical reactions of water with other salts such as calcium carbonate. For example, water which has passed through gypsum will have some calcium sulphate dissolved in it.

There are some advantages of hard water, such as 'nicer taste'. Also, less toxic metals are usually present in hard water (e.g. lead and copper compounds), and a glimpse at Fig. 3.65 shows one reason why. The chemicals causing hardness are deposited over the surface of the metal, providing a protective barrier between the water and the metal.

There are various disadvantages associated with hardness, including the following:

- 'Furring up' of boilers, washing machines and kettles means that more energy is wasted.
- Extra soap is required in washing.
- Many industrial processes are influenced by hard water.
- Deposits formed around sinks, baths, lavatory pans, etc., appear unsightly.

Bicarbonates in water form **temporary** hardness, whereas sulphates cause **permanent** hardness. The meaning of these terms is explained below.

Temporary hardness

Temporary hardness can be removed from water by boiling. Figure 3.65 shows deposits in a copper pipe. In the case of calcium bicarbonate (chemical formula $Ca(HCO_3)_2$), heat breaks up this salt into calcium carbonate (the material which makes limestone or chalk). Water and carbon dioxide are also produced in the decomposition process. As calcium carbonate ($CaCO_3$) is not soluble in water it is deposited as a solid. The reaction can be written as a chemical equation:

Figure 3.65 Deposits caused by temporary hardness are evident in this view of a copper central heating pipe

$$Ca(HCO_3)_2 \text{ (aq)} + \text{heat} \rightarrow$$
$$CaCO_3 \text{ (solid)} + H_2O \text{ (liquid)} + CO_2 \text{ (gas)}$$

(*N.B.* In this chemical equation, 'aq' means aqueous, or dissolved in water.)

Permanent hardness

As already mentioned, permanent hardness is caused mainly by calcium sulphate ($CaSO_4$) and/or magnesium sulphate ($MgSO_4$) dissolved in water. Permanent hardness *cannot* be removed by boiling the water.

One way of removing permanent hardness from water is by use of washing soda, chemically known as sodium carbonate:

calcium sulphate + sodium carbonate →
calcium carbonate + sodium sulphate

It is important to remember that this reaction is taking place in water. Using chemical symbols, the reaction can be written:

$$CaSO_4 \text{ (aq)} + Na_2CO_3 \text{ (aq)} \rightarrow$$
$$CaCO_3 \text{ (solid)} + Na_2SO_4 \text{ (aq)}$$

In this chemical reaction, calcium carbonate is **precipitated**. This means that this material is deposited as a solid as it is insoluble. The other chemical produced, sodium sulphate, remains dissolved. Sodium sulphate, however, does not cause hardness. With the removal of the calcium sulphate, the water is now soft.

Self-assessment tasks 3.48

1. Write down a chemical reaction, both in words and symbols, to show how washing soda (Na_2CO_3) removes the hardness caused by magnesium sulphate.
2. The hardness of water varies tremendously from region to region. For example, water in Durham is soft while the water in Luton is hard. In which area will it cost more to do equal amounts of washing? Why?

Water can be softened commercially by use of the *zeolite* process. Zeolites are complex compounds which react with the hardness-causing chemicals to produce soft water. As an example:

magnesium sulphate + sodium zeolite →
magnesium zeolite + sodium sulphate

The chemicals produced on the right-hand side of this equation do not cause hardness: the resulting water is soft. The sodium zeolite gets 'used up' in producing the soft water. It is easily regenerated by reacting the magnesium zeolite produced with sodium chloride (table salt):

magnesium zeolite + sodium chloride →
sodium zeolite + magnesium chloride

The sodium zeolite has been recovered in this process. It can now be re-used to produce more soft water.

Self-assessment tasks 3.49

1. Write down three advantages of soft water over hard water.
2. Natural mineral water is collected from springs and is sold in shops as drinking water. A typical analysis is shown below:

---

pH = 7.4
Analysis in mg/l:

Calcium 55 Magnesium 19 Sodium 24 Potassium 1 Bicarbonates 248
Chlorides 42 Sulphates 23 Nitrates <0.1 Iron 0 Aluminium 0

   (a) Is the water acidic or alkaline?
   (b) Does the water contain hardness-causing agents?
   (c) What does mg/l mean?

Water treatment

Throughout this section, we have seen that water can contain a huge range of impurities. The water used for public consumption must be *wholesome*. This means that it should be

- harmless to health
- pleasant tasting
- colourless
- odourless
- clear

Untreated water frequently contains a range of impurities in **suspension**. This means that the impurity is not dissolved but exists in the form of small particles, mixed in with the water. Such impurities include particles of silt and clay. The water often appears murky. Organic matter such as fungi is often present. Micro-organisms also need to be removed from water supplies because of the risk to health.

Storage of water

Reservoirs are used to **store** water. In reservoirs (see also page 144), the water treatment process begins 'naturally' provided that the water is stored for a reasonable length of time (e.g. 1 month):

- **Sedimentation** causes the natural sinking of the small particles in the suspension.
- Ultra-violet radiation from the Sun kills the bacteria (e.g. where pollutants may be present).
- Certain micro-organisms (which could cause diseases such as typhoid) also die because of the lack of nutrition in the water.

Unfortunately, the conditions in reservoirs allow the growth of undesirable, tiny plant-like organisms called algae. Various types of algae exist, and water which supports their growth is known as eutrophic. (Can you think of the type of chemical contaminants that might help these organisms to grow in water? Hint: see page 146.) The problem with algae is that their presence increases the difficulty of treating the water. Algae are killed by the controlled addition of certain chemicals.

Clarification of water

Clarification is chemically assisted sedimentation. In other words, it is a method used for the removal of the very fine silt particles which are still present after the naturally occurring sedimentation process occurs in reservoirs. There are three stages in the process:

1. The addition of the correct amount of chemical, such as aluminium sulphate (although certain salts of iron can also be used), and thorough mixing with water.
2. Stage 1 results in **coagulation** (or, using simpler words, a curd-like mass forms). This precipitate consists basically of aluminium hydroxide. The material flocculates into larger particles.
3. The sedimentation process now occurs. Specially built sedimentation tanks are usually employed to remove the clear water from the surface. The sludge which accumulates is continuously removed.

The clarification process removes about 90% of the suspended matter in the water. The remaining material is removed by **filtration**, of which there are two main types:

- slow sand filtration
- rapid gravity filtration

Slow sand filtration

In this process, the water in a very large tank flows downwards through a fine sand bed, followed by a supporting bed of gravel. The water is then collected by the pipes beneath (see Fig. 3.66).

It is important to note that the mechanism for purification here is not simply a straining action. Bacteriological action is the main reason why purification occurs.

Although slow sand filters can produce water of excellent quality, they have various disadvantages. They are very large, occupying much land and they operate slowly. The cleaning out of the large areas of filter can be laborious. They need to be taken out of service and cleaned at roughly monthly intervals.

Rapid sand filtration

Here, the tanks are much smaller, and the rate at which filtration occurs is at least 20 times greater than slow sand filters. With rapid sand filters, the filtration occurs mainly by *physical* action (although some chemical changes do occur in the water as it passes through the bed). Figure 3.67 shows a simple rapid (gravity) sand filter.

As with the slow sand filter, the water passes through sand followed by gravel. Note, however, that the filtration rate is much greater with the rapid sand filter. Because of these greater flow rates, the filters become clogged much more rapidly. Therefore, more frequent cleaning is necessary with these type of filters after one or two days' use.

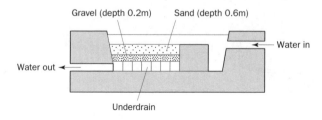

Figure 3.66 Section through slow sand filter

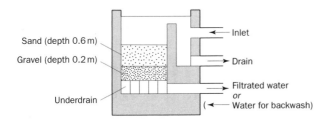

Figure 3.67 Rapid (gravity) sand filter

Cleaning occurs by first forcing compressed air to pass through the filter after drainage. This helps to dislodge the surface scum and the dirt from the same grains. Filtrated water is then pumped upwards through the filter so that the deposits are now washed away. The upward flow rate is about 10 times greater than the filtration rate and this action removes the impurities from the filter.

Rapid gravity filtration plants are designed, then, to filter water much more quickly than slow water filters. However, the rapid gravity filters cannot be relied on to provide water free of harmful organisms. The water must be further disinfected or sterilised.

Disinfection

Organisms in water include bacteria, viruses and low forms of animal life. Sterilisation usually means killing *all* of the organisms within the water although this is not usually necessary. Disinfection means reducing the organisms in the water to such low concentrations that infection (causing diseases) will not result when the water is consumed or used in other ways.

There are many ways to disinfect water. Earlier in this section, it was explained that storage, clarification and filtration all reduce the organisms in water. Boiling is a simple and effective method for disinfection. Sometimes, when water supplies have been contaminated, householders are requested to boil the tap water before using.

On the commercial scale, water supplies can be disinfected by, for example, the use of chlorine, chlorine dioxide or ozone.

Chlorine is extremely toxic. The way in which chlorine kills bacteria in water is not well understood. However, the action is extremely effective and so chlorine is commonly used for disinfection. Chlorine is normally a gas but is liquefied under pressure and stored in containers. The chlorination process is effected by injection of known quantities of this material into water under very carefully controlled conditions.

Note that swimming pools are also disinfected by chlorination, and most of us are familiar with the well-known smell of swimming pools. Chlorine is also present in ordinary household bleach, which is used for disinfection on a small scale.

Ozone is a highly reactive gas composed from three oxygen atoms (O_3), whereas the normal oxygen we breathe is made from two atoms (O_2). Ozone is an extremely efficient disinfectant. Its use is more expensive than chlorination but ozone has the advantage that fewer unwanted residuals remain in the water after the disinfection process.

> **Self-assessment task 3.50**
>
> Water from a certain river is to be used for public consumption. Briefly explain the various stages of treatment which result in a suitable supply.

Conclusion to Unit 3

There is no doubt that nineteenth- and twentieth-century science has revolutionised developments in the built environment. The use of science helps to improve our internal and external environments and provides better materials for our buildings. Understanding the science of water is helping to produce plentiful amounts of suitable water for consumption. Our electrical energy supply, which is so often taken for granted, has become available as a result of scientific enquiry, knowledge and, of course, curiosity.

Further reading

Useful further reading relating to the environmental science component of this unit:

McMullan R 1998 *Environmental Science in Building* (4th edition) Macmillan
Smith B J, Phillips G M and Sweeney M E 1983 *Environmental Science* Longman
Burberry P 1997 *Environment and Services* (8th Edition) Longman

Useful further reading more closely relating to the materials component of this unit:

Everett A 1994 *Materials* (5th edition) Longman
Lyons A R 1997 *Materials for Architects and Builders: An Introduction* Arnold
Taylor G D 2000 *Materials in Construction* (3rd edition) Longman

Structures, Construction Technology and Services

Des Millward

A glance backwards in time will show that buildings have been constructed in many shapes and sizes, and by using a variety of construction methods and materials (Fig. 4.1). The purpose for which a building was built was as varied as the method employed to build it. What is common to all those buildings is the fact that they had to be structurally safe and that all, in some way, would create an internal environment which had modified the external climate.

Present day building forms have evolved from practices and lessons learnt from the past. The particular behaviour of structures and the methods used to enclose or clad them have enabled designers, those responsible for the construction of buildings, and building users to develop a better more informed understanding of how a building performs throughout its life.

Further changes to the internal climate beyond that created by the external structure have become increasingly possible and sophisticated with installation and development of building services. Warm, healthy and hygienic spaces allow the occupants of buildings to enjoy controlled environments whatever the weather or building use.

This unit uses these themes to introduce the reader to the following:

- the different types of building elements
- the intended functions of the major building elements
- the form of the major building elements, including structural members and building services
- judging how well building elements perform their task

These themes will be described and explored thus providing an understanding of how the basic needs of structural stability, shelter and environmental comfort are met by buildings. The unit also has direct links with the other mandatory units, particularly those of Science and Materials, and Design. It will also provide a suitable base for further study of units in the progression routes, and related optional units.

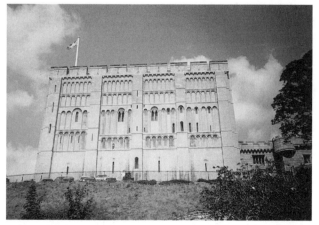

Figure 4.1 Buildings over the ages

4.1 Performance of building structure

Before discussing in greater depth the requirements of a building it is important that we understand what is meant by the term 'structure'. A structure can be defined as a **system for transferring loads from one place to another**. Designers would therefore expect certain features from a structure. These include:

- the building is capable of carrying its own dead weight
- foundations should remain stable under load
- excessive wind forces should not cause the building to collapse
- walls, floors, and roofs should not deflect unduly when loaded
- building frameworks should not deform, resisting excessive movement
- the building should be able to resist excessive movement

All building structures have to carry loads. What is important is how the structure will react to various types of load acting on different parts of the structure. Initially the strength of a building should allow it to carry loads without failure of the construction.

Types of load

The **primary loads** (Fig. 4.2), which a building has to carry and be strong enough and stiff enough to resist, are:

- dead loads
- imposed or live loads
- snow load
- wind load

Dead loads

Dead load is the sum of the weight of all the parts of the building, which are permanent and stationary. This includes such items as walls, beams, columns and floor slabs. To these may be added the weight of non-structural elements such as service pipes, suspended ceilings and floor finishes. Certain items of permanent machinery such as lifts, escalators and air conditioning equipment also fall within the definition of dead loads.

Imposed loads

Imposed loads are those loads which act on a structure during its use. These loads include items such as people, furniture, portable machinery, cars and food. Imposed loads may be sub-divided into **imposed floor loads** and **imposed roof loads**. British Standard 6399: 1984 Part 1 and Part 3 respectively provide typical loadings, which can be used as a benchmark for calculation purposes.

Snow loads

Snow that collects and rests on a roof can add a considerable load, which the roof structure has to carry. Location of the building is important when considering snow loads, the volume of snow being dependent upon the latitude and altitude of the building. The amount of snow being carried on the roof is also influenced by the pitch or steepness of the roof slope.

Wind loads

Wind loads can act on a building structure from many directions and can produce **positive pressure** or pushing and **negative pressure** or suction on different areas of the same building (Fig. 4.3). Lightweight structures such as framed buildings with cladding units are most at risk not only from possible instability and collapse, but also from uplift forces on roofs.

In addition there are other types of loads which do not fit into the previous categories, common ones being those of pressures from liquids and soils, which are important when

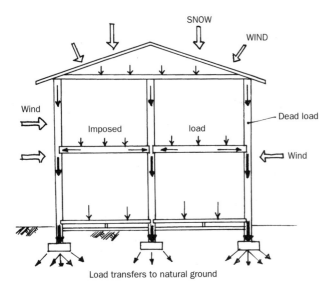

Figure 4.2 Loads on a building

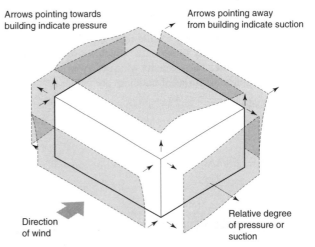

Figure 4.3 Pressure and suction due to wind. (*After* Foster & Harington 1993 *Structure and Fabric* Part 2, Addison Wesley Longman)

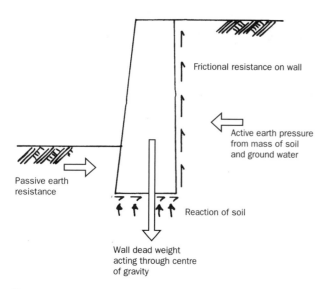

Figure 4.4 Forces acting on a retaining wall

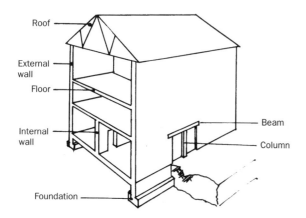

Figure 4.5 Elements of a building

constructing retaining walls (Fig. 4.4). Structures may also be subjected to more specialised **secondary loads**. In simple structures these are unlikely to cause a problem and are:

- temperature change
- shrinkage of members
- settlement of supports
- dynamic loads

Both primary and secondary loads have to be carried or resisted by the **elements** of a building (Fig. 4.5). Elements are able to resist and carry these loads, which assist the structure to fulfil its purpose. The **elements** which carry structural loads and are used in most forms of buildings are:

- foundations
- walls
- floors
- roofs
- structural frameworks (normally steel or concrete)

Requirements of building structures

Structural elements need to possess sufficient strength to resist pushing, pulling, and twisting forces. In order for a structure

to maintain its stability it will require sufficient bracing or stiffness to prevent toppling over or collapse. Reducing deflection of a floor, or the side sway of a building in order for it to function effectively will require adequate stiffness of the structure and its structural members. Therefore for a building structure to be considered a successful design it is essential that it fulfils strength, stability and functional requirements.

Early builders and designers had little knowledge of the characteristics of the materials that were used to construct buildings. They were not able to rely on mathematical calculations for determining the strength and size of structural members. Instead they relied rather more upon 'trial and error' methods, or knowledge which had been passed on from one generation of craftsmen to another. Inevitably this caused many structural failures of buildings, leaving the successful ones to stand as witness to the skill and intuition of those who designed and built them.

Today designers are more informed and are able to predict more accurately the behaviour of a building under a variety of loading conditions. The use of British Standard design codes has assisted greatly in this (Table 4.1), allowing designers to benefit from proven information to:

- increase safety standards
- use materials economically
- apply design criteria in a consistent way
- use standardised structural sections
- justify designs for statutory approval

Table 4.1 Principal British Standard Design Codes

Code	Title
BS 6399 : Part 1: 1984	Design loadings for buildings
BS 6399 : Part 3: 1988	Design loading for roofs
BS 648 : 1964 CP3: Chap V:	Schedule of weights of building materials
BS 648: Part 2: 1972	Wind loads
BS 5950: Part 1: 1990	Structural use of steelwork in building
BS 5268: Part 2: 1991	Structural use of timber
BS 5268: Part 1: 1978	Structural use of masonry
BS 5950: Part 1: 1990	Structural use of steelwork in building
BS 8004: 1986	Foundations
BS 8110: Part 1: 1985	Structural use of concrete

Structural stresses

Structural engineers will need to estimate the forces acting on a structure and its component parts. This is so that all the structural elements remain stable under primary and secondary loads. In order to understand how structural stability can be achieved the behaviour of the components should be known. This behaviour will be influenced by:

- structural loads and external forces
- materials used
- size and position of the components
- structural connections between the components

These factors will influence the type of structural stress, which may be:

- compressive (Fig. 4.6a)
- tensile (Fig. 4.6b)

- shear (Fig. 4.6c)
- torsion (Fig. 4.6d)

The results of these stresses may be:

- buckling in vertical members - walls, columns
- cracking in horizontal members - beams, floor slabs
- failure of members - ties in roofs, beams
- twisting of members - columns, beams, girders
- movement or collapse of the structure

Compressive stress

Compressive stress is produced when a structural member is being compressed or squashed by the forces acting on it. Excessive compressive stress will tend to cause the crushing of a material. Typical members which have to resist compressive forces, are walls, struts and columns.

Tensile stress

When a structural member is being stretched by the forces acting upon it produces **tensile stresses**. Too much stretching can cause a member to fail. Concrete, for example, without any reinforcement is weak in tension, whereas steel possesses a greater ability to resist tensile stresses.

Shear stress

Sliding occurs or tends to occur as a result of an application of forces on a structural member in opposing directions. These forces create a sliding tendency, which results in **shear stress** in the material. The shear forces acting on a structural member can cause excessive shear stress leading to deformation or breaking of the member.

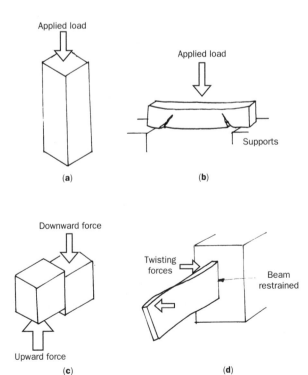

Figure 4.6 Types of structural stress (a) compressive; (b) tensile; (c) shear; (d) torsion.

Torsion or twisting

When a structural member is being twisted by the forces acting on it the material is said to be in **torsion**. An increase in torsional stress to a point where it becomes excessive will cause a member to twist leading to eventual failure by breaking.

Bending moment

Any structure that is subjected to loads must be provided with supports to prevent it from moving (Fig. 4.7). The forces which are created on the structure by these supports are called **reactions**. If the requirement is that the structure does not move then it is said to be in a state of **equilibrium**. This is when the net forces from the loads and reactions must be zero in all directions.

When a beam is placed under load it will have a tendency to deflect or bend (Fig. 4.8) until the beam's own internal forces balance the applied external load. This will lead to **bending stresses** causing the horizontal fibres to change in length. The top fibres become shorter being in compression and the bottom fibres become longer being in tension. Compression and tension are zero at the centre of the beam which is called the **neutral axis**.

In structural work the turning effect of a force is called the **moment of a force**. The turning effect or the moment of a force depends on the magnitude of the force and its distance from a turning point (Fig. 4.9). It is measured by multiplying the force by its distance from the turning point.

A moment of force that results in bending is known as a **bending moment**. Using a formula it is possible to calculate beam sizes and shapes that are capable of resisting bending moments. Fig. 4.10 shows a simply supported beam. If the beam is loaded at its mid-point bending will occur. This will cause bending in clockwise tendency to the left of the beam, and an anti-clockwise moment to the right of the beam. This will cause 'sagging' or bending of the beam in the centre.

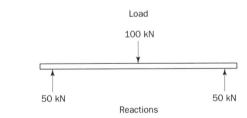

Figure 4.7 Beam in equilibrium

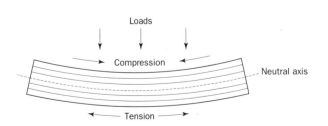

Figure 4.8 Bending moments in a beam

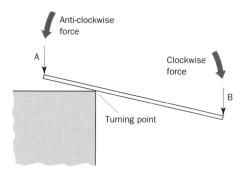

Figure 4.9 Moment of a force

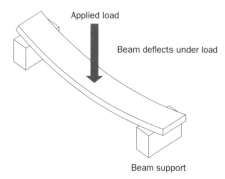

Figure 4.10 Simply supported beam

Strength and stiffness

Strength and stiffness are important properties when considering the suitability of a material for use in a structure. The strength of a material controls the determination of the collapse load of a structure. Stiffness is vital to ensuring that a structure will not deflect too much under load. It is also related to collapse as it controls the buckling load, which can lead to failure of members in compression.

Some building materials are **elastic**. This means that when they are stretched or shortened by a force they will revert immediately to their original dimensions when the force is removed. This is based on the assumption that the force is not too great.

When a load is applied to a beam it will deflect. If, when the load is removed, the beam reverts to its original position it will be behaving elastically (Fig. 4.11). This will happen no matter how many times the load is applied. Structural members in buildings are expected to behave in an elastic way, which means that no permanent deformation will be caused by the original design loads.

If the beam did not return to its original shape after a load has been applied and removed then **plastic deformation** is said to have taken place. Each time further load is applied to the beam an increase in plastic deformation will occur until it reaches a point where the beam will fail. This breaking point is called the **ultimate breaking point** of the material.

A property of an elastic material is that **stress** is proportional to **strain**. Strain is a measure of how much each millimetre length of the material deforms under stress. It is therefore related to the **stiffness** of the material rather than its strength. Strain, whose units are dimensionless, can be expressed as:

$$\text{strain} = \frac{\text{change in length}}{\text{original length}}$$

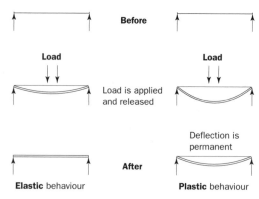

Figure 4.11 Elastic and plastic beam behaviour

It is possible for members to have internal and external forces. External forces result from applied loads and internal forces are produced in structural members because of applying the loads. Internal forces cause **stress**.

$$\text{stress} = \frac{\text{force}}{\text{cross-sectional area}} \text{ N/mm}^2$$

If stress is proportional to strain then for any given material stress divided by strain will be a constant. This produces a constant, which determines how much strain occurs for a given stress and is known as the '**modulus of elasticity**' (**E**) or **Young's modulus.**

$$E = \frac{\text{stress}}{\text{strain}} \text{ N/mm}^2$$

From the above

$$\text{strain} = \frac{\text{stress}}{E}$$

It can be seen that materials with high E values will have relatively small strains and can be described as **stiff**. If a material has a high E value it will be difficult to stretch or shorten it, and conversely a small value of E makes it easier to stretch or shorten it. Some typical E values are shown in Table 4.2.

Table 4.2 Typical modulus of elasticity (E) values

Material	Modulus of elasticity (N/mm^2)
Mild steel	205 000
High yield steel	200 000
Concrete	28 000
Softwood	7 000
Hardwood	12 000
Engineering brickwork	20 000
Aluminium alloy	70 000

Permissible or working stresses

In order to produce structures that will remain stable under design loads it is necessary to know the **permissible or working stresses** of materials. These have been based on figures for the **ultimate or failing strength** of materials, and will allow the size of structural members to be determined to resist compression, tension and shear, for example.

Permissible stresses are lower than the stress that would allow structural members to fail. In other words this creates a safety margin or **factor of safety**. Designers must ensure that the permissible stress is not exceeded at any point in the structure. This allows for compensation for errors in both loading and material strength.

Clearly the value of the factor of safety must be greater than 1 in order to prevent collapse of members or a structure. The magnitude of the factor depends upon the predictability of loading and material properties. Factors can range from 1.5 to 5.5.

Structural members

Concrete floors and slabs

Concrete is weak in tension and strong in compression. When used to form a ground floor slab it is supported from the ground, which reduces to an acceptable minimum the tensile stresses. In order that the floor remains stable it is cast on a bed of hardcore over the compressible topsoil. The slab will usually have a damp-proof membrane placed between it and the hardcore, or between oversite concrete and the floor screed (Fig.. 4.12) to prevent rising moisture entering the floor slab.

Concrete floors possess advantages of strength and fire resistance over timber suspended floors. In addition they also offer good resistance to airborne sound. This makes them particularly useful in most forms of multi-storey construction.

The simplest concrete floor is the **one-way spanning** slab between main beam supports (Fig. 4.13). It can be thought of as a large beam which when uniformly loaded will deflect in a similar manner, with bending and shear stresses (though these are minimal) being similar (Fig. 4.14). The floor is reinforced in one direction only by **main reinforcing bars**, which span the shortest distance. However, when floors are cast on site in one concrete pour, secondary stresses may cause cracks to occur due to temperature changes in the concrete and shrinkage.

In order to control and distribute these secondary stresses **distribution steel** is used. This steel does not carry any of the

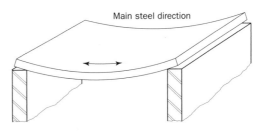

Figure 4.13 One way spanning slab

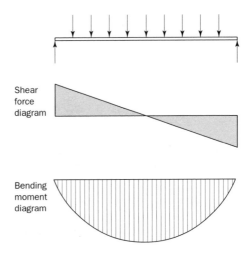

Figure 4.14 Sheer force and bending moment diagram

bending stresses, these being carried by the main reinforcing steel. This has the effect of forming a grid of reinforcement. Manufacturers can produce reinforcement meshes which are capable of resisting stresses in a floor slab.

Rectangular floor slabs are most likely to be considered as one-way spanning whereas square slabs are often **two-way spanning** (Fig. 4.15). Two spanning slabs are designed so that the main reinforcement spans in two directions with both sets of steel calculated to resist bending stresses. These floors are used where there is a need for larger spans or heavy loadings to be accommodated.

As the span of a flat slab floor increases so does the slab thickness, which in turn increases the overall building dead load. One-way spanning slabs are economical where spans do not exceed 5.00 m; floors with spans beyond this are designed to be hollow and therefore lighter in weight. Some typical examples of how this is achieved with one- and two-way spanning floors are shown in Fig. 4.16.

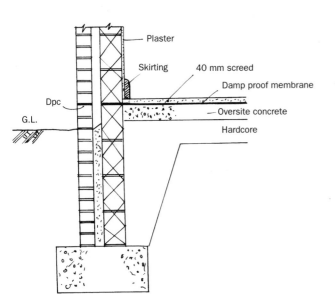

Figure 4.12

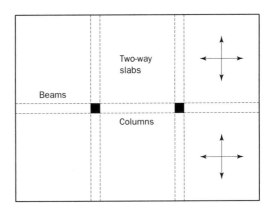

Figure 4.15

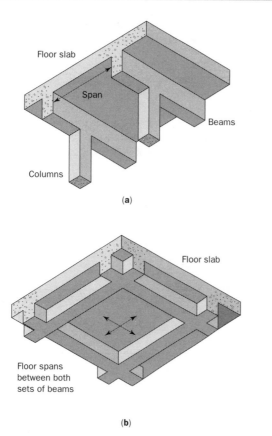

(a)

(b)

Figure 4.16 Floor spans: (a) one way spanning; (b) two way spanning

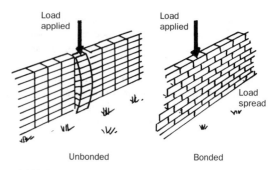

Figure 4.17 Bonding of brickwork

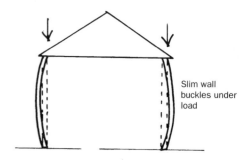

Figure 4.18 Buckling of brickwork

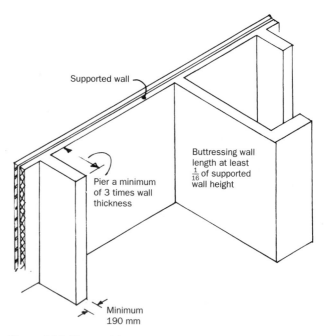

Figure 4.19 Piers and buttresses

Load-bearing walls

Walls are formed from bricks, blocks or stone and have to resist compressive stresses caused by dead and live loads. These stresses are resisted by the density of the materials used and by **bonding** the courses together (Fig. 4.17). Bonding allows the compression loads to be better distributed throughout the wall.

Cement mortar is used to allow the bricks to be laid and positioned to the correct alignment, and to take up any dimensional variations in the bricks. The mortar should not be stronger than the materials with which it is used to prevent their premature failure through cracking under load.

Compressive strengths of bricks range from 3.5 to $70 \, \text{N/mm}^2$ and concrete blocks from 2.8 to $35 \, \text{N/mm}^2$. The mean compressive strength of mortars ranges from 1.0 to $16 \, \text{N/mm}^2$.

As the length of a wall increases vertically between its supports, failure due to **buckling** is likely to occur (Fig. 4.18). This is due to the lack of stiffness in the wall, which will allow bending to occur, and introduces tensile stresses. The greater the height of the wall, the more the relationship of its height to its thickness increases in importance. This relationship is known as the **slenderness ratio**. As the ratio increases, the load carrying capacity of a wall and its stability decrease.

Increasing the stability of a wall by making it thicker is uneconomical in terms of the use of materials, and in addition it will increase the loading on the ground. **Lateral stability** can be provided by several means:

- piers
- buttresses
- lateral support from floors and roofs

Piers are columns of masonry which increase the thickness of the wall. They may also support the ends of beams.

Buttresses are built at right angles to a wall and may be formed by internal walls or returning external walls (Fig. 4.19). The buttresses are placed at predetermined intervals and will resist the wall's tendency to overturn. Walls may also derive **lateral support** from internal floors and the roof provided that an adequate connection is made. Figure 4.20 shows support from timber on a floor and roof.

Lintels and arches

Where doors, windows and other forms of openings are placed in walls they must not be allowed to carry the structural load. Two methods (Fig. 4.21) may be used to carry and divert the load:

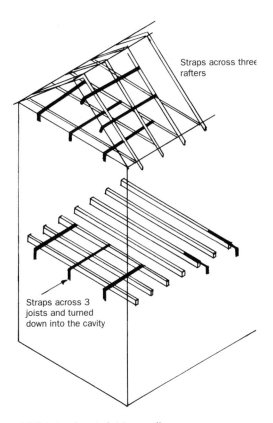

Straps across three rafters

Straps across 3 joists and turned down into the cavity

Figure 4.20 Lateral restraint to a wall

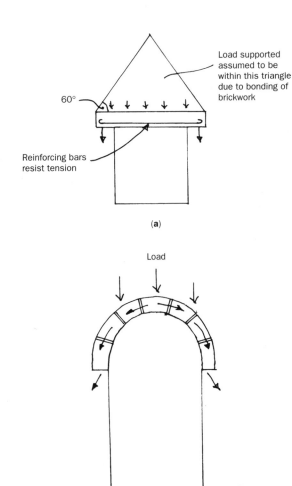

Load supported assumed to be within this triangle due to bonding of brickwork

60°

Reinforcing bars resist tension

(a)

Load

(b)

Figure 4.21 Brickwork load transmission

- lintels
- arches

Lintels are a form of beam, which span across an opening and provide support for the wall above. They are able to resist compressive and tensile stresses and are therefore able to transfer the structural load from the wall above to the wall at the sides of the opening. The lintels may be concrete, steel, pressed steel (Fig. 4.22) or a combination of materials.

In order to maintain the stability of lintels in use they need to have a bearing on the supporting structures at each end of at least 100 mm rising to 225 mm for lintels covering larger spans.

Door and window head openings are a potential source for moisture to penetrate through to the internal wall of a building. To overcome this the lintel should be manufactured from a material that is naturally moisture-resistant and has a profile that conducts cavity moisture to the external face of a building. Such a lintel made from pressed steel, is shown in Fig. 4.22. If the lintel is made from concrete then it is normal to include a damp-proof course on top of the lintel to assist in resisting moisture penetration.

In order to maintain the structural integrity of the wall when it suffers a fire, lintels should be able to resist the effects of heat for minimum periods. Concrete provides its own natural fire protection subject to minimum distances of concrete cover to the steel reinforcement. Steel lintels will require additional protection that can be provided by:

- encasement in concrete
- spraying with a fire-retardant finish
- plasterboard and skim coat
- other fire-retardant manufactured boards

Arches are created by using small units of brick or stone and are laid to a profile. If an arch is to fulfil its function it will need to be restrained by vertical flanking walls. These prevent the arch from spreading and allow the material from which it is made to remain in compression, thus allowing materials which are weak in tension to bridge openings (Fig. 4.23).

Beams

Beams play a major part in the construction work. In the broadest interpretation they support floors and roofs, assist in forming and stiffening frameworks, and create bridges and towers. Materials from which beams may be manufactured are:

- structural timber
- structural steel
- reinforced concrete

Beams are structural members that become subject to bending due to a load being carried by them. Bending causes curvature

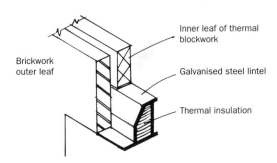

Brickwork outer leaf

Inner leaf of thermal blockwork

Galvanised steel lintel

Thermal insulation

Figure 4.22 Steel lintel in a cavity wall

Figure 4.23 Brick arches

of the beam, and varies according to the method used to support the beam. Beams are normally used in a horizontal position with loads being inclined vertically downwards, though occasionally a beam can be installed in an inclined position.

Beams may be:

- simply supported
- cantilever
- simply supported and cantilever
- continuous (Fig. 4.24)

The size of a beam will vary and will be principally determined by the:

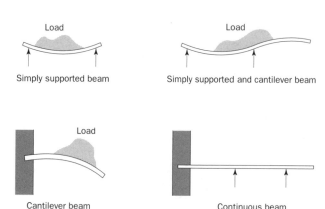

Figure 4.24 Beam supports

- material/s used for the beam
- span of the beam
- load the beam has to carry
- construction of the beam

Structural timber

Timber beams or joists

One of the simplest and earliest beams used by early builders was one made from wood. Early examples were whole branches or trunks of trees, but eventually timber trunks were converted into smaller section sizes. The usefulness of timber as a beam is limited by its structural strength, the distance it has to span, and the load it has to carry.

Beams of a rectangular cross-section size are common in timber. In order to resist bending the beam is used with the deepest dimension possible. This can be wasteful of solid timber and so beams can be fabricated by laminating timber together, and by forming box beams – the latter two forms being capable of carrying higher loadings and spanning larger distances (Fig. 4.25). Laminated timber sections can also be used to form portal frames.

A variety of softwoods are available for structural use in buildings. They behave elastically, and are good in tension, bending and shear. It is normal for designers to specify timber by strength and therefore **stress-graded timber** is used. Stress grading is easily carried out by machine, which measures the strength and stiffness of a piece of timber. There are four machine grades:

- M75 75% free of structural defects
- MSS special structural
- M50 50% free of defects
- MGS general structural

Structural steel

Structural steel is the product of controlled removal of carbon from cast iron, and therefore the strength of steel is determined by the carbon content. The larger the percentage

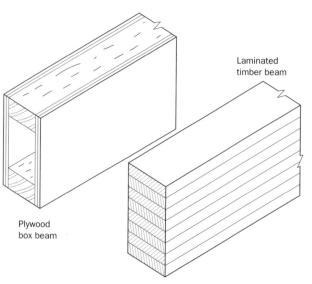

Figure 4.25 Types of timber beam

of carbon the higher the strength. Steels used for structural purposes contain up to 0.30% carbon.

A range of steel suitable for structural work is available in three basic grades:

- grade 43   mild steel
- grade 50 ⎫
- grade 55 ⎭ high strength steels

Each grade number represents the approximate minimum tensile strength of the steel. Fire causes steel to have a rapid loss of strength beyond a temperature of 250°C. At a temperature of 550°C the yield strength is reduced to two thirds of the normal, which virtually eliminates any safety factors.

Universal beams and columns

If red hot steel is passed through a series of rolling mills different cross-sectional profiles can be produced (Fig. 4.26). The profiles have evolved over the years and present designers with an acceptable range of standard sizes for use in a wide range of structural applications.

Joists and universal beams cover a range of applications from lightly loaded short span beams in a range of buildings to concrete-decked bridges for motorway traffic. Universal columns are suitable for load-bearing stanchions in multi-storey buildings. Channels, angles and tees can be used individually or built up into compound members such as roof trusses or braced columns.

Hollow steel sections

The hollow sections are welded up from steel strip or plate depending upon the thickness. The resulting circular section can then be hot rolled to form square or rectangular sections (Fig. 4.27). These sections are ideally suited to situations

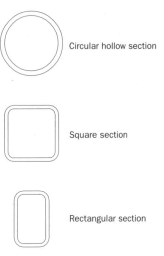

Figure 4.27 Hollow steel sections

where members are in compression and require good stiffness against buckling in all directions.

Castellated beam

These are formed from a universal beam, column or joist sections by slicing the web horizontally in the factory in a zigzag fashion and then welding the sections together. The depth of the beam may be further increased by adding a further plate into the web. This allows economy in the use of materials whilst letting them carry heavier loads than would be possible with the initial steel member. A further advantage is that building services can pass through the perforated web without affecting the performance of the beam.

Structural concrete

Mass concrete is strong in compression, but its shear and tensile strengths are low, its compressive stress being at least ten times its tensile strength. Therefore if a concrete beam, column or floor slab were made of plain concrete it would fail under lightly loaded conditions.

Steel bars called **reinforcement** are strong in compression, tension and shear and are therefore added to concrete to resist the shear and tensile stresses (Table 4.3). In order to resist these stresses efficiently the reinforcement must be placed in the concrete where the stresses are highest. It is normal practice for the steel to be placed to provide a minimum of 20 mm of concrete cover, which also assists in providing fire resistance.

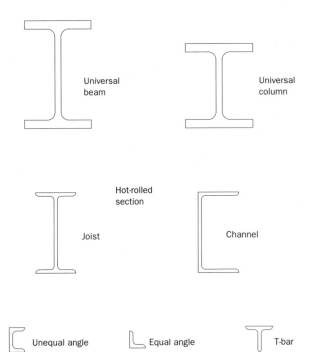

Figure 4.26 Steel profiles

Table 4.3 Types of reinforcement

Type	British Standard	Minimum yield stress (N/mm^2)
Plain round hot rolled mild steel	BS 4449	250
Hot rolled deformed (high bond)		460[a]
High yield stress bars	BS 4449	425[b]
Cold worked bars	BS 4461	460[a], 425[b]
Fabric hard drawn steel wire to BS 4482	BS 4483	485[c]

[a] Diameter not greater than 16 mm
[b] Diameter greater than 16 mm
[c] Diameter not greater than 12 mm

Structural concrete members may be manufactured on or off the building site. When the concrete members are made on site it is often referred to as **'in-situ'** concrete, and when brought to the site from a manufacturing plant is known as **'precast'** concrete. Whichever method is used reinforcement is still required. It should be noted that precast concrete would have additional areas of local reinforcement purely to resist stresses placed on the concrete caused through lifting and transporting the members to their final positions on site.

Beams

Concrete beams can be supported in similar positions to those illustrated in Fig. 4.24. In order for the beam to function effectively **tension reinforcement** is placed in the positions shown in Fig. 4.28. In a simply supported beam concrete would fail in tension at the bottom of the beam. The reinforcement is therefore placed below the neutral axis (Fig. 4.29) to take the tensile stresses, whilst the concrete above the neutral axis resists the compressive stresses.

Concrete beams will fail in shear near to support positions through diagonal tensile stresses. To resist these stresses **shear steel** in the form of inclined bars or vertical stirrups, or combination of the two, is used (Fig. 4.30)

When concrete beams are used in multi-storey frames they are classified either as **main beams** or **secondary beams**.

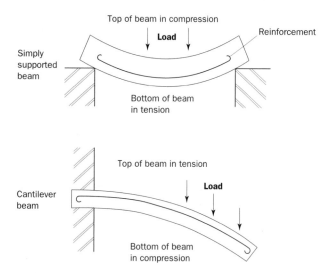

Figure 4.28 Tension steel in beams

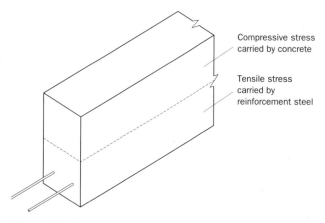

Figure 4.29 Simple beam reinforcement

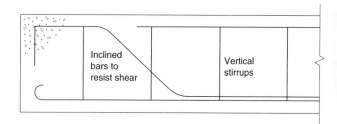

Figure 4.30 Shear reinforcement in a concrete beam

Secondary beams transmit floor loads to the main beams, which in turn transmit those loads to the columns and down to the foundations.

Columns

Columns are mainly subjected to compressive stress, the magnitude of the stress varying with the layout of the building, its use, and the position of a column. Where possible, columns are kept to uniform sizes. The load on a column decreases the higher up the building frame it is located. Consequently the amount of steel reinforcement will also decrease.

Concrete columns can fail either by crushing or buckling. In general fat short columns will fail by crushing and tall slender columns by buckling. The mechanism by which a column fails will depend upon whether it is a **short** or **long column** (Fig. 4.31), which in turn depends on the **slenderness ratio**. This ratio is a measure of the effective slenderness of the column and is:

$$\text{slenderness ratio} = \frac{\text{effective length or height}}{\text{least lateral dimension}}$$

The effective length will vary according to how the column is fixed at the top and bottom. The least lateral dimension refers to the smallest cross-sectional dimension of column's rectangular section.

Rectangular columns are described as short when the height to minimum width ratio is less than 15 if its top is restrained against lateral movement, and less than 10 if unrestrained. Most concrete columns in buildings are classified as short for buckling purposes.

Columns must always have a minimum specified area of reinforcement, and be provided with lateral links encompassing the main bars (Fig. 4.32). The minimum permitted area of cross-sectional steel is 0.8% of the total area of the cross-section of the column, and the maximum

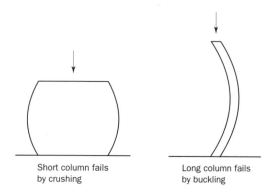

Figure 4.31 Short and long columns

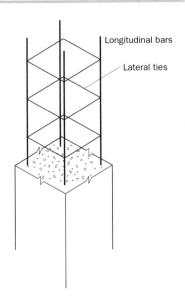

Figure 4.32 Column reinforcement

permitted area is 8%. This steel will assist in resisting any tensile stresses caused by buckling.

Roofs

Common roof forms are flat and pitched. Both must carry:

- their own self-weight
- wind load
- snow load
- applied roof coverings
- other imposed loads

Whichever roof form is used, it is necessary to reduce the dead load to a minimum to enable the imposed load to be carried with the greatest material economy. Low deadweight is important because the live or superimposed load is relatively small. Where the roof's own deadweight is less than the live weight then the structure is inefficient. This is because the roof would primarily be designed to carry its own weight rather than the load imposed on it. The smaller the deadweight is in relation to the live load, the more efficient and economic the structure. This is called the **dead/live ratio**.

In addition, the **strength/weight ratio** is also important. This relates the weight of a material to its strength, and is an indication of the efficiency of the material in terms of the weight required to fulfil the structural function. A high strength/weight ratio indicates a high level of efficiency because it denotes that a low weight of material is required to fulfil a particular structural function.

Any roof will need to be designed to span between supports. These may be walls, columns or beams. Where buildings are small or subdivided into small areas, or where columns are at reasonably close intervals, a light economic roof structure can be used. In most multi-storey buildings flat roofs similar in construction to suspended floors can be used. Where the span between supports is large the roof structure must be designed to be free spanning.

The supporting structure for flat roofs can consist of beams or roof joists made from timber, steel or concrete. A combination of realistic spacing of the joists and roof coverings, which are profiled and self-supporting, will produce a roof of relatively low deadweight. Alternatively it may be necessary to introduce purlins, which span between and on top of the joist positions to carry the roof decking material.

Pitched roofs will require careful thought with respect to the structural support. Portal and shed frame roof structures are illustrated in Figs 4.33 and 4.34. Shed frames rely on a triangulated frame or roof truss to be the structural load-bearing member (Fig. 4.35). Steel roof trusses may be welded or bolted (Fig. 4.36) together.

Roof rafters are prevented from spreading by being fixed firmly at the foot, and rigidity to the truss is provided by bracing from **struts** and **ties**. The trusses are joined together by purlins, which are designed as simply supported beams. Their purpose is to carry the enclosing roof sheeting and associated wind loads. **Wind bracing** may be necessary between the bays of the trusses or portal frames.

Steel roof trusses normally sit bolted onto mild steel plates on the top of columns. If the building structure is brickwork then brick piers will have been built with a concrete pad stone on the top to carry the load down to the foundation.

Pitched roof structures on houses and similar short-span structures are often fabricated from timber to form **trussed rafters** (Fig. 4.37). The trusses are spaced at 600 mm centres. Tile battens to the rafters carry the load of the roof covering firstly, and then the truss transmits the roof loads to a wall plate. This is bedded in mortar on top of the inner leaf of the wall in order to spread the load evenly. Galvanised steel straps fastened to the wall assist stability at the wall plate position.

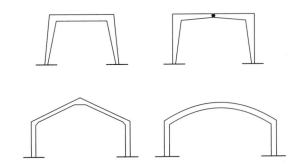

Figure 4.33 Types of portal frame

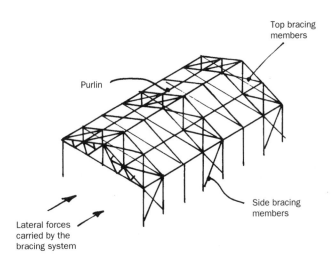

Figure 4.34 Steel roof turn with purlins and bracing

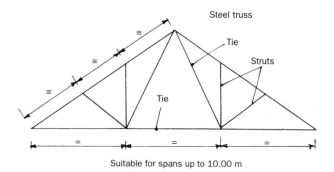

Figure 4.35 Triangulated roof frame

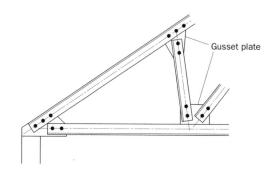

Figure 4.36 Bolted turns using gusset plates

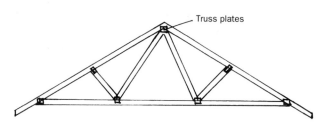

Figure 4.37 Trussed rafter

Self-assessment tasks

1. Within your locality identify a domestic residence, a factory and an educational establishment.
   (i) In each case list the various loads which each building would have to carry or resist.
   (ii) Produce simple sketches to show how the structural loads are transmitted to the earth.
2. Prepare a discussion paper on how timber, steel and concrete beams resist point loads.
3. Describe with the aid of sketches the effect of structural loads on:
   - suspended floors
   - external walls
   - columns
4. Describe how structural loads are carried around openings in walls, clearly explaining how moisture penetration is prevented.
   Describe how loads are carried in roof frameworks, clearly explaining the purpose of:
   - ties
   - struts
   - braces
   - wind bracing
   - joints

4.2 Performance of building elements

Building elements

Buildings are made up from a series of parts, which are called **elements** (Fig 4.5). Elements are able to resist and carry different types of loads which assist the building to fulfil its purpose. The **primary elements** used in most forms of buildings are:

- foundations
- walls
- floors
- roofs
- frames

The **loads** (Fig 4.2) that one or more of these elements have to resist are:

- wind
- snow
- dead
- imposed

Major dead loads will include the self-weight of the building structure and be made up of the load from the materials forming the primary elements. Imposed loads are a mixture of dead and live loads. Live loads can include people, and dead loads will include furniture, movable partitions and other equipment.

Designers know that certain things are expected of a building. These include:

- foundations should not sink into the ground
- the building should not fall down
- excessive movement should not occur
- floors should not deflect an undue amount
- roofs should not be blown off by the wind
- frames should not deform
- temperatures should be maintained

Limits and conditions can be applied to each of these to suit particular circumstances, according to the type of building and its structural form. In other words, the design will meet certain criteria for stated conditions. These criteria will in turn determine the structural **performance** of a building in use. Other criteria will be applied to the internal requirements.

In order to satisfy these performance criteria designers will need to relate the use of the building, the type of structure, and the materials used to each other. This in turn will affect the stability of a building. The appearance or aesthetics of the building may also need consideration. This is more so in the case of domestic properties and offices, though new cladding materials combined with different types of structural frames for industrial buildings can produce interesting profiles and colourful exteriors.

Factors that will affect the materials used to form the elements of a building are:

- loads to be carried
- height and length of walls

- clear span of roofs or floors
- degree of fire resistance required
- weatherproofing requirements
- aesthetics
- type of roof structure

Performance requirements define the functional requirements of building elements and components in order that the duty of each in particular circumstances can be clearly stated. This will then allow the selection of the most suitable construction method using the most appropriate materials and technological methods.

Whilst the elements that form the substructure and superstructure are described separately it must be remembered that the sum of all their performances will affect how users determine whether a building meets their needs. These requirements are shown collectively in Fig 4.38.

Substructure

The substructure is that part of the building situated below the damp-proof course (DPC). Its purpose is to transfer the dead and imposed loads of the superstructure to the ground. Essential parts of the **substructure** are the **foundations** and the **ground floor**.

Foundations

Foundations perform an important function in buildings. Their function is to carry the loads of the building and distribute them over the ground in such a way that movement of the building is minimal. Different types of foundations are used according to:

- building load
- structural form of the building
- type of subsoil

Foundations are constructed by using either mass or reinforced concrete. Mass concrete is used where the ground is able to support the foundation and prevent tensile stresses from causing movement or failure through shear. Two broad classifications for foundations are:

- shallow
- deep

For economic reasons shallow foundations should be used where possible unless the situation demands otherwise. The following foundation types have been described earlier:

- strip foundations
- pad foundations
- raft foundations
- short bored pile

Table 4.4 indicates the suitability of foundation types to soil and site conditions.

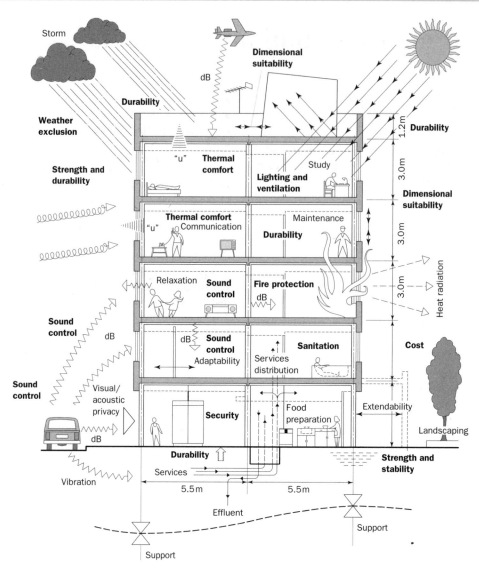

Figure 4.38 Performance requirements for a building. (*After* Osbourn 1997 *Introduction to Building*, Addison Wesley Longman)

Table 4.4 Choice of foundation type in accordance with soil and site conditions

Soil and site conditions	Possible type of foundation
Rock or solid chalk, sand and gravels	Shallow strips or pads
Firm stiff clay with little vegetation liable to cause shrinkage or swelling	Strips 1 m below ground level or piles with ground beam
Firm stiff clay with trees close to the building	Trench fill or piles and ground beam
Firm stiff clays where trees have recently been felled and the ground is still absorbing moisture	Reinforced piles or thin reinforced rafts in conjunction with a flexible building structure
Soft clays or soft silty clays	Wide strips; up to 1 m wide or rafts
Peat or sites consisting partly of imported soil	Piles driven down to a firm strata of subsoil
Where subsidence might be expected (e.g. mining districts)	Thin reinforced rafts

(*Source*: Ashcroft *Construction for Interior Designers* Addison Wesley Longman)

For the substructure to perform satisfactorily in use it should be able to:

- safely **transmit the dead and imposed loads** from a building to the ground such that movement is limited and the ground is not over-stressed;
- avoid damage from **swelling, shrinkage or freezing** of the subsoil;
- resist attack by **sulphates** or other harmful matter in the soil.

Stability of the substructure

The stability of the foundation and the associated structure up to the damp-proof course is subject to:

- the ground conditions
- the construction of the substructure

The way in which a subsoil behaves when it is under load can influence the behaviour of a foundation. Typical ground bearing capacities are shown in Table 4.5.

Table 4.5 Allowable bearing pressures

Classification	Bearing capacity (kN/m²)
Rocks	
Strong sandstone	4000
Schists	3000
Strong shale	2000
Granular soils	
Dense sand and gravel	>600
Medium dense gravel	200 to 600
Loose sand and gravel	<200
Compact sand	>300
Loose sand	<100
Cohesive soils	
Stiff boulder clay	300 to 600
Stiff clay	150 to 300
Firm clay	75 to 150
Soft clay and silt	<75

(*Adapted from*: Table 1, BS 8004: 1986; reproduced courtesy of BSI)

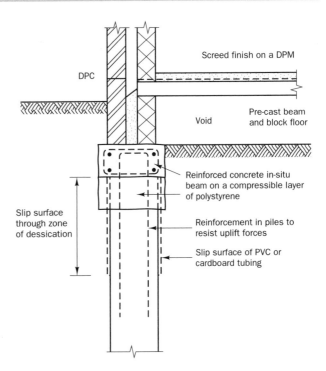

Figure 4.40 Pile and beam foundation to resist soil heave

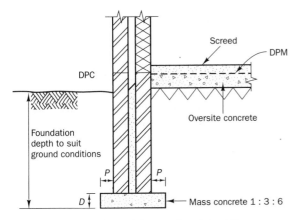

Depth *D* must be 150 mm minimum and must equal *P*.
P must be equal projection either side of the wall

Figure 4.39 Shallow strip foundation

In order to limit movement due to the ground shrinking and swelling because of climatic changes **strip foundations** are normally a minimum of 900 mm below ground level (Fig 4.39). Further precautions will be necessary when trees are close to foundation positions. **Short bored pile** (Fig 4.40) and **deep strip** foundations extend deeper and beyond the clay or compressible layers (Fig 4.41). **Raft foundations** are placed on the ground surface but their construction is such that they are able to accommodate shrinkage and swelling, subsidence and differential settlement (Fig 4.42). Failure of a strip foundation is shown in Fig 4.43

Load transmission and strength

Load transmission and strength of foundations relies on:

- quality of the concrete
- thickness of the foundation
- load-bearing ability of the ground
- type of building structure
- type of foundation

It is important to remember that with most types of foundation stability is increased when loads are placed centrally to the foundation to provide axial loading rather than eccentric loading.

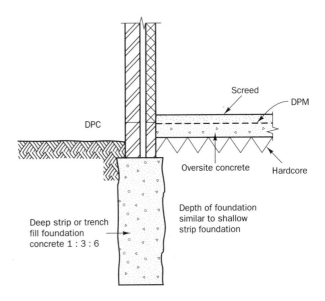

Figure 4.41 Deep strip foundation

Compatibility and durability

The successful performance of the foundation will depend upon the compatibility of the:

- foundation with the type of structure
- foundation with the ground load-bearing characteristics
- soil conditions with the foundation

The choice of foundation to match the structural load is an important one, as the transfer of the load must be effectively transmitted to the ground. Where the foundation is not matched, failure of the foundation through settlement or breaking up could be the result.

Where the ground load-bearing characteristics are known, for example a weak 2.0 m layer of soil near the surface, then deeper foundations will be required such as short bored piles to carry the load to a suitable load-bearing stratum. Again

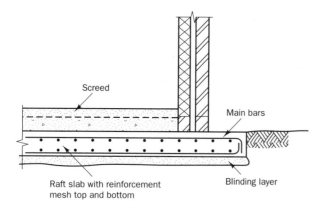

Figure 4.42 Thick reinforced concrete raft

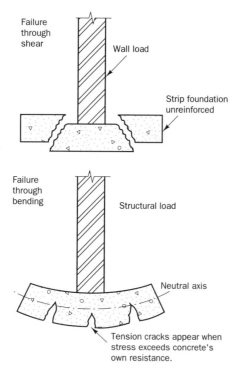

Figure 4.43 Failure of strip foundation in shear and bending

settlement of the foundation could result from an ill informed choice

Durability of foundations can be achieved by selecting and using the appropriate grade of concrete, and correctly constructing the foundation excavation. Dense concrete is the most widely used type of concrete for roof and floor slabs, foundations, lintels and structural frameworks. The density of the concrete will usually be in the range 2150–2500 kg/m³, with the 28-day compressive strength being between 15–60 N/mm². The proportion of cement to aggregate is usually expressed as cement : fine aggregate : coarse aggregate. Mixes of 1:3:6 are common for foundations and ground floor slabs, while mixes of 1:2:4 are used for general reinforced concrete work.

Concrete strength and durability also involves control of the water:cement ratio, too much water leading to the likelihood of the concrete being weak. Voids would be formed which would allow the concrete to be compressed under load. Voids could also be left if the concrete is not vibrated to remove pockets of air trapped while placing it. Generally water: cement ratios of 0.4 to 0.7 are adequate for most uses.

Foundation concrete and other materials used in the substructure construction must be able to carry the required loads without failure. Where the ground contains a sulphate that leads to deterioration and weakening of the foundation, appropriate **sulphate-resisting cement** should be used. Concrete made with this cement is more resistant to sulphate attack by the compounds which may be found dissolved in ground water, and which are present in seawater.

Self assessment tasks

1. What is the purpose of a foundation?
2. Why are different types of foundations needed?
3. As a result of your own research prepare a five-minute talk on the characteristics of clay soils.
4. Describe the factors that could cause a foundation to fail.
5. Explain how foundations can be constructed to resist the action of chemicals in the ground.

Ground floors

Floors are classed as **solid** or **suspended**. Solid ground floors are those that gain their support from the earth, and suspended are those floors that span between supports. Suspended floors may be at ground level or at intermediate levels within a building, for example in an office block or residential home.

Floors may be constructed from:

- timber beams or joists and sheet material as the decking or floor surface
- reinforced concrete
- concrete beams and infill blocks with a floor screed
- precast concrete floor panels with a floor screed

Whatever the type of floor construction used its ability to carry loads and resist excessive deflection is always required. In addition other properties such as fire, sound and thermal insulation may be needed.

The stability of a **suspended timber floor** will depend upon:

- its span
- the load/s
- depth of joists and their thickness
- spacing of the joists
- type and thickness of the covering forming the floor surface
- use and spacing of strutting
- timber species

Tables A1 and A2 in the Approved Document in the Building Regulations give guidance on acceptable spans for timber joists. These take into account the depth of the joist, which may have its **effective depth** reduced by notches and holes provided for building services if they are not within the restricted limits.

Some aspects of the **stability of timber floors** have been previously discussed. In addition to those points made there, suspended timber ground floors are able to gain intermediate support from sleeper walls that enable a reduction in the joist span and the size of the joist (Fig 4.44). Further stability is provided by the joists being built into the external and sleeper walls thus reducing the need for strutting.

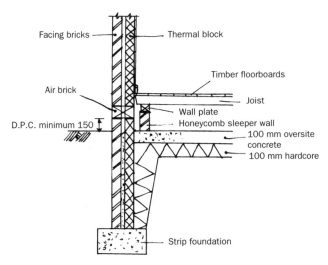

Figure 4.44 Suspended timber ground floor

Deterioration of ground floors can occur which in turn will affect their **durability**. To prevent this, damp-proof courses must be laid under all the joists where the wall is in direct contact with the ground, thus preventing a direct path for moisture to the timber. Ventilation of the air space in order to prevent dry rot is achieved by using **air bricks** and the intermediate honeycomb sleeper walls (Fig 4.44). Where joist ends are built into the wall a timber preservative should be used to prevent rotting.

Where external walls run parallel to internal floor joists **lateral support** can be provided. The support is in the form of galvanised mild steel straps of a minimum cross-section of 30 mm × 5 mm fixed across three joists at not less than 2 m centres (Fig 4.20). It is usually provided to properties not more than two storeys in height.

Concrete ground floors

Concrete is weak in tension and strong in compression. When used to form a **ground floor slab** it is supported from the ground, which reduces to a minimum the tensile stresses. In order that the floor remains stable it is cast on top of a bed of inert hardcore. This hardcore has replaced the topsoil which is a compressible material. The purpose of the damp-proof membrane (DPM) is to prevent the passage of ground moisture into the floor slab. It is essential this DPM be taken up to meet the DPC in the wall to prevent moisture bypassing the DPC (Fig 4.39).

Ground floors are required to meet **thermal insulation** requirements of the Approved Document L of the Building Regulations. The student is advised to refer to these for specific situations. Usually a **thermal transmittance** or *U* **value** of 0.35–0.45 W/m²K is required. The lower the *U* value, the less the heat transfer through the element or structure. Heat losses from ground floors are greatest at the perimeter as the heat flow to the external air is possible at this position. Little heat flow takes place from the centre of a ground floor as the ground itself acts as an insulator. It follows, therefore, that solid ground floors must have insulation along the edge of the slab as well as beneath it.

In certain parts of the country radon and methane gases are to be found in the ground. Radon is a naturally occurring radioactive gas, and methane occurs as a result of the concentration of gas from deposited decaying organic materials.

Where either of these gases is present it is common practice to use suspended precast concrete floors with provision for natural draught under-floor ventilation. The aim of using such ventilation is to minimise the gas concentration by dilution and, in conjunction with wire or fibre reinforced LDPE membranes, prevent the ingress of gases into the building.

Superstructure

The superstructure is normally taken to be that part of the building above the ground or the damp-proof course. Its purpose is to carry the loads imposed on the building as dead and live loads safely to the substructure, which then transmits them to the ground.

Elements of the superstructure include:

- walls, including door and window openings
- frames
- cladding
- floors
- roofs
- building services

Walls

Wall stability has been discussed previously; however the influence of the following on the wall should not be forgotten:

- type of materials used – brick, concrete, mortar
- construction of the wall – bonding, cavity ties
- design of the wall – slenderness ratio
- wall stiffening – piers, buttresses, lateral restraint ties
- type of load

External walls

Durability of walls is related to the degree of weather exposure they are subjected to in a particular location. The materials used to build walls are to some extent porous. The choice of brick and mortar is therefore important in order to minimise the amount of moisture entering the brickwork, which may then in turn become subject to frost action in winter (Table 4.6).

Bricks used for wall construction can be generally described as:

- commons – suited to general building work, with no special decorative effect
- facings – specially made or selected for an attractive appearance
- engineering – a brick which is dense and strong having well defined properties of strength and absorption, possessing low porosity levels

If moisture penetrates right through a wall it will cause the inner wall surface to exhibit varying degrees of dampness. Two major causes of dampness are moisture rising from the ground and rain penetration, followed by penetration around openings. Methods used to prevent moisture passing through or along an external 'wall' of a building are by:

Table 4.6 Performance requirements for external walls

Performance	Factors to consider
Stability	Type of foundation; brick/block types; bonding; solid or cavity construction; loading to be carried
Moisture resistance	Brick/block types; mortar; prevailing weather conditions; wall construction; openings; transmission routes; source of moisture; DPC/DPM positions; ground conditions
Sound insulation	Brick/block types; surrounding noise levels; openings and penetrations; wall construction; transmission routes; type of building structure
Thermal insulation	Brick/block types; surrounding temperature levels; openings and penetrations; wall construction; transmission routes; insulation techniques; U-value and Y-value
Fire resistance	Brick/block types; proximity of surrounding buildings; openings and penetrations; wall construction; fire risk; use of building or space

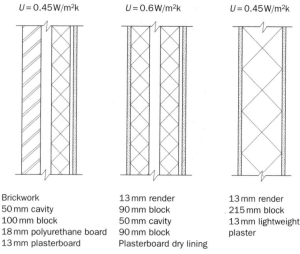

Brickwork
50 mm cavity
100 mm block
18 mm polyurethane board
13 mm plasterboard

13 mm render
90 mm block
50 mm cavity
90 mm block
Plasterboard dry lining

13 mm render
215 mm block
13 mm lightweight plaster

Figure 4.45 U-values of typical wall constructions

- providing a totally impervious barrier – glass in curtain walling, profiled steel or GRP sheeting
- providing a barrier that moisture cannot bridge – building walls with a cavity
- using impervious barriers in key positions – DPC around window and door openings

A **damp-proof course** (DPC) is used to prevent the passage of moisture from the ground up a brick wall (Fig 4.39). The DPC is placed at least 150 mm above ground level and in both leaves of a cavity wall. Damp-proof courses are also placed under copings on parapet walls and around door and window openings, and chimneys.

Fire resistance of walls involve two aspects:

- surface spread of flame
- inherent fire resistance of the wall

Ideally all materials should not assist with the spread of flame across their surface. Bricks have high non-combustible properties and are therefore Class O for surface spread of flame, meaning no spread will occur.

A wall's inherent fire resistance can fail when:

- the wall collapses under fire
- fire breaks through part of the wall
- heat insulation properties of the wall are destroyed

No material or form of construction is totally fireproof and therefore periods of fire resistance are quoted for specific building uses in specific situations. Minimum periods vary for load-bearing walls but range from 30 minutes to 120 minutes.

Internal walls may be required to be fire resistant, typical situations being:

- along designated fire escape routes
- protected shafts – lifts, staircases
- compartment walls between different use of spaces
- load-bearing walls

Thermal transmission through walls can be quite high because of the density of the materials used. The insulation value of a wall is measured by its **U-value**. The U-value is a measure of the thermal transmittance value of a building face, which is its rate of heat transfer through the construction from air to air. Typical constructions are shown in Fig 4.45. The lower the U-value the less the heat transfer through the wall. Currently a U-value of $0.45\,\mathrm{W/m^2K}$ is required for external walls.

This can be achieved by:

- careful selection of materials
- use of a cavity walls
- insulation in the cavity
- using thermal blocks on the inner leaf
- dry lining the internal leaf

Temperature swings inside buildings are affected by the **admittance or Y-value**. This is a property of an element or a room which controls inside temperature fluctuations. Small temperature swings are a result of a higher admittance value, and vice versa. Materials such as concrete, which is a dense material, have high admittance values, whereas less dense insulating materials will have lower values. Thus structures constructed of predominantly dense materials will have smaller temperature swings than lightweight structures.

Sound resistance of external walls does not normally present a problem unless a building is situated next to a major road, railway, airport or noisy industrial area. The use of dense materials, cavity walls with insulation, and double-glazing will assist. In severe locations it may be necessary for air conditioning to be installed to prevent noise through open windows.

Within the building, walls that separate semi-detached or terraced houses must be capable of keeping noise down between adjoining properties. Requirements vary according to the form of construction used so the Approved Document E to the Building Regulations should be consulted. Three typical methods used to control sound transmission are shown in Fig 4.46.

In simple situations where the mass of the wall is used to reduce airborne sound, the wall, including the finish, should have a density of $375\,\mathrm{kg/m^2}$, and concrete blocks or in-situ concrete a density of $415\,\mathrm{kg/m^2}$.

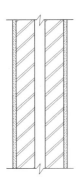

lightweight concrete blocks 600 kg/m³ in both leaves 5 mm cavity 2.5 mm plasterboard and kim coat

13 mm sand/cement render 50 mm cavity Brickwork 1800 kg/m³ in both leaves

Concrete blocks 1800 kg/m3 50 mm cavity 13 mm sand/cement render

Figure 4.46 Methods of controlling sound transmission between dwellings

Internal walls

Internal walls or partitions divide the interior spaces into areas to suit the use of the building or they may separate buildings such as terraced or semi-detached houses. Additionally, they may separate the same building into identifiable fire-risk areas, e.g. a block of flats, or an office block. Whatever the use, they will fall into two main categories:

- load bearing
- non-load bearing

Load-bearing partitions are designed to carry superimposed loadings and carry them through the foundation safely to the ground. These loads will include not only their own self-weight but loads from:

- floors
- roofs
- occupants
- furniture and fittings
- machinery
- services
- wind and snow loads

Non-loadbearing partitions do not act as part of the structural system of a building and will therefore not be used to carry structural loadings of the building. These partitions may be constructed from:

- brick
- block
- timber or metal stud
- panel and slab
- cellular core

Within each of these categories the partitions may be required to meet a range of performance requirements:

- provide a physical barrier
- control sound transmission
- reduce thermal transmittance
- prevent spread and penetration of fire
- remain stable
- resist impact
- carry loads – both self-weight and imposed
- allow for dismantling and re-erection
- accommodate openings and penetrations

Timber stud partitions may be used to form internal walls. Normally they are non-loadbearing but can be designed to carry structural loads. The construction is shown in Fig 4.47. Different forms of sheeting may be applied to the studs but where fire resistance is required, plasterboard and skim are used. The centre of the partition can be filled with insulating material, which will improve its thermal and acoustic properties.

Alternatively, **lightweight blocks** can be used to form partition walls. They possess inherent qualities of fire resistance, thermal and sound insulation. In order to maintain the structural integrity of the block partition they should be a continuation of the walls at ground-floor level, where design and layout allow. Other methods of support include steel or concrete beams or concrete floors. Timber wall plates or double joists in timber floors can also be used (Fig. 4.48).

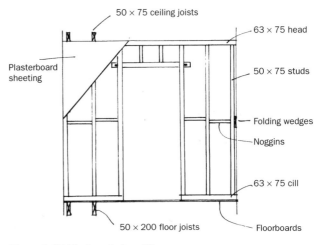

Figure 4.47 Timber stud partition

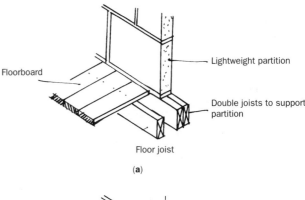

(a)

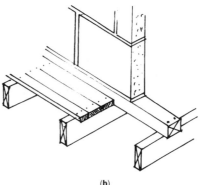

(b)

Figure 4.48 Floor support to a lightweight partition

Floors

Floors should be strong enough to:

- carry the required loads
- reduce deflection to a minimum
- afford support to other parts of the structure

In addition to the above, floors may be required to meet the following performance requirements:

- provide a physical barrier
- control sound transmission
- reduce thermal transmittance
- prevent spread and penetration of fire
- resist impact
- accommodate openings and penetrations

Timber floors

Suspended timber **upper floors** have to span from wall to wall and therefore they are deeper in depth to limit deflection and will require strutting (Fig 4.49) to reduce twisting and sideways movement of the joists. The joists may be built into the walls or suspended from joist hangers. The stability of the floor surface will depend on the spacing of the joists and the board or sheet material used. 18 mm is considered to be a minimum thickness for boards and sheets.

Often timber floors are required support a timber stud partition. This will bring an increased dead load in a particular area of the floor. In order to carry this load adequately, double joists are used often bolted together (Fig 4.48a). Where the partition runs across the joists a wall plate is used (Fig 4.48b).

Upper floors often have a staircase to accommodate. This will involve shortening some of the joists to create a **stairwell**. Figure 4.50 shows how the main bridging joists are cut and supported by a trimmer joist, which in turn is supported by trimming joists. The method of trimming the opening allows the remainder of the floor construction to satisfy its structural performance requirements.

Sound insulation is not normally a requirement with timber

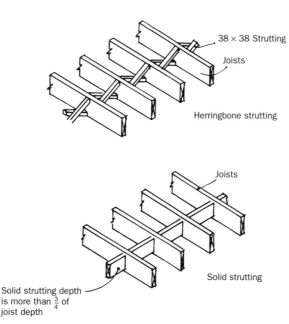

Figure 4.49 Strutting of a timber floor

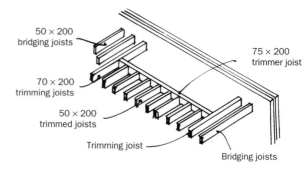

Figure 4.50 Stairwell in a timber suspended floor

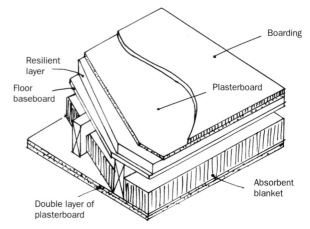

Figure 4.51 Sound insulation to suspended floors

suspended floors unless a property has multiple occupancy, say flats. In this case upgrading of the floor can be achieved by either creating a new ceiling with two layers of plasterboard to which are added layers of mineral wool and a floating insulation layer (Fig 4.51).

Fire resistance for timber floors requires that they are able to:

- continue to carry a load for a stated time
- prevent fire from breaking through
- resist excessive heat transfer

This may be achieved for example by using 12.5 mm plasterboard nailed to joists at 600 mm centres with 40 mm galvanised nails at 150 mm centres. The plasterboard must be fixed to every joist and the heading joints nailed to timber noggins.

Concrete floors

The structural characteristics of concrete floors have been discussed earlier. In addition to strength and load-bearing characteristics a floor may have to meet performance requirements for:

- fire resistance
- thermal insulation
- sound insulation

Fire resistance of concrete slabs is good initially up to 120°C but thereafter there is a progressive loss in strength. An important consideration is that the steel reinforcement must retain its concrete cover as long as possible. Once this cover is lost failure of the slab will be rapid. The minimum cover of concrete is specified according to the anticipated fire load on the structure. The minimum depth of cover is 25 mm.

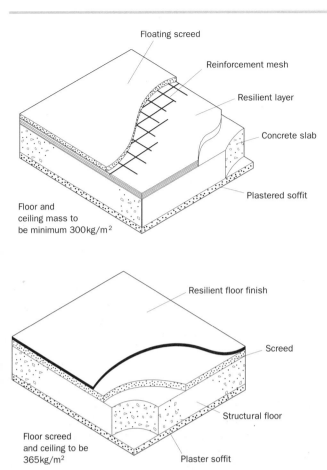

Figure 4.52 Sound insulation of concrete suspended floors

Concrete is not a good **thermal insulator**. In order to satisfy its load carrying requirements its density is most important. Unfortunately dense materials conduct heat at a faster rate than those with voids in them.

Floors, which separate dwellings from non-domestic use, must provide insulation against structure and airborne sound. Concrete does however have good **resistance to airborne sound** because of its mass, which is able to absorb the sound energy and poorer qualities with respect to **structure borne sound**. Provision will therefore have to be made to improve resistance to structure borne sound by using resilient layers and floating screeds (Fig 4.52)

Good sound insulation will depend on the following:

- density – which assists in reducing sound vibrations
- completeness – lack of gaps, e.g. service penetrations
- flexibility – not being too stiff which can cause loss of insulation
- isolation – having discontinuous structures

Cladding

Cladding is a term used to describe a method of enclosing a framed structure by fixing elements which are able to span between support points on the face of the building. This then eliminates the need for having a continuous background supporting structure.

Cladding elements will be strong enough to resist wind loads on the face of the building and transfer that load to the supporting structure behind. In addition the cladding should be able to resist driving rain or snow, and be able to accommodate thermal movement between a range of temperatures.

As claddings are manufactured off site their dimensions and tolerances are critical if they are to fulfil their performance requirements. Dimensional co-ordination is essential not only between cladding panels sizes but also to the structural frame, that is to support them.

Furthermore, the materials from which they are manufactured must be capable of allowing joints to be formed which will prove efficient in preventing the ingress of water. Claddings may be heavy elements formed from precast concrete, or lightweight structures made from metal or plastic profiled sheeting, or glass curtain walling.

Two systems of cladding are common. The first is an impervious skin attached to the frame of the building with sealed joints. The second consists of a weather-resisting layer with 'dry joints', which are designed to arrest the progress of water and direct it back out to the face of the building.

Stability of the cladding panels and their ability to transfer wind loads to the frame will depend upon the fixing design. Normally these are able to provide flexibility in terms of initial installation and fixing to meet tolerances. In use the fixings are able to allow controlled movement of the cladding caused by thermal expansion and contraction.

Three types of claddings are noted in Approved Document C4:

- impervious – metal, glass, plastic and bituminous products
- weather resisting – natural stone, cement-based products, fired clay, timber
- moisture resisting – bituminous and plastic products

It is essential that a vapour barrier or ventilated cavity is used behind the cladding as the last two types are permeable to water vapour. Typical joints used to resist water penetration are shown in Fig 4.53. If claddings are to satisfy thermal transmittance requirements it will be necessary to incorporate thermal insulation within the cladding system.

Self-assessment task

1. Floors, walls and claddings have to meet a range of performance requirements. Describe where appropriate how each element satisfies the requirements of:
   (a) sound reduction
   (b) thermal transmittance
   (c) durability and moisture penetration
   (d) resistance to fire

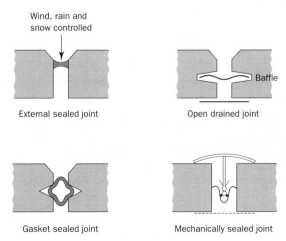

Figure 4.53 Types of cladding joints

Windows

Windows are used in buildings to:

- admit daylight and sunlight
- allow an external view
- permit ventilation of a space

In performing these functions the window may also be required to:

- exclude moisture
- minimise heat loss
- reduce sound transmission
- remain stable
- be durable for an acceptable period of time
- withstand fire for a minimum period

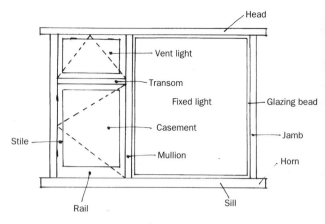

Figure 4.54 Window frame members

Table 4.7 Performance requirements for windows

Performance	Factors to consider
Resistance to weather	Controlling draughts and heat loss, preventing water penetration. Fit of the window sash into the frame, and the frame into the structure
Security	Type, location, and use of the building. Selection of glass and ironmongery.
Passage of heat	Draught strips and double glazing
Noise control	Location relative to source and type of noise. Thickness and spacing of glass
Affording privacy	Reason for privacy, e.g. an office or a bathroom, and the means for achieving it, e.g. opaque glass
Fire resistance	Locations such as flats, and protected routes. Use of wired glass
Stability	Minimising deformation due to expansion and contraction and use
Providing ventilation	Satisfying Building Regulations and Health and Safety Executive requirements

Windows can be classified as:

- casement
- sliding (horizontal or vertical)
- pivoted (vertical or horizontal)

Windows may be manufactured from:

- timber – hardwood or softwood
- metal – steel or aluminium
- rigid uPVC

Stability of windows is normally achieved by using a basic **framework** of members (Fig 4.54) called:

- sill – a horizontal member at the bottom of the frame
- head – a horizontal member at the top of the frame
- transom – an intermediate horizontal member
- mullion – an intermediate vertical member
- joints – used to connect the above members together

In order to allow ventilation to take place opening parts of the window called **sashes or casements** are used. In addition the firm fixing of the window frame into the structure is important.

Windows are built in to the external brick walls as the building is built, or fixed into prepared wall openings afterwards. In order to maintain support to the load-bearing structure above the window **lintels** are used (Fig 4.22).

The sides or **reveals** of the window opening between the cavity walls have to be closed. This is done by returning the inner leaf to the rear of the outer leaf. In order to prevent the passage of moisture from the outside to the inside of the building at this point a vertical damp-proof course is used.

As this is a potential **cold bridge** point between external and internal temperatures, modern developments allow the use of a DPC with polystyrene bonded to a polyethylene DPC (Fig 4.55). Alternatively a proprietary **cavity closer** can be used along the reveals and under the sill of the window (Fig 4.56)

Natural light is admitted to a space through glazed sashes. The amount of light and its distribution will be influenced by:

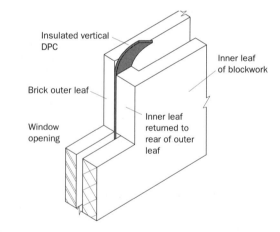

Figure 4.55 Closing the cavity with an insulated DPC

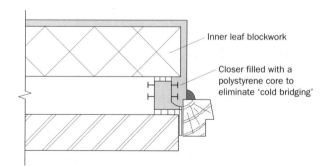

Figure 4.56 Plan view of a proprietary cavity closer

- area of glass
- type of glass
- orientation of the window
- position of the window in the wall
- external obstructions

In situations where excessive solar gain occurs, laminated solar control glass can be installed. Two types of glass are available which control solar gain by:

- reflecting and absorbing solar energy
- absorbing solar energy only

Durability of windows is achieved by:

- careful selection of materials – to reduce or minimise decay
- using watertight joints – to prevent moisture penetration
- using suitable preservative treatments – to enhance the life of materials
- protecting vulnerable parts – cills, bottom rails, transoms

Sound resistance is not often required except in special cases. Some reduction is achieved as a by-product of double-glazing for reducing thermal transmission. Sound reduction relies on the weight of the glass and distance between the panes and good seals being achieved between the sash and frame. An air gap of 100 mm upwards is usual to improve sound insulation properties. Laminated sound control glass in the correct combination of glass and interlayer thickness can provide insulation against traffic, factory and office noise.

Thermal transmission is controlled by using double-glazing with two panes of glass 10 to 20 mm apart (Fig 4.57). The sheets of glass are hermetically sealed at the edges using a metal spacer and bedded in a non-setting compound. Flexible sealing strips are used to prevent air leakage between the sash and frame. Window frames made from uPVC often have the cavity of the extruded section filled with polyurethane foam to reduce thermal transmission and condensation.

Resistance to moisture penetration will rely on:

- high-quality window construction
- the fit of sashes into the frame, and the frame into the opening
- weather-stripping in the rebates
- good cill and transom design
- careful design of opening sashes

Window frames will therefore be designed to prevent the passage of water to the inside of the frame. This is achieved by:

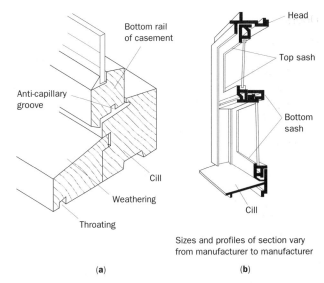

Sizes and profiles of section vary from manufacturer to manufacturer

(**a**)   (**b**)

Figure 4.58 Prevention of moisture penetration in windows. (*After* Ashcroft 1994 *Construction for Interior Designers*, Addison Wesley Longman)

- **weathering** or sloping of horizontal surfaces to prevent water lying on horizontal surfaces
- **anti-capillary grooves**, which prevent driving, rain passing through gaps between the sashes and the window frame
- **throatings** or drips, which prevent water being drawn underneath cills and transoms (Fig 4.58)

Building Regulations and Approved Documents require habitable rooms to be ventilated and in particular:

- kitchens
- bathrooms
- toilets
- living rooms
- bedrooms

Two forms of ventilation are required:

- rapid
- background

Rapid ventilation is usually provided by either a door or window. Windows should have at least part of them 1.75 m above floor level. The openable part of the window should have an area of at least one twentieth of the floor area. Background ventilation should be not less than 8000 mm^2. Kitchens and bathrooms will require half of this figure but must have a form of extract ventilation. There are further specific requirements for utility rooms and sanitary accommodation

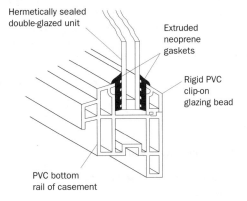

Figure 4.57 Double glazing to wood and metal windows. (After Ashcroft 1994 *Construction for Interior Designers*, Addison Wesley Longman)

Self-assessment tasks

1. Windows in a property are close to, and facing a busy road. What are the key performance requirements to consider?
2. Explain how a window can control solar gain.
3. State the air gaps between the panes of glass for sound and thermal resistance.
4. How is rapid ventilation provided by a window?
5. Research and prepare a paper for a group discussion on the sound and thermal properties of windows.

Doors

Doors are part of the enclosing and dividing function of a building and are fitted within walls or partitions. They are classed generally as internal or external doors. Within each of these classes are further types of doors which may meet one or more of the performance requirements in Table 4.8. Doors may be made from:

- timber – hardwood or softwood
- metal – steel or aluminium
- rigid uPVC

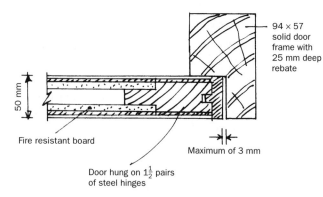

Figure 4.59 Fire door and frame detail

Table 4.8 Performance requirements for doors

Performance	Factors to consider
Access and egress	Who will use the door. Family, old or disabled people, general public, vehicles
Resistance to weather	Controlling draughts and heat loss, preventing water penetration. Fit of the door into the frame, and the frame into the structure
Security	Type, location, and use of the building. Selection of glass and ironmongery
Passage of heat	Draught strips and double glazing
Noise control	Location relative to source and type of noise. Weight of the door
Affording privacy	Reason for privacy, e.g. an office in a shop, and the means for achieving it, e.g. opaque glass
Fire resistance	Locations such as flats, garages, and protected routes
Stability	Minimising deformation due to expansion and contraction and use

Timber is commonly used for external domestic doors though aluminium and uPVC are being used increasingly. Metal doors are often used for shops and offices, industrial and commercial buildings. Stainless steel and bronze may be used for doors in prestigious buildings such as banks and building societies.

Doors are available in a range of co-ordinated sizes. Their frames correspond to the dimensions of brickwork courses into which the door will fit.

Aluminium doors may be hinged or sliding. They are made from extruded sections and can accommodate panels and double-glazed units. They are supported in hardwood timber frames fully weather-stripped.

Steel casement doors are made from rolled steel sections to British Standard profiles. Glazing units and sheet panels can be provided. Thermal insulation can be enhanced by using double-glazing and bonded insulation in panels.

Rigid uPVC doors use hollow extrusions, which may need reinforcement with internal metal sections in the hollow cores. Double glazing and weather-stripping are standard features used to control thermal transmission and moisture penetration.

Durability of doors is achieved by:

- careful selection of materials
- using watertight joints
- using suitable preservative treatments
- protecting vulnerable parts (using kicking plates)

Resistance to fire is achieved by:

- using materials resistant to penetration of flame or hot gases
- careful design of both door and frame (Fig 4.59)
- using Georgian wired glass in panels
- choice of ironmongery and fittings

Sound resistance is not often required except in special cases. Any reduction effect is normally achieved as a by-product of the materials used for the door construction. Specialist doors are available but are often for internal use only. Sound reduction relies on the weight of the door and good seals being achieved between the door and frame.

Resistance to impact will depend upon:

- the cause of the impact
- type of door construction
- materials used
- material used to cover the external surface of the door

Resistance to moisture penetration will rely on:

- high quality door construction
- the fit of the door into its frame
- weather-stripping in the rebates
- good threshold design
- the design of outward-opening doors

Doors in order to function must be supported in a frame. It is common practice in domestic building construction to hang external doors in **door frames** and internal doors in **door linings**, any load-bearing wall construction above being supported by lintels in a similar manner to windows. Likewise vertical DPC and cavity closers can be used around the opening to prevent moisture penetration.

Doors for industrial situations are required to satisfy a wide range of applications and performance requirements. Normally industrial doors satisfy two functions:

- to provide a durable and secure method of enclosing large openings
- to be easily operated and create a minimum of obstruction to 'traffic' when open

Performance requirements will include:

- security against unauthorised persons
- fire resistance
- sound reduction
- thermal insulation
- speed of operation

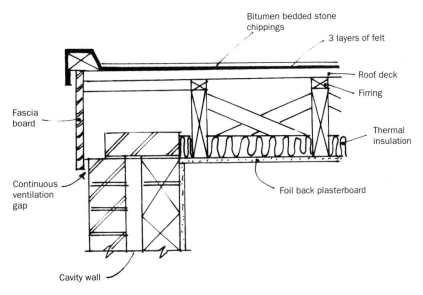

Figure 4.60 Flat roof construction

Approved specifications are available for interlocking shutter doors to meet the needs for an efficient fire check door. Energy conservation has led to an increase in the use of the insulated sectional overhead door. A polyurethane high-density foam infill provides a high thermal insulation standard, which can better that for structural walls.

Self-assessment tasks

1. What performance factors would be considered important for an external door to a house?
2. Produce simple sketches to show how moisture penetration is prevented around external timber doors.
3. Research and produce a matrix that shows the performance requirements for doors which represent one from each category of building shown in Table 4.65.
4. Research and prepare a paper for a group discussion on the sound and thermal properties of doors.

Roofs

There are many shapes of roofs but most falls into the two general categories of flat and pitched. A flat roof has its external face at less than 10° and a pitched roof over 10° to the horizontal.

Flat roofs

Flat roofs are very similar to timber floors in their construction. They have roof joists that support a decking, which in turn supports a water resistant roof covering. They also span between supports in a similar manner to a suspended timber floor (Fig 4.60). Openings for items such as roof lights can be trimmed in a manner similar to stairwells.

Stability of the roof is achieved by using:

- roof joists having an adequate cross-sectional size
- timber which is stress graded
- strutting to stiffen the joists laterally
- galvanised mild steel anchor straps

Concrete may also be used to form a flat roof slab. It is reinforced in a similar manner to a suspended floor slab.

Unless the concrete is of a very high quality it will need a weatherproofing membrane on its outer surface.

Timber flat roofs are not naturally **fire-resisting** constructions though the application of plasterboard and skim to the underside of the joists will provide at least half an hour's fire resistance. Where the flat roof passes over the party wall between dwellings fire stopping will be necessary to prevent fire spread between dwellings. A typical example is shown in Fig 4.61.

Roof finishes should ideally have a low spread of flame but a flat roof with a built-up felt finish with 12.5 mm bitumen bedded stone chippings will be acceptable. Concrete will possess sufficient fire resistance for most purposes.

Airborne **sound resistance** of a concrete flat roof is excellent, any weak points being where there may be roof openings. Timber roofs are not normally required to provide high levels of sound resistance.

Thermal transmission through flat roofs can be enhanced by the addition of thermal insulation. In the case of the timber flat roof the roof can either be a warm deck roof or cold deck roof construction. **Warm deck roofs** can have the insulation placed under the surface of the waterproofing layer, which is sandwich construction, or on top of the waterproof layer, which is known as **inverted construction**. **Cold deck roofs** have the insulation placed in the roof void between the joists (Fig 4.62).

All three decks have disadvantages, but the cold deck is considered to be the least desirable because of the risk of condensation and the variability of the wind speed which ventilates the roof.

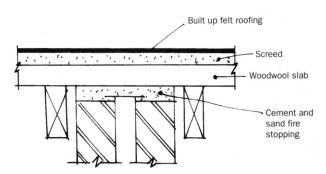

Figure 4.61 Fire stopping in flat roofs

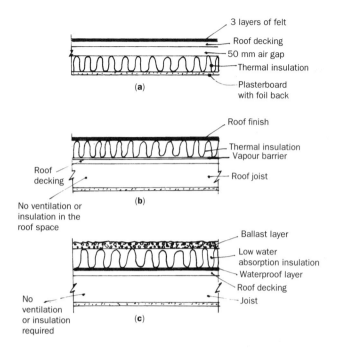

Figure 4.62 Flat roof decks

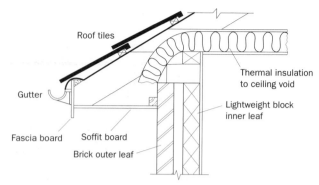

Figure 4.64 Typical roof eaves detail

Pitched roofs

Factors which affect roof construction and structural stability have been noted previously. Whether the roof is made up from steel or timber members it is still required to carry and transmit all the loads placed upon it safely.

All pitched roofs rely on **triangulated frameworks** for their stability. It can be seen from Fig 4.35 that there are several triangulated frames, which maintain the **stability** of the roof construction. The whole roof is in effect a series of parallel frames joined together by the binders, ridge board wall plates and wind bracing.

The trussed rafter (Fig 4.63) is the modern equivalent of the traditional cut roof. Every position has a braced truss that has led to timber economies and increased strength characteristics. These are spaced at 600 mm centres. Further **stability** is provided by wind bracing and strapping.

Steel roof trusses are constructed in a similar manner using angle section members to form rafters, struts, purlins and ties. These are connected together with bolted or welded gusset plates. The **load transmission** of the roof load is via the purlins to the trusses that are spaced at 3.0 to 4.5 m centres.

Fire resistance of pitched roofs will rely mainly on applied finishes to the roof surface and to the underside or soffit of the roof. Timber will tend to smoulder and char and therefore keep its structural strength for a long period of time.

Steelwork will remain stable until the fire reaches the steelwork and a temperature of 250 °C, beyond which there is a rapid loss of strength. Fire protection can be provided by applied cladding, intumescent paint or sprayed concrete. As for flat roofs, fire stopping is required to prevent spread between properties at roof level.

Thermal insulation can be installed to create either a cold or warm roof structure. Principles are the same as those outlined for flat roofs. Profile sheeting for warehouse and factory applications on steel trusses can incorporate a thermal sandwich, which will form a warm roof structure. Building Regulations expect minimum U values to be achieved. Approved Document L gives further guidance.

General

Roofs are required to prevent moisture reaching the inside of the building. Roof tiles in many materials and forms are used. Profiled PVC, metal, and sheet roof coverings are also available. Gutters and downpipes are used to collect the rainwater and carry it to a safe disposal point away from the building (Fig 4.64)

Figure 4.63 Trussed rafters

Self-assessment tasks

1. Use simple sketches to illustrate the terms warm and cold deck roofs.
2. What purpose does bracing serve in pitched roof construction?
3. How can the fire resistance of steel roof trusses be increased?
4. Describe with the aid of sketches how rigidity is achieved in roof frameworks.
5. Research and prepare a paper for a group discussion on the stability of pitched roofs.

Fire and buildings

Fire can destroy a building and kill any occupants very quickly. Destruction, death or injury by fire can create

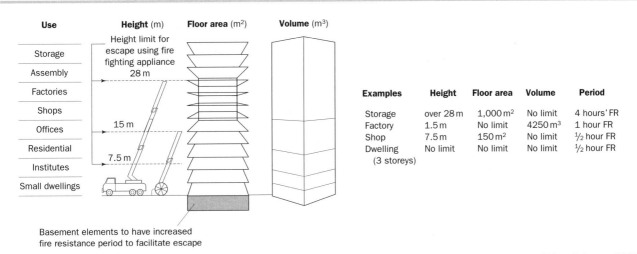

Basement elements to have increased
fire resistance period to facilitate escape

Figure 4.65 Factors which determine period of fire resistance for elements of structure forming part of a building. (*After* Osbourn 1997 *Introduction to Building*, Addison Wesley Longman)

Examples	Height	Floor area	Volume	Period
Storage	over 28 m	1,000 m²	No limit	4 hours' FR
Factory	1.5 m	No limit	4250 m³	1 hour FR
Shop	7.5 m	150 m²	No limit	½ hour FR
Dwelling (3 storeys)	No limit	No limit	No limit	½ hour FR

horrifying incidents. The design of a building and its component parts must therefore seek to safeguard first the safety of the occupants and secondly protect the property and any surrounding buildings.

In order to achieve a measure of protection for a property some degree of fire protection will be necessary. Initially this will involve designers ensuring that the structural elements of a building possess sufficient fire-resisting properties to prevent serious damage by fire for specified time periods. This action will safeguard the structural stability and integrity of load-bearing elements.

The use of non-combustible materials such as brick, steel and concrete will assist in this. It must be remembered that all materials have particular characteristics in a fire, which mean that even though a material is non-combustible it does not guarantee its stability. Structural steel, for example, is one such material, which loses its strength as the temperature of the steel is raised. The steel will require surrounding by other materials which will protect the steel for a given time period. Thus steel reinforcement is surrounded by concrete in floors, columns and beams.

Fire resistance is a term used to describe the ability of a building element to fulfil its function in a fire without assisting the growth and spread of the fire throughout a building. Often periods of fire resistance are required by designers to meet the requirements of building regulations. These notional periods are quoted according to time e.g. 1/2, 1, 2, 3, 4, 5, or 6 hours.

These times will be quoted having taken into account the:

- type of the building
- activity taking place inside the building
- the likelihood of fire risk
- the potential source and spread of fire

and will be sufficient to ensure the reasonable safety of the occupants and contents in a building. This will include the time taken to discover the fire and escape safely from the building. The period of fire resistance suitable for particular elements of a building depends on the function to be accommodated, and the volume and height of the spaces involved (Fig 4.65)

The spread of fire within a building can be restricted by recognising the fire hazards which the building may present and seeking to contain them according to the risk. This can be achieved by constructing fire-resisting compartments within a building (Fig 4.66)

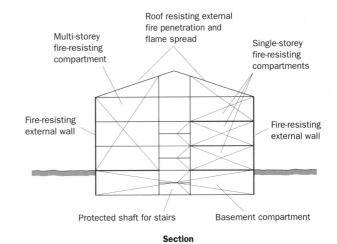

Section

Typical floor plan

Figure 4.66 The use of compartments to limit spread of fire in a building. (*After* Osbourn 1997 *Introduction to Building*, Addison Wesley Longman)

Compartmentation is the name given to dividing the inside of a building into designated enclosed spaces, which are separated by fire-resisting **compartment walls and floors**. Compartmentation aims to prevent the rapid spread of fire, which can trap occupants, and to reduce the risk of the whole building being at risk from a fire which could be contained within the space where it originates.

The Building Regulations Approved Documents give details of the maximum dimensions for compartments or whole buildings if appropriate. Minimum periods of fire resistance are also quoted according to building use and whether sprinkler systems are installed. The use of sprinklers permits a reduction in the resistance period.

Means of escape

People in buildings must be provided with well-defined escape routes should a fire break out. These routes should be:

- free from any obstructions
- easy for people to negotiate
- free from the effects of flame, heat and smoke

Escape routes should allow an individual to turn away from a fire and escape safely, and also have an alternative means of escape. Escape routes are protected, which means that they will provide protection from fire for a given period of time, which is normally sufficient to allow building occupants to escape.

The first part of an escape route is usually unprotected as it involves travel across a room and possibly along a corridor until a protected area is reached. This distance should be minimal. **Protected routes** are normally considered to be designated corridors and stairways – the stairways leading out to a place of safety outside the building. These routes should be clearly signed to show the direction of travel to the safety area. Flames, smoke and gases should be excluded from the protected stairway.

It will be evident that safe means of escape in case of fire will rely on a building being designed and constructed in such a way that the building elements possess appropriate periods of fire resistance. Where this is so, the relevant aspects of fire resistance have been discussed when considering the performance requirements of those elements.

Self-assessment tasks

1. Choose a building that is well known to you and describe using sketches the measures which have been taken to:
   (a) provide means of escape for the occupants
   (b) reduce fire spread throughout the building
   (c) provide minimum periods of fire resistance

Types of building structures

The way in which a building is constructed is principally influenced by the intended use for the building (Table 4.9). The student must also be aware that buildings should be designed to enable future changes of use. Change often brings with it the need to reorganise the internal division of space to provide required work areas to occur without demolition.

Table 4.9 Typical uses for a building

Residential	Industrial	Commercial
Houses	Factory	Shops
Flats	Warehouse	Cinema
Hospitals	Garages	Supermarkets
Hotels	Foundry	Offices
Care homes	Petrochemicals	Sports complex

Buildings may be classified as:

- low rise – not exceeding three storeys in height
- medium rise – between three and eight storeys
- high-rise – beyond eight storeys in height

Typical factors that influence the choice of structural form are:

- type of soil and its load-bearing characteristics
- use(s) of the building
- internal clear height
- clear uninterrupted floor area
- height of the building
- permanency of the building
- contemporary technology

Structural forms

Whichever structural form is used the primary purpose will be to ensure that the building remains in a state of equilibrium. This means that all the loads and forces that act on the building and are eventually transmitted to the ground are supported by soil reactions that will assist in keeping the building stable.

Structural forms can be defined in many ways, but here they are defined as:

- solid
- skeletal
- panel
- membrane

Solid structures

These structures normally use walls, which act in both an enclosing and load-bearing functions (Fig 4.67). As well as providing protection from the elements, the walls are able to carry the combined loads and forces through their construction down to the load-bearing ground. In this instance the walls are acting mainly under compressive stress.

Historically solid construction has used materials such as timber, stone and brick to provide an economic form of construction for low-rise buildings. Today brick, block, stone and concrete may be used. The stability of the structure is derived from each wall's weight and thickness and the additional support gained from the internal walls.

Skeletal structures

Skeletal structures use a framework of steel, concrete or timber members arranged in a regular form (Fig 4.68) to carry and

Figure 4.67 Example of a solid structure

Figure 4.68 Steel skeletal structure

transmit building loads through the foundation to the ground. The building load is carried and concentrated through columns or stanchions to the ground. Pad foundations are normally associated with frame buildings up to medium rise.

The wall is relieved of its load-carrying function allowing the design of a lighter structure, which can be erected more quickly than the solid structure. The enclosing function of the wall as a climatic barrier can now be undertaken by various types of thin lightweight cladding systems, reducing the total dead load even further.

The most common applications for skeletal forms are:

- single-storey structures
- two-way spanning structures
- multi-storey frames

Single-storey structures are in major demand by industrial users requiring workshop, storage, and warehouse and farm buildings. They are formed from two main types:

- truss and stanchion shed frames
- portal frames

Shed frames consist of stanchions and a flat or pitched roof truss or beam (Fig 4.68). They are normally made from structural steel, which is strong both in compression and tension and is also a stiff material. The stiffness of steel means that the structure and its members will not easily deflect under load. Steel also has a high strength to weight ratio, which makes it an efficient structural material.

Shed frames can be any length, but where a floor area needs to be increased sideways the floor area will be limited by the span of the roof structure. If the stanchion positions are not crucial to the internal use and layout of the building then multi-bay construction can be used. Where the stanchions are not acceptable within the floor area, then braced girders or lattice trusses can provide the increase in clear span.

When shed frames are formed they will require wind bracing in order to resist side sway collapse. This is achieved by using top bracing between the trusses and side bracing between the stanchions (Fig 4.34).

Portal frames These are a form of arch (Fig 4.33) that may have curved or straight members. Like the shed frame it is able to provide a clear floor space between the supports. Portal frames are described as rigid or hinged.

The **rigid frame** provides continuity of the of the portal because of the stiff restrained joints between the parts. Less material is also needed at the centre of the portal than with a simply supported beam (Fig 4.69).

The rigid portal is fixed firmly at the foundation points, whereas a **two-hinged portal** is fixed to the foundation by a sole plate but not prevented from rotating. This has the effect of moving the bending moment to the more rigid points of the frame. If a third hinge is used at the apex of the portal, bending moment is released which means the frame has to take more bending at the 'knees' (Fig 4.70).

Portal and shed frame buildings need to be designed to resist the wind pressures blowing from different directions. Wind blowing on the end of a factory building will produce an uplift situation and wind blowing on the side of the building will produce side sway (Fig 4.3). Methods by which these loads can be resisted are:

- the inherent stiffness of the joints – bolted or welded
- purlins and sheeting rails with their associated claddings
- bracing between portals at wall and roof positions – see Fig 4.33
- masonry panels built between portal frames acting as shear walls
- internal walls designed to resist loading from the frame

Two-way spanning structures As the span between supporting columns is increased it creates the need for heavier

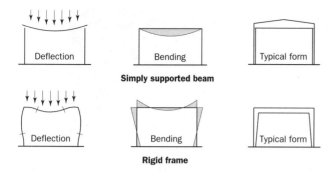

Figure 4.69 Comparison of rigid and beam construction. (*After* Foster & Harington 1993 *Structure and Fabric* Part 2, Addison Wesley Longman)

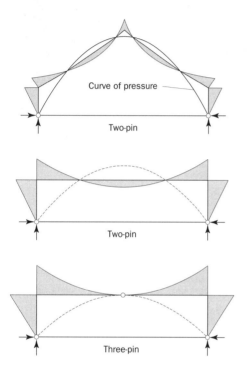

Figure 4.70 Variation of bending moment and thrust on a two- and three-hinged portal. (*After* Foster & Harington 1993 *Structure and Fabirc* Part 2, Addison Wesley Longman)

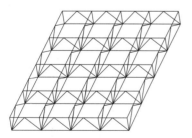

Figure 4.71 Space frame

Figure 4.72 Multi-storey frame

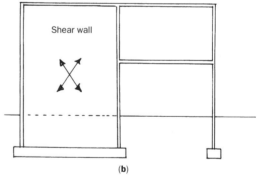

Figure 4.73 Frame bracing

and deeper structural members; consequently the cost per unit area covered increases. To overcome this a three-dimensional skeletal solution called a space frame is used (Fig 4.71). These are most efficient when covering plan shapes that are square, which then allows a general symmetrical arrangement.

Multi-storey frames These consist of a framework of horizontal beams and vertical columns (Fig 4.72). The beams have to resist compressive and tensile stresses in transmitting loads from the walls, floors and roof to the columns. The columns in turn have to resist largely compressive forces in transferring the beam loads down to the foundation and the soil beneath.

As the foundations are located at the base of the columns this causes the ground loading to be concentrated at these points rather than being more evenly distributed as with the foundations for a solid structure.

The building frame is enclosed by using infill panels to form the external walls. These panels are made from durable materials and apart from carrying their own self-weight, they

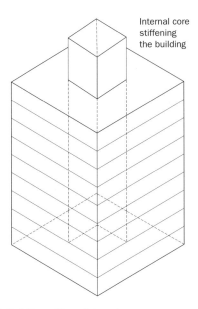

Figure 4.74 Building with an internal core

Figure 4.75 Panel structure

are designed to be structurally non-load-bearing. In addition the panels are designed to be able to transmit the wind loads back to the structural frame through their fixings.

Building frames will require some form of additional stiffness in addition to that provided by the connections formed between the frame members, because wind loads are likely to cause more structural failures than any other type of load. Designers therefore need to provide a structural load transmission route through a structure to the ground.

A building which is designed around supporting vertical loads only will eventually be subject to horizontal wind loads, which would lead to deformation or collapse of the structure. Frame buildings will require effective **lateral bracing** depending upon the stiffness of the joints between beams, columns and floor slabs.

Rigid joints are easily formed when using *in-situ* concrete frames, but are more difficult when using steel, though some rigidity of the joints can be achieved by welding joints *in-situ* or by using **high strength friction grip bolts**. These bolts produce a rigid connection by clamping the plates tightly together so that friction is created between the adjacent faces.

For low- or medium-rise frames independent means of creating the required stiffness are possible. These include using lift and staircase shafts or service ducts to provide stability. Other methods include:

- shear walls (Fig 4.73a)
- frame bracing (Fig 4.73b)
- internal cores (Fig 4.74)

Panel structure

Panel structures are able to carry and transfer building loads without the use of beams and columns (Fig 4.75). Load-bearing panels are used for the walls, floors and roof, each being designed to resist imposed loads as well as satisfying other performance requirements.

This form of construction lends itself to prefabrication techniques and site assembly. It is common therefore to find that the individual components have been dimensionally co-ordinated while retaining an element of choice for designers.

Figure 4.76 Membrane structure forming a sports hall

Membrane structure

A mixture of tension and compression members is often used to support thin non-structural membranes that form the walls and roof (Fig 4.76). Permanent structures use compression members (columns) and tension members (cables or ribs) to support an enclosing membrane. Closer examination of the structural concepts of these buildings is beyond the remit of this unit, but should the reader wish to pursue this further then *Structure and Fabric Part 2* by Foster and Harrington is a suitable starting point.

Self-assessment tasks

1. Describe how the use of a building might influence the choice of its structural form.
2. You are to be part of a group discussion concerned with the topic 'stability of buildings'. Make brief notes to enable you to participate in the discussion.
3. For each of the types of building structure described, explain how two structural members perform their intended function.

4.3 Evaluation of elements in buildings

The introduction to this chapter commented on the fact that buildings have been and will continue to be built in a variety of different ways while aiming to achieve a similar objective. This Vocational A Level unit requires the student to be able to examine the elements in a building, evaluate how well they meet the design function and where possible, suggest suitable alternatives. Tables 4.10 and 4.11 are the result of examining a domestic and a commercial building, identifying their present elements and associated performance requirements, and then suggesting suitable alternatives. Table 4.12 reviews building services with respect to their installation, performance and control.

Table 4.10 Detached house (see Fig. 4.67)

Element	Construction	Performance required	Alternative construction	Scientific principles and properties
Foundation	Mass concrete strip foundation	Carry imposed loads; resistant to moisture; resistance to chemical attack	Wide strip reinforced; short bored pile; reinforced raft	Durability; porosity; crushing strength; soil-bearing capacity; load transfer mechanisms; stresses
External walls	Cavity wall construction, with outer leaf of facing brick, inner leaf of load-bearing insulating block-work, dry lined with plasterboard	Moisture resistance; stability; load transmission; thermal barrier; climate control; durable; sound barrier; resistant to wind loads	Cavity wall construction, with common brick outer leaf clad with clay tiles; inner leaf load-bearing insulating block-work and plaster, cavity-filled with insulating material	Durability; porosity; load transfer; stresses; water/frost cycle; heat transmission; U-values; mass law; air tightness; fire resistance; moisture transfer; air pressures
Roof	Timber trussed rafters, supporting tile battens and interlocking roofing tiles	Climate control; moisture resistance; resistant to wind loads; thermal barrier; load transmission; sound barrier	Flat roof joisted construction; covered with proprietary roofing felt laid to a decking, with thermal insulation	Wind pressure;stability; stresses; U-values; heat transmission; air tightness; porosity; load transfer; convection; decay mechanisms
Internal walls	Timber load and non-load-bearing partitions clad with plasterboard and skim coat, with insulation for sound to bathroom and en-suite areas	Space division; load-bearing ability; provision to accept fixings and services; sound insulation	Lightweight block with plaster coat	Load transfer mechanisms; mass law; stability; air tightness; fire resistance; heat transmission; U-values; stresses
Ground floor	Mass concrete slab laid on hardcore incorporating a DPM and thermal insulation	Imposed load-carrying ability; resistance to moisture; thermal insulation; stability	Suspended floor of concrete beam and block, with non-structural floor screed	Load transfer mechanisms; heat transmission; decay mechanisms; ventilation; stability; stresses
Upper suspended floors	Timber joists with chipboard decking and plasterboard and skim to underside	Accommodate services; stability; limited deflection under load; ability to carry imposed loads to other structural elements	Suspended floor of concrete beam and block, with non-structural floor screed and plaster coat to underside	Load transfer mechanisms; mass law; stability; air tightness; fire resistance; heat transmission; U-values; stresses
Openings in walls	Steel lintels incorporating a DPC and thermal insulation, with reveals having a vertical DPC and cavity closers	Load-carrying ability; moisture resistance; thermal resistance	Concrete inner lintel supporting a profile steel lintel with brick outer skin	Load transfer mechanisms; stability; moisture resistance and transfer; heat transmission; stresses

Table 4.11 Multi-storey office block (see Fig. 4.72)

Element	Construction	Performance required	Alternative construction	Scientific principles and properties
Foundation	Mass concrete pad foundation	Carry imposed loads; resistant to moisture; resistant to chemical attack	Short bored pile and pad foundation	Durability; porosity; crushing strength; soil-bearing capacity; load transfer mechanisms; stresses
External walls	Concrete cladding panels with a thermal sandwich, and inner leaf of block-work with plaster coat	Moisture resistance; thermal stability; thermal barrier; sound insulation; climate control; durability; resist wind pressures	Curtain walling using an extruded aluminium frame and proprietary panels with waterproof surface and integral thermal sandwich	Durability; porosity; load transfer mechanisms; stresses; water/frost cycle; heat transmission; U-values; mass law; air tightness; fire resistance; moisture transfer; air pressures; dimensional stability
Structural frame	Structural steel beams and columns of standard cross-sections and bolted site connections	Resistance to bending, tensile and compressive stresses; stable frame construction; load transmission; resistance to corrosion; fire resistance	In-situ reinforced concrete frame with integral floor slabs	Load transfer mechanisms; structural stresses; stability; fire resistance; durability; degradation principles
Suspended floors	Precast concrete beams and infill clay blocks, with structural topping screed and plastered soffit	Resistance to bending moments and tensile stresses; fire resistance; sound insulation; load transmission; ability to support imposed loads; dimensional stability	Precast concrete floor planks with a non-structural topping and plastered soffit	Load transfer mechanisms; mass law; stability; air tightness; fire resistance; heat transmission; U-values; stresses
Internal walls	Lightweight block walling	Structural stability; ability to carry and transmit structural loads; thermal resistance; sound resistance; fire resistance; ability to accept and support fixings	Aluminium alloy frame and panel construction; panels from two sheets of plasterboard bonded to a honeycomb core	Load transfer mechanisms; mass law; stability; air tightness; fire resistance; heat transmission; U-values; stresses
Roof	Reinforced precast concrete slabs with screed laid to falls with an applied elastomeric finish	Resistance to bending moments and tensile stresses; fire resistance; load transmission; dimensional stability; moisture resistance	Reinforced concrete slab with thermal insulation, screed and hot mastic asphalt and granite chippings	Wind pressure; stability; stresses; U-values; heat transmission; air tightness; porosity; load transfer; convection; decay mechanisms

Table 4.12 Building services

Service	Application	Performance required	Controls	Intergration into the building
Water	Cold water supplies; hot water supplies; space heating	No contamination of supply; ability to isolate and drain down; not affected by low temperatures; adequate flow rates and recovery rates; minimal noise levels; economic use; economical installation; provision for storage; no leaks; low maintenance costs; corrosion-free; durable components; controlled temperatures	Valves; meters; ball valves; insulation; drain valve; pressure-reducing valves Air thermostats; thermostatic valves; diverting valves; timer/ programmer	In vertical ducts and either within floor construction or surface mounted within ducts; insulated pipe-work
Drainage	Soil and waste water removal	Prevention of odours; non-blocking; no leaks; minimal noise levels; adequate capacity; self-cleansing; disposed of in an environmentally friendly manner; accomodate variations in water temperatures; access for maintenance; flexible joints	Traps; air admittance valves	In vertical ducts and either within floor or roof construction, or surface mounted within ducts
Electricity	Lighting, heating and power supplies	Safety from shock; overload protection; voltage stability; adequate current; ease of control; local control; metered supply; individual circuit isolation; insulated supply	Consumer units; isolation switches; fuses; bonding; meters	Embedded in walls, ducts, floors and ceilings; conduits and trunking
Gas	Heating, cooking and process requirements	No leaks; constant pressure; ease of control; metered supply; access for purging and testing; bypass provision on large installations; accommodate thermal movement, isolation of circuits; corrosion-free	Governor; meter; gas cocks; thermocouples; gas valve; thermostatic controls	Fire protected ducts and compartments; surface mounted pipe-work

4.4 Building services

Most users of buildings will spend very little time considering just how the provision and maintenance of the environment in which they live or work has to do with building services – until one of the services fails to function correctly. It is taken for granted that

- **water** will run from a tap
- **gas** will be available to provide heating
- **electricity** will enable the bulb to light
- **communications** can be assured by use of a telephone

These services are taken for granted firstly because the environment in which we often find ourselves is considered to be safe, comfortable, hygienic and healthy and secondly because the building services which support these are economic, efficient and reliable. It is also assumed that buildings will be supplied with these services whether they are situated in isolated, rural or urban areas.

Self-assessment task

Before reading on, write brief notes on how you think the following services reach the property in which you live, and where they originate.

1. Cold water
2. Electricity
3. Gas
4. Telecommunications

Water supply

Water is an important primary service, as it not only provides a ready supply of cold water into a property for drinking purposes but it can also be:

- warmed to provide hot water supplies
- heated to provide space heating
- used as a means of removing various types of waste
- incorporated into industrial processes
- used as a liquid feed for plants

British Standard 6700 relates to the design, installation, testing and maintenance of services supplying water for domestic buildings, and British Standard 5546 relates to non-storage appliances. Water supply in England and Wales is largely controlled by the use of water bylaws. These were made by water undertakers under section 17 of the Water Act 1945. These bylaws aimed to prevent water being:

- **wasted** by flowing away unused from an appliance
- **unduly consumed** by using more water than is required for a particular purpose
- **misused** for purposes other than that for which it was supplied
- **contaminated** through use by any means

New water bylaws came into being in Britain on the 1 January 1989 and have been amended subsequently. Scotland has bylaws virtually identical to those for England and Wales.

Source of water

Rain is the primary source of water in this country, and in arid parts of the world desalination of seawater may be necessary. Above ground, rainwater falls into streams, rivers, and lakes as well as falling elsewhere on the earth's surface. The rain which falls on the surface finds its way into the ground by filtering through the porous strata until it reaches the impervious strata where it forms the underground water table. Occasionally this water may emerge at the surface as a spring. The depth of the water table from the surface will vary according to the topography, nature of the subsoil and the prevailing rainfall. In certain areas this groundwater may be extracted and treated to be used in water supply.

Treatment of water

A basic essential for water supply is that it should be free of harmful impurities and fit for drinking. Water which has been collected from above ground or extracted from below ground is unlikely to be acceptable as it may have become contaminated. It will therefore need to pass through a treatment process. (Fig 4.77).

Water supply to building

The supply to buildings may be from **public** or **private water supplies**. The great majority of buildings in urban areas take their supplies from public sources through the network of water mains. Private water supplies are used where buildings

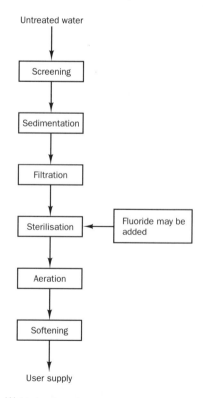

Figure 4.77 Water treatment processes

are situated in the more rural or isolated areas beyond the extent or economical reach of public supplies.

Water supply to urban areas

Wherever possible, water supplied from the public water main is distributed by gravity. The adequacy of the water mains supply will determine the number of properties and the volume of water that is capable of being supplied. This will depend upon:

- pressure of water in the mains
- size of the main
- demand upon the main

Pressure of water in the mains pipe is often expressed in terms of 'head' – this being the height to which water in the main would rise in a vertical pipe. A convenient mains head in the street is between 30 and 70 m, this being sufficient to supply buildings by gravity, and generate sufficient head to meet the requirements of fire-fighting forces. Pipework would also be within acceptable strength requirements and transmission noise would be limited.

As the vertical distance between the consumer and the reservoir can be considerably in excess of 70 m head, subsidiary service reservoirs are introduced to break the primary flow and serve local areas. It should be remembered that the head could be reduced by pipework frictional losses and demand from consumers (Fig 4.78)

In low-lying areas the source of water may be a river from which water will be pumped and stored into a settlement tank or reservoir. Subsequently the water will be treated using the processes previously described and pumped onwards to a service reservoir sited on high ground relative to the area which it would serve, or alternatively to a storage cistern on the top of a tower (Fig 4.79).

Distribution of water in urban areas

Water mains are used to carry the potable water from the service reservoirs to the urban area where it is needed. **Trunk mains** are used to carry the water in large volumes over long distances to urban areas. They are then subdivided into **street mains** and **submains** thus forming an urban water main grid. This grid would ideally be served by two trunk mains, which will enable isolation of individual sections while continuing to maintain a supply (Fig 4.80).

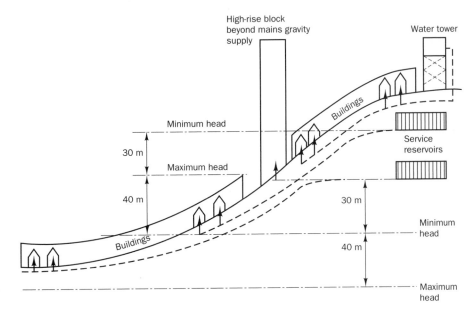

Figure 4.78 Service reservoir distribution

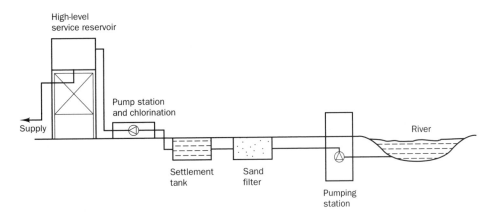

Figure 4.79 Pumped water distribution

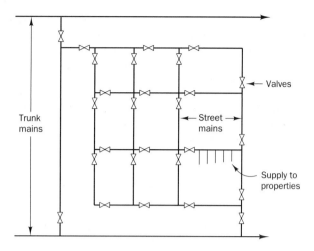

Figure 4.80 Typical water main distribution

Water supply in rural and isolated areas

Where piped water under pressure may not be available, alternative water supplies will have to be found. A supply may come from one of the following:

- lake
- river or stream
- well

This will usually involve water being lifted to a storage tank at high level from which water can flow by gravity to supply the building. Where an isolated settlement is to be served then the arrangement described previously for low-lying areas may be employed (Fig 4.79).

Where groundwater supplies will provide household water then a **well** can be constructed. It is advisable before water is used that it is analysed and reported upon. Likewise the regional water authority may need to be consulted with respect to the permitted extraction of water.

Wells may be classified as shallow or deep. Shallow wells do not usually exceed 7.5 m in depth and are normally worked by a simple suction pump. Deep wells are usually bored rather than dug and therefore known as **boreholes.** The greater the depth of the well the less the risk of water contamination. The analysis will determine whether treatment of water prior to use is necessary. In remote areas this may consist of a chlorination plant, or simply boiling the water before use. Ideally wells should not be situated near drains or cesspools.

Maintenance of water quality

It is important that water quality in the mains supply is protected, and that the supply to the user within building premises is uncontaminated. Preservation of water quality in four main areas is considered by BS 6700. These are:

- materials that come into contact with water
- stagnation of water supplies
- cross connection of water supply
- prevention of back flow from appliances or fittings

Key design information

It is important that the water supply in a building is capable of delivering acceptable flow rates with minimum noise levels.

This may be from the main or from a storage cistern. The cistern should have an adequate stored capacity for the appliances that it serves. Various sources of information are available to assist the services engineer to design an efficient and economical system.

Flow rates will vary according to the type of appliance being served and the type of premises within which the appliance is located. Table 4.13 gives some minimum recommended rates that have been found to be acceptable to consumers.

Table 4.13 Typical minimum rates of flow for appliances and fittings

Fitting	Flow rate (litre/s)
Spray tap	0.04 per tap
Wash basin tap	0.15 hot or cold
Bath tap nominal size $\frac{3}{4}$ in	0.30 hot or cold
Bath tap nominal size 1 in	0.60 hot or cold
Shower head	0.10 hot or cold
WC flushing cistern float-operated valve	0.10
Urinal flushing cistern	0.004 per position
Sink tap nominal size $\frac{1}{2}$ in	0.20 hot or cold
Sink tap nominal size $\frac{3}{4}$ in	0.30 hot or cold

Further information that will aid the designer can relate to the water consumption of appliances. Tables 4.14 and Table 4.15 give some typical details.

Table 4.14 Average water consumption of domestic appliances

Appliance	Average water consumption (litre/operation)
Wash basin	6
Bath	75–90
Shower	4 per minute
WC standard flush	9
Bidet	6
Washing machine	60–180
Dishwasher	30–70

Table 4.15 Average water consumption – domestic installations

Domestic installation	Litre/day/person
Washing up	10
Personal bathing and washing	25
Flushing WC	35
Laundry	15
Cooking, drinking and food preparation	20

It rarely happens in hot and cold water installations that all appliances are used simultaneously. It is therefore the practice to design for less than the maximum demand. The concept of using **loading units** can be applied to determine to a fair degree of accuracy the simultaneous demand of appliances. If the number of appliances is multiplied by the loading unit the total of the units can be used to determine the flow rate from a conversion graph. Table 4.16 gives typical loading units.

The pipe diameter necessary to achieve desired flow rates will depend upon:

- the head available
- smoothness of pipe bore used
- effective length of pipe run

Table 4.16 Appliance loading units

Appliance	Loading units
Domestic washbasin	1.5
WC 9-litre flushing cistern	2
Shower	3
Spray tap	0.5
Bath tap nominal size $\frac{3}{4}$ in	10
Sink tap nominal size $\frac{1}{2}$ in	3
Sink tap nominal size $\frac{3}{4}$ in	10

There will be a loss of head in the actual length of pipe to which must be added that caused by fittings such as tees and elbows, draw off taps, ball valves and stop valves. The relative discharging power of 15 and 22 mm diameter copper pipe is 0.44 and 1.40 litres/s respectively.

Connection of water supply to a property

Water supplies can be connected to a property from the mains supply provided that the building owner or occupier has complied with the requirements of the Water Act 1989, and that the installation as a whole satisfies water bylaw requirements.

The regional water authority will undertake to connect a property to the water main. Where a water main is in existence the connection will be made while the main is live using a stuffing box clamped to the main. This enables the water company to provide a mains tapping plug cock from which the **communication pipe** to the property can be connected. The communication pipe is that part of the **service pipe** which belongs to the water authority. The service pipe supplies water from the main to the building premises at mains pressure, subject only to the closing of the stop valve. (Fig 4.81)

The communication pipe will have a **stop valve**, which is a form of **globe valve**. It is used to control the flow of water at high pressure through the pipe work. The stop valve is capable of being closed slowly due to its internal construction and thus reduces the risk of causing water hammer.

Consumption of water has been on the increase and consequently new water sources have become more difficult to locate. It is no surprise therefore for the water authorities to consider and install **water meters** as a means of measuring the consumption of the user. They may also help with the tracing of leaks. The meters are usually situated outside the boundary of domestic premises, but may be within industrial and commercial buildings.

The position and depth of the service pipe should be such that the effects of frost, heavy traffic or building load are negated or minimised. Where the service pipe passes into the property it is housed in a protective duct suitably sealed and insulated. This will aid replacement of the service pipe if necessary. Suitable materials for service pipes are copper, polythene and PVC.

As the service pipe enters the property a stop valve and **drain down provision** are made for the consumer. This allows the consumer to isolate the water supply from within the premises in an emergency, and drain down the internal pipe work if required.

Distribution within the building should ensure that:

- the cold water is delivered at an acceptable temperature
- design flow rates are provided and maintained
- drinking water is provided directly from the main
- noise levels are kept to a minimum
- economical pipework layouts are used
- adequate support is given to pipework and storage cisterns
- appliances are connected in accordance with bylaw requirements e.g. air gaps
- isolation of appliances or delivery zones is possible

Table 4.17 Fittings and components used in water supply systems

Component/fitting	Purpose
Stop or globe valve	To regulate water flow and provide a means of isolation, normally fitted to the rising main
Non-return valve	To prevent the back flow of water into the main
Gate valve	To control or isolate water flow on the indirect cold water supply; acts as a service valve
Drain valve	Allows for the whole or part of a system to be drained down
Ball valve	Provides an automatic means of controlling the supply of water to a cistern
Taps	Used to control the flow of water at the outlet point
Pipework	Used to convey the water; can be copper, mild steel or PVC
Cistern	Used to store cold water prior to use; can be steel, GRP or polythene
Pressure-reducing valve	Reduces mains pressure to acceptable design pressures for the system

---

Self-assessment task

Make brief notes in answer to the following questions.

1. Describe the sources of water that are available to supply water to domestic consumers, and assess how they might affect the user.
2. Identify the various items that are associated with the water supply from the main to a consumer's premises.
3. Describe the control and monitoring methods used for domestic water supply, and comment on the effectiveness of each.

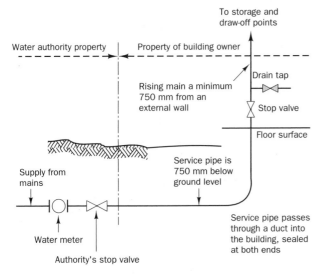

Figure 4.81 Cold water supply to a property

Water supply systems in other low-rise buildings

Where water consumption in small buildings is likely to be similar to that of a dwelling, then the features in Fig 4.82 or Fig 4.83 may be adopted. For other low-rise buildings such as hotels, office blocks and factories it will be preferable for all water except drinking water to be supplied from a cold water storage cistern.

Where a building's height or position determines that there will be insufficient pressure to supply the whole of a building then the possibility of a **pumped supply** to the cold water cistern should be considered. Situations will arise in non–domestic buildings where it becomes necessary to store large quantities of cold water. It would be impracticable to use only one storage cistern on the grounds of:

- size and space restrictions
- concentration of the load
- no supply can be assured during maintenance or replacement
- water may form local stagnation areas
- economic pipe distribution in a building with a large floor area

Where cisterns may be located close to each other they may be linked together (Fig 4.84). In order to avoid the risk of *Legionella* the cisterns should:

- conform to the requirements of Bylaw 30
- be regularly maintained and inspected
- have the inlet and outlet connections at opposite ends
- be of such a size that stagnation is prevented by rapid turnover
- have float valves that open and close together

Water softeners

Water softeners are increasingly being installed in domestic properties, but their primary use has been in properties where there are high volumes of hot water consumed. Their purpose is to reduce formation of scale in hot water systems and components where the water supplied from the main is hard. (Hard water is caused by a salt presence of calcium or magnesium.) It should be noted that water supplied for drinking purposes should not pass through a softening process.

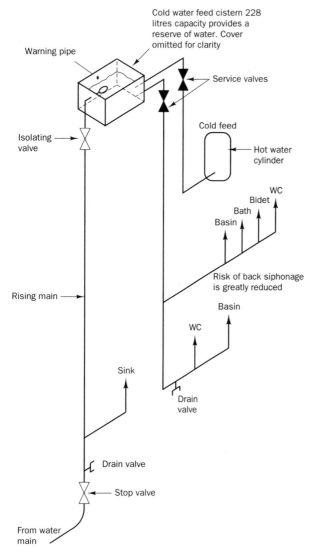

Figure 4.82 Indirect cold water supply

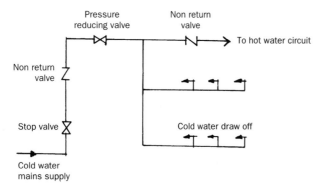

Figure 4.83 Unvented mains fed cold water supply

Self-assessment task

1. What factors must be taken into account when designing cold water supply?
2. Describe with the aid of sketches how water supplies in a town are distributed.
3. List the typical flow rates for appliances in a domestic property.
4. Why does an engineer design for less than the maximum water demand?
5. What factors influence the use of more than one storage cistern?
6. How may the risk of *Legionella* be reduced?

Hot water supply

Design and selection of systems

Systems providing hot water (Table 4.18) should take the following factors into consideration:

- the volume of hot water required
- temperature that the water will be stored at
- temperature required on delivery at the point of use
- installation and maintenance costs
- fuel energy requirements
- running costs
- economical use of water and energy
- nature and size of premises being supplied

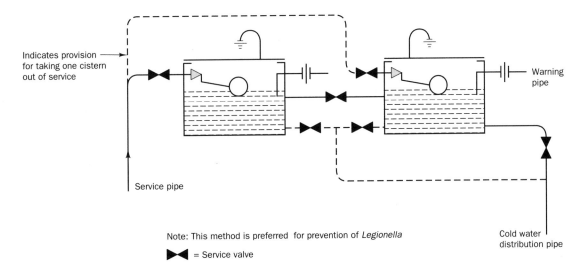

Note: This method is preferred for prevention of *Legionella*

▶◀ = Service valve

Figure 4.84 Cisterns connected in series

Table 4.18 Hot water temperatures and quantities

Fitting	Quantity (litre)	Temperature (°C)
Bath	100	40
or	60	60
plus	40	10
Shower	0.10	40
Lavatory basin	0.15	40–60
Kitchen sink	0.20	60
Hot water in dwellings	35–45 per person/day	60

(*Adapted from*: BS 6700; reproduced courtesy of BSI)

Standards

BS 6700 relates to the design, installation, testing and maintenance of services supplying water for domestic buildings and BS 5546 relates to non-storage appliances. Many aspects of hot water supply are also covered in the New Model Water Bylaws. These standards are a useful reference source for designers.

Types of system

There are two principal methods of providing hot water: **instantaneous** methods and hot water **storage**.

Instantaneous systems In instantaneous systems water is heated immediately as it passes through the appliance directly to the draw-off point. The flow of water will continue for as long as is required. The outlet temperature at any particular rate of flow will depend upon the heat input and inlet temperature of the water. These appliances are very efficient as standing heat losses are very low.

Storage systems These systems require the water to be heated some time before it is required and stored in an insulated vessel ready for use. The quantity of water available is limited by the storage capacity and the recovery period for reheating water. Correct design will allow desired requirements to be achieved. The temperature of the stored water is controlled by a thermostat.

The whole of the stored water volume can be drawn off at a relatively constant temperature regardless of the rate of flow, the flow being limited only by the frictional resistances

and the available head of water. For domestic, commercial and industrial applications, **vented** or **unvented** storage systems are available.

Centralised boiler heated water systems

The principal components of this system are the **boiler, cylinder and the cistern**. The boiler is to heat the water, the cylinder stores the heated water and the cistern provides replacement cold water. The boiler may be heated by gas, solid fuel, oil, or electricity. The systems may be:

- vented
- unvented

Controls for central hot water systems

Controls for hot water systems are necessary for:

- economy
- safety
- convenience

Table 4.19 Fittings and components used in hot water supply systems

Component/fitting	Purpose
Cylinder	Stores the heated water before use
Immersion heater	A form of heating element immersed in the cylinder and used to raise water temperature
Boiler	A source of heating water
Heat exchanger	Used in cylinders to provide efficient heat exchange and to separate primary and secondary circuits
Thermostat	Controls water temperature either in the boiler or in the hot water cylinder
Timer	Used to control the operation of the boiler or the immersion heater
Thermal insulation	Reduces the rate at which heat is lost from pipework or the cylinder
Circulating pump	Used to increase flow around systems and overcome gravity
Instantaneous heater	A form of water heater that raises the temperature of water as it flows through it
Vent and expansion pipe	Prevents a system from becoming pressurised and allows water to expand and contract on heating and cooling

Their purpose is to

- control starts and stop times of primary heating
- prevent overheating
- prevent a build up of pressure
- operate at temperatures that avoid *Legionella*
- control pump operation where applicable (Table 4.19)

Vented systems The vented system is fed with cold water from a storage cistern above the level of the highest water draw-off point to provide the necessary head of pressure in the system. The cistern will also accommodate any expansion of water when it is heated through an open vent pipe that runs from the cylinder to the cistern. The risk of explosion is therefore reduced by use of the open vent pipe and cistern. (Fig 4.85)

Unvented system Unvented systems remove the necessity for a storage cistern and are usually fed directly from the cold main supply pipe or via a pressure-reducing valve (Fig 4.86). Unvented system characteristics are:

- safety aspects are governed by the requirements of the Building Regulations
- safety devices provide protection from explosion
- no reserve of water is available
- risk of frost damage is virtually eliminated
- float-operated valve noise is eliminated

Protection from expansion

Water in domestic properties is not needed at temperatures above 100 °C. The Building Regulations require that there will be adequate precautions to prevent this temperature being exceeded in systems in excess of 15 litres capacity. Consequently three independent levels of protection for each source of energy are required. These are:

- a thermostat set not higher than 70 °C
- a temperature operated cutout acting on the energy supply at 85 °C
- a temperature-operated relief valve that opens at 90 to 95 °C

They are all designed to operate sequentially, so for the water to reach 100 °C all of them must have failed.

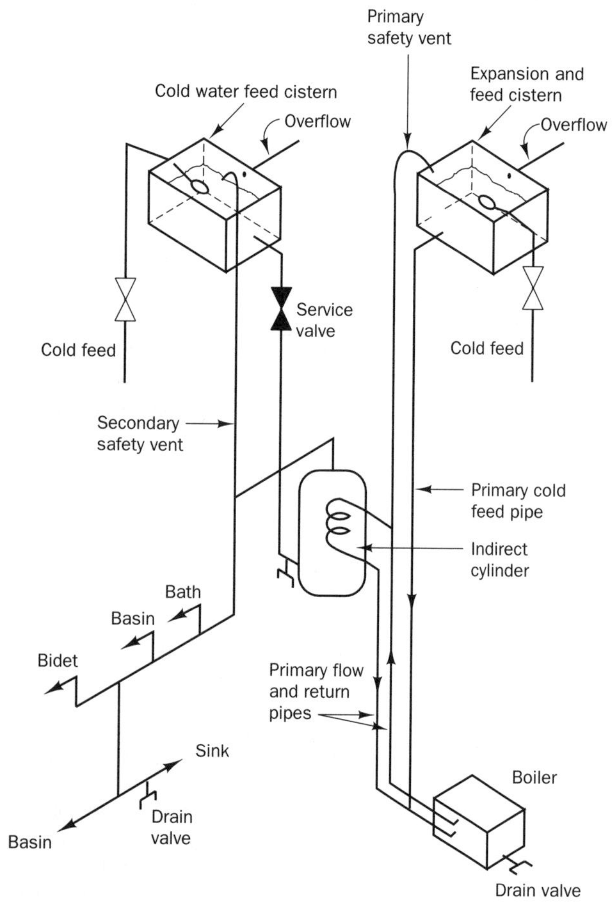

Provision for expansion

When cold water is introduced into a hot water storage vessel and heated it expands by 4% in volume. If this expansion were discharged to a drain it would contravene the Water Bylaws. In the majority of installations the expansion is accommodated by use of an expansion vessel. This must be sized to accommodate the maximum expansion expected in the system.

Pressure control

Mains pressure can vary widely and so the use of a pressure control device is required. This will be a pressure-reducing valve that should be able to cover a wide range of pressure variation.

Self-assessment tasks

1. Working in a small group discuss the advantages and disadvantages of vented and unvented hot water supply systems.
2. Prepare a 10 minute illustrated talk on safety mechanisms in unvented hot water installations.
3. Identify and describe the controls which are used to ensure economy, efficiency and safety of a vented hot water system.
4. Identify and describe the performance requirements normally required for hot and cold water supplies.

Gas supplies

Gas is a primary fuel supplied directly to gas installations in buildings for the purpose of providing one or more of the following:

- hot water
- heating
- cooking facilities
- process requirements

British Gas, through its regions, provides a national network for the transmission of gas. Again, like water, there is a hierarchy of pipe sizes in the network taking the gas from its source to the consumer. Natural gas is supplied to premises at pressures up to 5 kPa. Gas installations are controlled by the Gas Safety (Installation and Use) Regulations 1984 which amended the Gas Safety Regulations 1972 and the Gas Safety (Rights of Entry) Regulations 1983.

Figure 4.85 Indirect hot water system (vented)

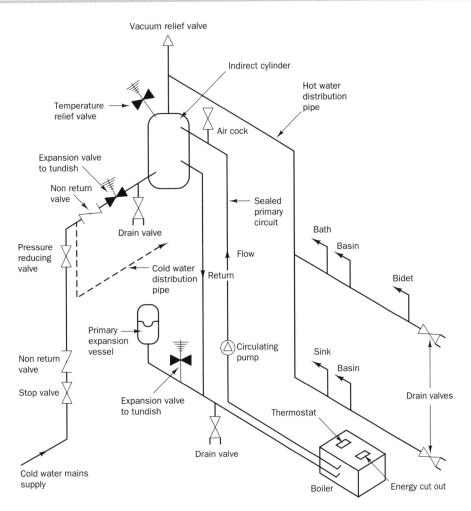

Figure 4.86 Indirectly heated unvented hot water system

Sources of gas

In the United Kingdom **natural gas** has virtually replaced town or manufactured gas. Around 90% of gas used for domestic applications is natural gas from beneath the North Sea, being directly derived from natural sources and mostly oil related. An alternative often used where supplies of natural gas are not available is **liquefied petroleum gas** (LPG).

Gas supply in urban areas

Gas supplies enter building premises through the **service pipe** that runs from the gas main in the street to the consumer's meter control. Service pipes should be situated where possible to enter buildings on the elevation nearest to the main, and avoid passing under the foundations of the building. The service pipe cannot run through an unventilated void space, or within a cavity though it is permissible to pass through a cavity by the shortest route (Fig 4.87).

Service pipes may be of copper or steel. Steel pipes should be protected with a bituminous wrapping or encased in plastic. It is common practice to install meter boxes in the external walls of buildings (Fig 4.88), but where this is not possible and the service pipe has to pass through the structure it will have to be sleeved and sealed. Pipes running on the face of walls will need to be securely clipped.

A meter installation includes a gas cock, governor, filter and a meter. A gas pressure test point will also be available.

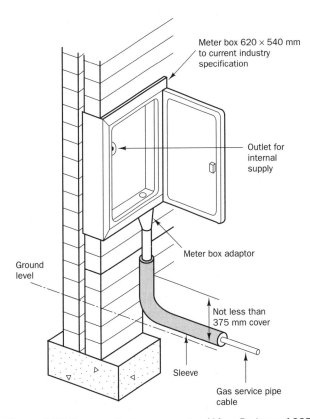

Figure 4.87 Gas supply to a property. (*After* Burberry 1997 *Environment and Services*, Addison Wesley Longman)

Figure 4.88 Gas meter box

The **gas cock** or valve allows the consumer or gas engineer to control the supply from the service pipe to the installation. It is positioned in the service pipe before the governor and meter and enables repairs or maintenance to be carried out.

The combined **governor** and **filter** is fitted at the service pipe connection to the meter. The function of the governor is to reduce the pressure of the gas in the main to a pressure more suited to the appliances being served. The delivery pressure of 5 kPa after being governed gives a nominal pressure between 2 and 2.5 kPa. This then ensures adequate pressure to serve the domestic appliances that are designed to operate at pressures between 1.75 and 2.5 kPa. The purpose of the **filter** is to collect the fine particles that would clog the gas jets of the appliances.

The **gas meter**, called a **primary meter**, is connected to the service pipe. As its name implies it is there to record the consumption of gas by the user. **Secondary** or **subsidiary meters** are used in buildings where there may be more than one tenant to establish individual consumption. Accuracy is important in the functioning of meters and they should not therefore be exposed to:

- the likelihood of physical damage
- excessive temperature changes
- the risk of contact with flame or sparks
- continuous wet or damp conditions

In new installations gas meters must not be installed under stairways or elsewhere if the stairway or other part of the building is the only means of escape in case of fire. Where meters are being replaced in alteration work for example, then the requirements of the Gas Safety (Installation and Use) Regulations 1984 must be complied with.

The **pressure test** point is to enable a check to be made on the pressures in the pipe work system after the governor and also allows the efficiency of the governor to be checked.

Gas installation

Careful consideration is required before installing the distribution pipe work in a building. The exact routeing of pipe work should be planned in order that indiscriminate cutting of beams and joists is reduced, and the integrity of walls and floors is not compromised.

Points to consider when planning distribution are:

- pressure drops can be minimised by reducing the number of sharp bends and angles
- means of disconnection for each run of pipework should be provided
- access to pipework should be possible without damage to finishes or structure
- incombustible material should be used to support pipework
- sleeves must be used where pipework passes through elements of structure
- all pipework should be adequately supported
- pipes should be protected from corrosion, heat and puncture
- joints should be of an approved type and allow easy disconnection
- a line diagram showing a layout of the system and position of cocks and valves should be provided

Gas cocks and valves

Gas regulations require a valve or cock to be positioned in an accessible position on the incoming service pipe to the primary meter, and to the installation pipework serving individual floors or self-contained areas within floors. Cocks should be protected against accidental operation and fitted as close as possible to the end of a pipe run. Where gas pokers, cookers and gas rings are to be used the provision of a plug-in point should be made to accommodate a wandering lead.

Table 4.20 Fittings and components used in domestic gas supply

Component/fitting	Purpose
Service pipe	The pipe from the main to a property
Gas cock	Allows the gas supply in the property to be isolated from the main, or an appliance in the property from its supply
Governor	Reduces the pressure from the main to a pressure more suited to the appliances being served
Filter	This collects the fine particles that could clog the gas jets of appliances
Meter	Records gas consumption
Pressure test point	Allows a check to be made on pressures and the governor efficiency
Meter box	Normally fitted in the external wall and contains the meter, governor and control cock

Bypass to gas meters

There will be instances where buildings such as hospitals, schools and factories will need to be fitted with a meter bypass in order to avoid interrupting the supply during meter

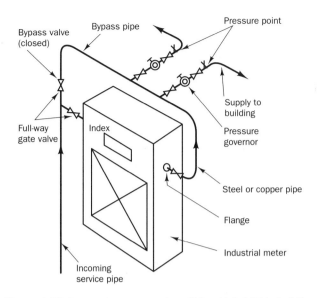

Figure 4.89 Bypass to a gas meter. (*After* Hall 1994 *Building Services and Equipment* Volume 2, Addison Wesley Longman)

replacement. In this case the bypass should still be subject to the pressure governor. A bypass valve will be fitted and sealed in a manner acceptable to the gas board. (Fig 4.89)

Installation in multi-storey buildings

Gas service to these buildings can only be installed in protected shafts to the requirements of the Building Regulations. Alternative methods of constructing a shaft are:

- a continuous shaft
- a vertical protected shaft

The **continuous shaft** should be ventilated at the top and bottom to the outside air. A fire-stopped sleeve will be required where a lateral service run will pass through the wall of the shaft. A **vertical protected shaft** may be required to be fire-stopped at intervals. In this instance the service pipe must be sleeved and fire-stopped both where it passes through the floor of each level and the lateral service pipe fire-stopped as for the continuous shaft. Ventilation is again required but for each isolated section (Fig 4.90).

The following additional points must also be observed:

- service laterals will have a service valve adjacent to the riser
- differential thermal expansion must be accommodated by a flexible connection
- in public areas where access to valves and riser is required, sealed fire-resistant panels will be installed
- gas services should be located to allow for maintenance and repair
- meters should have their controls close to them
- the gas riser must rise vertically up the shaft
- lateral service runs must not exceed 2 m from the riser or from a ring main supplied from the riser
- in blocks of flats, offices or commercial buildings where there is multiple tenancy, provision must be made for local disconnection. Secondary meters may be provided for each tenant.

In order that a sufficient quantity of gas is delivered to the appliances, care must be taken in the **sizing of the distribution pipework**. Items to consider when sizing are:

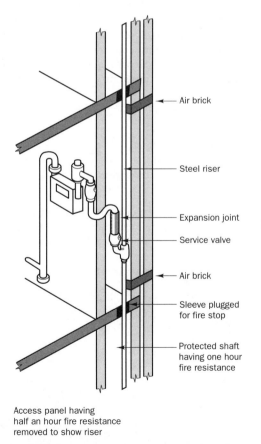

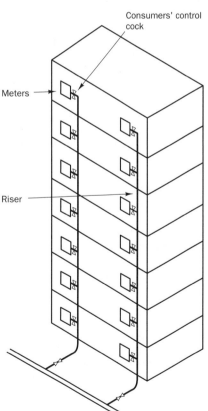

Figure 4.90 Gas service pipe in a multi-storey building. (*After* Hall 1994 *Building Services and Equipment* Volume 2, Addison Wesley Longman)

- gas pressure supplied
- number and type of appliances being served
- possibility of appliances being added to the system
- resistance to flow caused by pipe fittings
- gas flow rate
- intermittent or continuous use

Gas supply in rural or isolated areas

In areas where buildings are beyond the service provided by British Gas, the alternative gas supply can be by use of **liquefied petroleum gas** (LPG). LPG may be provided in two forms in cylinders or in bulk supply tanks. Two main liquefied petroleum gases are in use, these being commercial butane and commercial propane. Propane boils at -42° Celsius compared with butane at -0.5° Celsius. Propane is therefore more suited to freezing conditions. Butane cylinders should be protected from frost.

LPG storage in cylinders

Domestic installations that are permanently piped with a low off-take rating, such as a cooker, would require two 19 kg propane cylinders with a changeover regulator. Where a higher off-take rating is needed to serve central heating boilers and fires, then the installation will consist of four 47 kg propane cylinders.

Each cylinder is fitted with a **valve** to control gas flow and an excess **pressure relief valve**. **Pigtails** are used to connect the cylinders to the **changeover valve**, which incorporates a **regulator** to reduce the pressure prior to delivery to the appliances to 37 mbar. The changeover valve is connected to two cylinders and when these are empty the valve changes over automatically to the two reserve cylinders. Where cylinders are used in connection with portable domestic appliances butane is normally used.

LPG bulk storage

Storage vessels vary in size from 1200 to 24 000 litres. Single dwellings are supplied from individual tanks, whereas groups of dwellings can be supplied from a shared storage tank with a metered supply to each outlet. In order to ensure that gas supplies are continuous, particularly under adverse weather conditions, storage should be sufficient for six weeks, supply at maximum use. Tanks may be made unobtrusive by landscaping and planting provided that access for filling and maintenance is not impaired, and adequate air movement about the tank is maintained. Tanks need to be sited so a road tanker can approach to within 25 m of the valve inlet position. Refilling can be done to a predetermined schedule or to suit individual requirements.

The pressure of the vapour within the storage vessel is between 2 and 9 bar. Safety pressure relief valves protect against excessive pressure due to exposure to heat. A first stage regulator is mounted on the tank to reduce the pressure to 0.75 bar. A second-stage regulator reduces this pressure down to 37 mbar – this being the industry standard for propane serving domestic appliances.

The supply pipework is run underground from the tank to the building or buildings it will serve. The supply can be metered if necessary. Where the supply pipe rises up the outside of the building prior to entry a control valve will be installed to enable isolation. The service pipe then enters the building to serve the appliances.

Self-assessment task

1. What advantages are to be gained by planning the distribution of gas services in a property?
2. Describe the precautions to be taken when installing gas in multi-storey buildings.
3. What technique is used to maintain constant gas pressures?
4. What method is used to enable a gas supply to be isolated?
5. What forms of gas supply are available for urban and isolated areas?
6. Why must care be taken in the location of gas meters?
7. Sketch and describe the function of the components connected to the gas meter.

Electricity supplies

Electricity is generated at power stations and fed to the national grid system from substations operating at 400 000, 275 000, and 132 000 volts. Electricity is carried to grid supply points by transmission lines using overhead conductors (Fig 4.91). In heavily populated areas underground cables will be used instead of overhead lines. Bulk supplies of electricity are then taken from the grid at 33 000 volts for distribution to urban areas, industrial estates and groups of villages.

Transformers at intermediate substations reduce the voltage to 11 000 volts. These then distribute to local transformers, which further reduce the voltage to 400 volt 3-phase, four-wire supply (Fig 4.92). Here 240 volts single phase is tapped off to serve shops, commercial premises, schools and homes. There is no fixed pattern for local distribution, this being developed as a result of the requirements of the area (Fig 4.93).

Electricity supplies are used to provide power for:

- lighting circuits
- water heating
- space heating
- operation of machinery
- small electrical appliances

Electrical installations are controlled principally by the Electricity Supply Regulations 1988 (Amended 1990) and the *IEE Regulations for Electrical Installations*, 16th Edition.

Figure 4.91 Electricity transformers and transmission lines

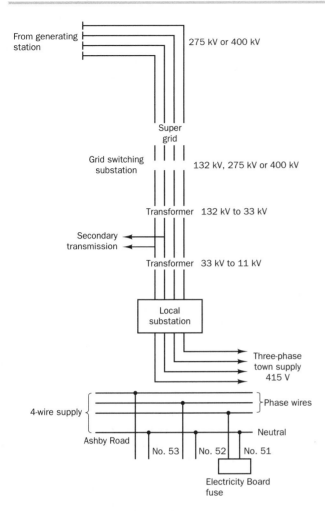

Figure 4.92 Distribution of power from generator to consumer

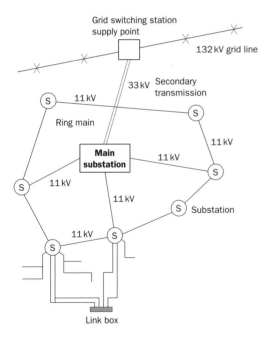

Figure 4.93 Local distribution of electricity

Electrical supplies to domestic properties

The point at which electricity supply is supplied to a building by the regional board is known as the **main intake**. The exact point of entry will be decided with the regional board but

Figure 4.94 Electrical supply box

within the building provision will have to be made for, and carefully planned around, the main intake.

The **service cable** brings the electricity up to the property from the supply in the street. Modern practice is to install a **meter box** at the intake position on the external wall. The service cable is then passed through a protective sleeve acting as a **duct** to serve the consumer board. The service cable terminates at the sealing chamber that contains the **service fuse** (60-100 A). This fuse is there to protect the electrical supply to the street should there be a serious fault in the property. A cable connects the sealing chamber to the **meter** that registers the power used (Fig 4.94).

Cable tails are then taken to the **consumer unit** (Table 4.21). The consumer unit is a box that incorporates the mains isolation switch and the individual protective devices which protect the circuits in the property. The **isolation switch** is a double pole switch and controls the phase (live). The protective devices, which protect the final circuits from overload and reduce the risk of fire, are miniature circuit breakers or cartridge fuses. (Fig 4.95)

Table 4.21 Fittings and components used in electricity supply

Component/fitting	Purpose
Service cable	The cable connecting the property from the main
Service fuse	Protects electrical supplies in the street
Meter	Records electricity consumption
Cable tails	Cables used to connect the meter to the consumer unit
Consumer unit	A box which incorporates the mains isolation switch and individual protective devices for circuits in the property
Isolation switch	A double pole switch which controls the phase (live)

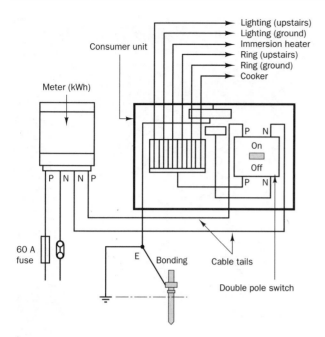

Figure 4.95 Domestic distribution board

Small power circuits

These circuits incorporate socket outlets or fused connection units for fixed items of equipment. Two types of circuit are permitted:

- ring circuit
- radial circuit

Ring circuits

A **ring circuit** uses twin and earth wire looped from one socket to another with both ends being connected at the consumer unit to the same 30 A fuse or circuit breaker. This permits the connection of a large number of sockets and fused connection units per 100 m² of floor area. **Spurs** may be added provided that their number does not exceed the total number of socket outlets and that there are no more than one single socket outlet, one twin socket outlet or one fixed appliance per spur. (Fig 4.96)

Theoretically the load on the ring could be many hundred amperes but not all sockets will be used at once. Also the load on any socket will only be a proportion of the maximum that can be provided through a plug. This is limited with plugs having a maximum rating of 13 A.

Socket outlets in bathrooms are forbidden by the IEE Wiring Regulations. Where a shower cubicle is installed in a room other than a bathroom then the socket outlet must be 2.5 m from the cubicle. Exceptions to this are shaver sockets and safety extra low voltage sockets.

Other fixed electrical equipment in the bathroom must not have switches within reach of a person using the bath or shower. This can be overcome by the use of pull cord switches. It should be noted that correct **earth bonding** is necessary for exposed metal parts in bathrooms.

In **non-domestic buildings** attention should be paid to the load of the equipment, which is to be connected, plus the likelihood of overloading the circuit from portable appliances. It may be necessary to reduce the number of sockets and the area served. Areas with specific loadings such as a kitchen should be allocated a separate circuit. Separate circuits must also be used for permanently connected appliances that are fed through fused connection units.

Radial circuits

Radial circuits may serve an unlimited number of BS1363 sockets provided that the area served does not exceed 50 m² and they are wired in 4 mm² PVC cable with a 30 A or 32 A cartridge fuse or circuit breaker respectively. For areas up to 20 m² the circuit protection is 20 A with 2.5 mm² PVC cables. Any type of overcurrent protective device may be used (Fig 4.97). Radial circuits are commonly used for showers, immersion heaters, cookers and instantaneous water heaters.

Small lighting circuits

For domestic properties lighting circuits will be radial and on the **loop-in** basis. These will be served from the consumer unit to individual lighting locations (Fig 4.98). Various switching arrangements are possible to suit the convenience of the user. A common one is **two-way switching** to a staircase, long room or corridor.

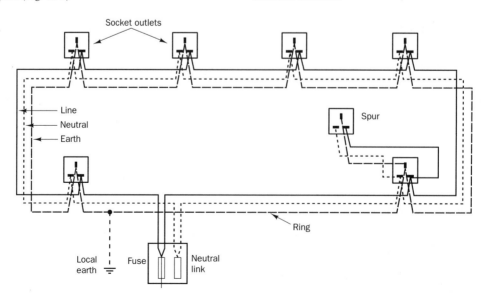

Figure 4.96 Small power ring circuit

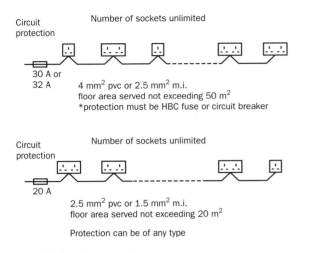

Figure 4.97 Radial power circuit

In non-domestic properties submain cables will serve distribution boards located around the building fed from the main low-voltage switch panel. These boards will have an isolating switch and fuses or MCBs to protect the outgoing circuits. The distribution boards may be either single- or, if many lights are to be served, three-phase.

Table 4.22 Typical fuse ratings and applications

Fuse rating (amps)	Application
60	Cooker
30	Ring main ground floor
30	Ring main upper floor
30	Radial circuit – kitchen
15	Immersion heater
15	Garage
5	Central heating controls
5	Lighting ground
5	Lighting upper floor

Electrical supply

A preliminary exercise prior to providing an electrical supply to a building is to assess the **load of the building** and the demand it would place on the supply network. In larger buildings this will have significance with respect to the space required for electrical equipment. When demand is assessed it is important that both present and future needs of the building are projected.

In general a single-phase 230 V supply will be provided for demands of up to 100 A. Beyond this up to 800 kW, 400 V three-phase supply will be required. Above 800 kW supply will be high voltage at 11 000 V three-phase.

Where a building takes a low-voltage electrical supply the incoming supply cable for domestic premises will be connected to a consumer unit, and in other premises to a low voltage switchboard. This unit then splits the incoming supply to serve smaller outgoing circuits (Fig 4.99). Individual isolation and overcurrent protection is therefore possible for each circuit.

The **overcurrent protection** is achieved by one of the following:

● re-wirable fuses
● high breaking capacity fuses
● miniature circuit breakers (MCBs)

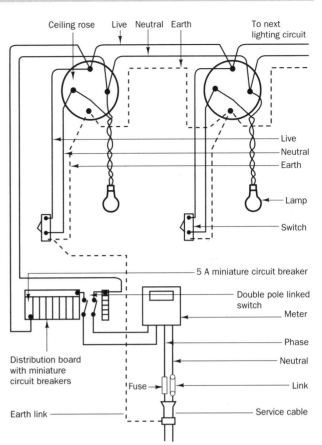

Note: A ceiling rose shall not be installed in any circuit operating at a voltage normally exceeding 240 volts (IEE Regs)

Figure 4.98 Loop-in method for lighting circuits

The Institution of Electrical Engineers recognises that MCB and certain types of cartridge fuse will provide more consistent and reliable protection against excess current than rewirable fuses.

The domestic circuits will be to lights, sockets, cookers, and immersion heaters and off-peak electricity provision. The outgoing circuits in larger installations will serve lighting, socket outlets and heavy current appliances.

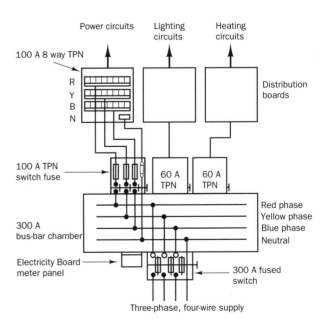

Figure 4.99 Typical small factory wiring distribution

Cable rating

The amount of current that a cable can carry is limited by the heating effect caused by the resistance to flow of electricity. The implication of this is that the maximum current load under normal conditions must not generate temperatures that would cause damage to cable insulation.

When choosing a conductor size for a particular load the following must be taken into account:

- maximum current rating the cable will carry
- voltage drop that occurs when current is carried
- whether the cable is enclosed or unenclosed
- grouping of cables that can cause heat build up
- temperature of the surrounding air
- type of protection device

Typical applications for conductor sizes in domestic properties are shown in Table 4.23.

Table 4.23 Typical cable size applications for domestic installations

Cable cross-section area (mm^2)	Typical application
1.0	Lighting circuits
1.5	Immersion heater
2.5	Ring circuits and radial subcircuits
4.0	Radial circuits
6.0, 10.0, 16.0	Cooker circuits

Earthing

Any earth fault current will try to find a low resistance path to earth. All services must therefore be bonded as near as possible to their entry into the building. Likewise the exposed metal surfaces of radiators, baths, sinks and tanks must be **bonded** together and to earth. This bonding will ensure that all the metalwork in the building will be at the same potential (i.e. no voltage difference) in the event of metalwork becoming live to earth.

Small non-domestic buildings

Many of the principles previously described will also apply to these buildings though the scale of the electrical services will be greater. Electrical supply may be either single- or three-phase and connected to a low-voltage distribution board. The location of this should not be open to unauthorised persons, but be available for periodic maintenance and testing.

Blocks of flats will be served by a three-phase supply that will rise up through the building. From this supply single-phase will be supplied to individual properties and separately metered. The space for these service runs should be negotiated early in the contract to ensure sufficient room is available. It is common practice to provide a separate circuit for the staircase and external lighting.

Office blocks will require a similar method of electrical supply. The number and position of meters will depend on whether the building will be single or multiple occupancy.

Distribution about the building

Distribution is by **armoured cable** to distribution boards for lighting and power requirements. Excessively long final circuits can be avoided by carefully siting the distribution boards. Power supply for mechanical plant items is three-phase. It should be remembered that the electrical supplies would have to be installed to suit the needs and use of the building. An example is given in (Fig 4.100).

Bus-bar trunking can be used to service lighting and power needs. This is a method that allows for a fair amount of

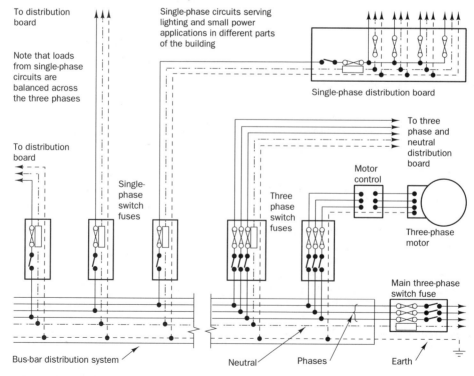

Figure 4.100 Typical arrangement of sub-main and final circuits to a large building. (*After* Burberry 1997 *Environment and Services* Addison Wesley Longman)

flexibility for relocation of lights or plant. Wiring of circuits in these buildings should consider:

- long-term use of the building
- need to alter and extend the electrical provision
- shock and vibration on equipment and cabling

These points are met by using single-core cable in conduit or trunking. This will provide resistance to mechanical damage and yet allow for extension of the system or rewiring.

Electricity supply in rural and isolated areas

In rural and isolated areas it is usual to find the electricity supply is delivered by overhead power lines rather than underground. When it reaches the property the intake will be as described for urban areas. For areas beyond the reach of mains supply, property owners are looking to electricity by wind generation, or use of local generators powered by petrol or diesel oil.

Self-assessment task

1. Explain the meaning of the following terms;
   radial circuit — bus bar
   over current protection — ring circuit
   bonding — spurs
   earthing — cable rating
   loop-in wiring — MCB
2. Describe how power and lighting circuits are distributed in a domestic property.
3. Explain how electrical supplies will be distributed in an office block.
4. Explain why care must be taken with electrical supply in bathrooms and describe the measures that can be taken to increase safety for the user.
5. Describe the purpose of the components that are to be found in the meter box.
6. How is the risk of current overload prevented in a domestic property?
7. Using your home and the centre where you are studying your Vocational A-Level as examples:
   (a) Draw a simple site plan to show where the services intake positions are to the two buildings.
   (b) Prepare a 10 minute illustrated talk on the control and monitoring devices installed on the services in your home. Your talk should explain the purpose of the devices identified.
8. Produce a matrix that will allow you to assess water, gas and electrical services in terms of convenience, capacity of the service, and quality given to the user.

Drainage installations

The use of water with various fittings and appliances in buildings creates a need for the efficient collection and discharge of the foul and waste water, whether it is contaminated or not. Similarly rainwater that falls on the building or the surfaces surrounding it, as well as the water in the subsoil, will need to be collected and discharged in a safe manner. For drainage purposes water may be classed as:

- surface water
- foul water

Surface water

Surface water may be collected from the roofs and faces of buildings, and the surface areas around them such as drives and paved areas. This water is normally considered to be safe and therefore its discharge may be directly into main sewers, convenient watercourses or soakaways.

Soakaways collect and store rainwater during a storm and then release it into the surrounding ground as quickly as the ground conditions will allow. The rate of this discharge is also influenced by the height of the water table. Soakaways are normally sited a minimum of 5 m away from a building to reduce possible settlement of the building's foundations. Small soakaways are filled with coarse granular material and hardcore. Larger soakaways are formed from dry-jointed perforated concrete rings (Fig. 4.101). The outside of the ring is backfilled with granular material to allow the water to percolate into the surrounding ground more effectively. The soakaway is covered with a concrete slab which will also allow access should it be needed.

Subsoil drainage

Subsoil drainage is provided to prevent the passage of moisture beneath a building, and to reduce possible damage to the fabric of the building. Subsoil drainage will also increase stability of the ground and its horticultural properties. A variety of methods are available, these being illustrated in Fig. 4.102.

Foul water

Foul water is waste-water from a sanitary convenience or other soil appliance, or water that has been used for washing or cooking. Building Regulations require that any system that carries foul water should be adequate. This applies to drainage systems both above and below ground. In this respect, a drainage system should:

- carry the foul water to a suitable discharge point
- minimise the risk of leaks or blockages
- prevent foul air from entering the building under normal operation
- be ventilated
- provide access for clearing blockages

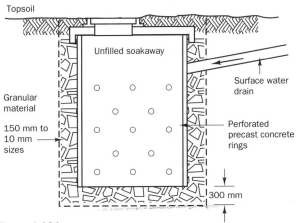

Figure 4.101

LEEDS COLLEGE OF BUILDING
LIBRARY

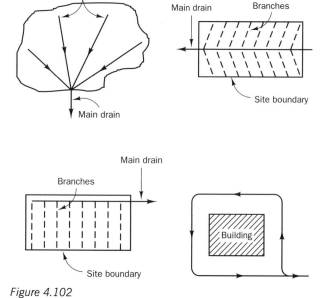

Figure 4.102

Table 4.24 Comparison of combined and separate drainage systems

	Combined system	Separate system
1	Foul and surface water served by one drain and sewer which reduces cost	Two sets of drains are needed which increases installation costs
2	Risk of making wrong connection is eliminated	Possibility of making wrong connection exists
3	Surface water can be used to flush the foul water through the drain	Foul water drain relies on self-cleansing gradient
4	Foul gases may bypass trap seals in rainwater gullies	No risk of polluting air through the surface water drain
5	Sewage disposal plant and treatment costs increase	Sewage plant is smaller and treatment costs are less
6	Pumping costs may increase but this depends on location of the sewage treatment plant	Surface water may be disposed of locally thereby reducing the cost of any pumping

Above-ground drainage

Above-ground drainage is commonly called sanitary pipework and should be designed, installed and maintained so that it minimises the risk to health that could arise through leakage, blockage or surcharge of the system as a result of discharge from waste and soil appliances.

In domestic properties soil and waste appliances are discharged to a single stack. The single stack (Fig. 4.103) is used in properties where the appliances are grouped closely together, and can be connected to the discharge stack to assist with efficient operation of the system. The system consists of a vertical discharge stack to which are connected soil or waste appliances via their own branch pipe. In order to prevent the penetration of sewer smells into the premises a water trap is used (Fig 4.104).

If a trap seal is lost there is a direct pathway for sewer or drain odours to enter the building. The water seal depth is 50 mm for WCs and 75 mm for all other appliances. There are three principal ways in which the seal may be lost (Fig. 4.105):

- self-siphonage
- induced siphonage
- backpressure

In addition to the main discharge stack a stub stack may be used. This allows connections from an unventilated stack (the stub stack) to a ventilated discharge stack or sewer. Conditions limit the connection of a branch to the stub stack to no more than 2 m above the invert and a WC branch should be no more than 1.5 m above the invert. The length of the unventilated stub stack should be no more than 6 m for a single appliance or 12 m for a group of appliances.

Below-ground drainage systems

The system of drainage used will depend upon the locality and the requirements of the regional water undertaking. Two principal methods are used (Table 4.24):

- separate system
- combined system

The separate system is commonly used. This collects surface water and foul water separately from a property and discharges them to separate sewers. The combined system collects foul water from appliances and surface water from paved and roofed areas by a single drain to a combined sewer (Fig. 4.106).

The design and installation of drainage systems should:

- be simple
- have few changes in direction and gradient
- sweep connections in the direction of flow
- be ventilated at the head of the drain
- have pipes laid in straight lines
- minimise the effects of settlement
- use a self-cleansing velocity of 0.75 m/s
- use impervious, strong and durable materials for pipes
- allow access for clearing blockages

Types of access and their spacing are contained in the Approved Document of the Building Regulations. Two typical ones are rodding eyes (Fig. 4.107) and manholes (Fig. 4.108).

Pipes for drainage fall into two categories:

- rigid
- flexible

Rigid pipes are manufactured from vitrified clay, concrete, and grey iron. Flexible pipes are manufactured from uPVC. Joints used in pipelines should be appropriate to the materials being used. Flexible jointing methods are preferred to minimise the effect of ground movement through settlement (Fig. 4.109)

Flexible pipes should be laid at a minimum depth of 900 mm under any road and 600 mm in fields and gardens up to a maximum depth of 10.00 m. Where depths are less than these then special protection of pipes will be required. Where drains pass alongside buildings the provisions shown in Fig. 4.110 should be observed. Figure 4.111 shows a method of accommodating a drain passing through a wall.

The choice of bedding and backfill to drains depends upon:

- the depth at which the pipes are laid
- their size and strength
- the nature of the ground excavated

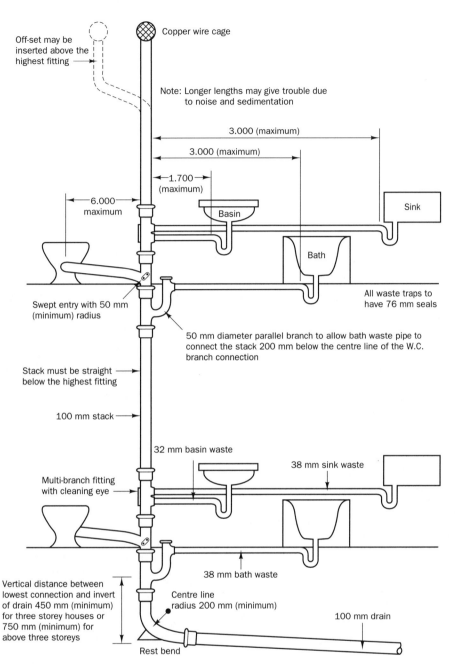

Off-set may be inserted above the highest fitting

Copper wire cage

Note: Longer lengths may give trouble due to noise and sedimentation

3.000 (maximum)

3.000 (maximum)

1.700 (maximum)

6.000 maximum

Basin

Sink

Bath

Swept entry with 50 mm (minimum) radius

All waste traps to have 76 mm seals

50 mm diameter parallel branch to allow bath waste pipe to connect the stack 200 mm below the centre line of the W.C. branch connection

Stack must be straight below the highest fitting

100 mm stack

32 mm basin waste

38 mm sink waste

Multi-branch fitting with cleaning eye

38 mm bath waste

Vertical distance between lowest connection and invert of drain 450 mm (minimum) for three storey houses or 750 mm (minimum) for above three storeys

Centre line radius 200 mm (minimum)

100 mm drain

Rest bend

Figure 4.103 Single stack drainage

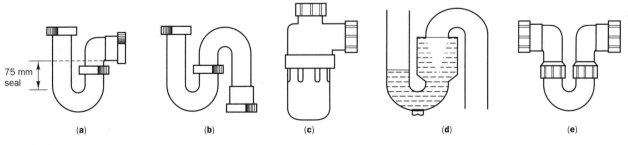

75 mm seal

(a) (b) (c) (d) (e)

Figure 4.104 Water traps

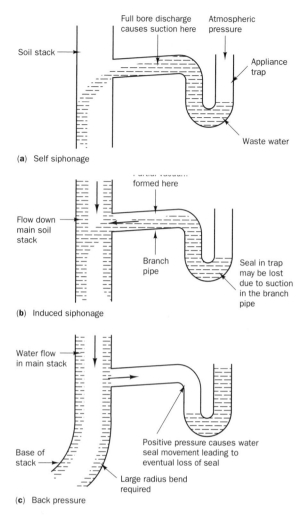

(a) Self siphonage

(b) Induced siphonage

(c) Back pressure

Figure 4.105

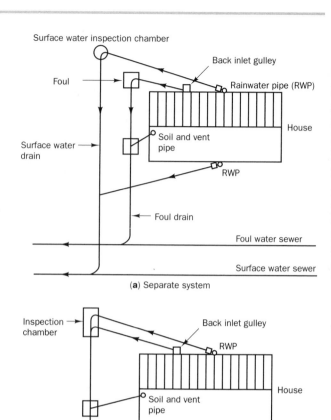

(a) Separate system

(b) Combined system

Figure 4.106

Details of different bedding to drains can be found in the Building Regulations Approved Document.

Sanitary fittings for domestic premises

A variety of sanitary appliances can be installed to satisfy the range of special applications (Table 4.25). Sanitary fittings can be viewed as:

- soil fittings
- waste fittings

Table 4.25 Sanitary fittings

Type	Fitting	Materials
Soil	WC	Vitreous glazed china
Waste	Washbasin	Vitreous china; glazed fireclay; plastic
	Bath	Enamelled pressed steel; enamel on cast iron; fibreglass-reinforced plastic
	Showers	Vitreous china; acrylic plastics; vitreous enamelled sheet steel
	Bidet	Plastic Vitreous china

Self-assessment tasks

1. State ways of disposing of surface water from a building.
2. Describe the purpose of a trap and how trap seal may be lost.
3. What is a 'stub stack' and where is it used?
4. Describe and illustrate the differences between combined and separate drainage systems.
5. State the performance requirements for an above-ground drainage system.
6. What are the advantages of using flexible pipe joints in foul drains?

Space heating

Buildings are heated for various reasons but in domestic properties they are heated for the health and comfort of the occupants. An individual's satisfaction with the heating in a space is often a matter for personal preference, and may be related to the type of activity being undertaken, or the amount of clothing being worn. In domestic properties the acceptable temperature range lies between 19 and 23 °C.

Heating systems commonly used in domestic properties usually serve to modify the air temperature and not humidity. This does not matter too much as humans can feel comfortable in a wide humidity range. For normal comfort conditions this is between 30% and 65% humidity.

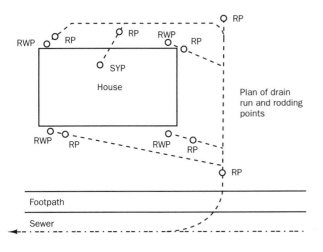

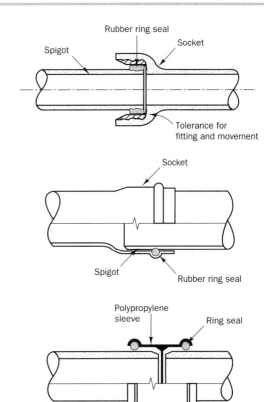

Figure 4.109 Rigid pipes

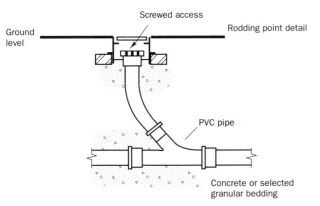

Figure 4.107 Rodding eyes

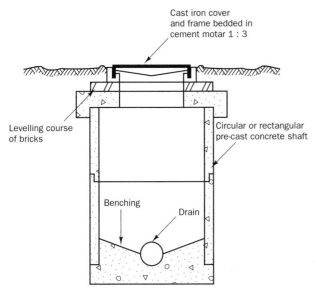

Figure 4.108 Manholes

Factors that influence heating installations

Apart from temperature and humidity, the following will also have an influence:

- the orientation of the room or building
- use of the room
- volume of the room
- number of people in the room

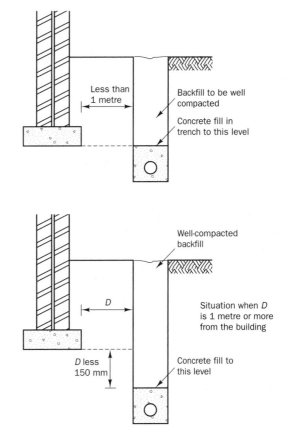

Figure 4.110 Flexible pipes

- number and area of external walls and windows
- heat transmission levels through the structure
- temperature differences
- heat gain from appliances

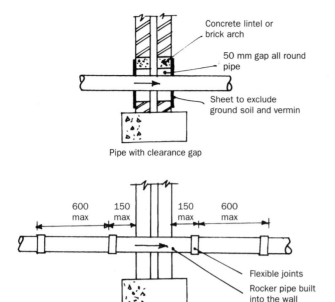

Pipe with clearance gap

Flexible jointed rocker pipes

Figure 4.111 Drain passing through a wall

Table 4.26 Fittings and components of a wet heating system

Component/Fitting	Purpose
Boiler	A source of heating water
Pipework	Used to carry the heated water
Control valves	Used to isolate or regulate flow
Motorised valves	Valves with electric motors allowing automatic regulation of flow
Radiators	Hollow metal heat emitters
Programmer	A control device; modern ones allow a variety of time settings throughout the day and week
Thermostat	Controls air temperature in a heated building or space

In addition these factors, the type of space-heating installation will be a major influence. Systems may be direct or indirect. Direct systems are those where the energy purchased is consumed within the space to be heated (e.g. a gas or electric fire).

Indirect systems involve the energy purchased being consumed outside of the heated space and then transferred to the space for distribution. Two common systems are:

- hot water heating
- ducted warm air systems

Water or 'wet' systems have an advantage in that the distribution takes place through pipes that are small in diameter and are easily routed around the property from downstairs to upstairs and even through timber floors. The pipes are therefore easily accommodated and may be completely out of sight or situated in positions that allow the pipes to be unobtrusive.

Warm air systems rely on the use of square, rectangular or circular ductwork to transmit the heated warm air to the individual outlets in the rooms. This ductwork is usually a minimum size of 100 mm diameter or its equivalent in other cross-section shapes. Planning of the duct distribution is important and occurs prior to building and installation. Future modification, while not impossible, is not as easy as with water systems.

Hot water heating

These systems use water that is heated in a boiler and then transferred to the heating circuit, which is called a primary circuit (Table 4.26). Water is moved around the system using a circulating pump. The use of the pump:

- allows efficient and effective control
- reduces pipe sizes
- provides quicker heat-up times
- increases flexibility of the installation

The pump provides a velocity of up to 3 m/s and reduces the warm-up time. Pipework layouts can be adapted to suit individual building styles and are normally installed in a two-pipe ring circuit (Fig. 4.112). The two-pipe system uses two pipes, called flow and return pipes, to feed the radiators. This system gives a balanced flow temperature to the radiators. Other forms of heat emitters can also be used, these being:

- fanned convectors
- skirting convectors

A variant of the system is the micro bore installation. It is similar to the system described above except that the pipework is of a smaller diameter, which allows the pipework to be accommodated more easily in both new and renovation installations. It also uses a manifold through which the flow and return pass (Fig. 4.113).

Self Assessment Tasks

1. State the performance requirements of a wet heating system.
2. Describe the controls that may be used to improve the efficiency of a heating system.
3. How may building user requirements influence the design of heating systems?
4. What factors will influence the installation of pipework for a wet heating system?

Installation and distribution of services

Buildings serving different purposes will require variations in the number, location and distribution of electrical, mechanical and sanitary services. In domestic premises this is not a problem, but where buildings become service-intensive it is important that the design team collaborate at an early stage to agree how the services will be distributed in a building.

Access to services is needed to allow for:

- installation and minimal disruption to other activities
- inspection and maintenance
- isolation of services
- testing and commissioning
- alteration and replacement

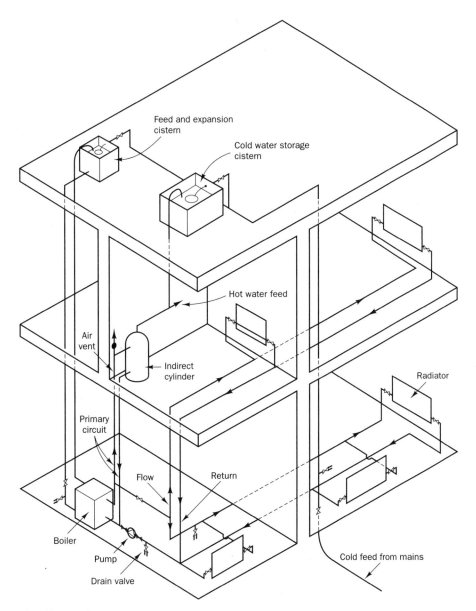

Feed and expansion
cistern

Cold water storage
cistern

Hot water feed

Air
vent

Indirect
cylinder

Radiator

Primary
circuit

Flow

Return

Boiler

Pump

Cold feed from mains

Drain valve

Figure 4.112 A two-pipe ring circuit

Distribution of services

Building services must be distributed about a building in an orderly and logical way. Two broad classifications for achieving this are structural and non-structural methods of accommodating them.

Structural accommodation can be influential in the design of the building, as it represents ducts and recesses accommodated within the fabric of the building. **Non-structural** methods involve attaching services to the building fabric and then enclosing them with secondary elements such as a suspended ceiling or raised floor.

Inevitably the distribution of services around a building will involve vertical and horizontal ducts. Additionally, from the main horizontal duct there will need to be lateral ducts to enable further distribution.

horizontal planes (laid to falls). **Space heating** will require more predetermined routes but often its path can be varied more easily than soil or waste pipes.

Hot and cold water supplies often use smaller pipe work than heating. This enables their distribution to be more flexible. As the operation of water supplies is not too dependent upon straight pipework lines they can be routed above or below other services. **Gas** services likewise present few problems.

Cable services for **electricity** and **communications** are very small and are often disposed of within wall or floor structures, or in suspended ceiling voids. Alternatively plastic or metal trunkings are used.

Closely associated with services distribution is their location and treatment with respect to preventing spread of fire, or enabling sound transmission from one area to another. Statutory requirements will also need to be observed.

Services requiring consideration

Waste and soil installations form a major limiting factor, as their efficient operation requires them to be in the vertical or

Access methods

The method by which access is gained must be related to the considerations outlined above. The principal techniques are:

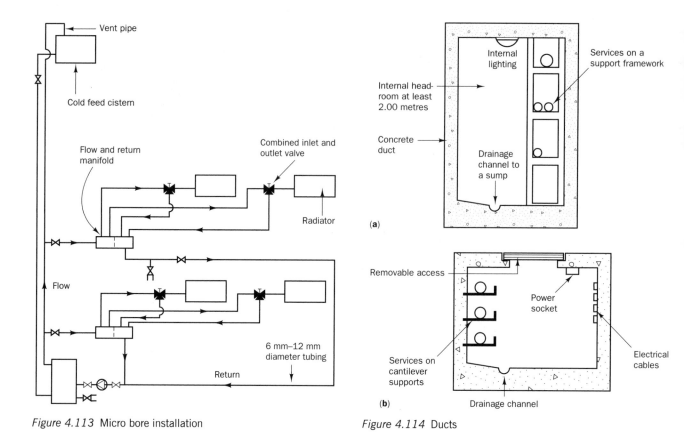

Figure 4.113 Micro bore installation

Figure 4.114 Ducts

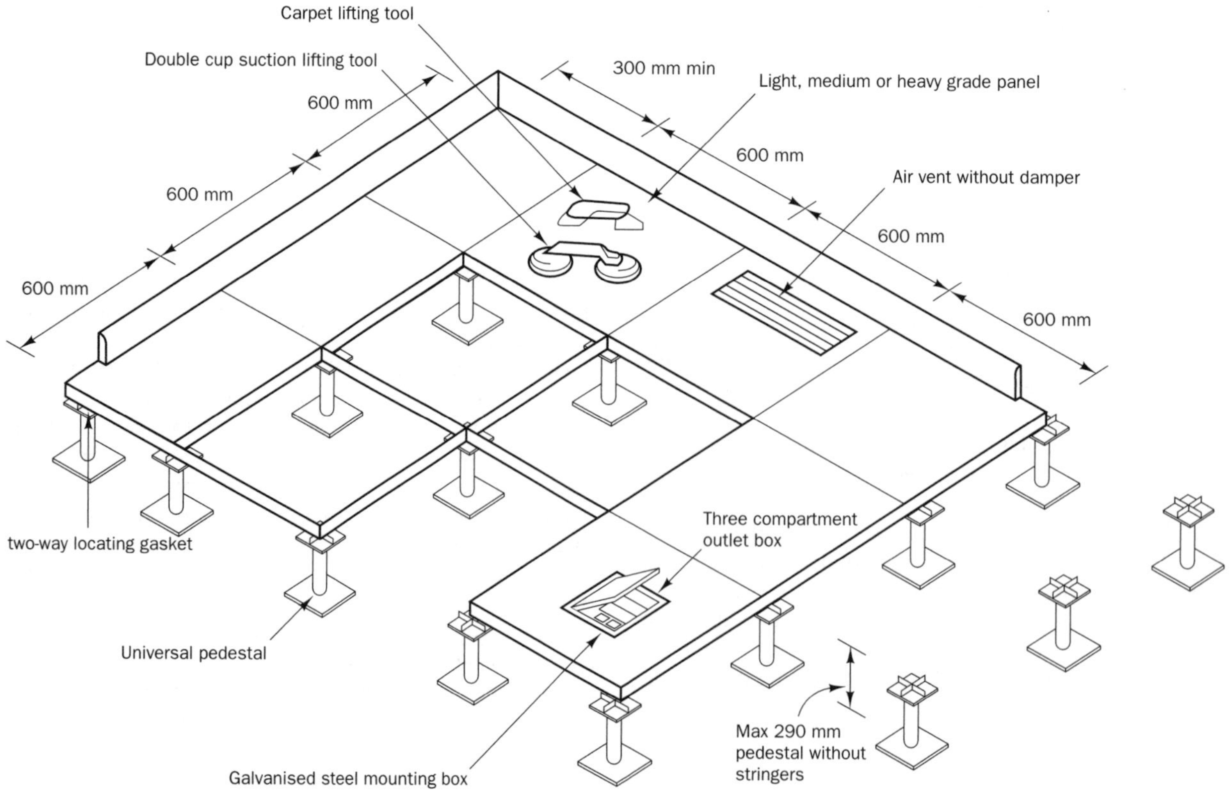

Figure 4.115 Raised floors with crawl way provision

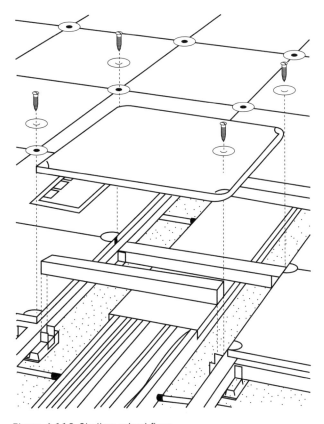

Figure 4.116 Shallow raised floor

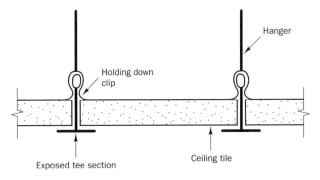

Figure 4.117

must be remembered that suspended ceilings are not a substitute for correct service support in ceiling voids. They are designed to carry their own weight plus lighting and associated services.

Frame and panel systems consist of panels that may be laid directly into an exposed grid (Fig. 4.117) or where the grid is partly or fully concealed (Fig. 4.118). The exposed grid will allow panels to be removed across the ceiling area but will not necessarily permit installation or removal of services without removal of some or all of the framework. Access to the concealed grid can be by screwed access (Fig. 4.119).

- ducts
- raised floors
- suspended ceilings
- access panels

Ducts

In buildings requiring extensive servicing it would be normal to distribute the pipe and cable services around the floor plan of the building, from which the vertical ducts will rise through the building. Ground floor ducts may be walkways or crawlways (Fig. 4.114). Access to walkway ducts will normally be from the boiler room or, as with crawlways, through lift-off covers strategically placed.

Raised floors

Raised access floors originally provided accommodation for cabling associated with computer installations or the electronic office. Their use has now been extended to general office areas and other serviced spaces. The construction of the floor can vary in height and means of access. Access is possible through every floor panel or at designated points of access. Deeper voids will allow crawlway provision (Fig. 4.115) whereas shallow voids will allow only surface access. (Fig. 4.116).

Suspended ceilings

The lateral distribution of services from vertical ducts can be achieved by either raised floors or suspended ceilings. The common ceiling types are jointless, and frame and panel. Jointless ceilings will require special access provision for services and would not be heavily serviced ceiling voids. It

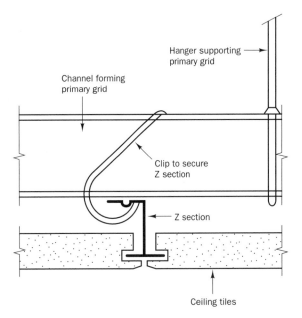

Figure 4.118

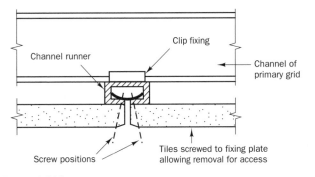

Figure 4.119

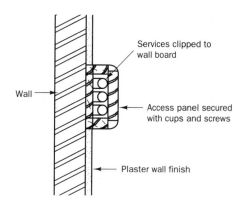

Figure 4.120

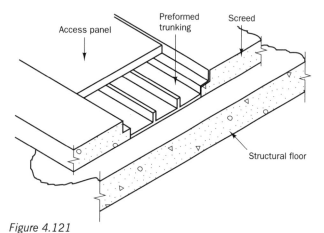

Figure 4.121

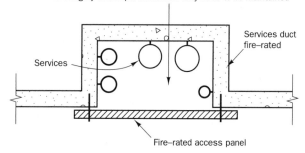

Figure 4.122

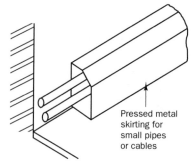

Figure 4.123

Access panels

Ducts that are to contain small pipes or cables are often provided on the surface of a wall (Fig. 4.120), or within the floor (Fig. 4.121), or wall construction (Fig. 4.122). Services may also be concealed in skirtings around the perimeter of a room (Fig. 4.123). In all cases, screwed access panels will be used.

Self-assessment tasks

1. Why must access to services be considered at the design stage?
2. Explain why some services will take priority over others when considering distribution.
3. Describe how suspended ceilings will allow access to the services.
4. Sketch details of how access can be gained to services in raised floors.
5. Explain how access to crawlways may be achieved.

Town Planning and Development

Clara Greed

Towns and cities have developed over many centuries, at different rates of growth and in different ways. This unit explores the main features and characteristics of urban areas. It identifies, within an historical context, the factors that have shaped development and city form and structure. Urban growth and change continue today, but nowadays development is controlled by the town and country planning system. Therefore it is important to understand the framework within which modern town planning operates. There is a range of legal, financial, political and environmental factors that influence and determine the nature of modern towns and cities. This unit investigates all these factors and explains the stages of the planning process. Town planning is a complex area but one that everyone in the construction industry should know about, because you cannot undertake development in most cases unless you have planning permission.

Students may be impatient to know how the system operates, but there is no point in knowing the 'rules' about the system if you do not understand the policies and reasons behind the regulations. Also it is important to appreciate the impact of planning and development policies upon the shape of our towns and cities, and the lives of the people within the community who live in them. In particular it is important to understand the effects of planning policy upon the natural and built environment for your project.

The unit is conveniently divided into sections corresponding to the required syllabus, but students and teachers are advised that the revised Unit 5 is now project-based rather than unit and element-based.

- Section 5.1 outlines the influences that have shaped the development of towns and cities from the Industrial Revolution onwards, i.e. through the nineteenth and twentieth centuries.
- Section 5.2 investigates the different patterns of urban form and the factors that have contributed to the end result, with reference to the effects of history, geography and government planning. This unit is concerned with city form and structure.

- Section 5.3 looks at the legal framework that has affected development, with particular reference to the town planning acts and other forms of state intervention over the natural and built environment. Attention is also given to the availability of grants and incentives for development in specific urban areas under present government policy. The wider context of financial, economic and political factors is considered.
- Section 5.4 outlines the stages in the development process, from the pre-site stages such as the initial decision to develop, and then gaining planning permission, through to site development considerations and the final disposal, management and maintenance stages.
- The last section, Section 5.5, discusses the impact of planning and development upon the community and the natural and built environment. Emphasis is put upon the question of the effect of development upon the quality of life and upon the differing needs of urban society. The impact of development upon the environment and the implications for the use of natural resources are discussed within the context of planning for sustainability.

Project Work

This unit is now project-based. You are required to produce a detailed case study of an urban area. This must contain images such as maps, plans, tables and other illustrations showing the main phases and characteristics of development. Supporting notes should describe the plan and development of the area chosen. The factors that have influenced development should be identified and explained. In particular, details of a current or recent local development project should be explained, with emphasis being given to the potential environmental impact of such a project.

In the course of reading the units it is recommended that each time you find an item or feature described which corresponds to the situation in your chosen area that you make a note of this and investigate it fully. Thus you will gradually build up your portfolio.

Summary

For your detailed case study of an area you must include the following:

- the plan and development features of a chosen town in the area
- the factors that have influenced the development of the chosen town
- the planning and development of a current or recent local project
- the potential environmental impact of such a project

5.1 Influences on the development of towns and cities

The development of towns and cities has been influenced by a variety of factors, both historical and modern. In particular, the introduction of town planning and other forms of state intervention have influenced development. Planning first became prominent in the nineteenth century (1800s) in response to the problems created by the Industrial Revolution and related urban growth. This section traces the development of urbanisation and the related growth of town planning and other forms of state intervention from the Industrial Revolution and through the twentieth century to today. It is worth checking Section 5.2 as well to make comparisons in respect of the factors from earlier historical periods which have shaped our towns and cities.

Project Work

As you go through this unit start looking for features that are described in the text which correspond to components of the town or city you are studying. Make a note of these as you go along and collect maps, data and documentary material to illustrate the phases and features of development. There are additional short test questions and tasks included in this unit to help you on your way.

Illustrations and tables are included, but students should aim at producing their own specifically related to the urban area being studied.

The Industrial Revolution

A whole new situation

Relatively speaking, both town planning and urbanisation itself 'started' in the nineteenth century, i.e. from the 1800s, during the Victorian period. At the beginning of the nineteenth century Britain was undergoing major economic and social change. There was already a long historical tradition of town planning before this period but it was concerned with much smaller populations and often only with the more affluent classes, set against a relatively static technological context. The demand for 'modern' town planning was called forth by a combination of the effects of three main factors, namely, industrialisation, urbanisation and population growth, and the related problems of overcrowding and disease.

The Industrial Revolution, as its name suggests, transformed Britain from a predominantly rural agricultural society to a modern industrial urban society. There had been an 'agricultural revolution' with changes in farming methods in the eighteenth century which had led to greater yields and fewer agricultural labourers. In some areas this created a surplus of workers, leading to a movement of the workforce to the towns, providing the necessary workforce for the Industrial Revolution, and leading to rural depopulation.

Development of new forms of technology, and in particular the creation of machinery that could produce manufactured goods more quickly than the human hand, led to major changes in the nature of work and the duties of the workforce. At first, industrial development occurred on a fairly small scale, fitting in with the surroundings with little disturbance because the early woollen mills and factories were powered by water power. The early industrial settlements were relatively rural, being placed alongside fast-flowing streams in hilly countryside.

Later, coal was used to fuel steam engines which could power many more machines at once by means of connecting drive belts running throughout the factory. New industrial settlements grew up alongside the coal mines, particularly in the North, the Midlands, and South Wales. The emphasis shifted from the production of textiles in rural areas, to iron and steel, and then manufactured goods in highly urbanised areas, as a result of technological developments. People flocked to the newly industrialising areas, resulting in rural depopulation and a complete regional redistribution of the population broadly from the South towards the North (the opposite of today) and from the West Country to South Wales.

In the later stages of industrialisation other forms of power, such as gas and electricity, were developed which could be transmitted anywhere nationally. In theory one could develop anything anywhere, provided one had the financial backing to do so (leading to the phenomenon of 'footloose' industry which went wherever it was the most economic to locate). However, development was inevitably attracted to areas that had already established themselves as industrial centres, because they offered concentrations of skilled workers, necessary infrastructure, and the commercial expertise to help run the businesses and market needed to sell the products.

Nowadays access to transport routes for distribution purposes, especially the need to be near motorway junctions, or within prestigious motorway corridors such as the M4, is likely to be more important than being near sources of local power because of the ubiquity of the national grid. Modern high-technology industries are so different in their education and skill requirements from those of the past that industrialists might find that suitable personnel are more likely to be drawn from the traditional office and 'quaternary' workers of the South and South East (who incidentally are less unionised), than among the skilled and unskilled manual workers of the North and Midlands. These social changes and classifications are discussed further in Section 5.5.

Figure 5.1 Industrial and residential townscape, Avonmouth, Bristol

Transport Revolution

The Industrial Revolution was accompanied by a revolution in transport. For centuries, cities had been relatively close-knit because the extent of cities and the distances between different land uses and amenities had been governed by the distances that people could comfortably walk. Industrial goods were first transported by turnpike road and then by canal, but with the introduction of mechanical means of transport, goods could be transported speedily across the country. People too could travel further, and more quickly than they could walk, and cities began to spread out horizontally. With the development of the railway system, those who were more affluent moved further out and commuted in, starting the trend of suburbanisation and decentralisation which has been such a major feature of urban development in Britain over the last 150 years. Many small towns owed their very existence and prosperity to the development of the railways, being blessed with a station which brought with it potential customers for local goods and services. Other towns were more directly involved as major interchange points on the railway system, e.g. Crewe, or as major producers of rolling stock, e.g. Swindon.

Self-assessment questions

1. What were the main technological changes that brought forth the Industrial Revolution?
2. What were the main aspects of the transport revolution?
3. What were the social changes that took place? (see next section for this)
4. What was the impact on towns? (see next section)

Project Work

Add details of transport systems – roads, railways, canals and docks – to your history portfolio. Are there any of these that used to exist but which have now fallen into disuse?

Urbanisation and population growth

The growth in industrialisation was accompanied by the growth of towns and cities, and also population growth (Tables 5.1 and 5.2).

Table 5.1 UK population growth 1801–1901

Date	Total Population
1801	8.9 million
1851	17.9 million
1901	32.5 million

Table 5.2 UK population in 1999

England	49 284 million
Scotland	5 123 million
Wales	2 927 million
N. Ireland	1 675 million
London	7.8 million (Greater London)
United Kingdom	59 million (rounded total)

(*Source: Social Trends* (ONS 1999). *Social Trends* is produced annually by the Office of National Statistics and contains information on every statistical aspect of urban society.

Table 5.3 shows the tremendous rate of urban growth that was occurring in the new industrial towns and cities during the nineteenth century; they were doubling and tripling in size.

Table 5.3 Urban growth 1801–1901

Date	Birmingham	Manchester	Leeds
1801	71 000	75 000	53 000
1851	265 000	336 000	172 000
1901	765 000	645 000	429 000

Table 5.4 Global comparison: the world's largest cities in 1950

New York	12.3 million
London	7.8 million
Tokyo	6.7 million
Paris	5.4 million
Shanghai	5.3 million
Buenos Aires	5.0 million
Chicago	4.9 million
Moscow	4.8 million
Calcutta	4.4 million
Los Angeles	4.0 million

Table 5.5 The world's largest cities in 2000

Mexico City	25.6 million
Sao Paulo	22.1 million
Tokyo	19.08 million
Shanghai	17.0 million
New York	16.8 million
Calcutta	15.7 million
Mumbai (Bombay)	15.4 million
Beijing	14.0 million
Los Angeles	13.9 million
Jakarta	13.7 million

Table 5.6 The largest British cities in 1999

Greater London	7.8 million
Birmingham/West Midlands	2.3 million
Greater Manchester	2.3 million
Leeds/West Yorkshire	1.5 million
Newcastle/Tyneside	0.88 million
Liverpool	0.84 million
Glasgow	0.66 million
Sheffield	0.64 million
Nottingham	0.61 million
Bristol	0.53 million

(*Source*: ONS 1999, Table 1.7.)

While there was an overall growth of population in the nineteenth century, there were also, as stated above, large movements of population from one part of the country to another, both on a regional basis, and in a general migration from the countryside to the towns. This may be summed up by the following statistics:

1801 – 80% of the population was rural.
1991 – 80% of the population was, and is, urban.

Not only were there changes in the quantities of people in towns and cities, but inevitably there was a decline in the quality of their lives owing to disease and overcrowding. Conditions and standards were not very different from the situation in rural areas of the time, but people could get away with fairly elementary methods of sewage disposal in small villages, whereas the sheer concentration of numbers in the new cities increased the likelihood of disease developing in the crowded alleyways and tenements. These problems could not be solved by personal individual efforts but required civic initiatives and national solutions.

Rural and regional perspectives

As a result of the development of the railways, Britain 'shrank' in that it became much easier to travel, and few areas were remote from a railway station. Indeed the urban/rural division was rapidly breaking down. Also some of the industrial settlements, while appearing very urbanised and concentrated around the mill or mine, were in fact near to the countryside. In the valleys of South Wales or parts of Derbyshire one only has to take a short walk to be out of the industrial environment and into the open countryside. The effects of industrial activity, especially mining, encroached to some extent on the surrounding countryside, spewing out slag heaps and pollution, and leaving an extensive burden of industrial dereliction. Such land is still being reclaimed, for example by the Welsh Development Agency (WDA) in South Wales, and as part of projects such as the Garden Festival project at Ebbw Vale in 1992.

This was very different from the situation in the south of England where large amounts of manufacturing industry developed within inner city areas, often as back-street business in erstwhile residential areas. Many houses on main roads were converted into shops or businesses. One can quite clearly see where the shop fronts were added, especially when looking down on the buildings from the top of a double decker bus while travelling through a shopping street. Urban development seemed to spread out, on and on in all directions with hardly a break, over many miles in the London region. In fact, some of the most industrialised, urbanised and commercialised areas of Britain were in the South, in the inner London boroughs with large working class populations to match.

In the South the office and commercial revolution followed hard on the heels of Industrial Revolution, creating a new 'proletariat' made up of clerks, typists, service industry workers and shopkeepers who were often mistakenly perceived as middle class (or 'petit-bourgeoisie') and unworthy of special attention, in spite of their low incomes and poor working conditions. Many would argue that the emphasis in regional economic planning policy in the 1960s, which favoured the 'depressed' northern areas, was actually at the expense of these other working groups of people in inner urban areas in southern cities. Some would argue that this was a contributory factor to the decline of the inner city today in which high levels of unemployment and poverty exist.

While it can be seen that the divisions within social classes and land uses are not as clear cut as the early urban theory-makers imagined, nevertheless many cities were replanned by means of strict land use zoning which separated out housing areas from industrial and other uses, and which made little allowance for the need for a mixture of land uses such as had existed in traditional, organic, planned settlements. Nowadays it is interesting that there is a move among some planning authorities towards a greater emphasis upon the acceptance of mixed land uses, if only to reduce the need to travel, and in order to provide employment and investment in local areas. However, in a sense this is shutting the stable door after the

horse has bolted because, as will be seen in the next section, twentieth-century planning has been firmly focused on zoning, decentralisation and dispersal of land uses and facilities. Likewise, private sector developers and businesses have welcomed the establishment of out-of-town shopping centres, and decentralised business parks, which have made it almost essential for people to have cars, particularly in the light of the decline of public transport. Indeed the average person living 100 years ago would have had a wider choice of public transport, and a more extensive rail network, than is the case today.

Reaction and reform

As a result of the changes and bad conditions found during the Industrial Revolution, a series of reforms were introduced, with an emphasis upon housing, public health and town planning measures. The spread of cholera and other water-borne diseases made intervention necessary, there being two major outbreaks in 1832 and 1849. Because cholera was a water-borne disease and no respecter of persons, although it might originate in working class districts it could spread anywhere along the insanitary water systems of the city. In 1854 a Dr Snow showed the relationship between a major cholera outbreak and a single polluted pump in the Soho district of London. Increased state intervention to provide sewerage and drainage systems was needed (Table 5.7).

Table 5.7 Main Pre-World War II planning acts

1835 Municipal Corporations Act (gave powers to local authorities)
1847 Sanitary Act (connection of houses to sewers)
1848 Public Health Act (minimum of 8 feet ceilings)
1868 Artisans and Labourers Dwellings Improvements Act
1875 Public Health Act (bylaw housing, against back to backs)
1875 Artisans Dwellings Act (slum clearance of streets)
1879 Public Health Act
1890 Housing of the Working Classes Act (council houses)
1894 London Building Act (London building regulations)
1909 Housing and Town Planning Act
1919 Housing and Town Planning Act
1932 Town and Country Planning Act
1935 Restriction of Ribbon Development Act

Then 1939–45 World War II

To implement reforms there was a need for an effective, administrative structure. The 1835 Municipal Corporations Act laid the foundations for this, enabling the creation of local authorities with relevant powers. Following a series of studies on public health conditions, the 1847 Sanitary Act required sewers and drains to be provided in all new residential areas. The 1848 Public Health Act went further, being one of the first acts intervening in *how* houses were constructed, and therefore potentially adding to the cost for the developers. This act required that all ceilings must be at least 8 feet (2.4 m) high. 1875 is a landmark in the development of state intervention into the built environment. Several important Acts were passed in that year. The Artisans and Labourers Dwellings Improvement Act of that year increased local authority powers to deal with whole areas, as against individual buildings, giving them compulsory purchase powers, and the power to build schemes that provided accommodation for the working

Figure 5.2 Viaduct tenements built in the Industrial Revolution

classes – this being a major step towards the modern-day power of local authorities to carry out compulsory purchases and to take control of the building of an area themselves. The 1875 Public Health Act was also a major landmark and set minimum standards on the design of houses and also on the layout of streets, so it is in a sense one of the first true town planning acts. This was achieved by giving local authorities the power to introduce bylaws controlling the layout of new streets and housing schemes. It required that every house should have a back access, which was meant to solve the problem of back to back houses. To summarise, in these Acts the three functions of local authorities were to clear existing areas, to build housing themselves, and to control the developments of others.

In 1890 the Housing of the Working Classes Act increased the power of local authorities to build new houses themselves, thus creating an early form of council housing. By this time developers were losing interest in building cheap housing for the working classes to rent, and were turning their attention to the more affluent emerging owner-occupied middle class suburban housing developments. Council housing was to go on to become a major feature of our towns and cities in the twentieth century. It is only since the 1980s that this sector has been in decline following various negative housing acts, and a push towards owner-occupation, which has now reached around 70%. Up until 1909, only 10% of people owned their own house and most of these were upper middle class people. Many perfectly respectable middle class people rented their housing, as is still the case to a greater degree in other European countries today. Nowadays over two-thirds of householders are owner-occupiers.

Model communities

Private initiatives: model communities

Government initiatives were augmented by a wide range of private reforming endeavours. There were already a number of early housing societies concerned with improving the conditions of the working classes. One of the most well known and productive was the Peabody Trust set up in 1862 by George Peabody, an American philanthropist. Many of his buildings can still be seen today in areas of

London such as Islington, Whitechapel, Vauxhall and Bethnal Green, and most of these are also in the style of walk-up tenements. Many of these schemes look fairly grim, judged by today's standards, but they were better than existing alternatives.

Robert Owen (1771–1858) was one of the earliest Industrial Revolution period 'town planners'. He developed New Lanark, in Scotland, to be a model industrial community. The mills have long since closed and nowadays 'The New Lanark Experience' is a tourist attraction – a heritage village. A second flowering of the model towns movement occurred in this area of rapid industrialisation. Colonel Akroyd, a rich mill owner, built two model communities, the first at Copley in 1849, and then Akroydon in 1859. Akroydon consisted of fairly modest terraced and town houses for the workers, based on a grid layout. Another key figure in the Halifax school is Titus Salt (1803–1876) who founded the village of Saltaire in 1851, on the River Aire. Saltaire is nowadays protected by conservation area policy.

The garden city movement

There is a marked change of style from these early relatively high-density developments of the early nineteenth century to the lower density, more luxuriant garden city schemes of the latter part of the century in which the housing consists of traditional cottages with gable ends and front gardens, rather than tenements or plain terraces. The leader in this field was Ebenezer Howard, the grandfather of British Town Planning.

Ebenezer Howard wrote the book *Tomorrow: A Peaceful Path to Reform* in 1898, this being renamed *Garden Cities of Tomorrow* in 1902, in which he put forward his main town planning ideas for the creation of an ideal community. Howard believed that although the Industrial Revolution had been accompanied by great problems of overcrowding, bad housing and environmental problems, at the same time it had brought many benefits. Therefore he sought to combine the best of the modern town and the new industrial society with the best of the countryside and the traditional way of rural village life in the town-country or garden-city as he called his ideal community. This idea is shown graphically in Fig. 5.3, in which the garden city is seen as a powerful 'countermagnet' that would attract people away from both the overcrowded industrial cities and the backwardness of the countryside.

Howard was not only a theorist but also man of action. In those days there was no adequate state system of town planning, and so whatever was to be done had to be achieved through private investment and development. He attempted to start the process off by setting up the first Garden City Company Limited before the First World War and started developments in Letchworth in 1903, and later in Welwyn Garden City in 1920, both on the edges of London (now well and truly in the commuter belt). These enterprises ran into business difficulties. However, the sites he had recommended for the rest of the ring of garden city countermagnets which he proposed, were later adopted by the planners under the 1946 New Towns Act as the location of the first phase of British **new towns**.

Howard was not working in isolation and others sought to create garden cities too. For example, George Cadbury (1839–1922) moved his chocolate factory out of Birmingham

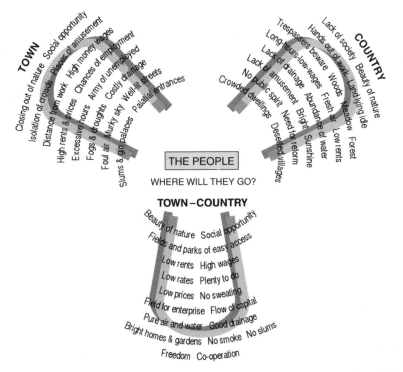

Figure 5.3 Ebenezer Howard's 'three magnets'. (*After* Howard E. 1898 *Garden Cities of Tomorrow*, (republished in 1960 by Faber and Faber))

to Bourneville in 1879, and built the main settlement around it from 1895. W. Alexander Harvey was employed as the architect. Harvey believed in designing the layout in sympathy with the topography, stating 'it is nearly always better to use the contour of the land, taking a gentle sweep in preference to a straight line'. This contrasted with the grid-iron type layouts of many of the earlier settlements, and is a precursor of the trademark of much English town planning of meandering and curving roads, and a generally 'natural' appearance. The houses were built at a very low density

(seven or eight houses to the acre), with large open space areas and trees.

Port Sunlight was built by Lever, the soap manufacturer, across the Mersey from Liverpool. He bought 52 acres on Merseyside, and started building his factory there in 1888, and then started his model village in 1889, which was not completed until 1934 (Fig. 5.6). Again the scheme is low density with five to eight houses per acre. Joseph Rowntree (1836–1925) is the third of the most notable philanthropic factory owners of the late nineteenth century who built a

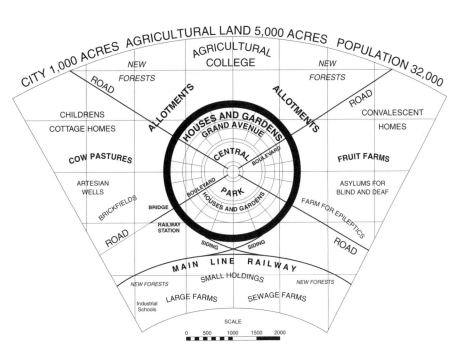

Figure 5.4 Howard's conception of the Garden City and its rural belt. (*After Howard E. 1898 Garden Cities of Tomorrow* (republished in 1960 by Faber and Faber))

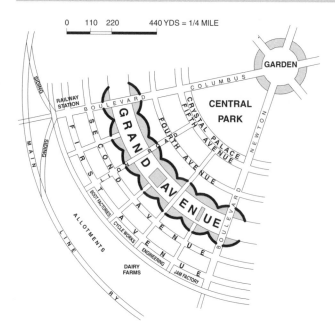

Figure 5.5 The neighbourhood of Howard's Garden City. (*After Howard E. 1898 Garden Cities of Tomorrow*, (republished in 1960 by Faber and Faber))

Figure 5.6 Garden City, Port Sunlight

model community, in this case at New Earswick near York. He employed Unwin and Parker as architects, again developing garden city type houses, which in this settlement were grouped around *culs de sac*.

The early Town Planning Acts

The style and space standards of the houses were to act as models for the council houses introduced under the 1909 and 1919 Housing and Town Planning Acts, and in particular the Tudor Walters standards for council housing design (later to be superseded by the Parker Morris standards in more recent times).

Both of these acts, as suggested by their titles, were more concerned with providing 'schemes' (as plans were called then) for setting out the council housing, than for planning whole towns in the modern sense. The 1919 Act enabled local authorities to draw up a land-use plan for the whole town or city, but as the powers of the Act were very weak and they were unable to enforce control over land use, they often drew the zones in after the developers had departed.

As will be seen, in the twentieth century, development plans, as they became known, were to become an important means of planning and controlling urban development in an effective manner, backed by legal powers. Relatively speaking, all the Acts prior to 1945 were quite weak, and it was not until the post-war reconstruction planning of the 1940s that a comprehensive town planning system was created.

Project Work

Continue to add features such as council estates, garden suburbs and, if you are lucky, model communities to your local history map.

If at all possible, visit one of the examples discussed above and make notes on it.

Self-assessment tasks

1. What were the main aspects of reform in response to the urban conditions created by the Industrial Revolution?
2. Name any three model communities and their creators.
3. What were the main features of the garden city?

The development of the modern town planning system

Town planning, in its present form, dates primarily from the post-war reconstruction period, i.e. from 1945 onwards. In particular, the 1947 Town and Country Planning Act was a milestone, introducing a comprehensive system of plan making and control of development.

The nature of the system under these acts will be explained shortly. But what is town planning? Here is one definition:

Town planning is the art and the science of ordering the land-uses and siting the buildings and communication routes so as to secure the maximum level of economy, convenience and beauty.

This definition was coined in the 1950s in the heyday of British town planning by a planner called Lewis Keeble during the urban reconstruction programme following the Second World War (1939–45). If you wish to follow through the 'story of town planning' in more detail, you should consult *Introducing Town Planning*, by C. Greed (1996), in which this and many other town plannning issues are discussed in greater depth.

Table 5.8 Main immediate post-war town planning related Acts

1945	Distribution of Industry Act
1946	New Towns Act
1947	Town and Country Planning Act
1949	National Parks and Access to the Countryside Act
1952	Town Development Act

(For a full list to end of twentieth century, see Table 5.11.)

We will now provide a brief linking section showing how the planning system developed in the first part of the twentieth century resulted in the present system.

The dimensions of the modern planning system

Evolution

By the beginning of the twentieth century the various aspects of built environment policy such as public health, housing management, building control and town planning were separating out into different functions of local government, as represented by different professions. The town planning movement had been developing throughout the latter part of the nineteenth century, increasingly occupying itself not just with dealing with the immediate crisis problems of disease and overcrowding in respect of working class housing, but formulating ideas on how to replan whole cities to accommodate the demands of modern, industrialised, urbanised society. The interests of town planners were not limited merely to housing or to working class areas by this time, but they were concerned with planning for all land uses and all the social classes. It was soon realised that urban problems could not be solved 'once for all' by producing 'the plan', but that planning was an endless process of policy-making, control and implementation, and 'survey, analysis, plan'.

By the inter-war period (1919–38) many of the town planning problems that confront us today were already beginning to develop. In particular, there was concern about the spread of the town into the countryside, particularly because of the growth of suburban housebuilding, of which 'ribbon development' was one aspect. This occurred when developers built alongside existing main roads to save building their own roads but in the process they created long tentacles of unplanned development radiating into the countryside. The 1935 Ribbon Development Act sought to halt this, but as mentioned above, planning legislation at this time lacked adequate powers.

There were also a whole range of regional planning issues related to the problems of growing unemployment in the areas of declining heavy industry such as the North East, and on the other hand, congestion, growth, and thus pressures for house building and development in London and the South East. Between 1930 and 1940, 2 700 000 houses were built and much of this was as urban sprawl and suburban growth in the South East and Midlands. Other land use matters included demands for greater control of, and access to, the countryside by a range of early environmental groups and countryside enthusiasts. Concern was also beginning to be expressed about the need to build more roads and plan for the motor car, although car ownership never topped 2 million before the war, whereas today there are over 20 million cars on the road.

Reconstruction planning 1945–52

After the end of the Second World War, the new Labour government put in place the framework of the Welfare State and other national reform programmes. The main components are described below. The main aspects of post-war reconstruction planning are outlined below. Specific aspects are dealt with in more detail later in the unit.

Figure 5.7 Post-war reconstruction: St Paul's Cathedral bombing, London

Development plan system

The main plank of post-war reconstruction planning was the 1947 Town and Country Planning Act. Under this act all development had to receive planning permission. Local authorities had to prepare **development plans** showing the main land uses by means of coloured zonings. The system was based on a 'master plan' or blueprint approach.

To make the new planning system work there had to be strong powers of development control and there was also a high level of taxation of profit from land and property development. There have been subsequent changes to the legislation but many of the policies and major decisions found in these early planning documents still shape planning practice today, not least a commitment to land use zoning. In the 1950s, many of these plans showed green belts which were intended to create a protective cordon of non-development around major cities to prevent urban sprawl. London was slightly ahead of other cities, in that it had its own green belt before the war and its development plan was published in 1944 under separate legislation.

The next major change was the 1968 Town and Country Planning Act, later consolidated into the 1971 Town and Country Planning Act, which introduced a new type of development plan, known as the **structure plan**. Then in the 1990s the current system was introduced.

The new towns programme

Much of the post-war housing and new development was located in the **new towns**. The 1946 New Towns Act in many respects fulfilled the original dreams of the late Ebenezer Howard. The new towns were developed in three main phases. The first phase (Mark I) was built immediately after the war and consisted mainly of satellite settlements around London on sites that were very similar to Howard's original ones. The 1952 Town Development Act introduced the idea of creating expanded towns, such as Swindon, rather than building complete new towns. This was followed by a much reduced second phase of Mark II new towns under the Conservatives in the 1950s, and then a third extensive phase known as Mark III new towns, built under the Labour government of Harold Wilson, in the 1960s, which included Milton Keynes (Fig. 5.8).

The early new towns were generally of a population of around 50 000 and consisted of a series of neighbourhood units of around 5000 population, each with local shops and a

Figure 5.8 The new towns of Britain

town centre. Milton Keynes was designed as a **new city**, based on a grid layout of roads, and was intended to have a target population of over a quarter of a million. It is located midway between London and Birmingham and is somewhat notorious for its peculiar design features and architecture.

Regional planning

The 1945 Distribution of Industry Act gave grants and incentives which encouraged firms to move to these areas, following the principle of taking work to the workers. However, some would say that this approach penalised businesses that wanted to develop and expand in the more prosperous areas. Also, even in the most prosperous cities such as London, there were distinct areas of unemployment and poverty which needed employment and could not compete with the more favoured areas.

There was a long series of regional planning Acts until the Conservative government took power in the late 1970s. Most of the acts have now been repealed, as the emphasis has shifted to other planning issues and inequalities, not least inner city revitalisation. Clearly, regional planning was concerned with tackling social and economic change as well as physical land use and locational issues.

National parks

Another related aspect of the post-war planning programme was the 1949 National Parks and Access to the Countryside Act within the context of a national land use strategy for Britain. There has been a subsequent development of a more complex range of types of protected areas, and new variations are still being considered, but the original legislation is still in force. This aspect is discussed further in Section 5.5 in the context of conservation of the natural environment.

Listed buildings and urban conservation

Post-war reconstruction planning in the twenty years after 1945 may be described as 'hit and run planning' or 'knock it all down and start again', with the emphasis being put upon new towns, new houses, and new town centre development. Planning, then, gave little attention to existing, older urban areas. Instead the emphasis was on decentralisation and removal of 'non-conforming uses' to green field sites. Also, what we would now see as historic buildings worthy of conservation, were being demolished to make space for new developments and new roads.

As will be explained in Section 5.3 in the discussion of architectural trends, there was great enthusiasm by the 1960s for high-rise blocks of offices and a veritable 'property boom' hit the country, fired by town centre redevelopment. Conservation groups became increasingly concerned with the visual effects (until then the highest buildings had been the church towers) and at the wanton demolition that was necessary to make space for new development. Many Victorian town halls narrowly missed destruction, and many a Georgian terrace was sacrificed.

As a result, the 1967 Civic Amenities Act gave powers for the creation of **conservation areas**, and the listing of buildings of historical and architectural importance became a major issue. Subsequently this legislation was elaborated upon and the 1990 Planning (Listed Buildings and Conservation Areas) Act is the most recent Act in force. Buildings are listed by the Department of the Environment. English Heritage is now the body responsible for listing buildings. Buildings are listed if they are seen to be of outstanding historic or architectural interest. Such buildings include all those built before 1700, most of those built between 1700 and 1840, some built between 1840 and 1914, a few built between 1914 and 1939 and even a few built after that. There are three main categories of listing. Grade I buildings must not be removed in any circumstances and are of national or even international importance. Grade II buildings fall into two subcategories: Grade II* (starred) – which means they have an asterisk * beside them on the list – cannot be removed without a compelling reason, and are usually of significant regional, if not national importance; Grade II (unstarred) are more ordinary buildings such as typical Georgian or Victorian town houses of more local importance. There are around half a million listed buildings in England and Wales, of which 5 800 are Grade I, and 15 000 are Grade II*, and there are more than 6 000 conservation areas.

Housing improvement

The 1957 Slum Clearance Act gave local authorities strong powers to carry out demolition, and this led to much criticism from communities living in the areas affected. The 1969 Housing Act introduced GIAs (General Improvement Areas) and also increased the availability of individual grants to improve older property in inner areas.

There have been many similar housing Acts introducing a complex variety of grants and incentives for the improvement of housing, as an alternative to slum clearance, such as the 1974 Housing Act which established Housing Action Areas. This marks a turning point in government policy and the beginning of a serious concern and recognition of what came to be known as the problems of the 'inner city'.

Now there is a whole range of initiatives both for older privately owned housing areas, and for council estates, such as the HATs (Housing Action Trusts), which give tenants and residents more say in decision-making and participation in the policy process. Since the 1980 Housing Act and the 1985 Housing Act, tenants were given 'the right to buy' their council houses and there has been a gradual rundown of this form of social housing.

Inner city

In spite of continuing regional planning policy, by the 1970s inequality was visibly re-emerging. The poverty and deprivation that were developing were not entirely explained by the rise in unemployment, but were the result of other social problems such as racial discrimination, family breakup, and an ageing population, and areas such as Handsworth in Birmingham, Everton in Liverpool, St Pauls in Bristol, Tottenham in London, and Sparkbrook in Birmingham were mentioned in the newspapers. The 'inner city' became the catch-phrase to describe the collection of neighbourhoods, social groups and urban problems located broadly within the poorer inner urban areas, corresponding to what traditional urban sociologists called the zone of transition (as discussed further in Section 5.2).

In 1968 the Home Office had initiated the 'Urban Programme' to investigate the emerging problems of the inner city, and in 1969 the Community Development Programme was set up. The 1978 Inner Urban Areas Act, which as its name suggests enabled the creation of special inner urban area policies, this time chiefly under the control of the town planners. The 1989 Local Government and Housing Act introduced the concept of **renewal areas**, with emphasis on partnership with the private sector. A variety of other national and local authority schemes have followed.

Enterprise Zones and Urban Development Corporations

The Conservative Government (1979–97) had put great emphasis upon solving both economic and social urban problems through stimulating local private sector investment and development, rather than directly through state subsidy as had been more common under Labour policy. The 1980 Local Government Planning and Land Act paved the way for EZs (Enterprise Zones) and UDPs (Urban Development Corporations).

EZs are relatively small areas, the size of a small industrial estate, and are administered via the existing local authority, whereas UDCs are much larger areas, such as the London Docklands, or the Bristol Development Corporation area. Considerable investment is put into infrastructure, as in the case of the Docklands light railway in London, and into road improvements. Subsequently the 1986 Housing and Planning Act introduced, among other things, SPZs (Simplified Planning Zones), and the Urban Grant programme was extended. Other revitalisation programmes for rundown industrial areas have included 'Garden Festivals', such as at Ebbw Vale in Wales. One of the more interesting, or at least most publicised sources, of funding for urban renewal is the Millennium fund and related Lottery, Arts Council and Sports Council funds. Many would argue that this creates a somewhat piecemeal approach which is not always linked back into the statutory planning system, and the debate continues. The funding aspect is discussed further in relation to development finance in Section 5.3.

Self-assessment tasks

1. List the main components of the post-war planning system.
2. How many of these components are still part of the planning system today? (Hint: most! but give reasons for your answer.)
3. How does pre-war planning contrast with post-war planning systems?

Project work

We have covered a vast area it is suggested that you choose one particular component of planning that is of interest to you, and develop project work on this with your supervisor in relation to your chosen urban area.

Further reading

Chapman D (ed) 1996 *Neighbourhoods and Plans in the Built Environment* E & FN Spon

Greed C 1996 *Introducing Town Planning* (2nd edition) Addison Wesley Longman

Greed C and Roberts M 2000 *Approaching Urban Design* Pearson Education

5.2 Town plan features

The purpose of this section is to identify the main features and characteristics of towns past and present. These include organic features of the relatively unplanned towns that developed naturally in medieval times, through to the more geometric, planned, formally structured towns that developed in later times. Therefore this section is tackled in chronological order. The development of town planning since the Industrial Revolution has already been covered in Section 5.1 and readers are advised to reread this when they reach the references to the nineteenth century in this section.

In the course of the discussion, attention will be given to factors such as human need and social considerations, technological change, and governmental influence in the development of town planning, and thus the shape of towns and cities. Clearly, there are a complex range of factors that contribute towards 'what is built', and which therefore shape our towns and cities, but the suggested activities for project work and self-assessment questions are intended to encourage readers to explore some of the key issues in more depth for themselves.

As a result of studying the first section the student will be able to identify the key components and features of town form, both historical and modern. Although the historical phases are fundamental, in many towns the bulk of urban development occurred in the twentieth century. A whole range of planned features such as shopping centres, industrial estates and recreation areas have been developed,

many of which have been built in the last 50 years. Also in modern times controls on town form have been introduced, such as green belts to restrict outward growth and prevent urban sprawl. In particular, zoning, i.e. the separation of land uses, and the creation of distinct residential, commercial and industrial areas has been the key factor shaping urban form during the second half of twentieth century (Fig. 5.9).

Historical development of town planning

Organic development

Most towns in Britain evolved gradually rather than being planned. For example, a small settlement would develop beside a river and gradually tracks would develop into roads that meandered down the valley side to a bridge. From time to time houses would be built alongside the roads where and when the residents felt the need. Gradually other facilities – artisan quarters, houses, paddocks and market places – would develop, often centring around a well or a crossroads. Roads would follow footpaths, creating the typically irregular street pattern characteristic of medieval towns (Figs 5.10–5.13).

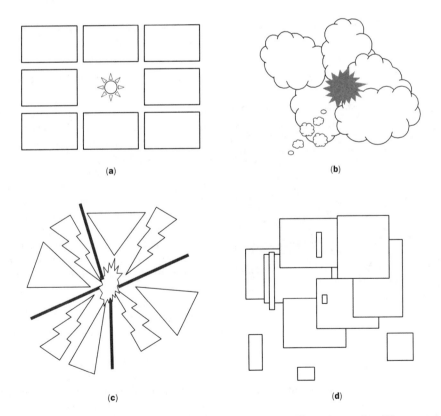

(a)

(b)

(c)

(d)

Figure 5.9 Main types of city form and urban patterns. (a) The formal grid layout settlement, usually military or colonial in purpose, e.g. Roman towns. (b) The organic town which grew naturally, usually with a centre around a bridge and a market, e.g. a medieval town. (c) A radial city based on rail and road networks, usually a nineteenth or early twentieth century town. (d) A modern city, characterised by the effects of town planning, zoning and decentralisation, e.g. Los Angeles

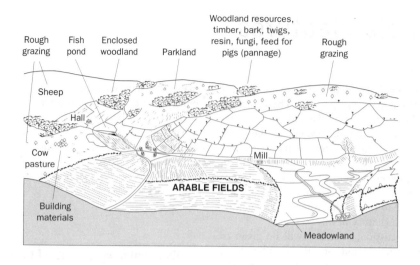

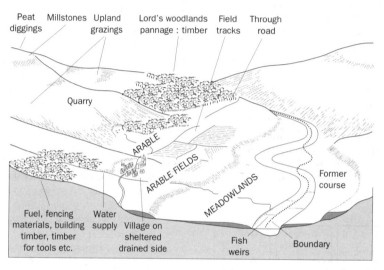

Figure 5.10 Siting constraints. (*After* Roberts 1994 *The Making of an English Village*, Addison Wesley Longman)

Figure 5.11 Typical medieval town form

Early planned towns: Greek and Roman

While in Britain many historical towns grew in an unplanned manner, this was not always the case in other parts of Europe. The Ancient Greeks had developed theories on town planning, many of which they put into practice in the building of their city states and the colonial towns in their empire. Most Greek settlements were based on a grid layout (streets at right angles to

each other) but they combined this with a flexibility of design which took into account the particular features of the site, creating natural amphitheatres in the hillsides.

Greek settlements centred on a central market square (the agora) which was surrounded by the main public buildings such as the town hall. Not only did the Greeks build magnificent streets and buildings, they took into account the need for sanitation, drainage and a water supply. Lewis Mumford, a famous commentator on town planning (*The City in History*, 1965), stated that the quality of a civilisation should be judged by the way in which it disposes of its waste material.

Likewise the architecture and town planning concepts of Ancient Rome were highly influential on the work of subsequent centuries. The Roman Empire was also a vast city building enterprise and 'Every Roman soldier had a town plan in his knapsack'. Indeed the army did most of the construction and many of the town planners, civil engineers and architects were military men.

Roman towns were more standardised than Greek ones, and were based on a simple grid layout with a square in the centre which was called the **forum**, and several other standard public amenities were provided around the town such as baths, latrines, an arena, etc. (Figs 5.14 and 5.15). There was an element of land-use zoning based largely on the social rank differences and occupations of the residents, with distinct

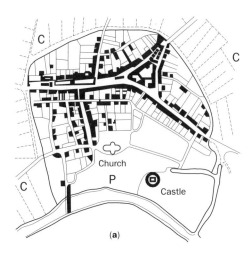

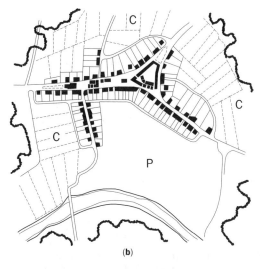

Figure 5.12 Development of a typical village into a market town – common fields (C) and pasture (P): (a) c. 900; (b) c. 1100. (*After* Morris 1994 *History of urban forms*, Addison Wesley Longman)

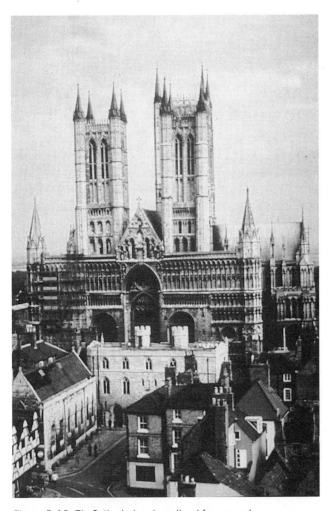

Figure 5.13 Ely Cathedral and medieval foreground

retail (merchants) and industrial (artisans) areas. As with most ancient and classical civilisations, a very high proportion of the population would be slaves. It is important to remember that when the Greeks talked about the ideal city consisting of 5000 people they meant the people that mattered (slaves, women, tradespeople, etc., were marginal categories).

The greatest building engineering achievements of the Romans were the perfection of the arch and the dome, elements that were not features of earlier styles. The Coliseum in Rome is a good example of arch construction, as are the many aqueducts and viaducts dotted throughout the Empire all over Europe and North Africa.

Defensive walls were also a feature of many Roman settlements. Indeed for centuries most towns and cities had walls, and town planning was in certain respects a military exercise to ensure effective defensive measures.

The Romans first invaded England under Julius Caesar in 55 BC, and by AD 43, under Claudius, had conquered most of England, Wales and southern Scotland. Indeed much of what is now Western Europe was part of their far-flung Empire. The Roman towns and interconnecting roads established the basic national land use and settlement pattern for Britain's subsequent development. Today many main roads, such as the

A1, follow Roman routes. Many of the main towns and cities (especially those ending in 'chester', or 'cester') are of Roman origin for example, Colchester in Essex, Chester, Winchester, and many others (Fig. 5.16).

There are many other examples of grid layout cities. Some of the most well known are the 'bylaw housing' areas of nineteenth-century British industrial cities, such as Manchester and Leeds, where all the housing was built to minimal standards for the workers on a formal street layout. Mostly North American cities (Fig. 5.17) were also laid out as a vast grid, New York being a good example. Also Milton Keynes new town is based upon a grid pattern of major roads for the cars, but at the local area level is based on a more traditional street layout for pedestrians. In fact anywhere where there is colonisation, military government or the need to organise and house large numbers of people rapidly one is likely to find planned settlements based upon grid layouts, whether it is Roman Britain, North America, or in rapidly industrialised towns.

Self-assessment tasks

1. What are the differences between organic and grid-iron towns? Give examples of each.
2. Find examples in your area of each type. If you cannot do so, explain why. For example, if you live in a large industrial town you may only find formally laid out grid housing, and no organic areas. If you live in a small rural market town you may only find organic development and no formal grid layout. Describe and explain.

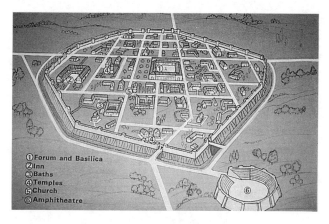

Figure 5.14 Roamn grid plan town

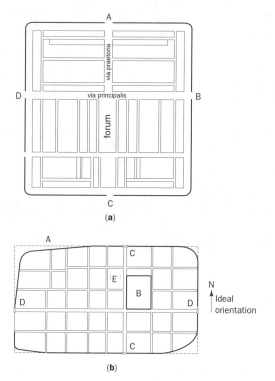

Figure 5.15 Urban plans: (a) the typical Roman army castra layout; (b) the component parts of a typical imperial urban plan – the defensive wall (A), rectangular in theory but characteristically of curving outline when constructed around an existing city; the Forum (B) at the intersection of the Cardo (C) and Decumanum (D); the theatre (E). (*After* Morris 1994 *History of Urban Design*, Addison Wesley Longman)

Project work

Continue with your local history portfolio and look for the features discussed above such as churches, public buildings, different types of street layout, and date, draw and describe these. Perhaps your local history society has some books on the topic.

The Romans left Britain in the fifth century, and what are known as the Dark Ages began. There were a series of other invasions but in general Britain reverted to a more rural society in which towns were market centres and local administrative centres rather than imperial, fortified Roman outposts. By 1086 (as recorded in the Domesday Book), there were approximately

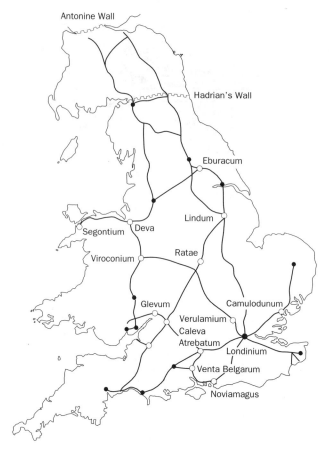

Figure 5.16 Roman towns in Britain

13 000 villages in England alone, many of which were to grow naturally into larger towns, originating in the Anglo-Saxon period of the fifth to the tenth centuries. The Norman Empire, which was extended to Britain by William the Conqueror in 1066, had a major effect on the land use patterns of Britain. Large feudal estates were created and large sectors of the population were serfs and agricultural labourers.

Right through this period and into medieval times (up until Georgian times in the 1700s) most of British society and economy was predominantly agricultural and rural in nature, although London and a few other regional cities, such as Bristol, York and Chester remained important. Even by the fourteenth century most towns had a populatation of less than 10 000. An exception to this was London, which had a population of 40 000. Other large towns were York (8000), Lincoln (6000), Thetford (5000), and Ipswich (3000).

Medieval towns and cities generally exhibit a more unplanned, organic, natural type of city form and structure, in contrast to the formally planned Greek and Roman grid-iron layouts, in which the design was imposed from above by colonial forces on the population. Generally, medevial towns are dominated by a cathedral or large church around which the town is clustered, with adjacent market square and public buildings. These features together comprised what we would now call the central business district, where trade took place and where government was centred.

Renaissance and Georgian town planning

Towards the end of the Middle Ages in Europe the influence of the Church became less dominant in the more prosperous

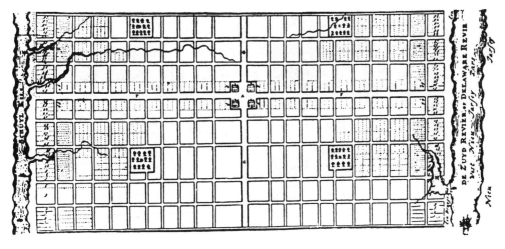

Figure 5.17 Plan of Philadelphia, United States, late nineteenth century

city states that were developing, particularly in Italy. Self-made businessmen and merchants rather than traditional feudal powers took control. There was a rebirth (a **renaissance**) of interest in the ideas and culture of the classical civilisation of the Greeks and Romans, which were considered more appropriate to modern needs than the mystical other worldly emphasis of the Middle Ages.

The Renaissance began in Italy where there was enthusiasm for the use of classical features in the development of new public buildings and palaces to express the wealth of the merchant princes, e.g. the Medicis in Florence. Splendid new town planning features were introduced in Italian cities, such as a formal central square or piazza (along the lines of the forum, or agora). Most Mediterranean settlements have always had market squares which often act as 'outdoor living rooms' where people meet and eat in the pavement cafés, and walk around in the cool of the evening. Later Renaissance piazzas often incorporated a colonnaded walkway in the classical style along one side, with fountains and statues tastefully arranged in the centre. This is very different from British town planning but, as we shall see, elements of the town square were adopted into Georgian cities from the 1700s. (A fuller account of Renaissance town planning and architecture in Italian and other European cities is to be found in Chapter 8 of *Introducing Town Planning*) by Greed).

While Georgian planning and architecture was a result of the impact of the Renaissance influence on Britain, the style, scale and whole approach was significantly different from the knock-out scale found in continental Europe. The Georgian style (broadly parallel to the period when a series of King Georges sat on the throne) is a mixture of classical Italian Renaissance features with other influences from northern Europe. In particular, the Dutch had developed a distinctive domestic (housing) architectural style, as expressed in the neat but restrained symmetrically proportioned brick town houses in Amsterdam, with sash windows and gabled façades. Brick was a relatively expensive building material in Britain and was usually only used in great houses, being imported from the Low Countries (Holland and Belgium).

The Great Fire of London in 1666 was a landmark in British architectural history. London's population in 1530 was 50 000 and by 1605 had grown to 225 000, as a result of migration from the countryside, owing in part to an early form of Enclosure Act (you may have heard of these in your history lessons). At the same time, London was developing into the major British exporting centre, providing unlimited

job opportunities. London in 1666 was a typical medieval town with narrow meandering streets and lanes. Most buildings were of timber construction with thatched roofs. Overcrowding was made worse by an early planning law passed in 1588 under Queen Elizabeth I, which prohibited building around London and other towns unless each house had a plot of 4 acres (1.6 hectares). The law was passed to satisfy the wealthy merchants, but constricted the nature of urban growth, and was an early form of zoning, and green belt (see Section 5.2). (A green belt is a protective area around a city where development is not permitted, to discourage the town from spreading into the countryside.)

These conditions contributed to the devastating plague of 1665, which killed 90 000 people, one-third of London's population. This disaster was followed by the Great Fire of London in 1666, which started in a baker's shop in Pudding Lane, near London Bridge, in the early hours of Sunday 2 September 1666. It eventually destroyed 373 acres of property inside the city walls: only 75 acres remained undamaged.

Following the devastation of the plague and the fire, the King, Charles II, made a proclamation for 'present and future plans' which prescribed that buildings should be constructed of fire-resistant materials and the important streets widened to form fire breaks. Brick became more commonly used following the Great Fire, and brick fields were developed around London, where the raw materials were available. Many public buildings and churches were constructed of stone.

The Fire provided an opportunity to rebuild the capital using a Comprehensive Master Plan approach to planning, and Christopher Wren prepared one such plan based on a formal grid layout on a grand scale with formal vistas and squares (Fig. 5.18). However, there was much opposition from individual landowners. The monarchy did not have the power of some of its European counterparts to impose a plan from above. Individual real property rights and a growing parliamentary democratic approach to government prevented this. Note again how the political and social structure of society, i.e. human factors, influence the shape and design of cities as much as technology or geographical factors.

In the end a series of individual speculative developments emerged, many of which took the form of town squares with Georgian town houses facing onto grass and trees in the middle of the square. The houses themselves, aimed at the new affluent classes, were a mixture of Dutch features, including use of brick and sash windows, along with classical elements such as Greek pediments and columns. The squares

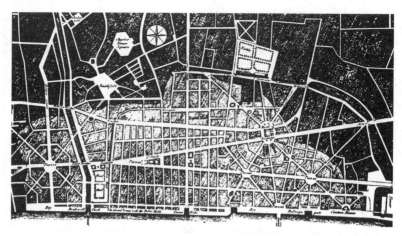

Figure 5.18 Wren's master plan for London after the fire of 1666. (*From* John Gwynn 1766 *London and Westminister Improved* (republished in 1969 by Gregg International Publishers Ltd))

were no doubt inspired by the Italian piazza but had a soft grass centre rather than a hard paved surface. Individual front gardens were not favoured, being considered rather 'common', rural, and peasant-like, but there were often long walled back gardens, and separate mews at the back for the servants and the horses.

Names such as Bedford Square, Grosvenor Square and Sloane Square bear witness to the property development abilities of the ducal landowners who possessed estates in what is now the West End, Kensington and Chelsea. The main city churches and St Paul's Cathedral were rebuilt by Sir Christopher Wren following the Fire. St Paul's is in the style of St Peter's in Rome, using a dome construction, whereas many of the other Wren churches are more English yet still classical in design.

London continued to grow throughout Georgian times, developing as a prosperous capital and eventually, in the nineteenth century, as the world capital of the British Empire. This role was reflected in the architecture of individual buildings in Georgian and Victorian times (the nineteenth century), but with the following exception there was no comprehensive replanning in the Grand Manner. Indeed, there were still districts which reflected earlier historical phases of town form, of the more organic, vernacular, medieval format.

In the early nineteenth century in Regency times (named after the Prince Regent) part of the Crown Estates just to the north of the centre of London, namely Regent's Park, was developed as a series of upmarket town houses by John Nash the architect. Further developments, namely Regent's Street, Mayfair, Trafalgar Square, the Mall, Piccadilly Circus, Oxford Circus and Buckingham Palace, were all part of this grand design. In fact, the scheme developed over many years, with the Victorians altering and enlarging various elements of the original Regency scheme.

It is significant that many of the streets comprising this scheme were designed specifically as shopping areas, reflecting the increased prosperity and manufacturing growth of the nation, and the development of a distinctive retail and service 'tertiary sector', which was to become even more important in the twentieth century.

In Georgian and Regency times a whole series of provincial towns and resorts were developed to meet the needs of the new affluent leisured classes. The early ones were mainly inland and centred on spas where people could 'take the waters', most notably in Bath, Cheltenham and Harrogate, but also at Epsom (hence the racecourse), Hotwells in Bristol and Brixton in south London (Fig. 5.19). Later, sea bathing became the fashion, and a second series of resorts was developed, e.g. Brighton (Regency Pavilion), Skegness and Weston-super-Mare.

Bath is one of the most famous Georgian spa towns. It was put on the map when Queen Anne 'took the waters' for her rheumatism in the 1720s. However, it was Beau Nash who really popularised and publicised the city when he was made the Postmaster for Bath. He has been compared with Billy Butlin in creating the holiday industry, in this case encouraging wealthy people to come for 'the season' (Fig. 5.20).

Figure 5.19 Georgian development in Clifton, Bristol

Figure 5.20 Typical Georgian development at Lansdown Crescent, Bath

Thus the holiday and leisure industry was born. This was to become an important sector of the economy in the twentieth century, with its own land use demands, special buildings and town planning needs. However, it was not until the development of the railways that these became more working class resorts for the ordinary people. Today, with the development of mass air travel, the whole tourist and holiday industry has developed far more than could ever have been imagined in Georgian times.

Self-assessment tasks

1. How did British Georgian town planning differ from the mainstream European renaissance version of town planning?
2. Name two Italian renaissance cities and two British Georgian cities.
3. How were town planning and use of building materials in London affected by the Great Fire of 1666?

Project work

It is recommended that you look around your own town or city and find out if you have any Georgian or Regency buildings. If so describe them and add them to your map.

Do you have a town square or other 'renaissance' type public space in your town? How is it used? For example, is it a public meeting place? Does it have pavement cafés? Or is it used as a car park or a place for sleeping rough? Make a diary of the use of the square during the week. If there is no square, look at a map of your town and discuss where one might be located and what it might be used for.

Chronological phases of city development

Table 5.9 gives a summary of the main historical periods. It should be stressed that the dates given reflect the main start date from which each phase is dominant and that phase continues until superseded by new civilisations and architectural styles. Readers should consult related history books and their teachers for fuller information, as this list is simply intended as a basic guide through the centuries, with some key words for each. Do not worry if you do not recognise all the words.

Nineteenth century

As a result of the Industrial Revolution in the nineteenth century, many people moved into the new industrial towns as explained in Section 5.1. Readers are recommended to familiarise themselves with that section before continuing with this unit.

Changes in transport transformed cities in the nineteenth century. For centuries, cities had been relatively close-knit because the extent of cities and the distances between different land uses and amenities had been governed by the distances which people could comfortably walk. With the introduction of mechanical means of transport, people could travel further, and more quickly than they could walk, and cities began to expand. With the development of the railway system, those who were more affluent moved further out of town and commuted in, starting the trend of suburbanisation and decentralisation that was to become a major feature of urban development in Britain.

Table 5.9 Chronological phases of architectural style and city development

Date	Period, Style, Civilisation	Key words
BC 5000	Ancient civilisations	Mesopotamia, Tigris–Euphrates Valley
3000	Egypt	Cairo, pyramids, Nile
1000	Early Greek	Knossos, Mycenae
500	Greek	Athens, Parthenon, columns
400	Roman	Rome, grid-layout towns, roads
AD 400	Byzantine	Constantinople
500	Dark Ages	Anglo-Saxons,
600	Islam	Moslems, mosques, cities
900	Norman, Europe	France, churches, defence
1066	Norman, English	William the Conqueror, cities, castles
1200	Gothic	Organic towns, Medieval, churches
1450	Renaissance	Italy, Venice, Florence
1550	High Renaissance	Rome, Classical, Art
1666	Great Fire of London	Rebuilding London, Wren
1700	Georgian	Bath, London, Edinburgh
1800	Regency, Classical	Brighton, Colonial cities
1820	Victorian	Industrial Revolution
1900	Modern Architecture	America, international
1945	Post-war Reconstruction	New towns, planning system
1960	High-rise	Town centre redevelopment, flats
1970	Reaction, conservation	Conservation areas
1980	Post-modernism	Out-of-town centres
1990s	Green environmental movement	Sustainable buildings

Thus as a result of the changes in the transport systems cities spread out and distinct social zones developed. Also as a result of the state intervention in respect of controlling housing development, the beginnings of a land-use zoning system began to develop, further differentiating the different types of land use and housing areas within the industrial cities.

While many of the new working classes in the cities were suffering from bad housing, poor health and overcrowded conditions, there was also an increase in national prosperity. There was a tremendous amount of building of commercial premises, town halls, libraries, and the beginnings of modern high street development, with long rows of individual shops

Figure 5.21 Typical 1930s low-rise detached suburban housing

Table 5.10 Historical population growth

Population	Reign	Year of Census	England	London
William I	1066–1087			
William II	1087–1100	1100	1 500 000	17 850
Henry I	1100–1135			
Stephen	1135–1154	1150	1 750 000	20 000
Henry II	1154–1189			
Richard I	1189–1199			
John	1199–1216	1200	2 000 000	22 500
Henry III	1216–1272	1250	2 500 000	25 000
Edward I	1272–1307	1300	3 300 000	30 000
Edward I	1307–1327			
Edward II	1327–1377	1348	4 000 000	40 000
Richard II	1377–1399			
Henry IV	1399–1413	1400	2 500 000	35 000
Henry V	1413–1422			
Henry VI	1422–1461	1450	3 000 000	50 000
Edward IV	1461–1483			
Edward V	1483			
Richard II	1483–1485			
Tudors				
Henry VII	1485–1509	1500	3 500 000	65 000
Henry VIII	1509–1547			
Edward VI	1547–1553	1550	4 000 000	80 000
Mary	1553–1558			
Elizabeth	1558–1603	1600	4 500 000	150 000
Stuarts				
James I	1603–1625			
Charles I	1625–1649			
Commonwealth	1649–1660	1650	5 500 000	400 000
Charles II	1660–1685			
James II	1685–1688			
William III	1689–1702	1700	6 000 000	600 000
Anne	1702–1714			
Hanoverians				
George I	1714–1727			
George II	1727–1760	1750	6 400 000	750 000
George III	1760–1820	1800	8 900 000	950 000
George IV	1820–1830			
William IV	1830–1837			
Victoria	1837–1901	1850	18 000 000	2 300 000
Edward VII	1901–1910	1900	32 500 000	4 500 000
Windsors				
George V	1910–1936	1930	39 750 000	8 000 000
Edward VIII	1936			
George VI	1936–1952	1950	43 700 000	8 350 000
Elizabeth II	1952–			

Figure 5.22 Example of a Victorian public building with classical features: Birmingham Town Hall

increased state intervention and national wealth. There was also emphasis on the building of town parks and playing fields, which nowadays are often seen as a luxury by both developers and local authorities. Many are in danger of development, as they are often located in what are today central area sites with high land values.

Not all residential development consisted of substandard working class housing and slum properties. The nineteenth century was a period of the most massive amount of house building, and this included the construction of middle class villas, town houses and substantial terraces which still occupy large tracts of our cities. Also there were large areas of better quality, skilled artisan and respectable working class housing consisting of miles of little terraced houses built on a grid layout. Much of this is ideal building stock even today. The problems of the time occurred chiefly in areas where there was a concentration of large numbers of working class people in poorly built housing around the new factories and mills. They located there because at the beginning of the Industrial Revolution there was very little money or time for commuting and the transport systems had not yet developed, so people were huddled together in proximity to their workplace. At first it was a matter of converting existing housing. For example, larger inner city town houses were subdivided into seperate dwellings: in some cases whole families were living in one room and some people were even living in cellars.

Many local builders made a large profit by building substandard tenements and terraces, which were 'jerry built' (a phrase thought to derive from the reputation of the work of a particularly bad builder of that name). Houses were often 'half a brick thick' (i.e. thin, substandard walls) and 'back to back'. This means that what appeared to be a terrace of ordinary houses in fact contained twice the number of dwellings, because the houses were divided at the ridge of the roof, and backed onto each other, creating two 'rows' of houses, one facing onto the street and the other facing onto the back alleyway.

Suburbanisation and transport

First railways and then tramway systems contributed to decentralisation, followed by omnibuses; eventually these lost out, albeit not completely, to the motor car. With the invention of the internal combustion engine, public transport was augmented by omnibuses, which were not limited to a fixed linear track as in the case of trains and trams, and could

and early department stores, all these buildings toegether creating the foundations of the modern CBD (central business district). The Victorians also put a vast amount of investment into infrastructure, in the form of sewers and drains, as a result of the public health reforms. By the end of the nineteenth century, the city fathers, having made their pile, could now sit back and distribute their bounty in the form of public works. Civic pride and public building works went hand in hand with reform which often took the form of what was called 'gas and water socialism', i.e. investment in public works to build up the necessary infrastructure. While there is still much criticism of this period it must be remembered that many cities are still dependent on Victorian sewers, and that they left an immeasurable heritage of public investment which has not been continued into the present day, in spite of go anywhere. The buses, and of course the subsequent development of the private motor car, led to a veritable explosion of suburbanisation, for, provided there were passable roads, people could for the first time in history travel anywhere they wanted at considerable speed. The bicycle became popular in the late nineteenth century and is having a comeback today. These changes in transport technology further encouraged cities to grow and to segment into distinct land use zonings; in particular, the industrial and residential (the work and the home) areas separated out. At the same time the traditional central business district (i.e. the centre with all the offices, shops and civic buildings) remained pivotal, expanding and acquiring increased importance in servicing the needs of trade and finance which had expanded as a result of the Industrial Revolution.

The logical conclusion in order to create maximum efficency was to abandon the traditional radial concentric form of cities and build linear developments along the main routes, with concentrations of housing ideally located at relatively high-density clustering around each railway station or tramway stop. It was important to have enough people living close to each stop, within walking distance, in order to make the developments viable in enabling passengers to reach them without them having to use a secondary form of transport each time. This led to various theories developing in Europe. For example, Arturo Soria y Mata suggested the concept of the linear city, which he visualised stretching right across Europe (Fig. 5.23). The linear form could also be joined up to form a circular 'ring' city, or be turned in on itself as a figure of eight such as in the Runcorn New Town Plan in the 1960s. However, Soria y Mata only succeeded in building a few kilometres outside Madrid.

The motor car was not limited to a fixed track and gave much greater flexibility anywhere there were roads. Paradoxically as the motor car grew, public transport receded. Nowadays people without cars in some areas are probably worse off in terms of transport than their ancestors were in the nineteenth century. The motor car caught on quite early in the USA even among relatively low-income people, thanks to the cheap mass production methods of Henry Ford.

Frank Lloyd Wright (1869–1959), an American architect, developed the idea of a city planned entirely for the motor car, 'Autopia', as proposed for Broadacre City in the 1930s. This was to be based on a very low-density grid with every house being like a homestead with a one acre plot in which they would grow their own food. The settlement would not have a centre in the traditional sense but the districts would be focused around the gas station (petrol station). This vision is how some American cities actually developed, e.g. Los Angeles where everybody drives rather than walks. Those who do not have cars – e.g. the poor, or those who are unable to drive such as the young and old – are at a severe disadvantage, and have to depend on limited public transport or the goodwill of others. This is a form of grid, as discussed earlier in this unit, but the car-based version is on a much larger scale.

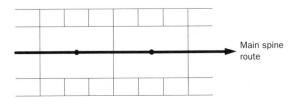

Figure 5.23 Linear city

While it can be seen that the divisions within social classes and land uses are not as clear-cut as the early urban theory-makers imagined, nevertheless many cities were replanned by means of strict land-use zoning which separated out housing areas from industrial and other uses, and which made little allowance for the need for a mixture of land uses such as had existed in traditional, organic, planned settlements. Nowadays it is interesting that there is a move among some planning authorities towards a greater emphasis upon the acceptance of mixed land uses, if only to reduce the need to travel, and in order to provide employment and investment in local areas. However, in a sense this is shutting the stable door after the horse has bolted because, as will be seen in the next section, twentieth-century planning has been firmly on the side of zoning, decentralisation and dispersal of land uses and facilities. Likewise, private sector developers and businesses have welcomed the establishment of out-of-town shopping centres and decentralised business parks, which have made it almost essential for people to have cars, particularly in the light of the decline of public transport. Indeed the average person living 100 years ago would have had a wider choice of public transport, and a more extensive rail network, than is the case today.

A tale of two cities

'How do you want to live?'. This is a fundamental question that has inspired and motivated town planners for the last two hundred years. Town planning is always concerned with two aspects of existence:

- trying to solve problems and improve conditions, i.e. reacting and responding to change; and
- seeking to create new, creative ways of designing towns and cities, i.e. proactively and innovatively seeking to create change.

For example, as we have seen, in the nineteenth century many of the problems experienced in cities were related to poverty, bad housing, overcrowding and disease, and the solutions were in the area of public health and housing policy, land-use zoning and greater regulation. But at the same time town planners sought to rise above these problems and 'dream' of 'how things might be', as in the case of Ebenezer Howard.

Howard's solution to the problems of the time was to water down the worst effects of the town with the good effects of the countryside by creating 'garden cities', low-density settlements with lots of trees and gardens. However, as is so often the case in the world of town planning and architecture, there were many that criticised his work for being 'anti-urban', escapist and sentimental. In particular, the whole 'English Garden City Movement' was challenged by the work of some European town planners and architects who subscribed to the ideals of what is called the 'Modern Movement'.

Let us look at their ideas because, in seeking to understand the likely development of trends in the future, we must appreciate the rivalry between these two main schools of thought, which together encapsulate many of the issues and problems that still plague town planning.

Techno fix?

Le Corbusier (1877–1965), a French–Swiss architect working at the beginning of the twentieth century, is generally seen as the main figure in the European movement. Like Howard he was seeking alternatives to the overcrowding and poor conditions of nineteenth-century industrial cities, but his solution was quite different. He suggested that rather than moving people out 'horizontally' into low-rise (two or three storey), low-density houses in garden suburbs, instead he would apply the most modern technology and build upwards, creating high-rise vertical cities; he even suggested mile-high skyscrapers. This would in turn free the space at ground level, and thus reduce congestion.

He believed that applying modern technological solutions and science to the urban situation would be the solution. He was very impressed by what he had seen in North America, where cities such as New York and Chicago were already going upwards, building towards the sky. Also he was impressed by the production line method of assembly of motor cars pioneered by Henry Ford. He decided that applying prefabrication and mass production to dwellings as well as cars would create efficient housing. He is famed for saying, 'a house is a machine for living in'. This attitude, as we shall see later, was much criticised, particularly by those who were more concerned with the social aspects of planning than the purely technological aspects.

Le Corbusier is also known as being a member of the functionalist movement who expressed their beliefs in statements such as 'form follows function' and 'function is beauty, beauty is function'. At the beginning of the twentieth century architects wanted to cast off all the clutter and decoration and heavy stonework of Victorian architecture and build pristine, plain structures that reflected the new spirit of progress, science and engineering. Changes in technology, especially the development of steel-framed structures which supported a building without the need for heavy, thick, load-bearing walls, and also the development of electric elevators (lifts), meant that the sky was the limit (Figs 5.24–5.26). No longer was building height limited by the fact that the average person could only be reasonably be expected to climb up six floors of stairs at the most, nor was building floorspace limited by the need to be near a window now that natural lighting was superseded by gas and then electricity.

Corbusier envisaged entire vertical cities, as expressed in his books written in the 1920s *The Radiant City* and *The City of Tomorrow*. He imagined that people would live in vertical neighbourhoods with all the facilities, including shops,

Figure 5.25 High-rise building, Manchester, built during the 1960s property boom

Figure 5.26 High-rise development, Moscow

schools, sports and other facilities, located in high-rise blocks alongside homes and workplaces, and where people would commute up and down the escalators. The ground level would be devoted to parks, leisure and also to a futurist vision of motorway provision and air travel facilities, with additional ground level zoning of other industrial, employment and some residential provision. We are talking here about high-rises over 100 storeys high, not the little high-rise blocks of around 12 to 15 storeys that we find in Britain.

Supporters of Corbusier say that his ideas would have worked if there had been sufficient money and enthusiasm to implement them. Indeed in North America there are many successful high-rise buildings in which people live and work, such as the World Trade Centre in New York, and the Sears Tower in Chicago, but a great deal of money is put into their maintenance, servicing and running. The tallest building in the world is now the Petronas Towers complex in Kuala Lumpur, Malaysia, which contains offices, residential apartments, car parking, shops, mosques and leisure facilities, all within a massive 18 million square feet of floor space.

Social ecology

It is helpful in understanding the nature of city form and structure to refer to what are known as the 'social ecology' theories of the city, first developed in Chicago in the 1930s

Figure 5.24 Early steel-framed structure in a high-rise building in the 1880s

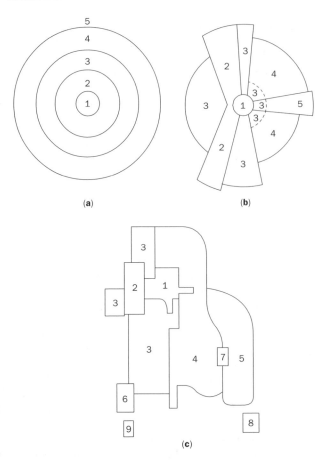

(a)   (b)

(c)

Figure 5.27 Three social ecology models (generalised explanations of the land use patterns of cities): (a) **concentric zone concept** – 1: central business district; 2: zone of transition; 3: zone of working-men's homes; 4: zone of better residences; 5: commuters' zone; (b) **sector concept** – 1, central business district; 2: wholesale light manufacturing; 3: low-class residential; 4: medium-class residential; 5: high-class residential; (c) **multiple nuclei concept** – 6: heavy manufacturing; 7: outlying business district; 8: residential suburb; 9: industrial suburb. (*From* Harris and Ullman *The Nature of Cities*, in Annals of the American Academy of Political and Social Science, November 1945)

and since developed further in Britain up to the present day. Ecology is the study of plants and animals in relation to their environmental setting, and in particular is concerned with the process of competition for living space and territory. It was intended that such theories could be used also to explain the ways in which different social groups settled in fast-expanding North American cities. The theories themselves, it must be stressed, are somewhat questionable in respect of modern British cities, but the diagrammatic representations of the structure of cities are still a useful starting point in analysing town plan features (Fig. 5.27).

The first model – the **concentric zone model** – developed by Burgess and Park was originally intended to explain how new migrant groups to a city tended to locate in inner city areas where prices were cheaper and where there were fewer barriers to settling in and becoming part of the community. The concentric zone model is not meant to be static but dynamic. The concentric zones should be seen like ripples on a pond continuously moving outwards (Fig. 5.27a). The city grows outwards and expands as each of the zones within it grows, owing to immigrant pressure in the centre causing the inner area to expand and thus put pressure on the next zone out.

The concentric zones model *is* only diagrammatic as Chicago is built alongside Lake Michigan and thus takes the form of a semi-circular city. It is not intended to be a land-use plan of how cities should be, but rather a diagram to illustrate a theory of what cities have been observed to be like. The zone of transition around the central business district is of particular interest. This is the area where the older rundown cheaper housing is found, but it is also the area where the CBD is expanding, leading to rapid changes in land values and types of development. Many British cities possess an historical central area and inner ring of housing, some of which has declined and may fit the description of the zone of transition, but other central areas might consist of higher class housing and nowadays be designated as conservation areas. The zone of transition has become virtually synonymous with the inner city and is often associated with high concentrations of ethnic minority populations. Many other European cities are quite different from British and North American cities, haveing much higher concentrations of people of all classes living in the city centre, and less suburban development, although different 'districts' still have very distinct class connotations. Meanwhile in North America's large cities, particularly in New York, one can still observe the ongoing conflict for 'space' between competing groups, nowadays made more visible by the use of graffiti to mark territories between street gangs, many of whom are black or Hispanic ethnic groups, rather than European immigrant groups as in the days of Burgess in Chicago.

The other zones on the diagram are fairly self-explanatory and broadly applicable to the British situation. The zone of working class homes might consist of small terraces around older factory areas, but in Britain, because of state intervention in housing and town planning, one might also find working class council estates out on the edge of the city where the land is cheaper, or where industry has been decentralised and re-zoned.

The zone of better residences is where the 'normal' average family is meant to live, in a deviance-free area. In reality, the suburbs have proved to be the source of many problems, especially for people without cars, as they are separated from the rest of the city by land-use zoning and poor transport links. Furthermore the suburbs and zoning generate traffic commuting and parking problems back in the centre of the city.

The next circle, the commuter zone, is meant to be the 'best' area in the model, and is entirely dependent on the

Figure 5.28 inner city area, Bristol

motor car (note it has no outer boundary). In Britain one often finds a planned green belt around the edge of the city, and so the suburbs leapfrog the green belt and form a secondary ring.

The ideas of Burgess and Park (see above) were modified in a series of subsequent models. The **sector concept** developed by Homer Hoyt in the 1930s put emphasis upon the importance of transport routes, and upon parallel linear wedges of development, superimposed over the concentric structure (Fig. 5.27b). Sectors of better development can develop on one side of the city because of the direction of the wind (from the east in America, from the west in Britain) as more affluent people prefer to live in less-polluted areas. The working classes are seen as being more likely to have to live downwind from the industry, with all the smoke drifting over them. Many cities have a distinct East and West End or side, but nowadays all areas are probably equally polluted by gases and sediments in the atmosphere.

Other geographical factors, such as the existence of an attractive hillside ideal for development of higher quality housing, or the presence of a river or valley, will also create natural sectors. Roads and railways can also act as barriers. In North America working class people are often described as living 'the wrong side of the railroad tracks'.

The **multiple nuclei concept** was developed by Harris and Ullman in the 1950s (Fig. 5.27c). This theory reflects many of the realities of contemporary metropolitan land use, allowing for decentralisation, land-use zoning and state intervention. These theories have been developed further over the years, by sociologists such as Mann in Britain, and the alternatives are endless (Bulmer 1984) *The Chicago School of Sociology*, London: University of Chicago Press.

The growth of a typical city

In conclusion to the explanation of the way in which the historical development of cities affects their form and structure, a summary description of a typical British city will be given, to aid students in the preparation of their project.

Typically in the centre of the city there will be a small area of streets that still reflect the Roman grid-layout pattern, or the subsequent medieval organic form of urban development. However, the chances are that these areas will be limited because of the effects of centuries of wars, including bombing during the Second World War. The centre is likely to have originally been located at a crossing point or a bridge across a river, and this focus may have been retained over the centuries.

Surrounding the historical core, there may be an area of smart town houses, possibly Georgian or Regency terraces and squares, and around this another ring of substantial Victorian villas. Since these properties survived the redevelopment activities of the planners in the post-war period they may now be the subject of urban conservation area policy, and may be used either as up-market office accommodation or as an up-market residential area. Such an area hardly corresponds to the zone of transition delineated by Burgess's concentric zone theory. However, in some cities such areas have not 'gone up the world' and remain as seedier areas, where the classic features of bed-sit land, subdivided and run-down properties are to be found.

Depending on the regional location of the city in question, and upon whether it has been highly industrialised in the past, one will also find large areas of small terraced houses, and working-class bylaw housing in the centre. Such housing is likely to be located on the industrial side of the town, downwind of the pollution. These inner residential areas may now be criss-crossed by inner ring roads or urban motorways, and parts of them may have been redeveloped for a range of twentieth-century uses, including high-rise council flats, small precinct shopping developments and car parking areas. Some inner city areas are characterised by problems of unemployment, crime and poverty but it is unwise to generalise as some are the homes of prosperous ethnic minority communities who have breathed new life back into previously depressed inner urban areas.

Further out, one is likely to find the beginnings of suburbanisation, and what Burgess termed the zone of working class homes, though these are no longer necessarily family homes. It is estimated (readers can check this for themselves in *Social Trends*) that less than 25% of families now fall into the traditional category of a married couple with dependent children. It may be argued there is no longer one typical type of family or household: a household may comprise a single-parent family, an adult couple with no dependent children, or an elderly single widow or widower. The housing market implications of this are that there is a greater demand for smaller units, particularly within inner urban locations where people want to live nearer to their work to avoid commuting pressures.

Further out again, one begins to see distinct suburban districts, starting with 1930s 'semi-detached suburbia', much of which is still linked to local railway stations to take workers into the city centre. There are also likely to be areas of newer infill, and again vast amounts of land are likely to have been used in the 1960s for road widening and the construction of urban motorways. Beyond this, the urban structure is punctuated by distinct areas of green, including parkland and the beginnings of surrounding agricultural land. The outer fringe of suburbia is likely to contain at least three distinct types of housing development: council housing estates located on the edge of the city; large detached suburban houses for more affluent commuters; and cheaper, smaller, owner-occupied housing for younger and lower-income commuters.

The outer edges of the city are also likely to be cluttered with a series of out-of-town shopping centres, decentralised hospitals and new university campuses, science parks and high-tech industrial developments. One is also likely to find purpose-built 1930s industrial estates, built as a result of decentralist regional policy, or because of past attempts at strict zoning of industrial 'non-conforming uses' away from inner city housing. Such areas may now be surrounded by a sea of newer development, and be in need of refurbishment or redevelopment. Surrounding all of this in larger cities there is likely to be a green belt, which is making a valiant and somewhat unsuccessful attempt to prevent urban sprawl.

In conclusion, if looking at the city in question 'from above', looking down on the urban development plan (say, from an aeroplane) the viewer would possibly be struck by the noticable effect of past zoning policies under the various planning Acts. In many districts this has created an artificial patchwork effect with strict divisions between residential, industrial and green public open-space areas. Also, as a result of green belt policy, or possibly natural topography, there will be a distinct 'stop' to urban development on parts of the edge of the city, making the countryside suprisingly close to relatively built-up areas. Cutting through the green belt, dissecting the city and skirting around the edges of the city there are likely to be a range of major roads, and possibly urban motorways, ring roads and major national motorways, as well as railway lines. Glinting on the horizon one might be able to make out reservoirs which provide water to the city, and an array of masts, pylons, radio transmitters and other prominent features, all of which form part of the infrastructure of the modern city.

Further reading

Ashworth W 1968 *The Genesis of Modern British Town Planning* Routledge

Chapman D (ed) 1996 *Neighbourhoods and Plans in the Built Environment* E & F N Spon

Greed C 1996 *Introducing Town Planning* (2nd edition) Addison Wesley Longman

Morris A E J 1972 *History of Urban Form: Prehistory to The Renaissance* Godwin.

5.3 Legal, financial and political factors affecting planning

The purpose of this section is to explain the legal framework under which the statutory planning system works. In addition, you need to be aware of the controls on new and existing development which exist under building control, housing, environmental, property and European Union legislation.

You also need to appreciate the influence of financial factors on the decision to develop in the first place. In this section, attention is therefore given to the role of regional and urban grants and regeneration initiatives under the planning Acts. Material on the wider taxation, economic and fiscal aspects is to be found in Unit 8 Finance and the Built Environment, especially in Section 8.1 Project Finance. Further material on the feasibility and commercial development aspects of planning is to be found in Section 5.5 within the context of the explanation of the process of property development.

Town planning legislation

Town planning, in its present form, dates primarily from the post-war reconstruction period, i.e. from 1945 onwards. The 1947 Town and Country Planning Act was a milestone, introducing a comprehensive system of plan making and control of development. This legislation was subsequently updated by the introduction of a more sophisticated system under the 1971 Town and Country Planning Act. Nowadays the main town planning Acts are:

- 1990 Town and Country Planning Act
- 1991 Planning and Compensation Act

The nature of the system under these acts will be explained below. To give you an idea of the vast scope and extent of planning legislation which affects just about every aspect of planning and development, Table 5.11 gives a list of some of the main pieces of legislation since 1945, most of which still shape planning practice.

Table 5.11 Main post-war town planning related Acts

1945 Distribution of Industry Act
1946 New Towns Act
1947 Town and Country Planning Act
1949 National Parks and Access to the Countryside Act
1952 Town Development Act
1954 Town and Country Planning Act
1967 Civic Amenities Act
1968 Town and Country Planning Act
1970 Community Land Act
1971 Town and Country Planning Act
1972 Local Government Act
1974 Housing Act (Housing Action Areas)
1975 Community Land Act
1975 Development Land Tax Act
1976 Local Government (Miscellaneous Provisions) Act
1978 Inner Urban Areas Act
1980 Local Government, Planning and Land Act
1982 Local Government (Miscellaneous Provisions) Act
1981 Minerals Act
1982 Derelict Land Act
1985 Housing Act
1986 Housing and Town Planning Act
1988 Housing Act
1988 Local Government Act
1989 Local Government and Housing Act
1990 Town and Country Planning Act
1990 Environmental Protection Act
1990 Planning (Listed Buildings and Conservation Areas) Act
1990 Planning (Hazardous Substances) Act
1991 Planning and Compensation Act
1992 Local Government Act
1993 Housing and Urban Development Act
1994 Local Government (Wales) Act
1995 Environment Act
1995 Disability Discrimination Act
1996 Housing Grants, Construction and Regeneration Act
1998 Housing Act
1998 Regional Development Agencies Act

The present-day planning system

Development plans

The shape and design of towns and cities is not accidental or natural; there is a need for policies to be developed and implemented. Therefore planners need to produce Development Plans for a town, city or county, showing the main policies and proposals over the next 5–10 years. The nature and titles of these plans vary somewhat according to the locality and the date when they were approved.

In general you will find two types of development plan systems and related plans in operation. First, under the 1971 Town and Country Planning Act (and still in force across many parts of England and Wales) there are what are known as **Structure Plans** which, as their name suggests, show the overall urban 'structure', including land uses, transport routes, and a whole range of development issues (both for urban areas and rural counties). These therefore provide overall high-level policy guidance. They are complemented by a series of **Local Plans**, which give details of how the high-level policies will work out in detail in relation to a particular area in the short term. This type of development plan system is known as a two-tier system because it deals with both the overall urban 'structure' and 'local' detailed planning policy.

Secondly, there are what are known as **Unitary Development Plans** (known as UDPs), which were introduced more recently under legislation that was consolidated under the 1990 Town and Country Planning Act. These are being phased in nationally but at present they mainly cover large metropolitan areas and conurbations in the Midlands, and are also the form of plan found in each of the London Boroughs (Fig. 5.29).

Examples of planning issues in some of these boroughs are discussed in Part V of *Implementing Town Planning*, edited

Figure 5.29 London boroughs

1 City	12 Merton	23 Waltham Forest
2 Westminster	13 Sutton	24 Haringey
3 Lambeth	14 Croydon	25 Enfield
4 Southwark	15 Lewisham	26 Barnet
5 Tower Hamlets	16 Bromley	27 Brent
6 Hackney	17 Greenwich	28 Harrow
7 Islington	18 Bexley	29 Ealing
8 Camden	19 Newham	30 Hillingdon
9 Kensington & Chelsea	20 Barking & Dagenham	31 Hounslow
10 Hammersmith & Fulham	21 Havering	32 Richmond upon Thames
11 Wandsworth	22 Redbridge	33 Kingston upon Thames

Helpful hint: Most 'plans' do not consist of a single map or a 'plan on the wall'; they generally consist of a set of reports, policy documents and several actual 'plans'. Nowadays some of these may also be prepared using computer techniques and by combining GIS techniques (Geographical Information Systems), as many local authorities store all the information about an area on computer using Ordnance Survey Grid References to access data for a particular site, on planning policy, current land use, planning applications, rateable values, population density, air quality, traffic flows etc.

Second hint: Since this whole section is very much about explaining, describing and developing an understanding of what town planning today is all about, do not expect there to be only one precise right answer to some of the questions. Much depends upon the locality where you live, and the nature of the local issues and urban problems. As we shall see, it gets even more complicated when it comes to considering possible solutions to many of our modern urban and rural problems.

by C. Greed (1996). The unitary (or single-tier) planning system combines, in one plan and related policy documentation, features of both the Structure Plan high-level policy component, and the more detailed Local Plan component, with a view to making the system more efficent and easier to understand and operate.

Basically all the Acts mentioned above have been concerned with two aspects of planning:

- Development Plans and policy
- Development Control and regulation

Project work

It is suggested, for a school or college group undertaking this section, that the teacher approaches the local planning department and asks for information about the type of plans in use in their town, city or county. Many authorities have educational liaison officers and are helpful, and they may also have leaflets and other information. It is not advised that individual students or pupils should approach such sources themselves, but information may also be obtained from the local library or information centre.

Self-assessment tasks

In conjunction with this section and optional task undertake the following self-test (1–3 are easy, but 4 requires more work).

1. What is the main legislation in force in relation to town planning nowadays? (List at least two Acts.)
2. What are the two main functions of the planning system?
3. What are the main types of Development Plan?
4. What is the nature of the Development Plan system in operation in your area? What are the 'plans' composed of? How have they influenced development and town form? And what do you personally think of them?

Development Control

As explained above, the town planning system has two main components: Development Plan production (of which there are two types), and secondly, what is known as **Development Control**. This term refers to the process of dealing with planning applications and deciding whether to give planning permission, in the light of the policy requirements enshrined in the Development Plans themselves, and in respect of additional national town planning laws and regulations. Development Control is normally undertaken at the local district level within the local planning authority, whereas strategic policy issues are dealt with at the county or unitary authority level. Therefore, before builders can even think about undertaking development on a particular site they must obtain planning permission! Also, as we shall see later there are a range of other statutory controls and financial factors that need to be taken into account long before the proposal reaches the desk of the local planning officer.

But what is 'development'? 'Development' is defined in planning law under section 55 of the 1990 Town and Country Planning Act as: *the carrying out of building, engineering, mining, or other operations in, on, over or under land, or the making of any material change in the use of any buildings or other land*.

Therefore 'development' includes both new buildings and a change in use of existing buildings, as will be explained.

A planning application form from the local planning office must be completed and submitted in order to obtain planning permission. In 'determining' (deciding) a planning application the local authority must consider the nature of Development Plan policy for the area. Obviously if there is a proposal for a new housing estate in the middle of a 'green belt' area, which is an area of protected land around the edge of a town or city, then it is unlikely to be granted.

Other situations are more complex; for example, if new development is proposed in what is known as a 'Conservation Area', i.e. an area of special historical or architectural importance, then the nature of the proposed development must be considered very carefully and special 'conditions' (as they are all called) may be put upon the scheme.

In summary, therefore there are three types of likely answer to an application:

- yes
- no
- yes, but provided conditions are agreed

In practice, normally, for any significant sized development a developer or owner would put in what is known as an 'Outline' application first to see what the planners think of the overall nature of the development, and then, subject to approval, a 'Detailed' (or 'Full') application would be put in later detailing the design features, such as access, design and appearance, details of use, parking and landscaping factors.

When 'determining' a planning application, the planners must also consider national legislation and rules. These are mainly contained in what are known as the GDO (General Development Order) and the UCO (Use Classes Order) which are statutory regulations accompanying the Acts, and which (warning!) are frequently updated. Therefore the following details are given for illustrative purposes, to give you an idea of what it's all about, but it is likely they will be amended in the future – such is the nature of planning law.

Legal aspects of development control

First, the GDO gives details of what is 'permitted development', i.e. development that does not require planning permission. This includes:

- house extensions up to 15% for detached properties and 10% for other properties
- the building of small front porches
- painting buildings and such like (see p. 195 of *Introducing Town Planning*)

These 'facts' should not be used for any purpose beyond this study unit because, as stated, they are subject to change. Indeed the legal aspects of town planning cannot be underestimated. As readers may be aware, it is a very litigious area, with endless planning appeals taking place (when applicants have disagreed with the planning decision they have been given) and much case law. Town planning law is another aspect of 'land law' which itself is a very fraught area because we are dealing here with land, which in our culture means property, wealth, investment and development profits. Although town planning policy might appear to be socially and environmentally progressive, the legal, economic, political and financial implications and results of planning decisions are often immense.

Secondly, the UCO provides a list of categories of land use. Basically if there is what is known as a 'change of use' between one land use to another 'worse' one (e.g. commercial to industrial) then planning permission is required. If, on the other hand, the change is within a use class, e.g. to a different type of residential development, then it may not need planning permission.

Self-assessment tasks

1. What are the two aspects of the definition of 'development'?
2. What are two types of planning application?
3. What are three likely types of answer?
4. What is the difference between the UCO and the GDO?

Project work

Ask your teacher to obtain copies of the planning application forms, and have a look at them, discuss them, and see what you make of them. Perhaps do a practice application for a piece of land, but do NOT send it in, because (i) there is a charge for all forms submitted and (ii) you are not likely to be the owner, or have a valid interest in the land.

Table 5.12 Summary of the Use Classes Order

Class A1	Shops of all types including superstores and retail warehouses; also includes hairdressers, sandwich bars, etc., not car showrooms
Class A2	Financial and professional services, including banks, building societies, estate agents and betting offices
Class A3	Food and drink, including restaurants, pubs and take-aways
Class B1	Business use, includes offices, research and development, general industrial use provided it is not detrimental to the area
Class B2	General industrial
Class B3–7	Special industrial uses
Class B8	Storage and distribution, including wholesale cash and carry
Class C1	Hotels and hostels
Class C2	Residential homes and institutions
Class C3	Use as a dwelling houses (a) by a family (b) by not more than six persons living together as a household (including those under care)
Class D1	Non-residential institutions including religious buildings, museums, medical, public halls, creches, nurseries
Class D2	Assembly, leisure, cinemas, bingo halls, casinos, indoor sports

Sui Generis Many uses do not fall into any class and are therefore in a class of their own literally. For example, theatres, car hire, petrol stations, car showrooms and various innovative uses have been seen to be *sui generis* (i.e. in a general category). This gives the planning office discretion to decide on the basis of planning policy whether a change of use has occurred or not

Property Law

Town planning powers are, contrary to popular opinion, quite specific and arguably limited in extent, with greater emphasis upon land use zoning and change of use regulations than upon detail. In addition to planning controls there is a need to be aware of the laws concerning private property as regards ownership, tenure, easements, covenants and rights of way. Land law, offically called 'real property law', existed for many centuries prior to planning law, and provides, by means of covenants on the use of land, a range of provisions regarding the design, density, height and use of buildings, especially in respect of residential areas.

Also many aspects of development will be controlled by a range of other public laws such as Housing Acts, Environmental Health Acts, Noise Abatement, Pollution, Parking Controls and Building Regulations. This aspect is discussed further within the context of the process of property development in Section 5.4.

Other planning controls

In addition to the requirements described above there is a whole range of other legal and policy factors which the local planning department must take into account. These include the following:

- **Urban Conservation.** If an individual building is 'listed' it is protected from demolition, extension or repair in most circumstances. Also any building in a conservation area, listed or not, is subject to various controls. Regulations are more concerned with external townscape and architectural factors but internal features are also subject in control in certain instances. This is a complex area and it suggested that if you wish to study this area in more depth you obtain the appropriate forms and guidance leaflets from your local planning department.

- **Rural Conservation.** Generally all protected areas, such as national parks, are subject to special development control powers. Also since the introduction of the 1995 Environment Act and related European Directives (relating to all countries within the European Union) enacted under earlier Acts and EC Directive 85/337, in many cases nowadays new development in the countryside is subject to EIA (Environmental Impact Assessment) procedures in relation the environmental and ecological implications of development. Also there are now many environmental controls on pollution, industry and minerals extraction both in town and country, as discussed further in *Investigating Town Planning*.

- **Nature conservation.** In addition there are a variety of minor regulations (but often disproportionate in effect) in relation to vegetation, flora and fauna. In particular, TPOs (Tree Preservation Orders) prevent the lopping or felling of designated trees, and this may form a major 'problem' for site developers. In the past one often heard tales of builders 'accidentally on purpose' backing their lorry into such obstructions to demolish them, but nowadays the legal situation has been tightened up. In contrast, there is no control on the height or nature of trees planted, especially in private gardens, although many other countries ban non-native intrusive species such as *Leylandii* and *Eucalyptus* trees. Paradoxically, under the GDO, boundary walls over 2 m (6'6") require planning permission but not hedges, and there is no right of light or view, although there is political and public pressure to increase the scope of criminal powers to cover such cases. Currently there are hefty fines and the threat of imprisonment for demolition of protected trees or listed buildings.

Building regulations

Town planning is also 'only' officially concerned with the 'outsides' as against the 'insides' of buildings; it is not responsible for construction detail or internal details. These matters are dealt under the Building Regulations, and enforced by building inspectors, not town planners. From the town planning viewpoint there is concern for people with disabilities to ensure adequate access is designed into buildings. These matters often seem to fall between two stools – between the roles of the architect and planner. The standards embodied in the Building Regulations are based, to a degree, upon the requirements set by regulatory bodies such as the British Standards Institution. Table 5.13 shows the differences between town planning and building control.

The 1995 Disability Discrimination Acts increases controls in relation to access to public buildings, shops, educational institutions and ordinary housing. Also the Town and Country Planning Act 1990, section 76, requires that local authorities give attention to the question of the level of accessibility for the disabled when determining a planning application. This particularly relates to access to individual buildings, especially offices, shops and other public buildings, by virtue of the *Code of Practice for Access of the Disabled to Buildings* (BS 5810) and Design Note 18, *Access for Disabled*

Table 5.13 Differences in the planning and building control processes

Planning control process	Building control process
Local policies and planning variations (this may result in varying provision and uncertainty for users)	National objectives and standards (people know what to expect)
Standards measured against approved plan	Measured against national criteria
Applies to most types and ages of land use and development	Only applies to new build, rebuild and major extensions: various exemptions.
Developers/builders need to find out planning requirements	Developers know what is expected nationwide
Long approval process before work starts	Once plans are deposited work can start or can start with simple provision of notice
Work in progress is seldom inspected	Work in progress is inspected
Public can inspect plans and plan register	Plans are not open to public
Clients and public involved and think they know about planning	Decisions seen as technical and unlikely to be understood
Consultation and public participation	No such outside liaison
Councillors must approve decisions	Officers make final decision
Planners must consult with many groups	Only consult with fire service
Concerned with physical, and various social, economic and environmental factors and other on- and off-site issues.	Concerned with structural factors, fire and safety
Mainly land-use control and external design control.	Mainly internal and structural design control
Must advertise major (changes)	Can make changes, relaxations
Can approve phases of plan	Must approve whole scheme
Some control over future provision/ fate of conditions	Cannot control future management or maintenance of access features

People to Educational Buildings, published in 1979 by the Department of the Environment.

Thus there are a range of controls under the Building Regulations and British Standards related to increasing access and safety for disabled people. For example, BS 5810 *Access for Disabled People*, last updated in 1992, sets out the principles, and Linked Document M of the Building Regulations translates these standards into design requirements. (You will find further information on the nature of Building Regulations in Sections 2.4 and 5.4). Other relevant regulations on disability include BS 5588 Part 8: *Code of Practice on Means of Escape from Buildings*, BS 6465 on toilets, BS 5776 on powered stairlifts, and BS 6460 *Lifting Platforms* for when a lift cannot be used in an emergency or fire. (The topic of town planning and disabled groups is discussed by L. Davies in C. Greed (ed.) *Implementing Town Planning*).

In addition there are a range of other health, safety, design, environmental and practical considerations that have to be taken into account, and which will require approval from the relevant department of the local authority. It must be stressed again that just because something has got planning permission does not mean it has got building consent and vice versa. Also there are an increasing range of European Directives coming on line which the developer will need to take into account.

Finally, it used to be said of town planning, 'it all comes down to sewers in the final analysis'. By this is meant the fact that, particularly with new development on the edges of towns, it is most important to ascertain what the local infrastructural and services position is before even contemplating development, particularly in respect of sewerage systems, water supply and road building.

In the 'good old days' before privatisation and the emphasis upon a market economy rather than a public service ethic among statutory undertakers, developers might have assumed to get infrastructure provided 'free' or in return for an agreement to contribute towards provision. Now, particularly on sites that are currently not connected up, this should not be assumed.

Self-assessment tasks

1. What town planning controls need to be taken into account in development?
2. What other built environment regulatory and infrastructural factors must be considered?

The levels and framework of planning

The purpose of this section is to provide an overview of the levels and framework of planning already referred to in the above description of the functions of the planning system. This section will also provide an opportunity for a discussion of the political aspects of planning. Following this, in the final section, stages, and the roles of the participants, within the development process will be set out. In the final section a short case study will be presented that will bring in the financial factors involved, as well touching upon the social, physical, environmental and functional aspects already highlighted in the above account.

Central government

There are two main levels of town planning in Britain, central and local government (Fig. 5.30). The Department of the Environment, Transport and the Regions (DETR) is the main central government department responsible for town planning. When the new Labour Government came to power in 1997 they combined the previous Department of the Environment (DoE) with the old Department of Transport (DOT) to create the DETR. This was done in order to integrate planning and transport policy more closely in order to deal more effectively with traffic problems and to promote environmental sustainability. The DETR is headed by the Secretary of State for the Environment who is a politician (*not* a planner), with cabinet status, who is supported by three, or sometimes four, junior ministers with specialist responsibilities.

The Secretary of State has overall responsibility for shaping and guiding national planning policy, particularly the approval of Development Plans. He or she also has the

final say on individual controversial planning decisions. Some 500 000 planning applications were received by English planning authorities in 1990, of which 80% were allowed. Some 26 000 planning appeals were received by the Secretary of State, of which 33% were allowed. Current statistical updates and information on the DETR publications and policies can be obtained from the following Web pages:

http://www.open.gov.uk
http://www.planning.detr.gov.uk

The Secretary of State is advised by professionally qualified staff, including town planners, surveyors, architects, environmentalists and housing managers. The Secretary of State does not have to accept their advice if it is not politically acceptable to the government. The divisions between the planners and their political masters, and between the private sector developers and public sector controllers of development, run all the way through the planning process. In the past, planners had a stronger role (and arguably more power and funding) in carrying out development, as in the case of the post-war new towns.

Town planning is in a sense 'neutral' as it can be used in the service of any political party's solutions to urban problems, the perception of the 'right way' to plan being influenced by the underlying political viewpoint of the planners' masters. It should be stressed again that town planning is a very political process, because it is all about power, money and how people live. For example, if you are a rich property developer looking for sites 'ripe for development' you may have a very different view of an inner city location threatened by office development, from that of a local community worker concerned with retaining shops, schools and houses for the local residents. Also, if you are a car driver you will have a different view of how a city ought to be planned than if you are dependent upon public transport, and fed up with having to walk vast distances and with not being able to reach out-of-town shopping facilities.

The DETR is a very large department within which many other functions related to policy-making for the built environment are carried out, such as aspects of housing, transportation, building and construction, inner cities, environmental health, conservation and historic buildings, and many other matters. A range of DETR policy documents are produced, such as government white papers, circulars, consultation papers, guidance notes and directives. PPGs (Planning Policy Guidance notes) cover a range of strategic issues; for example, PPG6 deals with policy on major retail development proposals.

There are also several *ad hoc* bodies in planning, these being any of the numerous government-sponsored agencies or authorities with independent planning powers. Among the most well known of these are the UDCs (the Urban Development Corporations – not to be confused with UDPs or Unitary Development Plans!, such as the BDC (Bristol Development Corporation), and the LDDC (London Docklands Development Corporation). The main aim of the LDDC was not so much to build new development itself (as was the case with the old, post-war New Town Corporations) but rather to engender development, to provide the infrastructure, especially roads, and the famous Light Railway, and to encourage private developers to come in and build and invest in the area.

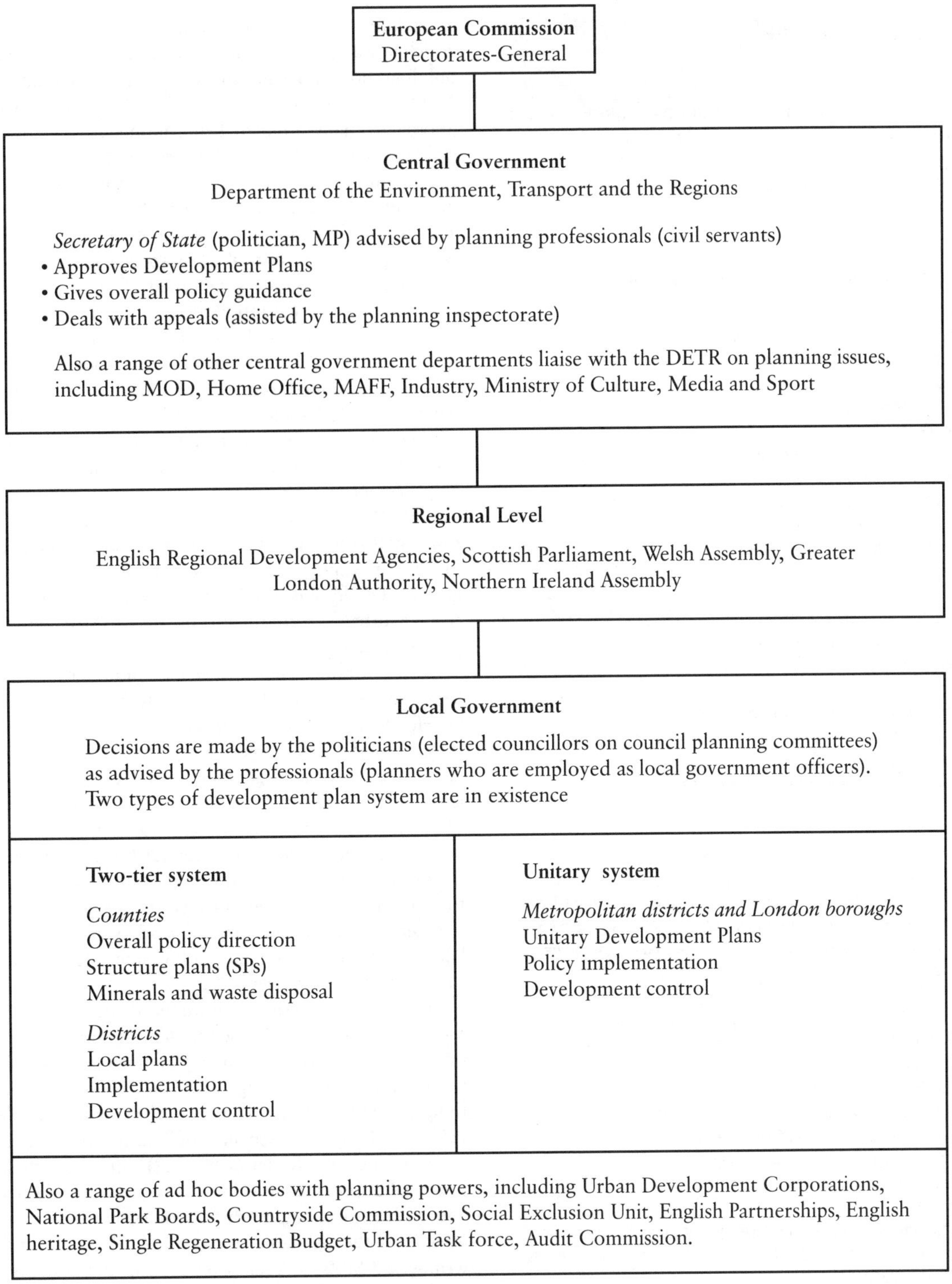

```
┌─────────────────────────────────┐
│      European Commission        │
│      Directorates-General       │
└─────────────────────────────────┘
                 │
```

Central Government

Department of the Environment, Transport and the Regions

Secretary of State (politician, MP) advised by planning professionals (civil servants)
- Approves Development Plans
- Gives overall policy guidance
- Deals with appeals (assisted by the planning inspectorate)

Also a range of other central government departments liaise with the DETR on planning issues, including MOD, Home Office, MAFF, Industry, Ministry of Culture, Media and Sport

Regional Level

English Regional Development Agencies, Scottish Parliament, Welsh Assembly, Greater London Authority, Northern Ireland Assembly

Local Government

Decisions are made by the politicians (elected councillors on council planning committees) as advised by the professionals (planners who are employed as local government officers). Two types of development plan system are in existence

Two-tier system	**Unitary system**
Counties	*Metropolitan districts and London boroughs*
Overall policy direction	Unitary Development Plans
Structure plans (SPs)	Policy implementation
Minerals and waste disposal	Development control
Districts	
Local plans	
Implementation	
Development control	

Also a range of ad hoc bodies with planning powers, including Urban Development Corporations, National Park Boards, Countryside Commission, Social Exclusion Unit, English Partnerships, English heritage, Single Regeneration Budget, Urban Task force, Audit Commission.

Figure 5.30 The levels of town and country planning

FINANCIAL FACTORS

Enterprise Planning

A range of initiatives have been created to bring back business and investment to the inner city, and to facilitate urban renewal. The Local Government Planning and Land Act 1980 consolidated previous legislation and change in this respect and provided the enabling powers for a range of other programmes and measures. For example, Enterprise Zones (EZs) were introduced which were meant to attract investment to run-down areas by means of reducing planning controls and suspending ordinary planning law within their boundaries. Urban Development Corporations (UDCs) were established in inner areas under the 1980 Act (Cullingworth and Nadin 1997: 238–9). Various other grants, loans, rates, holidays and incentives were introduced, including the City Grant for the redevelopment of areas and repair of buildings that were too deteriorated to be of interest to the developer. Such measures, along with a continuing enthusiasm for urban conservation, led in many cases to increased gentrification rather than meeting the needs of the inner city poor.

EZs are relatively small areas – the size of a small industrial estate – and are administered via the existing local authority,

Environmental assessment

Nowadays all major planning applications require environmental assessment.

Table 5.14 Categories of development requiring environmental assessment

Schedule 1

This includes the following 21 categories of development:

1. Crude-oil refineries
2. Thermal power stations, nuclear power stations
3. Installations for processing nuclear fuel or waste
4. Iron and steel smelting works
5. Asbestos processing works
6. Chemical plants
7. Construction of railways, airports, motorways and express roads
8. Ports, piers and waterways
9. Waste disposal installations involving incineration, landfill, hazardous waste and chemical treatment
10. Non-hazardous waste disposal installations over 100 tonnes per day
11. Groundwater extraction works
12. Water resource transfer works
13. Large waste-water treatment plants
14. Petroleum and natural gas extraction
15. Dams and other large water storage works
16. Pipelines for gas, oil or chemicals
17. Installations for intensive poultry or pig rearing
18. Industrial plans for timber, paper and pulp production
19. Quarries and open-cast mining
20. Construction of overhead electrical power lines
21. Storage of petroleum and chemical products

Schedule 2

These are uses not included in Schedule 1, which may not appear to be so environmentally problematic, but which because of their size, intensity or ecological aspects require special attention. Each of the 13 sections covers many types of development. Aspects which have caused comment are given for illustrative purposes.

1. Agriculture, silviculture and aquaculture, e.g. fishfarming
2. Extractive industry e.g. underground mining
3. Energy industry, e.g. wind turbines
4. Metal procesing, e.g. shipyards
5. Mineral industry, e.g. manufacture of ceramic roofing tiles
6. Chemical industry, e.g. manufacture of paint
7. Food production, e.g. brewing and malting
8. Textile, leather, wood and paper industry, e.g. cellulose
9. Rubber industry
10. Infrastructure projects, e.g. urban development projects, where the ground covered is more than 0.5 hectares, such as shopping centres and multiplex cinemas
11. Other projects, e.g. slaughter houses
12. Tourism and leisure developments, e.g. theme parks
13. Any change or extension of the projects listed in 1–12 above.

whereas UDCs are much larger areas, e.g. the Bristol Development Corporation area and the London Docklands Development Corporation area (LDDC). The London body was established separately from the existing local authorities in their area (much to their chagrin) and employed its own army of planners, surveyors, architects, etc. Its main aim, however, was not so much to build new development itself, but rather to provide the infrastructure, especially roads, and the famous Docklands Light Railway, to encourage private developers to come in and build and invest in the area. This is

a very different approach from the New Town Corporations which always took a much more active role themselves in building both housing stock and industrial units for rent. There are arguments to support both approaches – the approach finally adopted being influenced by the underlying political viewpoint of the planners' masters.

Both the EZs and the UDCs have a limited life expectancy of around 10 years, after which they will be de-designated. This is already happening to some of the early ones. The aim was simply to give critical areas special status while they find their feet and become established. Considerable investment has been put into infrastructure, as in the case of the Docklands Light Railway in London, and into road improvements. Although many firms took up the offer, as with old-fashioned regional planning it is debatable as to whether new jobs and new prosperity were really created, or whether firms simply moved across the boundary in order to catch the grant, and thus deprived other areas of existing employment.

Under UDC policy, vast areas were reclaimed for upmarket residential and business use within the old London Docklands, in close proximity to the City of London, attracting a new social class to the old 'East End' and convenient for 'Yuppies' (i.e. the 'young urban professionals' of the 1980s). However, this process created considerable resentment among some of the original working class residents. Although the inner city legislation was originally purported to be on their behalf, it has benefited the middle class groups far more. People remember how difficult it was in the past even to get the council to put on an extra bus service to get them to work, whereas now expense is no object. Meanwhile, because of high house prices, and lack of council or cheap rented accommodation, many working class people who also have jobs in central London (on the Tube, in the hospitals, cleaning in the offices, in the shops) find they have to commute further and further out, while many managers wonder why there is no longer a ready supply of working class labour to do all the essential, yet low-status, jobs upon which the running of the capital depends.

In 1985 the Government introduced the White Paper *Lifting the Burden* which emphasised minimising perceived restrictions on economic growth created by planning controls. Subsequently the Housing and Planning Act 1986 introduced, among other things, Simplified Planning Zones (SPZs) which supplement the EZs and UDPs, but are smaller and the criteria for their location are more flexible. Rydin (1998:212) notes that these were of historical importance in being a move towards a blanket zoning approach to planning, in which permission for development was inherent in the area designation of SPZ. There are, at the time of writing, 13 SPZs, as against 35 EZs, in the UK. The need for their designation was subsequently superseded by the introduction of a range of other measures which sought to 'lift the burden' from developers.

The main principle of such initiatives was to attempt to simplify and speed up the planning system or to create an organisational framework tailor-made for the special circumstances of a particular situation without disrupting the existing planning system. Meanwhile, in non-special category areas planning law became more complex, and the Conservatives introduced planning charges for applications in the late 1970s. The proliferation of *ad hoc* bodies only serves to weaken the existing planning system, and increase the powers of central government. In spite of other 'gimmicky' schemes such as 'Garden Festivals', and various other inner city initiatives, unemployment continued to rise, inner city problems continued and regional disparities became even greater. Many argued that it was time to bring back regional planning, though it needed to be based upon more sensitive criteria than it had in the past. For example, it should take into account women's employment as well as men's, and demonstrate awareness of the great social disparities that can exist within a region such as the South East between run-down inner city areas and the more prosperous suburbs and market towns.

A range of urban renewal initiatives were created, including 'Action for Cities' and the 'Urban Programme' and in 1991 under 'City Challenge'. This was superseded by the Single Regeneration Budget (SRB) in April 1994, which is still in force. The SRB initially combined over 20 existing programmes, including Estate Action, City Challenge, Urban Programme, Safer Cities, and TEC Challenge. The SRB also seeks to coordinate the input of different government departments, such as the DETR, the Home Office, the Employment Department, local authorities, and other bodies concerned with the social, economic and physical regeneration of inner city areas, through a system of integrated regional offices. The SRB programme is continuing at the time of writing, in spite of the fact that so many other new initiatives have come on line too. It would seem that in order to manage such a vast initiative the government finds that it cannot do without 'planning' and 'planners' – who are planners in all but name, as nowadays these words have such negative connotations that alternatives are often used. For example, advertisements in the Wednesday edition of the *Guardian* each week are for professionals qualified to undertake urban regeneration, not 'planners' *per se*.

Development finance

Having outlined the governmental and legal aspects of the planning system, it must be stressed again that the planners are not the same as the developers. They are two different groups. The developers are mainly private sector people who initiate, coordinate and implement new building schemes, while the planners exercise control over these schemes to ensure they comply with the public interest. The developer's main aim is to get the best return from the site, to make sufficent profit to justify the investment in the scheme in the first place. The planner is concerned with a wider range of issues on behalf of society.

However, as described above, the planning system today does offer various grants and incentives to develop, particularly in the inner city and in economically depressed areas. Private developers and local authority planners may co-operate and enter into a 'partnership scheme', for example on large developments which are seen to be to the benefit of the community. The local authority has powers of compulsory purchase and land assembly to enable a site to be acquired. The developers can offer additional benefits which may not be available from public sector resources, (e.g. the provision of additional sports facilities) through what is known as 'planning gain'.

The private developers are likely to be advised in their decision to develop by chartered surveyors and valuers as to the feasibility of the scheme. Indeed the areas of investment, taxation, valuation and economic policy all have their own professionals and experts, over and above the role of the planners. Within an increasingly commercialised environment, in which the profitability of a development is the key consideration, clearly town planners have to be more commercially aware, as well as being concerned with environmental, social and practical land use considerations.

The private sector is motivated to invest in development because of the likely financial yield it will return, and not because there is necessarily a human need for a particular type of development. The decision to invest is influenced by the current situation regarding taxation, and the existence of likely purchasers and investors in the scheme. Developers often possess an entire portfolio of property investments, and their choice of properties is influenced by the state of the market, and by the evaluation and appraisal recommendations of their professional advisors. After all, property is just one type of investment among many possibilities, including, for example, race horses, oil, equities and bonds. But it also happens to make up the towns and cities in which we live and move and make our homes.

Developers are influenced by the likely level of risk and the likely rate of return in deciding whether or not to go ahead with property projects. The developer's aim is to maximise returns and minimise risk. Such factors influence decision-making and the timing of development. Likewise changes in government and shifts in emphasis in taxation policy, for example on capital gains tax or corporation tax, strongly influence development. Levels of interest rates, for both borrower and investor, will also influence the decision to develop, particularly in respect of new private housing development, where most of the occupiers are likely to be mortgage payers.

For example, in the town you are studying you may find examples of development projects which started and then stopped, or were delayed, as a result of the financial backers pulling out or going bankrupt. You may also find examples of planning gain and compulsory purchase controversially influencing the nature of a development scheme. There are huge regional contrasts in development activity. In economically depressed regions such as the North East property values are low, as are house prices, because there is limited demand for new development, and many incentives will be given to encourage businesses to move there. In contrast, in the South East and especially in London, property values are very high, and investors, developers and contractors are all keen to build, because the likely returns are so high. Because of the competition the planners can specify much stricter requirements for the developer in terms of planning conditions, planning gain and public facilities. Clearly it is impossible to separate the operation of the planning system from the surrounding economic and political context.

New levels of power

European planning

A new level of power

Overarching the national central government level of planning, as embodied in the DETR, the pan-European level of planning powers will now be discussed. Policies and issues that have featured strongly in European planning, such as environmental sustainability, will discussed.

The implementation of European environmental legislation is overseen by the European Environmental Agency (EEA) which seeks to ensure that member-state planning agencies and local authorities are actually aware of the requirements. The European Commission (EC), through 24 Directorates-General, produces policy guidance, directives and regulations which must be taken on board by all the member states of the

European Union (EU), which together have a population of over 380 million, rivalling North America (Davis 1992; Ludlow 1996; Williams 1996, 1999). The Directorates of particular relevance to town planning are:

- DG XVI Regional Policy
- DG XI Environment, Nuclear Safety and Civil Protection
- DG V Employment, Industrial Relations and Social Affairs
- DG VI Agriculture
- DG XVII Energy
- DG XXIII Tourism

Foremost, EC Directive 85/337 on the Environmental Assessment of certain categories of new development must be complied with. This was subsequently updated and expanded as EC Directive 97/11.

Regional planning

There was no significant regional level of planning between the national and the local authority level for nearly 20 years. The new Labour Government has sought to re-establish a foundation to rebuild the regional level of planning. Regional Development Agencies were created on 1 April 1999. Their brief is to establish regional strategies to deal with economic development, regeneration and regional competitiveness.

Local government reorganisation

The local government system in England and Wales has been based upon a two-tier system, consisting of counties and districts, for the last twenty years. Long-awaited local government boundary reorganisation took place in 1996 (following the 1992 Local Government Act), creating a system of unitary authorities. This involved breaking up many of the large super-counties such as Avon (around Bristol) created under the last major boundary reorganisation in 1974, and restoring some of the original historical boundary demarcations. Elsewhere larger erstwhile second-tier district authorities were restructured as unitary, single-tier authorities in their own right. The map of Britain now constitutes a confusing mixture of single and two-tier authorities. Nevertheless the nature of the plans produced still conforms to the description given above, with counties producing Structure Plans, unitary areas producing Unitary Development Plans, and so forth.

Project work

Check the situation in your area.

Devolution

The devolution of power from Westminster, in 1999, to a Scottish Parliament in Edinburgh and a Welsh Assembly in Cardiff, along with arrangements for the devolution to an elected assembly in Northern Ireland, have signalled fundamental changes in the government of the United Kingdom. These changes have important consequences for planning. The main legislation for Scotland is now contained in the Town and Country Planning (Scotland) Act 1997 and

the Planning (Listed Buildings and Conservation Areas) (Scotland) Act 1997. These are consolidating Acts rather than introducing anything new. Scotland also has provisions similar to those in England on permitted development and changes within particular use classes.

Wales

Welsh affairs were previously dealt with by the Home Office but a separate Welsh Office was created in 1964 with its own Secretary of State for Wales. The Welsh Office produces all of its planning publications in both Welsh and English, but the planning systems have been virtually the same. Welsh authorities had already been reorganised under the Local Government (Wales) Act 1994. Now a greater independence is being achieved, with a new Welsh Assembly being established in 1999, but at present the Assembly has only limited powers; for example, it has some tax distribution powers but no tax raising powers. The new Welsh Assembly also has planning powers that will allow for the development of planning in Wales to move forward separately from that of England in future, but this will be more of a transitional process than in Scotland.

Circular 53/88 on 'The Welsh Language: Development Plans and Development Control' recognised the importance of the Welsh language as part of the cultural and social fabric of Wales and allowed it to be taken into account in plan production. It also recognised that language was a material consideration in determining planning applications. This has been the subject of controversy in Wales, with some authorities attempting to apply strict restrictions on house building in an attempt to limit the influx of English speakers.

London

The organisation of the planning system for London has been undergoing radical change. Greater London has a population approaching 8 million. Following the abolition of the GLC in 1986, remaining planning advisory functions were taken over by the London Planning Advisory Body, with the London Residuary Body being responsible for administering its gradual demise. The GLC's powers were devolved to the 33 London Borough Councils (Heap 1991:38). The new Labour Government is committed to the new strategic authority for the governance of London, namely the Greater London Authority (GLA), to start in July 2000. A new mayor and assembly has considerable powers to 'run London' rather along the lines of the North American 'city manager' (Hambleton and Sweeney 1999). As to town planning powers, major applications from the London boroughs have to be referred to the GLA, and overall policy guidance will be given by a mayoral spatial strategy, which is particularly concerned with urban renewal and economic regeneration.

All change

It is clear that a great many changes are occurring to the town planning system at present. Therefore it is important for students to check what the current situation is in their own area when assembling up-to-date material for their project portfolio.

Further Reading

Cullingworth J B and Nadin V 1999 *Town and Country Planning in Britain*, Routledge
Davies L 1992 *Planning in Europe* RTPI
Greed C (ed) 1996 *Implementing Town Planning* Addison Wesley Longman (and others in the same series)
Greed C (ed) *Social Town Planning* Routledge
Rydin Y 1998 *Urban and Environmental Planning in the UK* Macmillan, London
Hambleton R and Sweeting O 1999 *Planning* issue no 1347

Head D 1996 *Outline of Planning Law* Sweet and Maxwell
Williams R 1996 European Union Spatial Policy and Planning Paul Chapman

Those students who wish to pursue the valuation, investment and taxation aspects of property development are advised to consult the following:

Hargitay S and Yu S 1993 *Property Investment Decisions* E & F N Spon
Lumby S 1994 *Investment Appraisal and Financing Decisions* Chapman and Hall

5.4 The development process

The purpose of this section is to explain the sequence of the development process and the role of town planning. The stages in the development of a hypothetical scheme by a private sector development company will now be outlined. Current standards for designing a housing estate layout will be given, including the pre-site development sequence and the site development.

The stages

Finance

Before we even get to the planning stage, let alone the site development stage, there is a vast amount of pre-contract, pre-planning application activity going on in the world of property development. In particular, 'finance' is a primary factor, economic trends need to be taken into account, particularly since the property market has strongly manifested 'boom and bust' features over the last ten years. Further details on this may be found in *Implementing Town Planning*, 1996 Chapter 2, 'The market economic context of town planning' by P. Hobbs, and Chapter 4, 'Regenerating cities' by

N. Oatley. Unit 8 of this book should also be consulted for further financial details.

A project may be directly financed by pension funds, insurance companies, trusts, etc., who choose a development company to undertake the scheme for them. They will naturally be concerned that their shareholders' and investors' money is being invested wisely. Now many insurance companies have their own in-house property advisors, these often being surveyors and valuers who ensure that the 'portfolio' of property investment is well balanced, and that any actual development project is carefully evaluated.

There may be an actual human need for better facilities in an area, but the extent of need is not the overriding criterion as developers are only interested if there is a profit to be made from the scheme – which is the main reason for developing. That is why, in Figure 5.31, the first box is not the decision to develop, but rather the analysis of the property investment situation, as property (to the market) is no more than a commodity like racehorses and oil.

However, if developers do not take into account and respond to human need they are unlikely to find themselves with a viable scheme. Students should also be aware of the changing taxation situation in respect of capital gains tax, corporation tax and property taxes in general. It is difficult to specify details here as this is a vast field, and regulations change with each Budget, but

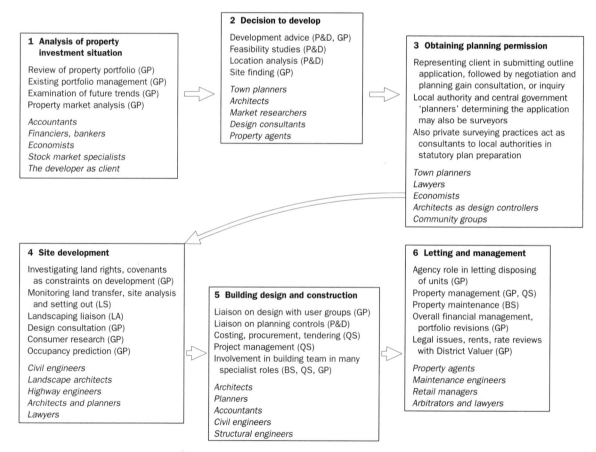

Figure 5.31 The process of property development, showing the sequence and aspects of the process – different divisions of surveyors contribute to an archetypal example of a new scheme for a developer as client. Contributing professions other than surveying are shown in italics – GP: general practice; P&D: planning and development; LS: land surveying; LA: land agency; MS: minerals; QS: quantity surveying; BS: building and surveying divisions of the RICS. (Greed 1996. *Introducing Town Planning* Longman)

in the course of undertaking the project work specified for this unit on site development you can find out what is involved; you should also refer to Unit 8 in this book. The property industry employs vast numbers of valuers, accountants and investment analysts to deal with just such matters because they are so complex. Chartered surveyors (those surveyors who are members of the RICS) often act as financial advisors to the private sector. Many professions are involved in the development process (Table 5.15).

Table 5.15 Membership of the property professions 1996

Body	Student members	Full members	Total members
Royal Town Planning Institute (RTPI)	2196 (43.0%)*	13689 (22.0%)	17337 (23.0%)
Royal Institution of Chartered Surveyors (RICS)	8193 (15.5%)	71865 (7.0%)	92772 (8.7%)
Institution of Structural Engineers (ISE)	4358 (13.4%)	10114 (1.3%)	21636 (4.4%)
Institution of Civil Engineers (ICE)	8353 (11.7%)	42658 (1.8%)	79480 (4.3%)
The Chartered Institute of Building (CIOB)	9859 (6.2%)	10244 (0.9%)	33143 (2.7%)
Architects and Surveyors Institute (ASI)	—	—	5046 (2.5%)
Royal Institute of British Architects (RIBA)	3500 (31.0%)	22670 (8.0%)	32000† (12.0%)
Association of Building Engineers (ABE)	327 (10.4%)	2292 (1.7%)	4577 (2.3%)
Chartered Institution of Building Services Engineers (CIBSE)	2196 (5.3%)	6275 (1.1%)	15264 (2.0%)
Chartered Institute of Housing (CIOH)	4190 (63.0%)	8258 (41.0%)	13490 (47.0%)
Architects Registration Board, ARCUK (UK only)	—	—	25153 (11.5%)
British Institute of Architectural Technology (BIAT)	—	—	5495 (3.3%)

Of 1.3 million in construction 15% are professional – of these 6% are women (0.9% of total); approximate total for all is therefore: 195000 (6.0%)

*Female percentages are given in brackets
†RIBA figures are approximate due to new format of presentation of figures on education statistics and membership
Note: In some cases there are other intermediate or honorary categories which make up the remainder of the total, who are not, strictly speaking, either fully qualified members or students, such as probationers, technicians, international members, graduate associates. Also categories of data may be redefined by professional bodies.
Source: The professional bodies.

Feasibility

Before proceeding, the developers might carry out a feasibility study to ascertain the potential catchment area and turnover of the scheme, and may bring in the specialist skills of a development surveyor and property researcher to do so, possibly using the in-house expertise of one of the large London companies of chartered surveyors, who produce property market analysis reports. They will also need to consult with the local authority planners in the area to find out what the zoning and overall policy is for that area.

It is likely that in large or controversial schemes, planning consultants for the developers will produce a planning brief setting out the proposals as a basis for negotiation. The local planning authority may have already have drawn up its own development brief or policy statement as to what is acceptable in the area – particularly if they are located in an area such as parts of London where there is already demand to develop, and 'site finders' are scouring every square inch of the territory looking for development potential. The planning authority and developers are unlikely to see eye to eye at their first meeting but by a process of negotiation they can move closer towards defining a scheme that will be acceptable to both parties. It is quite likely that an element of 'bargaining' will take place to get the best 'planning gain' possible, through what was known as a 'planning agreement' – now known as a 'Section 106 Agreement' under the 1990 and 1991 Town and Country Planning Acts – in return for certain concessions in development control.

Planning applications

In considering whether or not to give the scheme planning permission (box 3, in Figure 5.31) the planning authority are not only concerned with the nature of the development itself, but with the additional traffic and car parking it is likely to generate, and with the visual townscape impact.

Planners do not look at a site in isolation but in relation to its effect on the surrounding area, and the impact of this new development on the existing mix of uses. Are there already too many offices in this area? Would the use of the site for shops preclude its use at a later date for more social uses and provisions of facilities that are lacking? Would the development of a particular site prevent surface mineral extraction at a later date? Planners are therefore concerned with balance and adjusting all the land uses together. The fact that it is profitable to the developer does not necessarily mean that it is right from a town planning viewpoint.

All development has to get planning permission, whether it be private sector residential development or public sector council housing. Permission is not a foregone conclusion, although there are special mechanisms for one local authority department to get planning permission from another.

Housing is a major land use and therefore is a strategic issue in the Structure Plan, which will have implications for the whole nature of the city, both physically and socially. New housing has major implications for the transportation policy of the urban area, and means increased demand for basic supporting services such as schools, shops and leisure facilities as housing generates people. This is over and above the immediate concern of the housing department to meet housing need, or to rehouse people on their waiting list.

The planners need to look not only at the detailed nationwide planning controls of planning law, but also they need to consider central government policy statements, the implications of Structure Plan policy, as well as any specific Local Plan statements for that area. Any decisions the planners make must be based on these sources, and not be arbitrary decisions. Since the planners are only the professional advisors of their political masters, the councillors, any planning decision must be discussed and approved by the planning committee of the local authority council. Certain matters may also have to be passed up to the county level, and even to central government. Depending on the scale and nature of the scheme it may also be necessary to advertise the nature of the scheme to the general public and undertake public participation, and carry out consultations with statutory undertakers, related government departments and other official groups.

The development process must be placed within the wider political context of the planning system. In reality the relationship between the planning professionals, their political masters, 'the members', (i.e. the councillors on the planning committee), and the community is much more complex, and may be subject to the vagaries of different personalities and interest groups fighting it out to the bitter end. The system is highly political because land and property are involved, although it is believed that only in a minority of cases are overt bribery and corruption attempted.

On major schemes there may be a great deal of lobbying from community groups, and from pressure groups concerned with the issue in question. There are provisions in many cases for public participation and consultation on statutory plans, but the situation is far less amenable in the case of separate planning applications where only limited advertisement of the proposals may be required. The perceived lack of openness, obscurity, and paucity of communication associated with the planning process is one of the reasons why there has been so much conflict, dissatisfaction and pressure group activity surrounding the planning system (Reade 1987). Every political and legal tactic will be used by different interest groups to promote or prevent a planning decision being made, and proposals for planning schemes can drag on for years, and still result in a decision that pleases no one.

Delays in gaining planning permission can cost a development company millions of pounds in interest payments, for 'time is money'. In some cases a scheme may go to public inquiry to deal with objections from the general public; or to appeal if the scheme is refused and the developer appeals to the Secretary of State. One should not see the planners and the developers as necessarily being adversaries; in some cases the local authority and the developers will enter into a partnership scheme together.

The local authority planners have powers that can help the developers, such as land assembly and compulsory purchase, and the developers have expertise in getting the scheme off the ground which is of use to the local authority. It depends, to some degree, on the location, and more particularly the region, as some areas are keen to attract developers whereas in the South East planners can afford to be more choosy as there is so much competition between developers for the right to develop on different sites. It has even been suggested that the planners ought to hold auctions and sell the right to develop to the highest bidder, as in California.

Design considerations

When it comes to the design and building of the scheme a whole range of other property professionals come into play (boxes 4 and 5 in Fig. 5.31). Clearly the actual design, costing, tendering and ultimate construction of the scheme relate to major aspects of the work of the construction industry as described in other units within this book. First of all there is the architect who designs the scheme; nowadays it unlikely to be just one person but a whole team of skilled people. Also there are likely to be interior designers, particularly if it is a shopping mall type of development, to create the right lifestyle image for the consumers.

The planners, both public and private, will be involved in the overall layout, and the relationship with the surrounding buildings, particularly if it is in or adjacent to a conservation area. There is the major question of the car parking, goods vehicles servicing, public transport if there is going to be any, and the overall circulation, access and general road layout. This will involve the specialist skills of transportation planners and also, ultimately, highway engineers.

The design process is likely to go on for many months, because of a thousand and one constraints and the question of the 'cost factor'. Quantity surveyors in particular are responsible for costing out the 'price' of the building. It must be pointed out that the actual cost of materials and construction is only a small part of the final value of the property. There is also the cost of the land, the acquisition of the site in the first place, which can be a very substantial part of the overall investment outgoings. The value of the development once built is dictated more by market forces than by construction or land costs. There may be statutory requirements for public participation and community consultation on the scheme, and there is usually likely to be a level of public opposition to larger schemes.

The property lawyer will deal with easements across the site (rights of way), restrictive covenants (private legal controls against certain uses or types of development on the land) and the confusing maze of land titles that need to be dealt with. Also, separately, people who specialise in building contract law and 'project management' (who may be senior quantity surveyors, general practice surveyors or even architects) will need to sort out the contracts, tenders, and all the legal details of dealing with the large numbers of people, contractors and suppliers involved in building the scheme.

Once the architect has worked out the design, the quantity surveyor must work out the cost, and the project manager or architect in control of the project must put it out to tender and get the contractors in to build it. There are a multitude of detailed design factors and legal factors that need to be taken into account. The actual construction will involve a vast range of professionals, including civil and structural engineers, heating and ventilating engineers, etc. as well as a range of building trades workers and labourers, all with their foremen, managers and back-up administrators.

The land surveyor also has an important role both at the beginning in setting out the site, and at the end when the development is completed, at which time it is likely that the Ordnance Survey will send someone along to add the new scheme to their maps ready for the next revision. However, it is also likely that they will have been sent copies of the new layout beforehand.

Disposal and management

When the development is built it has to be let or sold (box 6 in Fig. 5.31). Following this the building and site has to be cared for, and managed. Again this is the job of the surveyor (Cadman et al. 1990; Scarrett 1983; Stapleton 1986). There are maintenance aspects to be considered, but beyond this janitorial role there are all the other financial and legal matters to deal with; the development is not just bricks and mortar but an ongoing investment, so matters such as rent reviews, dealing with existing tenants (such as chain stores or commercial office takers) and ongoing letting policy have to be dealt with. In larger schemes specialist facilities management professionals may be used.

At a later date questions of alterations or redevelopment of the scheme, or indeed the question of whether the original client owner wishes to sell his interest in the property for something more financially viable have to be considered. It should be pointed out that the vast majority of all office and shopping developments are not owned by the users, but rented to them. The freehold, or headlease, belongs to a variety of financial interests including insurance companies, pension funds and investment consortiums, and sometimes affluent individuals.

Project work

For the GNVQ, you are required to undertake a project that looks at the development of a project, in a similar way to what we have described above. A new road, shopping development or housing scheme may be a useful example. In association with your teacher or lecturer, you may be able to access local planning policy information from the local planning department, or at least from your local reference library, as most libraries keep a set of current development plan and local plan documents.

For guidance on this it is recommended that you look again at each of the stages identified in Fig. 5.31, and see if you can gather information in relation to your chosen scheme for each of these stages. In addition, you should look more carefully at the policy context of the scheme you are studying. Identify what the local plan policies are, what the highways proposals might be, and whether there any special grants or planning initiatives in place in the area.

You should illustrate your project with maps, plans, diagrams, elevations and other visual material as appropriate. In particular, if you can get a 'before' and 'after' set of plans, or better still produce some tracing paper overlays showing how the site developed in stages, this would be very worthwhile and give you a better insight into how the different stages, participants and functions of the development process come together on site.

Planning standards and design principles

Understanding the basics

This section explains the design principles and layout factors that must be taken into account in the development of an actual site layout scheme. It is important to be aware of the main, practical considerations that need to be taken into account in the process of planning at the local estate design level, before embarking upon a discussion of the wider urban design agenda. Therefore in this section the main considerations are summarised with reference to the development of a new housing estate. Housing constitutes 70% of all development, and 75% of all new development. Many of the principles given could be applied to other types of development also. Some additional material will be provided, where appropriate, in relation to other sorts of land uses. Some commentary on how the situation is changing as a result of the renaissance in the urban design movement, environmental assessment requirements, sustainability policy and community considerations will be provided en route. Also, key changes in government guidance which shape the main planning standards will be highlighted.

Client considerations

Some firms of private house builders and some local authority housing departments still have a standard pattern of house type and estate layout which they will seek to impose whatever or wherever the site right across the country. However, good design should take into account the special characteristics of the specific site in question and seek to meet the needs of those who will live in the layout. First, quite 'who' the development is aimed at should be considered carefully. In the private sector this question is directly linked to working out the type of people who, it is envisaged, will buy the houses – in terms of class, income, family size and age group. For example, in a desirable area near a golf course it might be advisable to build just a few really expensive houses at a low density and get a good financial return. In a suburban infill site the best solution to capitalise on market trends would be to build for young married couples wanting starter homes at the cheaper end of the price range, and so the developer would build more houses, at a higher density. Alternatively, in a fashionable inner city area that has already been gentrified, new development may be ill-advised, and instead conversions might yield a greater return.

The above paragraph is written from the developers' viewpoint. The planners might also have specific policies in the Structure Plan, or Unitary Development Plan, and in greater detail in the Local Plan affecting the area, as to the level of social mix, density, accessibility, and land use combinations sought in this area. They may look favourably on a planning application for the development of a site that includes a local shop or pub, or a scheme which does not develop the whole of the site but leaves some land undeveloped for amenity purposes. All of this would have to be negotiated and may be the subject of planning gain agreements. How far the developer will go all depends on how desperate they are to develop, and whether they also have their eyes on another comparable site elsewhere, where the planning authority is less fussy. After all, the developer is in the business basically for the financial return from building houses, and not because they are necessarily interested in producing good urban design or housing the homeless. Clearly financial rather than aesthetic or social considerations often predominate in this branch of planning.

Site constraints

Whatever the nature of the development, or the funders, certain basic 'physical' factors need to be taken into account. In designing a scheme for a site, an initial site analysis must be undertaken of its main natural and artificial characteristics. The slope and aspect of the site needs to be noted, not only with regard to drainage constraints, but also to see whether there are any good views out of the site that might be capitalised upon. The planning authority may be more concerned about views in, as that they do not want a development stuck on the skyline or half way up a hill which might constitute an eyesore. In the past, developers used to be unwilling to build on slopes of more than 1 in 7, but nowadays much of the remaining available infill land is sloping and so a range of styles of split-level housing has emerged to use this land. The level of the water table should be investigated as well as whether there are any areas liable to flooding. Attention should also be paid to the microclimate of the site, in particular whether there are any frosty hollows to be avoided, or any areas that receive more sun towards which the houses might be orientated.

It used to be said, in more leisurely times, or in respect of building for more affluent clients, that houses should be designed so that the bedrooms face the sun in the morning, and the living rooms and the garden at the back of the house get the sun in the evening. This is virtually impossible to achieve on more than half of the houses on an estate if the houses are built along roads facing each other (unless the internal layout is reversed). However, reasonable levels of sunlight and daylight penetration should be sought where possible (Littlefair 1991).

Wind direction is another important factor that should be taken into account, especially on high, exposed ground. This affects the orientation of the road layout in residential areas and passageways might become mini wind-tunnels. The power of the wind is an even greater problem in central area commercial developments of high-rise office blocks which can increase the effects of wind eddies and air streams around the buildings. Most pedestrians have had the experience of fighting their way through the elements along the pavement at the bottom of a high-rise building on a windy day. This principle also applies to council high-rise blocks of flats, which are notorious for being windswept, with accompanying swirling litter. Indeed, it is noticeable that as such schemes have been privatised, wind buffers and subtle planting have been introduced to deal with this problem (Roberts and Greed 2000).

A technical survey of the site will need to be undertaken to ascertain soil type, the load-bearing qualities of the site, and the likelihood of subsidence. This is particularly important in mining areas. A special legal 'search' can be made with the relevant coal authority to establish the whereabouts of old tunnels and shafts. A wary eye should be kept on nearby spoil tips where imperceptable solifluction (soil creep) can threaten a development. For example, the Welsh Development Agency has done a commendable job of greening the valleys and covering much of the dereliction and slag heaps, but much of this land is unstable, and unsuitable for construction purposes at present. In industrial locations, possible noise and smells from adjacent sites should be considered. The location of cables, drainage pipes and sewers should be established in consultation with the relevant companies or statutory undertakers.

Site development potential may be limited by the availabilty of adequate sewerage and storm drainage facilities, all of which cost money to install. As stated earlier, the developer will normally pay substantially towards these services, but even so, if a site is several kilometres from the next phase of proposed main sewer extension then it is unlikely to be built upon. Likewise, water does not flow up hill unless it is pumped, and therefore the cost of developing a site may be prohibitive simply because of the lack of services. Some aggrieved owners on new housing estates would also point out that it is equally important to them that there is adequate television reception and that houses are not built in shadow areas or where reception is poor. This affects house sales once word gets around, although cable television may provide the answer. Nowadays digital cables are being installed as standard in many new housing developments to meet demands for fax, telephone, television and computer connections.

Vegetation and visual factors

The existing visual qualities of the site and of the surrounding area need to be investigated. The vegetation of the site should be recorded. Many local authorities require the retention of existing trees and hedgerows on new housing developments,

and many would-be buyers are thrilled at the idea of real country hedges in their back gardens. Much green-field site development on the edge of the city is on erstwhile farmland. Of course, it may be that the planners on principle are against such suburban invasion of the countryside, but the DETR often favours such developments on appeal nowadays. Some trees may have Tree Preservation Orders (TPOs) on them. Therefore they cannot be removed, or if they are, replacement trees of a similar species must be put in their place.

As to new planting, fashions vary, though the traditional principles found in books such as Keeble (1969) are still to some extent applicable. Ash, beech, blackthorn and spruce used to be recommended as windbreaks (but take decades to grow). Ash, elm, oak, yew, poplar and willow are good for open spaces, but require a wide radius for their roots, and so should not be planted near walls. Cedar, chestnut, lime and walnut are good for town squares, but are unsuitable for small gardens. Acacia, birch, horse chestnut, plane and laburnum are suitable for wide roads, and almond, cypress, holly, lombardy poplar and rowan for narrower roads. Trees with flowers and berries, especially flowering cherry, are often seen as rather kitsch or suburban in taste. Trees that are likely to drop leaves over cars and pavements should not be used.

Many developers prefer 'instant', fast-growing, maintenance-free trees. Local authorities like to use vandal-proof trees, or prickly bushes that keep people on the footpaths and off the gardens, and dense plant cover which discourages weeds and dogs. On the other hand, women's groups and crime prevention groups advise against putting tree cover, high walls or screening near to footpaths as they may obscure visibility and act as a haven for muggers. Railings, or walls of spaced bricks or blocks that can be seen through, are preferred where possible, provided this does not reduce privacy within gardens.

There are wider issues of the protection of the wildlife, wild flowers, etc., that may be located in some out-of-town development locations. There have been several well-publicised incidences of science parks and other commercial developments having to be relocated a short distance from the preferred location to allow rare species of frogs and newts to remain undisturbed in their ponds. Drainage of development sites without a preliminary ecological analysis is seen as a thoughtless approach to development. Environmental assessment is now required on larger schemes, including residential schemes, under Schedule 2 as described in Section 5.5. Additionally, planners are unwilling for developers to develop on high-grade agricultural land. However, such development is often inevitable.

The characteristics of the local building materials, style and colour should also be investigated to ensure that the new scheme blends in with the surrounding area, especially in urban infill sites and rural locations. In many instances the use of materials will be controlled by the planners, especially in conservation areas. Existing gates, fences, walls and other townscape features may be incorporated in the design to good effect.

Legal factors

Many other factors need to be taken into account in the design process; indeed any one of these 'little' issues may put the developers off altogether. The legal rights over the land must be checked, and normally a **local search** would be undertaken with the local authority in question by the purchaser's or developer's solicitor before the land was bought. The search will reveal any existing 'charges' on the land, such as unexpired planning permissions, listed building designations, etc. An **additional enquiries** form would also reveal wider planning issues related to the structure plan, sewer availability, road widenings, etc., affecting the site.

A typical site is likely to be criss-crossed by a range of public and private rights, footpaths and other rights of way. There may be private rights over the land, such as easements which give people, their cables and drains, and even their animals, the right of passage over the land. The tenure situation of the land must be established: who owns what rights, and whether there are any outstanding restrictive covenants over the land, over and above any zoning controls the planners may have on it. For example, some Victorian houses with large back gardens, which look like ideal sites for infill development, are still governed by restrictive covenants which prevent an increase in density – a condition put on when they were built to preserve the quality of the area. Application can be made to the Lands Tribunal for the extinguishment or modification of such covenants. Even if the application is granted, the applicant may be required to pay compensation. It is of interest that in the USA the planning and zoning law is as much related to density as it is to land use, thus ensuring the separation of income groups and the preservation of property values.

Layout principles

Once all these factors have been mapped on to the site plan, a possible design solution to the layout might already be suggesting itself because of the constraints of the site (such as gradients or the requirement to retain protected trees). The house-type required by the developer or the planners may itself determine the likely layout of the site. To save time, preliminary discussion with the planners is advisable, with the presentation of a draft 'brief' of what is in mind, before an application is made in the case of larger-scale developments. Some say it is important to start the design process by sketching in the roads (taking into account their relationship with any existing sewers, etc.) and then arrange the houses around them. Others block in the main areas of housing first, subdivide them to the density required, and then add the roads. Some designers go for the 'creative intuitive leap' and cannot explain quite how they come to the final design.

If there are going to be houses at 30 dwellings per hectare (dph), i.e. that is 12 dwellings per acre (12dpa), house plots will be about 12 m (40′) wide, with a total plot depth of around 36 m (120′). This will be composed approximately of a 15 m (50′) back garden, 10.5 m (35′) depth of house, 6 m (20′) front garden, 2 m (6′) pavement and say 3 m (10′) to the white line in the middle of the road. Housing plots are usually measured to include half the estate road width, with pavement. Having given typical dimensions it should be stressed that housing layouts are seldom this regular, as there is likely to be considerable variation in plot size across the estate because of topographical factors and other constraints.

Residential densities measure the number of dwellings, i.e. the number of habitable units per hectare (or per acre), and not just the number of buildings. These two may coincide in a new housing suburban housing estate, but the two are not the same in the case of older houses which have been subdivided into flats. In fact, crude density is not always a good measure of actual plot coverage, which may need to be measured by other criteria for design purposes. For example, the planners may stipulate that not more than 50% of the site is developed. A particular awareness of these factors is necessary in respect of tall residential buildings where there may be an apparently high net density but low plot coverage because all the dwellings are piled up on top of each other. Nor is density, in itself, a measure of the quality of the area, as some conservation areas consisting of Georgian town houses and mews may have a high density.

There are two main types of residential density: net and gross. **Net density** is based on the dimensions given above, i.e. the width of the house plot multiplied by the length of the total plot made up of the house standing within its front and back garden plus the distance up to half way across the estate road. If all these blocks were put together they would cover the whole area of the housing estate. **Gross density** includes all of the above, plus the land taken up for local shops, schools, amenity space, and distributor roads. In other words, the gross density is a neighbourhood density, and therefore may appear to be lower than the net density. It is important to check which type of density the planners require in respect of a particular site.

The word 'dwellings' rather than houses is usually used in density definitions, as this includes not only houses, but also flats and bedsitters. This is an important distinction for planners seeking to estimate the number of people that will live in an area and for whom they will need to provide a certain level of shopping or school provision. It is particularly important where there are areas of large Edwardian houses which may only be about 4 houses per acre (10 per hectare), but when all the flats that they have been subdivided into are counted, then the number of actual dwellings might be five times the number of houses, i.e. 50 dwellings per hectare (50 dph), which is approximately 20 dwellings per hectare (20 dpa). Some planning authorities operate density controls, to stop an area being too built up; for example, they may refuse an extension on a house, or refuse the subdivision of a house into more than two units. This can be most insensitive to the actual residents of the house who might want a granny flat for a relative, but the planners have to take into account the fact that once granted, the 'permission runs with the land'. This means that it attaches to the property rather than the family in question, who may move later on – and they cannot take the extension with them! In fact, the answer might be to make sure that the flat is linked to the house without its own separate entrance, so that it does not count as a 'new' dwelling (i.e. development), fire regulations permitting.

Here are some illustrations of the sort of densities that are likely to be found in different types of housing area. Note that an acre is 0.405 hectares and a hectare is 2.471 acres. Both the persons per hectare (pph) (or persons per acre, (ppa), and the dwellings per hectare (dph) (or dwellings per acre, (dpa) are given, but for simplicity's sake after the first few examples only the dph will be given. Pph (or ppa) is normally three times dph (or dpa). Large detached houses in big gardens on the edge of the city are likely to be built at 2.5–10 dph (1–4 dpa) which is the same as 8–30 pph (3–12 ppa). Typical inter-war detached houses are nearer 20 dph (8 dpa), whereas semi-detached suburbia was normally built to around 30 dph (10–12 dpa). Council housing used to be built to around this figure, but the densities became higher on new schemes as the years went by.

Moving further into the city, terraced housing averages around 37 dph (15 dpa), as does patio housing, which was much used in some new towns and inner locations where there is little garden space, the house forming an L shape around an internal courtyard. Three-storey terraces and maisonettes come out around 50–70 dph (20–30 dpa). A maisonette comprises one self-contained dwelling above another, but, unlike flats, each has its own separate entrance. Maisonettes are known as duplexes in the USA. Six-storey blocks of flats result in around 90 dph (40 dpa), and may be termed, according to British usage, as medium-rise development.

Levels of 200 dph (80 dpa) can be achieved in high-rise developments of 10–15 storeys, provided little ancillary space is allowed around the base of the blocks. However, in Britain, unlike Hong Kong where densities go far beyond this, it is impossible to achieve really high densities by going high-rise because of the sunlight and daylight regulations which require that space must be left around the block, so little is gained by building higher.

Very high densities are also achieved in older areas where there has been a great deal of subdivision into individual bedsits or studio flats, in what are moderate medium-rise buildings, such as six-storey converted Victorian town house mansions. Using linked and clustered low-rise dwelling forms, such as patios, quite high densities can be attained without going high-rise. It is important, therefore, not to confuse or conflate high-rise and high-density as they can exist separately.

Roads, parking and circulation

Government guidance on parking standards has changed radically because of pressures to create environmentally sustainable cities. The Planning Policy Guidance Statement (PPG3) on Housing (1998: para. 42) specifies that car parking standards in any new development should not exceed 1.5 to 2 car parking spaces per dwelling off street, and that it should be significantly lower where possible. It also recommends that densities should be raised to above 25 dwellings per hectare. This is a great change from even ten years ago when the principle 'predict and provide' ruled in all aspects of transport planning and at least two off-street parking spaces per house was the ideal standard set, with additional parking for residents.

When assessing a site's potential, access and circulation within the site need to be considered, with regard to existing road and other transport connections. There are some sites that look ideal on a map, but on closer investigation they prove to be completely landlocked, i.e. surrounded by other properties. Sometimes there will be just one possible access point through a strip of land, which because of the exorbitant price the owner is likely to ask for it, is called the ransom strip. Nowadays, lack of motor car access is not necessarily a major deterrent to development, in the light of government guidance on the need to restrict motor car usage. More attention is being given to providing adequate footpaths, and bicycle path access, something which was often given secondary importance in the past when it was assumed that everyone would have a car.

Developers used to build alongside available roads, creating ribbon development as was discussed in earlier chapters. It is now unlikely that a through road will go right across a new housing estate because of road safety considerations. Likewise, planners and highways engineers

do not want cars coming out of lots of little access roads, or driveways from individual houses all coming out onto a main road and thus slowing down the through traffic. Today's layouts more commonly emphasise the use of *culs de sac*, and the safety of pedestrians.

The principles of residential layout are all determined by the answer to the question 'how you want to live?' (DoE, 1972,a). This branch of planning, which is meant to make people's homes and lives better, has sadly developed a mechanical, restrictive, technological image, no doubt because of its association with site engineering and road planning. Of course, there do have to be practical standards to ensure, for example, that the fire engine can reach every house, or to enable the dustcart to get through without the dustmen having to walk more than a certain distance, as laid down by their union (normally set at 25 m).

By way of guidance it is normal for local authorities to specify varying widths of road according to their capacity, desired speed and function. For example, local distributor and residential spine roads will be in the region of 7.3 m wide, with a maximum intended speed of 20 km/h (30 mph), whereas smaller access roads and *culs de sac* may be down to 6 m or less. Roads and driveways giving access to small groups of houses are likely to be down to around 4 m, although in the new *Essex Design Guide* widths as low as 2.7–3.4 m are stipulated (Essex County Council 1997). Such narrow access roads are combined with a mixture of chicanes (zig-zags), road narrowings, speed bumps and other traffic-calming devices to reduce the velocity of vehicles in residential areas. Such devices are also interspersed on the wider distributor roads, to narrow the carriageway, and thus slow the traffic. It is not envisaged in the *Essex Design Guide* that the traffic speed will reach above 50 km/h (30 mph), even on peripheral and distributor roads within the neighbourhood.

Highways engineers also set standards as to the radius of the curves on all roads, and the dimensions of junctions, turning spaces, and hammerheads. Again, these vary from area to area, but 6–9 m radii on the inner turning bends of hammerheads are common. However standards have generally been revised down in order to achieve higher densities and to impede rather than facilitate motor car movement within residential areas (Essex County Council 1997: 72).

Likewise for many years it was general policy to provide extensive visibility splays, with generous dimensions (Fig. 5.32). Visibility splays are also called sight splays. These are triangles of land kept free from development on the corners of junctions to enable drivers to have unobstructed vision along the main road. For example, imagine a Pythagorean triangle of $9 \times 12 \times 15$ m comprises the visibility splay. This might be set out so that the 9 m side runs along the white line in the centre of the side road out to where it meets the white line of the main road, creating a right angle with the 12 m which runs from this point along the white line of the main road to the right. The 15 m hypotenuse side of the triange slices off part of the right-hand corner plot to ensure visibility (as described in *Roads in Urban Areas*, (DoE 1990). Further details are to be found in Unit 2, Fig. 2.16.

Subsequent updates, such as described in *Residential Roads and Footpaths Design* Design Bulletin 32 (DETR 199b) and within the *Essex Design Guide* (Essex County Council 1997) propose smaller sight splays on residential access roads, and put greater emphasis upon pedestrian safety too. For example, Essex recommends a triangle of $2.4 \times 3.6 \times 4.3$ m, and also

Figure 5.32 Generous junction layouts allow drivers good visibility

suggests simple $1.5 \times 1.5 \times 2.2$ m chips off the corners. In all cases vegetation should be limited so as not to impede visibility. Ground cover should not be higher than 6 cm. The calculation of exact visibility splay dimensions is a complex issue generally undertaken by traffic engineers in consultation with the planners, in the light of local road conditions and likely traffic speed. Nowadays the addition of traffic bumps and other traffic-slowing devices on the approach to junctions can reduce the need for extensive splays (Fig. 5.33).

Traditionally, footpaths and pavements have been 6′ in width, this being based originally on the fact that it enables two prams to pass. A width of 2 m (6′6″) is now taken as the minimum, and a width of 3 m is often designated for paths that are shared by cycles and pedestrians, with a white line drawn down the middle. This arrangement has proved both dangerous for pedestrians and unpopular with cyclists, and in an ideal situation the two should always be provided with separate 2 m wide paths.

Conversion

To convert inches to centimetres multiply by 2.54; feet to metres multiply by 0.3048; yards to metres multiply by 0.9144. To convert centimetres to inches multiply by 0.3937; metres to feet multiply by 3.2808; metres to yards multiply by 1.0936.

For area measurements which are used in indicating floor space, e.g. for retail development, 1 square foot = 0.0929 m²; and 1 m² is 10.764 square feet, i.e. divide or multiply by 10, plus or minus a bit.

Cubic measurements which are of relevance to development control, e.g. when assessing the size of house extensions, are as follows: to convert cubic feet into cubic metres multiply by 0.0283, and to convert cubic metres into cubic feet multiply by 35.314.

An acre = 0.405 ha and 1 ha = 2.471 acres (multiply a hectare by 2.5 to turn it back into acres).

In social housing, e.g. housing association housing for single people, the elderly or the disabled, a minimum of one car parking space per dwelling is often permitted. At present there are 35 orange badge holders (designating disabled drivers) per 1000 population (ONS 1999, table 12.13). Ordinary car parking spaces are 2.4×4.8 m, while disabled parking spaces should be 4.8×3.6 m. Alternatively, an additional strip of 1.2 m should be provided between each of two standard parking spaces, even if this means redrawing the lines and losing spaces overall (Palyfreyman and Thorpe 1993: 3). When

Figure 5.33 Traffic calming

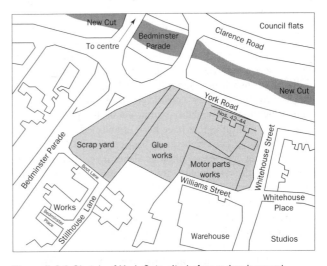

Figure 5.34 Sketch of York Gate site before redevelopment

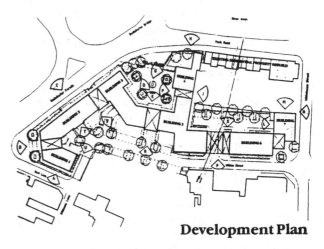

Development Plan

Figure 5.35 Planned development shown in a publicity leaflet

calculating the capacity of urban car parks, allowance must be made for aisles between the rows and for the provision of access roads.

Increasingly local authorities are writing into their plans and design guides wider controls on the unnecessary uses of steps and changes of level, and the need for dropped kerbs in all layouts, to help the disabled, the elderly, and also mothers with prams and pushchairs. All these groups may find steps an

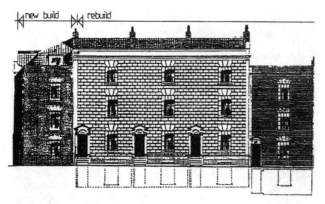

Figure 5.36 Artist's impression of refurbished façade on York Gate site

insurmountable barrier to getting about, or even to getting in and out of their own front door. Gradients on ramps should not be more than 1 in 12, but ideally there should be no steep areas throughout the housing scheme. To achieve such an objective is indeed a challenge, but one that is being tackled even in historic housing areas, e.g. in urban conservation areas in hilly locations within London (CAE 1998).

Related to this, it is now considered good practice to ensure adequate lighting and visibility within public footpath systems. Many of the principles that have been established and adopted in respect of inner city regeneration projects, in which there has been a strong emphasis upon collaborative, participatory planning with the community, are now working their way into new developments too. In particular, the concept of 'lifetime housing' is becoming widespread (Rowntree 1992), this housing designed to be adaptable for all age groups in the household.

The question of how much ordinary parking space is to be allowed on non-residential development, such as offices, industry and retail developments, depends on what the developer wants to achieve. For example, where there are no space restrictions one parking space per $19\,m^2$ of office space may apply, e.g. on a purpose-built business park. This means that in schemes where one parking space per $19\,m^2$ of office space is allowed, the total space alocated to parking will be as much as the original office space itself!

However, in a central area location where the planners want to discourage congestion, and where land is limited, figures of one parking space per $284m^2$ or even $475\,m^2$ of office space may apply. There are currently proposals to charge for workplace parking, ostensibly to encourage employees to use public transport. As stated earlier, such an alternative is not viable for many commuters living in areas poorly served by public transport.

The 1997 revision of PPG1 (DETR 1997) on general planning principles included a new section (S.55) on the disabled which states, 'the development of land and buildings provides the opportunity to secure a more accessible environment for everyone, including wheelchair users, and other people with disabilities, elderly people and people with toddlers or infants in pushchairs'. Therefore this is a consideration that local authorities must take into account in determining a planning application (Manley 1999). Such external and internal pressures are reshaping the nature of urban design, and the creation of accessible environments, both in respect of new and old areas of cities (Palfreyman and Thorpe 1993; CAE 1998).

Project work

It can be seen that there is a series of stages and phases in the property development process. See which of these phases you can identify for your project portfolio.

Further reading

The following cover the process of property development:

Seeley I 1997 *Quantity Surveying Practice* Macmillan, London

Greed C (ed) 1996 *Implementing Town Planning* Addison Wesley Longman

Material on design guidance, site development and housing layout includes:

Essex County Council 1997 *The Essex Design Guide* Essex County Council

Bentley I (ed.) 1992 *Responsive Environments: A Manual for Designers* Architectural Press

Greed C and Roberts M 1998 *Introducing Urban Design* Longman

A case study of the development of York Gate, Bristol is given in *Implementing Town Planning* (Greed 1996).

Cadman D and Topping R 1995 *Property Development* Spons

DoE 1972 *How Do You Want To Live?* Department of Environment Report

DETR 1999a *Residential Roads and Footpaths Design* Design Bulletin 32

DETR 2000 *Urban Design in the Planning System* – Towards Better Practice

DoT 1999 *Roads in Urban Areas* Department of Transport

Littlefair P 1991 *Site Layout Planning for Daylight and Sunlight: A Guide to Good Practice Building* Research Establishment

ONS (Annual) *Social Trends* Office of National Statistics

Reade E 1987 *British Town and Country Planning* Open University Press

Rowntree 1992 *Lifetime Homes* Joseph Rowntree Foundation

Roberts M and Greed C 1998 *Introducing Urban Design* Longman

Roberts M and Greed C 2000 *Approaching Urban Design* Longman

Stapleton T 1986 *Estate Management Practice* Estates Gazette

5.5 The impact of planning and development

The purpose of this section is to help you understand the impact of planning and development upon the built and natural environment, and the implications for quality of life for the community, both at city-wide and local development project levels.

Key considerations include:

● quality of life for the community
● infrastructural changes
● changes in usage and land use patterns
● changes in the use of resources such as energy and water
● conservation of the built environment
● conservation of the natural environment

Quality of life for the community

The community

A community may be defined as a group of people who have something 'in common', in this case the area where they live. Cities are generally also made up of a collection of smaller communities in different distinct local areas, comprising neighbourhoods and districts (Fig. 5.37). Britain is highly urbanised – nearly 80% of the population live in urban areas – yet it contains substantial areas of open countryside between the towns and cities. The UK has a population of 59 million, but nearly 80% of the total 24 410 000 hectares of land is agricultural (ONS 1999, table 1.2).

One of the reasons that town planning is not a simple process in which there is one 'obvious' right answer is that different groups of people have different needs and preferences: what is right for one person may be wrong for another. For example, people who drive cars often have a

Figure 5.37 Typical shopping centre street scene

very different idea of how cities should be planned compared with those who travel mainly by public transport, and those who are concerned with protecting the environment. Cities based on walking distances and public transport are likely to be much higher density (i.e. a higher number of houses to the acre or hectare) and less extensive than cities based on the motor car, such as Los Angeles which is around 50 by 80 km across, with extremely low-density housing (houses are spread out on large plots) and vast areas taken up for car parking and road building. (Check Section 5.1 for concepts of the neighbourhood unit and community spirit in New Towns.)

Planning for diversity

The demand for land use and development is influenced by changes in human activity, demands, needs and social patterns. Some of the main factors that communities are likely to want of an urban area include:

● satisfactory housing provision
● adequate transport
● good local facilities, including shops, schools and amenities
● local employment opportunities
● a pleasant and safe environment
● social, recreational and leisure facilities

Town planning is concerned with the city-wide scale as well as with the local detailed layout of an individual neighbourhood or district. At a more detailed level still, it is concerned about the details of the development of a particular building site, and thus about density, urban design, housing, architectural factors and all the so-called 'little' issues which contribute to the success and good planning of an area, such as access, car parking and local facilities. The scope and nature of planning, with reference to the present-day statutory town planning system, is described in earlier sections within this unit.

The community does not consist of a single group of identical people. People differ on the basis of the following factors:

● age
● class
● ethnicity
● disability
● gender

Planners need to take all these factors into account. The above percentages are intended to give a general picture. Much depends on how the categories are defined, and also there are considerable regional differences. To find out more about the composition of society readers are advised to consult *Social Trends*, an annual statistical report produced by the Office of National Statistics (ONS).

Social class

Some of the biggest social changes and trends in recent years have been in relation to the sort of work that people do,

Table 5.16 Economic activity rates: by ethnic group, gender and age, 1997–82 (Source adapted from ONS 1999)

	Males				Females			
	16-24	25–44	45–64	All aged (16–64)	16–24	25–44	45–59	All aged (16–59)
White	79	93	78	85	71	76	70	73
Black Caribbean	68	92	72	82	65	78	72	75
Black African	57	85	76	77	—	62	—	56
Other Black groups	68	85	—	78	—	71	—	71
Indian	54	94	73	81	53	70	48	61
Pakistani	54	88	60	72	41	28	—	32
Bangladeshi	58	90	—	70	—	—	—	21
Chinese	40	87	75	71	—	63	—	60
None of the above	54	84	83	76	49	58	63	56
All ethnic groups	77	93	78	85	69	75	69	72

where they do it, and by what means. Whereas in the nineteenth century, as a result of the Industrial Revolution, a large urban 'working class' developed who were mainly employed in factories, mills and mines, in the twentieth century we entered the post-industrial phase of society's development. Nowadays the largest single sector of employment is the office and services sector, and women as well as men are a major component of the workforce. Whereas in 1901 only 20% of women worked outside the home, todays over 65% do so, and this percentage continues to rise.

The workforce may be classified as follows:

- Primary workers are those engaged in basic industries such as agriculture, mining, heavy industry
- Secondary workers are those involved in manufacturing
- Tertiary workers are those involved in office work and service industry.

Increasingly a further category is recognised, namely quaternary workers – those involved in research and development, higher professional work and the creation of knowledge (basically, the thinkers and innovators). One can see a gradual progression across the last two centuries from an emphasis on primary workers as the key sector, across the other categories, until today quaternary workers are seen as the prime sector for the future.

All this has implications for the land use requirements in cities, with less land being needed for industrial sites and more land being needed for offices, educational institutions and science parks.

Market researchers use similar categories as the Registrar General (Table 5.17), but mix them in slightly different ways. In particular, market researchers want groupings that will indicate a certain level of income (and therefore buying power) rather than just occupation (Table 5.18). For example, a developer may use such data to establish what the market and likely profitability of a certain type of development will be in a particular area. If most of the residents are unemployed or on low incomes, it will not be an economically worthwhile place to create new development, even if *socially* there might be great demand for better facilities. One of the most commonly used classifications is the **Social Grading Scale**. This scale was invented by NOP (the

Table 5.17 Socio-economic groupings
N = Non-manual and M = manual.

I	Higher professional and managerial
II	Lower professional and managerial
III N	Supervisory and lower/routine non-manual
III M	Skilled manual
IV	Semi-skilled manual
V	Unskilled manual

National Opinion Polls people), and runs from A to E. Classes A, B, CI and CII correspond to I, II, IIIN and IIIM given in Table 5.17, with class D covering IV and V. A sixth class, E, is used for the unemployed, pensioners, housewives not in paid employment, and the permanently sick and disabled. This scale is therefore more concerned with spending power than with social class. NOP Market Research Limited classification is shown in Table 5.18.

Table 5.18 Social grading scale

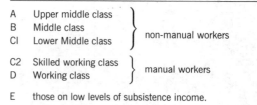

A	Upper middle class	
B	Middle class	non-manual workers
CI	Lower Middle class	
C2	Skilled working class	manual workers
D	Working class	
E	those on low levels of subsistence income.	

Self-assessment tasks

1. Name two types of social class grouping, and explain one.
2. What are the implications for town planning of employment changes? Name at least three.
3. Describe the employment situation in your town, and as an additional activity indicate to how you see these future trends affecting your life!
4. What do you see as the future trends in employment, and what are the implications for town planning and the built environment? (A very big question for discussion.)

Gender

It is now acknowledged by town planners and property developers that 'gender' differences must be taken into account in policy-making. Women are still less likely to be car drivers, although this is changing among the younger age groups where possession of a driving licence is becoming more evenly matched among people in their late teens and early twenties. Also more women are working outside the home. However, it remains a fact that most women are still the ones responsible for caring responsibilities, in terms of looking after babies, children, the elderly and the infirm, and for doing most of the housework and shopping. 'Gender' is normally taken, therefore, to mean the role and duties given to women, as against 'sex' which simply describes the biological differences. Many women find great difficulty combining their traditional roles with work outside the home, not least because of childcare responsibilities. Some town planning departments now have policies in their development plans on creches, nurseries and childcare, but implementation is still difficult.

Therefore, it is not enough to say that 'planning is for people' and to assume that we can plan 'equally' and the 'same' for everyone without closer inspection of how needs differ. In particular, because more women work part-time than men, and because many have responsibilities for shopping and for taking children to and from school, they are likely to have different and more varied travel patterns. They often travel outside of the rush hour, when public transport is often at its worst. Also women with babies and small children may encounter real mobility problems in town centres designed for able-bodied grown-ups who are not accompanied by pushchairs and toddlers, in terms of steps, toilets, access, shops and public transport. One of the trends in town planning, particularly at the detailed design level of planning, is to take into account the needs of women and children more carefully.

Self-assessment tasks

1. What town planning issues and trends are of particular concern to women?
2. What policies can town planners introduce to improve the situation for women?

Project work

It is suggested that, as a means of collecting primary data by means of survey methods, you undertake an observation of the gender of the people using your local town centre (which should include both shops and offices or other employment in order for this to 'work'). Observe the gender, age and other characteristics (as directed by your teacher) of people at four times during the day:

- morning rush hour
- mid-morning
- lunch hour
- after school.

As a hint, you will probably find that about 60% of the people on the streets in the rush hour are men, that 80% of shoppers mid-morning and at lunch-time are women, and that in afternoon, you will get more of a mixture plus more young people coming home or going round the shops after school. Make sure that you get permission from the relevant authorities if you are doing this study in an enclosed shopping mall or where there might be questions from shopkeepers.

Disability and age

It is estimated that around 5 million of the population, or around 1 in 10 of the population, is disabled in some way or other. Only 2% are actually wheelchair users. Hidden impairments, such as epilepsy, heart disease, asthma and other respiratory disorders, are less likely to be included on the official data including the Census itself, and yet many of these impairments can affect personal mobility.

Even official estimates for the number of disabled people in the UK population vary between 6.1 million and 9.3 million (OPCS 1988). The Royal National Institute for the Deaf estimated in 1989 that 7.5 million people in the UK have experienced hearing loss, which amounts to 17% of the total population. The Royal National Institute for the Blind estimates indicate that in 1987 there were 959 000 people registered blind and a further 740 000 with a sight disability.

It is well known that the prevalence of disability increases with age, although many elderly people would not contemplate being considered to be disabled. Perhaps the first generation to have experienced high-levels of personal mobility are now approaching retirement age. If this group, pregnant women, small children, and people who have a temporary mobility impairment are added to the list of people who need a barrier-free environment it might be wondered why the consideration of ensuring good access is considered to be a minority interest.

As can be seen it is often difficult to come up with precise figures. However, some trends are recognisable. The proportion of people over 55 in the population currently stands at 17% of the total, and this is likely to rise to 19% by 2025. But in some retirement areas, such as the south-west of England, the percentage of persons over 60 may be between 25 and 35%. Clearly, planners need to take these trends into account when planning for the 'average man in the street'.

Likewise there is a general decline in population levels among the younger age groups and at present the population in Britain is maintaining 'replacement levels' only. The population booms of post-war years are now far behind, in Britain and the West, and although worldwide there is still tremendous population growth, some predict signs of this declining too. People in Britain are living longer, 75 is easily the average life expectancy, and significantly the majority of elderly people are women.

As to statistics, *Social Trends* is not so strong on 'disability' as such and you need to consult more specialist material such as the government's 'Disability Unit', but your teacher will be able to advise of more local sources of material, or simply ask in your library.

Self-assessment tasks

1. What are the main groups who make up the disabled?
2. What particular town planning problems are encountered by the elderly?

Ethnicity

Not only do people vary on the basis of age, class, gender and family, they also vary on the basis of ethnic origin. Ethnic minorities themselves vary greatly in terms of class, occupation, origin, education, and of course colour, culture

Table 5.19 Population by age in the UK

	Under 16	16–24	25–34	35–44	45–54	55–64	65–74	75 and over	100% (millions)
					Percentages			All ages	
Mid-year estimates									
1961	25	12	13	14	14	12	8	4	52.8
1971	25	13	12	12	12	12	9	5	55.9
1981	22	14	14	12	11	11	9	6	56.4
1991	20	13	16	14	11	10	9	7	57.8
1997	21	11	16	14	13	10	8	7	59.0
Mid-year projection									
2001	20	11	14	15	13	10	8	7	59.6
2011	18	12	12	14	15	12	9	8	60.9
2021	18	11	13	12	13	14	11	9	62.2

Source: ONS (1999). Adapted from *Social Trends*.

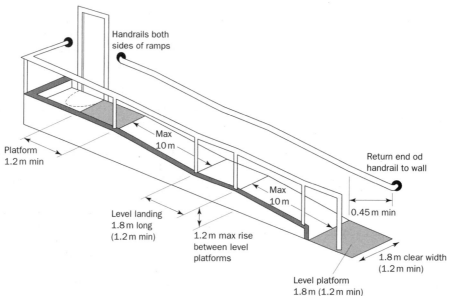

Handrails both sides of ramps

Platform 1.2 m min

Max 10 m

Return end od handrail to wall

0.45 m min

Level landing 1.8 m long (1.2 m min)

1.2 m max rise between level platforms

Max 10 m

1.8 m clear width (1.2 m min)

Level platform 1.8 m (1.2 m min)

Figure 5.38 A typical ramp for wheelchair access

Figure 5.39 Postbox accessible for wheelchair users, Italy

and language. Nowadays approximately 5% of the population are of ethnic origin, although it should be stressed that over half were born in Britain. However, this ethnic minority is not evenly distributed throughout the country, being mainly centred in the Midlands. Bradford has over 40% Indian and Pakistani communities in some parts of the city, and in inner London, boroughs such as Tower Hamlets and Lambeth have more than 50% Afro-Caribbean communities in some parts. There are vast ranges of types and groups of ethnic minorities, but because many of these are 'white' and/or 'European' and/or 'Christian' in background they are not as likely to be 'noticed' and seen as 'different'.

Town planners are increasingly seeking to take into account ethnic diversity in relation to planning policy, not least because of problems of alleged discriminatory development control, and insensitive development plan policy. Particular problems have revolved around getting planning permission for ethnic 'hot food takeaways' and restaurants and religious buildings. Also there have been problems related to requests for permission to extend dwellings to accommodate the traditionally larger 'extended' family units – perhaps including grandparents, aunts and uncles – found in some Indian and Pakistani communities. In particular, strict controls on housing extension may actually lead to a ethnic minority group looking elsewhere for accommodation, thus undermining the community identity of an area.

Table 5.20 UK households by size

| | **Percentages** | | | | |
	1961	**1971**	**1981**	**1991**	**1992**
1 person	14	18	22	27	28
2 people	30	32	32	34	35
3 people	23	19	17	16	16
4 people	18	17	18	16	14
5 people	9	8	7	5	5
6 people	7	6	4	2	2
All households (= 100%) (millions)	16.3	18.6	20.2	22.4	23.6
Average household size (no. of people)	3.1	2.9	2.7	2.5	2.4

Source: ONS (1999). Adapted from *Social Trends*.

Self-assessment tasks

1. What are the main factors that town planners need to be aware of in relation to planning for ethnic minorities?
2. Find and give figures and percentages on the situation using either *Social Trends* or local information.

Crime and design

Crime and demands for greater social control have become major issues. There is considerable concern about the changing and often increasing levels of crime and violence in cities. It has been shown that town planning, and indeed the construction industry as a whole, through the role of building design can have some effect on deterring crime, by adopting sensitive layouts that do not include blind corners or public spaces that are 'no man's land' and open to

Figure 5.40 Security shutters on shops in Bedminster, Bristol

vandalism. Also, the installation of CCTV (closed-circuit television) systems in many town centres may deter crime, or at least move it elsewhere. Others would argue that much of this is somewhat limited in effect, and what is needed is increased employment and educational opportunities, and a greater sense of community and social responsibility, which perhaps, to some extent, can be fostered by sensitive town planning policy.

It can be seen that while town planning and property development are in one sense part of the construction industry, and therefore concerned with no-nonsense issues related to land use, design and development, they also have a heavy social responsibility to respond to human needs and to create responsible and responsive environments.

Infrastructure changes

Infrastructure may be defined as the system of roads, rail and other transport links which serve an urban area, plus the services and public utilities provided, such as gas, water, electricity, telephones and other cabled services. Clearly all these are essential to the functioning of the city and the quality of life of its residents.

Town planning is not just a technical process concerned with arranging buildings and different land uses, e.g. zoning and separating residential areas from industrial districts. *Planning is for people*; it is a means to an end. Therefore human and social factors need to be taken into account. But these can only be met within the technological constraints and advances of the time. For example, in ancient times people built cities where there was an abundant local water supply to support the urban population, and thus many cities were near rivers. Rivers also provided good communication, and if a settlement was located at the main crossing point of the river, this gave military and trading advantages too.

In contrast, with today's national provision of energy sources and utilities such as water, gas and electricity, town planners are far less restricted by natural factors. Also, with the advent of the motor car and the related road system, most areas are highly accessible, and therefore, in theory at least, you can build anything anywhere – provided there is the money available, and that building does not take place on environmentally sensitive areas. In the building industry there is much competition and change as a result of technological innovation and international trends. The methods and technologies used in construction owe much to factors such as human resource management, available labour and skills. Other factors are also coming into play, especially at the professional and technical levels, such as widespread use of computer technology such as CAD (computer aided design).

Technology has brought progress and higher living standards, but it has also brought problems for town planners. For example, increased car ownership has led to traffic problems, increased urban sprawl and demands for road-building solutions. As described in Section 5.1, there were many changes in the transport systems of cities during the twentieth century. Many town planners now see traffic as the main problem in our cities. Up to 40% of the average city ground surface is taken up by roads, car parks and other car-related uses.

Table 5.21 UK Households with regular use of a car

	Percentages			
	1 car only	2 or more cars	No car	Total
1961	29	2	69	100
1971	44	8	48	100
1981	45	15	40	100
1991	45	23	32	100
1997	45	25	30	100

Source: Department of the Environment, Transport and the Regions.

There are over 22 million cars on the road. Over 75% of households own at least one car, and over 25% own two or more cars (ONS 1999, tables 12.6 and 12.7). Yet, it does not follow that everyone in the household will have equal access to a car. Large concentrations of households without cars, particularly among the elderly, can also be found. Over 80% of single-person pensioner households are carless.

Nationally over 85% of males and over 55% of females hold a driving licence, but it is estimated that only about 20% of women have access to a car during the day, only 8% of women use their cars to participate in the school run, and over 70% of all car journeys are still made by men.

It remains true that over 75% of all journeys are *not* by car, i.e. they are on foot and by public transport (cf. RTPI 1991; Barton 1998). Yet, in *Planning Week* (23 November 1995), it was commented that a Department of Transport source had discounted walking as a form of transport because 'transport is something you get **in**'. To plan for the motor car as if it were the main means of transport for everyone is an extremely biased approach, and a more socially-aware attitude is already in evidence at the newly created DETR. There are considerable differences in the land use and transport needs of people in respect of their age, gender, income, disability, mobility and ethnicity.

Likely future trends are increased public transport, more traffic-calming measures, more cycle paths, extensions to park and ride, and motorway tolls (Fig. 5.42). Some say we do not just need land use planning, we need 'time planning'; that in order to reduce congestion and to harmonise opening and closing times of workplaces, shops, schools and social facilities, we need to co-ordinate the use of time in our cities, as is being pioneered in Germany and northern Italy.

Changing patterns of usage of towns and cities

Life-style and work patterns

In post-industrial society there continue to be major changes in working patterns. This includes increasing unemployment, especially in inner city areas. There is a growth of part-time, short-term employment, and of self-employment and service and retail sector jobs, especially for women. There is a decline in traditional male employment, in primary and secondary work, but much of this continues in the developing world.

There are demands among some town planners for development plans which reflect these changes, especially the need for more local employment and more acceptance and allowance for 'telecommuting', home-based offices, working from home, and local childcare provision in the development control regulations.

Figure 5.41 Motorway viaduct cutting across a valley

Figure 5.42 To encourage more cycling, there needs to be adequate provision for locking up bicycles

Not only are social class divisions changing, but the nature of work itself is altering, not least because of the introduction of new technologies and more flexible working patterns, all of which will have implications for land use and development. For example, much is made of the likely effects of **tele-working**, i.e. people working at home on their computer, linked up to their office by a modem. However, it is estimated that less than 4% of the workforce actually do so at present, and many of these people are self-employed rather than employees. Judging by trends in North America, it may become more common for routine office work to be relocated to the home, but suggestions that high-rise office blocks in city centres will one day become redundant buildings, as outdated as Victorian warehouses and mills from the last century, is open to debate.

There has been an increase in leisure time, and spending power (disposable income) among some groups, which has resulted in people participating in a wider range of recreation, sport, leisure and hobby activities. As indicated earlier, market researchers are also keen to link life-style, class, area and income to assess development potential, and nowadays one will find Geographical Information Systems (GIS) that show

Table 5.22 Journeys per person per year in the UK, by mode and journey purpose, 1995–97

| | Percentages | | | | |
	Car	Bus and coach	Rail	Walk	Other
Social/entertainment	26	18	18	20	27
Shopping	19	32	10	24	13
Other escort and personal business	21	11	8	14	10
Commuting	18	18	47	7	26
Education	3	15	6	11	11
Escort education	4	1	1	8	1
Other, including just walk	—	—	—	15	—
Business	5	1	6	1	4
Holiday/day trip	4	2	4	1	8
All purpose	100	100	100	100	100

Source: National Travel Survey, Department of the Environment, Transport and the Regions.
Adapted from *Social Trends*, ONS (1999).

Table 5.23 Participation in the most popular sports, games and physical activities

| | Percentages | | | | | |
| | Males | | | Females | | |
	1987	1990–91	1996–97	1987	1990–91	1996–97
Walking	41	44	49	35	38	41
Snooker/pool/billiards	27	24	20	5	5	4
Cycling	10	12	15	7	7	8
Swimming	—	14	13	—	15	17
Darts	14	11	—	4	4	—
Soccer	10	10	10	—	—	—
Golf	7	9	8	1	2	2
Weightlifting/training	7	8	—	2	2	—
Running	8	8	7	3	2	2
Keep fit/yoga	5	6	7	12	16	17
Ten-pin bowls/skittles	2	5	4	1	3	3
Badminton	4	4	3	3	3	2
At least one activity	70	73	71	52	57	58

Source: General Household Survey, Office for National Statistics.

such data on an Ordnance Survey base map. Likewise, town planners incorporate these aspects into development plan-making and thus eventually into what is actually built.

It is estimated that on average, less than a quarter of car journeys are work-related, but all are no doubt seen as essential by the drivers concerned with the school run and the trip to the supermarket, which compete with the journey to work as vital expeditions. British town planning has been obsessed with the dangers of out-of-control suburban sprawl. The outward growth of our towns and cities, and decentralisation and dispersal in general, have become even stronger trends over recent years (Fig. 5.43).

Solutions suggested include rearranging the land uses so that people need to travel less, to create a city based on walking distances, mixed land uses and at a human scale. Perhaps the biggest town planning mistake of the 1990s was to allow an increase in out-of-town retail and office developments, and a general dispersal and decentralisation of land uses and facilities – making everyone more and more dependent on the motorcar – when at the same time we have increasing numbers of elderly people who cannot drive, lots of people who cannot afford cars, and when we are meant to be fighting pollution. What alternatives are there? Where do we go from here?

Self-assessment tasks

1. What are the main trends affecting retail development?
2. How would you deal with the problems of planning for the motor car?

Sustainability and use of resources

Conserving Resources

The depletion of non-renewable resources such as energy and water has meant that the need for sustainability and the need for conservation have become integral components in planning policy. In particular, as discussed above, there is a changing attitude towards planning for the motor car, moving away from a 'predict and provide' approach to road-building, and towards one of 'let the polluter pay'. The motor car is dependent upon fossil fuels and emits CO_2 and other dangerous gases into the atmosphere, with implications for the ozone layer and the entire ecology of the planet.

Also there is concern with the way in which water is often

Figure 5.43 main regional out-of-town retail centres in the UK

Figure 5.44 Environmental issues: pollutiion

health of the biosphere, and the health of humanity, are indivisible; one is nature orientated and the other is concerned with the social aspects of planning, but the two are interdependent.

There are two foundational international reports which set the agenda for sustainability:

* *The Rio Declaration* United Nations Conference on the Environment, Rio de Janiero, 1992
* The Bruntland Report *Our Common Future* 1997.

According to these documents, sustainability comprises three components:

* social equality
* economic self-sufficency
* environmental balance

Bruntland defines 'sustainable development' as follows: 'development that meets the needs of the present generation without compromising the ability of future generations to meet their own needs'. Reference is made to the importance of sustainability in DETR policy documents such as PPG1 (Planning Policy Guidance Note 1, 1997) on *General Planning Principles*. In Britain, the emphasis has generally been especially upon the environmental aspects of sustainability.

Arising from the Rio Conference, Agenda 21 was established, and subsequently local Agenda 21 initiatives were established with local authorities. Agenda 21 documentation states that 'good health depends on social, economic and spiritual development and a healthy environment, including safe food and water'. Likewise the World Health Organisation (WHO) has endorsed the importance of sustainability and promotes a Healthy Cities Programme internationally.

wastefully used in our society, not least traditional sewerage systems which are based upon 'flush and forget' rather than 'recycle and remember' approaches to the disposal of human waste. There is concern too about the continuing emphasis upon mineral extraction, aggregate depletion, and the effects of surface working upon the landscape and environment (Fig. 5.44).

The Environment Act 1995 has introduced measures relating to abandoned mines and contaminated land, and a new regime for reviewing and updating longstanding mineral permissions. The Act introduced changes in the responsibilities of national park authorities, strengthened control over water resource management, flooding and pollution, and established a National Environment Agency (NEA) for England and Wales, the Scottish Environment Protection Agency, and separately the Alkali and Radioactive Inspectorate in Northern Ireland. It should be noted that the Environment Agency incorporates the previous National Rivers Authority (NRA).

Planning for sustainability

Sustainability in a nutshell:

* Horses eat grass, manure the ground to feed more grass, and give birth to little horses: sustainabiity achieved.
* Motor cars run on fossil fuels, pollute the environment, and end up as rusting hulks: this is not sustainable, and it cannot last forever.

There are two main perspectives on the significance of sustainability. One perspective is human-centred: we must be kind to the Earth so that the Earth is kind to us. The other is nature-centred: we must respect the Earth because the Earth and its creatures have as much right to exist as we do. The

---

Project work

Is there a Local Agenda 21 group or programme in your town or city? If so, what are the implications for town planning policy and urban development?

Planning for urban conservation

Protecting the urban heritage

In parallel with the above measures there has been a concern for the preservation of the past, of the heritage of the built environment, which can so easily be destroyed by demolition or thoughtless redevelopment. Compared with the past, much of today's town planning is not concerned with new development and new towns; it is much more likely to be concerned with the redevelopment of existing areas, the urban conservation and preservation of historical districts, the improvement and refurbishment of rundown areas, and a multitude of detailed planning issues.

Also there is increasing concern for the protection of the countryside from urban development and the spread of towns, and thus within the twentieth century a range of controls and policies were aimed at protecting and conserving the countryside, such as green belts, national parks, and environmental impact controls. We live in a small set of islands with a relatively limited amount of land space, yet a large population, and therefore control and allocation of land has long been a key area of government policy in Britain.

Post-war reconstruction planning in the twenty years following the Second World War may be described as 'hit and run planning' or 'knock it all down and start again', with the emphasis being put upon new towns, new houses and new town centre development. Planning, then, gave little attention to existing, older urban areas; rather the emphasis was on decentralisation and removal of 'non-conforming uses' to green field sites. Also what we would now see as historic buildings worthy of conservation were being demolished to make space for new developments and new roads. As mentioned in Section 5.1 there was great enthusiasm in the 1960s for high-rise blocks of offices and a veritable 'property boom' hit the country fired by town centre redevelopment. Conservation groups became increasingly concerned at the visual effects (until then the highest buildings had been the church towers) and at the wanton demolition that was necessary to make space for new development. Many Victorian town halls narrowly missed destruction, and many a Georgian terrace was sacrificed.

As a result, the 1967 Civic Amenities Act gave powers for the creation of Conservation Areas, and the listing of buildings of historical and architectural importance became a major issue. Subsequently this legislation was elaborated upon and the 1990 Planning (Listed Buildings and Conservation Areas) Act is the most recent act in force. Buildings are listed by English Heritage, which is an agency of the Department of Environment, Transport and the Regions (DETR).

Buildings are listed if they are seen to be of outstanding historical or architectural interest: all buildings before 1700, most 1700 to 1840, some 1840 to 1914 and a few 1914 to 1939 and even a few after that. There are three main categories of listing. Grade I must not be removed in any circumstances and are of national, even international importance. Grade II comes in two sub-categories. Grade II * (starred) which means they have an asterisk * beside them on the list, cannot be removed without a compelling reason, and are usually of significant regional, if not national importance. Grade II unstarred are more ordinary buildings such as typical Georgian or Victorian town houses of more local importance. There are around half a million listed buildings in England and Wales of which 5800 are Grade I, 15 000 Grade II *, and there are more than 6000 conservation areas.

Urban conservation or modern architecture?

There is still a great deal of debate about what our towns and buildings should look like. Nowadays the conservation movement has become quite powerful and vast areas of cities

are covered by conservation area policy. However, at the same time a reaction is setting in. Great interest is found, especially among influential architects, in a return to the modern movement and high-rise development. For example, Norman Foster, the international architect, wants to build the London Millennium Tower at 435 m high, which would be twice the height of the NatWest Tower and would be the tallest in Europe. Richard Rogers is famed for the building of the Lloyds Building in London, the Pompidou Arts Centre in Paris and the Millennium Dome, all of which are in modern styles. What do you think about this type of architecture? Are people fed up with too much conservation and listing of buildings?

Table 5.24 Notable high-rise structures

Structure	Date of completion	Height (m)
TV Tower, Delhi	1988	235
Eiffel Tower, Paris	1889	300
Empire State Building, New York	1931	381
Sears Tower, Chicago	1974	443m
Menara TV Tower, Kuala Lumpur	1996	420m
Petronas Towers, Kuala Lumpur	1996	452 (tallest building)
TV Tower, Moscow	1967	540
CN TV Tower, Toronto	1976	553 (tallest mast structure)
London comparisons		
Canary Wharf		243
NatWest Tower		182
BT Tower		176
Nelson's Column		56

Source: The Concrete Society, 1997.

Conserving the natural environment

Environmental and green issues

There is now a vast range of protective legislation ensuring conservation of the natural environment (especially the countryside) and sustainability. As a result there are extensive controls on where a developer can build, particularly in respect of new housing (Fig. 5.45).

National parks

The National Parks and Access to the Countryside Act 1947, as its name suggests, set up a series of national parks and also opened up a series of footpath networks throughout the countryside. The aim of the national parks was to preserve the natural beauty of the countryside and provide access for the general public, along the lines of the recommendations of the Scott, Dower and Hobhouse Reports, and so they were part of the overall national land use planning strategy of the post-war period (Hall 1992). Most of the National Parks were established straight after the act in 1949, with the exception of the Norfolk Broads which was designated in the late 1990's. In 2000 the South Downs were declared a National Park.

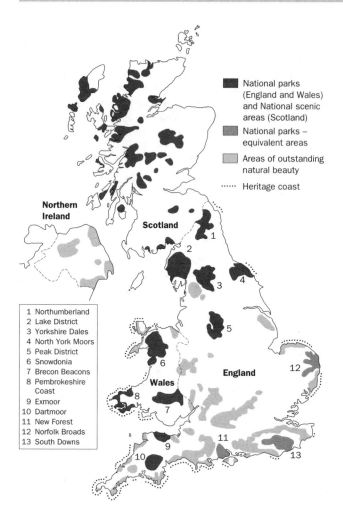

Figure 5.45 Areas of rural control

National parks (England and Wales) and National scenic areas (Scotland)

National parks – equivalent areas

Areas of outstanding natural beauty

Heritage coast

1 Northumberland
2 Lake District
3 Yorkshire Dales
4 North York Moors
5 Peak District
6 Snowdonia
7 Brecon Beacons
8 Pembrokeshire Coast
9 Exmoor
10 Dartmoor
11 New Forest
12 Norfolk Broads
13 South Downs

AONBs

The 1949 Act also established Areas of Outstanding Natural Beauty (AONBs), which are smaller, more accessible areas than the national parks, e.g. the Quantock Hills in Somerset. Grants of up to 75% were available to the local authorities whose job it was to administer them for maintenance and improvement of amenities. Both in national parks and AONBs there are strict planning controls on new and existing development. This is comparable to the situation in urban conservation areas.

Country parks

The Countryside Act 1968 established country parks, which were meant to enable people to enjoy the countryside without having to travel too far, to ease pressure on remote and solitary places, and to reduce the risk of damage to the countryside. This was achieved by creating small, managed park areas near to urban concentrations, with ample provision of car parks, toilets and amenities such as picnic sites and transit sites for campers and caravans. Local authorities received 75% grants from central government to create country parks, which were seen as 'honey pots' drawing people away from a more dispersed use of the countryside. Emphasis has continued to be put upon preserving non-agricultural uses and ecology within the countryside.

SSSIs

Sites of Special Scientific Interest (SSSIs) are small areas often in the middle of farmland. Such sites can be endangered by thoughtless farming practice, by careless tourists, and of course by development. Controls also exist in nature reserves and a range of other ecologically significant locations under the 1981 Wildlife and Countryside Act.

Green belts

Green belts are protective circular zones established around the edges of cities or towns. They are not designated for their landscape value, but to prevent urban sprawl in areas of development pressure; more broadly, they have also been seen as the 'green lungs of the city', and as having recreational and agricultural value. In fact, substantial parts of approved green belts are not really very green, with a diversity of gravel workings, glass houses and infill sites, and yet they still contain 20% of all agricultural land.

Certain uses are seen as being suitable for green belt location such as golf courses, hotels and leisure facilities, and, in the past, hospitals and similar government institutions. Some would argue that green belts do not prevent development in any case. All that happens is that development 'leapfrogs over the greenbelt' leading to a second ring of housing, and greater commuting distances for its inhabitants further out into the countryside.

Brown land

This term is used to describe land that was previously developed but which is now vacant, and usually located within the existing built-up area. For example, demolition areas within inner city locations, derelict docklands, or infill sites within existing residential areas are brown land. The planners are keen to see these areas filled in, as an alternative to outward expansion.

White land

White land is a term with no legal significance. It just means land that was not designated a particular land use under the old style of development plan. It is often on the inside edge of the green belt. Developers saw these areas as ideal for

Figure 5.46 Greenfield site sold for development

housing, and in some cases the government appeared to go along with this presumption in the past. Nowadays most white land areas have subsequently been covered by Structure Plan policy. In addition there are often wedges of white land marooned on the urban–rural interface which would cut into the countryside if developed. For example, awkward little bits are often left between the edge of an urban area and a passing motorway: a prime site for development if there is also a motorway intersection nearby. Motorways themselves cut right through established green belts often attracting a corridor of planning applications alongside their path.

Planning Policy Guidance Notes

By way of illustration, a list of PPGs is given in Table 5.25, showing the range of topics which in turn reflect trends and policies of concern to the government.

Table 5.25 Planning Policy Guidance (PPGs)

1. General Policy and Principles
2. Green Belts
3. Housing
4. Industry, Commercial Development and Small Firms
5. Simplified Planning Zones
6. Town Centres and Retail Development
7. Countryside and Rural Economy
8. Telecommunications
9. Nature Conservation
10. Waste
11. Regional Guidance (to be replaced)
12. Development Plans and Regional Planning Guidance
13. Transport
14. Development on Unstable Land
15. Planning and the Historic Environment
16. Archaeology and Planning
17. Sport and Recreation
18. Enforcing Planning Control
19. Outdoor Advertisement Control
20. Coastal Planning
21. Tourism
22. Renewable Energy
23. Planning and Pollution Control
24. Planning and Noise

The DETR constantly updates these notes which cover most aspects of planning. It is not intended to produce more than the present 24, and other policy issues are dealt with through White Papers (Command Papers) or Green Papers (Consultative Papers) produced by the DETR on current planning issues.

Table 5.26 Command Papers (White Papers)

1977	WP 6485	Policy for Inner Cities
1985	WP 9517	Lifting the Burden
1989	WP 569	Future of Development Plans
1966	WP 2928	Leisure in the Countryside
1990	WP 1200	This Common Inheritance
1994	WP 2426	Sustainable Development: The UK Strategy
1994	WP 2427	Climate Change: The UK Programme
1994	WP 2428	Biodiversity: The UK Action Plan
1995	WP 3471	Projections of Households in England to 2016
1996	WP 3234	Transport: The Way Forward
1996	WP 3188	This Common Inheritance
1997	WP 3814	Building Partnerships for Prosperity
1998	WP 3897	A Mayor and Assembly for London
1998	WP 3950	A New Deal for Transport: Better for Everyone

Self-assessment tasks

1. Name three data sources relevant to trends in town planning.
2. What is the difference between qualitative and quantitative data?
3. What percentage of households had cars in 1951 and what percentage have cars now?
4. Does walking count as transport?
5. What are the transport problems associated with out-of-town development?

Project work

It would be valuable to look at the retail development changes that have occurred in your town or city. Collect information on this, provide data and maps and use these as part of your portfolio with your teacher's approval and guidance.

6 UNIT

Surveying Processes

Chris Longhorn

This unit covers the skills and knowledge of general evaluation and surveying relevant to all career pathways in Construction and the Built Environment and prepares students for progression, either simultaneously or at a later stage, for the more practical and specialised optional units of surveying. On studying this chapter, students will:

- learn to select and use data sources such as maps, to investigate environmental features relevant to projects in land management, planning, building, civil engineering, structural engineering and building services engineering;
- have the opportunity to incorporate essential skills into their portfolio work through completion of self-assessment tasks discrete to the area under study, or through a task that provides sufficient opportunities to present work which meets the assessment criteria for the whole unit which is compulsory and the optional units of surveying;
- gain the underpinning knowledge of the processes and techniques required when undertaking a site survey and taking practical measurements in the field. The work undertaken to meet the assessment evidence for this unit has useful links with compulsory Unit 1: The Built Environment and Its Development and Unit 2: Design for Construction and the Built Environment. There are also links with optional units in the pathways of civil engineering, building and building services and housing studies. The content of this Unit also covers the knowledge requirements for the optional units of surveying at intermediate level.

The key areas covered by this unit are:

- use and understanding of maps

- principles of surveying measurement, recording data and plotting information
- surveying calculations in the determination of length, area and volume
- site evaluation from information contained in a site report
- site investigation case studies.

After reading this chapter you should be able to:

- select cartographic material (maps) for an environmental investigation of a chosen area
- recognise the main features shown on a map
- use Cartesian co-ordinates and Ordnance Survey grid references to identify features on maps
- describe the significance of map features for projects in construction and within different pathways of construction and the built environment
- relate the significance of map features to a selected project
- define terminology associated with linear measurement, angular measurement and height control
- explain and demonstrate techniques and processes related to the determination of length, height and angle, in the field
- measure and record, in an appropriate format, the key features of a site
- present plotted surveys in an appropriate format
- calculate lengths, areas and volumes from measurements taken in the field and from sketches and drawings
- describe the objectives of a site evaluation and the contents of a site report

6.1 Use and understanding of maps

Topics covered in this section include:

- map studies
- use of environmental data as part of a site and soil investigation
- the significance of map features and information obtained from a site report in selecting design criteria for projects in the built environment

In this section the investigatory processes undertaken as part of the desk studies and site and soil investigation will be examined in relation to proposed projects in the built environment. A significant amount of information can be obtained by an understanding of topographical maps, geological maps and soil profiles obtained from borehole and trial pit information.

Map studies

The Ordnance Survey is responsible for the surveying and mapping of Great Britain and publishes maps to widely differing scales for different purposes. Maps are issued at scales of $1:1250$, $1:2500$, $1:10000$, $1:25000$, $1:50000$ and $1:250000$.

Symbols, signs, colours and abbreviations are used to identify features on these maps. Ordnance Survey benchmark values are identified at their particular locations on the larger scale maps. The use of these benchmarks will be reviewed in the second section of this chapter and it is sufficient to say that the number next to the symbol representing the benchmark is the height in metres above Ordnance Datum Newlyn.

You should familiarise yourself with these symbols by studying the key of a map of your area. There are many other different types of maps such as:

- large scale foreign maps
- street plans
- road maps
- atlas maps
- maps provided by estate agents and local authorities
- underground railway maps
- bus route maps
- maps showing places of interest to tourists, 'you are here' maps and increasingly visual display unit maps in public places

It may be only a short time before a small screen linked to a central traffic controller is installed in a new car for monitoring traffic hold-ups.

Scale

Which map is selected for a task depends on the scale. The larger the map scale the greater is the amount of detail that can be shown, but the smaller the land area shown and vice versa. The scale of maps can be shown in one of three ways.

1. A statement of the map scale, e.g. 1 centimetre represents 1 kilometre.

2. A ratio between a single unit of length on the map and the actual distance that the unit of length represents on the ground, e.g. $1:1250$. On the map a length of 1 mm represents 1250 mm on the ground or 1.25 m. The actual unit of measurement is not so important as, at the scale of $1:1250$, a length of 1 m represents 1250 m or 1.25 km. The ratio stated always remains the same and is sometimes called a representative fraction. The scale of $1:2500$ can be written thus $\frac{1}{2500}$, which means that on the map any measured distance is $\frac{1}{2500}$th the length of its actual distance on the ground.

3. A linear scale. This is a line on a map which has been graduated into smaller sections, each section representing an equal distance on the map. On the $1:25000$ map, a distance of 10 centimetres represents 10×25000 centimetres on the map or 250000 centimetres $= 2500$ metres $= 2.5$ km. A linear scale on the map could be drawn by ruling a line 10 centimetres long and marking it off with five equal 2-centimetre graduations and labelling them 0.5, 1.0, 1.5, 2.0, 2.5 kilometres respectively. This technique is useful when photocopying from plans or maps, as some distortion always occurs with the process. Any distortion will be reflected not only in the plan but in the scale length itself.

Orientation

The top of a map usually points north and only in exceptional cases, if it is more convenient due to the shape of the area, is it necessary to have some other compass point at the map top. On Ordnance Survey maps the grid lines point to grid north, which is nearly but not exactly the same as true north. The north found by a compass is the magnetic north, and this is not true north either.

Grid references

All Ordnance Survey maps use the National Grid, which is a network of squares that cover the whole of Great Britain. Further information on the National Grid system is included more appropriately in the next section. It is, however, necessary to locate features, such as a church, on a map using the system of grid lines shown on an Ordnance Survey map. This is known as identifying a feature on a map using Cartesian coordinates, which are basically two fixed axes at $90°$ to each other. The grid lines increase in number as you travel east (called the eastings) and likewise increase in space as you travel north. The grid square is identified by the grid lines which form the southern and western sides of the square, e.g. grid square 64 shown in Fig. 6.1.

A feature on an Ordnance Survey map is almost always identified by a six-digit grid reference number such as 546213. The easting is identified by 546 and the northing by 213. Figure 6.2 shows the relationship of this grid reference to an assumed feature of a church. Students should note the method of dividing a line into equal parts – a useful technique when working with linear scales.

The largest squares used by the Ordnance Survey are $100\,km \times 100\,km$ and these can be identified by discrete

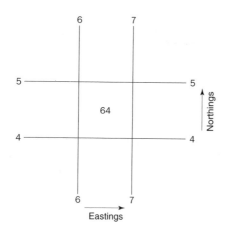

Figure 6.1 Eastings and northings

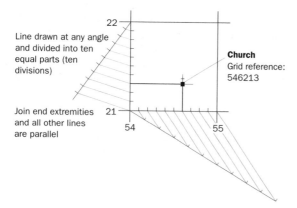

Figure 6.2 Grid reference

two-letter references such as TQ in the London region. If, in the above example, the letters SP were used, this would identify the 100 km square of the National Grid, while the six-digit reference identifies a square 100 m × 100 m on that map and the church located within the square. Any other feature may also be related to a map reference. For example, if a source of building material for a development such as face gravel used as the sub-base material for a road can be obtained from a local quarry, that location can be recorded on a map.

Summary of procedure in finding a six-figure grid reference

1. Locate the number of the easting grid line (first two digits) which runs vertically from top to bottom down the map.
2. The third digit in the grid reference gives the position of an imaginary grid line some tenths of the way between the two grid lines on the map.
3. Run a line some tenths eastwards from the easting grid line until you fix this position.
4. Repeat procedures 1 to 3, substituting the word northing and using the last three digits.

Map symbols

On very large-scale maps, such as the Ordnance Survey 1:1 250 and 1:2 500 series, buildings and roads are exactly to scale. On smaller maps, the mapmakers use points, lines and patches. These points, lines and patches can be identified

by reference to a panel on the map, known as the map key or legend.

- points, such as a cross for a chapel, are used to identify features whose position can be identified by a single grid reference
- features which are identified by area, such as a woodland or lake, are generally shown as patches of colour or as shaded areas on the map. They may also be identified by a symbol
- linear features, which have length but little breadth, are shown in different colour lines of often varying thickness depending on their importance. The line is often coloured such as a contour line which identifies positions on a map which have a stated equal height.
- abbreviations, such as PH for public house, are used to identify specific map features.

Aerial photography

Relating a map to a vertical aerial photograph can be useful if one can be obtained. They can, however, be difficult to interpret as they are often taken at an oblique angle of view which does not correspond to a map square. Features in the foreground are often seen in detailed close up although they may be only a few metres wide, while features on the horizon appear to be several kilometres wide. In working out an angle of view shown by the camera, it should be remembered that all the features depicted close to the left-hand side of the photograph must lie on a straight line on the map and, similarly, this is true of the right-hand side. This fact can be used to work out where the photograph was taken, since by identifying two or more features on or close to the edge of each side of the photograph, you will be able to find two converging lines on the map, with the photograph being taken from the point where the two lines meet. The use of photogrammetry in surveying is beyond the syllabus for this book, but students should be aware that the use of aerial photographs and the expert interpretation of 'light and dark' can often identify such things as areas of contaminated land and old tipping sites which have previously been unrecorded.

Map reading

Map reading is when you identify points, patches and lines on a map, when you draw cross-sections or longitudinal sections, make selective tracings and find the gradients between various points. There are often links to be identified when you look at a map. The distribution of settlements such as towns, villages and farms are often related to the geography of the area. The relationship of the settlements to the spread of high land, the drainage pattern, the geology of the area, the road network, distribution of industry and tourism attractions can all be identified. Distribution maps using lines which join places having a common similarity are called **isopleth** or **isoline** maps. A contour map is an example of this type of map. Maps which use colours or shading to show areas of land, say, between different levels are called **chloropleth** maps. Maps using points and symbols are known as **dot distribution** maps produced by making selective tracings from Ordnance Survey maps.

Map interpretation

Map interpretation is used when reasons, for example, the growth of an industry, are identified such as the distribution of archaeological remains on upland rather than lowland sites. Drawing cross-sections is often a useful tool to pick out drainage patterns, uplands, settlements or woodland. The close examination of a map at a site in a chalkland area, such as the East Yorkshire Wolds, may reveal the location of a string of villages at the foot of an escarpment, all at approximately the same height above sea level and all at a point where springs issue from the chalk, as at Millington near Pocklington, East Yorkshire. These are called **spring-line** settlements and in seeing a relationship between relief, underlying rocks, drainage and settlement patterns, the map is interpreted to find out features of significance. It is essential that students adopt a systematic approach to map interpretation.

Summary

The interpretation of any map should be undertaken systematically. If the interpretation is part of a site investigation at desk-study it is useful to highlight the key features that might influence whether the site is suitable for a particular purpose. For example, a small residential development on a steeply sloping site may require a significantly larger storm water sewer than that required just for the development, as the drainage would be for a much greater area than just the site. Substantial excavation works and possibly earth-retaining walls may also be needed, all adding to the eventual cost of the infrastructure required if the development is to proceed. It may be necessary to refer to the local library or local authority archive office to review how the area under study has developed over, for example, the last hundred years. Old maps and associated historical data should be available and by perusal of the 1908 edition of the old 1:500 scale maps much useful information may be gained.

> **Self-assessment task**
>
> Obtain a 1:2500 scale map for an area with which you have some familiarity, e.g. a town centre or small village. Systematically study the map by reference to the following summary points and produce an appraisal of the area, giving reasons why it has developed in the way it has.

1. Draw sketch sections to identify the rise and fall of the land.
2. Identify the principal compass directions to find the direction of any prominent slopes on the map. North-facing slopes get little sun and south-facing slopes get most sun, which is an important factor in the orientation of buildings on planned developments.
3. Relate the evidence shown on the map to evidence shown on any aerial or ground level photographs that you may have. The information gathered from a below-ground survey will be covered later in this chapter and borehole logs are often available for a particular area, especially if significant development has been undertaken in previous years. In this way a picture of the below-ground soil strata can be collected.
4. Identify evidence on how local people get a living. Place names and farm names often have links with the historical development of the district. Check on industry which has developed. A cement works may be in a location because of the naturally occurring chalk which is available at that particular locality. A coal-fired power station is likely to be situated where cooling water is available. Any underground water sources may attract water abstraction for public supplies.
5. What do symbols on the map reveal about existing topographical features of an area? An identification of a 132 kV overhead electricity transmission line may negate proposals for domestic housing development as it would be virtually impossible or too costly to divert. Road, rail, airports, ports and other routes of communication may feature in the development plans of an area and require infrastructure provision which requires detailed costings to be produced at feasibility stage in the work.
6. Investigate the relationship to each other of villages and towns and the public services infrastructure which may exist.
7. Identify which areas are designated settlements appropriate for development and any evidence to suggest features of the area which may attract development grants, e.g. tourism or industry.
8. Can spring-line settlements be identified? Towns located at the crossing points of a river or estuary or towns and villages on a dry site above damp land may be subject to periodic flooding from, say, a river.

Geographic information systems (GIS)

There are many definitions for GIS which, when analysed, mean methodologies for the organisation and analysis of geographic information. In the past few years, the cost and time required for data capture have put off potential users. There is now a wide range of satellite-borne and airborne remote-sensing systems available which have created a source of geographic information for GIS. GIS is best known for its map presentation ability and, for many, the sole use of GIS is to produce maps.

Within GIS there is a wide range of cartographic functions and presentation can go beyond the planimetric overview. Three-dimensional views, hyper maps, fly-throughs and virtual reality displays are other modes of presentation of geographic information. The results from retrieval can also include text.

Ordnance Survey digital maps have been produced since 1970, initially as a means of producing hard copies of a map. The information is now available as computer data and in this form they can be used in Geographical Information Systems, computer-aided design packages and as a base for a client's command and control system, e.g. recording the location of underground pipes and cables. The digital map consists of strings of coordinates of all salient features stored digitally on magnetic media, which can be viewed and edited on the computer screen or hard copied at the plotter. The information is copyright and can only be reproduced by users under licence. It is particularly useful in the preparation of hydrographic maps and charts for tidal estuaries and as an aid to navigation.

The Ordnance Survey map provides an ideal base for a GIS operated by a local authority. The basic database would cover the topography and land usage for an area, which could be used to provide line information plus contour and spot height data on similar lines to a conventional plan. It could also be used to produce thematic plans for town planning purposes and each department could have an overlay plan or database containing relevant details. For example, the finance department may wish to record the details of a land owner and property valuation, while the planning department may record details of planning applications. Any information could be recalled by displaying the map on a computer screen and then 'pointing and clicking' with a mouse.

Applications of the technology are only limited by financial restraints and legal requirements relating to confidentiality of data. The engineering context would allow data to be stored and retrieved relating to, say, a single street, e.g. overlay maps showing the location of services, street lamps, street furniture, traffic accidents, etc. This usage would ultimately allow for more effective excavation and reinstatement programmes involving the utilities.

Use of environmental data as part of a site and soil investigation

Environmental data obtained from topographical maps, geological maps and geographical information systems, which are covered by text and examples in the next section, should be referenced to the features as defined by the range of syllabus. Much of this data and the features above ground can be obtained from maps and a site investigation. Subsoil conditions can only be determined from an accurate below-ground soil investigation and, if necessary, a detailed analysis of samples of soil obtained from various depths in the ground. The site and soil investigation is often undertaken separately but the information comes together in a site report. Before the significance of map features to projects in the built environment can be fully analysed the process of undertaking a site and soil investigation should be fully understood.

Scope of a site investigation

The understanding of the physical make-up, engineering and chemical properties of the subsoil strata of a site is essential in determining the safe design of a structure. To determine this information a soil investigation is undertaken. The object is to obtain a comprehensive picture of a civil engineering site

below the ground surface, i.e. a subsoil survey. This involves the determination of the positions of natural features although information on foundations to structures, public utilities (gas, electricity, water, telephones, etc.) may be recorded for future reference. Two British Standards are relevant to this work. BS 5930: 1981 *Site investigation* and BS 1377: 1990 *Methods of test for soils for civil engineering purposes.*

It is important to understand the relationship between engineering and non-engineering soils and this is shown in Fig. 6.3.

The term **subsoil** is used to describe the layers of strata that lie between the top soil and the bedrock. It is these layers that usually support or in the case of tunnels surround a structure. It is now standard practice to examine any site on which a structure is intended to be erected in order to determine:

- the suitability of the site for the proposed works
- an adequate and economic foundation design
- the difficulties that may arise during the construction period
- the occurrence or cause of all changes in site conditions

The scope and extent of soil investigation depends on:

- the type and importance of the structure to be built
- the existence of any previous knowledge of the subsoil
- the cost of the investigation relative to the cost of the proposed structure

Cheap sources of information which can reduce cost include official publications, mining records, geological maps, local knowledge particularly from the Local Authority Building Control section. The soil investigation report should contain sufficiently detailed information on:

- the nature and thickness of the subsoil strata
- the mechanical properties of each stratum layer or up to an underlying strata that is to support the foundations of a structure; this information could include: density, permeability, compressibility, bearing capacity, shear strength, moisture content which would include seasonal variations
- the chemical and physical properties, e.g. are sulphates present in the groundwater which could attack concrete in foundations and should any steelwork buried in the ground be afforded with a degree of protection?
- natural groundwater level of the particular site

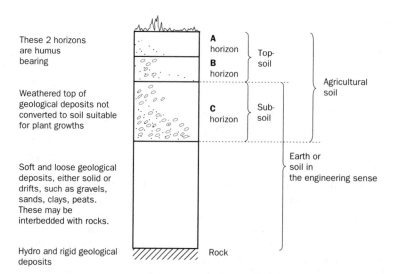

Figure 6.3 The relationship between engineering and non-engineering soils

Conclusions can be drawn on the behaviour of soil during excavation, construction and the working life of the structure. The report will influence the type of foundation a structure will require.

A site investigation may not always be for new construction. An investigation of defects or failure of existing works may necessitate a site investigation. In the case of water-retaining structures of significant capacity, constant monitoring of ground conditions is necessary to ensure the continued safety of existing works. Firms may also specialise in investigations relating to the suitability and availability of materials for construction purposes.

Investigation methods

Before samples of soil can be taken, access must be made to the various levels of soil strata. The choice of method used depends on the nature and type of ground. An investigation of the ground consisting of running sand will be entirely different from that in stiff clay. The topography of the ground and, to a certain extent, surface features of a site may also influence the choice of method, as will the comparative cost of available methods. The most commonly used methods are (a) trial pits, (b) borings, (c) headings.

Trial pits (Fig. 6.4)

By excavating a hole large enough for a person to work in, a section through the ground will be exposed revealing the soil strata for examination and sampling. This method is usually used for shallow investigations up to a depth of about 3 m, although some trench sheeting or battering of the pit sides may be required to ensure ground stability; above 3 m deep the cost of the pit increases appreciably compared with borings. The pits can either be hand or mechanically excavated. Problems occur in water-bearing soils. In dry conditions pits are particularly valuable since they allow hand-cut samples to be taken which minimises the disturbance of the sample. Trial pits are the most suitable method of exploring back-filled areas and sites overlain by variable natural deposits.

Borings (Fig. 6.5)

Hand or mechanical auger borings are cheap methods of subsurface exploration for soils which can stand unsupported. Holes can be sunk to about 3 m providing there are no obstructions such as boulders. The diameter of the boreholes are usually 150 or 200 mm. This is sufficient diameter to allow soil sampling tubes to be used easily. The mechanical auger is used in gravelly soil (non-cohesive) which involves the use of casing to prevent collapse of the boring.

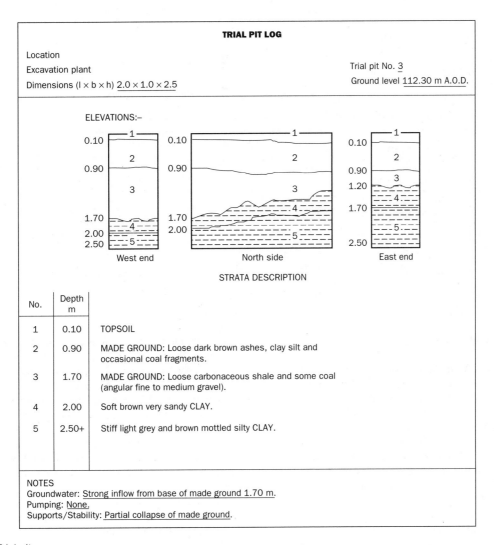

Figure 6.4 Trial pits

Scheme/location		Borehole no. 1 Sheet 1 of 1
Equipment and methods Light cable tool percussion rig. 200 mm dia. hole to 7 m, casing 200 mm dia. to 6 m		
Carried out for	Ground level: 9.9 m (AOD) Coordinates: E350 N901	Date: 17–18 June 1994

Description of strata	Reduced level	Legend	Depth & thickness	Sample/tests Depth	Sample No.	Test	Field records
Made ground (sand, gravel, ash, brick & pottery)	9.40		(0.50)	0.20	D 1		
				0.50			
Made ground (red and brown clay with gravel)	9.10		(0.30)	0.80			
				0.70–1.15	U 2		24 blows
					D 3		
Firm mottled brown silty clay (flood plain gravel)	7.90		(1.20)	1.15			
				2.0			
Stiff brown sandy clay with some gravel (flood plain level)			(1.65)	2.10–2.55	U 4		50 blows
				2.55	D 5		
	6.25			3.60–4.05			
			3.65	3.65	D 6 U	5 N27	No recovery
Medium dense brown sandy fine to coarse gravel (flood plain gravel)			(1.65)	4.00–4.30			
				4.00–5.00	B 7		
	4.60		5.30	5.30	D 8	S NIL	Standpipe inserted 5.30 m below ground level
Firm becoming stiff to very stiff fissured grey silty clay with partings of silt (London clay)			(2.15)	6.00–6.45	U 9		35 blows
				7.00–7.45	U 10		44 blows
			7.45				
End of borehole							

Sample/test key
D Disturbed sample
B Bulk sample
W Water sample
Piston (P), tube (U) or core sample length to scale
S Standard penetration test
V Vane test
C Core recovery (%)
r Rock quality designation (RQD%)

Water level observations during boring					
Date	Time	Depth of hole (m)	Depth of casing (m)	Depth to water (m)	Remarks
18 June	1615	7.00	0.00	3.65	Casing withdrawn
24 June	1200	0.00	0.00	2.37	
27 June	0915	0.00	0.00	2.33	
27 June	1420	0.00	0.00	2.11	Standpipe readings
28 June	1000	0.00	0.00	2.46	
1 July	1015	0.00	0.00	2.46	

Figure 6.5 Borehole data

Types of boring equipment

- **Post hole auger.** A simple hand-operated tool that is suitable for depths of up to 3 m in soft ground. In some cases, such as gravels or loose sands, the bore may be lined but the placing of the lining may need mechanical assistance (Fig. 6.6)
- **Shell and auger boring.** This tool can be hand operated in soft soils up to a depth of about 20 m. For greater depths a mechanical tool will be used. Casings if needed are positioned by means of a 'monkey' suspended from the winch (Fig. 6.7)
- **Percussion.** The operation of a percussion borer is by repeated blows breaking up the ground formation to sink the borehole. Water is added to the borehole as the work proceeds and the soil is removed at intervals. Due to the action of the borer the collection of undisturbed samples must be carried out with care, and for detailed investigations the rotary method is preferred
- **Wash boring.** A tube is sunk by a strong jet of water. The jet of water disintegrates and displaces the soil and returns the disturbed soil by way of the returning water. Progress downwards is made by either the tube sinking under its own weight or driven by a 'monkey' (Fig. 6.8)
- **Rotary borings.** This method is divided into three categories:
  - **Core drilling.** Used in rock this technique produces a continuous core of rock. The broken rock which results is displaced by the core cutter and removed by the wash-boring method.

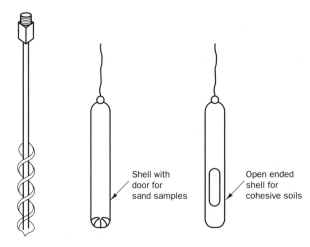

Figure 6.6 Post hole auger

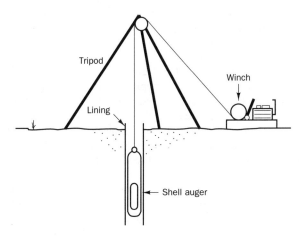

Figure 6.7 Shell and auger boring

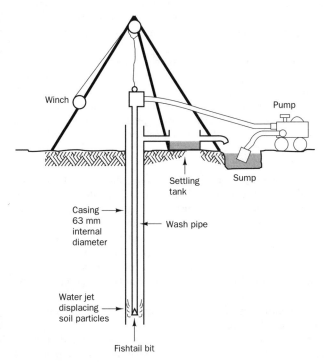

Figure 6.8 Wash boring

- **Mud rotary drilling.** This method employs a drilling action with a rotating bit. As the hole is sunk a mud laden fluid is injected into the borehole through hollow rods connecting the bit to the rig. The fluid carries the disturbed soil up the borehole to the surface as well as providing a support to the hole sides, avoiding the need for a casing. Samples are obtained by use of a core-cutting tool.
- **Shot drilling.** With shot drilling the head consists of chilled steel shot which is fed down the bore as an abrasive in place of the normal drilling head. The course cuttings do not flow to the surface but accumulate in a special cut above the cutting head.

Headings

Where suitable topographical conditions exist the use of headings driven horizontally or inclined may be employed. Where the strata dip appreciably it is a method often employed. In tunnelling work it is usual practice to drive a pilot tunnel ahead of the main tunnel to explore the ground conditions. This is a type of heading.

Collection of soil samples

Two types of soil sample can be obtained from boreholes and trial pits.

Disturbed samples

These are recovered from boring equipment such as the parings from an auger, the contents of a shell, sludge brought to the surface by wash boring or small deposits hand dug from trial pits. Usually the soil structure has been changed by the method of removal and the particles may not be representative of how they existed in the ground. They are suitable for grading and sulphate content tests and the samples should be placed in airtight tins to ensure that the moisture content remains largely unchanged. The sample should be labelled to identify its location.

Undisturbed samples

This is a sample where the constituent structure and moisture content are identical to that existing in the *in situ* soil. Hand-cut samples of soils taken with a knife from a trial pit enable samples to be taken with the minimum of disturbance although these should be prevented from drying out by coating in wax and storing in a cool room with high humidity. Samples largely undisturbed can also be obtained by driving a thin-walled steel tube into the soil and withdrawing it. Undisturbed samples from a borehole investigation are obtained using a variety of techniques which are reflected in the cost of obtainment. The cheaper methods lead to a degree of disturbance which may provide spurious results when tested in the laboratory. The use of an open-drive sampler for clays and silts (cohesive soils) provides samples of 100 mm diameter and 450 mm long. In this case the sampler is attached to boring rods and penetrates the soil by percussion drawing or jacking after which rotation causes the sample core to be broken off and brought to the surface. A piston sampler can also be used in soft and silty clays. The sampler is jacked down into the soil from inside the borehole casing. The tube and piston are pushed down together to the desired depth and when a sample is required the piston is held stationary by the boring rods and the tube is driven into the soil. Sampling of fine sand below the water table uses a compressed air sampler consisting of a sample tube that moves within an outer tube. The inner tube is driven into the soil by the boring rods and compressed air is pumped into the bell. This in turn forces water out from around the sample and as the tube is withdrawn the compressed air exerts pressure on the underside of the sample to retain it in the tube. Unfortunately the sample is usually disturbed.

Site and laboratory testing of soils

The detailed methods of testing soils for engineering purposes is beyond the scope of this chapter and reference should be made to BS 1377: 1990 for full descriptions. It is necessary to have some understanding of the purpose of the more common tests.

Shear strength

The shear strength of a soil is used in foundation design and may be determined by both laboratory and *in situ* testing. The shear strength of a soil is defined as the maximum shear stress applied to the soil at the point of failure.

Vane test. This test is used for obtaining the shear strength of soft and silty clays and involves pushing a bladed vane into the soil and applying a measured twist which is then converted to a shear strength by substitution into an equation.

Standard penetration test. This test is used for foundation design in granular soils. It involves drawing a tube into the bottom of a borehole by repeated drops of a known weight which is referenced to the penetration of the tube into the soil. The higher the number of blows to effect penetration, called the SPT 'N' value, the denser the soil.

Dutch cone test. This test is often used where piled or shallow foundations are anticipated as there exists a correlation between the results obtained from the electrical resistance at the point of the cone and the skin resistance of the sides as it is forced into the ground.

Plate loading test. This test is used where the likely settlement of a proposed foundation needs to be known. A load is applied to the plate by jacking against kentledge (rigid mass) and measuring deflection for increments of load.

California Bearing Ratio test. This is an important test used by highway engineers for determining the thickness of road pavements by measurement of the strength of subgrade or road formation. The test can be carried out either in the laboratory or *in situ* and consists of noting the loads required at various penetrations to cause a plunger to penetrate into the sample at a constant rate. With this test a curve is plotted, and the loads required to produce penetrations of 2.5 mm and 5 mm are expressed as percentages of standard loads. These percentages are then referenced to the thickness of road pavement layers for different constructions.

Wet sieving. This test involves removing the finer fractions of clay and silt by washing and then determining the particle size distribution of the remainder by dry sieving.

Dry sieving. This test is used for determining the particle size distribution of a sample of material down to find sand.

Wet analysis. The determination of fractions of fine particles in the clay and silt ranges is obtained by a sedimentation (settling out) process. This test is the basis of Stoke's law, which relates the settlement time of fine particles to the actual particle size. The purpose of all grading tests is to classify a soil sample from which it is possible to (a) analyse the suitability of the material for embankment construction; (b) determine the likely (permeability) properties of a soil behind an earth-retaining wall; (c) consider groundwater lowering methods as some methods are more suitable for particular soil types than others, e.g. well point dewatering is suitable for fine gravels and sand whereas electro-osmosis is only suitable for silts.

Sulphate content test. Sulphates in the ground attack concrete and mortar and the test should be employed to determine the need for sulphate-resisting cement in concrete construction.

Groundwater level test. To monitor the changing groundwater conditions during the investigation requires the sinking of steel or plastic standpipes. The bottom 1 m is perforated and filled with gravel to prevent the entry of silt which may block the tube.

Undrained triaxial test. This laboratory test suitable only for cohesive soils is used for establishing the strength of an undisturbed soil sample. The test involves the sample being placed in special apparatus called a cell which is maintained at a constant pressure. An axial load applied at the top of the cell is applied at a constant rate until the specimen fails. The test is repeated several times and results applied graphically.

Consolidation test. This test is similar to the *in situ* plate-bearing test and is used to determine the compressibility of a sample and the coefficient of consolidation.

Bulk density test. This test is used to determine the weight per unit volume of a soil including the effect of any voids filled with air and water. The dry density is the weight of dry solids per unit volume of soil. The density of a material is important in the stability of slopes, earth dams, embankments, earth pressure on retaining walls and excavation support.

Compaction test. The optimum compaction of materials is obtained at a given combination of dry density and moisture content. The sample of material is mixed with water and, after compaction with a standard rammer, a graph of moisture content against density gives an indication of the best density that is likely to be achieved at a given moisture content.

Site investigation. So far the investigation has concentrated on the below-ground soil make up. The site investigation should include a full appraisal of the ground topography and other above-ground natural and man-made features. Early maps often found in libraries, museums or local authorities may indicate the presence of springs, wells or shafts which are not shown on later maps. Aerial photographs can often provide information to the trained observer which may not be recorded otherwise. Slight discoloration on the photograph can identify such things as ground contamination or previously filled areas.

Meteorological records which go back over a hundred years can provide representative information on rainfall and temperature.

Local authorities may have information on buildings which have been on the site previously. These buildings may include basements which, if the site is to be developed, may require demolishing or filling in. Local authorities can also advise on the existence of Tree Preservation Orders or Listed Buildings. Region Water Authorities and Environment Agency hold records of main river and watercourses and can also identify areas which are prone to floodings as well as give details of the height of known flood levels related to Ordnance Datum. The National Coal Board have detailed records of coal seams and the location of mine shafts and tunnels. Records may also be held on likely subsidence areas. Other mines for extraction of minerals and clay may also exist in the area under investigation and in some cases, like the lead mines of the Yorkshire Dales, may have been derelict for some time. The public utilities responsible for services such as electricity, gas, water, telephones should be able to locate or position the pipes and cables which may cross the site. It is a requirement of the Public Utilities Street Works Act to consult these organisations prior to any development. Main drainage and public sewer records held by the local authorities generally as an agency agreement from the water authorities will show the presence of drains across the site. It is a requirement of the Building Regulations Approved Document C to investigate the likelihood of contaminated land which may prove a danger either during or after construction. Specialised knowledge may be required in the identification of methane gas or hazardous waste on the site and the local Environmental Health Department will provide guidance on procedure. Areas of grassland or shrubland where vegetable growth is stunted provide essential information to the trained observer. Public rights of way and bridle paths which, if the site is to be developed, may require diverting need accurate positioning during the site reconnaissance. On land, particularly in suburban areas, there may be a covenant which restricts the type of development designated and it is not unusual to find an easement running across the site under which is a major service such as a trunk water main and over which development is not permitted.

It can be seen that the knowledge attained during a site and

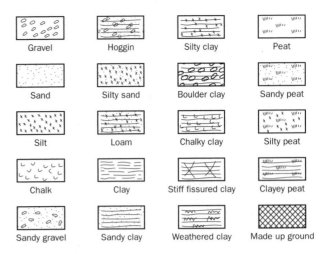

Figure 6.9 British Standard soil symbols

soil investigation is extensive and usually this information is collected and brought together as a site report.

The site investigation report

The information gained from the site investigation, which would include both desk studies and the soil investigation incorporating results from any testing of soil samples, is brought together in the site report. This is used by the client for the proposed works, to confirm (or otherwise) the suitability for development of the site for a specific purpose. If the scheme progresses to the next stage, information contained in the site report would be used for design and costing purposes.

1. **Preamble** – giving client, job, terms of reference. Usually the report will be prepared by a specialist company having expertise in soil investigation and the taking and testing of samples.

Legend	Description	Depth & thickness (m)	Reduced level (m)	Water level (m)	Casing & progress (m)	Sample range (m)	Type	Natural moisture content (%)	Liquid limit (%)	Plastic limit (%)	Plastic index (%)	BSCS	Bulk density (Mg/m³)	Cohesion (kN/m²)	ι	SPT CPT N value	Mv (m²/MN)	Notes
	TOPSOIL and ash	(0.30) 0.30	99.67															
	Orange-brown and grey Sandy stony CLAY – firm – large boulders between 1.50 and 2.00	(1.75) 2.05	97.92			0.30 to 0.50	BD	19	40	22	18	CS CI	2.07	40	8		0.64	Water added from 0.30 to 4.00 to assist boring
						0.50 to 1.00	U100 (32)											
						1.00	SD	18										
						1.00 to 1.50	BD					C(G/S) CI	1.91	–	–		–	Insufficient core recovery for triaxial compression or consolidation testing
						1.50 to 2.00	U100 (110)											
						2.00	SD	18 17	36	20	16							
	Brown and grey stony CLAY – firm	(0.95) 3.00	96.97			2.05 to 2.50	BD					GC						Triaxial compression test not possible due to stony nature of core sample
						2.50 to 3.00	U100 (59)	15	31	17	14	CL	2.20	–	–		0.23	
	Weathered SANDSTONE with clay bands – dense – hard at 4.00	(1.00) 4.00	95.97	DRY		3.00	SD	14				(G/S) WC						Triaxial compression and consolidation tests not possible due to friable nature of soil
						3.00 to 3.50	BD											
						3.50 to 4.00	U100 (146)	12	33	20	13	CL	2.16	–	–		–	
						4.00	SD	10										
	Borehole backfilled from 4.00 to ground level with surplus excavated material	Stopped																

Table header:
County council of	Highways Laboratory	Borehole record
Scheme PROPOSED FOOTBRIDGE, KIRKELLA		Borehole no. 1
Driller KL JW — Boring started / Boring finished 7.4.89	Type 150 mm percussive	Ground level (SITE DATUM) 99.97 m Nat. Grid ref.

Figure 6.10 Data for proposed footbridge, Kirkella

2. **General description of the site** – this will usually include a plan giving grid references and other essential information relating to topography, above-ground features and public utilities and restrictions.

3. **General geology of the area** – this will often include Ordnance Survey and geological maps highlighting any unusual features pertinent to the site.

4. **Description of soil in boreholes or trial pits** – these are presented as scale drawings of the information obtained from a borehole survey. They give descriptions of the soil types at the respective depths and indicate the positions of the samples on which either laboratory or *in situ* tests were carried out. The borehole logs are presented at the beginning of the results sections of a site investigation report and the results of any detailed tests usually follow. An example of a borehole log is shown in Fig. 6.5 and a trial pit in Fig. 6.4. Symbols used in the borehole log follow recommendations contained in the British Standard. These recommendations are reproduced in Fig. 6.9 for the three primary soil types: cohesive, non-cohesive and organic. The descriptions given for the soils are also in accordance with the British Standard and made in the following sequence:
   (a) Consistency and structure for cohesive soils or density for non-cohesive soils
   (b) Colour
   (c) Size of particles
   (d) Type of soil: e.g. soft (a); laminated (a); grey (b); clay (d); uniform (a); brown (b); fine (c); sand (d).

5. **Laboratory test results**: Fig. 6.10.

6. **Discussion of results.** This would include comment on such things as type of foundation, type of cement, sources of local materials for construction, disposal of waste materials, i.e. distance to and availability of spoil tips. Some contractors use pre-printed forms to be filled in as the information is gained and this will help to avoid costly omissions.

7. **Conclusion and final recommendations.**

Self-assessment tasks

1. Differentiate between a site and soil investigation and show by an example how data obtained from a borehole can be recorded on a drawing.
2. Indicate the two categories of soil sample that can be obtained during a soil investigation and briefly outline the types of test that would be carried out on samples to provide information for design.
3. Explain the purpose of each column of the borehole log (Fig. 6.5) and trial pit log (Fig. 6.4) and give one practical example of how each column would be used at the design stage for a proposed development.
4. Compare the strata identified in Fig. 6.10 with the strata shown in Fig. 6.5 and select, with reasons, suitable foundations for a lightly loaded medium-rise office block in each type.

Case study

The following is an actual site report for a small development of residential housing proposed for the centre of a small rural village. The site plan has been omitted. Figure 6.11 provides a

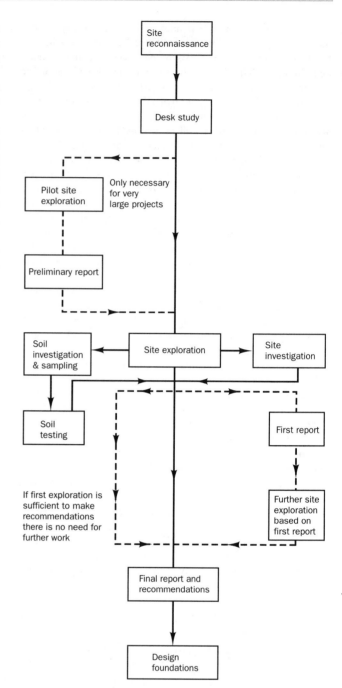

Figure 6.11 Sequence diagram for the design of a foundation

sequence diagram tracing the steps to be taken from the initial site reconnaissance stage to the design of the foundation. Refer to Fig. 6.12 for the borehole log.

PROPOSED RESIDENTIAL DEVELOPMENT KERRY CLOSE, KIRKELLA, E. YORKSHIRE

1. *Introduction*
   At the request of XYZ Construction Ltd, a site investigation was carried out at the above site on 24 April 1986, in order to ascertain the subgrade bearing strength beneath the proposed access roads to serve the development.

2. *The site*
   The proposed development area consists of a grass field lying to the north of the existing Kerry Close. Access to the new site will be from Kerry Close at one end and from Valley Drive at the other. The site lies on a hillside, with a

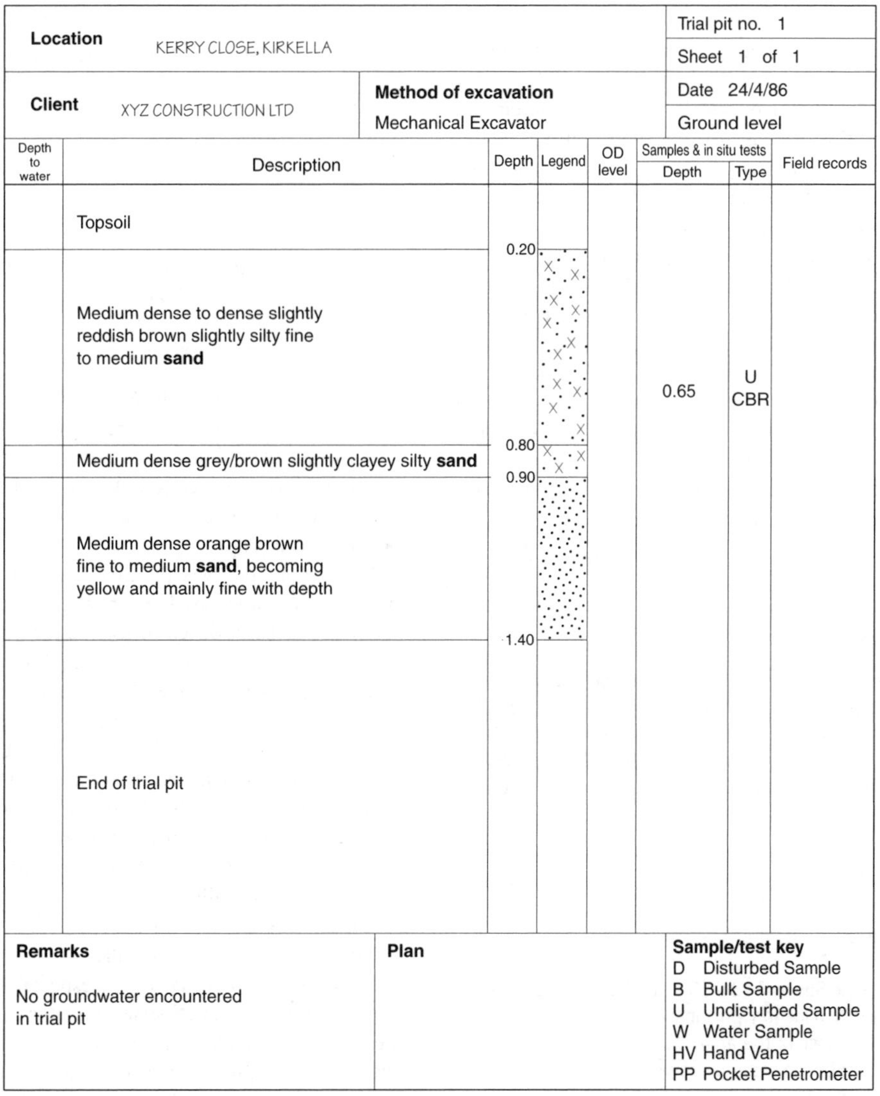

Location	KERRY CLOSE, KIRKELLA				Trial pit no. 1			
					Sheet 1 of 1			
Client	XYZ CONSTRUCTION LTD	**Method of excavation**			Date 24/4/86			
		Mechanical Excavator			Ground level			

Depth to water	Description	Depth	Legend	OD level	Samples & in situ tests		Field records
					Depth	Type	
	Topsoil						
		0.20					
	Medium dense to dense slightly reddish brown slightly silty fine to medium **sand**				0.65	U CBR	
		0.80					
	Medium dense grey/brown slightly clayey silty **sand**	0.90					
	Medium dense orange brown fine to medium **sand**, becoming yellow and mainly fine with depth						
		1.40					
	End of trial pit						

Remarks	Plan	Sample/test key
No groundwater encountered in trial pit		D Disturbed Sample B Bulk Sample U Undisturbed Sample W Water Sample HV Hand Vane PP Pocket Penetrometer

Figure 6.12 Borehole log

general slope of between 1 in 25 and 1 in 30. Approximately 170 m of A2 class road are to be constructed, with a further approximately 280 m of A4 class roads leading off. (Site location, OS Grid Reference TA 920 314.)

Available records from the British Geological Survey indicate this site to lie within an area of outcrop of rocks of the Redbourne Group of the Middle Jurassic.

3. *Fieldwork*
Five trial pits were excavated at positions identified on the site plan. These showed that the likely formation level will lie on a variety of materials, including clay, limestone and sand. Undisturbed CBR samples of sand and clay materials were taken from trial pits 1, 4 and 5 and returned to the laboratory for testing. Full details of the trial pits, including depths at which samples were taken, are attached.

Groundwater was encountered in trial pits 4 and 5 at depths of 0.65 m and 0.70 m respectively.

4. *Laboratory testing*
California Bearing Ratio tests to BS 1377: 1975, Test 16, were carried out, and gave the results shown in Table 6.1.

Table 6.1 California Bearing Ratio Test

Location	Depth (m)	Moisture content (%)	Bulk density (kg/m^3)	Dry density (kg/m^3)	CBR (%)
TP1	0.65	18.1	1871	1584	3
TP4	0.65	26.5	1930	1526	2
TP5	0.70	19.5	1979	1656	2

5. *Discussion and recommendations*
The results obtained are considered consistent with the materials as seen on site. The limestone seen in pits 2 and 3 will have a CBR value in excess of 5%, but is considered likely to be susceptible to prolonged frost action and will thus require a minimum construction thickness of 450 mm. The sand material seen in trial pit 1 contained occasional thin bands of slightly clayey material, and as a result it is considered that a CBR value of 2% is more appropriate for design purposes for this material. The area of clay outcrop at the western end of the site showed several small areas of standing water, as the time of investigation followed a period of heavy rainfall. As a

result it is felt that, provided the subgrade is treated with care during the construction period, further softening of the clay is unlikely and a CBR value of 2% is thus acceptable for design purposes. It is recommended that the subgrade in this area is not excavated and then left open to the elements for any excessive period. Any soft areas exposed at any point on the site should be excavated and backfilled with suitable material.

To summarise, a CBR value of 2% is acceptable across the site, requiring a subbase thickness of 400 mm. Around trial pit 3, where the limestone outcrops within 450 mm of the surface, with a bed thickness of more than 600 mm, the construction can be such that a total thickness of 450 mm (surfacing plus sub-base) is used. The minimum flexible surfacing thickness required by the Estate Roads Design Manual is 155 mm, which means that the formation level over the remainder of the site will be at a minimum depth of 555 mm below finished level.

Materials Engineer

Self-assessment tasks

Select a small parcel of land near to home or college and undertake a site investigation. A borehole log may be acquired from the local authority or if the site is one which is under development the contractors' site agent may be able to provide you with one. If difficulty still exists you may use the one in this unit.

1. Produce a site report in a recognised format outlining the suitability of the site for a proposed development of your choice.
2. Identify the location of the site with a six-figure grid reference.
3. Obtain the Ordnance Survey 1 : 1 250 or 1 : 2 500th scale plan of the selected site and identify principal features of the area.
4. Make a selective tracing of the area.
5. Produce a dot distribution map to show:
   (a) residential premises
   (b) commercial premises
   (c) industrial premises
6. On a separate tracing produce a contour plan of the area and comment on the topography of the area.
7. Outline any problems related to water supply and waste water disposal if a high-rise development was to be proposed.

Geology

The geology of an area influences the scenery of a district and the suitability for development. **Igneous rocks** were once molten magma deep inside the earth. They may have cooled inside the crust, in which case they are **plutonic rocks**, or out on the earth's surface as **volcanic rocks**. **Sedimentary rocks** were formed from mud, sand or shells which dropped down to the bottom of rivers, lakes and seas. **Metamorphic rocks** have been changed from their original state by heat or pressure.

The characteristics of the different rock types (Fig. 6.13) affect how useful they are. Characteristics of the rock include hardness, permeability and mineral content. The pattern in which rocks are arranged in the earth is called **rock structure**. Earth movements often fold (or bend) or create a fault (or break) rock layers to create distinctive landscapes. The characteristics of common rock types and their use are shown in Table 6.2.

Table 6.2 Characteristics of common rock types

Rock type	Hardness	Permeability	Minerals	Uses
Granite	Very hard	Low	None	Building stone
Slate	Hard	None	None	Roofing tiles
Sandstone	Hard	Some	None	Building stone e.g. lintels, cills
Limestone	Moderate	High	Impure $CaCO_3$	Road, gravel, concrete aggregate
Chalk	Moderate	High	Pure $CaCO_3$	Cement
Clay	Soft	None	None	Bricks, pottery
Coal	Moderate	Some	Carbon	Fuel

Rocks are not often found in flat layers and can be folded or faulted. **Anticlines** are upfolds and **synclines** are downfolds. Anticlines are not as resistant to erosion or wearing away as synclines. When this happens the anticline is said to be 'unroofed' with an example being the scarplands of Britain and Europe.

There may be two parallel faults in the earth where the land to each side has been pushed upwards and the land in between has sunk down to form a rift valley.

The steep valley sides are called **fault scarps** and usually there is an association with volcanic activity. Britain's largest rift valley is the Scottish Central Lowland lying between the Grampian Highlands and the Southern Uplands.

Soft rocks, which are easily washed away with river and stream water, leave lowland valleys and plains. Clay is a typical example. It is usual for most people in a country to live in the lowlands, especially the central parts of plains and the gaps between hills.

Hard rocks are not so easily eroded by rivers and streams and can be left standing as hills.

Chalk is not very hard but, especially if it is well fissured, acts like a giant sponge soaking water into it and – except for the depth of chalk near the surface which can break down into a kind of putty – is not easily eroded. Chalk rocks often form gently sloping uplands which in England are often called 'downs', although this is a misnomer. Chalk and the usually harder limestone often form good **aquifers** for a source of public water supply which is achieved through the sinking of boreholes and wells. As the water has been well filtered as it soaks through the chalk, only sterilisation by chlorination is usually required to make the water fit for drinking, which makes it the cheapest source when compared to river abstraction, dams or desalination.

Uplands are cooler, windier and wetter than surrounding lowlands and in high latitudes, like Britain, this is a disadvantage, which is why uplands are left as moorland for sheep rearing. In hot countries, however, highlands often have the water that the lowlands lack.

Rocks are made of minerals, which offer exploitation opportunities for people who live in the area. Figures 6.14–6.17 inclusive show the significance of different rock formations and associated industries.

Chemical weathering

Rocks may be broken down by chemical weathering, which is the first stage of soil formation. This is particularly noticeable in areas where there is carboniferous limestone, where the reaction of acid rainwater with limestone has created **clints**, **grikes**, potholes, underground caverns, **stalagmites** and **stalactites**. Grikes are really deep fissures and the limestone blocks between grikes are clints.

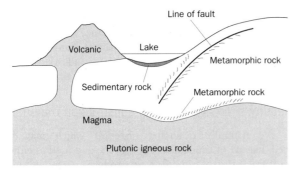

Figure 6.13 Types of rock

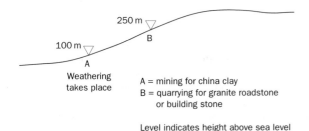

A = mining for china clay
B = quarrying for granite roadstone
or building stone

Level indicates height above sea level

Figure 6.14 Granite

In granite uplands chemical weathering may have helped to form the granite which can be seen on moorlands such as Dartmoor.

Many other chemical reactions affect the minerals in rocks, causing them to disintegrate into smaller pieces. Hydrolysis and oxidation are two of these processes.

Mechanical weathering

Mechanical weathering occurs when water freezes in the cracks of a rock face, causing fragments of rock to break off and collect on mountain sides as scree, which is marked on large-scale Ordnance Survey maps. Areas around the three peaks of Yorkshire, Whernside, Ingleborough and Pen-y-ghent, have considerable amounts of hillside scree, which increases each year with not only the natural processes mentioned but with the amount of tourists who wish to climb these peaks. These weathering processes shape hillsides which, with other processes, eventually create soils.

Soil profiles

As previously mentioned, the thickness of the different below-ground soil strata can be plotted from the results of a detailed below-ground soil survey undertaken by specialist geotechnical companies. Simple soil profiles, albeit relatively shallow, may be determined from areas where bare rock is exposed at the side of a river or at a coastal cliff. Where soil erosion has taken place, aerial photographs often provide clues as to the underlying strata as the whiteness of chalk may often show through thin coverings of soil. Where there has been movement of soil downhill, this can be identified by distorted or bulging walls and trees tilted towards the bottom of a slope. Soil trapped behind a wall may also be indicative of soil movement. Evidence of past use such as the disused lead mines of the Yorkshire Dales may also be identified from maps and topographical features.

Soil testing

The testing of soils is an activity that should be undertaken by specialists, and results interpreted from samples carefully taken in the field. The student, however, can gain a simple appreciation of the constituents of a soil by completing a simple test. Take a handful of soil and examine it carefully:

- Is the soil coarse and gritty to the touch? Does it include particles of sand? Is it possible to make it stick together to form a ball? Can it be rolled to form a thread without breaking? Does it leave the hand relatively clean after it has been handled?

If the answer to these questions is 'Yes', the soil is probably sandy.

- Is the soil smooth and sticky when wet? Can it be easily shaped into a smooth round ball? Does it leave the hand dirty after it has been handled?

If the answer to these questions is 'Yes', the soil is probably a clay.

- Is the soil silky to the touch, neither coarse and gritty, nor smooth and sticky? Can it be shaped into a fragile ball? Does it leave the hand slightly soiled after being handled?

If the answer is 'Yes', the soil is probably a loam.

In practice, however, many soils lie between the three categories. The Building Regulations Approved Document A also provides some assistance in the field interpretation of soils for their load-bearing characteristics, when the need for an assessment of the width of a strip foundation for a house is required. Finally, when all information is to hand it is necessary to confirm from Ordnance Survey maps patterns of level which allow the visualisation of land features (Figs 6.18–6.20).

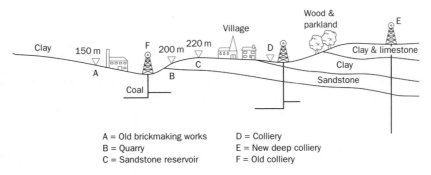

A = Old brickmaking works
B = Quarry
C = Sandstone reservoir
D = Colliery
E = New deep colliery
F = Old colliery

Figure 6.15 Clay and sandstone escarpments

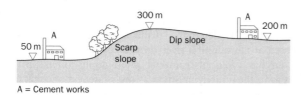

Figure 6.16 Chalk

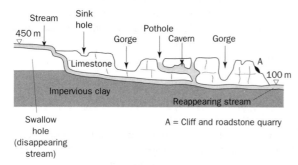

Figure 6.17 Carboniferous limestone

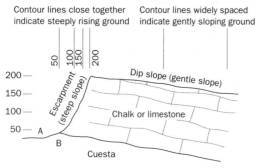

A = Villages often sited here because of springs
    (spring line settlements)
B = Springs at foot of slope

Figure 6.18 Contour lines

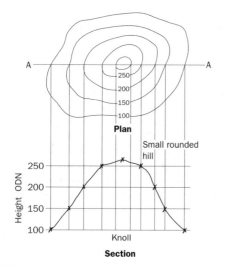

Figure 6.19 Contour lines for hill

Map features

Map features and information obtained from a site report are significant when selecting design criteria for projects in the built environment.

After reading the following text the student should have gained some understanding of the significance of map studies and the interpretation of information gained from reading a site report. This significance is summarised as follows.

Availability of local sources of construction materials

These are naturally occurring materials which may be quarried, blasted or dredged as appropriate and used in either their natural form or modified to produce a new product either at source or by transportation to a manufacturing centre. Examples of materials which are used in their natural form would include granite and non-frost-susceptible limestone for use as roadstone sub-base or base materials. The same materials may be coated by tar or bitumen to produce a material suitable for the base and wearing course of a road. Sandstone may be quarried for use as local stone for building. Limestone can be used for cement production and clay for brick production where the natural mineral colouring produces a distinctive brick, discrete to the locality from which the clay was dug. The effect of the derivation of these materials has a significant environmental impact on an area and has serious implications on the balance of the topographical features of the natural environment. Erosion, pollution and the products of waste produced by mining operations are major considerations for the planners when analysing and licensing the abstraction of materials from the ground.

Transport of construction materials

The transport of materials, particularly by large heavy vehicles, creates pollution of many different types. Apart from the fact that these heavy vehicles accelerate the deterioration of roads – many of which were not designed to take such traffic – noise, dust and dirt seriously affect the quality of life for people living along the route taken by these vehicles. The transportation of limestone from quarries is a particular example where noise, dust and slurry create significant problems of control.

Much of the transport of materials does, however, in an indirect way, create employment in different localities and it is a difficult balance that needs to be achieved when measuring the effects of pollution against people's livelihood.

There is much more legislative control of pollution now and areas which have previously been used for, say, mining are being regenerated by lighter manufacturing industries. Waste tips from mining are slowly being reclaimed and planted although communities which were originally based on a single major employer have in many cases experienced high unemployment, when that employer has ceased production.

Availability of water supplies

Analysis of the ground strata will identify water-bearing aquifers which can be used as sources of both public and private supplies. All ground-water abstraction has to be licensed by the Environmental Services Agency in the interests of the environment.

River abstraction of water for water supply purposes is a sensitive issue, particularly after the 1996 drought, when a number of Drought Orders were issued allowing water

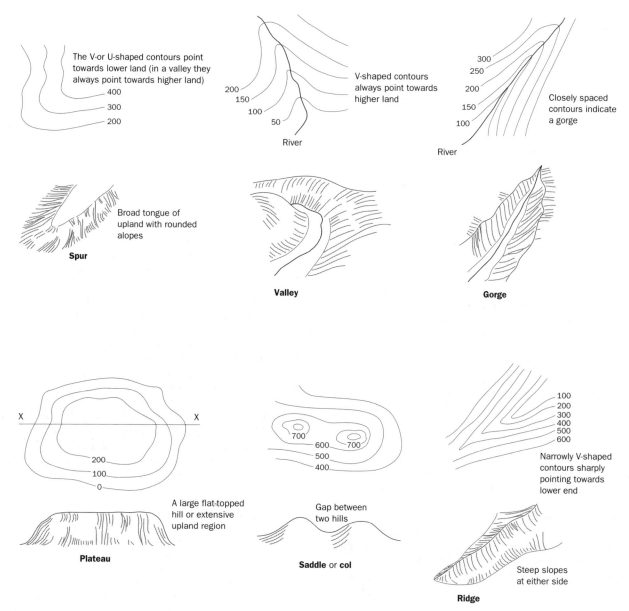

Figure 6.20 Contour lines for hilly area

undertakings to abstract quantities of water sometimes far in excess of their original licence.

Rivers are also used as open pipelines so that, by regulation, abstraction can take place near the major conurbations to avoid the necessity for the laying of large-diameter pipelines from the headwaters of a river, over great distances.

At the turn of the century many impounding reservoirs were constructed as a source of water supply in suitable localities. Many of these constructions had a serious impact on the regime of the river where the reservoir had been constructed and few new reservoirs, apart from Kielder in Northumbria, have been constructed in recent years. Features such as rivers, reservoirs, wells and boreholes are shown on published maps.

Services design

High-voltage overhead transmission lines are also identified on the published maps from the Ordnance Survey. Although having less of a visual impact, the laying of underground pipes and cables create issues which need identification. The constituents of soil may be such that iron pipelines may require protection to avoid accelerated corrosion from acids and sulphates contained in soils such as peat. The encapsulation of ductile iron pipes in polythene sleeves is now commonplace and the use of selected bedding material for pipes and cables is essential for the longevity of the service.

The jointing of pipes and the selected pipe material should be influenced by characteristics of the ground. Where setttlement can be anticipated and predicted, the use of flexible pipes with flexible joints and the appropriate pipe bedding, is essential. Where high loads may be transferred to a pipe due to its excessive depth or from a building, rigid pipes and joints may be more suitable.

Major pipelines are identified on maps and the statutory utilities usually keep records of pipe and cable positions on the 1:1250 and 1:2500 scale Ordnance Survey sheets.

The production of longitudinal sections from a level survey along routes is also needed when it is proposed to lay trunk gas or water pipelines. In water pipelines and sewers a level survey is essential to ensure that working pressures and pipe gradients are within the capability of the pipe for the anticipated design flow.

Foundation design

Earlier in this section the tests undertaken on soil samples have been reviewed. When determining the most suitable foundation for a building the chemical constituents of the ground and its bearing capacity are major considerations.

Sulphates in groundwater attack concrete, and an analysis would reveal the necessity for using a sulphate-resisting cement in production of the concrete.

Low-bearing ground capacities, or those locations where the ground is of variable strength across the site, may require the design of specialised foundations, such as piles and reinforced concrete rafts.

- Localised loading from the columns of a multi-storey building needs to be accommodated by foundation design related to the prediction of behaviour of the soil that the load is ultimately transferred to.
- Characteristics of sliding of foundations due to, say, a building being located in a water-lubricated clay may cause serious deterioration or even failure of a retaining wall.
- Localised settlement under a foundation may result in the need for expensive underpinning.
- The presence of a high water table may create an unacceptably high uplift pressure on a lightly loaded building which may cause uplift of the building itself.
- Well-lubricated clay can create what are called 'slip-circles' resulting in the movement of earth embankments where the centre of the radius of potential slip is outside the mass of the embankment.

Clay is a notoriously variable material to have beneath a foundation. In summer it may shrink as it dries out and in winter it can swell as it takes up moisture. Specialised foundations may be required in these circumstances. Many buildings constructed in the 1930s and 1940s failed to take account of the clay shrinkability and have settled either uniformly or differentially, particularly in recent times after successive years of below-average rainfalls. A borehole log or trial pit is essential to identify the strata available for locating a foundation and the most economical depth at which to place it.

Drainage design

Pipe materials available for drainage would be selected as previously discussed. Surface-water drainage depends to some extent on the permeability of the ground and the impervious area being drained. The rate of rainfall is the other major design factor influencing the size of pipe required. Roads and roofs of houses are largely impermeable; grassland, verges and soil are each allocated permeability factors with which the likely prediction of drainage requirements can be made. Permeable soils such as chalk and limestone will absorb water, clay will artificially 'hold up' in some situations the level of water in the ground. This is called a perched water table. Subsoil drainage may be required with some developments where embankments and cuttings are to be constructed.

With new road design schemes it is essential that rainfall is taken away quickly and effectively and discharged either at the sewage works or, if of an appropriate quality, into a suitable ditch, stream or other watercourse, without polluting the environment.

The prediction of flooding is an ongoing concern as more and more land is developed. Flood alleviation schemes may be needed to avoid flooding of valuable commercial developments.

This may result in the widening of rivers or the laying of large-diameter pipelines to prevent this.

Perusal of maps and consideration of ground topography will identify where flood plains can be utilised when it is predicted that a river will not overtop its banks or where it is feasible to raise the level of river banks. In rural villages designated as selected settlements it may be necessary to dispose of surface water by suitably constructed soakaways and again by reference to the geology of the area it would need to be confirmed as to whether this was practicable or not.

Likelihood of contaminants

It is a statutory requirement for premises holding dangerous or toxic substances to be licensed. In addition, the company has to complete a risk assessment identifying the risks of the chemicals that they use and the precautions required to minimise the risk. The Building Regulations Approved Document C also details contaminants of land which may be naturally occurring or the result of previous land or building use. Special precautions may be needed to treat these hazards and monitor potential long-term problems.

Some landfill sites produce large quantities of methane gas which should be adequately vented to atmosphere in a suitable way to prevent explosion.

Radon gas created in grounds such as granite can permeate into buildings, and special precautions may be needed to prevent this if development is anticipated on ground where this occurs. The geology of the area should be familiar when dealing with this latter case and monitoring of gas discharges should be undertaken, if possible, over long periods.

Possibility of subsidence

Subsidence has been considered earlier when it was related to the differential settlement of a building. Old mine workings can create settlement of roads, particularly if they cannot be accurately located beneath the ground.

When planning the route of a new road the position of mine ventilation shafts, which should be shown on the Ordnance Survey map, are a useful guide to the location of perhaps derelict mine workings. Swallow holes in the ground can also be positioned and whether or not their depth would be a potential problem for a proposed construction can be determined.

Tree effects

Deciduous and coniferous woods are identified on Ordnance Survey maps. Individual trees of particular beauty, interest or aesthetic appeal may attract a Tree Preservation Order. This prevents the felling or pruning of the tree without prior permission of a local authority who has the invested powers of control from the Department of the Environment. Hedges may also attract a Tree Preservation Order and a recent decision by the High Court has set a precedent about any wholesale 'grubbing-up' of hedges by a developer.

Trees are large water consumers. Willows and oak trees in particular have extensive root systems which search out water. If they are planted in clay soils this can accelerate the shrinkage of the material and create settlement problems for the buildings located close by. The location of piped services may also be affected by the presence of tree roots. Conversely the laying of service pipes and cables through the tap roots of a tree can damage or kill the tree.

Foundation and services design should consider the proximity and species of mature trees and take the appropriate action to avoid future problems of building settlement. Root barriers and other methods to prevent root incursion close to buildings now form a requirement of planning and building regulation approval.

Summary

In this section there are many areas of investigation that can be pursued by a student to satisfy the assessment evidence that needs to be produced for both the compulsory and optional units of surveying. The following exercise covers the requirements of the assessment criteria E1, E2, C1 and A1 of 'what you need to produce'.

Project work

The work for this project can also be used to claim evidence for key skills, Communication Level 3. The appropriate process work in obtaining maps and other information needs to be kept and you should be aware that a Crown Copyright exists on Ordnance Survey map reproduction. Appropriate permission needs to be obtained if you intend to photocopy sections of maps.

1. The Ordnance Survey now produce maps using digital data.
    (a) Contact the Ordnance Survey and request information on the Superplan system of digital mapping.
    (b) Explain how the Superplan system of digital mapping works and to what scales are the maps available.
2. (a) Obtain the following Ordnance Survey maps (you may be able to borrow some of the maps from your local lending library): (i) 1 : 250 000; (ii) 1 : 50 000; (iii) 1 : 25 000; (iv) 1 : 2500; (v) 1 : 1250.
    (b) Compare the detail and information contained on the maps and write a brief report identifying the level of information contained on each.
    (c) Outline the main purposes of each map type and state the advantages and disadvantages in use for each map.
    (d) Identify ten features on a (I) 1 : 250 000 and (ii) 1 : 1250 scale map and provide 6-figure grid references for each.
    (e) From one map showing ground contour intervals, describe the topography and justify the description of the area.
    (f) Explain how the road network is likely to have developed for a selected area and the features of topography which have had an influence.

Self-assessment tasks

1. Prepare a report describing the purpose of the triangulation and National Coordinate system used by the Ordnance Survey.
2. Explain the use of scales used for mapping and indicate the type of plan usually prepared at the following scales: (a) 1 : 1000; (b) 1 : 500; (c) 1 : 2500; (d) 1 : 1250; (e) 1 : 100; (f) 1 : 50; (g) 1 : 10; (h) 1 : 5.
3. Using the coordinates on your local Ordnance Survey map, identify the following features: (a) settlement, (b) mine; (c) spring or beck; (d) road; (e) railway; (f) cairn; (g) pot-hole; (h) reservoir; (i) spot height; (j) contour-line; (k) footpath; (l) cave; (m) telephone box.
4. Describe how the features identified in task 3 are significant (or otherwise) in the development of the area.
5. Figure 6.21 shows a site survey for a proposed office and factory. Complete parts (a) and (e) after studying Section 6.1; leave parts (b), (c) and (d) until you have studied sections 6.2 and 6.3.
   (a) Describe the main features of the site.
   (b) Produce a longitudinal section showing existing and proposed levels along the route of the sewer from IC1 to IC4.
   (c) Determine, by calculation, the volume of excavation for the office and factory 1 if the formation level for dig is 450 mm below the finished floor level shown on the drawing.
   (d) Produce a traverse table for the four-sided figure ABCD.
   (e) Explain possible problems to services and foundations from the mature trees shown on the drawing.

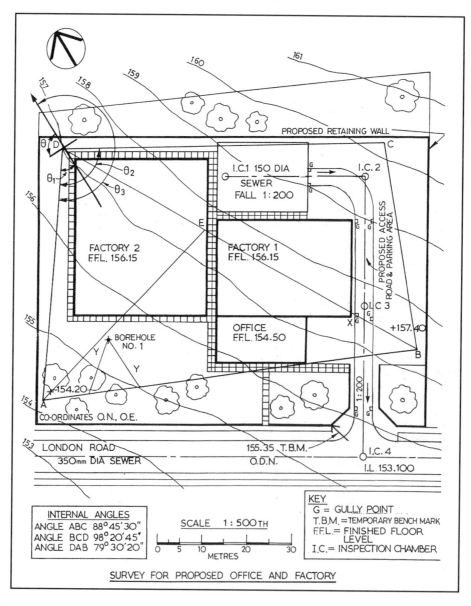

Figure 6.21 Self-assessment exercise

6.2 Principles of surveying measurement, recording data and plotting information

Topics covered in this section are:

- Imperial and metric measurement
- Equipment used for linear measurement
- Terminology used for linear measurement
- Techniques used with linear measurement
- Purpose and applications of height control
- Terminology used with height control
- Level and ancillary equipment used for height control
- Techniques and principles associated with the levelling process
- Applications of levelling and associated setting out
- Purpose and applications of angular measurement
- Terminology used with angular measurement
- Equipment used for angular measurement
- Techniques and principles associated with angular measurement
- Numerical processes normally undertaken in the field

Linear measurement: imperial and metric

How long? How wide? How deep? How high? We can answer all these questions to varying degrees of accuracy because measuring instruments are commonplace, and standard systems are accepted throughout the world. This was not always so because ancient standards were based principally on people's limb measurements and, of course, varied from person to person. Today with modern scientific instruments we can measure small and large distances quickly and accurately. It was not until just over 600 years ago, however, that under a statute of Edward I an attempt was made to secure uniformity of English measure by law. In 1624, an English mathematician, Edmund Gunter, invented a new measuring device, the chain, which is still used today for surveying.

In most countries of the English-speaking world the **metric system** of measurement is now used, although the old British **imperial system** is still partly used in the United States of America. Sometimes measurements of an old building being surveyed are required to be undertaken using imperial measure. Imperial measurement, with its metric equivalent, is shown in Table 6.3.

Table 6.3 British linear measurement with metric equivalent

Imperial							Metric
Inches	Feet	Yards	Poles	Chains	Furlongs	Miles	
1							2.54 cm
12	1						30.48 cm
36	3	1					91.44 cm
	$16\frac{1}{2}$	$5\frac{1}{2}$	1				5.03 m
		22	4	1			20.12 m
		220		10	1		201.17 m
		1760			8	1	1.69 km

Similarly, metric linear measurement with its imperial equivalents is shown in Table 6.4.

Table 6.4 Metric linear measurement with imperial equivalent

Metric			Imperial
10 millimetres	=	1 centimetre	0.394 inches
10 centimetres	=	1 decimetre	3.937 inches
10 decimetres	=	1 metre	39.37 inches
10 metres	=	1 decametre	32.808 feet
10 decametres	=	1 hectometre	109.361 yards
10 hectometres	=	1 kilometre	0.621 miles

Equipment used for linear measurement

The fundamental principles of surveying are few and simple. On any area of land it should always be possible to select two points and to measure the distance between them either directly or indirectly. Sometimes a very long measure is needed and other times obstacles such as trees or ponds may obstruct the ease of measurement. If the two points on the line to be measured are called A and B, this line after measurement can be drawn to scale on paper. Other points of detail can be located relative to this line by taking two other measurements which can also be drawn to scale on the paper. In this way a map or plan is constructed. The two measurements can consist of **two distances, one distance and an angle**, or **two angles** (Fig. 6.22).

For small surveys the above approach could well suffice, with C representing the point of detail to be located from line AB, which would be known as the base line. When the whole area to be surveyed cannot be seen from the one line, as is the case with most surveys, additional lines require to be defined, relative to the first using such pairs of measurements. The points of the junctions of these lines are called control points and together with the lines they constitute a skeleton framework for the survey. Normally the control points always need to be visible. In addition to locating points of detail by further angular and distance measurements, engineering features such as roads can be set out from the framework in the same way.

Because the rest of the mapping or setting out work is based on this framework it has to be surveyed to greater accuracy than the detail. The relative positions of points can be calculated more accurately than they can be directly plotted, and, except for the simplest survey, a significant amount of calculation is required and the positions of control points can be given in terms of **coordinates**, which is similar to the plotting of points on a graph.

Method		Use
Measure AC, BC		Tape and offset surveys, ties

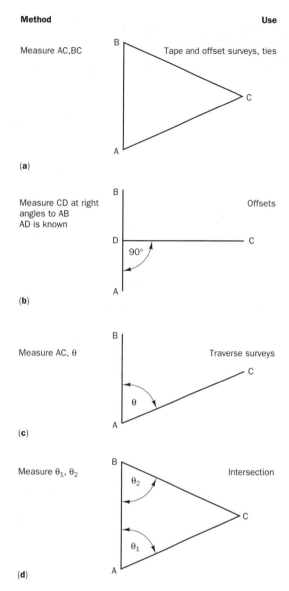

(a)

Measure CD at right angles to AB
AD is known — Offsets

(b)

Measure AC, θ — Traverse surveys

(c)

Measure θ_1, θ_2 — Intersection

(d)

Figure 6.22 Measurement of lines and angles

Reliability of a survey

All measurements are subject to unavoidable error and surveyors must be aware of the sources of error and how these can be minimised. The surveyor must ensure that the techniques chosen will produce a result that is sufficiently accurate for the intended purpose. After completion of the survey a check must be made to ensure that the required accuracy has been attained.

Accuracy required

When the intention is to produce a plan the accuracy is defined as the **scale** used for the drawing of the plan. The smaller the scale used in production of the plan, the less the accuracy of the survey requires to be. A draughtsperson can plot a length to within about 0.25 mm and if a plan is required at a scale of 1:1000, which means that 1mm on the plan represents 1m on the ground, the smallest plottable distance is 0.25 m. Thus for a survey at 1:1000 scale, all measurements must be taken such that the relative positions of any point with respect

to any other must be determined to 0.25 m or better. The specification of surveys for other purposes such as engineering works, e.g. tunnelling, or property boundary definition might well be determined by engineering tolerances or legal standards.

Orientation of plans

Apart from being able to measure distance by scaling from a plan, it is also important to establish **direction** or **orientation**. This can only be obtained by measuring the angle the line makes with some fixed reference direction. Every map should be referenced towards the top of the sheet, and should be one of the following: (a) the direction of **true north**, (b) the direction of **magnetic north**, (c) the direction of any arbitrary line between two features on the drawing.

Achieving the specification

Equipment and methods must be chosen to ensure that the correct specification accuracy is achieved. There are several types of error that occur and an understanding is required to appreciate the limitations of measurement techniques. The types of error are

- mistakes
- systematic errors
- random errors

Mistakes

The **miscounting** of the number of tape lengths when measuring a very long line or **transposing** numbers when booking are two common mistakes that are frequently made. These types of mistake can occur at any stage of the survey – when observing, booking, calculating or plotting – and may well result in the survey being done again. By working to a recognised procedure and by building independent checks into each stage as the survey progresses, mistakes should be easily detected.

Systematic errors

These arise from sources which act in a similar manner on observations. The method of measurement, the instruments used and the physical condition at the time of measurement must be considered. Expansion of steel tapes and the stretching of fibre glass tapes all affect the true length of a line. These systematic errors have a significant effect on long line lengths as the error tends to be cumulative and is difficult to detect unless different measuring equipment is introduced intermittently as a check.

Random errors

These errors do not fall into the other two categories and are caused by limitations of instruments and observers. They are seldom large and as they are of a random nature can be equally **positive** or **negative** and can often cancel each other out. These errors can be reduced by repetition of readings and the taking of additional measurements as a check.

Checking the survey

On completion of all the work the **dimensional coordination** of the survey should be confirmed in the field by inspecting the completed map and comparing measurements scaled off the plan with their equivalents on the ground.

Tape and offset surveying (chain surveying)

This branch of surveying derives its name from what originally was the principal item of equipment used, i.e. the **measuring chain**. It is a complete method of surveying, especially useful when large-scale maps of relatively small areas are required to be produced. Some of the operations of tape and offset surveying are also used in traverse surveying where the chain and tape are often used to survey details.

Equipment used in tape and offset surveying

The equipment falls under four broad headings:

- used for linear measurement
- used for measuring right angles
- used for measuring ground slope (only plan dimensions are plotted on a map)
- ancillary equipment

Equipment used for linear measurement

The chain (Fig. 6.23). Normally 20 or 30 m long, produced from tempered steel wire, 8 or 10 SWG and made up of links which measure 0.2 m from centre to centre of each middle connecting ring. Swivelling brass handles are fitted at each end and the total length is measured over the handles. Tally marks made of plastic, are attached at every whole metre position and those identifying 5 m positions are of a different colour. Older chains may have brass tallies marking every tenth link. The chain is fairly robust and easily read although care has to be taken when reading the tallies. It can vary in length owing to wear on the metal-to-metal surfaces, bending of the links and debris between the bearing surfaces.

The surveyor's band (or drag tape) (Fig. 6.24). The steel band is a much more accurate measuring instrument than the chain. It is manufactured from strip steel, some 6 mm in width, and is carried on a four-arm open-frame winder. A handle is fitted for returning the band into its frame after use and this also

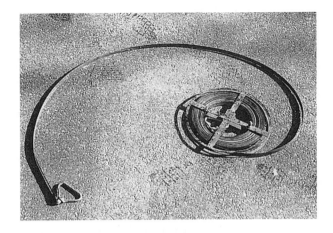

Figure 6.24 The surveyor's band

provides a locking device for retaining the band. Handles or rawhide thongs allow the bands to be pulled or straightened. Lengths of 30 or 50 m are readily available and 100 m bands are also produced. BS 4484: Part 1:1969 requires that metres, tenths and hundredths of metres should be marked, with at least the first and last metre also subdivided into millimetres. The operating tension and temperature for which the band was graduated should be indicated on the band as this information is required when undertaking calculations related to precise surveying.

Tapes (Fig. 6.25). Tapes may be made of **synthetic** material, glass fibre being typical, coated steel or plain steel. BS 4484: Part 1 suggests 10, 20 or 30 m as the desirable lengths. For the synthetic types the British Standard requires major graduations at whole metre positions and tenths, with minor graduations at hundredths, and 50 mm intervals indicated. Those manufactured of glass fibre have a PVC coating. They are graduated every 10 mm and figured every 100 mm; whole figures are shown in red at every metre. These tapes are used for relatively short dimensions as they have a tendency to stretch with use.

Steel tapes may be provided with a vinyl coating or may be plain. The former type has sharp black graduations on a white background. They can be obtained graduated every 5 mm and figured every 100 mm; the first and last metre lengths are also graduated in millimetres. Whole metre figures are again

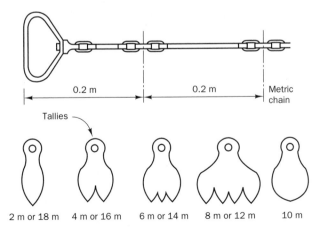

Figure 6.23 The chain

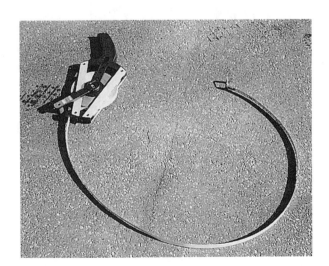

Figure 6.25 Typical measuring tape

shown in red at every metre. The latter type have graduations and figures etched on to the steel and they present the same subdivisions as the vinyl-covered types. They are generally wider and are usually contained in a leather case as opposed to a plastic one. The steel tape is vulnerable and is brittle and has a tendency to break if stood upon or if traffic passes over it. It is essential that tapes and bands be wiped clean and be dry before being rewound into their cases or frames. Steel tapes also require occasional treatment with an oily rag to prevent rust formation. An additional problem with steel as a tape material is that it has a relatively large **coefficient of expansion**, about 0.000 011 per °C, and errors due to expansion and contraction affect the reading accuracy. **Invar**, an alloy of nickel and iron, has the lowest coefficient of expansion of any metal, about 0.000 000 2 per °C. Small errors in establishing the temperature of an invar tape make little difference to its length. Unfortunately they are more delicate than steel tapes and are not robust enough for everyday use. Principally used for accurate base line measurements, they provide a degree of accuracy that is not normally needed in everyday surveying work.

There are three main methods of making linear measurements: (i) by direct measurement; (ii) by optical means known as **tacheometry**, which is outside the syllabus of the Surveying Processes unit but is briefly covered in the section on height control; (iii) by **electromagnetic distance measurement** (EDM), which is briefly covered in the section on angular measurement.

Equipment used for measuring right angles

The **cross staff** (Fig. 6.26) The instrument consists of two pairs of vanes set at right angles to each other with a wide and narrow slot in each vane; alternatively it consists of an octagonal brass box with slots cut into each face so that opposite pairs form sight lines. The instrument is mounted on a short **ranging rod**, and to set out a right angle, sights are taken through any two pairs of slots whose axes are perpendicular. The other two pairs then enable angles of 45° and 135° to be set out.

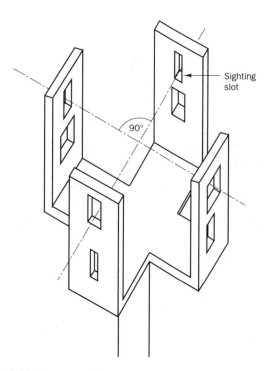

Figure 6.26 The cross staff

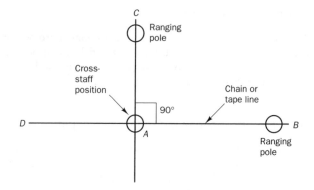

Figure 6.27 Procedure for using the cross staff

The procedure for using a cross staff is outlined below (see Fig. 6.27).

1. Set up on chain line DB at point A, the position where the right angle is to be set out.
2. With a ranging pole at B on line DB, sight the instrument upon it and then, without moving the cross staff, sight through the second pair of vanes in the direction of C and direct a chainman with a second ranging pole until this pole appears in the sights. Line AC will be at right angles to DB.

The optical square   This is similar to the cross staff but has a greater degree of accuracy. There are two types of optical square: one using two mirrors and the other using a prism. The instrument is small, rarely measures more than 75 mm in diameter and is about 20 mm thick.

The mirror type makes use of the fact that a ray of light reflected from two mirrors is turned through twice the angle between the mirrors, which is derived using the principles of reflection of light. Mirror A is completely **silvered**, while mirror B is silvered to half its depth, the other half being left plain. Thus an eye looking through the small eyehole will be able to see half an object at O_1. An object at O_2 is visible in the upper (silvered) half of mirror B, and when angle O_1XO_2 is a right angle (where X is centre of the instrument), the image of O_2 is in line with the bottom half of O_1 seen directly through the plain glass.

The procedure for using an optical square is outlined below (see Fig. 6.28):

1. The surveyor stands at X and sights O_1, directing an assistant to move O_2 until the field of view is, as shown in Fig. 6.28, angle O_1XO_2 for, considering any ray from O_2, incident on mirror A at angle α to the normal, it will emerge at the same angle to the normal

$$XAB = 2\alpha$$

and from a consideration of the angles

$$\text{angle } XBA = 90° - 2\alpha$$

$$\therefore \qquad \text{angle } AXB = \text{angle } O_1XO_2 = 90°$$

and the result is independent of α.

The prismatic type of optical square employs a pentagonal-shaped **prism**, cut so that two faces contain an angle of exactly 45°. It is used in the same way as the mirror square but is more accurate. A variant of this model has two such

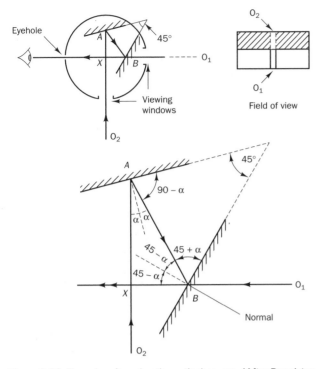

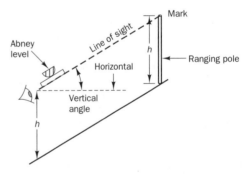
Field of view

Figure 6.28 Procedure for using the optical square. (*After* Bannister, Raymond & Baker *Surveying* Longman)

prisms, one mounted above the other. For setting out right angles the top one only is used, but the prisms are so positioned that both of them can be used to set out two points O_1 and O_2 such that angle O_1XO_2 is $180°$.

Equipment used for measuring ground slope (Fig. 6.29)

The Abney level. This versatile instrument can be used either as a hand level or for the measurement of vertical angles. It consists of a sighting tube, to which is attached a graduated arc. An index arm, pivoted at the centre arc, carries a small bubble tube whose axis is normal to the axis of the arm, so that as the tube is tilted the index moves over the graduated arc. By means of an inclined mirror mounted in one-half of the sighting tube, the bubble is observed on the right-hand side of the field of view when looking through the **eyepiece** of

the sighting tube. The milled head is used to manipulate the bubble. The arc itself is graduated in degrees from 0 to $+90°$ indicating that the sighting tube is looking up or in elevation and 0 to $-90°$ indicating that the sighting tube is looking downwards or in depression.

The scale is read by the vernier on the index arm to 10 minutes. Also engraved on the arc is a gradient scale giving gradients from $1:10$ to $1:1$. In using the instrument for measurement of vertical angles when measuring mean ground slope and if the sight is taken on to a point whose height above ground is the same as the observer's eye, then the line of sight will be parallel to the mean ground surface. A ranging pole with a mark on it makes a suitable target.

The procedure for using an Abney level is outlined below (see Fig. 6.30):

1. To measure an angle a sight is taken on to a mark on a ranging pole.
2. The bubble is brought into the field of view by means of the **milled head** to be bisected by the sighting wire at the same time as the wire is on the target.
3. The angle is read on the **vernier**.

Watkins clinometer (Fig. 6.31). This instrument which comes in several forms is used for measuring the angle of ground slope. The most common type consists of a counterweighted scale freely suspended so that the line OX is always horizontal. The scale is divided from $0°$ in both elevation and depression.

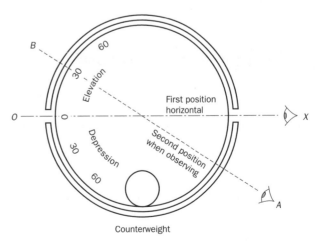

Figure 6.30 Procedure in taking an angular reading. (*After* Bannister, Raymond & Baker *Surveying* Longman)

Figure 6.29 The Abney level

Figure 6.31 The Watkins clinometer

The procedure for using a Watkins clinometer is outlined below:

1. To measure the ground slope for a line *AB*, the surveyor stands at *A* while the chainman stands at *B* with a pole clearly marked at a point at the eye level of the surveyor.
2. This point is observed through the instrument at *A* and if it is at a higher level than *A*, the instrument will be tilted upwards. As the scale is freely suspended its position in relation to the horizontal will not alter and the **angle of elevation** may be read upon the scale from a fixed mark on the **clinometer** case.

Ancillary equipment

Ranging rods or **ranging poles.** These are poles of circular section 2, 2.5 or 3 m long, painted with distinctive red and white bands which are usually 0.5 m long. The poles are tipped with a pointed steel shoe to allow them to be driven into the ground. They are used for the measurement of line with the tape and for marking any points that always require to be visible. A sectional tubular type is also available, the short bottom section of which is often useful where headroom is restricted. When using ranging rods on pavements and other hardstanding, a **tripod restrainer** is used to support the rods.

Arrows. When measuring the length of a long line, the tape or chain is required to be laid out a number of times and the positions of the ends are marked with a short steel arrow having a circular handle. The arrows are usually about 400 mm long and a piece of red ribbon tied to the handle enables them to be seen easily.

Pegs. Positions which require to be more permanently marked, such as intersection points of survey lines, are marked by nails set in the tops of wooden pegs driven into the ground with a mallet. If they are intended to form permanent control stations for the survey, they are often concreted to avoid being dislodged by the passage of site traffic. Steel **dowels** may also be used in hard ground while in tarmac or asphalt roads small *square brads* are used.

Field books (Fig. 6.32). Dimensions of measurement are recorded in a field book about 100 × 200 mm. The book opens lengthways and entries are started at the back and continued towards the front. Thus the surveyor records measurements forward in the same direction as that in which he is walking. Dimensions are recorded at the centre of each page between two ruled lines about 15 mm apart, which represent the survey line.

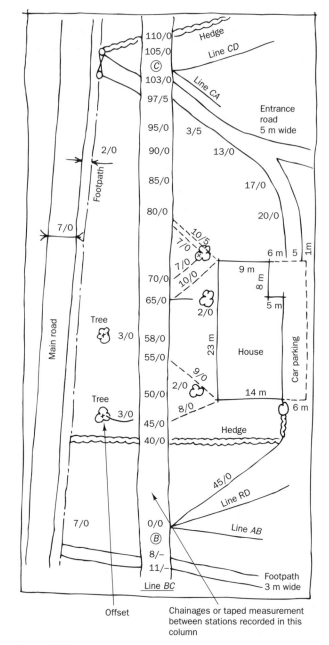

Figure 6.32 The field book

Terminology used with linear measurement

Chaining

This is the process of the direct measurement of a line, though today it is not necessarily carried out with a chain. Three kinds of chain are in existence, although the first two are rarely seen today.

The Gunter's chain. This is 66 feet long and divided into 100 links each 0.66 feet or 7.92 inches long.

The engineer's chain. This is 100 feet long and divided into 100 links, each 1 foot or 12 inches long.

The metric chain. This is usually 20 metres long and is divided into 100 links, each 200 mm long. A metric link is always 200 mm long and a 30 metre chain will therefore contain 150 links.

Taping

The terms taping or banding are often used in preference to chaining. Strictly, however, taping is the process of direct measurement of a line using a suitable band or tape from the wide range of steel, invar, linen, glass fibre or plastic types which are available for selection.

Ranging

This is a basic procedure in tape and offset surveying and is more commonly referred to as the ranging of a line. The operation is carried out by two chainmen (note the traditional

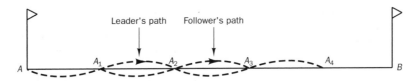

Figure 6.33 Ranging of a line. (*After* Bannister, Raymond & Baker *Surveying* Longman)

use of the word 'chainmen' although it is more likely that a tape or band will be used for the measurement today). One person acts as the leader and the second person the follower.

The procedure for ranging is outlined below (see Fig. 6.33).

1. The chainmen each take one end of the steel band and the band is pulled out full length and examined for defects.
2. The leader equips himself with ten steel arrows and a ranging rod and the follower also takes a ranging rod to measure the line AB, having previously located A and B and positioned ranging rods appropriately.
3. The leader drags his end of the band forward to A_1, and holds his ranging rod about 0.3 m short of the end.
4. The follower holds his end of the band firmly against station A and the surveyor lines in the leader's pole between A and B by closing one eye, sighting poles A and B, and signalling the leader until he brings his pole into line AB. A system of signalling is usually adopted as follows: swing the left arm to the left as an instruction to the leader to move his pole in that direction and, similarly, for the right arm. Both arms extended above the head indicate that the pole is on line. It is essential during this operation to ensure that the poles remain vertical in the ground or tripod restrainer.
5. The leader straightens the band past the rod by sending gentle 'snakes' down the band.
6. The follower indicates that the band is straight and the leader puts an arrow at the end A_1 (at this stage offsets or ties may be taken from known chainages to positions of required detail).
7. The leader then drags his end of the band A_2, taking nine arrows and his pole.
8. The follower moves to A_1, and puts his pole behind the arrow, and the surveyor then again lines in from here or from A. If a choice of direction is available it is easier to sight downwards on a gradient where the ground is sloping.
9. The above procedure is repeated with the follower picking up the first arrow before he moves from A_1. The leader moves to A_3, carrying eight arrows and the follower moves to A_2 carrying the arrow from A_1. If the line measured is longer than ten times the band length, the leader will exhaust his supply of arrows, so that when the 11th band length is stretched out, the follower will have to hand back the ten arrows to the leader. This fact is recorded by the leader in his field book with the number of arrows held by the follower acting as a check as to the number of band lengths measured during the work.

Baselines (Fig. 6.34)

The basic principle of measurement is that if two points A and B are fixed, a third point C can be located by measuring AC and BC. With the length of three sides of the triangle being

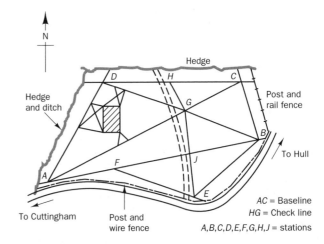

Figure 6.34 Survey baselines (backbone)

known, the triangle can be plotted on a plan. Any area of land required to be surveyed may be divided into a series of triangles which form a framework. The accuracy of any survey will be increased if the framework of triangles is founded on a '**backbone**' or **baseline**, bearing in mind that the smallest number of 'well-conditioned' triangles usually gives the most satisfactory results. All intersections should be clear for plotting giving approximate equilateral triangles if possible, for where points are plotted by striking arcs with beam compasses, representing the measured tie lengths, the determination of intersections at angles of much less than 30° is difficult. For every survey there should be one long 'backbone' or baseline to the survey upon which the surveyor founds the triangles. In high-precision work various corrections may require to be made in the determination of the accuracy of the line length.

Stations

The intersection points of survey lines are called stations and these are established initially by placing ranging rods (and, later, pegs if permanency is required) after a preliminary reconnaissance survey of the site has been made by the survey team. Ancillary points on a survey line are known as **line points**.

Witnessing

All **station points** require witnessing in the event that the position gets displaced after the survey gets underway. Station points should be referenced to adjacent permanent features such as telephone poles, street lamps or other street furniture and dimensions to at least two features carefully taken and recorded. If the station point gets moved it can be accurately repositioned from the recorded dimensions.

Check lines

Additional survey lines, not absolutely essential for the recording of detail, should be incorporated where necessary to confirm measurements taken, hence ensuring that errors in measurement will not go undetected, e.g. line HG in Fig. 6.34 When features such as buildings are to be included in the survey, their positions are fixed by setting out a series of secondary lines running as closely as possible to the features from which offsets are taken.

Offsets (Fig. 6.35)

To locate topographical and man-made features relative to the survey framework, measurements are made of the distances at right angles from the chain or tape line to the boundary or other feature which is required to be recorded. From a series of these offsets the shape of a field boundary or a footpath may be recorded and later plotted. The correct angle of short offsets is judged by eye and should not constitute distances greater than 5 m. Where offsets of a greater length are required other methods must be used.

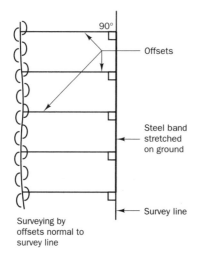

Surveying by
offsets normal to
survey line

(a)

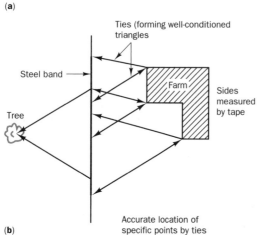

(b)

Accurate location of
specific points by ties

Figure 6.35 Line measurement terminology. (*After* Bannister, Raymond & Baker *Surveying* Longman)

Tie lines

To locate, for example, the corner of a building, a key feature for many surveys, random dimensions from convenient positions along the chain or tape line may be taken. At least two 'ties' should be taken in this instance.

Fieldwork

When considering the basic principles of surveying, if two fixed points A and B are located then a third point C can be formed by measuring AC and BC and the triangle can be subsequently plotted. Any area of land can be divided into a series of 'well-conditioned' triangles (all angles ideally about 60°) which form a framework. To locate topographical and man-made features relative to this framework, measurements are made with the tape from the lines during the course of the survey.

Triangulation

Triangulation is a method of control surveying. In its simplest form the area is divided into a series of standard figures, such as braced quadrilaterals or polygons with central points, the corners of which form a series of accurately located control stations. In Fig. 6.36(a) by the measurement of angles A, B and C and knowing the length of side AB, the length of sides BC and CA can be calculated. In Fig. 6.36(b) the angles marked are measured and the lengths of all the other sides of the whole triangulation and the coordinates of the stations are worked out from these observed angles, the length of the initial side (the baseline) the coordinates of A and the orientation of AB. Measurement of the one line provides the scale of the survey, while the angular observations define the shape. If all of the 20 angles were measured, rather more information would be available than required, but these are used to improve the precision of the final result. Using this system distance measurement by tape is kept to a minimum with the main framework being obtained by good angular measurement. Because of the advent of electromagnetic distance-measuring techniques in recent years the determination of lengths to a higher accuracy previously unobtainable with tapes can be achieved and the layout of the control scheme need not now be restricted to braced quadrilaterals and the centre point polygons. By measuring line lengths only a **trilateration**

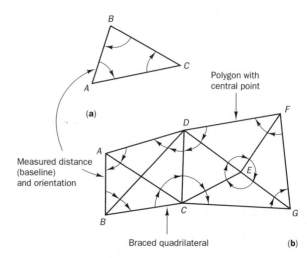

Figure 6.36 Triangulation

framework results. Most modern control schemes involve both angular measurement and the measurement of selected, or all, sides and so should not be simply called triangulation or trilateration surveys, but, by convention, the name triangulation generally applies.

Techniques used with linear measurement

As part of the requirements of the surveying processes unit it is necessary to undertake a site survey. Various techniques and processes are required which are essentially techniques associated with linear measurement. At this stage it is useful to be aware of the procedures and in this section reference will be made to the problems that are likely to be encountered when distance measuring, as it is possible that these will be faced when undertaking an actual survey.

Dealing with obstacles

Technique
To range a line over a hill between two control points or stations which are not visible from each other (Fig. 6.37).

Procedure
1. Set up ranging poles at A and B. An assistant with a ranging pole is stationed at D_2 which is a random point

approximately on the line AB, and from where he can just see the pole at A.
2. The surveyor with a ranging pole walks from A towards D_2 until he can just see B. He is then lined in between A and D_2 by the assistant and places his pole at C_2.
3. The assistant is then lined in between C_2 and B by the surveyor, his position now being at D_3 where he can just see A.
4. The surveyor is then lined in by his assistant to position C_3 on the line D_3A, where he can just see B. This process by the method of **repeated alignment** is continued until all ranging poles are in a straight line.

Technique
Setting out a right angle from a chain or tape line by the 3, 4, 5 unit method (Fig. 6.38).
   This method is based on the mathematical relation that a triangle having sides whose lengths are in equivalents of 3, 4, 5 is a right-angled triangle.

Procedure
1. To set out a right angle A on tape line XY between stations, measure back 12 m from A to point C.
2. With the end of the tape held at A and the 48 m held at C (12 + 16 + 20 m), hold the tape at the 16 m mark and pull taut. This will locate position B at right angles to XY.

Technique
To survey a lake or thickly wooded area (Fig. 6.39).

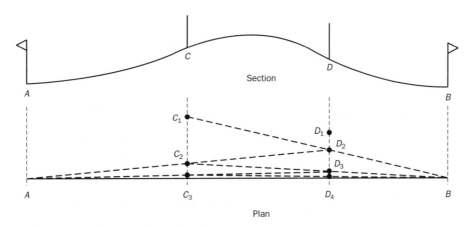

Figure 6.37 Ranging over a hill. (*After* Bannister, Raymond & Baker *Surveying* Longman)

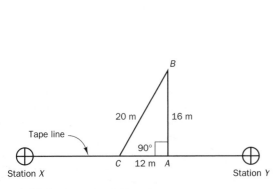

Figure 6.38 Setting out a right angle

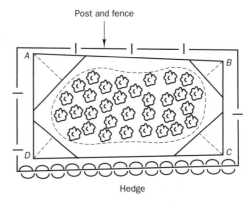

Figure 6.39 Survey of a wooded area. (*After* Bannister, Raymond & Baker *Surveying* Longman)

Procedure

1. A framework of lines is set out around the area and the corners triangulated. Each corner triangle should be checked by suitable check lines shown dotted.
2. Detail of the wood or lake perimeter can be recorded by taking offsets. The method is not very accurate and is called **chain traversing**.

Technique

To measure the length of a chain or tape line across a pond (Fig. 6.40).

Quite often obstacles do not obscure vision but do prevent measurement, and the usual method employing careful mathematical and measuring techniques is shown in Fig. 6.40.

Procedure

1. Two equal offsets *EC* and *FD* are set out perpendicular to *AB* using a tape to construct the right angles. The techniques described for Fig. 6.38 should be used for setting out the offsets.
2. *EF* is measured to supply the missing length *CD*. As a check, *GK* and *HL* may be set out on the other side, if possible, and *KL* measured.

Technique

To measure the length of a chain or tape line across a river (Fig. 6.41).

Using the method illustrated in Fig. 6.41(a):

Procedure

1. Set a ranging rod *H* on the far bank of the river.
2. *CE* is set off on the near bank perpendicular to *AB*, and a pole is ranged in to point *F* between *E* and *H*.
3. A perpendicular is dropped from *F* on to *AB*, meeting at *G*.

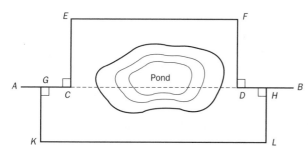

Figure 6.40 Measuring a line across a pond. (*After* Bannister, Raymond & Baker *Surveying* Longman)

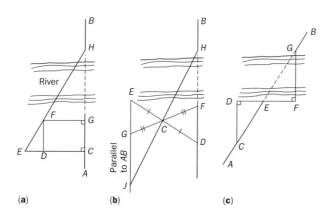

(a)   **(b)**   **(c)**

Figure 6.41 Alternative methods of measuring distance across a river. (*After* Bannister, Raymond & Baker *Surveying* Longman)

4. Distances *CE*, *FG* and *CG* are measured and by the mathematical technique of similar triangles the distance across the river can be found in the following way:

$$\frac{FD}{ED} = \frac{HG}{FG} \text{ by similar triangles}$$

$$\therefore \quad \frac{FD \times FG}{ED} = HG \text{ [equation 1]}$$

but $FD = GC$ and $ED = EC - FG$; substituting into equation 1:

$$HG = \frac{CG \times FG}{EC - FG}$$

Using the method illustrated in Fig. 6.41(b) gives the answer directly and does not involve setting out any angles:

Procedure

1. A line *DE* is set out on the near bank and bisected at *C*.
2. The line *FCG* is now set out such that *FC = CG*.
3. With a pole *H* on the far bank and on the line *AB*, a pole can be set at *J* on the intersection of lines *EG* and *HC* produced backwards, *JG = FG*.

Using the method illustrated in Fig. 6.41(c), where the line crosses the river obliquely:

Procedure

1. Place ranging poles on the line *AB* at *E* and *G* on the near and far bank respectively.
2. A line *DF* is set out along the bank so that *GF* is perpendicular to *DF*.
3. A perpendicular from *D* is constructed to meet *AB* at *C*. The distance across the river can be found in the following way:

$$\frac{EF}{EG} = \frac{DE}{EC}$$

$$\therefore \quad EG = \frac{EF \times CE}{DE}$$

If *DE* is made equal to *EF*, then triangle *EFG* = triangle *DEC* and *CE = EG*.

Adjustment for sloping ground

All measurements in surveying must either be in the horizontal plane, or be corrected to give the projection on this plane. Lines measured on sloping ground must be longer than lines measured on the flat. If the slope is steep, then a correction must be applied. Any slope greater than 3° should be adjusted by either of the following methods.

Stepping (Fig. 6.42)

On ground which has variable slope this is the most satisfactory method which requires no calculation. The measurement is done in short lengths of between 5 and 10 m, the leader holding the length horizontal. The point on the ground below the free end of the band or tape is best located by plumb bob, as illustrated in Fig. 6.42. When 'stepping', it is easier to work downhill than uphill, the follower then having the awkward job of holding the band taut, horizontal and with the end vertically over the previous arrow. The leader has therefore to line himself in.

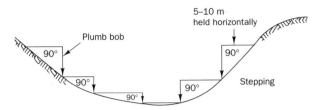

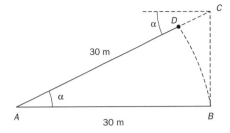

Figure 6.42 Stepping technique for measurement adjustment on sloping ground. (*After* Bannister, Raymond & Baker *Surveying* Longman)

Figure 6.44 Correction to be applied to tape length on sloping ground

Measuring along the slope

This method is most suitable where the ground runs in long regular slopes. The slope is measured with an **Abney level** or **clinometer**, or by **levelling**, a procedure which gives the surface height at points along the slope. Knowing the length of one side and the angle of slope, the correct or plan measurement of the distance between two points can be determined using **trigonometrical** formulae.

Many surveying techniques require the use of the **sine**, **cosine** and **tangent** formulae (Fig. 6.43). These are usually abbreviated to **sin**, **cos** and **tan**.

In triangle *ABC*:

$$\text{sine } \alpha = \frac{BC}{AC} = \frac{\text{opposite}}{\text{hytpotenuse}}$$

$$\text{cosine } \alpha = \frac{AB}{AC} = \frac{\text{adjacent}}{\text{hypotenuse}}$$

$$\text{tangent } \alpha = \frac{BC}{AB} = \frac{\text{opposite}}{\text{adjacent}}$$

In Fig. 6.43, where the slope angle α has been measured by a suitable instrument and the slope length with a tape:

$$\cos \alpha = \frac{\text{correct length}}{\text{slope length}}$$

$$\therefore \quad \text{correct length} = \cos \alpha \times \text{slope length}$$

$$= \cos \alpha \times L$$

$$\text{correction to be subtracted} = \text{slope length} - \text{correct length}$$

$$= L - (\cos \alpha \times L)$$

$$= L(1 - \cos \alpha)$$

This method corrects only the total length of the line, and if intermediate measurements are to be made correctly, adjustments must be made during measurement. In Fig. 6.44 *AD* represents one tape length say 30 m, measured along the slope. What we require is the point *C* beyond *D* such that a plumb bob at *C* will cut the horizontal through *A* at *B*, where *AB* is 30 m on the horizontal, i.e. we require the correction *DC* which is to be added to each tape length measured along the slope.

It can be shown that the correction $DC = \frac{1}{2}\alpha^2 \times AD$, where α is measured in **radians**. A radian is an angle at the centre of a circle subtending an arc whose whole length is equal to the radius of a circle (57° 17′ 45.6″).

Slope can also be expressed as 1 in *n*, which means a rise of 1 unit vertically for *n* units horizontally. For small angles $\alpha = 1/n$ radians.

Figure 6.45 shows the relationship between corrections and slopes for 20 m lengths.

The height difference *h*, between the end positions of a sloping line can be found by using a level. In Fig. 6.46 the

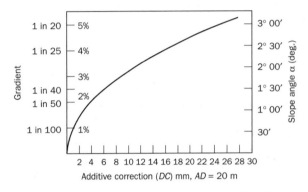

Figure 6.45 Gradient/slope angle corrections. (*After* Bannister, Raymond & Baker *Surveying* Longman)

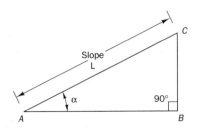

Figure 6.43 The right-angled triangle

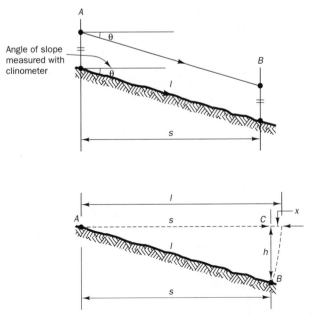

Figure 6.46 Indirect slope correction using height difference

difference between the slope measure α and the horizontal distance s is the slope correction x.

By applying Pythagoras Theorem to triangle ABC

$$\ell^2 = s^2 + h^2$$

but $\qquad s = (\ell - x)$

$$\therefore \quad \ell^2 = (\ell - x)^2 + h^2$$

$$= \ell^2 - 2\ell x + x^2 + h^2$$

$$\therefore \quad 2\ell x = h^2 + x^2$$

$$x = \frac{h^2}{2\ell} + \frac{x^2}{2\ell}$$

Usually the second term is small enough to be ignored and the slope correction reduces to $x = h^2/2\ell$.

Maintaining accuracy during linear measurement

Errors in taking dimensions fall into three classes, namely **mistakes**, **cumulative errors** which accrue in one direction and **compensating errors** which may balance each other by varying techniques.

Mistakes
1. Forgetting to record and book one or more chain, tape or band lengths during a long survey.
2. Confusing the tallies when using a chain.
3. Miscounting the links when using a chain.
4. Confusing 6 m and 9 m when using a tape.
5. Incorrect marking of the end of a chain, tape or band line.
6. Incorrect booking of dimensions in the field book.
7. Mistaking or mishearing dimensions being called by the surveying assistant.

Cumulative errors
These can be **positive** errors which cause the measurement to be **too large** or **negative** errors which cause the measurement to be **too small**. The former category includes:

1. Using a short chain due to bent links, or knots in the connecting rings or using an inadequately repaired tape or band which had previously been broken.
2. Not allowing for slopes when the incline exceeds $3°$ per tape length.
3. Incorrect alignment between stations.
4. The bellowing out of the tape due to wind.
5. Chain links clogged with mud or other debris.

The latter category includes:

1. The flattening of the chain connecting rings.
2. The stretching of the tape which can be significant with some tape materials.

Compensating errors
1. Holding and marking.
2. Variation in tension.
3. Temperature variations which may be positive or negative.

Precise measurement and techniques for adjustment of errors

The principal source of error in precise length measurement when, for example, the baseline of an important survey is being measured is the expansion and contraction of the equipment caused by temperature changes. For long precise measurements tapes are hung in **catenary** clear of the ground (Fig. 6.47). This has the advantage that the ground does not have to be flat and the temperature of the tape can be more conveniently recorded with a thermometer.

Even when suspended the temperature cannot be precisely established, although invar tapes having a low coefficient of expansion are used.

Procedure
1. Measuring tripods are set out along the line to be measured and measuring heads attached which can be accurately levelled and possess fine index marks. The tape is strung between the heads and known weights are attached to wires passing over pulleys on the straining trestles. These provide the tape with even tension. A number of readings of the tape are made through reading glasses attached to the measuring heads.
2. Every measurement in a baseline requires to have certain corrections applied to it.

Temperature correction

Tapes and bands supplied by the manufacturer are at their nominal length under criteria of temperature and tension which are stamped on the case. Tapes stretch with use and quickly lose their **nominal** length. A correction may be applied but it is more convenient to combine tension and temperature together as the field temperatures of the latter rarely coincide. Hence the change in tape length due to temperature, required to bring the tape to its nominal length, is calculated from the temperature correction formula:

$$\text{correction} = \alpha L (t - t_s)$$

where α = coefficient of linear expansion (per $°C$)
$\qquad L$ = length measured (m)
$\qquad t$ = actual temperature ($°C$)
$\qquad t_s$ = standard temperature ($°C$)

As the temperature increases above the standard, the tape expands, the reading becomes too small, and the correction must be added to the observed reading, and vice versa.

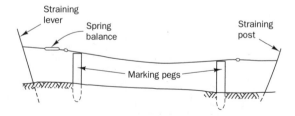

Figure 6.47 Base measurement using a tape in category. (*After* Bannister, Raymond & Baker *Surveying* Longman)

Tension correction

If the tension applied to a tape is different from the standard, a correction will also have to be applied:

$$\text{correction} = (P - P_s)\frac{L}{AE}$$

where
 P = field tension (N)
 P_s = standard tension (N)
 L = length measured (m)
 A = cross-sectional area of band (mm²)
 E = Young's modulus of elasticity for the band (N/mm²)

As the tension increases above the standard the tape expands, the reading becomes too small, and the correction must be added to the observed reading and vice versa. Sometimes the standard tension is recorded in units of kilogram force (kgf). To convert to newtons (N) multiply by 9.81. Young's modulus of elasticity for steel tapes is 200 000 N/mm², and for invar tapes 150 000 N/mm².

Slope correction

This correction, as previously indicated, is always negative as the slope distance is always longer than the horizontal plan dimension required:

$$\text{correction} = \frac{h^2}{2L}$$

where h = difference in level between line extremities (m)
 L = slope length (m)

Sag correction

If a tape is standardised lying along flat ground, a negative sag correction is needed if it is supported in catenary in use, as the chord distance across the bay required is always less than the distance along the tape:

$$\text{correction} = \frac{W^2 L^3}{24 P^2}$$

where W = weight per unit length of the tape (N)
 L = length of tape between supports (span) (m)
 P = tension applied to the tape (N)

If the tape has been standardised in catenary, no correction is necessary as long as the **field tension** P is the same as the **standard tension**.

Height above sea level correction (Fig. 6.48)

Owing to the curvature of the earth, a length ℓ measured at sea level between two points will increase to a length greater than ℓ as these points are produced to a height H above sea

level, each normal to the earth's curve. This correction is always a deduction and therefore **negative**.

$$\ell = (R + H)\theta$$

$$\ell_1 = R\theta$$

$$\therefore \quad \ell_1 = \ell\frac{R}{R + H}$$

$$\text{correction} = \ell - \ell_1 = \ell\left(1 - \frac{R}{R + H}\right)$$

$$= \ell\frac{H}{R + H}$$

$$\text{which is approximately} = \ell\frac{H}{R}$$

where ℓ = length of measured line (m)
 ℓ_1 = length of line at mean sea level (m)
 θ = angle subtended at the centre (radians)
 H = height above mean sea level (m)

The radius of the earth (R) may be taken as 6.367×10^6 m. The above correction is not normally necessary unless it forms the basis of a national triangulation system or if the height above sea level is large and the survey is to be connected into an existing triangulation network.

Scale factor

To understand this correction fully a knowledge of **map projection** is needed. A map projection is a means of representing lines of longitude and latitude of the globe on a flat sheet of paper. The network of lines formed is called a **graticule** and since it is impossible to represent the curved surface of a sphere on a plane, flat surface, there is no perfect projection. Certain projections are correct in some respects and scale may be correct along certain lines. The Ordnance Survey of Great Britain have adopted the Transverse Mercator projection using longitude 2° West as origin. The scale of a map is therefore correct along this line, with increasing scale distortion east and west of this line. This magnification of error, amounting to about 1/1250 in the limits of the British Isles, is cut by reducing the scale along the origin by half this amount. The correct scale would then be obtained along parallels 180 km on either side of 2° West. The maximum scale error is then only 1/2500, which is too small to be scaled on any one Ordnance Survey map.

$$\text{scale factor} = \frac{\text{grid distance}}{\text{ground distance}}$$

The National Grid network is based on the longitude origin of the projection, 2° West. Lines are established parallel at right angles to this line 100 km apart. Measurements east of the origin are referenced **positive** and west **negative**, and for this reason a false origin was created 400 km west of 2° West and 100 km north of latitude 49° North. As a result, all grid coordinates of points in the British Isles are positive **eastings** and **northings**. The scale factor along the central meridian is 0.999 601 3. The local scale factor is 0.999 601 3 × $[1 + (1.23E^2 \times 10^{-8})]$ where E is the distance in km from the central meridian.

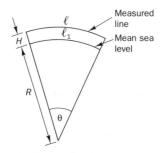

Figure 6.48 Correction for height above sea level

Example

During the measurement in catenary of a survey line of four bays, the information shown below was obtained.

Bay	Measured length (m)	Temp (°)	Difference in level between ends (m)	Tension (N)
1	29.899	18.0	+0.064	178
2	29.901	18.0	+0.374	178
3	29.882	18.1	−0.232	178
4	29.950	17.9	+0.238	178

The tape has a mass of 0.026 kg/m and a cross-sectional area of 3.24 mm^2. It was standardised on the flat at 20 °C under a pull of 89 N. The coefficient of linear expansion for the material of the tape is 0.000011/°C and Young's modulus is 20.7×10^4 N/mm^2. The mean level of the line is 26.89 m above sea level.

Determine the absolute length of the survey line reduced to sea level.

Bay	L	L^3	h	$h^2/2L$
1	29.899	26 728.22	+0.064	0.0001
2	29.901	26 733.58	+0.374	0.0023
3	29.882	26 682.65	−0.232	0.0009
4	29.950	26 865.23	+0.238	0.0009
	119.632	107 009.67		0.004

Tension correction:

$$(P - P_S)\frac{\Sigma L}{AE} = (178 - 89) \times \frac{119.632}{3.24 \times 20.7 \times 10^4}$$
$$= +0.016\,\text{m}$$

Sag correction:

$$\frac{W^2 \Sigma L^3}{24P^2} = \frac{(0.026 \times 9.806)^2 \times 107\,009.67}{24 \times 178^2}$$
$$= 0.009\,\text{m}$$

Temperature correction (based on average of 18 °C, since there is little variation):

$$\alpha \Sigma L(t - t_S) = 0.000\,011 \times 119.632\,(18{-}20)$$
$$= -0.003\,\text{m}$$

Slope length:

$$\Sigma \frac{h^2}{2L} = -0.004\,\text{m}$$

Reduction to mean sea level:

$$\Sigma L \times \frac{H}{R} = -119.632 \times \frac{26.89}{6\,367\,000}$$
$$= -0.001\,\text{m}$$

Absolute length = 119.632 + 0.016 − 0.009
  −0.004 − 0.003 − 0.001
  = 119.631 m

Sources of error: Summary

Wrong length of tape

- If the tape is too long, the measured distance is too short and the correction must be added (and vice versa).
- To obtain an accuracy of 1 : 5000, one end of a 30 m band may be in error by ±0.006 m.

Poor ranging

- If only the distance is required, fine accuracy ranging is not needed, but any offset measurement taken at right angles to the line of the tape will be in error by the amount the tape lies off the correct line.
- To obtain an accuracy of 1 : 5000, one end of a 30 m band may be 0.6 m off line.

Poor straightening

- To obtain an accuracy of 1 : 5000, the centre of a 30 m band may be 0.3 m off line.

Example

After completing a survey, the 30 m band used was checked and found to be 30.056 m long.
(a) What is the length of the line *AB*, observed to be 120.681 m long?
(b) The area of the site calculated from the observed measurements was 2.870 ha. What is the true area of the site?

Answer

(a) Band too long, dimension too short.

$$\text{true distance} = \left(\frac{\text{measured}}{\text{distance}}\right) \times \frac{\text{actual length of band}}{\text{nominal length of band}}$$

$$= 120.681 \times \frac{30.056}{30}$$

$$= 120.906\,\text{m}$$

(b) true area $= \left(\dfrac{\text{measured}}{\text{area}}\right) \times \left(\dfrac{\text{actual length of band}}{\text{nominal length of band}}\right)^2$

$$= 2.870 \times \left(\frac{30.056}{30}\right)^2$$

$$= 2.881\,\text{ha}$$

It should also be noted that 10 000 m^2 = 1 hectare.

Slope

- To obtain an accuracy of 1 : 5000, one end of a 30 m band may be 0.6 m higher or lower than the other end.
- The angle of slope to the horizontal which may be ignored to maintain the above accuracy, is 1°9′.

Sag

- To obtain an accuracy of 1 : 5000, the centre of a 30 m band should not be allowed to sag by more than 0.3 m.

Temperature variation

- To obtain an accuracy of 1 : 5000, the temperature should not vary from standard by more than 18 °C when taping with a steel band.

To complete an understanding of the requirements of linear measurement determination it is necessary to have a clear knowledge of the field procedures to ensure that all data that is required to be recorded is done, so as to avoid repeated visits to the site which could have been avoided if more care had been taken with the preparatory work. After completion of the fieldwork, data is required to be plotted and maps produced to recognised drawing standards.

Fieldwork procedure

1. After a preliminary reconnaissance of the site, make a sketch showing the location of the chosen stations and survey lines.
2. Witness the control stations and note sufficient information to enable each station to be relocated if necessary.
3. Take the bearing from true or magnetic north of at least one of the lines.

Principal features involved in booking lines and recording the data.

- Begin each line at the bottom of a clean page in the field book.
- Use plenty of room and make no attempt to scale the bookings.
- Exaggerate any small irregularities which are capable of being plotted.
- Make clear sketches of all detail, inserting explanatory matter in writing where appropriate. Do not rely on memory.
- Book systematically, proceeding up one side of the survey line and then the other, starting with the side having more detail and hence more offsets.
- Accuracy of measurements depends on the scale to which the survey is to be plotted. Bearing in mind that the scale might be increased after completion of the survey it is better to be more accurate than may appear necessary. Main survey lines should generally be measured to an accuracy of 20 mm and offsets to the nearest 50 mm.
- The perpendicularity of short offsets is normally judged by eye or by swinging the tape, but with longer offsets instrumentation should be used.
- Where the offset would be longer than one tape length, a subsidiary triangle should be employed to ensure accuracy (Fig. 6.49).
- Whole metre values can be written with or without decimal values, e.g. 21.00 or 21.

Office and plotting procedures

1. Preliminary calculations and checking must first be carried out before plotting can commence, e.g. if any survey lines have been measured along regular slopes, the projection of these lengths on the horizontal must be calculated. Check line lengths must also be calculated to confirm measured lengths. Any errors which are revealed may need to be measured again in the field before plotting can start.
2. Many surveys are plotted by **computer-based plotters** where the data is downloaded from a logger. Hand-produced surveys are still satisfactory for the small site and a good

draughtsman can plot a length to within 0.25 mm. Thus, if the scale used is 1 : 500, i.e. 1 mm represents 500 mm on the ground, then 0.25 mm represents 0.125 m on the ground.

3. Surveys should be plotted on good-quality paper, or holland cloth to reduce shrinkage. **4H hardness** pencils are used for drawing the framework and **2H** pencils used for plotting detail. **Waterproof Indian ink** is used for inking in the completed survey.
4. Ancillary equipment, which should be 'on hand' before starting plotting, includes
   - beam compasses for striking large radius arcs
   - a steel straight edge 1 or 2 m long
   - a set of railway curves
   - set squares, protractor, French and flexi-curves
   - colour brushes and a set of stick water colours
   - scales for plotting.
5. Scales are usually cross-referenced to plan purpose and Table 6.5 provides a guide for selection.

Table 6.5 Preferred metric system scales

Small-scale maps	Large-scale maps	Site plans	Detail plans
1 : 1 000 000	1 : 10 000	1 : 500	1 : 20
to	to	to	to
1 : 20 000	1 : 1000	11 : 50	1 : 1 (full size)

- **Topography surveys** are undertaken to produce maps and plans of the natural and man-made features. A plan is generally used where a detail is required to be drawn true to scale while a map has many features represented by symbols. Into this category fall plans which are used for engineering design and administration purposes and maps which have a multitude of uses: navigational, recreational, geographical, geological, military, exploration. Generally the scale of these maps and plans is in the range 1 : 25 000 to 1 : 1 000 000.
- **Engineering surveys** (e.g. Fig. 6.50) are undertaken to produce maps required before, during and after any

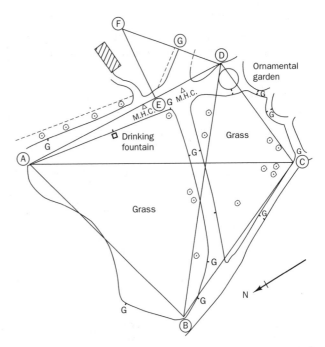

Figure 6.50 Peel Park survey. (*After* Bannister, Raymond & Baker *Surveying* Longman)

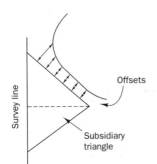

Figure 6.49 The use of subsidiary triangles. (*After* Bannister, Raymond & Baker *Surveying* Longman)

engineering works: roads, railways and in addition volumes of earthworks and curve setting out data is needed to be determined. Generally the scale of these maps and plans are as follows:

- architectural work, building work, location drawings: 1 : 50, 1 : 200
- site plans, civil engineering works: 1 : 500, 1 : 1000, 1 : 1250, 1 : 2500.
- town surveys, highway surveys: 1 : 1250, 1 : 2000, 1 : 2500, 1 : 5000, 1 : 10 000, 1 : 20 000, 1 : 50 000
- **Cadastral surveys** are undertaken to produce plans of property boundaries for legal purposes: 1 : 500, 1 : 1250, 1 : 2500.

6. It is good practice to draft out the survey lines on tracing paper so that by overlaying this on the paper to be used the survey may be properly centred on that sheet. The 'North' point should always be shown and preferably pointing towards the top of the sheet.

7. A line to represent the longest survey line is drawn and the length scaled off. By striking arcs usually with beam compasses the other stations are established and the network of triangles drawn. Check lines are scaled off and compared with actual distances. Offsets and ties are systematically plotted in the same order in which they were booked, i.e. working from beginning to the end of each line up one side and then the other. The right angles for offsets may be set out by set square or by using an offset scale.

8. When the points are plotted the detail is drawn in, using, wherever possible, **standardised symbols**. Some flexibility is needed: e.g. a feature of 4000 mm width on a 1 : 500 scale plan can be shown by two fine parallel lines 0.8 mm apart while on any plan of scale smaller than this a single line is sufficient.

9. After the detail has been drawn in, the plan should be taken to the site and checked. If no detail has been omitted and no error found, the plan is inked in, North point drawn and any necessary lettering and titling carried out. A scale line should be drawn on the plan, relating plan length to ground length, which gives in the future an indication if any plan shrinkage has occurred. If it is necessary to photostat the detail, some distortion of scale occurs.

Fig. 6.50 shows the plotted survey in Peel Park, Salford, and sample pages from the field book used for the plotting of the survey are illustrated in Fig. 6.51.

Self-assessment tasks

1. Define each of the following terms: (a) baseline; (b) chain line; (c) detail line; (d) check line; (e) offset; (f) tie line.
2. What is meant by the term 'well-conditioned triangle'?
3. The plan of a field having an area of 34 872 hectares covers 55 800 mm^2 of paper. Determine the scale.
4. A field measurement with a 30 m tape was found to be 10 hectares. The tape was later found to be 29.86 m long. What is the true area of the field?
5. Five bays of a line *AB* were measured under a tension of 53 N and the following data recorded:

Length of span (m)	Rise between ends of span (m)
29.149	0.027
29.944	0.196
29.474	0.126
29.514	0.055
29.690	0.336

Field temperature $= 10\,°C$

Tape standardised on the flat under a pull of 89 N and at a temperature of 20 °C. Tape data:

Coefficient of thermal expansion $= 0.000\,011/°C$
Young's modulus of elasticity $= 207\,kN/mm^2$
Density $= 7700\,kg/m^3$
Cross-sectional area $= 6\,mm^2$

Determine the length of line *AB*.

6. Draw up typical field book entries for the lines of a tape and offset survey illustrated in Fig. 6.52.
7. Produce referenced sketches to show how the following operations are undertaken:
   (a) Record of a boundary hedge curving rapidly away from a survey line.
   (b) Measure a line where a rise in the ground prevents visibility between the stations.
   (c) Set out a right angle from a survey line.
   (d) Measure a line which crosses a river of 50 m width.
8. Practical work: Site survey by linear measurement. Brief:
   (a) Select a small area of public land close to your place of study.
   (b) Working in groups of three, select, position and witness at least five control points for the completion of a small survey.
   (c) By practical application and use of tapes, chains or bands record the features of the site in a field book in accordance with recognised procedures.
   (d) From the field book produce a drawing to a recognised scale showing the site features.
9. Calculate the scale of a plan where 1 mm represents 0.5 m.
10. An area was measured on a plan using a linear scale and found to be 125 mm × 275 mm. Calculate the ground area in square metres if the scale is (a) 1:1250, (b) 1:500, and check your answers using mathematical proportions.
11. Plot the position of a tree Z, to a scale of 1:200 from the following data obtained through a chain survey:
    (a) Trilateration
    length XZ = 17 m, length YZ = 11.8 m, length XY = 25 m
    (b) Offsets
    length OZ = 7 m, length XO = 15.5 m, length OY = 9.5 m
    The tree is deciduous and has a 2.5 m radius spread of branches.
12. A survey line AB was measured along a 8° gradient. The slope distance was measured as 52.55 m. Calculate the plan length of the line to one significant figure.
13. A survey line AB is interrupted by a river which has a width that cannot easily be measured. On the near bank a right angle is set out at point C for a distance of 20 m and a point D is established. At point E, 40 m back from C on the line AC, a second right angle is set out to F on the same side of AC as point D. Point F is aligned with B and D. Line EF measures 31 m. Calculate the width of the river BC.

Height control: history

An early form of levelling instrument consisted of a glass U-tube filled with water, the tube being firmly fixed to a stand held on the ground. An observer viewing the **imaginary** level line between the two columns of water was able to sight on to a graduated rod some distance away from the U-tube. By

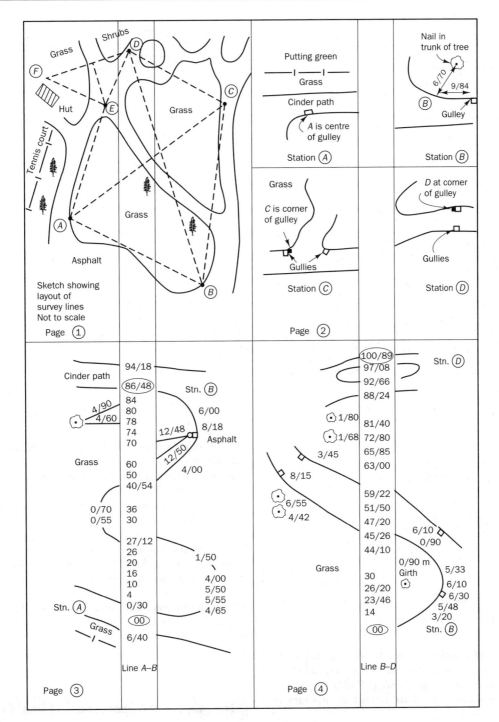

Figure 6.51 Field book – Peel Park survey. (*After* Bannister, Raymond & Baker *Surveying* Longman)

recording differences between this level line at different positions of the graduated rod, relative differences between ground levels could be determined.

Principles and definitions

Levelling is the operation required in the comparison of heights of points on the surface of the earth. A **level surface** or **line** is one which is at a constant height relative to mean sea level, and since it follows the mean surface of the earth it must be a **curved** line.

A **horizontal surface** or **line** is a plane flat surface or straight line which passes through a point at right angles to

the pull of gravity at that point. It is therefore a **tangent** to the curve of a level surface. Over short distances a level and horizontal line are taken to coincide, but over long distances a correction for their divergence becomes necessary.

A **datum surface** is any level surface to which the elevations of points can be referred. The surface most commonly adopted as a datum is the mean level of the sea. The present datum of the Ordnance Survey levelling of Great Britain is the Newlyn datum, often referred to as Ordnance Datum (OD). It is the mean level of the open sea at Newlyn in Cornwall and was computed from hourly observations taken over a period of six years from 1915 to 1921. Some areas around the British Isles have ground levels below the mean sea level at Newlyn and they are said to have negative levels.

LEEDS COLLEGE OF BUILDING LIBRARY

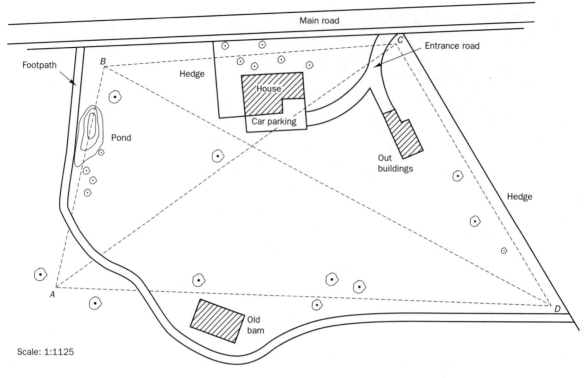

Figure 6.52 Survey of Hill House

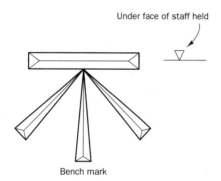

Figure 6.53 Ordnance Survey bench marks

A reduced level of a point is its height above or below the surface adopted as a datum. Most surveys of any substance are related to Ordnance Datum Newlyn (ODN) but where only relative differences in level are needed an arbitrary or local datum can be used.

Bench marks are stable reference points, the reduced levels of which are accurately determined by the process of levelling. Bench marks can be defined as points of known elevation above Ordnance Datum which have been established by the surveyors of the Ordnance Survey. The commonest type of bench mark is illustrated in Fig. 6.53. This type is usually chiselled in the form of a broad arrow on permanent features such as bridge parapets and house walls.

The centre of the bar across gives the level (to 0.01 m indicated on the 1:1250 and 1:2500 scale maps) at which the foot of the staff should be held. Values of bench marks are related to Ordnance Datum Newlyn (ODN). **Temporary bench marks,** which are of a less permanent nature, are often established on a construction site to control the level of, say, an excavation. These are usually related to a permanent bench mark which may be some distance away with the level transferred to site by a technique called 'flying levelling'.

Three other types of Ordnance Survey bench mark may be encountered:

Fundamental bench marks. These form part of the main levelling network of the British Isles and consist of 225×225 mm granite or concrete pillars built into rock with a metal bolt set on top.

Flush brackets. These are metal plates mortared into the face of buildings. The reduced level refers to the small platform at the point of the broad arrow mark.

Bench marks on horizontal surfaces. These occur less frequently and consist of bolt bench marks, rivet and pivot bench marks.

The purpose and applications of height control

There are five main applications of levelling or **height control:**

1. The determination of the relative vertical heights between two stations or points on the ground.
2. Contouring, which, when completed, provides a picture of the ground topography related to vertical heights above a datum, usually Ordnance Datum. A contour is defined as a line representing the earth's surface along which all positions are of equal elevation.
3. Planning of roads and railways to ensure that gradients, curve alignment and levels are within the set design limits produced by the appropriate controlling authority.
4. Planning of underground services such as pipelines to ensure that correct gradients and levels can be integrated into the design and the pipeline excavation controlled at the correct depths during excavation for installation.

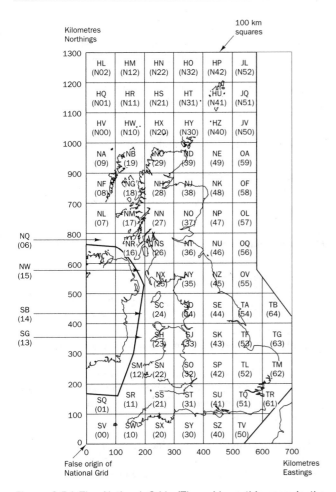

Figure 6.54 The National Grid. (The grid on this map is the National Grid taken from the Ordnance Survey map with the permission of the Controller of the Stationery Office, Crown copyright)

5. Fixing site levels to ensure that road levels are related correctly to the components of building construction such as correct position of foundations, damp-proof courses, etc.

Each of these applications will be covered in greater detail after an understanding of the terminology, instrumentation and procedures of height control has been gained.

Terminology used with height control

Ordnance Survey

The Ordnance Survey produce maps and are responsible for the plan referencing system for the British Isles. The country has been gridded to form the basis of a **rectangular coordinate system** devised for plotting and providing a unique reference for any feature shown on the maps they produce. All the maps produced can be fitted into the grid system and the reference of any point on the map is the same as for any other map drawn to a different scale. Figure 6.54 illustrates the **National Grid** referencing system.

The grid network is based on the longitude origin of the projection 2° West, previously referred to in the discussion of linear measurement. Lines are established parallel and at

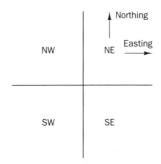

Figure 6.55 The four quadrants

right angles to this line 100 km apart. To avoid dealing with positive and negative measurements a false origin was created in the sea, south-west of the Scilly Isles, 400 km west of 2° W and 100 km north of latitude 49° N. Figure 6.55 illustrates the layout of the 100 km grid lines and to prevent the need for large coordinate values each square is identified by a pair of capital letters. The grid is initially divided into 500 km squares, each being identified by a letter. The major squares are then subdivided into twenty-five 100 km squares, each being lettered alphabetically commencing from the right-hand corner. Every 100 km square has a unique alphabetical reference, e.g. Hull lies in TA and London in TQ.

All the maps produced by the Ordnance Survey are based on this grid.

1 : 25 000 scale maps

At this scale the 100 km grid square is divided into 10 km squares, each representing the sheet limit of the map. The maps are identified in terms of tens of kilometres, e.g. SE47. SE identifies the particular 100 km square in which it is located and the 4 and 7 indicate that its south-west corner lies 40 km east and 70 km north of the south-west corner of grid square SE.

1 : 10 000 scale maps

At this scale, using the previous SE47 as an example, the area is covered by four maps, each of which is identified by the quadrant in which it lies. To obtain the reference for the 1 : 10 000 map, add the quadrant to the map reference. The four quadrants are identified in Fig. 6.55.

Therefore the map reference might be SE47 NW.

1 : 2 500 scale map

This is a popular scale map used by planners, local authorities and statutory undertakers for recording information such as positions of drains, sewers and water pipes in rural areas. At this scale, plans cover an area of 1 km² and are identified by dividing the 100 km square into 1 km squares numbered from 1 to 99. The grid reference of the south-west corner identifies the plan. South-east again identifies the 100 km grid square and the number, say 4872, indicates that its south-west corner lies 48 km east and 72 km north of the south-west corner of the 100 km grid square SE.

1 : 1 250 scale map

This is the most popular scale map for use in urban areas. At this scale such plans cover one of the four quadrants illustrated on Fig. 6.55 with the plans being identified by their quadrant of the relevant 1 : 2500 scale plan, say SE4872 NE.

Summary

SE47	–	two letters and two numbers, 1 : 25 000 scale map
SE47 NW	–	two letters, two numbers and a quadrant, 1 : 10 000 scale map
SE4872	–	two letters and four numbers 1 : 2500 scale map
SE4872 NE	–	two letters, four numbers and a quadrant, 1 : 1250 scale map

Every Ordnance Survey map is printed with grid lines spaced 1 km apart but the 1 : 2500 and 1 : 1250 scale plans have grid lines at 100 m intervals. To define a specific point such as a house within the 1 km grid, it is necessary to divide the sides into tenths or 100 m sections. The house may then be given a six-figure reference, e.g. SE485726 NE indicating an easting of 48.5 km and a northing of 72.6 km. Note that the eastings are always quoted first. For further accuracy a grid reference of eight or ten figures may be quoted.

The popular 1 : 2500 and 1 : 1250 scale maps are uncoloured topographical plans. Spot heights of roads and other relevant points are indicated and the position and value of bench marks related to Ordnance Datum Newlyn are shown.

Levelling terminology

The following terminology is illustrated in Fig. 6.56.

Bench mark (BM). A fixed point on the earth's surface whose level above Ordnance Datum is known.

Ordnance Datum (OD). Mean sea level to which all other levels are related. Set by the Ordnance Survey and related to Newlyn in Cornwall. The term **A.O.D.** stands for 'above ordnance datum'.

Backsight. The first sight taken after the levelling instrument has been set up. A sight taken usually on a levelling staff at a point whose height is known or can be calculated.

Foresight. The last sight taken to a point whose height is usually required to carry on the line of levels from another instrument set up.

Intermediate sight. Any sight taken on a levelling staff other than the first or last from any instrument set up.

Reduced level (RL). The calculated level of a point above or below the datum being used, usually Ordnance Datum Newlyn (ODN).

Height of collimation or **Height of instrument (H of I).** The height of the horizontal line as seen through the eyepiece of the instrument telescope above the datum.

Rise and fall. The method of booking staff readings during a level survey which gives a full mathematical check on the reduction of levels to Ordnance Datum. The advent of calculators has made this method of booking the most time consuming.

Collimation. The method of booking which relates staff readings to the height of instrument when determining the reduced level of any point. The most popular and quickest method of booking.

A level line. This is a line which is at a constant height relative to mean sea level, and since it follows the mean surface of the earth it must be a curved line.

A horizontal line. This is tangential to the level line at any particular point, since it is perpendicular to the direction of gravity at that point.

Change point. This is the point at which both a foresight and consecutively a backsight are taken during work which requires a significant number of instrument position changes. At each instrument movement, readings on the change point ensure a continuity of levels from a single position of known level.

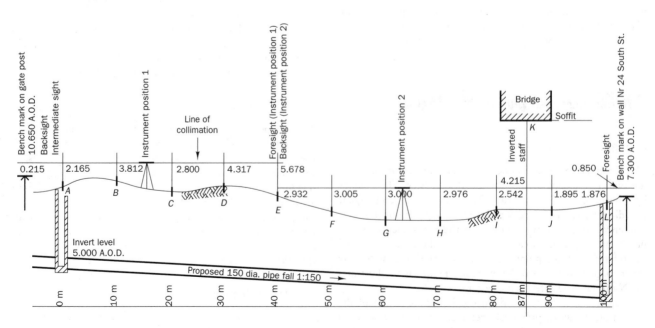

Figure 6.56 Levelling terminology

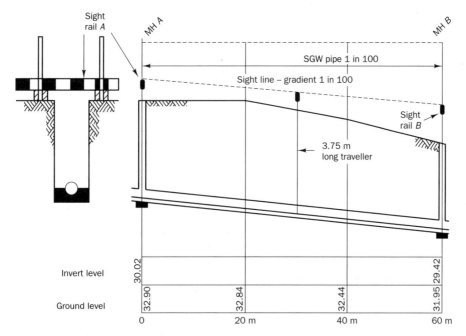

Figure 6.57 Sight rails and travellers. (*After* Bannister, Raymond & Baker *Surveying* Longman)

Sight rail (Fig. 6.57). This consists of a board fixed horizontally to two stout pegs driven into the ground. The rails, sometimes referred to as profiles, are established by the engineer to define the plane of the finished work relative to a level above the ground.

Traveller (or **boning rod**). This is a portable sight rail with a vertical support whose length defines the level of the finished work below the sight rail plane. Used extensively when excavation of trenches is being carried out. An observer sighting the top of the traveller from a sight rail some distance away can quickly ascertain whether or not the trench excavation is at the required depth.

Curvature and refraction (Fig. 6.58). From the terminology of level and horizontal lines, the line of collimation is not a level line but is tangential to the level line. When sights are long, corrections must be applied, i.e. when the deviation of the tangent from the circles becomes significant. Taking a level line as being the circumference of a circle whose centre is the earth's centre, the required correction can be deduced as follows.

Let L be the position of the instrument which is directed towards a staff held vertically at X, i.e. held along the extension of radius $OX (= R)$:

$$(OY)^2 = (OL)^2 + (LY)^2 \text{ by Pythagoras}$$

and $\qquad OL = OX' = R \text{ (approximately)}$

$$(R + X'Y)^2 = R^2 + (LY)^2$$
$$R^2 + 2RX'Y + (X'Y)^2 = R^2 + (LY)^2$$
$$2RX'Y + (X'Y)^2 = (LY)^2$$
$$X'Y (2R + X'Y) = (LY)^2$$

$$X'Y = \frac{(LY)}{2R + X'Y}$$

Since $X'Y$ is small compared to XY the expression approximates to

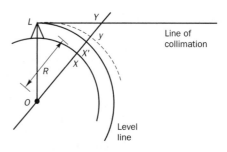

Figure 6.58 Curvature and refraction

$$X'Y = \frac{(LY)^2}{2R} \text{ km [or } 0.078 \times (LY)^2 \text{ m]}$$

where $\quad X'Y =$ curvature correction (km)
$\quad LY =$ distance (km)
$\quad 2R =$ diameter of the earth (km)

Rays of light are refracted by differing conditions of the atmosphere. As air density reduces with altitude, light rays from a higher altitude are refracted downwards as they pass through progressively denser air, so that the line of collimation actually cuts the staff at y. If R_1 is taken as the radius of curvature of that line, then

$$Yy = \frac{LY^2}{2R_1}$$

and the total correction for refraction and curvature is

$$X'Y = (LY)^2 \left(\frac{1}{2R} - \frac{1}{2R_1} \right)$$

and the coefficient of refraction is

$$K = \frac{\text{radius curvature of earth}}{\text{radius of curvature of line of collimation}} = \frac{R}{R_1}$$

$$\therefore \quad X'Y = \frac{(LY)^2}{2R} (1 - K)$$

Conventionally $K = \frac{1}{7}$ over land

$$\therefore \quad X'Y = 0.078 \left(1 - \frac{1}{7}\right)(LY)^2$$

$$= 0.67 D^2 \text{ m (where } D = (LY) \text{ km)}$$

Parallax. When viewing a levelling staff through the telescope of a level the apparent movement of the image of the objective (the staff) relative to the cross-hairs of the eyepiece is known as **parallax** and is caused by the image not being in the plane of the cross-hairs. If a slight movement in the position of the eye, while viewing, results in this apparent movement, it indicates that the telescope is not properly focused.

Level and ancillary equipment used for height control

Level equipment

Six basic types of levels are in common use.

Dumpy level (Fig. 6.59)

In a dumpy level the telescope and vertical spindle are cast as one piece. The levelling head consists of two plates, the telescope being mounted on the upper plate while the lower plate screws directly on to a tripod. The two plates are held apart by three levelling screws (**footscrews**) and adjustments to these enable accurate levelling of the instrument to be carried out. When levelling has been effected using the bubble attached to the telescope, the instrument should remain level regardless of the direction in which the telescope is pointing.

Tilting level (Fig. 6.60)

With this instrument, and unlike the dumpy level, the telescope is not rigidly fixed to the vertical spindle and is capable of a slight tilt in the vertical plane about an axis placed immediately below the telescope. The movement is controlled by a fine setting screw at the eyepiece end of the telescope and the bubble is brought to the centre of its run before each reading by means of this screw. Tilting levels are robust and capable of the highest accuracy and many modern levels, whether for precise work or for ordinary levelling, incorporate the principle.

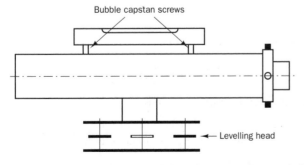

Figure 6.59 The Dumpy level. (*After* Bannister, Raymond & Baker *Surveying* Longman)

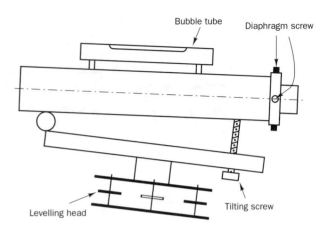

Figure 6.60 The tilting level. (*After* Bannister, Raymond & Baker *Surveying* Longman)

Automatic level

There is currently a large range of levelling instruments available for hire or purchase with no precise bubble attached. The telescopes of these instruments need only be approximately levelled and then a compensating device, usually based on a pendulum system inside the telescope, corrects for any residual mislevelment. These levels are popular because of the ease of use.

Precise level

Precise levels possess a high magnification and measure to the highest accuracy. They are principally used in geodetic surveys, generally carried out on a national basis, which provide survey stations, precisely located, long distances apart. An account is taken of the earth's curvature and the accurate measurements taken form part of the science of geodesy in which the size and shape of the earth is examined. The precise level can also be used to measure small vertical displacements of structures and in the checking and alignment of machinery. An essential feature of these instruments is a parallel plate micrometer. The device consists of a parallel glass plate fitted in front of the object lens and given a tilting motion by the rotation of a micrometer head at the eye end of the telescope. The unit enables the interval between the horizontal cross-hair and the nearest staff gradation to be read directly to 0.1 mm rather than be estimated.

Cowley level

This instrument is such that neither lenses nor a bubble tube is used in its construction. Owing to the absence of any form of magnifying device, its range is limited to around 30 m, with its accuracy over that distance being in the order ±5 mm. It was used for coarse levelling in building work but is not often seen on site today.

Laser level

Two types of laser are in common usage: the **rotating laser** where the laser beam spins out a horizontal beam of light or on some units a sloping plane and the **pipe laser** where a beam of laser light defines the line or gradient of a pipeline or tunnel. Laser safety is covered by BS 4803: 1983, 'Radiation safety of laser products and equipment'. Rotating lasers can use a variegated range of light-emitting equipment to produce the visible beam of red laser light emitted from the tube mounted vertically in the unit and shining on the prism head which can be rotated at varying speeds. The range of most instruments is between 100 and 300 m and some units have a self-levelling facility. Most instruments operate from a 12-volt rechargeable battery, although 6-volt models using an infra-red laser diode, which produces an invisible beam of light, are available. Photoelectric sensors may also be used with visible-beam lasers and some manufacturers produce 'laser wands' that are special staffs with driven sensors that automatically seek and find the level of the laser plane.

Ancillary equipment used for levelling work

Tripod

The timber or metal mounting has a machine platten on which the instrument is fixed via a screw which passes through a hole in the centre of the plate and onto the instrument. Some tripods incorporate a levelling bubble.

Levelling staff (Fig. 6.61)

Staffs used for ordinary levelling work are sectional and are assembled either telescopically or by slotting onto one another vertically. Most staves are now manufactured in an aluminium alloy for lightness although wooden staves made of mahogany are available. BS 4484: Part 1: 1969 requires lengths of either 3 m, 4 m or 5 m on extension, upon which the closed lengths depend. Staves having an extended length of 4.267 m may also

be encountered, being the equivalent imperial dimension for the **Sopwith staff.** The British Standard requires upright figuring with graduations 10 mm deep spaced at 10 mm intervals, the lower three graduations in each 100 mm interval being connected by a vertical band to form an E shape, natural or reversed. The 50 mm or 100 mm intervals are located by these shapes. Readings can be estimated to 1 mm over short sighting distances or use of a parallel plate micrometer can be made.

To assist in holding the staff in a vertical position, a small circular spirit level is often incorporated at the rear of the staff.

When using a precise level a special staff is required which incorporates a graduated invar strip fitted into a wooden frame. This is fastened at the bottom and spring mounted at the top so that the calibrated length is unaffected by temperature effects on the frame. Two folding handles and a circular level are also provided. The staff is always set up on a steel base plate and may be supported by a pair of struts, hinged to the top and of adjustable length, so that the staff can be maintained in a vertical position. The invar strip has two sets of graduation lines at 10 mm intervals, but these are displaced and numbered differently so that two different readings can be obtained for each sighting.

A field check is possible because the two readings must differ by 3.0155 mm. Figure 6.62 shows a close-up view of part of the levelling staff. The reading observed by a surveyor looking through the eyepiece would be 2.035 m.

Level books

In the same way that linear measurement is recorded in a **field book** when undertaking a site survey, a level book is used to record and reduce staff readings to levels. Figure 6.63 illustrates a typical layout where the readings are to be reduced by the **rise and fall method**. Figure 6.64 illustrates the layout where the **height of instrument** (collimation) method is used.

Figure 6.61 Levelling staff

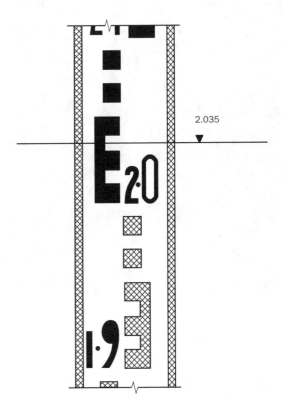

Figure 6.62 Levelling staff reading

Date:						Name & Location of site:	
Name of Surveyor:						....	
Backsight	Intermediate	Foresight	Rise	Fall	Reduced level	Distance	Remarks

Figure 6.63 Booking by rise and fall

Date:					Name & Location of site:	
Name of Surveyor:					....	
Backsight	Intermediate	Foresight	Height of instrument	Reduced level	Distance	Remarks

Figure 6.64 Booking by height of collimation

Figure 6.65 Digital level

Digital level data logger (Fig. 6.65)

With the advent of information technology and the increasing use of automatic instruments, much work has been devoted to the automatic registration of levelling observations. Recent advances in digital electronics have facilitated the design and production of digital levels. Using electronic scanning, the instrument evaluates staff images. By use of a keyboard, information relating to levels or the features of a site can be loaded into a **data logger** where the information stored can be down-loaded back to the office using appropriate software. In this way a survey or level plot can be produced relatively quickly.

Tapes and bands

The use of tapes and bands for linear measurement has been covered in the previous section and the same techniques and processes are used when linear measurement is incorporated into levelling work.

Personal protective equipment

Health and safety legislation covers the use of surveying equipment in the field and it is sufficient to say that care and repetitive safe working procedures should be incorporated into all surveying operations. If the surveyor can sequence surveying activities into regular order then accidents should not happen. Simple tasks such as carrying ranging rods with the point downwards and not throwing items of equipment between surveyor and chainman are all parts of good working practice. BS 4803: 1983, 'Radiation safety of laser products and equipment' covers the aspect of safety when using laser level devices.

The surveyor's telescope (Fig. 6.66)

Although not part of the syllabus for the surveying processes unit, any student studying and using surveying instrumentation should be aware of the mechanics of telescope lenses.

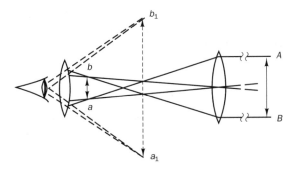

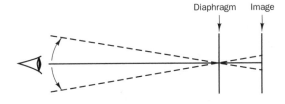

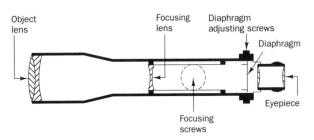

Figure 6.66 The surveyor's telescope. (*After* Bannister, Raymond & Baker *Surveying* Longman)

The **Kepler type** of telescope, consisting of two convex lenses mounted so that their principal axes lie on the same line to form the optical axis of the instrument, is the one used in surveying. The converging object lens *AB*, which is the one nearest to the object, forms a real image *ab*, the rays from which pass on to the **eyepiece** where they are refracted again and form a vertical image a_1b_1 inverted and magnified, at some convenient distance in front of the eye. **Magnification** is an important property of surveying telescopes. The field of view diminishes with increase in magnification and in order to obtain a bright image of the staff, the clear aperture of the objective needs to be increased as magnification increases.

The diaphragm (Fig. 6.67)

To provide positive and visible horizontal and vertical reference lines in the telescope, a **diaphragm** is inserted in front of the eyepiece in a plane at right angles to the optical axis. There are a number of forms of diaphragm (also called **cross-hairs**, **graticule** or **reticule**) but nowadays it is usually a thin glass plate on which the lines are engraved. The imaginary line passing through the intersection normal to the cross-hairs and through the optical centre of the object glass, is called the line of collimation of the instrument and all level readings are taken to this line.

Internal focusing instruments and parallax (Fig. 6.68)

The eyepiece and object lens are on modern instruments mounted in a tube of fixed length, a movable concave lens moved by rack and pinion gearing inserted between them. Many variations of the telescope exist but the main purpose remains the same, i.e. to define precisely a line of sight and to magnify the target. When focusing the telescope, the real image formed by the objective lens is made to lie in the same plane as the diaphragm. If this is not done errors in staff reading will result due to the phenomenon of **parallax**.

The bubble tube (Fig. 6.69)

Whereas the telescope of a level gives extended lines of sight in the horizontal plane, the bubble tube enables those lines to be brought horizontal. The tubes are between 50 and 125 mm and are ground to circular profile in longitudinal section. The sensitivity of the bubble is increased as the radius increases. The top surface of the tube is graduated symmetrically about its centre with individual graduations usually at 2 mm spacing. The angular value of one division is indicated on the tube. When in correct adjustment the bubble should remain central about its centre regardless of movement of the telescope in the horizontal plane.

Figure 6.67 The diaphragm. (*After* Bannister, Raymond & Baker *Surveying* Longman)

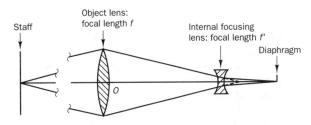

Figure 6.68 Internal focusing telescope. (*After* Bannister, Raymond & Baker *Surveying* Longman)

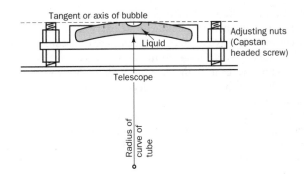

Figure 6.69 The bubble tube

Techniques and principles associated with the process of levelling

Setting up the level (Fig. 6.70)

(i) Screw the lower plate of the instrument on the head of the tripod whose legs have been opened to about 60° and firmly fixed in the ground.

(ii) The circular bubble should be brought to its central position, using the footscrews or 'ball and socket assembly'. The usual procedure is illustrated in Fig. 6.70.

(iii) Rotate footscrews 1 and 2 in opposite directions, at the same time the bubble can be set on the line 1–2. The bubble will move in the direction of rotation of the left thumb, i.e. if the left thumb is rotating footscrew 1 clockwise, the bubble will move to the left.

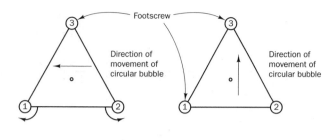

Prisms reflect an image of both ends of the bubble into the eyepiece: Image split down centre. As the telescope is tilted, the two halves appear to move in opposite directions. The instrument is levelled up when the two halves of the bubble are coincident.

Figure 6.70 Levelling the instrument

(iv) By rotation of footscrew 3 only, the bubble can be centred in the target ring.

(v) To eliminate parallax turn the telescope to the sky and focus the eyepiece so that the cross-hairs are clear and distinct. This is achieved by turning the eyepiece, which is threaded into the telescope barrel. After this has been completed, sight the levelling staff and focus the image with the focusing screw so that when the eye is moved slightly there is no relative movement between the image and the cross-hairs.

(vi) If the instrument is a tilting level, centre the sensitive bubble using the tilting screw prior to the taking of every reading. Ensure that the tripod remains untouched when taking readings.

Steps (ii) to (vi) are regarded as temporary adjustments. There is only one permanent adjustment necessary for a tilting level to ensure that it is in good adjustment, i.e. to ensure that the bubble tube axis is parallel to the telescope axis so that when the bubble is central the line of sight is horizontal. The procedure for the adjustment, which is usually carried out in the field, is described later after the procedure for taking and recording readings has been reviewed. Two permanent adjustments are required for the dumpy level, the first being the same as for the tilting level and the second to ensure that the bubble tube axis is set perpendicular to the vertical axis.

This test and adjustment are the same for the plate bubble on a theodolite and are described in the section dealing with angular measurement.

Procedure in levelling (Fig. 6.71)

To find the difference in ground level between points *A* and *F*.

(i) Assume the level is in perfect adjustment and set up correctly at instrument station 1.

(ii) With the staff positioned at *A* take a reading – this will be a **backsight**.

(iii) Transfer the staff to *B* and take a reading – this will be a **foresight**.

(iv) Move the level to instrument station 2 and set up as previously.

(v) Take a second reading on the staff at *B* from the new instrument position – this is a **backsight**. The lengths of the backsight and foresight at any instrument position should be approximately equal to eliminate the possibility of instrument error.

(vi) Transfer the staff to *C* and take a reading – this will be a **foresight** again.

(vii) The above process is repeated, preferably working between bench marks of known level.

(viii) Where a number of staff readings are taken between the foresight and the backsight, these are known as **intermediate sights**, as indicated at instrument position 3 and staff position *D*.

Reducing levels

There are two methods of reducing levels in the level or field book:

- collimation method
- rise and fall method

Collimation method (also known as height of instrument)

Booking and reducing the levels shown in Fig. 6.71 is carried out as follows. The first reading with the staff on the bench mark is a backsight (staff reading 3.752) and this is entered in

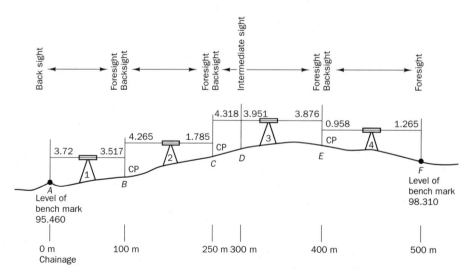

Figure 6.71 The levelling procedure

the backsight column. The reduced level of the bench mark is 95.46 and this is entered in the reduced level column on the same horizontal line as the backsight.

The sum of the backsight and the reduced level gives the height of instrument 99.212 (95.46 + 3.752) and this is entered in the height of instrument column. The next sight on the staff at B is a foresight (staff reading 3.517) and this is entered in the foresight column on the next horizontal line in the field book. The foresight is subtracted from the height of instrument to determine the reduced level of position B, 95.603 (99.212 − 3.517) and this is entered in the reduced level column.

When the instrument is set up at location 3 and sighted onto the staff at D, this sight is neither a foresight nor a backsight, but an intermediate sight and its value 3.951 is entered in the intermediate sight column. It is reduced in the same way as the foresight.

The full tabulation is shown in Table 6.6.

To check the mathematical accuracy of the determination of the reduced levels (not a check on the accuracy of the readings) the calculation is as follows: The difference of the sum of the backsights and foresights should equal the difference between the first and last reduced levels.

Rise and fall method

The terms 'rise' and 'fall' mean the rise or fall of a station relative to the preceding station, i.e. rise in consecutive readings means a fall in level between those stations and a fall in consecutive readings means a rise in level between those stations. The rise or fall of a station is added or subtracted to the reduced level of the preceding station to obtain the reduced level of the station.

The 'tabulation' is shown in Table 6.7 and each step should

be compared with the previous method to gain an understanding of procedures.

To check the mathematical accuracy of the determination of the reduced levels (not a check on the accuracy of the readings), the calculation is as follows: The difference of the sums of the backsights and foresights should equal the difference of the sums of the rises and falls and the difference between the first and last reduced level.

It should be noted that the check with the rise and fall method picks up the intermediate sights since they affect the rise and fall columns, whereas in the collimation method only backsight and foresights are included in the mathematical check.

Although it is useful to commence and terminate levelling work on a bench mark as this serves as a check on the readings, it is not absolutely necessary to do so. If relative levels are required an arbitrary datum of, say, 100.000 may be assumed when commencing the work.

When several pages of levels require to be recorded it is useful to commence and terminate each page respectively with a backsight and foresight to allow checking to be carried out as the work progresses. Bench marks, which are provided throughout the country at densities of 5 per km^2 for rural areas and 40 per km^2 for urban areas, should also be integrated into the survey as a check wherever possible.

Inverse levelling

It is not infrequent that to obtain a staff reading, the staff has to be held in an **inverted** position. This is the occurrence when a bridge soffit or height of a boundary wall needs to be recorded (Fig. 6.72). The inverted staff reading is booked in the appropriate column of the level book with a negative sign,

Table 6.6 Booking by height of instrument

Backsight	Intermediate sight	Foresight	Height of instrument	Reduced level	Distance (m)	Remarks	
3.752			99.212	95.460	0	Bench mark at	A
4.265		3.517	99.960	95.695	100		B
4.318		1.785	102.493	98.175	250		C
	3.951			98.542	300		D
0.958		3.876	99.575	98.617	400		E
		1.265		98.310	500	Bench mark at	F
13.293		10.443		98.310			
10.443				95.460			
2.850				2.850			

Table 6.7 Booking by rise and fall

Backsight	Intermediate sight	Foresight	Rise	Fall	Reduced level	Distance (m)	Remarks	
3.752					95.460	0	Bench mark at	A
4.265		3.517	0.235		95.695	100		B
4.318		1.785	2.480		98.175	250		C
	3.951		0.367		98.542	300		D
0.958		3.876	0.075		98.617	400		E
		1.265		0.307	98.310	500		F
13.293		10.443	3.157	0.307	98.310			
10.443			0.307		95.460			
2.850			2.850		2.850			

so that when reducing this reading from the height of collimation of the level we have the equation:

reduced level = height of instrument − (−staff reading)

If an inverted staff reading is booked in the backsight or foresight column during levelling, it is necessary to deduct the readings identified by a minus sign when undertaking the mathematical checks. These readings are shown in Table 6.8.

Reciprocal levelling

By means of reciprocal levelling the need to apply corrections to long sight readings becomes unnecessary. It is a technique which is also used where equalisation of length of backsights and foresights is not possible in instances such as when a line of levels is interrupted by a wide stream or ravine. The principle is that two sets of differences are averaged to give the true differences. With this method it is most convenient to use two instruments which should be in correct adjustment. The procedure is as follows (see Fig. 6.73):

1. With the instrument at A and staffs at B and C, read levels at B and C.
2. Move the instrument to D (or use similar second instrument) and read B and C again.
3. The mean of the two differences of level is the correct difference.

Table 6.8 Inverse levelling

Backsight	Intermediate sight	Foresight	Height of instrument	Reduced level	Distance (m)	Remarks
0.795			101.295	100.500	0	Bench mark
	−2.450			103.745	100	Bridge soffit
		1.801		99.494	170	Bench mark C
0.795		1.801		100.500		
		0.795		99.494		
		1.006		1.006		

Self-assessment tasks

1. Using the collimation method, reduce the listed staff readings in Table 6.9 and show the appropriate mathematical checks.

Table 6.9

Backsight	Intermediate sight	Foresight	Height of instrument	Reduced level	Distance (m)	Remarks	
1.300				50.000	0	Bench mark	A
	1.580				20		B
	1.615				40		C
	1.415				60		D
2.400		2.000			80		E
	2.20				100		F
	1.500				120		G
	1.675				140		H
	1.600				160		I
		1.700			180		J

2. The figures in Table 6.10 were extracted from a level book, some of the entries being illegible owing to exposure to rain. Insert the missing figures and check the results.

Table 6.10

Backsight	Intermediate sight	Foresight	Height of instrument	Reduced level	Distance (m)	Remarks	
?			100.786	98.763		Bench mark on gate	
	5.930			?	0	Bench mark at	A
	?			97.716	30		B
	3.216			?	60		C
8.194		?	?	97.570	90		D
	6.920			?	120		E
	3.718			?	150		F
	?			102.208	180		G

3. The readings shown in Table 6.11 were taken during a levelling exercise to determine the clearance between the bed of a stream and a bridge that crosses it. The chainages are measured from the left-hand bridge abutment. Calculate the reduced levels and apply the usual mathematical checks.

Table 6.11

Backsight	Intermediate sight	Foresight	Reduced level	Distance (m)	Remarks
1.110			100.00	0	Ground level, abutment left hand
	−0.950			0	Bridge soffit
	1.020			2	Ground level
	0.980			4	Ground level
	1.450			6	Bank water level
	1.850			8	Stream bed
−1.550		−1.450		8	Bridge soffit
	1.710			10	Stream bed
	1.900			12	Stream bed
	−1.550			12	Bridge soffit
	1.660			14	Stream bed
	1.560			16	Stream bed
	1.350			18	Bank water level
	0.910			20	Ground water, abutment right hand
		−1.050		20	Bridge soffit

4. The following list of readings was taken sequentially during a levelling survey: 1.250 (BM, 1.435 m OD), 1.295 (peg A), 1.296 (peg B), 0.810 (change point), 0.910 (change point), −1.715 (inverted staff reading taken to underside of bridge), −1.890 (inverted staff reading on underside of bridge projection), 1.255 (peg C), 0.665 (change point), 1.915 (change point), 0.075 (peg D).

   Transfer the staff readings onto a standard booking form, reduce the levels to Ordnance Datum and undertake appropriate mathematical checks.

5. Table 6.12 shows the readings taken to determine the clearance between the river level and the soffit of a road bridge. Reduce the levels and determine the clearance between the river level and the bridge soffit which has the lowest reduced level.

Table 6.12

Backsight	Intermediate sight	Foresight	Reduced level	Remarks
0.872			21.550	O.B.M.
0.675		3.950		
	2.850			River level at A
	−1.335			Soffit of bridge at A
	−1.312			Soffit of bridge at B
	−1.295			Soffit of bridge at C
	−1.280			Soffit of bridge at D
	−1.350			Soffit of bridge at E
	−2.920			River level
4.250		0.597		
		1.255		O.B.M.

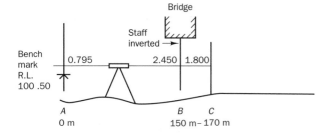

Figure 6.72 Inverse levelling (see Table 6.8)

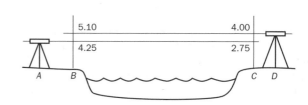

Figure 6.73 Reciprocal levelling

True difference in level $= \frac{1}{2}$ (sum of apparent differences)
Readings with instrument at A:

$B = 4.25$, $C = 2.75$ Difference $= 1.5$

Readings with instrument at D:

$B = 5.10$, $C = 4.00$ Difference $= 1.1$

Correct difference $= \frac{1}{2}[1.5 + 1.1] = 1.3$ m

Self-assessment task

In levelling across a river, reciprocal levelling observations gave the following results for staves held vertically at X and Y from level stations A and B on each bank, respectively:

Staff reading of X from $A = 1.753$ m
Staff reading of X from $B = 2.080$ m
Staff reading of Y from $A = 2.550$ m
Staff reading of Y from $B = 2.895$ m

If the reduced level of X is 90.37 ODN, obtain the reduced level of Y. (Students will find a sketch helpful in determining the relationship of level between X and Y.)

Checking for errors

Sources of error can be divided into three classes
- errors due to incorrect setting up
- instrument error and correction
- mistakes

Incorrect setting up

- Bubble not being central when the reading was taken. The bubble should be checked before booking.
- Staff not held vertically. Use a circular or target bubble at the rear of the staff face.
- Instrument moved during readings of foresight and backsight.
- Staff not correctly extended. Ensure extension lengths are 'clicked' into place and check continuity of graduations at the staff face.
- Parallax. Adjust the eyepiece and focusing screw as previously described.
- Movement of staff while reading is being taken or settlement of instrument tripod.

Instrument error and correction

- Collimation error. Check frequently and equalize lengths of foresight and backsight wherever possible.
- Errors in staff graduation. Check before using.
- Loose tripod head. Repair before using.
- Telescope not parallel to bubble tube. Permanent adjustment needed.
- Telescope not at right angles to the vertical axis. Permanent adjustment needed.

Reading errors depend on (i) magnification and image clarity afforded by the telescope; (ii) the clarity of staff graduations and the way in which they are marked and (iii) the length of sight. The maximum permissible length of sight with an ordinary instrument is in the order of 100 m and where climatic conditions dictate, e.g. heat haze, poor light, the length of sight should be reduced.

Mistakes

- Incorrect level readings taken
- Incorrect level readings booked. Follow the procedure: take reading, book reading, check reading, check booking

Permissible error

In work on building sites the permissible error is ± 0.0006 on the closing bench mark. BS 5606: 1990, 'Code of practice for accuracy in building' quotes the normally accepted maximum misclosure for the accuracy of engineer's levels $\pm 10\sqrt{k}$ mm, where k is the length of the circuit measured in kilometres.

Permanent adjustment of the tilting level

The only permanent adjustment is achieved by undertaking the **two-peg test** which confirms that the bubble tube axis is parallel to the telescope axis so that when the bubble is central the line of sight is horizontal (Fig. 6.74).

1. On a flat site establish two pegs A and B about 50 m apart and set up the instrument at P, a position midway between them.
2. After levelling and focusing, sight on the staff held vertically at A and take reading a_1.
3. Repeat with the staff held at B and record reading b_1. Assuming that the line of collimation is not horizontal but inclined at an angle e, the collimation error, then the true difference in height between A and B is given by

$$\Delta h_{AB} = (a_1 - d_1 \times e) - (b_1 - d_2 \times e)$$

And since the instrument is midway between A and B, d_1 and d_2 are equal and so

$$\Delta h_{AB} = a_1 - b_1$$

4. Move the instrument to Q, a point which extends the line AB by d_1 (about 25 m). Repeat the observations on to a staff at A and B, recording the readings a_2 and b_2. The line of collimation will again be inclined to the horizontal by the angle e. The true difference in height between A and B is given by

$$\Delta h_{AB} = [a_2 - (d_1 + d_2 + d_3)e] - [b_2 - d_3 \times e]$$
$$\Delta h_{AB} = (a_2 - b_2) - (d_1 + d_2)e$$

By equating the two measures of the height difference

$$(a_1 - b_1) = (a_2 - b_2) - (d_1 + d_2)e$$

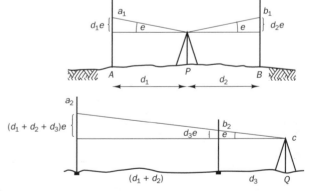

6.74 The two-peg test. (*After* Bannister, Raymond & Baker *Surveying* Longman)

and

$$e = \frac{(a_2 - b_2) - (a_1 - b_1)}{(d_1 + d_2)}$$

For a tilting level of average precision, e should be less than $\pm0.000\,05$ rad (equivalent to a height error of ±0.5 mm per 10 m). If the error is greater than this the level should be adjusted.

5. With the instrument set at Q a horizontal line of collimation would give a reading on the staff at A of

$$a_2 - (d_1 + d_2 + d_3)e$$

Using the tilting screw the line of collimation is lowered (or raised if e is negative) to the correct staff reading and then the bubble is brought to its central position using the capstan screws, which alter the alignment of the bubble with respect to the telescope.

The student should, as part of the fieldwork for the surveying process unit, follow the two-peg test procedure in the field to confirm the accuracy of the level prior to use.

Permanent adjustment to the Dumpy level

The test is the same as for the tilting level but the adjustment procedure is different. Any change to the line of collimation must be made by a vertical movement of the horizontal crosshair using the diaphragm adjusting screws since the bubble-tube axis has been positioned and set perpendicular to the vertical axis. This is the second of the permanent adjustments to the dumpy level.

Procedure

1. Set up and level the instrument.
2. Turn the telescope over any pair of footscrews and centre the bubble exactly.
3. Reverse the tube (turn through 180°). If the bubble runs off centre, bring it half way back with the footscrews and the remainder of the way with the capstan headed adjusting screw on the bubble tube.

Applications of levelling and associated setting out

Apart from the general problems of determination of level differences between two points, the principal uses of levelling are:

- contouring
- setting out levels
- the taking of longitudinal sections
- cross-sections

Contouring

A **contour** is a line joining points of equal altitude. Contour lines are shown on plans as full lines, often in distinctive colour overlaying detail. The contour line divides the land which is higher than the given height from that which is lower. Figure 6.75 illustrates the contours of a piece of

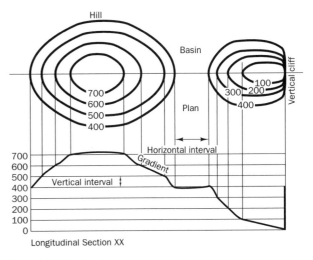

Figure 6.75 Contouring

land. When contour lines are close together, **steep gradients** exist, and as they get further apart the gradient becomes **flatter**.

The vertical or contour interval is the difference in height between one contour line and the next. The magnitude of the contour interval depends upon the purpose of the map, the nature of the site and the scale of the map. It is recommended that the contour interval for small sites is 1 m and larger sites 2 – 4 m. The horizontal equivalent is the distance between one contour line and the next measured on plan:

$$\text{slope or gradient} = \frac{\text{contour interval}}{\text{horizontal equivalent}}$$

Properties of contours

- Contour lines cannot cross
- Contour lines must form continuous lines
- Contour lines can only join at vertical sections, e.g. cliffs

Methods of contouring

Gridding. The method is ideal on relatively flat land on small sites. Grids of squares of 10 to 20 m width are set out and levels taken at the corners. To avoid setting out all the squares, two sets of lines may be established using ranging rods, as illustrated in Fig. 6.76 and to locate any particular square corner the staff man lines himself in, using pairs of ranging rods. For booking purposes the staffman is for example at E_1 and this would be recorded in the remarks column of the level book. The reduced levels are plotted on plan which has been gridded to a scale in the same manner and by any suitable means of interpolation, such as by the use of radial dividers, the required contours are plotted.

When plotting the contour from the calculation results it is assumed that the ground rises or falls uniformly between points. This may of course not be so, and if the topography is undulating the grid intervals should be smaller.

Example

It is required to plot the contour line of 100.00 shown in Fig. 6.76. The calculation sheet is shown in Table 6.13.

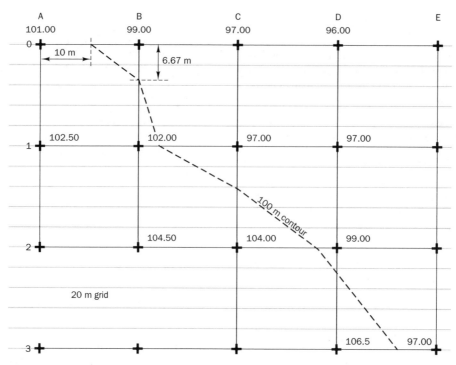

Figure 6.76 Contouring by gridding

Table 6.16 Calculation sheet

Stations	Rise/fall		Contour rise/fall	Distance	From	to
A_0–B_0	101–99	= 2	101–100 = 1	$(1/2) \times 20 = 10$ m	A_0	B_0
B_0–B_1	99–102	= –3	99–100 = –1	$(1/3) \times 20 = 6.67$ m	B_0	B_1
B_1–C_1	102–97	= 5	102–100 = 2	$(2/5) \times 20 = 4$ m	B_1	C_1
C_1–C_2	97–104	= –7	97–100 = –3	$(3/7) \times 20 = 8.57$ m	C_1	C_2
C_2–D_2	104–99	= 5	104–100 = 4	$(4/5) \times 20 = 16$ m	C_2	D_2
D_2–D_3	99–106.5	= –7.5	99–100 = 2–1	$(1/7.5) \times 20 = 2.67$ m	D_2	D_3
D_3–E_3	106.5–97	= 9.5	106.5–100 = 6.5	$(6.5/9.5) \times 20 = 13.69$ m	D_3	E_3

Direct contouring

This is the best method for hilly terrain. The actual contour is located on the ground and marked with coloured laths. The level is set up and levelled at some convenient position, and the height of collimation established by a backsight on a point of known level. In Fig. 6.77 this gives a height of instrument of 33.99 AOD. Thus any intermediate sight of 0.99 means that the staff is on a point $33.99 - 0.99 = 33$ m AOD. The surveyor then directs the staffman until the staff reads 0.99 and on a given signal a lath, of a particular colour to represent a contour line, is stuck into the ground. A series of staff readings enables the relative contours to be established. The positions of the

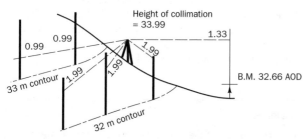

Figure 6.77 Direct contouring. (*After* Bannister, Raymond & Baker *Surveying* Longman)

laths are later surveyed by either tape and offset, traverse survey or by tacheometry.

Tacheometric methods

Although outside the surveying processes unit syllabus, students should be aware that by applying a multiplying constant, usually 100 (and with old instruments an additive constant), the distance of a staff position from a level can be readily determined with a correctly set up instrument. The constants for all telescopes can be obtained from the handbook for the instrument. When viewed through the eyepiece, three horizontal hairs spaced equidistantly can be seen. These are often referred to as the upper, middle and lower stadia. The middle stadia reading provides the level sighting for recording in the field book when undertaking levelling work. If the upper and lower stadia readings are also recorded, and a subtraction made, this gives the stadia interval. By application of the instrument constants the distance of the staff from the level may be determined, e.g. if the multiplying constant of the instrument was 100 and the additive constant was 0, then a stadia difference of, say, 0.439 would tell the surveyor that the staff was 43.9 m away (0.439×100). This method of distance measurement is usually sufficiently accurate for contouring work.

Determination of the average level of a grid

To determine the average level of a grid of ground levels, the reduced level at each grid point is multiplied by a factor which depends on the point's position. The sum of the multiplications is then divided by four times the number of squares. The factor depends upon the number of squares meeting at the grid point. In Fig. 6.76 at grid point A_0 there is only one square, therefore the reduced level is multiplied by 1, at B_0 there are two squares, and so on.

Uses of contour maps

- location of possible routes for roads, pipelines, etc.
- laying out building sites
- calculation of volumes of earthworks (using **Simpson's rule** or the **Trapezoidal rule**)
- determination of intervisibility for tunnel surveys or vertical and horizontal curves for roadways

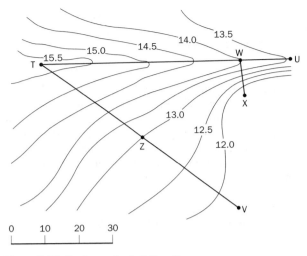

Figure 6.78 Contours of a building site

The taking of longitudinal sections

An example of such a section is illustrated in Fig. 6.79 from which it can be seen that the object is to produce on a drawing the existing ground profile along a particular line which is often the centre line of a proposed road or pipeline. Staff readings to 0.01 m are usually sufficiently accurate for this purpose.

The accuracy with which the ground profile is presented on the section is dependent on the selection of staff stations. As a general basis levels should be taken at:

- every 20 m
- points at which the gradient changes, e.g. top and bottom of embankments

---

Self-assessment task

Figure 6.78 shows contours at intervals of 0.5 m over a building site, drawn at a scale of 1:500.
(a) Using the linear scale shown on the map, calculate the gradient between (i) points W and X, and (ii) points Y and Z.
(b) Describe the type of ground terrain between (i) points T and U, and points T and V.
(c) Draw a section to suitable scales of the ground levels between T and V.

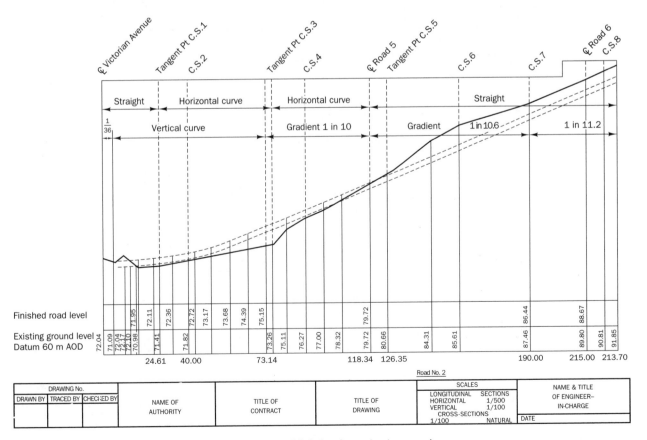

Figure 6.79 Longitudinal sections. (*After* Bannister, Raymond & Baker *Surveying* Longman)

- edges of natural features, e.g. ditches, ponds
- sections which cross roads, e.g. back of footpath, kerb, channel and centre of the road

The procedure for taking longitudal sections is as follows:

1. Commence work from an Ordnance Survey bench mark and make use of any bench marks along the length being levelled.
2. Keep backsights and foresights approximately equal in length to minimise errors which will occur if the line of collimation is not parallel to the bubble-tube axis.
3. Make all change points on firm ground (preferably on identifiable features such as manhole covers, surface box lids).
4. Take the final foresight on a bench mark or close back on the starting point by a series of 'flying levels' (levels of sighting between 40 and 60 m).

5. Do not work with the staff extended in high wind.
6. Take care when setting up the level.

Cross-sections (Fig. 6.80)

Works of narrow width such as pipelines require only one line of levels along the proposed trench centre line. Wider works such as road, railways, cuttings and embankments necessitate the use of ground on either side of the proposed centre line, and information regarding relative ground levels is obtained by taking cross-sections at right angles to the centre line. The width of these must be sufficient to cover the proposed works.

The procedure for taking cross-sections is as follows:

1. The centre line is first set out, pegs being placed at points where cross-sections are needed and the cross-sections

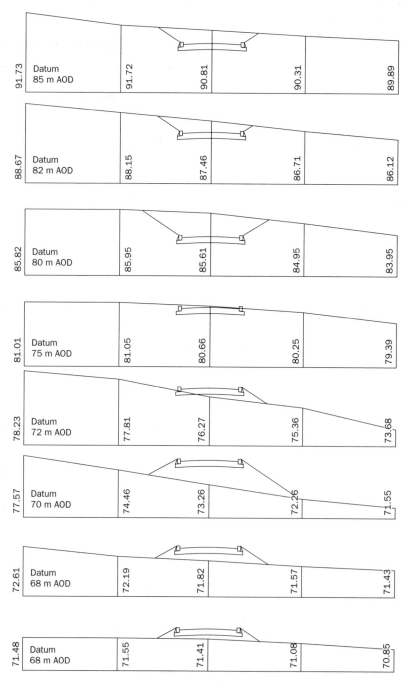

Figure 6.80 Cross-sections. (*After* Bannister, Raymond & Baker *Surveying* Longman)

themselves may be set out using an optical square or lower order instrument.

2. Cross-sections may be plotted one at a time, but the method is laborious and it is often convenient to record levels on an ad hoc basis, taking care to identify the reference position and distance in level book.

Plotting of sections

Longitudinal sections

Scales should preferably be in the ratio of 1 to 10. Scales which are distorted with 1 : 1000 **horizontally** and 1 : 100 **vertically** are popular. For pipeline sections through urban and rural areas it is often convenient to use a horizontal scale of 1 : 1250 with a copy of the Ordnance Survey sheet directly above the longitudinal section. The height of the datum for the vertical scaling work should be fixed so that there is a 100 mm space between it and the lowest level to be plotted (at a scale of 1 : 100, 10 mm represents 10 m level).

Cross-sections

The vertical and horizontal scales should be preferably the same as this facilitates the area measurement of the cut or fill for volume calculations although with the availability of **digital planimeters** (instrument for direct measurement of area from a plan) this is of less importance than in the past.

Summary of procedure for planning a new road

Requirements are:

- **alignment** – straighter the road, less land for construction, less materials for construction, the faster the road design speed
- **level** – ground ideally should have gentle slopes, gradients kept to a minimum, cut to balance fill (volume excavated = volume filled).

1. Choosing the route – decided by reconnaissance, rough traversing and sectioning, preparation of strip maps and sections for alternative routes, followed by an accurate survey of the selected route.
2. Set out the centre line of the selected route using a theodolite.
3. Set out grid lines parallel to the centre line at $\frac{1}{2}$ and $1\frac{1}{2}$ times the road width on either side of the centre line.
4. Take levels at the grid points.
5. Plot longitudinal sections.
6. Determine the road level ensuring that maximum and minimum gradients are not exceeded.
7. Draw cross-sections.
8. Determine earthwork volumes.
9. Draw a plan showing the heel of any embankment and the toe of the cutting.

Vertical control of construction activities

Having recorded site levels and prepared plans and sections it is necessary to convey to the construction workforce the

information necessary to complete the work, whether it be the excavation levels for a pipeline or the slope stakes for an embankment or cutting. The traditional method of doing this is to use sight rails (profiles) and travellers. The sight rails and travellers are defined in the section dealing with terminology (Fig. 6.57).

Consider a length of sewer being laid from manhole A with an invert level (lowest inside point on the pipe barrel) of 30.02 m to manhole B, 60 m away, the gradient from A to B being 1 in 100 and falling from A to B. If two rails are fixed over stations A and B and about 1 m above ground level, and at a fixed height above invert level, then an eye sighting from rail A to B will be sighting down a gradient which is parallel to the sewer gradient. In Fig. 6.58, a convenient height above invert would be 3.75 m so that a traveller of this length, held vertically so that its sight bar just touched the line of sight between sight rails A and B, would give at its lower end a point on the sewer invert line.

To fix the sight rails for use with a 3.75 m long traveller it is necessary to drive two posts on either side of the manholes and nail the rails between these at the following levels:

sight rail A,
$$
\begin{aligned}
\text{reduced level} &= \text{invert level} \\
&\quad + \text{length of traveller} \\
&= 30.02 + 3.75 \\
&= 33.77 \text{ m AOD}
\end{aligned}
$$

distance $AB = 60$ m $\quad \therefore \quad$ fall gradient $= 1$ in 100

$$
\frac{1}{100} = \frac{x}{60}
$$

$$
\therefore \quad x = \frac{60}{100} = 0.60 \text{ m}
$$

$$
\begin{aligned}
\text{invert level at } B &= \text{invert level } A - \text{fall } AB \\
&= 30.02 - 0.60 \\
&= 29.42 \text{ in AOD}
\end{aligned}
$$

$$
\begin{aligned}
\text{and sight rail } B, \text{ reduced level} &= 29.42 + 3.75 \\
&= 33.17 \text{ m AOD}
\end{aligned}
$$

If a level set up nearby has a height of collimation of say 34.845 m AOD, then the staff is moved up and down the post at manhole (MH) A until a reading of 1.075 m is obtained (34.845 − 33.770). Marks are made on each post and the sight rail is nailed in position. For rail B, the staff reading with the same instrument position would be 1.675 m (34.845 − 33.17).

As a general rule, if the top of the traveller appears above the line of sight, additional excavation is required; and, conversely, below the line of sight, the excavation is too deep. Three sight rails are required to define a line in a particular plane. For roadworks, sight rails are often in pairs on each side of the working area to reflect the cant or super elevation of the road. The viewing across the sight rails to determine the cut or fill necessary is called 'boning'.

Self-assessment tasks

1. Using the rise and fall method of booking and the data below; (i) draw up a typical level book page and reduce the levels obtained; (ii) determine the depth to invert at each manhole; (iii) decide the staff readings necessary to set up sight rails at each manhole. Traveller 3 m long to be used. Backsight of 1.505 onto nearby bench mark of reduced level 40.550 m.

Invert level of sewer at MH1	39.650
Staff reading at ground level for MH 1	1.205
Staff reading at ground level for MH 2	1.200
Staff reading at ground level for MH 3	3.000
Staff reading onto a TBM (temporary bench mark)	3.440
Gradient MH 1 falling to MH 2	1 : 50 distance 75 m
Gradient MH 2 falling to MH 3	1 : 75 distance 100 m

2. Figure 6.56 shows the profile of a length of ground, levelled for the purpose of producing a longitudinal section.
   (a) Book the staff readings by a recognised method.
   (b) Determine the difference in value of the bench mark at *Y* and the actual value obtained from the staff readings, accounting for any discrepancy.
   (c) Calculate the gradient of the 150 mm diameter pipeline
   (d) Determine the height of sight rails at *A*, *F* and *L* if it is intended to use a 4 m long traveller.
   (e) Sketch and describe how sight rails and travellers are used to control the depth of excavation.

Sight rails for cuttings

The slope of cuttings and embankments could be defined by sight rails up the slope, but it is normal practice to erect *batter rails* (Fig. 6.81) which define the excavation surface with a sloping rail.

The procedure for erecting batter rails is as follows:

1. Establish the plan location of the top of the cutting or bottom of the embankment.
2. Measure 1 m away from the excavation and drive in a stake.
3. Measure a further 1 m and put in a second stake.
4. Decide upon the traveller length such that the top edge of the batter rail will not be too high for cuttings or too low for embankments to be sighted upon.
5. If the excavation slopes at 1 in *x*:
   (a) for a cutting – on the first stake mark the level corresponding to the reduced level of the cutting top + traveller height + (1/*x*); on the second stake mark the level corresponding to the reduced level of the cutting top and traveller height + (2/*x*).
   (b) for an embankment – on the first stake mark the level corresponding to the reduced level of base + traveller height – (1/*x*); on the second mark the level corresponding to the reduced level of the base + traveller height – (2/*x*).
6. Nail on the sloping rail so that its top edge is in contact with the two marks and this sloping timber will define a plane at the traveller height above the finished formation.

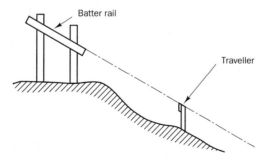

Figure 6.81

While sight rails are still used for road works, their use has diminished for drainage work and that on level compact surfaces due to the advent of construction lasers. In particular, the rotating laser where on some models the beam can spin both horizontally and inclined, is particularly useful.

Example

Calculate data to establish batter rails that define a cutting that is to slope downwards at 1 in 2 from a point of reduced level 50.457 m.

Answer

If a 0.4 m traveller is selected, drive in two stakes at 1 m and 2 m from the cutting top, then

$$\text{level mark on stake 1} = 50.457 + 0.4 + \frac{1}{2} = 51.357 \text{ m}$$

$$\text{level mark on stake 2} = 50.457 + 0.4 + \frac{2}{2} = 51.857 \text{ m}$$

Check the height of the upper edge of the batter rail, assuming that the ground is level at 50.457. Height of upper edge = 51.857 − 50.457 = 1.4 m, which is satisfactory.

Setting out

This is the process of using surveying instruments and techniques to transfer information from a plan to the ground or to convert calculations to information which can be used in construction. The procedures will be reviewed in more detail in the next section, but it is important to note this application and the equipment and procedures which are used.

Let us imagine a small residential development served by a roadway, with the drainage being provided by a storm water drain and a foul sewer. The site survey would have been completed using a closed traverse and the coordinates of the control stations would have been calculated. The proposed positions of the road, sewers and drains can be measured on a plan relative to the survey points using a scale rule and protractor, or more accurately by calculations using the coordinates. This information would be taken into the field by the surveyor and these scaled or calculated dimensions are set out from the survey pages to establish the ground positions of the proposed works.

On any construction site, it is general practice to firstly construct the roadways and sewers, in order to provide access to the site and main drainage to all buildings. The standard setting out equipment for the works would comprise the following:

Steel tapes. These should always be used for setting-out purposes and if a high degree of accuracy is required they should be standardised before use. The accuracy of setting out work is dependent upon the condition of the tape and the skill of the user.

Levels. Automatic levels are generally used as the setting-out work is quicker than with other levels.

Theodolites. The more automation that can be introduced, the greater will be the accuracy of setting out. It is therefore good practice to use theodolites with optical plumbing, automatic vertical circle indexing, electronic readout and electronic two-axis levelling.

Total station instruments. Most setting out work is most accurately accomplished by the method of coordinates. An EDM instrument is needed to set out distances and total stations can be used to set out horizontal distances easily.

Autoplumb instruments. These are used to set out vertical lines in high-rise buildings and are more convenient than conventional theodolites.

Pegs. These are usually wooden $50\,mm \times 50\,mm \times 500\,mm$ long stakes for use in soft ground or $25\,mm \times 25\,mm \times 300\,mm$ long steel angle section for hard ground. Pegs may be colour coded for their purpose to avoid confusion. Centre lines are usually coloured white, offset pegs yellow and level pegs blue. In setting out the road and sewers, centre line pegs are firstly established. As these get displaced during excavation, offset pegs are located 3–5 m to the right and left of centre lines.

Profiles and travellers. These have been described earlier in the section and are usually erected over the offset pegs. The length of the traveller equals the sight rail level minus the sewer invert level. Their lengths should be kept in multiples of 0.25 m and should have a desirable length of about 2 m.

Corner profiles. These are described in more detail in the next section. During the construction of buildings these pegs denote the corners of the building and are removed during construction work. The corner positions are usually removed some distance back from the excavations onto new corner profiles which are constructed from wooden stakes $50\,mm \times 50\,mm$, onto which wooden boards $250\,mm \times 25\,mm \times 1.00\,m$ long are nailed.

Angular measurement

The history of height control

The inventor of the name 'theodolite' was Leonard Digges and his description of the instrument under the title 'The Construction of an Instrument Topographical Serving most commodiously for all Manner of Mensurations' was published in the sixteenth century. From this time the instrument developed, with the first telescope theodolite being used in 1787 for the tie-up between the English and French triangulation systems. The instrument was only able to measure horizontal angles and it was not until the nineteenth century that instruments which could measure both were produced. From these early instruments 'transit' instruments were developed with initially **vernier** reading systems, largely replaced by 'glass circle' instruments. Electronic and electromagnetic instruments are now in common use. These instruments, used correctly, are not only able to measure horizontal and vertical angles but also distance. Currently the most modern type of electronic instruments now available are called '**total station instruments**', which incorporate a theodolite with electronic circles and an

EDM. With these instruments a microprocessor converts angles and distance to a digital display. These instruments can interface with other computers or data loggers to store information which can be later downloaded to plot a survey.

Principles and definitions

The theodolite is essentially a telescope whose line of collimation can usually be revolved through 360° horizontally and revolved through 360° vertically and appropriate angles measured. Revolution of the telescope is known as **transiting** the telescope.

Purpose and applications of angular measurement

Traverse surveying

A **traverse** is a continuous skeleton framework of lines connecting a number of stations or control points, the lengths of the lines and their angular relationships to each other being measured. The distance between the stations are known as **leg lengths** and the lines as **traverse lines**. Traverse surveys are used when site conditions are such that simple triangulation with a band or tape is impractical, such as the survey of a very large area.

Closed traverse

When the survey framework forms a closed figure, or when it starts and finishes at points of known coordinates, then a **closed traverse** has been obtained. This type of traverse is suitable for surveying woods, lakes or areas where ties and check lines cannot be used. Figure 6.82(a) illustrates a **closed loop traverse** and Fig. 6.82(b) a **closed line traverse**. It is useful to remember for a closed traverse that the angle sum of all the internal angles should equal $(2n - 4) \times 90°$, where n = number of control points. For consideration of the external angles, the equation changes to $(2n + 4) \times 90°$.

Open or unclosed traverse

A traverse whose starting and finishing points do not coincide or are not both fixed or known points is an **unclosed traverse** and is shown in Fig. 6.82(c). It is principally used for surveying rivers, overland pipelines or railway routes. Consideration should be given to referencing the control stations into Ordnance Survey trigonometrical stations as a check as work proceeds.

Traverse types are identified by the equipment used or accuracy required. A first-order traverse might have leg lengths of up to 50 km measured by microwave EDM, and angles measured by a geodetic theodolite having an accuracy of 1 in 100 000. Where precise control surveying is not needed, an instrument having an accuracy of 20 seconds may be more appropriate.

Triangulation

When considering linear-measuring techniques the principal of dividing an area into a series of standard geometrical

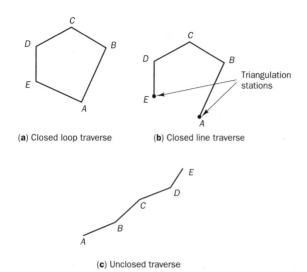

(a) Closed loop traverse **(b)** Closed line traverse

(c) Unclosed traverse

Figure 6.82 Traverse types

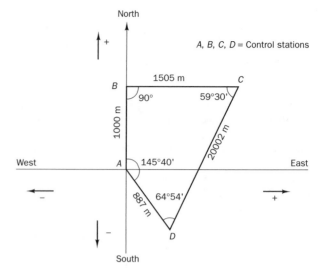

Figure 6.83 Theodolite closed traverse

figures (braced quadrilaterals or polygons) was discussed (Fig. 8.34). By measurement of angles and leg lengths between accurately located control stations the area can be conveniently surveyed from this framework. When undertaking a survey by triangulation methods, the area must be carefully reconnoitred to select the most suitable positions for the control stations. Existing contoured maps are of assistance at the desk studies stage of this work. When selecting stations the following should be borne in mind:

- Every station should be visible from the adjacent stations.
- Rays passing close to the ground should be avoided as they may be refracted due to air temperature.
- Triangles should be well-conditioned with triangles approximately equilateral.
- The size of the triangles depends on land configuration and the type of theodolite proposed for use. Long sights may require correction for the earth curvature and refraction. The use of a prism for the reflection of a signal is often the most satisfactory arrangement.

Once the framework has been established the control station positions must be marked and beaconed. A nail in a 50×50 mm wooden peg may suffice, or a metal pin set in the upper surface of a concrete pillar may be required if the instrument is to be mounted on the pillar. To make the station visible to a distant theodolite, a pole, prism reflector, luminous beacon or tripods with conical tops may be employed.

The triangulation procedure is as follows (see Fig. 6.83).

1. Fix the station.
2. Set up at A. Take the bearing line AB with a compass. This line is known as the meridian of the traverse. An arbitrary meridian may be established by setting up the instrument over station A and directing the telescope on to a permanent land mark which is temporarily called the **traverse meridian**. This can later be converted into the true meridian of the traverse by reference to an Ordnance Survey sheet.
3. Measure the angle BAD. Since the horizontal circle is graduated **clockwise** it is more satisfactory to measure the angles in a clockwise direction.
4. Measure the line AB. Depending on the instrument being used, the lengths of the various legs should be measured.

The accuracy of leg length measurement should, if a tape or band is being used, reflect the accuracy of the instrument used for measuring the angles.

5. Measure the angle CBA. Continue around the loop in a clockwise direction measuring the internal (and external) angle at each control point.
6. Plotting the traverse. Draw a line east–west across the paper and at a convenient position on this line draw a north–south line to reflect the orientation of the traverse and the control point A. To plot the position B in Fig. 6.83 measure 1000 m at the scale selected upwards from A on the north–south line. From B, set out at right angles to the north–south line a distance of 1505 m to scale and fix the position of C. Although control station D could be set out using a protractor, it is usual as the angles have been measured accurately to fix the station D by calculating coordinates.

Coordinates

The fixing of coordinates involves the following steps:

1. Check and correct the angles at the stations (internal and external).
2. Convert the angles to reduced bearings, although this is not necessary when using a calculator.
3. Calculate the latitudes (north–south) and departures (east–west).
4. Calculate the coordinates.
5. Correct the coordinates.

Using Fig. 6.83 for reference, the following steps would be followed:

1. Check and correct the angles at the stations

   The sum of the internal angles $= 145° \, 40' + 90°$
   $$+ 59° \, 30' + 64° \, 54'$$
   $$= 360° \, 04' \, 00''$$

   sum of internal angles *should* $= (2n - 4) \times 90$
   $$= (4) \times 90°$$
   $$= 360°$$

   The internal angles of the traverse shown in Fig. 6.83 are too large by 4′. This requires distributing equally between all the readings i.e. $01'$ per angle; as the error is positive, each angle requires reducing by 01′. The angles then become

angle $DAB = 145° 39′$
angle $ABC = \ \ 89° 59′$
angle $BCD = \ \ 59° 29′$
angle $CDA = \ \ \underline{64° 53′}$
$\qquad$ Sum $= 360° 00′$

2. Convert the angles to reduced bearings. The reduced bearing of a traverse leg is the smallest angle it makes with the north–south meridian (Fig. 6.84).

Line $AB =$ North
Line $BC =$ North 90° East or 90° East

Line CD lies in the third quadrant of a circle and will be $360° - (59° 30′ + 90° + 90° + 90°) =$ South 30° 30′ West

Line DA lies in the fourth quadrant of a circle and will be from mathematics of the angles

$64° 54′ - (90° - 59° 30′) =$ North 33° 24′ West.

3. Calculate the latitudes (northings and southings) and the departures (eastings and westings). From Fig. 6.83, B is 1000 m directly north of A. Thus if A has coordinates of its origin 0 North, 0 East the coordinates of B will be 1000 North, 0 East. C is 1505 m directly east of B. Thus using the previously determined coordinates for B the coordinates of C will be 1000 North, 1505 East. D is South 30° 30′ West and forms a triangle, as shown in Fig. 6.85.

The latitude of a station is its distance north or south (northing or southing) of the preceding station; positive latitude being north and negative latitude being south of the preceding station. The departure of a station is its distance east or west (easting or westing) of the preceding station; positive departure being east and negative departure west of the preceding station (Fig. 6.85).

To calculate the latitude of D, the leg length is multiplied by the **cosine** of the reduced bearing. Similarly, to calculate the departure of D, the leg length is multiplied by the **sin** of the reduced bearing.

Latitude of D relative to $C = 2002 \times \cos 30° 30′$
$\qquad\qquad\qquad = 1724.982$ m
Departure of D relative to $C = 2002 \times \sin 30° 30′$
$\qquad\qquad\qquad = 1016.092$ m

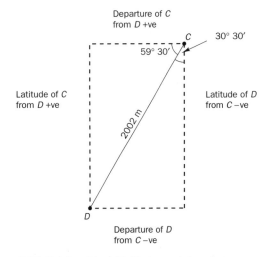

Figure 6.85 Relationships of latitudes and departures

4. Calculate the coordinates. The coordinates of a control station fix its position relative to an origin which, for a local traverse, is usually the first station of the traverse. The coordinates are the algebraic sum of the latitudes and departures respectively.

From step 3, the coordinates of C are 1000 N, 1505 E. The coordinates of D will be:

Latitude $= 1000 - 1724.982 = -724.982$ m
Departure $= 1505 - 1016.092 = 488.908$ m

Working in a clockwise direction we can check whether the coordinates of A are indeed 0, 0. Repeating the procedure in step 3, illustrated in Fig. 6.86.

Latitude of A relative to $D = 887 \times \cos 34° 24′$
$\qquad\qquad\qquad = 731.878$ m

Departure of A relative to $D = 887 \times \sin 34° 24′$
$\qquad\qquad\qquad = 501.126$ m

Coordinates of A will be:

Latitude $= -724.982 + 731.878 = +6.896$
Departure $= 488.908 - 501.126 = -12.218$ m

It can be seen that the coordinates of A have not returned to 0, 0. This indicates quite a significant error.

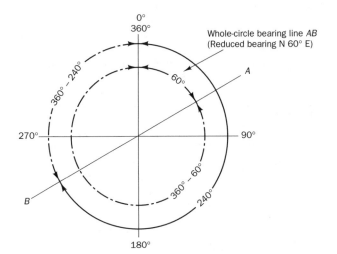

Figure 6.84 Measurement of angles

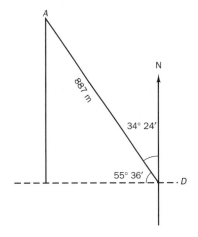

Figure 6.86

Table 6.14

Station	Leg	Length (m)	Latitude		Departure		Coordinates	
			+N	−S	+E	−W	N	E
A	AB	1000	1000		0		0	0
B	BC	1505	0		1505		1000	0
C	CD	2002		−1724.982		−1016.092	1000	1505
D	DA	887	731.878			−501.126	−724.982	488.908
A							+6.896	−12.218
Totals		5394	+1731.878	−1724.982	+1505	−1517.218		
				+6.896		−12.218		

This may have occurred due to errors in
(a) measuring lengths
(b) measuring angles
(c) calculation of latitude and departures and rounding up figures; the error should be distributed proportionally between the two coordinates

5. Correction of coordinates. The error is distributed proportionally between the coordinates and the correction is completed, as shown in Table 6.14.

The traverse shown in Table 6.14 does not close; the error in latitudes being +6.896 and the error in departures −12.218. This means that the latitudes are too great and require reducing by 6.896 and the departures too small and require extending by 12.218. Bowditch's method of correction, based only on mathematical proportioning, requires a correction to be made to each latitude and departure as follows:

$$\text{correction} = \frac{\text{closing error}}{\text{total length of traverse}}$$

Latitude corrections

AB $1000 \times \dfrac{-6.896}{5394} = -1.279$

BC $1505 \times \dfrac{-6.896}{5394} = -1.924$

CD $2002 \times \dfrac{-6.896}{5394} = -2.560$

DA $887 \times \dfrac{-6.896}{5394} = -1.134$

Departure corrections

AB $1000 \times \dfrac{+12.218}{5394} = +2.265$

BC $1505 \times \dfrac{+12.218}{5394} = +3.409$

CD $2002 \times \dfrac{+12.218}{5394} = +4.535$

DA $887 \times \dfrac{+12.218}{5394} = +2.009$

A corrected coordinates table can be produced and is illustrated in Table 6.15. It should be noted that care needs to be taken when applying each correction to the latitude and departure particularly when negative signs are employed.

Terminology used with angular measurement

Bearing. The term refers to the angle between the line and the north–south meridian (defined as a great circle passing through celestial poles and zenith of any place on the earth's surface or passing through the poles and any place on the earth).

Whole-circle bearing (Fig. 6.87). The bearing from north to the leg measured in a clockwise direction and the angle from the north line right round to the leg is known as a whole-circle bearing (WCB).

Forward and back bearings (Fig. 6.88). With the direction of the survey clockwise from A, the angle between north and AB at A (50°) is the forward bearing of AB. The angle between north and AB at control station B is known as the back bearing of line AB. The forward and back bearing should differ by 180° except where 'local attraction' occurs. The presence of metal, metallic ores or electric currents will divert the compass needle from the north–south line and cause the

Table 6.15 Corrected coordinates

Station	Leg	Length (m)	Latitude		Departure		Coordinates	
			+N	−S	+E	−W	N	E
A	AB	1000	998.721		2.265			
B	BC	1505		−1.924	1508.409		998.721	2.265
C	CD	2002		−1727.542		−1011.557	996.797	1510.674
D	DA	887	730.744			−499.117	−730.745	499.117
A							−0.001	0.000
Totals		5394	+1729.465	−1729.466	1510.674	−1510.674		
				−0.001		0.000		

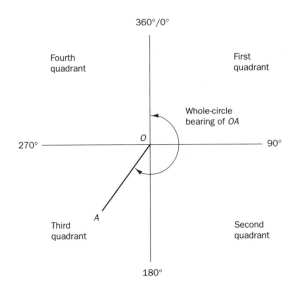

Figure 6.87 Whole-circle bearings

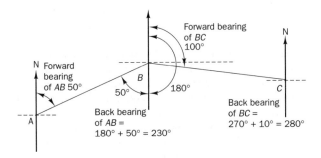

Figure 6.88 Forward and back bearings

readings to be inaccurate. When this occurs it is necessary to work from stations not affected by 'local attraction' and make adjustments as necessary.

Reduced bearings. The reduced bearing of the leg of a traverse is the smallest angle it makes with the north–south meridian. Various rules exist in the calculation of a whole-circle bearing and it is best to calculate this first before determining the reduced bearing.

Rule

(i) The WCB of a traverse leg is equal to the WCB of the previous leg plus 180° minus the internal angle at the station, or
(ii) the WCB of a traverse leg is equal to the WCB of the previous leg plus the measured external angle with the following proviso:
 (a) if the sum obtained is below 180°, then add 180° to it;
 (b) if the sum obtained exceeds 180°, then deduct 180° from it;
 (c) if the sum obtained exceeds 360°, then deduct 360° from it.

Azimuth angle. This is a horizontal angle between the direction of true north and the direction to the sun, clockwise for a morning observation and anticlockwise for one taken in the afternoon. A bearing to the sun can be established and if the horizontal angle between a line and the sun is observed then the bearing of that line can be determined.

Meridian. This can be defined as a great circle passing through celestial poles and zenith (point of sky directly overhead) of any place on the earth. The grid or projection bearing of a line depends upon the projection coordinate system in use. In great Britain the transverse Mercator projection, which is the most suitable for mapping, is used using longitude 2°W as the origin. By adopting this line, scale is correct only along the line, with increasing scale distortion to the east and west. This magnification of error amounting to about 1 : 1250 in the limits of the British Isles is cut by reducing the scale along the origin by half this amount. The meridians of longitude and parallels of latitude are projected as orthogonal curves which intersect at right angles, the central meridian being straight. In practice lines are established parallel and at right angles to the 2°W line, 100 km apart. Measurements east of the origin are positive and west are negative. As this could lead to difficulties, a false origin was created 400 km west of the origin. This is south-west of the Scilly Isles, 400 km west of 2°W and 100 km north of latitude 49°N. All grid coordinates of points in the British Isles are positive eastings and northings. When using some electronic theodolites, adjustments of angular readings being converted into coordinates require to be made by use of a scale factor. The local scale factor is determined from the equation:

$$0.999\,601\,3\,(1 + 1.23E^2 \times 10^{-8})$$

where 0.999 601 3 is the scale factor along the central meridian and E is the distance in kilometres from the central meridian. The scale factor is thus the grid distance divided by the ground distance.

Equipment used for angular measurement

Theodolite (Fig. 6.89)

The theodolite is an instrument that is used to measure horizontal and vertical angles to an accuracy varying from 1 to 60 seconds of arc. It is usually classified according to the method used to read the circle and although there are five principal types of instrument and methods of reading, the basic principles of construction between each are similar. The main components of a theodolite are illustrated in Figure 6.89 and comprise the following:

- **Tripod.** This provides support for the instrument and is usually made from aluminium. Tripods usually have telescopic (sliding) legs which assist in the levelling of the instrument, particularly on sloping ground.
- **Trivet stage.** This is the flat foot plate of the instrument which screws on to the tripod and carries the feet of the levelling screws.
- **Tribrach.** This is the instrument body which carries all the other parts. It has a hollow cylindrical socket into which fits the remainder of the instrument. All modern theodolites have hardened steel cylindrical axes, with a cylindrical ball race between the tribrach and the alidade taking the weight of the upper part of the instrument.
- **Levelling arrangement.** Levelling screws are fitted between the tribrach and the trivet stage. Movement of the footscrews as shown in Figure 6.95 centres the bubble of the plate spirit level located on the cover plate of the horizontal circle.
- **Horizontal circle (lower plate).** This is a graduated 'protractor' numbered from 0° to 360°. Modern

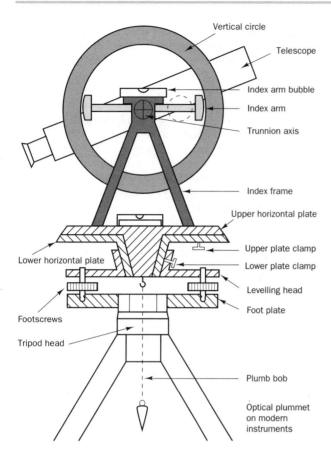

Figure 6.89 Older pattern of theodolite showing construction

instruments have glass circles which are mounted on cylindrical axes that fit around the outside of the tribrach. The circle is free to rotate around the tribrach and can be stopped in any position by applying the lower plate clamp. A limited amount of horizontal movement can still be obtained via the slow motion screw attached to the clamp, which only operates when the lower plate clamp is locked.

- **Alidade (upper plate).** This is the remainder of the theodolite, comprising the uprights which support the telescope, vertical circle and spirit levels. The alidade is free to rotate with respect to the horizontal circle, which is itself free to rotate around the tribrach sleeve.
- **Controls for measuring horizontal angles.** There are three main control systems for measuring horizontal angles and it is recommended that the student becomes familiar with each, initially by identifying the component parts of the theodolite and then by checking the movement of the horizontal circle by reference to the angular graduations. The three systems are:
  - (i) double centre screw, which employs upper and lower plate clamps
  - (ii) circle-setting screw, where the theodolite is not fitted with a lower plate clamp
  - (iii) repetition clamp system where the theodolite is fitted with a repetition clamp instead of a lower plate screw
- **Index marks.** As the alidade is rotated the index mark moves over the horizontal circle. When the alidade is locked, the index mark is read against the circle.
- **Transit axis or trunnion axes.** The transit axis rests on the standards and is securely held in position by a lockout. Attatched to the transit axis are the telescope and vertical circle, with all three being free to rotate in the vertical plane. They can be clamped in any position in the plane

by a telescope clamp, which when clamped can be moved a small amount by use of a slow motion device.

- **Telescope.** The telescope allows rays of light to pass through and should comprise components with a specification that reflects the accuracy of the optics and therefore the instrument. The magnification is usually ×30, with a shortest focusing distance of about 2 m. The vertical circle is attached to the telescope and may be graduated in different ways. The angle measured in the vertical plane may be referenced to the zero degree reading which indicates the horizontal position of the telescope or a zenith angle where the zero degree reading indicates the vertical position of the telescope.
- **Altitude spirit level.** Angles measured in a vertical plane must be measured to a truly horizontal line which passes through the centre of the transit axis and is maintained in a horizontal position by the altitude spirit level. The spirit level and index mark is attached to a 'T' frame which is made horizontal by activating the clip screw against the standards. On most new instruments automatic indexing is employed where the spirit level is replaced with either a pendulum device, which operates in a similar manner to an automatic level, or the surface of a liquid is used.
- **Centring motion.** As the theodolite must be accurately located over a survey control station, it is fitted with a centring motion fitted above the tribrach, which allows the whole of the instrument above the tribrach to move relative to the tribrach. A common difficulty experienced by students is the initial setting of the instrument above the central station and survey mark, and it should be remembered that the total movement or adjustment during the centring procedure is only 40 mm.
- **Optical plummet.** An optical plummet is incorporated in modern instruments which aids centring. When the theodolite is correctly set up and levelled, the observer is able to view the ground station through the eyepiece of the optical plummet, where the line of sight is deflected vertically downwards through a 45° prism. Movement of the centring motion allows the theodolite to be placed exactly over the control station.

Types of theodolite

- **Vernier.** This is rarely used today. The vertical angles are determined using vernier scales on the index arm against the vertical circle. The horizontal angles are determined by using vernier scales on the upper horizontal plate. Modern instruments incorporate developments in lens magnification, automatic vertical collimation and centring accuracy. These can be classified by either the angle reading system or by precision.
- **Optical scale theodolite.** This employs a transparent scale graduated over a whole glass circle division, normally one degree (Fig. 6.90).
- **Single reading micrometer theodolite** (Fig. 6.91). These instruments rely on a parallel plate micrometer to deflect light to read an index mark. The amount of deflection is read on the micrometer scale.
- **Double reading micrometer theodolite** (Fig. 6.92). These instruments have a light system which reads the opposite sides of the main circle and reflects them together. Rotation of the micrometer brings the readings into coincidence. This gives a reading free of eccentricity error.
- **Electronic theodolite.** These instruments have the graduated circles replaced by coded ones and readings

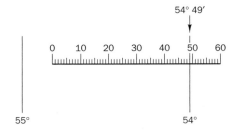

Figure 6.90 Optical scale theodolite reading

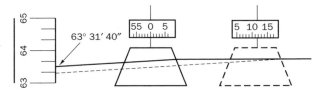

Figure 6.91 Single-reading optical micrometer

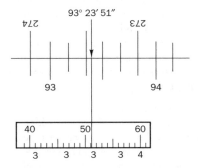

Figure 6.92 Double-reading optical micrometer

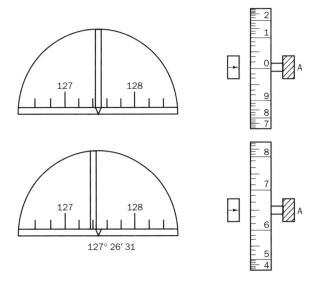

Figure 6.93 Drum micrometer reading

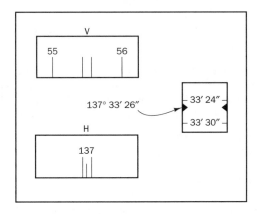

Figure 6.94 Three-window digital micrometer

appear on a crystal display. Readings can be collected in an integral data logger and downloaded into a computer back at the office.

The accuracy of an instrument selected depends on the type of work for which it is to be used. Low-order instruments reading to an accuracy of $20''$ are used for general construction and setting-out work where high accuracy is not essential. Middle-order instruments reading directly to $1''$ are used by land surveyors for large-scale surveys and third-order triangulation work. Geodetic theodolites reading directly to $0.2''$ are used for primary and secondary triangulation and first-order traverse work. Other micrometer reading systems are shown in Figs 6.93 and 6.94.

Techniques and principles associated with angular measurement

The levelling procedures for setting up a theodolite are similar to those for the level and are repeated as follows (Fig. 6.95):

Tripod

1. Ensure that the tripod is stable with points firmly in the ground.
2. Ensure that the tripod head is horizontal and that the fixing screws are tight.
3. Place the tripod approximately central over station peg.

Levelling

4. Position the telescope parallel to the footscrews A and B.
5. The footscrews should be rotated in such a way that thumbs on each hand rotate inwards or outwards. The plate bubble will follow the direction of movement of the left thumb.
6. Centralise the plate bubble.
7. Rotate the telescope through 90°.
8. Using only footscrew C, centralise the bubble. The bubble will follow the movement direction of the left thumb.
9. Repeat the procedure to confirm that the bubble remains central in both positions.
10. Check to confirm that the bubble remains central at telescope position 180° to that of step 4. If the bubble remains central there is zero bubble error. To remove any error at this position, reduce by half by turning the footscrew. In this way the plane will be perfectly horizontal even though the bubble will be off centre for the whole of the 360°.

Setting up above stations using optical plummet

11. Place the legs equidistant from the ground marker and level up the tripod head by eye.
12. Place the instrument on the tripod and locate the marker by sighting through the optical plummet.

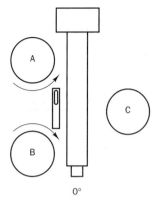
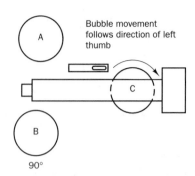

Figure 6.95 Levelling of plate bubble

13. Using footscrews, centre above mark.
14. Level using sliding legs.
15. Fine level using footscrews.
16. Release the centring clamp and centre above mark.

Measurement of a horizontal angle *CAO* with instrument at *A*

When an observer looks through the eyepiece the vertical circle of the instrument will be either to the right or left. If the vertical circle is on the left the readings taken from the position will be booked face left. The readings on each face differ by 180°.

1. Level up the instrument at *A*.
2. Clamp the lower plate.
3. With the upper plate unclamped, sight *O*.
4. Clamp the upper plate and using the fine adjustments screw obtain fine intersection of *O*.
5. Read the angle using the scale to give the face reading at *O*.
6. Unclamp the upper plate sight *C*.
7. Clamp the upper plate and using the fine adjustment screw obtain a fine intersection of *C*.
8. Read the angle using the scale to give the face reading at *C*.
9. On the other face intersect *C* in the same way and book on line *O*.
10. On the other face intersect *O* in the same way and book on line *O*.

A set of readings is then obtained, as shown in Table 6.16. Since the instrument is rotated 180° when changing face, the difference between face left and face right readings is 180°. If this difference is not exactly 180° the difference is known as the collimation error. The mean is obtained by applying 180° to the face right value and averaging the value obtained with the face left value. The angle *CAO* is the difference of the means.

Table 6.16

Instrument at	Station	Face left	Face right	Difference
A	B	63° 25′ 20″	243° 25′ 40″	180° 00′ 20″
	C	156° 48′ 40″	336° 49′ 00″	180° 00′ 20″
Difference		93° 23′ 20″	93° 23′ 20″	

Measurement of vertical angles

Vertical angles are measured with respect to a horizontal datum and the pattern of the vertical circle varies with different theodolites. Older instruments are fitted with an altitude bubble on the vertical circle which may be levelled with a clip screw, the bubble being centralised prior to taking readings. Modern theodolites have an automatic vertical indexing facility provided by a damped pendulum device. Electronic theodolites are normally automatic and will enable the operator to set zero either at the horizontal horizon or the zenith at the touch of an internal switch. Vertical angles should always be referenced to an elevation or depression with respect to the horizontal, with the instrument placed in position.

1. Level up through 360°.
2. Level the index arm spirit level in older instruments or accept automatic horizons with newer types.
3. Sight approximately onto *A* and clamp the circle.
4. Using the fine adjustment, sight *A* accurately.
5. Read the angle using the scale.
6. Repeat the procedure, using the opposite face.
7. Reduce the angles and determine the mean.

Typical horizontal and vertical angle recordings are shown in Fig. 6.96.

Theodolite adjustments are beyond the scope of this unit and suffice to say that if an error is suspected the instrument manufacturers' instructions should be consulted for the correcting action required. There are five adjustments that may be required, which should be completed in the following order:

1. Plate level adjustment: similar to the first adjustment of the Dumpy level, this confirms whether the bubble retains its central position irrespective of telescope rotation in the horizontal plane.
2. Horizontal collimation or vertical hair adjustment: this is to set the line of sight perpendicular to the trunnion axis.
3. Trunnion axis adjustment: this is to set the trunnion axis perpendicular to the vertical axis so that it will be horizontal when the instrument is levelled.
4. Vertical circle index adjustment: this is to ensure that the readings on each face are 0° or a multiple of 90° according to the circle graduations when the line of sight is horizontal.
5. Optical plummet adjustment: as the plummet can be located in the plate or tribrach, adjustments differ with the object of ensuring that the vertical line of sight coincides with the vertical axis of the levelled theodolite.

Sources of error in use when measuring angles are:

1. Inaccurate centring when measuring angles.
2. Inaccurate bisection using a plumb bob.
3. Parallax (see errors in levelling).
4. Line of collimation set at right angles to horizontal axis.
5. Line of collimation not in centre of telescope.

Instrument:	Surveyors:	Contract No: ....
Number:	Observers:	Title: ....
Station reference A:	Booker:	Job No.: ....
Station height: 1.42 ODN	Date:	

Position	Horizontal angles				
	Face left	Face right	Left and right mean	Angle with respect to X	
X	00°09′30″	180°09′10″	00°08′50″	00°00′00″	
B	64°16′50″	244°17′10″	64°17′00″	64°08′10″	
C	123°24′30″	303°24′20″	123°24′25″	123°15′35″	
D	184°36′40″	04°37′30″	184°37′05″	184°28′15″	

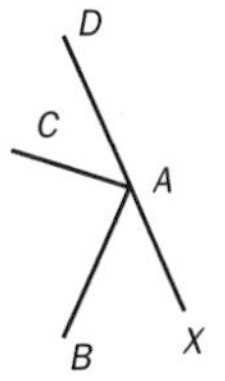

Difference X	180°09′10″		Difference B	244°17′10″
	000°08′30″			64°16′50″
	180°00′40″			180°00′20″

Angle XAB	64°16′50″		Angle XAB	244°17′10″
	00°08′30″			180°09′10″
	64°08′20″			64°08′00″

∴ Angle with respect of X = 64°08′10″

Position target height	Vertical angles				
	Face left	Face right	Face left correction	Face right correction	Average
B 1.42	93°04′10″	266°53′40″	−03°04′10″	−03°06′20″	−03°05′15″
C 1.42	87°42′20″	272°20′50″	02°17′40″	02°20′50″	+02°19′15″
D 1.42	86°18′40″	273°43′20″	03°41′20″	03°43′20″	+03°46′20″

Figure 6.96 Horizontal and vertical angle recordings

6. Imperfect graduations of circles.
7. Vertical instrument axis not truly vertical.
8. Horizontal axis not at right angles to the vertical axis.
9. Slip on bearings when using slow-motion screws.
10. Eccentricity of plate bearings.
11. Personal reading errors.

Safety in use:

1. The surveyor is responsible for the safety of the personnel and equipment.
2. Potential hazards and dangers should be anticipated, particularly when working close to moving construction traffic and adjacent to the public highway.
3. The instrument should be set up so that it is stable with the tripod legs secured in the ground.
4. If the instrument is set up on a smooth or hard surface, a tripod restrainer should be used to prevent slippage.
5. The instrument in use should be protected against extremes of weather.
6. Clamps and adjusting screws on the instrument should not be over-tightened.
7. On removal from its case the position or lie should be noted to make replacement easier after use.
8. Ensure that the instrument is clean and dry after use.
9. Clamps on the instrument should be locked after replacement.
10. There should be a daily check on the plate bubble and approximately monthly checks made on the trunnion

axis error, collimation axis error, index error and optical plummet.

Self-assessment tasks

1. A four-sided closed traverse has the following internal angles:

   Angle *DAB* 101° 30′ 00″ instrument at *A*
   Angle *ABC* 95° 30′ 00″ instrument at *B*
   Angle *BCD* 60° 00′ 00″ instrument at *C*
   Angle *CDA* 103° 00′ 00″ instrument at *D*

   Stations are lettered anticlockwise and angles measured clockwise. Length of sides of the traverse are:

   AB 65 m
   BC 110 m
   CD 98.5 m
   DE 70 m

   The whole circle bearing of line *AB* is 154° 30′ 00″.

   (a) Check and adjust the angles.
   (b) Determine the reduced bearings of the traverse.
   (c) Calculate the coordinates required for plotting the survey.

2. The results of a closed traverse survey lettered anticlockwise *ABCDA* are given below. Taking the coordinates of *A* as 1000.00 m east, 1000.00 m north and *AB* as the meridian:

   (a) Calculate the coordinates of *B*, *C*, and *D*.
   (b) Set out calculations and results in a standard tabular form with arithmetical checks.

Internal angle $DAB = 208° 25'$
Internal angle $ABC = 46° 20'$
Internal angle $BCD = 82° 40'$
Internal angle $CDA = 22° 35'$
Lengths: $AB = 82.46$ m
$BC = 127.50$ m
$CD = 218.13$ m
$DA = 162.41$ m

3. Working in a small group select a piece of land suitable for demonstrating the ability to complete the following tasks:

(a) Set up a theodolite over a given point.
(b) Measure, record and accurately calculate an angle between two given points.
(c) Set out precisely a given angle from one point.
(d) Obtain the reduced level of a point from a given temporary bench mark.
(e) Explain verbally the most suitable method to adopt in order to determine the height of a building using a theodolite and tape.

4. Figure 6.97 shows a theodolite set up to measure the zenith angle of slope of the ground. With the theodolite directed to point X the face left and face right readings were respectively $76° 31' 40''$ and $283° 21' 20''$. Determine the correct zenith angle if the vertical angle measures $23° 21' 20''$ uncorrected.

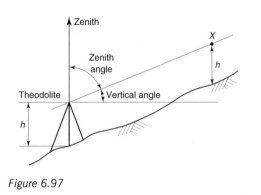

Figure 6.97

The versatility of the modern scientific calculator can be shown through many examples related to the calculation of coordinates and bearings of control stations. Students should work through the following example to identify the procedural steps.

Example

Using the rectangular–polar conversion facility on a scientific calculator, determine the bearing of B from A and its distance from the following information:

Coordinates of A 400.60 N, 300.80 E
Coordinates of B 605.80 N, 425.50 E

Difference in northings between
$B - A = 605.80 - 400.60 = +205.60$

Difference in eastings between
$B - A = 425.50 - 300.80 = +124.70$

On the calculator:

Enter 205.20, press ⟨INV⟩ ⟨R→P⟩ enter 124.7, press ⟨=⟩

Display shows: 240.119 m = length A to B

Press ⟨X ↔ Y⟩

Display shows: 31.287042° = bearing A to B decimalised

Press ⟨INV⟩ ⟨° ' ''⟩

Display shows: 31° 17' 13.3'' = bearing C to H

Using rectangular–polar angular conversion and memory facilities, the complete calculation is as follows:

Enter 425.50 − 300.80
Display shows: +124.7

Press ⟨M in⟩ to enter into memory

Enter 605.80 − 400.60
Display shows: +205.20

Press ⟨INV⟩ ⟨R→P⟩

Press ⟨MR⟩ ⟨=⟩

Display shows: 240.119 m = length A to B
Press ⟨X ↔ Y⟩
Display shows: 31.287042° = bearing A to B decimalised

Press ⟨INV⟩ ⟨° ' ''⟩

Display shows: 31° 17' 13.3''

Calculations associated with linear measurement, angular measurement and height control

The techniques of linear measurement, height control and angular measurement each attract calculations which have been integrated into the text at the appropriate section.

The calculations in this section are a significant part of the integrated mathematics for this GNVQ and by appropriate cross referencing many of the key skills outcomes at level 3 can be covered in the portfolio of evidence.

In this section the techniques for assessing the most suitable method of calculating areas will be covered to allow the necessary calculations to be made to find the areas for construction works projects. On most sites calculations of areas and volumes will require to be made for many purposes including setting out and contractual payments. Areas need to be calculated for land purchase and planning. Volumes need to be calculated for the earthworks to be allowed for in cuttings and embankments to hopefully have a situation where the 'amount of material cut' is balanced by the 'amount of fill required'.

All the data for calculations has to be obtained by some method to allow calculations to be made. The data can be obtained from a site survey and the calculations made directly from the field notes. The data can also be converted into coordinates of latitude or longitude or a plotted plan from which the area is computed. Some data may also exist in the form of a map or an Ordnance Survey plan. Areas which are regular in shape can be calculated by the direct application of the accepted mensuration formulae.

Regular areas

The regular areas are shown in Fig. 6.98. Trigonometry may also be used to determine areas of regular figures, and Fig. 6.99 is given as a reminder for a right-angled triangle.

A reminder for a non-right-angled triangle is shown in Fig. 6.100:

$$\frac{a}{\sin A} = \frac{b}{\sin B} = \frac{c}{\sin C}$$

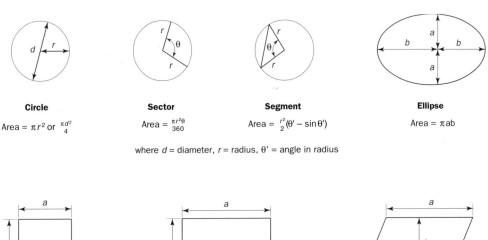

where d = diameter, r = radius, θ' = angle in radius

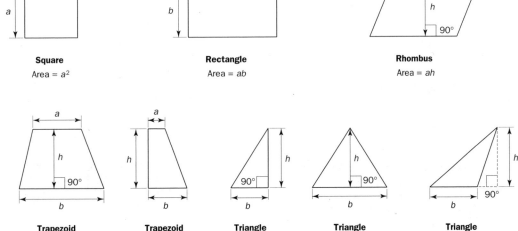

Figure 6.98 Regular areas

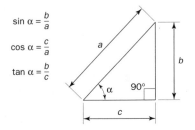

Figure 6.99

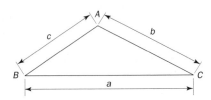

Figure 6.100

$$a^2 = b^2 + c^2 - 2bc \cos A$$

$$\cos A = \frac{b^2 + c^2 - a^2}{2bc}$$

$$\text{Area} = \tfrac{1}{2} ca \times \sin B \quad \text{or} \quad \text{Area} = \frac{c^2 \sin A \sin B}{2 \sin C}$$

Knowing only the length of sides, the 's' rule may be used to find the area of a triangle:

$$s = \frac{a + b + c}{2}$$

and

$$\text{Area of a triangle} = \sqrt{s(s - a)(s - b)(s - c)}$$

In work associated with the determination of land boundaries it is often useful to be able to calculate the perimeters and the curtilage of a parcel of land.

Perimeters

$$\text{Circle} = 2\pi r \quad \text{or} \quad \pi d$$

where r = radius of the circle

and d = diameter of the circle.

$$\text{Ellipse} = \pi(a + b) \quad \text{refer to Fig. 8.98.}$$

$$\text{Sector arc length} = \frac{\theta^\circ \times 2\pi r}{360} \quad \text{refer to Fig. 8.98.}$$

This last equation is used in connection with circular curve ranging, a technique covered by the Optional or Additional unit of surveying.

Examples of calculations of regular areas

The calculations would also form part of the requirement of key skills coverage at level 2 and 3 in Application of Number.

Example 1

An area of land has been split into six figures for convenience of calculation. Determine the total area of land shown in Fig. 6.101.

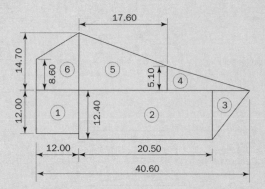

Figure 6.101 Example 1 (all dimensions in metres)

Students may also find it useful to produce Fig. 6.101 to scale on graph paper or using a computer.

Answer

Area ① Square   Area $= 12 \times 12 = 144\,m^2$

Area ② Rectangle Area $= 12.40 \times 20.50 = 254.2\,m^2$

Area ③ Triangle   Area $= \frac{1}{2}[40.6 - 32.5]\,12.40 = 50.22\,m^2$

Area ④ Triangle   Area $= \frac{1}{2}[40.6 - 12.0 - 17.60]\,5.10$
                            $= 28.05\,m^2$

Area ⑤ Trapezoid Area $= \frac{1}{2}[14.70 + 5.10]\,17.60$
                            $= 174.24\,m^2$

Area ⑥ Trapezoid Area $= \frac{1}{2}[8.60 + 14.70]\,12.00$
                            $= 139.80\,m^2$

Total area $= 790.51\,m^2$

Although this calculation has been made in m^2, land areas are often calculated in hectares:

$$10\,000\,m^2 \equiv 1\ \text{hectare}$$
(which is about 2.50 acres in the old imperial measurement)

$$100\ \text{hectares} \equiv 1\,km^2$$
(which is the area of one Ordnance Survey 1 : 2500 scale map)

Example 2

An area of land is shown in Fig. 6.102. Calculate (i) the total area of the site in hectares and (ii) the perimeter of the site.

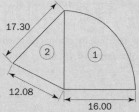

Figure 6.102 Example 2 (all dimensions in metres)

Area ① Quarter circle Area $= \dfrac{\pi \times 16^2}{4} = 201.062\,m^2$

Area ② Triangle   Area $= \sqrt{s(s-a)(s-b)(s-c)}$

$$s = \frac{a+b+c}{2} = 22.69$$

$a = 12.08$	$s - a$ =	10.61
$b = 16.00$	$s - b$ =	6.69
$c = 17.30$	$s - c$ =	5.39
	Check	22.69 ✓

Area $= \sqrt{22.69\,(10.61)(6.69)(5.39)}$

     $= 93.171\,m^2$ or 9.317×10^{-3} ha

Self-assessment tasks

1. Figure 6.103 shows the dimensions of a patio which is to have a raised flower bed.
   (i) Calculate the total area to be covered with concrete slabs $600 \times 600\,mm$. (The area should be initially superimposed on graph paper, to assist the calculation.)
   (ii) Assuming the flower bed profile shows the external face of the raised wall, calculate the perimeter of the raised bed.
   (iii) Using an appropriate computer software program, transfer the data shown on Fig. 6.103 to produce a computer-generated image of the area.

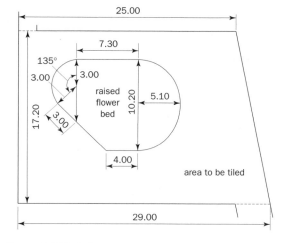

Figure 6.103 Self-assessment task 1 (all dimensions in metres)

2. Calculate the area of plate required for the ventilation duct shown in Fig. 6.104.

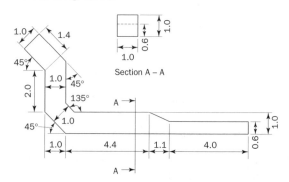

Figure 6.104 Self-assessment task 2 (all dimensions in metres)

3. Calculate the area of roof to be tiled from the dimensions shown in Fig. 6.105.

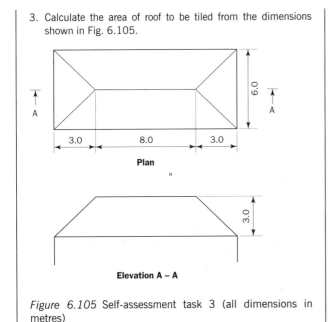

Plan

"

Elevation A – A

Figure 6.105 Self-assessment task 3 (all dimensions in metres)

Irregular areas

A plot of ground having at least one curved side is referred to as being irregular in shape, unless the curved side forms part of an arc of a circle. The curved sides preclude the use of the geometric formulae considered earlier and other methods are used for the area calculations for these shapes.

Area and boundary terms

Boundaries of areas on plans and drawings may be made up of straight lines (a rectangular boundary) or of irregular lines (curvilinear boundaries). Where the boundary is curvilinear, straight 'give and take' lines may be drawn on the plan to replace actual boundaries for calculation purposes (Fig. 6.106). These lines should be placed so that the areas excluded by them are approximately equal to the areas taken in by them. When the boundaries have been averaged out the figure becomes rectilinear.

Areas from plotted plans or other drawings

Subdivision into triangles Any straight-sided or rectilinear figure may be subdivided into triangles by drawing appropriate straight lines. The figure area is then the sum of the areas of the triangles. Trapeziums can also be used.

Counting squares or dots The squares method uses a transparent overlay with a grid drawn on the overlay, each grid square representing a unit of square measure, e.g. 2 mm

squared paper with each 10th line in a heavier gauge. At 1:500 scale each small square represents $1\,m^2$ and large square $100\,m^2$. At 1:2500 scale the areas would be $25\,m^2$ and 0.25 hectare respectively.

The transparency is placed over the area to be measured so that as many large squares as possible fall within the boundary and a line of the grid made to coincide with one or more of the rectilinear boundary. The squares are counted with part squares being judged by eye. This method should be done twice. An alternative method is to replace the squares by dots at the same spacing.

Ordinates overlay (Fig. 6.107) This method is similar to counting squares or dots.

Mean ordinate rule (Fig. 6.108) A line is drawn through the centre of the area to be measured (d). The line is divided into equal intervals of length l and ordinates drawn at right angles to the line, the length of the ordinates being scaled as O_1, O_2, $O_3, \ldots, O_n$.

The mean ordinate rule states that the area is equal to mean ordinate length multiplied by the total length of the line:

$$\text{Area} = \left(\frac{d}{n}\right)(O_1 + O_2 + O_3 + \ldots + O_n)$$

where d is the total line length, n is the number of ordinates and the ordinates are O_1, O_2, O_3, etc.

Trapezoidal rule In this method, the shape formed between each pair of ordinates is considered to be a trapezium; then summing the area of each trapezium gives:

$$\text{Area} = \left(\frac{l}{2}\right)(O_1 + 2O_2 + 2O_3 + \ldots + 2O_{(n-1)} + O_n)$$

Total area equals the common distance apart multiplied by the sum of half the first and last ordinates plus all the others. This method is more accurate than the mean ordinate rule.

Simpson's Rule This is similar to the trapezoidal rule but assumes that the irregular boundary consists of a series of parabolic arcs between the ordinates rather than straight lines.

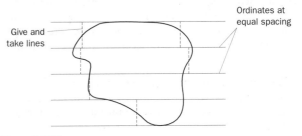

Give and take lines

Ordinates at equal spacing

Figure 6.107

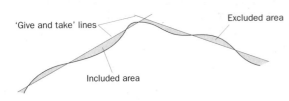

'Give and take' lines

Excluded area

Included area

Figure 6.106

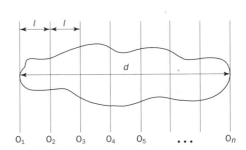

Figure 6.108

The area must be divided into an even number of strips by an odd number of ordinates. If there are an odd number of strips, then the last strip area must be calculated separately and added to the area calculated for the even number of strips:

$$\text{Area} = \left(\frac{l}{3}\right)(O_1 + 4O_2 + 2O_3 + 4O_4 + \ldots$$
$$+ 2O_{(n-2)} + 4O_{(n-1)} + O_n)$$

That is, the total area is equal to one-third the strip width multiplied by the sum of the first and last ordinates, twice the sum of the remaining odd ordinates and four times the sum of the even ordinates.

Example

A strip of land is 960 m long. This length is marked off into 8 equal divisions and the consecutive breadths are scaled off at the ends of the intervals as follows:

5, 13, 15, 18, 20, 24, 12, 6 and 5.

Find the area in hectares by (a) trapezoidal rule and (b) Simpson's rule.

Answer

(a) Each interval is $\dfrac{960}{8} = 120\,\text{m}$

Half sum of first and last ordinates $= \dfrac{5+5}{2} = 5$

Sum of remaining ordinates:
$13 + 15 + 18 + 20 + 24 + 12 + 6 = \underline{108}$
$\text{Total} = \overline{113}\,\text{m}$

$\text{Area} = 120 \times 113 = 13\,560\,\text{m}^2 = 1.356\,\text{ha}$

(b) Sum of first and last ordinates $\qquad\qquad = 10$

Twice the sum of all other odd ordinates:
$[2(15 + 20 + 12)] \qquad\qquad\qquad = 94$

Four times the sum of all even ordinates:
$[4(13 + 18 + 24 + 6)] \qquad\qquad = \underline{244}$
$\text{Total} = \overline{348}\,\text{m}$

$\text{Area} = \dfrac{120}{3} \times 348 = 13\,920\,\text{m}^2 = 1.392\,\text{ha}$

The planimeter (Fig. 6.109) The planimeter is a mechanical device for integration, i.e. the calculation of an area under the curve of a function. Area measurement from drawings by planimeter is efficient and fast. Accuracy is similar to that of counting squares.

1. The pole arm has a needle-pointed weight at one end, the pole weight sometimes being separate. The other end of the pole arm carries a pivot resting in a socket in the tracer arm.

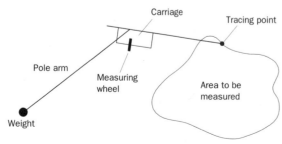

Figure 6.109

2. The tracer arm is fitted at one end with a tracing point with an adjustable support.
3. The carriage, which may be fixed to, or may slide along, the tracer arm, has a measuring wheel and a counting scale or dial.
4. The counting dial records the number of revolutions made by the wheel, which may also be fitted with a vernier scale.

Example

Using a fixed-arm planimeter with a pole block outside the figure, the following readings were recorded, where one revolution of the measuring wheel represented $100\,\text{cm}^2$ when measuring an irregular area on a plot to a scale of $1:500$. What was the ground area?

Answer

Initial reading	Final reading	Difference
0.160	2.173	2.013
2.173	4.188	2.015
4.190	6.204	2.014

Mean reading is 2.014. Each revolution $= 100\,\text{cm}^2$. Therefore, area on plot $= 201.4\,\text{cm}^2$.

At a scale of $1:500$:

$1\,\text{cm}^2 = 500 \times 500\,\text{cm}^2$

or $\quad = \dfrac{500 \times 500}{100 \times 100} = 25\,\text{m}^2$ on the ground

Therefore area on ground $= 201.4 \times 25$
$= 5035\,\text{m}^2 = 0.504\,\text{ha}$

Sliding bar polar planimeters (carriage slide along the tracer arm) have a scale on the tracer arm so that the carriage may be set at some particular map scale so that one revolution of the wheel will equal one specific unit of area.

Example

In measuring an irregular area of a $1:2500$ scale plot, the planimeter carriage was set such that one revolution of the wheel represented 5 ha. The constant of the instrument at this setting was 26.102. What was the area measured if the mean of three readings taken was 7.341 and it was noted that the initial readings were greater than the final reading each time?

Answer

The instrument recorded a backward movement, therefore the area measured was less than the area of the zero circle. The reading must therefore be subtracted from the constant.

Constant	26.102
Less reading	7.341
	18.761

$\therefore \quad \text{Area} = 18.761 \times 5\,\text{ha} = 93.805\,\text{ha}$

Example

Calculate the area shown in Fig. 6.110 from the data obtained from the chain survey.

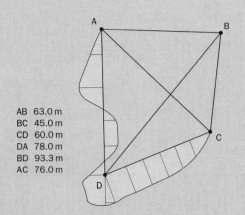

AB 63.0 m
BC 45.0 m
CD 60.0 m
DA 78.0 m
BD 93.3 m
AC 76.0 m

Figure 6.110

Answer

Figure 6.110 shows the rectilinear area ABCD which is calculated first; their regular strips between the chain lines and the boundary must be separately evaluated and either added or subtracted as necessary from the main rectilinear area calculation result.

AB and BC are straight boundaries. Offsets to the irregular boundaries are given in Table 6.17.

Table 6.17

Chainage AD		Offset	Chainage CD		Offset
A	0.0	0.0	C	0.0	0.0
	16.0	6.0		10.0	4.2
	33.0	7.0		20.0	6.4
	40.0	0.0		30.0	8.1
	49.0	7.0		40.0	10.3
	61.0	7.0		50.0	11.3
	68.0	0.0	D	60.0	13.2
D	78.0	11.0			
	89.0	5.0			
	93.0	9.0			

The rectilinear area from $A = \sqrt{s(s-a)(s-b)(s-c)}$

Area of $\triangle ACD$ $= \sqrt{107(31)(47)(29)}$

$= 2126.3\,\text{m}^2$

Area of $\triangle ABC$ $= \sqrt{92(29)(47)(16)}$

$= 1416.4\,\text{m}^2$

$\therefore$ Area of $\triangle ABCD = 2126.3 + 1416.4 = 3542.7\,\text{m}^2$

Check: Area of $\triangle ABD = \sqrt{117.15(54.15)(39.15)(23.85)}$

$= 2433.8\,\text{m}^2$

Area of $\triangle BCD = \sqrt{99.15(39.15)(54.15)(5.85)}$

$= 1108.9\,\text{m}^2$

$\therefore$ Area of $\triangle ABCD = 2433.8 + 1108.9 = 3542.7\,\text{m}^2$

Area of trapezoids on **AD**

Plus		Minus
$\dfrac{0+6}{2} \times 160 = 48.0$		
$\dfrac{6+7}{2} \times 17 \ = 110.5$		
$\dfrac{7+0}{2} \times 7 \ \ = 24.5$	$\dfrac{0+7}{2} \times 9 = 31.5$	
$\dfrac{0+11}{2} \times 10 = 55.0$	$\dfrac{7+7}{2} \times 12 = 84.0$	
$\dfrac{11+9}{2} \times 15 = 150.0$	$\dfrac{7+0}{2} \times 7 = 24.5$	
$\overline{388.5}$	$\overline{140.0}$	

388.5
-140.0
$\overline{248.5}$

Total (plus) area on $AD = 248.5\,\text{m}^2$

Area by the trapezoidal rule on CD

$$\text{Area} = 10\left(\frac{0.0+13.2}{2} + 4.2 + 6.4 + 8.1 + 10.3 + 11.3\right)$$

$$= 469.0\,\text{m}^2$$

The area of the omitted triangle can be calculated from the formula

$$\text{Area} = \frac{1}{2}\binom{\text{base on } AD}{\text{produced}} \times \binom{\text{perpendicular height from offset}}{\text{of 5 m at chainage 89.0 m}}$$

$$\text{Area} = \frac{15}{2} \times 5 = 37.5\,\text{m}^2$$

The total site area equals the sum of the individual parts being the following:

Rectilinear area (3542.7) + Irregular area on AD (248.5)
  + irregular area on CD (469.0) + omitted triangle (37.5)
  = 4297.7 m².

$\therefore$ Total area $= 0.4298\,\text{ha}$.

Digital planimeters

Mechanical planimeters have been largely replaced by digital planimeters such as the Tamaya Digital Planimeter, Planix 7, which incorporates integrated circuit technology. It has a tracer arm with a tracer lens and tracer point, but the pole and pole arm have been eliminated and there are now rollers, with contact rings, on an axle.

Firstly, the tracer arm is set on the approximate centre line of the area to be measured and after the power, which may be either battery or mains, is switched on the unit of measurement is selected from the available range. The scale or scales can be fed in via the relevant keys on the keyboard. A reference start point is selected on the perimeter of the area to be calculated and the tracer arm positioned thereon. The 'start' key is activated, causing the display to register zero, and the tracer point moved clockwise around the perimeter of the area to return to the reference point. Motion of the system is sensed by an electro shaft-encoder generating pulses which are processed electronically so that the measured area is displayed digitally. Some planimeters possess two rotary encoders which facilitate the evaluation of coordinates and can compute areas and line lengths. This instrument can be interfaced to a computer. (A photograph of a digital planimeter can be seen in *Surveying* by Bannister, Raymond and Baker, 277.)

Areas by coordinates

Where traverse surveys are plotted from coordinates it is often convenient to calculate the area from the coordinates themselves. Figure 6.111 shows a closed traverse $ABCDEA$ whose stations have coordinates E_A, N_A; E_B, N_B; etc., relative to two axes whose origin is O.

Area $ABCDEA = [ABPT + BCQP + CDRQ - DESR - EATS]$

$$= \left(\frac{N_A + N_B}{2}\right) \times (E_B - E_A) + \left(\frac{N_B + N_C}{2}\right)$$
$$\times (E_C - E_B) + \left(\frac{N_C + N_D}{2}\right) \times (E_D - E_C)$$
$$- \left(\frac{N_D + N_E}{2}\right) \times (E_D - E_E) - \left(\frac{N_E + N_A}{2}\right)$$
$$\times (E_E - E_A)$$

This can be simplified to:

$$\text{Area } ABCDEA = \frac{1}{2}\left[\sum_{i=1}^{n} N_1(E_{i+1} - E_{i-1})\right]$$

This is difficult to remember, especially as the formula can be developed by projecting the traverse legs onto the northing rather than the easting axis. The formula will give negative answers if the figure is lettered anticlockwise. Students may remember the equation more easily if it placed as words:

Area = [sum(easting of station × northing of preceding station) − sum(easting of station × northing of following station)]

and the array can be shown as follows:

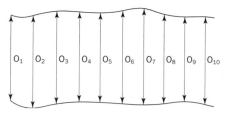

and the following is the sequence of operations in the calculation of the area of any polygon:

1. Write the array of eastings and northings as shown.
2. Multiply the departure of each station by the latitude of the preceding station and find the sum.
3. Multiply the departure of each station by the latitude of the following station and find the sum.
4. Find the algebraic difference between steps 2 and 3.
5. Halve this figure to give the area of the polygon.

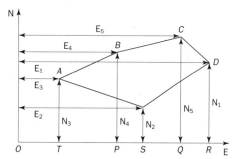

Figure 6.111 A closed traverse

Example

Calculate the area in hectares and m² enclosed by the line of a closed traverse $ABCDE$ from the following data.

Station	E(m)	N(m)
A	100.00	200.00
B	206.98	285.65
C	268.55	182.02
D	292.93	148.80
E	191.74	85.70

Answer

Table 6.18

Station	N_i	E_{i+1}	E_{i-1}	$N_i(E_{i+1} - E_{i-1})$
A	200.00	206.98	191.74	3 048.00
B	285.65	268.55	100.00	48 146.31
C	182.02	292.93	206.98	15 644.62
D	148.80	191.74	268.55	−11 429.33
E	85.70	100.00	292.93	−16 534.10
			Total	38 875.50/2
				= 19 437.75 m²

$10\,000\,\text{m}^2 \equiv 1\,\text{hectare}$ ∴ Area = 1.944 hectares

---

Self-assessment tasks

1. Using the trapezoidal rule calculate the area of the plot of land shown in Fig. 6.112.

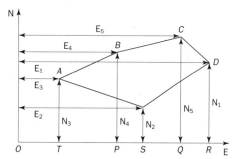

Figure 6.112

Offset: O_1 33.52 m, O_2 39.62 m, O_3 40.84 m,
O_4 37.18 m, O_5 33.52 m, O_6 35.36 m,
O_7 35.36 m, O_8 34.74 m, O_9 33.52 m,
O_{10} 35.36 m

The offsets are taken at every 15 m.

2. In a tape and offset survey the following offsets were taken to a fence from a survey line. Using Simpson's Rule calculate the area between the fence and the survey line.

Chainage (m)	0	15	30	45	60	75	90	105	120
Offset (m)	0	6.56	10.21	8.53	10.75	13.40	9.80	4.70	1.90

NB: Simpson's Rule is applied when there is an ODD number of ordinates. Any residual area between in this case a ninth and tenth offset is calculated separately.

Chainage (m)	135
Offset	0

3. Figure 6.113, the survey of a proposed cutting, shows that the depths at 15 m intervals are 0, 1.8, 3.0, 6.4 and 6.6 m respectively. Given that the roadway is to be 9 m wide and that the cutting has 30° side slopes, calculate:

   (a) the plan surface area of the excavation *ABCD*.

   (b) the actual area of the side slopes *ABE* and *CDF*.

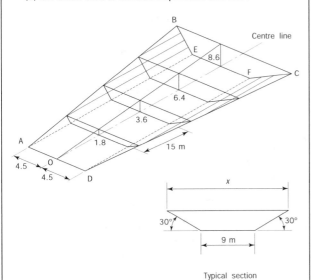

Figure 6.113 Survey of a proposed cutting

HINT: Some preliminary calculations are needed at each section to determine dimension *x* at each section.

4. (i) From first principles derive Simpson's rule for the calculation of axes.

   (ii) Measurements made from a base line to an irregular boundary were as follows:

Chainage (m)	Offset (m)
0	5.5
10	6.5
20	8.2
30	7.9
40	8.5
50	6.5
60	4.9
70	3.0
80	3.0
90	3.2
100	0

   Calculate the area between the base line and the boundary.

5. The coordinates of a six-sided area of land are as follows, in metres:

   A (0, 0); B (40, −30); C (120, −45); D (200, 15);
   E (150, 70); F (60, 102); G (−13, 28); A (0, 0)

   (i) Calculate the area of the land.
   (ii) If the land is to be divided into equal halves, calculate the coordinates of a fence commencing at *A* (0, 0) and terminating along one side of the land, if the fence is straight.

Volumes

While not forming part of the syllabus for the Surveying Processes unit, it is appropriate that students are able to make simple volumetric calculations for works which involve excavation, loading, hauling, dumping and disposal of earth, particularly as payment for this type of work is usually on a volumetric basis.

Volumes are usually calculated in one of three ways:

1. By cross-sections. Generally used for works such as roads, railways and pipelines. Calculations are from standard formulae or from first principles.
2. By contours. Generally used for larger areas such as reservoirs, and redevelopment sites. Contour interval requires to be 1 or 2 m at the most.
3. By spot heights. Generally used for smaller sites and basements.

The calculations for 1 and 2 are beyond the scope of this section but the method of spot heights should be well within the scope of student knowledge if this section has been read carefully. The site is divided into squares or rectangles, preferably with sides of equal lengths. The volumes are calculated from the product of the mean length of the sides of each vertical truncated prism and the cross-sectional area. The size of the rectangles or triangles is dependent on the degree of accuracy required with the aim to produce areas such that the ground surface within each can be assumed to be plane.

Example

Figure 6.114 shows the reduced levels of a rectangular plot which is to be excavated to a uniform depth of 7 m above datum. Calculate the mean level of the ground and the volume of earth to be excavated. Note that the mean level of the ground is the mean of the mean heights of each prism.

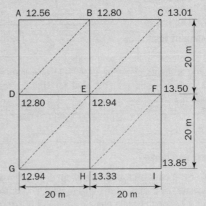

Figure 6.114

Answer

Calculation from triangles for the plot are shown in Table 6.19.

Table 6.19

Station	Reduced level	Number of times the reduced level is used (*n*)	Product reduced level × *n*
A	12.56	1	12.56
B	12.80	3	38.40
C	13.01	2	26.02
D	12.80	3	38.40
E	12.94	7	90.58
F	13.50	2	27.00
G	12.94	2	25.88
H	13.33	2	26.66
I	13.85	2	27.70
		$\sum n = 24$	313.20

Depth of excavation = 13.05 − 7 = 6.05 m
Volume = 6.05 × 40 × 40 = 9685 m³

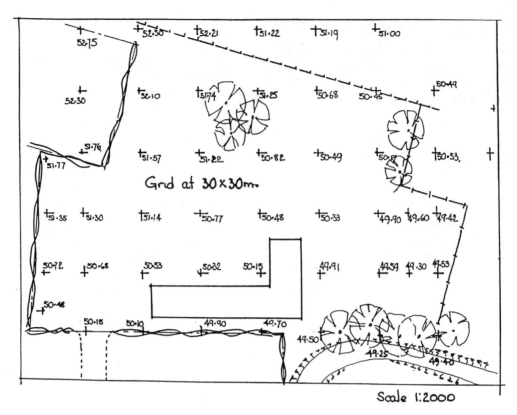

Figure 6.115 Site survey

Self-assessment task

Figure 6.115 shows a site survey plotted to a scale of 1 : 2000. The plan should be used to determine areas and volumes for excavation purposes and students preparing a portfolio of evidence to satisfy Unit 6 should supplement the data shown on the plan with their own design data which could also be used for Unit 2 Design for Construction and the Built Environment and Unit 5 Town Planning and Development.

Self-assessment tasks

1. A pipeline trench is excavated to a width of 750 mm along a line *XY* between, chainage 0 and 140 m..
   (i) Calculate the volume of material to be removed from the vertical-sided trench.
   (ii) If the pipeline to be laid has a diameter of 600 mm, calculate the volume of material that will be surplus to backfilling requirements.
   Data:

Chainage (m)	0		20		40		60		80		100		120		140
Depth (m)		1.20		1.50		0.90		2.20		2.5		0.90		1.80	

2. The areas within the contour lines at the site of a reservoir are as follows:

Contour (m)	Area (km²)	Contour (m)	Area (km²)
170	0.48	160	0.150
168	0.43	158	0.080
166	0.38	156	0.010
164	0.30	154 (reservoir base)	0.001
162	0.22		

   (i) Calculate the volume of water in the reservoir when the water level is 170 m.
   (ii) Calculate the water level when the resevoir contains 1 500 000 m³.

6.3 Site evaluation

Topics covered in this section are:

- Objectives of a site evaluation
- Measurement of the key features of a site
- Use of height and angular measurement in determining the key features of a site
- Presentation, plotting and analysis of the key features of a site
- Setting out features of new construction on a previously surveyed site

In this section, the terminology, techniques, instrumentation and processes for linear measurement, height control and angular measurement developed in Section 6.2 will be consolidated in a series of practical exercises which can form the basis of a portfolio of evidence which, if developed correctly, would satisfy the evidence requirements of not only this unit but also the relevant Edexcel and AQA optional units.

Candidates preparing portfolios of evidence for Unit 4, 'Structures, construction technology and services' and Unit 5 'Town planning and development' should be able to develop the material to produce a progression portfolio covering many of the objectives of the evidence indicators for these units. The surveys contained within this section could also be used for area determinations using the methods described and demonstrated in the previous section.

Objectives of a site evaluation

The purpose of a site evaluation is to obtain information about the site, to ascertain its suitability for a given purpose, to confirm boundaries and responsibilities for ownership and maintenance purposes and in the calculation of areas of land within the site.

The site evaluation is closely linked with the information contained in the Site Report, which includes information related to above- and below-ground characteristics which may influence design or allow the prediction of possible difficulties during construction. The overall object is in the maximisation of site potential. The Site Report contains information about the nature and properties of the subsoil insofar as they influence the design and method of construction of the proposed works. In particular the purpose of the investigation is:

1. To determine the most suitable types of foundations for the proposed structures and the depth at which they should be placed.
2. To determine the maximum safe bearing pressure that may be imposed on the ground.
3. To estimate the probable amount of settlement of the proposed structure.

4. To determine whether special precautions will be required during excavation of the foundations.

When small and relatively unimportant buildings are to be sited on an area of land where there is much practical experience of the nature and behaviour of the soils, a site investigation may not be necessary. Unfortunately, however, all too often a decision to excavate is made blindly in comparatively unknown ground and often 'bad' ground of low bearing capacity is encountered resulting in financial claims by the contractor and a compromise in the design of the work.

It should be emphasised that the Site Report contains much useful information on the ground topography and features above the surface in the section dealing with the site investigation. Information on utilities can also be obtained as part of this type of investigation, as can the position of ditches and other watercourses which may cross the site under investigation. Positions of public footpaths, bridleways or other 'rights of way' and Tree Preservation Orders which may exist all form part of the work associated with the site evaluation.

The soil investigation is usually the most expensive component of a site evaluation, but it is essential that the ground is explored to a sufficient depth. Shallow test pits taken out to a proposed foundation level have been a popular method of cheap site investigation in the past. Information obtained in this way can be misleading. The ground is stressed to a depth equal to $1\frac{1}{2}$–2 times the width of the foundation below this level, and although there may be an apparently good bearing stratum within a metre of the ground surface, the presence of a softer stratum below can very seriously affect the stability of a structure.

In clay soils there is generally a metre or so of relatively dry firm material at the top, below which the clay becomes wetter and softer. A geological reconnaissance has therefore to support the topographical information which can be plotted as a site survey and it is usual on works, other than the most minor, to have a pictorial view in the form of a borehole log to identify changes in the below-ground soil characteristics.

If it is found that a site is likely to be overlain by thick deposits of gravel or firm clay it will normally be necessary to put down only one or two confirmation boreholes to a shallow depth, from which samples can be taken for examination and testing. If the geological reconnaissance indicates that the subsoil is likely to vary over the site, or that deposits of soft clay or loose sand may be present, a more detailed programme of boring and sampling will be needed.

Often the necessary geological information can be obtained quickly by reference to *HM Geological Survey* covering the area in question, although it is always desirable and sometimes mandatory to make a brief survey of the site. The methods of soil investigation are dealt with in section 6.1 although it is sufficient to say, regardless of the method, that the objective is to identify characteristics of a soil strata, obtain samples and undertake tests to confirm or be able to predict the performance of the material after the development of the site. In this connection the components of the site evaluation related to the geological or soils investigation are summarised as follows:

1. **Identification of classification of soils.** This deals with the size and distribution of soil particles and moisture content.
2. **Site investigation and soil sampling.** This deals with the boring methods, equipment and techniques used in obtaining the properties of soils *in situ*.
3. **Engineering properties of soils.** This relates to the shear strength, moisture, density and interrelationship of permeability and compressibility when subjected to engineering conditions.
4. **Soil mechanics problems.** These are the conditions to which the soil would be subjected, covering problems of equilibrium, stability, elasticity and plastic deformation.
5. **Engineering classification of problems.** This governs (i) retaining walls and earth slopes, (ii) foundations, (iii) roads and runways, and (vi) drainage.
6. **Local knowledge and experience.** This involves the study of accumulated local knowledge of long tradition and from many aspects.

The interrelationship between the site survey information and the results of the geographical investigation link in the evaluation of proposals for the future development of a site. Some of the information obtained is used in different ways, many associated with linear measurement, vertical central and horizontal alignment, requiring use of surveying techniques covered in Section 6.2 of this book. A summary of information obtainable from a soil survey is provided as an example in Table 6.20.

As can be seen from Table 6.20, many of the design requirements, when implemented into the actual construction, require application of surveying processes. In particular the use of surveying instruments is essential and the student should review the main design requirement column of the table and list the equipment which would be needed for the setting out of the works. With any site evaluation it is possible to collect essential basic information by using a standard proforma and a set of questions. In this way essential information relating to the site cannot be overlooked. Many of the questions can be answered by reference to local information and this detail usually forms part of the desk studies component of the site investigation. Other information would be determined by reference to the local authority and the public utilities and it is essential to obtain the 1 : 1250 or 1 : 2500 scale Ordnance Survey sheets covering the site area to identify at the very least the location of Ordnance Survey bench marks and their values. Care should, however, be exercised in the use of the sheets in the site evaluation as detail may have changed since the survey was carried out. The Ordnance Survey sheet does, however, provide at the very least a useful basis for an initial visit to the site, especially if a photocopier is used to enlarge the area under investigation. If this technique is to be used a linear scale needs to be drawn on to the sheet prior to photocopying as the process does cause a distortion of scale.

Measurement of the key features of a site

The approach to all surveys, whether it be to produce a topographic map or the plan for an engineering project, is to establish a control framework, and then to fix detail or engineering features by measurements with respect to this framework.

There are four basic ways in which detail can be fixed with respect to a known line.

- offsetting
- tie lines
- radiation
- intersection

The procedure chosen for a particular job will depend on the personnel, availability of equipment and its appropriateness to the task. The accuracy needed must also be considered. It is suggested that measurements should be taken to 10 mm rather than the limits implied by the scale of the finished plan and any specification to which it must comply. Distance and angular reading precisions must be matched accordingly. If a point of detail has to be plotted within 0.25 mm at a scale of 1 : 100, then over a distance of 80 m this is equivalent to an angle of 60 seconds of arc. Thus the angles could be observed to that limit. It is always better to record measurements to a higher accuracy than required for plotting in case they are needed for other design purposes at a later stage.

You may also hear the terms 'hard' and 'soft' detail. The former refers to well-defined points on a survey such as the corner of a building or a wall and other man-made features. 'Soft' detail generally refers to river banks, hedgerows and other features of the natural environment which are difficult to define. Usually great care is needed in 'picking up' the 'hard' detail, but often measurements can be 'relaxed' when recording soft detail.

The processes of offsetting and measuring tie lines have been covered in Section 6.2. On small traverse surveys the tape can be used to measure the leg lengths and the detail is usually collected during the course of measurement of each leg. The lengths of each traverse leg should always be measured first, however, and some check undertaken on the primary dimensions.

Radiation is most suitable for rapid detail collection and it is a popular technique when contouring. The process consists of measuring

(i) the internal or external angles at a control station between the directions to another central station and the points of detail
(ii) the respective distances from the central station to the points of detail (which can be achieved using tacheometric techniques)
(iii) the respective vertical angles subtended at the central station by these points (for height control and tacheometry)

The theodolite and tape may be used in combination to position detail by radiation but it is only really viable if the detail to be recorded lies within one tape length of the instrument. Height differences can be found by measuring vertical angles to a mark on a ranging rod held at the detail point, and it is useful if this mark is at the same height above ground as the trunnion axis of the instrument.

An EDM has now become increasingly popular to position detail by radiation, with the prism reflector mounted on a pole at the matching height above ground. Use of a total station instrument will allow direct readings of horizontal distance and height difference to be computed which makes the 'radiation' process of determining ground level spot height relatively quick. The majority of these instruments, as well as some electronic theodolites, have the facility to download to a datalogger such as the one manufactured by Psion.

Back in the office, with the correct equipment, the stored information could be directly plotted as a plan.

The fourth method of intersection is now less popular and requires great care when recording observations of detail to ensure that the direction from one station is matched with the corresponding direction from the other, since the two are usually observed at different times. The principal use of this method is for the location of well-defined detail that is inaccessible from the control stations.

Use of height and angular measurement in determining the key features of a site

In Section 6.2 the terminology, instrumentation, techniques and process of height control and angular measurement have

Table 6.20 Information obtainable from a soil survey

Main design requirements	Particular requirements	Information obtainable from a soil survey	Information obtained from additional investigations
1. Suitability of selected location	(a) Suitability of horizontal alignment	Data for avoidance of unsuitable ground such as peat, soft clay, areas subject to landslips or to rockfalls, or to waterlogging in winter	
	(b) Suitability of vertical alignment	Data for avoidance of high embankments on weak foundations or unstable strata. Data for reduction or avoidance of cuttings in rock or unstable strata. Data for maintenance of formation level at a suitable height above water-table level	
	(c) Stability of foundations under embankments	Need for further investigations. Possibilities of increasing the bearing capacity of the subsoil. Indication of probable settlement of pipes and culverts	Shear strength determinations necessary to check designs. Consolidation tests necessary for closer estimates of likely settlement
	(d) Stability of rock strata	Visual inspection and preliminary geological information give indications of possible land slip and rock slides	
2. Selection of materials for embankment construction	Suitability of excavated material for embankment construction. Selection of 'borrow' pits	Soil type gives: (i) Quality of material as filling, probable moisture contents for compaction (ii) Indication of compacted densities (iii) Suitability for winter construction (iv) Desirable types of earthwork equipment	Field and laboratory compaction tests necessary to give definite information. In conjunction with density tests information on probable bulking or shrinkage of material
3. Earth slopes	Cross-sections of cuttings and embankments	Indication of safe slopes in cut and fill	In cohesive soils, shear strength of soil required to check design in doubtful cases
4. Earthwork quantities	Volume of excavation	Volumes of peat or rock excavation Allowances for bulking or contraction which depend on compacted densities (see 2(ii))	Field and laboratory compaction tests desirable for more detailed estimate
5. Drainage	(a) Subsoil drainage	Ground water studies indicate need for subsoil drainage and location of drains and interceptors. Spacing of drains depends on soil type	
	(b) Surface drainage	Drainage or diversion of ponds, streams and springs. Location of catch water drains	
6. Preparation of subgrade	Need for subgrade treatment and work required	Depends on nature of soil and season in which construction is to take place	
7. Design of pavement	Type and thickness of base	Indications of thickness required given by soil type and wheel loading proposed	Special investigations needed for closer estimates of required thicknesses (CBR tests)
8. Stabilisation	Suitability of local materials for construction of flexible bases	Indications given of practicability of various forms of stabilised construction	Special ad hoc investigations needed for detailed study

been covered. The principles, which should now be understood, can be consolidated by a series of multiple-choice questions and short answer questions associated with the records of a site survey shown on Fig. 6.116. These plans and answers to the questions could form the basis of a portfolio of evidence which will satisfy the evidence indicators of some of the elements of the mandatory Unit 6, and relevant Edexcel and AQA optional units.

Self-assessment tasks

Figure 6.116 shows the site survey undertaken as a prerequisite to the construction of Guilds House and associated outbuildings. Students should study the site plan and then attempt the following questions:

1. Describe the main site features and topography of the land.
2. Using the linear scale on the plan, measure the overall lengths of sides of Guild House and calculate the internal area.
3. Calculate, using two different methods, the overall area of the site.
4. Describe the general slope of the ground from north to south and east to west across the site.
5. Using a photocopy of the plan, sketch the 50.00 contour and 50.50 contour line.
6. Calculate the gradient of the slope of the ground between points E and F.
7. Calculate the invert level of the pipe at manhole 2 and manhole 3.
8. Explain how the length of line AF would be obtained accurately on the site (note the pond as an obstruction to measurement).
9. Draw a field book entry for the survey line BG.
10. Using the bench mark value of 52.45 ODN produce a simulated level book page for at least ten spot levels.
11. Using a protractor for the measurement of angle, determine the reduced bearing of A from F.
12. Calculate the coordinates of F from the following information:
    Coordinate of E: 0N, 0E
    Whole circle bearing of EF: $90°$
13. Select and justify equipment for carrying out the site survey of the plot of land for Guilds House.
14. The proposed position of Guilds House has a national grid reference of SJ873237. Explain what this means.
15. Using the linear scale on the plan and a protractor for measuring the internal angles of closed traverse $ABCDEFA$, produce a traverse table and calculate the coordinates of stations $ABCD$ and F (coordinates of E are 0N, 0E.
16. List ten objectives in undertaking the site evaluation of the land for the proposed development.
17. Identify four potential problems revealed by the site survey and the produced plan.
18. Using the linear scale and interpolated spot levels shown on the plan, draw to suitable vertical and horizontal scales a longitudinal section between manhole 1 and manhole 3.
19. Determine the volume of excavation of the sewer trench between manhole 1 and manhole 3. Assume the trench width to be 750 mm.
20. Using the 's' rule, calculate the area contained by the triangle DEF and determine the proportion of this area which will be occupied by the garage and outbuildings.

Presentation, plotting and analysis of the key features of a site

The presentation, plotting and analysis of the key features of a site requires the use of many skills from a technician in ensuring that information is displayed and written in a clear and concise manner. The following tasks will allow demonstration of these skills.

Self-assessment tasks

The contoured plan (Fig. 6.117) shows a surveyed stretch of countryside. A straight road is to be constructed from point A to point B, a distance of 366 m. The design data for the road is as follows:

- The formation level of the road at A is 21.328 ODN.
- The road has a constant rate of fall from A to B of 1 : 40.
- The roadway construction is to be 10.60 m in width, comprising 2 No. 3.30 m width carriageways and 2 No. 2.00 m width footways.
- Cuttings and embankments are to have side slopes of 1 vertical : 2 horizontal.
- Levels are to be interpolated on the proposed road centre line and at 15 m either side (which dimensions shall be taken as the contract extremities).
- The depth of road pavement to formation is 500 mm.
- The depth of footway to formation is 300 mm.
- The top of footway is 125 mm above carriageway channel level.
- There is to be a cross-fall from the centre line of the carriageway to each side channel of 1 in 40.
- Kerbs to have a cross-section of 250 mm × 125 mm.

1. Prepare a plan and longitudinal section of the proposed road.
2. Prepare cross-sections at intervals of 30.5 m showing existing and proposed features.
3. Identify on the longitudinal section and cross-sections, in suitable colours, areas that will be in cut and in-fill.
4. Calculate by any appropriate method the volume of material required for road construction in embankment.
5. Calculate by any appropriate method the volume of material to be cut in forming the required profiles.
6. Calculate the volume of 'out of balance' material and state whether it is required to be imported or disposed of.

Students are recommended also to progress this portfolio to cover the requirements of evidence indicators in mandatory Unit 2 and in the civil engineering optional units produced by each award body. The following additional tasks would allow a textual analysis to be produced as an analysis of the site.

7. Identify the civil engineering components of the work in constructing the road.
8. Describe features of the topography which are likely to create problems during and after construction.
9. Explain with the assistance of referenced sketches how a culvert could be constructed under the completed road at a later date.
10. Outline alternative drainage provision which could be considered for the removal of surface water from the road and run-off from the embankment.
11. Select and justify with reasons plant that would be required for construction of the road and embankments.
12. Explain the 'setting out' procedures that would be needed during the contract works.

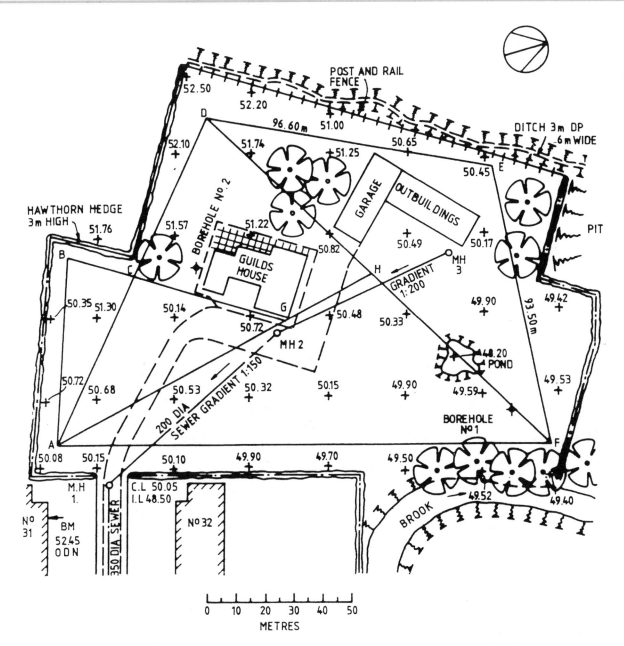

Figure 6.116 Survey of Guilds House

Setting out features of new construction on a previously surveyed site

Setting out is the process of using surveying instruments and techniques which have been described previously to transfer information from a plan to the ground or to convert calculations to information which can be used in construction. The tasks are usually undertaken by site engineers supervising the construction of new work. There are three components to the task:

- horizontal control to ensure that the new works are in the correct place
- vertical control to ensure that the new works are at the correct level

- vertical alignment to ensure that the faces of walls or basements are plumb

The accuracy achieved with equipment in good working condition and correct adjustment is tabulated in Table 6.21, as recommended in BS 5606: 1990, 'Code of practice for accuracy in building'.

Basic principles

Information from a plan transferred to site ground must be undertaken in such a way that it is understood by the construction workforce using it, so that the system is standardised from site to site. Three types of point can be defined.

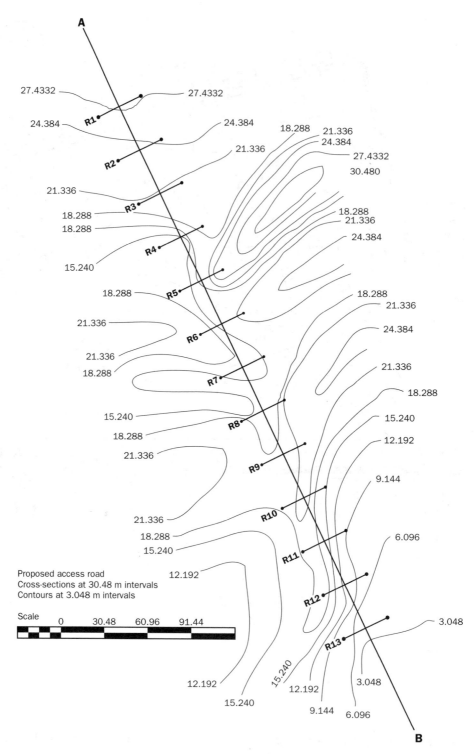

A

27.4332 — • — 27.4332

24.384 — • R1

18.288 — 21.336
24.384

24.384 — • — 24.384

R2 •

21.336 — • — 21.336

27.4332
30.480

21.336 —

R3 •

18.288 —
18.288 —

18.288
21.336

R4 •

24.384

15.240 —

18.288 — R5 •

18.288
21.336

21.336 —

24.384

R6 •

21.336 —
18.288 —

21.336

R7 •

18.288

15.240 —
18.288 —

R8 •

15.240

21.336 —

12.192

R9 •

9.144

21.336 —
18.288 —
15.240 —

R10 •

6.096

R11 •

Proposed access road
Cross-sections at 30.48 m intervals
Contours at 3.048 m intervals

12.192

R12 •

Scale

| 0 | 30.48 | 60.96 | 91.44 |

3.048

R13 •

12.192

15.240

15.240

12.192

3.048

15.240

9.144   6.096

B

Figure 6.117 Cuttings and embankments

Primary stations or setting out points (Fig. 6.118)

These are principal stations on the control traverse or triangulation system which may, if the work is important enough, be referenced to the National Grid for orientation if needed. The station should be permanent for the life of the works and typical construction could range from a brass plate or stud set in concrete to a road nail driven into a carriageway. The stations should be clearly marked and protected so that they remain undamaged by construction traffic and can be used easily for the accessing of setting up of instruments.

Secondary setting-out points

These are established closer to points of detail on the proposed works and are usually referenced by measurements from the primary points. They may be points in a grid surrounding a building and should be constructed in a similar manner to primary control points.

Table 6.21 Achievable equipment accuracy

Measurement	Instrument	Deviation
Linear	30 m steel tape, general use	±5 mm up to 5 m ±10 mm, 5 to 25 m ±15 mm, above 25 m
	30 m steel tape, precise use	±3 mm up to 10 m ±6 mm, 10 to 30 m
	EDM (standard infra-red type)	±10 mm, 30 to 50 m* ±10 mm + 10 ppm, above 50 m
Angular	30 m steel tape on uneven ground	±5′ ±25 mm in 15 m
	30 m steel tape on flat ground	±2′ ±10 mm in 15 m
	20″ Glass-arc theodolite	±20″ (±5 mm in 50 m)
	1″ Glass-arc theodolite	±5″ (±2 mm in 80 m)
Verticality	Spirit level	±10 mm in 3 m
	Plumb bob, freely suspended	±5 mm in 5 m
	Plumb bob, damped in oil	±5 mm in 10 m
	Theodolite with optical plummet and diagonal eyepiece	±5 mm in 30 m
	Laser (visible)	±7 mm up to 100 m
	Optical plumbing device	±5 mm in 100 m
Levels	Spirit level	±5 mm in 5 m
	Water level	±5 mm in 15 m
	Laser (visible)	±7 mm up to 100 m
	Laser (invisible)	±5 mm up to 100 m
	Optical level (builder's)	±5 mm per sight
	Optical level (engineer's)	±2 mm per sight ±10 mm per km
	Optical level (precise)	±2 mm per sight ±8 mm per km

* not recommended for distances less than 30 m

(*Source*: BS 5606:1990 'Code of practice for accuracy in building', reproduced courtesy of BSI)

Detail points

These points mark the location of features on the works such as the edge of an embankment or corner of a building. These marks will be lost as construction progresses and a 50 × 50 mm pointed stake with a nail in the top is usually sufficient.

Vertical control (Fig. 6.119)

Temporary bench marks (TBM) are used to provide a level of known value and are usually related to Ordnance Datum Newlyn. They are provided close to the works and daily use should only involve setting up an instrument and taking a backsight onto the TBM and a foresight to the work. The bench mark should be regularly checked and consist of 600 mm long steel dowels driven into the ground and set in concrete to ensure that they are not readily disturbed by the movement of site traffic.

Horizontal control

The four methods used for the location of a point, covered in an earlier section and illustrated in Fig. 6.1 are equally appropriate when setting out a point from control stations.

Site grid (Fig. 6.120)

A grid of secondary points is established around the site perimeter. The spacing of the grid can coincide with features

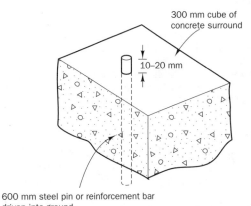

Figure 6.119 Typical temporary bench mark construction

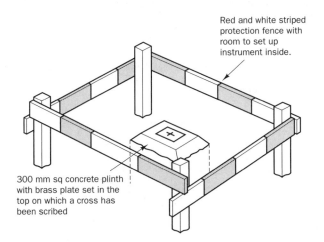

Figure 6.118 Primary setting-out station. (*After* Bannister, Raymond & Baker *Surveying* Longman)

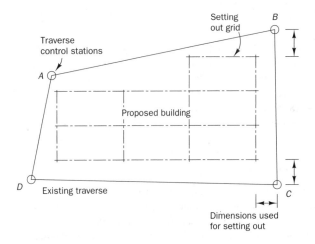

Figure 6.120 The site grid

of the permanent construction such as columns or piles. The grid should be outside the construction area to avoid disturbance. On large sites the survey data can be used to establish two conveniently situated lines, mutually at right angles, which are used to fix secondary points at appropriate intervals.

Coordinates from control points

On sites such as motorways or pipelines it is usual to have a system of control points on a traverse that was established at the survey stage. The works will have been designed by using advanced mathematical techniques on computer and coordinates will be available to fix main points of detail. These can be set out by **bearing** (angular measure) and **distance** (linear measure) using EDM equipment from one of the control points. Industrial sites and shopping centres can be set out conveniently using secondary setting out stations such as S and R, V and W, located from the primary control traverse by intersection methods, each pair being related to one or more structures as shown in Fig. 6.121. Other methods of fixing the random location of an instrument are available, including the taking of angular and distance readings onto a number of control stations and, by calculation, determining the coordinates from which further points may be set out.

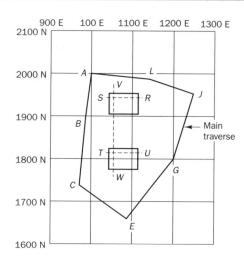

Figure 6.121 Coordinates from control points. (*After* Bannister, Raymond & Baker *Surveying* Longman)

$\oplus A$ 1000 E, 2000 N

$\oplus S$ 1025 E, 1950 N

$B \oplus 986.72$ E, 1897.46 N

Figure 6.122 Relationship of the points

Example

Two primary control points, *A* and *B*, have coordinates 100.00 m E, 2000.00 m N and 986.72 m E, 1897.46 m N respectively. Calculate data to set out points S, 1025.00 m E, 1950.00 m N by two measurements.

Before commencing the calculation it is useful to draw a sketch to show the relationship of the points, in the correct orientation (Fig. 6.122).

Answer

angle $BAS = \tan^{-1}\left(\dfrac{1025 - 1000}{2000 - 1950}\right) + \tan^{-1}\left(\dfrac{1000 - 986.72}{2000 - 1897.46}\right)$

$\qquad = 33°\ 56'\ 40''$

clockwise from direction $AB = 360° - 33°\ 56'\ 40''$
$\qquad\qquad\qquad\qquad\qquad = 326°\ 03'\ 20''$

angle $ABS = \tan^{-1}\left(\dfrac{1025 - 986.72}{1950 - 1897.46}\right)$

$\qquad + \tan^{-1}\left(\dfrac{1000 - 986.72}{2000 - 1897.46}\right)$

$\qquad = 28°\ 41'\ 50''$

clockwise from direction $BA = 28°\ 41'\ 50''$

$AS = \sqrt{(25^2 + 50^2)} = 55.9\,\text{m}$
$BS = \sqrt{(38.28^2 + 52.54^2)} = 65.01\,\text{m}$

---

is a corner of a building it will need to be set out for the centre line of excavation, foundation and brick or blockwork. At each stage the marker will be removed by the undertaking of the construction process. **Offset pegs** may be located close to the works but outside the area of excavation so that after each stage of the works the detail point may be replaced (Fig. 6.123). Offset markers may be constructed from 50 mm square wooden stakes with a nail in the top. The nail can be used with a string line to locate a specific line between points.

This leads to the use of **profile boards** (which should not be confused with sight rails). Profile boards are constructed from horizontal timber rails of sufficient length to cover the excavation width. Saw cuts or nails can be placed to represent lines of construction. The construction of profile boards is shown in Fig. 6.124.

Local control

Usually the corners of a building are square and, when setting out, sufficient checks should be carried out, e.g. measuring the diagonals, to ensure that, for a rectangular structure, the opposite sides are of equal length. In some cases detail points are required to be located more than once. If the detail point

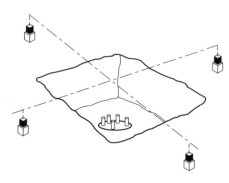

Figure 6.123 Use of offset pegs for a pile cap. (*After* Bannister, Raymond & Baker *Surveying* Longman)

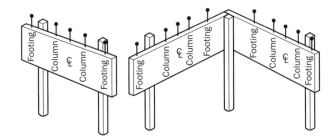

Figure 6.124 Use of profile boards. (*After* Bannister, Raymond & Baker *Surveying* Longman)

Procedure for setting out a rectangular structure using a simple angular measuring instrument and a tape

1. Establish the line of the building from data.
2. Set up the theodolite on this line and locate two corners of the building and two offset pegs or profile boards (Fig. 6.125(a)).
3. Set up the theodolite at one corner and sight onto the second corner. Turn the theodolite through 90° and establish a third corner of the building the appropriate distance away along the line of sight, plus further offset pegs or profile boards (Fig. 6.125(b)).
4. Repeat step 3 at the second corner.
5. Check the length of the furthest side and the diagonals (Fig. 6.125(c)).
6. Set up the theodolite on the third corner, sight the fourth corner and establish the remaining offset pegs or profile boards.

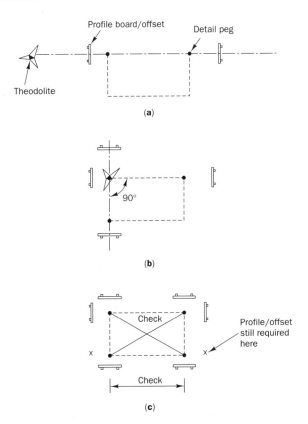

Figure 6.125 Setting out a rectangular building. (*After* Bannister, Raymond & Baker *Surveying* Longman)

Setting-out equipment

On most construction sites it is usual to construct as a first priority, roads and sewers, to ensure that site access is provided and that drainage facilities exist to all buildings. Surveying equipment used for this setting out has been detailed elsewhere in this unit, but it is useful to summarise the equipment that would usually be selected on all but specialised jobs.

1. **Steel tapes.** While the accuracy of setting out linear dimensions is principally dependent upon the expertise of the user and the condition of the tape, steel tapes are to be preferred, as they are not subject to the degree of 'stretch' as are Fibron tapes. Expansion characteristics of invar steel tapes reflect the more favourable characteristics of this material compared with plastic or glass fibre when high accuracy setting-out measurements need to be made.
2. **Levels.** Automatic levels are sufficient for most above-ground setting out. They are simpler and therefore easier to use than optical levels and are reliable in as much as with careful use, little adjustment is needed.
3. **Total station instruments.** Most setting out, particularly roadways, can be accomplished by the method of coordinates. An EDM instrument would be appropriate for setting out both angles and distances, and use of a total station instrument would provide the facility for additional computations to be made in the field.
4. **Theodolites.** Particularly with new technology removing much of the surveyor's traditional expertise, it has to be said that the more automation that can be

provided, the greater the likelihood of the accuracy of setting out. Theodolites with optical plumbing, automatic vertical circle indexing, electronic reading and two-axis levelling are to be preferred.

5. **Automatic instruments.** These instruments are more convenient than theodolites for setting out vertical lines in high-rise buildings, and have none of the disadvantages of plumb-bobs which oscillate in wind.
6. **Pegs.** Colour-coded softwood or steel pegs at least 500 mm long should be used to establish the key positions of construction. Centre line pegs are usually white and are established first; and offset pegs, which remain during any excavation process, are usually yellow, and distinguished from level pegs which are blue.
7. **Profiles.** Profiles as shown in Figs 6.57, 6.81 and 6.125, are erected over the offset pegs. Profiles serve one of two purposes: (i) sighting for the purpose of controlling excavation depths when laying pipelines; (ii) setting out the corners of buildings.

Computer programs and spreadsheets

The use of computer programs is advocated for the solution of repetitive surveying calculations. Budget-priced vectorisers with text recognition allow maps, site plans or scanned drawings to be converted to CAD. Simple programs for the computation of level readings are readily available. Alternatively, students will find additional enhancement to the study of the surveying units if they understand the rudiments of programming in the BASIC code (Beginners All-purpose

Symbolic Instruction Code). Instructions to the computer are written in this code which is in-built into the computer, which in turn interprets the basic code instructions and converts them into electrical signals which are acted upon. The user presents the computer with the data for a problem, called the input, and is then given the instructions for the solution of a problem through the provision of an equation. The computer solves the problem and stores it in its memory until the user instructs the machine to present a solution of the problem, either on the screen or via a print-out.

Example 1

The sum (S) and the difference (D) of two numbers, A and B, need to be calculated. In a BASIC program the user has to:
(a) Input A.
(b) Input B.
(c) Instruct the computer that the sum(S) of A and B is
$S = A + B$ and that the difference (D) of A and B is
$D = A - B$.
(d) Instruct the computer to print the answers on the screen by instructing it to print S.

(e) Print D.
The computer needs to handle the data sequentially and each separate instruction is usually numbered in increments of 10. The program would be keyed in as follows:

```
10      INPUT A
20      INPUT B
30      S = A + B
40      D = A − B
50      PRINT S
60      PRINT D
```

The computer is instructed to operate by typing the word RUN and asks for data through a question mark appearing on the screen.

If a hard copy of the results is required, the computer is instructed to print the results via the printer onto paper and lines 50 and 60 are respectively replaced by 50 L PRINT S and 60 PRINT D.

If appropriate computation is required the instruction RUN is again needed and if appropriate the program may be made to repeat itself, by using a GOTO statement which refers the computer to a line on the program where it is required to restart.

Example 2

Calculate the coordinates of an open traverse ABCDE from the following information:

Line	AB	BC	CD	DE
Bearing (°)	N 38° E	S 75° E	S 40° W	N 75° W
Distance (m)	48	72	85	39

The traverse is calculated manually to provide guidance. It may also help if you sketch out the location of each control station on graph paper

Table 6.22

Line	Quadrant bearing	Distance (m)	+E	−W	+N	−S	Dep (x)	Lat (y)	Station
							00.0	00.0	A
AB	N 35° E	48	27.532		39.319		+27.532	+39.319	B
BC	S 75° E	72	69.547			18.635	+97.079	+20.684	C
CD	S 40° W	85		54.637		65.114	+42.447	−44.430	D
DE	N 75° W	39		37.671	10.094		+4.771	−34.336	E

Sample calculation of coordinates of station B.

$$\sin 35° = \frac{HORIZ}{48} \qquad HORIZ = 48 \times \sin 35° = 27.532 \text{ (departure)}$$

$$\cos 35° = \frac{VERT}{48} \qquad VERT = 48 \times \cos 35° = 39.319 \text{ (latitude)}$$

∴ Coordinates of B = coordinates of A ± partial coordinates
 Departure B = 00.0 + 27.532 = 27.532
 Latitude B = 00.0 + 39.319 = 39.319

Using BASIC and the following symbols:
p = plan distance (in m); b = quadrant bearing

```
10    INPUT p
20    INPUT b
```
30   Computer calculation; b is changed to radians. $X = p * \sin\left(\dfrac{b * 3.141593}{180}\right)$

40   Computer calculation; b is changed to radians $Y = p * \cos\left(\dfrac{b * 3.141593}{180}\right)$

```
50    PRINT X (partial coordinates departure)
60    PRINT Y (partial coordinates latitude)
70    GOTO 10 (computer goes back to line 10 to receive instructions for next line of the survey)
```

This program can be enhanced by adding the station designation or reference, e.g. 'B', and further headings, e.g. 'DIFF EAST', 'DIFF NORTH'.

As already mentioned, new technology has increased the ease of use of surveying instrumentation and computation. Many software programs can be purchased at relatively modest cost. Many students are now able to produce simple spreadsheet programs for solving mathematically repetitive tasks such as reducing levels and calculating bearings. The following program may be of interest for those students who are wishing to integrate key skills IT level 3 into a surveying context. Table 6.23 shows a booking page for level readings taken during a survey. The readings have been reduced manually using the now not commonly used method of 'rise and fall'.

Self-assessment task

Using the attached sheets as a guide, convert the basic field data to a completed level book format incorporating a mathematical check on the reduced levels.

Table 6.23 Rise and fall method of levelling

	BS	IS	FS	Rise	Fall	RL	Dist	Remarks
1	2.001					3.000		
2	1.000		2.000	0.001		3.001		
3	1.500		0.500	0.500		3.501		
4		1.000		0.500		4.001		
5			2.00		1.000	3.001		
6								
7								
8								
9								
10								
11								
12								
13								
14								
15								
16								
17								
18								
19								
20								
	4.501		4.500	1.001	1.000	3.000		
	−4.500			−1.000		−3.001		
	0.001			0.001		0.001		

This is a screen shot of the spreadsheet with the relevant formulae listed below. Be careful when you input the formulae that you put the relevant formula in the correct cell before you copy the formula down. For example, the formula in E5 needs to be copied down to E23, and F5 copied down to F23 and G5 copied down to G23.

E5 =IF(AND(C4◇0,C5◇0),IF(C4-c5>0,C4-C5,""),IF(AND(B4◇0,C5◇0),IF(B4-C5>0,B4-C5,""),IF(AND(B4◇0,D5◇0),IF(B4-D5>0,B4-D5,""),IF(AND(C4◇0,D5◇0),IF(C4-D5>0,C4-D5,""),""))))

F5 =IF(AND(C4◇0,C5◇0)IF(C4-C5<0,ABS(C4-C5),""),IF(AND(B4◇0,C5◇0),IF(B4-C5<0,ABS(B4-C5),""),IF(AND(B4◇0,D5◇0),IF(B4-D5<0,ABS(B4-D5),""),IF(AND(C4◇0,D5◇0),IF(C4-D5<0,ABS(C4-D5),0),""))))

G5 =IF(AND(E5=F5,D5=""),"",(G4+E5-F5))

B24 =IF(AND(E5=F5,D5=""),"",(G4+E5-F5))

B25 =D24

B26 =B24-B25

D24 =SUM(D4:D23)

E24 =SUM(E4:E23)

E25 =F24

E26 =E25-F24

F24 =SUM(F4:F23)

G24 =G4

G25 =OFFSET(G23,-COUNTBLANK(G4:G23),0,1,1)

G26 =OFFSET(G23,-COUNTBLANK(G4:G23),0,1,1)-G4

6.4 Site survey exercise

The assessment evidence for the compulsory Unit 6: Surveying processes, and the optional AQA Unit 18: Surveying practices in Construction and the Built Environment, are shown in Figures 6.126 and 6.127. Students in undertaking study and producing a portfolio of evidence for both units are required to complete a site survey and associated evaluations. Practically, it is sensible to combine both units to consolidate surveying techniques, processes and terminology. Students usually have the greatest difficulty in completing site work because they have not fully mastered the underpinning knowledge related to procedures processes and the recording of information. Figures 6.126 and 6.127 provide an opportunity for consolidating the underpinning knowledge and producing assessment evidence prior to site work being undertaken.

Self-assessment tasks

1. Figure 6.126 shows the layout of a small office/industrial site and parking area off Loatley Lane for which Outline Planning Permission has been granted for construction of buildings, the associated access road and parking area. To maximise the potential of the site and surrounding land a footbridge is to be constructed across Loatley Lane, prior to the road being upgraded when the full development of the area is completed.

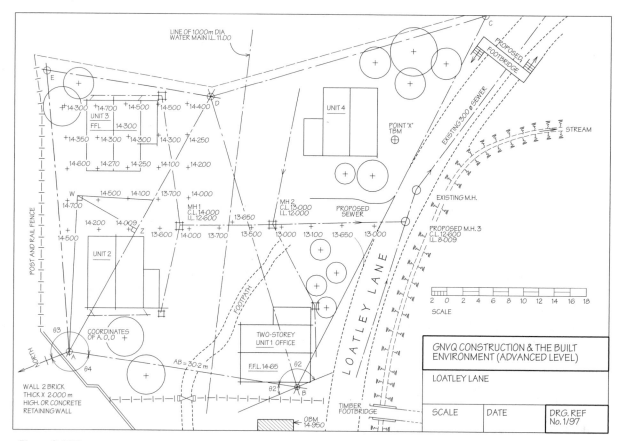

Figure 6.126

Evidence may be generated for the following:
- evaluating features of the site to ascertain suitability for the given purpose
- preparing specimen field books for recording topographical data
- preparing specimen field books for recording of spot levels
- contouring of the site
- producing longitudinal sections
- preparing a field book of angular measurements for the calculation of bearings and station coordinates
- producing mathematical calculations relating to linear measurements, angular measurements, areas, volumes, setting out of buildings and services to line and level
- design of building and civil engineering features shown on the site
- comparing areas of land shown on a variety of maps, identifying and selecting suitable land for incorporation of the features shown in Figure 6.126
- selection of equipment and, where appropriate, comparison of alternatives, which may have been used for the collection of data and the setting out of features of the site

2. Figure 6.127 shows the proposals for a small conference centre on a plot of land.

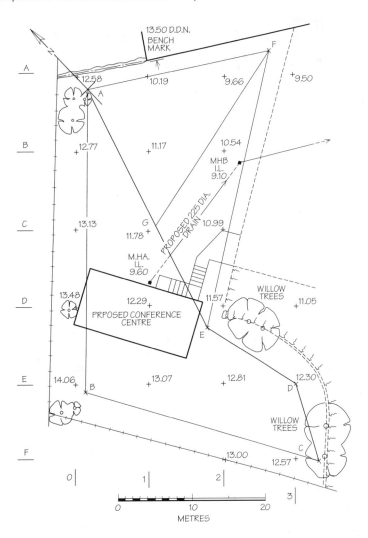

Figure 6.127

(i) Assuming that the value of the bench mark shown is 13.50 ODN, convert the spot levels to staff readings in apropriate level book format.

(ii) Using a protractor, measure the internal angles of the closed traverse ABCDEFA and book them in an appropriate format (remember that the total angle of the closed figure can be determined from the equation $(2n - 4)90$).

(iii) Assuming the coordinates of A are 0, 0, determine the value of coordinates B, C, D, E, F (line lengths may be scaled from the drawing).

(iv) Explain why the coordinates of A are unlikely to be 0, 0 after completion of the calculations to determine the coordinates.

(v) Explain with the use of sketches how the proposed 225 mm diameter drain would be set out by using sight rails and a traveller to control excavation depths.

(vi) Produce a longitudinal section between A and B manholes and calculate the volume of excavation needed to lay the drain, if the trench width is to be 400 mm.

(vii) On the drawing provided, show contours at intervals of 0.50 m.

(viii) Evaluate features of the site and explain possible influences that the presence of willow trees may have on the building foundations for the proposed conference centre.

(ix) Superimpose a proposed access road and car parking area for the site, if access is to be obtained from the east side between $A3$ and $B2$.

(x) Using sketches, show landscaping proposals for the site.

(xi) using at least two methods, determine the likely site and explain why the areas may be different.

(xii) Using features of the site layout, produce a glossary of surveying terminology for linear measurement, angular measurement and height control.

UNIT 7

Resource Management

Keith Roberts

The builder has to convert the design solution for the project into a completed building, and this calls for considerable skill and judgement. To maintain profitability the builder must deploy materials, plant and labour efficiently. From the builder's point of view the success of the project depends on resource management.

The key areas covered in this unit are:

- organisations and roles
- resource planning
- selection of resources for a project
- monitoring and controlling resources

After reading this unit the student should be able to:

- describe different organisations in the construction industry

- describe the purpose and benefits of project planning and the procedures involved
- describe the effect change has on project planning
- explain the effects of accommodating change on project planning
- describe work study techniques used in the construction industry
- plan and organise construction activities
- produce method statements and construction programmes for planning and organising construction work
- calculate the resource requirements for a construction project
- describe processes used for managing materials, plant, labour and safety on construction sites
- describe methods for monitoring construction work

7.1 Organisation and roles

Topics covered in this section are:

- types of construction companies
- types of organisational structures
- job roles in the construction industry

Sectors and types of firms

The construction industry can be split into the following sectors

- planning
- designing
- producing
- controlling

Each sector is moulded by the types of activity and the constraints imposed by clients. There may be specialist companies working independently yet with a project team coordinated by a project manager to achieve the client's aims and requirements. Another project may require a more cooperative venture using a national multi-discipline design team and one principal contractor. Often the type of organisational structure for the venture is decided by the method of procurement. This is explored in Unit 8, 'Financing the built environment'.

In Unit 1, 'The built environment and its development', the job types and qualifications were identified for working in the construction industry. In this unit we are concerned with how the different personnel interact and cooperate. This is called the **organisation framework**. How the people are formally controlled depends also on the type of company. For example, a small building company will have an entirely different method of organising the management functions to an international contracting company. The small building company will be a **sole trader**. This means that the builder is the owner of the company and the type of work and risks involved are at the discretion of the owner of the business. The international contracting company will most likely be a **public limited company**. To finance the company's workload private and institutional investors buy shares in the company, becoming shareholders. The company directors are responsible for the day-to-day running of the company, yet the shareholders demand a return on their investment.

Between these two extremes are a variety of types of business and organisational frameworks. The overriding requirement is to make a profit and keep the business a viable concern. To do that means obtaining work.

All businesses must obtain a satisfactory workload; the **private architectural practice** who may be a sole trader has to obtain some design work. If the workload of the practice grows beyond the ability of one person, staff may be recruited to join the practice. Another private architectural practice may share the workload for a particular project. This cooperative venture may be formalised into a **partnership**. A partnership is defined by the Partnership Act of 1890 as 'the relation which subsists between persons carrying on a business in common with a view of profit'. There may be between two and twenty partners who share the risks and rewards of the business venture. The partnership is governed by the **deed of partnership**.

In the building cycle the design team may be sole traders or partnerships. The large international multi-discipline consultants would be a **limited company**. The business risks are too demanding for a sole trader or partnership, so a **private limited company** is established. A limited company has a separate legal identity from its owners, so anyone taking legal action proceeds against the company and not the individual shareholders. This is in stark contrast to the sole trader or partnership where legal action can be taken against the individual or the partners. If, for example, the partnership goes into receivership the partners' assets can be seized and sold to pay off the debts. The same applies to the sole trader. Shareholders in a private limited company will only lose their investment. The Companies Act 1985 stipulates that certain annual financial statements must be filed with the **Registrar of Companies**.

Successful building businesses are usually private limited companies or **public limited companies**. The company raises capital (money) by requesting public investment and shareholding often through the **stock market**. The risks taken by the company are spread over a wide range of people called shareholders.

The type of business often depends on the owners and current business legislation, but all businesses must operate efficiently to survive in a very competitive marketplace. How the business operates is defined in the **organisational framework**. The principles will apply to all types of business activity.

Organisational structures

Job analysis will define the roles and responsibilities of the individual members of the organisation. For the business to function effectively all the different roles must be integrated into an organisational framework. The individuals must know their roles and responsibilities. This is written down in the **job description**. The job title should reflect the tasks performed, but different companies use different job titles to define roles within their company. For example, a surveyor in one company may be the same as a resource manager in another. The tasks are important, the job title often reflects the value attributed to the role by the company executives. In a medium-sized building company there will be several activities carried out by office staff supported by site staff.

These activities will include:

- **estimating** – obtaining a satisfactory workload for the company
- **buying** – obtaining materials, subcontractors, plant and equipment
- **accounting** – payment of bills, wages, banking money, bookkeeping
- **quantity surveying** – obtaining payments from the client and completing the final account for a project

- **contract managing** – running several projects from the office supported by the site staff; making sure the project is completed on time and within budget

These functions in a sole trader organisation are carried out by the principal, so it is easy to communicate, but a larger company will need a method for communication. The organisational framework will define the formal links between job roles (see Fig. 7.1).

There is a relationship between the managing director and the estimator. This **direct relationship** means that orders are issued by the managing director and the estimator reports to the managing director about the workload and other job functions. Some of the estimator's job will involve working with the quantity surveyor, not on a direct relationship but on a cooperative relationship or **lateral** relationship as they are both on the same management level. Preparing an estimate will also involve liaison with the buyer. This type of relationship is neither direct nor lateral as the buyer reports directly to the quantity surveyor. Also the buyer is on a lower tier of management compared to the estimator, who is more senior in the **organisational hierarchy**. But these two people must work together to achieve the corporate aims and the estimator's responsibility is to achieve a satisfactory workload. This is a **functional** relationship.

The roles of the various personnel in the organisational framework are categorised into **service management** and **line management**. Only the contracts manager in Fig. 7.1 is in line management – that is, directly controlling production. The other job roles of estimating, surveying and accounts are all service management.

You can imagine the number of management tiers in a large multinational company. This is called a **hierarchical organisational structure**, whereas a flat management structure would be called a **non-hierarchical organisational structure**. This type of organisational structure allows a larger number of personnel to share in the decision making of the company. The organisational framework for the site activities is dealt with later. The job roles may be categorised into type of activity. The contracts manager is in line management and might have professional status if he is qualified to degree level

and is a member of the Chartered Institute of Building. The structural engineer on the design team will also be a **professional**, usually trained to degree level and a corporate member of the Institute of Structural Engineers. If the structural engineer works for a consulting engineering practice, possibly as a partner, it will have a flat or non-hierarchical organisational structure.

Some functions in the office are technical. The safety officer in a building company or the planner may be classified as having **technical** functions within the organisation.

Self-assessment tasks

1. Using either the local business directory, classified directory or information supplied by the Building Employers Confederation, obtain a list of local building firms. Make sure that you have some private limited companies (they have the name of the business with Ltd after the name, e.g. Brown Contractors **Ltd**) and, if possible, some public limited companies (public limited companies have plc after the company name, e.g. Brown Contractors **plc**).
   (a) List at least **six** small building or civil engineering companies by name and with addresses.
   (b) List at least **three** private building companies.
   (c) List at least **three** public limited civil engineering or building companies.
   (d) List **three** architectural practices by name and with addresses.
   (e) List **one** example of each of the following with the practice name and address:
      – quantity surveyor
      – structural engineer
      – consulting engineer
      – town planning consultant
      – estates management consultant
      – facilities management company

2. (a) Based on your selected career, obtain information on **one** of the above companies which will allow you to write notes on the following:
      – type of business
      – sector of operation
      – geographical area of operation
      – organisational structure
      – main management functions and the job titles
   (b) Prepare a report (word processed) describing this company.
   (c) Illustrate the organisational framework and state if the organisational structure is hierarchical or non-hierarchical.
   (d) From your research about the job roles available in this company, write your perceived views on how the business operates. Further information about the job roles can be obtained from the relevant professional institute or the Career service. Whichever one you use, make sure you file as evidence your notes, interviews, telephone calls or letters you have used to obtain this information.

Figure 7.1 Organisational framework

7.2 Resource planning

Topics covered in this section are:

- purpose of project planning
- project planning procedure
- method statement

Purpose of project planning

Project planning is concerned with maximising the use of resources and minimising cost. The resources available to the contractor are

- labour
- materials
- plant and equipment
- space
- money

As far as site planning is concerned, the aim of project planning is to ensure that the resources are available at

- the right time
- the right quantity
- the right location

The data used needs to be as accurate as possible. Once the plan has been decided, then the programme can be prepared. The programme is a graphic form of communication, explaining the planning strategies. The estimator and the planner have produced the **tender programme** based on the tender documents and site reconnaissance.

Labour

To ensure efficient use of labour, the right type of labour must be available. Building labour has traditionally been classified by operation or trade. A **tradesperson** was traditionally time served, completing an apprenticeship and passing an examination such as the City and Guilds 'Bricklaying' craft examination. This meant that additional work was necessary to serve these craftspeople, and this was done by the **labourer** or **general operative**. The **gang size** also varied from craft to craft. A bricklaying gang went in multiples of two bricklayers to one labourer, hence a 2/1 gang. The craftsperson always comes first. Carpenters and joiners are also craftspeople but the serving arrangements are different, often 8/1. The joiner's labourer would 'load out' the work area with materials, clean up after the work and generally assist, keeping the more expensive labour working constantly.

Plasterers and painters are also craftspeople, but the drainlayer is **semi-skilled**, like the scaffolder and steelfixer. These are seemingly arbitrary groupings, but the wages and payment structure of the construction industry is based on this demarcation of labour. The type of labour is split into

- skilled operative, e.g. craftsperson
- semi-skilled operative, e.g. scaffolder
- unskilled operative, e.g. labourer or general building operative (GBO).

Specialism in a trade often means higher efficiency or output, so the aim of project planning would be to have the right grade of labour for each activity. It would be inefficient to have a carpenter or joiner sweeping up the estate road when a general building operative could do it as well, and more cheaply. Certain types of activity belong to a particular trade. One of the aims of project planning is to maximise resource deployment. Repair and maintenance work often involves several trades visiting the site. Each visit costs money in transport time and familiarisation of the site. That may be inefficient, so the project planner would allocate a multi-skilled operative to this work, thereby achieving the aim of efficient deployment of resources.

Materials

The bill of quantities describes and quantifies the project. The composition rules and framework of the bill is governed by SMM7. For example, a work-in-place item in brickwork is shown in Fig. 7.2. The rules in SMM7 clearly state that the quantities are measured net or **as fixed**. The buyer orders sufficient cavity ties for $50\,m^2$ of walling, but the bricklayers cannot finish the work because of a lack of materials as some of the cavity ties were lost or stolen. The buyer has missed the point of project planning: resources at the **right quantity** to carry out the operation.

Plant and equipment

To ensure maximum profit the overall building time has to be reduced. There must be a **breakeven point** at which the short project duration is more expensive. That is contrary to project planning ideas. The resources are carefully balanced to achieve a maximum workload with a minimum outlay or cost.

Mechanisation has helped the project planners, but the balance has to be achieved for overall success, and that requires the right plant and equipment in the right quantity and in the right location. The **method statement** (Fig. 7.3) will show the labour, plant and equipment considered necessary to carry out the operation efficiently.

The plant selected, the mixer capacity, the size of the tower crane and the five general operatives or concretors will be balanced to achieve **maximum output** for **minimum cost**. The control operation is the concern of the project planner.

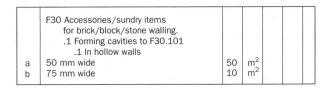

Figure 7.2 Part of the specification for a work-in-place item in brickwork

METHOD STATEMENT						
					Job no. 543/123	
Operation	Quantity	Method	Output	Gang size	Gang output	Remarks
Concrete	150 m³	Site mix 280/200R mixer Tower crane 5 operatives				

Figure 7.3

Space

Project planning is concerned with **utilisation** of resources, thus a well-prepared site, with material stacks at the point of final fix, are important. Travel routes should be well planned to minimise travel lengths and avoid blockages. The tower crane must be sited so that it covers all of the building activities.

Some work with rebar or steel reinforcing bars may be fabricated on site and **cost comparisons** have proved that cutting and bending steel reinforcement on site is the cheapest method. As the supplier delivers straight bars, the project planner must allocate an area for cutting, bending and temporary storage. The location of this area may cause these activities to be disadvantaged for the benefit of the overall project, but finding solutions to such problems and calculating the cost benefits are part of the project planner's role.

Money

Money is the final method of selection for the planner. All the other construction methods are costed and discounted except the cheapest. However, there must be a compromise; for example, the operation 'excavate to reduced level' if taken in isolation should be carried out by a bowl scraper. But the top soil must be stored in a spoil heap, and the reduced level dig spoil must be removed from the site. With these other activities taken into consideration, the bowl scraper method would not be the most economical.

The holistic method puts the overall project as the overarching factor. Contracts are single activities for the building company and the company's aims must take priority over contract benefits. For instance, the use of a tower crane with a reach of 30 m is the best equipment for the job, but that has to be hired from a plant hire company, and the rates paid are external plant hire rates. Within the company's plant pool there may be a crane with a reach of 40 m. This crane may be over-capacity but to leave it in the company's plant yard would be an inefficient use of plant. The site will therefore have the internal hire crane rather than the external crane, even though the hire charges may be greater. Compromises are always needed, which is why project planning is concerned with optimising efficiency. Now that the tender has been won, these decisions need to be reviewed.

Project planning procedures

The type of tender programme chosen by the contractor is called a **bar chart** programme. The activities or operations are listed in order of completion. The **bar duration** for each operation is calculated on the main quantities in the tender bill or as percentages of the overall time. Using percentages is similar to the quantity surveyor's elemental cost plan.

The tender programme or master programme in Fig. 7.4 shows an eight-week project duration. On signing the contract, the tender programme becomes the contract programme and the project duration becomes the contract duration and a critical contractor's obligation. The specific performance by the contractor is to complete the project in eight weeks. If the project is not completed within the contract period, then the contractor is in breach of contract and the employer (client) through the architect can deduct the agreed moneys. The deducted money is a set amount, usually per week, for non-completion and is called **liquidated and ascertained damages**.

Each operation has been **workloaded** to establish the resources necessary to complete within the bar duration. For example, for the operation 'Excavate' the bar duration was two weeks, but to achieve the completion of the activity within that bar duration, resources such as labour, plant, equipment and materials were necessary. The amount of labour, plant, equipment and materials is called the **resource requirement**. When establishing the tender strategies the estimator identifies risks. Some management risks involve the plant and equipment. If the contractor's plant breaks down, who will pay for the lost time and expenses? That is a risk that is taken by the contractor.

Project planning aims to utilise the resources to the optimum and costs are kept as low as possible by evaluating alternative construction methods against costs and duration. The contractor is committed to the **project duration**. The site planner's role will be to ensure that the right quantity of labour or plant or materials are available in the right place at the right time. The **right time** is the commencement date for each operation.

Space or land is another resource that needs to be utilised to the maximum. On a **restricted site** such as an inner city site, where will the sites offices or the canteen be positioned? How much space is available for the storage of materials? Is there sufficient space for the total delivery of the materials, or

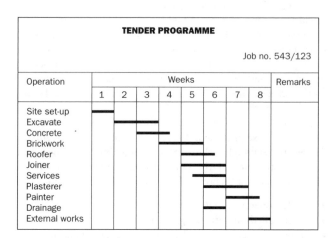

Figure 7.4

will the material deliveries need to be phased? The scheduling of material deliveries relies on the supplier, and this is another tender risk that the estimator must quantify. The utilisation of site space, location of temporary facilities, such as the site office and messrooms, is called **site layout**. All these decisions were taken by the estimator, contracts manager and planner at the tender stage, and now that the contract has been awarded, these decisions will need to be reviewed.

There was a risk that the contractor would not be successful in bidding for this work, and the tender decisions now need to be reviewed, confirmed or amended because of the definite agreement of the contract. Some of those tender decisions are mentioned below.

Subcontractors which the contractor will use need to be appointed and subcontracts signed, based on the **main contract conditions**. The **domestic subcontractor's** quotations, time required and sequence of construction all need to be agreed. A **pre-contract meeting** is necessary to coordinate and agree construction strategies and these strategies need to be published to all interested parties. The **works programme** or **contract programme** is the controlling document on site, detailing the number of subcontractor's operatives that will be required. The start and finish dates, based on the tender programme, will become subcontract conditions.

- What key activities need to be completed before the commencement of the subcontractor's work?
- What plant and equipment will the subcontractor require?

This will entail standing scaffolding, hoists, storage areas for temporary offices, materials and plant. The member of the contractor's staff who deals with the subcontract placement is the **buyer**, in consultation with the site planner and site agent (site manager or general supervisor).

Materials

Orders need to be placed with the suppliers. This is one of the jobs that the buyer will do. **Supplier selection** is not a random affair. **Supplier evaluation** is a constant activity and the suppliers selected will have to meet **delivery dates** and **minimum quality standards**.

- What is the **lead time** on the delivery of materials to site?
- Are part load deliveries possible?

The site planner has to ensure that the materials are delivered on time, and at the right quality and quantity. With this cooperation the site management staff can complete on time and within budget.

Labour

In the tender programme decisions were made regarding deployment of labour. The planned requirement of labour needs to be analysed according to the company's workload.

- Will the labour be available for the commencement of the operation?
- How many operatives will be available?
- Are the operatives capable of producing the contractual standard of workmanship?
- The site planner has to organise the labour resource to ensure that labour is available in the right place at the right time and in the right quantity.

Site layout

The tender strategy allowed for certain temporary facilities and work flow patterns.

- Are these decisions still acceptable?
- What alternatives are available?
- Which site layout will allow the site management the best possible opportunity to achieve the contract aims, on time completion and costs within budget?

The temporary offices, health and welfare provisions need to be checked against current legislation. Under the Health and Safety at Work, etc., Act the employer has a legal duty to ensure a safe working environment.

- Are the proposed methods of working acceptable?
- What dangers to site personnel do these working patterns create?
- How will a safe site be maintained?

The sequencing of activities will be crucial in ensuring a safe working environment.

Sequencing of the work

The **construction sequence** is the order for carrying the activities. The sequence is obtained by asking three questions to each activity:

- What job or activity precedes?
- What jobs or activities can be done at the same time?
- What activity must follow?

The answer to those questions can be seen on the bar chart programme shown in Fig. 7.4. No operations precede the activity 'site set-up'. There are no jobs at the same time or concurrent and the operation 'excavate' follows. The decision on the three questions stated above is usually based on **technical judgement**. For example, the painter cannot paint the plastered walls until the plasterer has completed plastering the walls. But in a rush, you might temper that decision. Therefore, we have a technical reason for the operation sequence and personal reasons for the work order.

A traditional sequence for a house might be:

1. Site set-up: erect temporary facilities and set out
2. Excavate: topsoil; reduced level dig: foundations
3. Concrete: foundations
4. Brickwork: walls to damp-proof course
5. Concrete: ground floor or oversite
   – base course including blinding; insulation; damp-proof membrane; concrete ground floor
6. Brickwork: to first floor
   – walls, external and internal: form openings; build in door and window frames
7. Carpenter and joiner: first floor joists
8. Brickwork: to roof or eaves
   – walls: form openings; build in window frames
9. Carpenter and joiner: roof carcass
10. Roofer: roof tiling, (often a domestic subcontractor)
11. Building watertight

The following operations could be concurrent:

1. Carpenter and joiner (called joiner first fix): first floor boarding and stairs; stud partition to first floor rooms; door linings

2. Plumber and heating (called plumber first fix or carcass): pipe runs; tanks; cylinders; boiler
3. Electrician (called electrical first fix): wiring in floor and roof; light drops

The following operation is not concurrent with any other:

- Plasterer: ceilings boarded out and skimmed; walls plastered

The following operations could be concurrent:

1. Carpenter and joiner (called joiner second fix): skirting boards; architraves; window boards
   - doors and door ironmongery
   - kitchen units
   - builder's work in connection with services
2. Plumber and heating (called plumber and heating second fix): install sanitaryware
   - radiators
   - balance and commission scheme
3. Electrician (called electrical second fix): wire in accessories
   - wire in boiler and controls
4. Drainlayer: excavate and lay foul drains including inspection chambers and connection to public drain
   - test drain runs
   - excavate and lay storm drains
5. External works: excavate and lay driveway; drop access to highway
   - excavate and lay paths; soft and hard landscaping

The following operations are not concurrent:

- Painter: internal paint
  - mist coat
  - walls and ceilings
  - joinery
- Painter: external paint
  - fascia, barge boards and soffits
  - joinery – windows and doors
- Handover: testing and commissioning heating
  - final clean of building and site.

There will be differences of opinion over the sequences since the list was only a guide. Each project will be divided into activities and the three questions will be asked for each activity: What precedes? What activities are concurrent? and What activities succeed? That will determine the sequence and the setting out of the method statement.

Method statement

Decisions are being taken at a pace during the preparation of the **works programme**. Information needs to be recorded and filed and sometimes retrieved to reconsider earlier decisions. The information held could be used to debrief contract staff, such as the site agent, general supervisor, trades supervisor. The method statement has such uses.

The method statement outlines the sequence of activities, the planned resource requirement and the planned duration for the main activities. For example, in the activity 'brickwork to first floor', the quantities need to be measured off the plan.

The bill of quantities gives the total quantities for work-in-place items and is used to check the total quantities used in the method statement. 'Brickwork to first floor' will involve

- outer skin of brickwork
- cavity and insulation
- inner skin of blockwork
- forming openings
  - closing the cavity and vertical DPC
  - lintel and DPC

The time it will take a craftsperson to do each job is called the **output** and is measured in hours per operative. The work will be set out in the method statement, as shown in Fig. 7.5.

The method statement is used by the site staff to monitor the performance of operatives. The contract programme or works programme is based on the method statement.

Bar chart contract programme

Apart from the site costing and management accounts the contract programme is the key control document for site staff. The overall construction time has been calculated from the method statement. Overlaps of activities are planned and outpacing of previous activities avoided. **Key dates** will be added to the works programme and the planned labour resources indicated on the bar durations.

This **long-term programme** will be used as the basis for **short-term planning**. The three-monthly **stage programme** will be based on key dates and durations from the works programme. To control the site activity further programmes are prepared. The **monthly programme** is based on target dates set in the three-monthly programme. **Weekly** and **daily programmes** will be necessary to ensure maximum utilisation of resources, especially of labour and plant. Delivery of materials will be phased from the three-monthly programme and start dates for subcontractors confirmed from the three-monthly programme.

This document will be used to measure the site performance. The actual progress will be compared with the planned progress weekly to achieve on-time completion. This is not the only measure of site performance. The estimate will

METHOD STATEMENT

Job no. 543/123

Operation	Quantity	Method	Output	Gang size	Gang hours	Remarks
Outer skin	100 m²	2/1 gang	1 h/m²	2	50	

The gang hours is calculated from this formula

$$\frac{quantity \times output}{labour \ or \ plant \ resources \ allocated} = 50 \ gang \ hours$$

$$\frac{100 \times 1}{2}$$

The servicing gang, i.e. the labourers, is not used in this calculation

| Cavity & insulation | 100 m² | | 0.2 h/m² | 2 | 10 | |
| Inner skin | 100 m² | | 0.6 h/m² | 2 | 30 | |

Figure 7.5

also measure the site management's skills on deploying resources. Not only time but, more importantly, costs need to be compared with the budgets established in the estimate.

Tender feedout – estimate breakdown

The estimate submitted to the architect included all the costs likely to be incurred by the builder and payment for risks taken – that is, profit and mark-up. To measure the site's performance and to update the data bank of constants the estimator requires some **site feedback**. The estimate has to be broken down to show the anticipated cost of **work-in-place items** and **preliminaries**. The feedout should allow the site staff to monitor their performance against the estimate.

Site staff have responsibility for labour and plant and equipment. The other estimating constants – materials and overheads – are outside their control. The purchase of materials and placement of subcontracts are the tasks of the buyer. The buying proficiency will be periodically monitored against the materials cost in the estimate. The overheads – that is, head office overheads not site overheads – are monitored and established by the accountant.

Site overheads are incurred by assigning staff to the site on a full-time basis. This will include the following line management staff:

- site agent
- site general foreperson
- trades forepersons (full-time supervision).

Other **line management** staff are usually part-time supervisors and are allowed for in the **all-in hourly** rate. A typical trades supervision structure would be:

- **Chargehand.** A tradesperson having to look after several gangs and reporting to the trades foreperson. The amount of supervision time allocated will depend on the project and the operatives involved.
- **Leading hand.** A tradesperson having responsibility for two or three gangs and reporting to the chargehand.

The usual ratio of operatives to a supervisor is six to eight. General operatives or labourers have a different authority structure. The full-time supervisor is called a **walking ganger** while the labourers' gang will have part-time supervisors called **gangers**. The management structure depends on the company's management philosophy and the company's adherence to management ratios. The bill unit rate quantifies the site costs involved in the work-in-place item.

Unit rate constants

The gross price was built up from several unit constants plus the profit margin and the mark-up. The estimator has built up a databank of items usually in **work-in-place** order as described in SMM7. The **labour constant** is recorded in hours per unit of measurement. For example, the bricklayer will lay in 1 hour 1 square metre of half-brick wall pointed. This output or **labour constant** is stated as: 'half-brick wall in facings, pointed as work proceeds 1 h/m².' The output is for

the bricklayer craftsperson and does not include the labourer serving the bricklayer.

The **plant constant** is similar: 'JCB excavate trench not exceeding 1.00 deep, over 300 mm wide, tipped to lorry 0.10 h/m³.'

The **material constant** is often expressed as a conversion factor. For instance, the brickwork is measured net, according to SMM7 and the unit of measurement is square metre of wall. The buyer purchases bricks per thousand, or per pallet or wagon loads and the quantity as fixed requires converting to bricks – hence, a conversion factor. All data used must comply with the unit of measurement in the bill of quantities. For example, the bill of quantities may specify 100 m² of brick wall (Figs 7.6 and 7.7), but how many bricks are required? That is not the form of measurement used in the bill and the answer requires a conversion factor. The purchase unit of measurement stated in the bill must be used by the buyer.

Based on a square metre of wall (since the bill states m²) the brick manufacturer's size is $215 \times 65 \times 102$ mm thick; but the brick wall size, including the mortar bed and perpendicular joint, is $225 \times 75 \times 102$ mm thick. Therefore, the conversion factor will be:

$$\frac{\text{area of wall}}{\text{brick wall size}} = \frac{1.00 \times 1.00}{0.225 \times 0.075} = 59.26 \text{ bricks/m}^2$$

The total quantities in the bill are measured as fixed or net, so an allowance for waste must be made. The waste percentage must include design waste, where the architect cannot coordinate the dimensions to modular brickwork and construction waste.

The **overhead constant** is calculated by the accountant as a percentage addition to the labour constant. The overheads are for head office overheads and visiting staff to site, such as the quantity surveyor, the plant manager, or the buyer. Staff on site full time are included in the **preliminaries cost** as a **time-related charge**. The unit rate is compiled from the four constants mentioned above.

a	F10 Brick/block walling .1 Walls to F10.109 .1 Half-brick thick .1 Vertical	100	m²	31.23	

Figure 7.6 Example from the bill of quantities

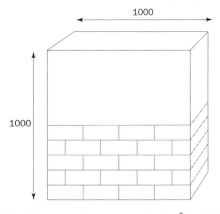

Figure 7.7 Calculating bricks required for 1 m² half-brick wall

A work-in-place item

Net pricing will allow the estimator to assess the financial risks.

Labour constant

Bricklayer	1 h/m² at £9.50 (all-in rate) £9.50	
Labourer (2/1 gang)	½ h/m² at £8.50 (all-in rate) £4.25	
Labour constant		£13.75

Plant constant

Mixer	½ bag	hire rate	£1.00 per h	
Dumper	¼ m³	hire rate	£1.00 per h	
			£2.00 per h	

[Using the labourer output rate in this instance]

| Plant constant | (½ h/m² at £2.00/h) | £1.00 |

Material constant

Purchase price: £240 per 1000 delivered
1 m² of brickwork = 59.26 bricks

$$\text{Purchase price} = \frac{\text{price per unit of measure}}{\text{conversion factor}}$$

$$= \frac{240}{60 \times 100} = \text{£4.00 per m}^2 \text{ of wall}$$

| Add waste percentage | £0.40 (10% waste) | |
| Material constant | £4.40 | £4.40 |

Overhead constant

| 50% of labour constant = 0.50 × £13.75 | £6.88 |

	Net unit rate	£26.03
	Add profit	2.60
	Add mark-up	2.60
	Gross unit rate	**£31.23**

The priced unit rate for the item will be as shown in Fig. 7.6.

The control of the site's performance against the gross unit rate is calculated by the management accounts prepared every quarter. Each week the site performance must be monitored against the estimate. The net unit rate includes material and overhead constants which are outside the control of the site agent. The estimate should be split up for this site monitoring.

What breakdown is needed?

Control of labour is certainly the responsibility of site staff. The operatives will be paid according to the national wages agreement – the **Working Rule Agreement** (WRA) produced by the National Joint Council for the Building Industry. An alternative wages agreement is produced by **BATJIC**, the Building and Allied Trades Joint Industrial Council. The WRA defines the pay structure according to status:

- skilled hourly rate
- semi-skilled hourly rate
- unskilled hourly rate

The difference in pay per hour is called a **wage differential**, that is, the pay rate used for the operatives on site, not the **all-in hourly rate** as used in the unit rate build-up. So for site, the estimate feedout needs to reflect the basic pay to operatives, not the all-in hourly rate.

Labour constant

| Bricklayer | 1 h/m² at £5.00 (basic pay) | £5.00 |
| Labourer (2/1 gang) | 1 h/m² at £4.00 (basic pay) | £2.00 |

Plant constant

Mixer	(½ bag)	£1.00/h (hire rate)	
Dumper	(¼ m³)	£1.00/h (hire rate)	
		£2.00/h	
Plant constant (½ h/m² at £2.00/h)			£1.00

| *Budget for site costing* (per m² of wall) | £8.00 |

Monitoring site actual costs against the labour and plant feedout from the estimate will help the site agent and the planner to achieve the aim of project planning – on-time completion and within budget. To ensure this performance is monitored, weekly, monthly and accumulative actual costs are compared to the budget in the estimate.

Work study

Method study

The contractor's management team is only as good as the information they possess. If the information is inaccurate then no amount of managerial skill will rectify the situation. Accurate information is therefore vital for the success of the project. Contractor's data has already been used to establish the bid or estimate, but how accurate was the base data for the estimate? The method statements that outlined the tender strategy were based on certain assumptions:

- Was the best method of doing the work used?
- Was there a balance between gang size and plant?
- Were the materials stacked in the best position?
- Was the static plant located in the best position?
- What are the controlling operations?

These questions can all be answered by using a work study technique called 'Method study'.

Aim of method study

Method study is a systematic analysis of actual and proposed work methods with the aim of finding an **improved method** of working. The method study technique tries to establish the **best method** of doing the work. It is not initially concerned with time as that is dealt with under work measurement or time study.

The builder under the Health and Safety at Work, etc., Act is required to establish and maintain **safe working practices**. The Control of Substances Hazardous to Health requires the employer (not the *client*, but the *builder*) to prepare work statements to reduce the risk of injury to the employees. The legislation focuses attention on the work patterns used by the operatives. Site management's aim is to ensure that the work patterns used are the most effective. That could mean observing existing methods and retraining operatives in safer, more productive work patterns, and this must be done systematically.

Steps in a method study

The procedure must be **systematic** or vital work patterns could be missed and the best method not obtained. There are six steps in method study:

- select
- record
- examine
- develop
- install
- maintain

Often the work is carried out by a specialist, trained in these observation and analysis techniques. Often the initial prompt comes from the site management, who are having difficulties meeting the deadlines imposed on the project by the contract period. The problems may also be self-inflicted and meeting the estimate's budget is proving extremely difficult.

Select   The operation to be studied must have a proved return for the money and time to be invested. The job must be repetitive and sufficiently important to affect the overall success of the project. The improved method of working should be transferable to other operatives and sites, thereby maximising the benefits. There are some questions that will guide the site staff into analysing the key operations.

- Is the operation a one-off?
- How many times will the operation be repeated:
  - on this project?
  - on other projects?
- Will the activity increase operative motivation?
- Estimate the hours taken to carry out the method study.

The use of these questions will help to select an operation that is suitable for method study. Finally, the choice will focus on:

- technical considerations
- economical considerations
- human reactions

There are obvious indicators for selection, such as:

- repetitive work
- long haul material movements
- bottlenecks, which hold up production

Record   The existing operation must be observed. The work study practitioner must record the activities as they occur. Often charts and diagrams are used to record the actual activities, usually without reference to the time scale. Some work patterns are of short duration but are very repetitive. **Micromotion study techniques** will be chosen to record the actual work patterns. The **SIMO** chart, or more correctly the simultaneous motion cycle chart, is a micromotion study using film analysis. Ordinarily method study charts and diagrams are used to obtain the best method of working: charts can indicate the sequence of operations or involve time, while diagrams indicate the movement of plant, operatives and materials. **Charts** can be

- outline process charts
- flow process charts – operatives, materials or plant and equipment
- two-handed process charts. Whichever type of chart is used the method study will focus on the sequence of activities.

Diagrams can be

- flow diagrams
- string diagrams
- cyclegraphs, usually involving filming techniques
- chronocyclegraph, usually involving filming techniques

The type of recording technique is determined by the operations being recorded. Sometimes a chart and a diagram are both used to record the facts.

Five standard symbols are used to illustrate the type of activity being carried out when recording work patterns (Fig. 7.8). The types of activity are:

- operation
- inspection
- transport
- delay
- storage.

Operation. This indicates the main stage in a process, method or procedure. The operation brings the work nearer to completion.
Inspection. This symbol indicates an inspection of work for quality/safety/quantity.
Transport. This symbol shows the movement of workers, materials and or plant and equipment.
Delay. This symbol indicates a temporary stoppage of work activity
Storage. This symbol indicates the permanent storage of finished goods.

Let us assume that the concrete batching plant has been selected for a method study. The work is repetitive and there could be a return on the investment in work study. The flow diagram (Fig. 7.9) will be used to record the activities as they occur.

As the diagram does not indicate the sequence of activities, a **flow process chart** is prepared (Fig. 7.10).

The purpose of this stage in method study is to obtain the facts as they occur, recording these activities in an unbiased manner.

The **outline flow process chart** uses also the symbols for operation and inspection. The outline flow process chart gives a quick overview of the operation.

The aim of method study is to obtain the **best method** of doing a job, so there is a need to consider both hands in some activities, for example, a joiner using a cross-cut saw in the joiner's compound. In order to obtain an unbiased view of the joiner's activity, the work study practitioner must use a two-handed process chart to record what one hand is doing in relation to the other (Fig. 7.11).

Symbol	Activity
○	Operation
▢	Inspection
⇒	Transport
D	Delay
▽	Storage

Figure 7.8 Standard symbols for activities

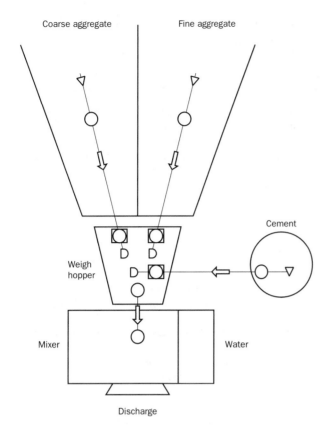

Figure 7.9 Flow diagram of joiner's compound

FLOW PROCESS CHART

Operation:	Concrete weigh batching and mixing
Plant:	240/200R mixer
Plant operator:	mixer driver
	batching operative

Date: 20/8/94

Activity	Quantity	◯	⇒	D	□	▽	Remarks
Charge hopper	3						
gravel bin						✓	
load shovel		✓					
transport		✓	✓				
discharge		✓					
weigh					✓	✓	
Charge hopper	3						
sand bin						✓	
load shovel		✓					
transport		✓	✓				
discharge		✓					
weigh					✓	✓	
Charge hopper	1						
cement silo						✓	
load hopper		✓					
transport		✓	✓				
discharge		✓					
weigh					✓	✓	
Raise hopper	1	✓	✓				
Operate mixer	1	✓					
Charge water	1					✓	
part discharge		✓	✓				
Inspect mix					✓		
final water added	1	✓	✓				
Inspect mix					✓		
Discharge mix	1	✓	✓				
Total	11	11	7	3	5	4	

Figure 7.10

TWO-HANDED PROCESS CHART

Operation:	Cutting to length using a jig
Plant:	300 m cross cut
Plant operator:	C. Saw (wood machinist)

Date: 30/8/94

Left hand	◯	⇒	D	▽	◯	⇒	D	▽	Right hand
								✓	Pick up wood
Offer wood to bench	✓				✓				
Hold wood against block	✓								
					✓				Cut piece to length
					✓				Pick up offcut
							✓		Throw to bin
Pick up cut length	✓				✓				Pick up two-handed
Transport to stack		✓				✓			Transport to stack
Stack cut length			✓					✓	Stack cut length
Total	3	1	1	0	4	2	2	0	

Figure 7.11

Recording of the work patterns by video has many advantages, especially with short cycle operations.

- gives greater detail than eye observations
- allows scrutiny without bias
- gives a permanent record of the activity
- gives an accurate record of operations

Having recorded the existing method the next step is to undertake a critical examination of the activity.

Examine This stage of method study is a systematic series of questions to establish the basic facts and reasons for the activity. Most jobs can be divided into three categories:

- make ready activities, e.g. loading out bricks and mortar
- do operations, e.g. lay bricks in wall
- put away activities, e.g. clean up after the operation

The 'make ready' and 'put away' activities are indicated, predominantly, by transport, storage and inspection symbols, whereas the 'do' operations are indicated by either operation or inspection symbols. The question or critical examination is structured to avoid unnecessary work. The following structure or pattern of questions is adopted:

- **Purpose** What is the reason for the activity?
- **Place** Where does the activity occur?
- **Sequence** What is the time or order of the activity?
- **Person** Who does the activity?
- **Means** How is the activity carried out (e.g. tools)?

This **primary** series of questions will secure the **facts** regarding the activity. The **reasons** for the activity and its present method are especially valuable in the search for the one best method of doing the job. The series of questions asked are:

Purpose	What? (facts)	Why is it necessary? (reasons)
Place	Where? (facts)	Why there? (reasons)
Sequence	When? (facts)	Why then? (reasons)
Person	Who? (facts)	Why that person? (reasons)
Means	How? (facts)	Why that method? (reasons)

Having established the facts and reasons for the present method the next step in method study is development, i.e. establishing of the best method of work patterns.

Develop A series of secondary questions leads to acceptable alternative methods. Each method must be technically acceptable, safe and non-hazardous to the operatives and the general public. The type of **personal protective clothing** and equipment will be introduced to ensure that all alternative methods produce a safe working environment. The structure is the same as in the critical examination stage:

Purpose	What else can be done?
	What **should** be done?
Place	Where else can it be done?
	Where **should** it be done?
Sequence	When else can it be done?
	When **should** it be done?
Person	Who else can do it?
	Who **should** do it?
Means	How else can it be done?
	How **should** it be done?

The final series of questions lead us to the best method. The best method of doing the job is:

- *What* work should be done?
- *Where* should the work be done?
- *When* should the work be done?
- *Who* should do the work?
- *How* should the work be done?

The operatives should be involved in the critical examination stage and their contributions welcomed since they have a deep understanding of the activity. It also helps in the next stage of method study if there is worker participation.

Install The best method has been established. All that is required now is for the workforce to adopt the new best method.

There are five stages in installing the new method. All are made easier by worker and staff participation in the development of the new method.

Stage 1: Acceptance by supervisors
Stage 2: Acceptance of the new method by the senior management
Stage 3: Gain acceptance by the operatives and their union
Stage 4: Retrain the operatives in a non-threatening situation
Stage 5: Monitor closely until the new method is firmly established

The use of videos will allow operatives to analyse their work patterns and reinforce the new operating standard. The important activity is to make a **habit** of the new method. The use of **written standard practices** will allow the operatives to become familiar with all the procedures and safety checks. The work standard practice should include the following:

- tools and equipment to be used
- work layout
- sequence of operations
- inspection stages

- safety precautions
- quality standards that are measurable and achievable

The final step in the method study is to maintain the job standard.

Maintain The best method was obtained against a set of conditions, and if the conditions change then the method might need to be reviewed. A well-written standard practice or operating procedure will prove valuable in maintaining the correct working patterns. Sometimes operatives become too familiar with the methods and do not obey all the rules and safety precautions. For example, if the inspection checks are omitted, the quality may suffer; or new work patterns may creep in, known as **foreign elements**, just for a change of routine. Monitoring is best carried out by the operative and the supervisor. If there are changes in the conditions, such as the purchase of higher quality materials or better plant, then the job standard must be adjusted.

There are a lot of useful work study techniques which the site planners can use as they try to maximise resource utilisation while minimising cost.

Work study techniques

Flow diagrams

The layout of the joiner's compound (Fig. 7.12) could be a work of art but is it a workshop. The storage of materials, position of woodworking machinery and work space should be ideal for making the formwork. By converting the scaled layout plan, and by using cutouts to indicate the storage areas, worker movements and machinery, the planner can design the best layout for the joiner's compound.

Another work study technique that will be useful to the planner in deciding the best location of storage areas, temporary facilities, hardstandings and temporary roads is the string diagram.

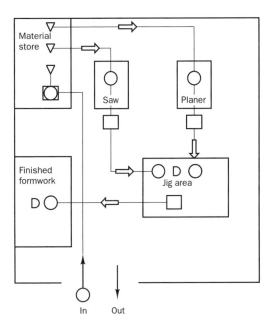

Figure 7.12 Diagram of joiner's compound

String diagram

A string diagram is a scaled plan which traces the movement of operatives, plant or materials using a thread or piece of string. The length of the string can be measured and converted to travel distance. Reducing the travel distance is an obvious area for improvement in the site layout (Fig. 7.13).

The string diagram also illustrates the potential **bottlenecks** in the transport flow.

Another technique that is very useful to the site planner is the multiple activity chart.

Multiple activity chart

A multiple activity chart illustrates on a common timescale the different yet simultaneous activities of operatives and/or plant. The multiple activity chart will identify the **controlling operation** in a gang, and is a very useful technique for gang balancing. The data used to workload the gang activity needs to be extremely accurate and only work study standard times should be used.

The suggested method for site concrete mixing is for batching to be carried out by one operative while another operative acts as the mixer driver. The tasks are divided as shown in Table 7.1.

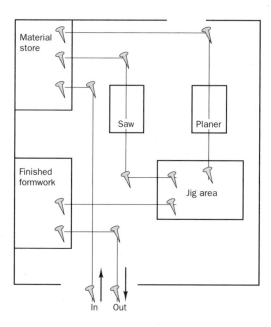

Figure 7.13 String diagram of joiner's compound

Table 7.1 Division of tasks for concrete mixing

Operative 1	Operative 2
Loads and charges the hopper	Operates the hopper and mixer
Loads gravel to hopper	Checks weight of gravel
Loads sand to hopper	Checks weight of sand
Loads cement to hopper	Checks weight of cement
	Operates hopper and discharges into mixer
	Mixes the batch
	Inspects the mixing
	Discharges the batch

MULTIPLE ACTIVITY CHART

Concrete batching and mixing

Time	Operative 1 batching	Operative 2 mixer driver	Mixer
	Load gravel Batch 1		
	Load sand Batch 1		
1.00	Load cement Batch 1		
2.00			
		Operate hopper	
			Mixing batch 1
3.00	Load gravel Batch 2		
4.00			
5.00	Load sand Batch 2		
6.00	Load cement Batch 2	Discharge Batch 1	
		Operate hopper	
7.00			Mixing batch 2
	Load gravel Batch 3		
Working time	$5\frac{1}{2}$	$1\frac{1}{2}$	4
Total cycle time	$7\frac{1}{2}$	$7\frac{1}{2}$	$7\frac{1}{2}$
% working time	73%	20%	53%

Figure 7.14

The job definitions in Table 7.1 seem to form a reasonable arrangement, and those activities are translated into a multiple activity chart in Fig. 7.14.

With a little rearranging the 'gang' can be reduced to one and the output is not decreased. The control operation is the mixer. The multiple activity chart should be carried out for one day to establish the work cycle and introduce break and lunch times.

The gang balancing has been achieved by the use of the multiple activity chart and work study standard times. The standard times are a product of work measurement.

Work measurement

Aim

Work measurement establishes the time for a **qualified worker** to produce one unit of production at a **defined level of performance**. The method study gave the best method, now the trained operatives are studied to establish the time taken in performing the tasks. Work measurement is concerned with **eliminating ineffective time**, whether due to management's or operative's inefficiencies.

Definitions

Time study is a work measurement technique for recording the times taken by a qualified worker, working at a defined level of performance, to produce one unit of production.

Qualified worker is a representative worker fully trained to perform a specified job at the right quality and adhering to all the safety procedures.

Rating is an assessment of the qualified worker's rate of work compared to standard performance.

Normal performance is the qualified worker's effectiveness under capable supervision but not motivated to work harder. Activity is continuous throughout the day.

Standard performance is the qualified worker's effectiveness, under capable supervision and motivated to work hard throughout the working day.

Time study methods

The purpose of observation of the qualified worker is to establish the minimum time taken to obtain one unit of production. There are two main methods of timing operations:

- flyback timing
- continuous timing (cumulative timing)

Both methods have their advantages and disadvantages, but the flyback method is preferred. To control the accuracy of the time study an external time is taken, called **elapsed time**. The start of the time study and the finish of the time study (called **check times**) are both noted:

time on:	10.00 (check time)
time off:	10.30 (check time)
elapsed time:	30 minutes

The activity chosen for the time study is first observed to check the work pattern and establish **elements**. The activity is broken down into elements to allow accurate assessment of allowances and to identify any foreign elements. The element should have a definite start point and finish point called **breakpoints**. Elements are classified into:

- **constant element**: the basic time remains constant irrespective of when it is performed
- **foreign element**: an element that is not necessary in performing the activity
- **occasional element**: an activity that is necessary for the work but does not occur every cycle, e.g. inspection or receiving instructions
- **repetitive element**: an element that occurs every job cycle
- **variable element**: a repetitive element but the basic time may vary as the element is repeated

Once the elements have been agreed the time study observation can take place. The number of observations is calculated statistically to a predetermined confidence limit and margin of error. For example, a confidence level of 95% with a margin of error of ±5% of the sample size of observations may vary from 10 to 200. The larger number is for short cycle time operations. During the observations the work study practitioner will rate the operative against a rating scale. The factors affecting rating are:

- variation in quality of materials being used
- changes in the operating efficiency of the equipment
- changes in the environment
- variations in mental attention

The rating scale allocates a numeric value of 75 for **normal performance** and 100 for **standard performance** (Table 7.2).

Table 7.2 Rating scales for work measurement

Rating	Description of industriousness
70	Steady slow activity with some wasted effort
75	**Normal performance.** Steady deliberate activity, appears slow but no intentionally wasted effort
90	Steady, deliberate activity, methodical and brisk
100	**Standard performance.** Brisk activity, deliberate movements, acceptable quality, all inspection checks and safety rules adhered to
125	Very fast, high degree of proficiency, dexterity and coordination
130	Short burst of very intense activity but not sustainable over working day

There are several rating excerises to help the work study practitioner establish the concept of standard performance. The next step is to observe the qualified operative at work. (Fig. 7.15)

TIME STUDY FORM

Operation: Laying bricks to first lift facing wall . .
        Part of 2/1 gang

Operative: B. Rick   Weather: Fine, overcast
Works No.: 124   Locations: Housing development
         Time on: 10.00
         Time off: 10.45

         Elapsed time: 45 mins

Element	Rate	Observed time	Basic time	Remarks
1. Roll mortar	100	0.50		
2. Spread mortar	90	0.75		
3. Pick brick	95	0.50		Includes select
4. Mortar head	100	0.25		
5. Lay brick	95	0.80		
6. Wipe joint	100	0.20		
1. Roll mortar	90	0.56		
2. Spread mortar	95	0.79		
3. Pick brick	95	0.50		
4. Mortar head	110	0.23		
5. Lay brick	100	0.76		
6. Wipe joint	100	0.20		
1. Roll mortar	80	0.63		
2. Spread mortar	85	0.89		
3. Pick brick	100	0.52		
4. Mortar head	100	0.25		
5. Lay brick	95	0.80		
6. Wipe joint	100	0.20		

Figure 7.15

Once the time study is completed the check times are used to establish the accuracy of the study.

$$\frac{\text{elapsed time} - \text{total observed time}}{\text{elapsed time}} \times 100$$

$$\frac{45.00 - 44.80}{45.00} \times 100 = 0.4\%$$

This is within the $\pm2\%$ tolerance allowed on the time study. The work study practitioner now calculates and compiles the basic time for each element.

Basic time

Basic time is the time taken by an operative working at standard performance to complete an element.

$$\text{basic time} = \text{observed time} \times \frac{\text{rate}}{\text{standard performance}}$$

If the work study practitioner has accurately carried out the time study, the basic time for the same element should be a constant numeric value. A slight variance will occur due to rating in increments of 5 units (Fig. 7.16).

The basic element times are now averaged and the job basic time obtained. All foreign elements and time have been discarded so the job time is the basic time taken by a **qualified worker** working at **standard performance** to achieve one unit of production, complying with all safety rules and achieving the right quality. However, the operative would not be able to maintain this rate because fatigue and relaxation allowances have not been included.

Allowances

The aim of time study was to obtain the time it takes an operative to perform jobs throughout the day, so allowances must be added to the basic time. The allowances are dependent on the tasks performed and the stress and strain of the quality specification.

Relaxation allowances have two major components:

- personal needs, for which 5–7% is usually added
- basic fatigue, for which 4% is commonly added

Variable allowances are determined by the operation and are usually categorised into:

- physical strains
  - force
  - posture
  - vibration and noise
  - restrictive clothing
- mental strains
  - monotony
  - eye strain
  - noise
- working conditions
  - humidity
  - temperature
  - ventilation
  - dust
  - wet
  - fumes

Contingency allowances which take into account variations in the quality of materials used, the environment and a *supervision allowance* as the operative must be under capable supervision and time must be allocated for receiving instructions and inspection checks.

Standard time

Standard time is the basic time obtained by observation of the qualified worker plus an allowance for all necessary ancillary duties needed to perform the operation.

Standard time is achieved by the qualified worker working at standard performance, under capable supervision, and observing all the safety procedures and producing one unit of production at the correct quality. The standard time is expressed as:

- standard minutes   (smin)
- standard hours   (sh)

and is the culmination of the work measurement. Work measurement gives accurate data on production times and is of assistance to the estimator when preparing the bid. It also provides valuable data that the site manager can use to control labour output.

Incentive payment schemes

A site manager requires accurate reliable data to measure an **operative's performance**, and work study standard times will provide that measurement. The standard time is achieved by the operative working at a standard performance. The definition of standard performance was:

'the qualified worker's effectiveness, under capable supervision and *motivated* to work hard throughout the working day'.

Standard time does not include any **motivation** for the operative to work harder. The bonus motivation is often monetary, i.e. the harder the operative works the more money is earned. A **bonus** allowance is added to standard time, and the total is called **bonus time**.

Element	Rate	Observed time	Basic time	Remarks
1. Roll mortar	100	0.50	0.50	$0.50 \times \frac{100}{100}$
1. Roll mortar	90	0.56	0.504	$0.56 \times \frac{90}{100}$
1. Roll mortar	80	0.63	0.504	$0.63 \times \frac{80}{100}$

Figure 7.16 Averaging the values in Fig. 7.15

There are two types of bonus incentive schemes based on work study standard times:

- direct incentive
- geared incentive

Both types of incentive pay the same bonus for work at standard performance, but the **direct incentive** rewards the quicker operative. The **geared incentive** favours the slower worker. This is illustrated in the following comparision of the two schemes. The geared scheme is a 50/50 and the operative working at standard performance will earn an additional one-third pay as an incentive. The hours saved on the bonus target will be used as the bonus payment. Hours saved on the direct incentive scheme will be paid at £4.00 per hour (basic pay). The 50/50 geared incentive will pay hours saved at £2.00 per hour (50% of basic pay). If the operative achieves standard performance there should be no difference in bonus payment (Table 7.3).

Table 7.3 Comparisons of bonus payments in direct and geared incentive schemes

	Direct incentive	Geared incentive
Standard time	9 sh	9 sh
Add bonus incentive at one-third of basic pay	3 (9/3)	6 (9/3 × 100/50)
Bonus target	12 bh	15 bh
Actual hours taken by the operative	9	9
Bonus hours saved	3	6
Bonus paid to operative	3 × £4.00 = £12.00	6 × £2.00 = £12.00

There is no difference on the incentive payment schemes when the operatives work at standard performance, but not all operatives are so consistent. Some are quicker and the quality is still acceptable (Table 7.4).

Table 7.4 Comparison of bonus payments in direct and geared incentive schemes.

	Direct incentive	Geared incentive
Bonus target	12 bh	15 bh
Actual hours taken by the operative	7	7
Bonus hours saved	5	8
Bonus paid to operative	5 × £4.00 = £20.00	8 × £2.00 = £16.00

The direct incentive payment scheme, sometimes called the 100% scheme, benefits the quicker more capable worker. Introducing a bonus incentive scheme based on work study standard times will allow the site management to concentrate on planning and organising the site to maximise the resources available. The use of an **incentive payment scheme** is predominantly about labour **control of output** and not 'take home pay'. For the incentive scheme to be effective the operatives should know the bonus target prior to starting the operation.

Issuing bonus targets

There are two ways of issuing bonus targets.

- individual bonus targets
- bulk targets

The latter is preferred but the cost and bonus surveyor will have to **premeasure the work** prior to the operation commencement (Fig. 7.17).

BULK TARGET BUILD UP SHEET

Operation: brickwork to first floor (external walls only)

Job No. 123

Operation	Quantity	Bonus target	Bonus hours
Brick to outer skin	45 m²	1.38 bh/m²	62.10
Cavity and insulation	44 m²	1.16 bh/m²	7.04
150 mm block inner skin	43 m²	1.88 bh/m²	37.84
Form openings			
– Block closing at sill	10 m	0.22 bh/m	2.20
– Ditto at jamb	25 m	0.17 bh/m	4.25
– Vertical DPC at jamb	25 m	0.06 bh/m	1.50
– Lintel steel combined	11 m	0.12 bh/m	1.32
– Horizontal DPC	11 m	0.08 bh/m	0.88
		Bulk target 3	117.13

Figure 7.17

The **bulk target** should be issued to the gang before commencement of the operation. This will maximise the incentive and allow the site management team to concentrate on planning future work, knowing that the labour output is controlled by the bonus incentive scheme. The cost and bonus surveyor will physically measure the work carried out with the gang, or leading hand bricklayer, noting any changes to the bulk target specification.

Planning programme methods

Bar charts

The tender programme was illustrated using the bar chart technique. Another similar programming method is the **Gantt chart** (Fig. 7.18).

There are some terms that need to be defined.

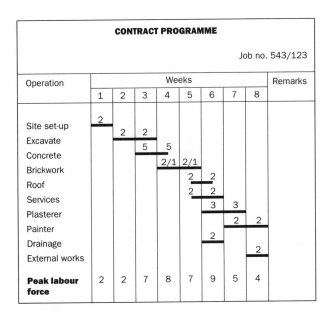

Figure 7.18 Gantt chart

Terms

- **Bar duration.** That is the programmed time to complete the operation. The bar duration is calculated from workloading, as follows

$$\text{bar duration} = \frac{\text{quantity} \times \text{output}}{\text{resources}}$$

- **Finish date.** The week number when the operation is planned to be completed.
- **Method statement.** A form showing the sequence, selected method of working and work loading for the project.
- **Peak workforce.** The highest number of operatives employed on the site in any week of the project.
- **Resources.** Labour, domestic and nominated subcontractors, plant and equipment.
- **Resource histogram.** A graph showing the total number of operatives on site each week. Used for resource balancing and welfare facilities.
- **Resource requirement.** The amount of labour, plant and equipment needed to complete the operation within the bar duration. It is usually indicated above the bar duration (see Fig. 7.18).
- **Resource scheduling.** Sometimes called resource balancing. The resource requirement is adjusted (levelled) to maintain a constant workforce.
- **Overlap.** The amount of time that a following operation can run concurrently with a preceding operation. For example, in the bar chart shown in Fig. 7.18, the excavate and concrete operations overlap.
- **Sequence.** The order for carrying out the work.
- **Start date.** The week or day number when the operation begins.
- **Workloading.** Calculating the bar duration and resource requirement for an operation.

The thinking and gathering of information start with the method statement.

Method statement

Part of working load is the preparation of the method statement (Fig. 7.19) by which the planner builds the project on paper. All the alternatives have been analysed and the best methods, work patterns and plant have been decided. This is the planning element.

The material quantities now have to be obtained, which is called **taking off**. The unit of measurement used has to be compatible with the **bonus target item bank** and the bill of quantities for site costing purposes. The **operational quantities** are calculated as fixed or net, with no allowance for waste. Any cutting to waste will have been included in the work measurement study used to prepare the bonus target.

The best method based on method study must be used and the resources required are for the individual operation. No attempt is made to balance resources at this time. Gang size is dependent on activity space and size of equipment, and gang balancing for the individual operation is achieved by using the multiple activity chart.

The output is the bonus target for the operation or a built-up **operation target** based on several targets. For example, the joinery second fix work will include the following activities:

skirting boards	straight fixing mitres fitted ends
architraves	straight fixing plinth blocks
window boards	fixing return ends
doors	hanging door furniture

All these activities can be calculated as a **bulk target** and used as such in the method statement. The bulk target can also be issued to the operatives as the bulk bonus target. The method statement would just summarize the bulk target (see Fig. 7.20).

Since the outputs are based on work study standard times, the quality checks, gang supervision and safety precautions have all been included. Confidently the method statement can be used for Mr Average craftsperson. The method statement data needs to be produced on the bar chart. This is called 'programming'.

Programming

The bar chart or Gantt chart presentation is easy to interpret and update, but it has severe limitations. At the moment we are discounting constraints such as time and costs, which in real life have to be considered. The contract period might dictate the overlapping of operations and the resource allocation.

There are some technical reasons to consider when overlapping operations; for example, the operation 'Concrete' and the following activity 'Brickwork'. The brickwork cannot start until the concrete has hardened, hence there must be a delay in starting the brickwork operations. The same is true of *in situ* concrete operations.

METHOD STATEMENT					
Operation	Quantity	Method	Output	Gang size	Gang hours
Excavate foundations (order or sequence of activities) e.g. joinery 2nd fix	Net as-fixed quantity see bulk target 43	Best method described resource requirement 2 joiners	Work study times 64.10	2	32.05

Figure 7.19

WORKLOAD SHEET				
			Bulk target 43 Job no. 543/123	
Operation	Quantity	Bonus target	Bulk target	Remarks
Joiner 2nd fix				
Skirting boards	110 m	0.35 h/m	38.50	
Mitres	12 no.	0.12 h/no.	1.44	
Fitted ends	6 no.	0.20 h/no.	1.20	
Architraves	30 m	0.15 h/no.	4.50	
Plinth blocks	6 no.	0.25 h/no.	1.50	
Window boards	12 m	0.55 h/m	6.60	
Return ends	8 no.	0.17 h/no.	1.36	
Doors	3 no.	1.15 h/no.	4.50	
Door furniture	3 no.	1.50 h/no.	4.50	
		Bulk target	64.10	

Figure 7.20

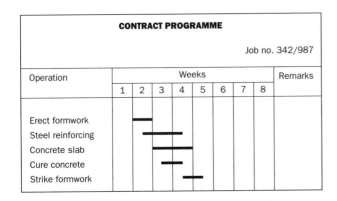

Figure 7.21

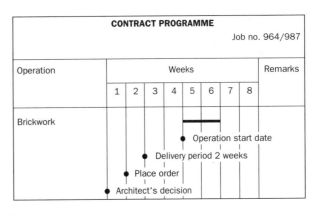

Figure 7.22

The programme (Fig 7.21) should explain how the project is to be built.

Information available

To control the work and keep to programme the site agent will want to know:

- the start date of the operation
- the planned resources and resource requirements
- the bar duration
- the finish date of the operation
- the sequence of activities

All that information is available from the bar chart programme. When the builder won the contract it was placed under the JCT Standard Form of Building Contract, 1980 edition. There are some contractual obligations placed on the main contractor. Clause 23, 'Date of possession, completion and postponement', says in part '... contractor who shall ... regularly and diligently proceed ... complete ... before the completion date'. Clause 5, 'Contract documents – other documents – issue of certificates' requires the contractor to provide the architect with a **master programme**. Contract condition clause 5.4 states, 'As and when from time to time may be necessary the architect ... provide ... 2 copies of further drawings.' So the contract or works programme must do more than coordinate the main contractor's work and the subcontractors' work (both nominated and domestic), but now also must **coordinate the release of further drawings**. At present the bar chart contract programme does not coordinate the architect's release of information. Based on the contract programme a further bar chart is prepared called the **information control chart**. Specific information is applied to the works programme dealing with the placement of material orders and the release dates for the architect's information. For instance, if the architect asks for sample approval on the architectural bricks before a firm order is placed, the information control chart would programme that information. The materials are not ex-stock so there will be a delivery period of two weeks. If the buyer requires one week to process the negotiations with the builder's merchant and place the order, how long before starting the operation must the architect decide on the type of facing brick? (Fig. 7.22).

Abbreviations are used on the information control chart (Fig. 7.23) to indicate the latest release and action dates by staff and design team:

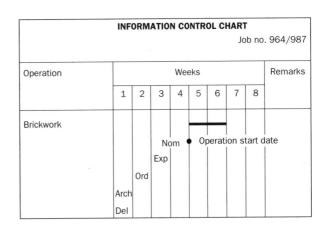

Figure 7.23

- exp   chase delivery by buyer to ensure on time delivery
- del   delivery
- nom   nominate subcontractor.

The chart would be monitored and updated weekly. The information would also form part of the **architect's site meeting**. Even all this planning and monitoring has not indicated the critical operations to the site agent. That is highlighted in another programming technique.

Critical path analysis

This planning technique clearly identifies the critical operations. The critical activities show the site agent what operations to monitor closely if an on-time completion is to be achieved. The workloading and method statements are similar to the bar chart, but the method of presentation and programming are completely different.

Terms

Operations are known as **activities**. The symbols used are given in Fig. 7.24.

With those symbols and their definitions in mind, the planner will prepare the arrow diagram.

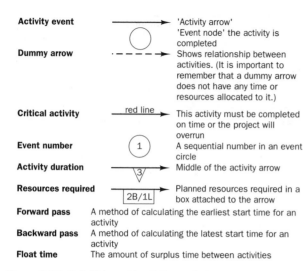

Figure 7.24 Definitions and activity symbols

Techniques

The arrow diagram shows the sequence of activities based on three questions asked about each activity:

- What activity precedes?
- What activities are concurrent?
- What activities succeed?

In preparing the arrow diagram it is best to list the activities in approximately the correct sequence, and number them. For example, when concreting a reinforced concrete column, the activities involved are:

- cut and bend reinforcement
- cast kicker
- make column formwork
- position steel reinforcing
- fix column formwork
- blow out column (clean out)
- concrete column
- strike and clean formwork

It may be best to think of the activities as a flow diagram. The three questions are now put to each of the activities, as shown in Fig. 7.25.

Next prepare the arrow diagram to illustrate the planning logic shown in the activity listing. The length of arrow is not significant; the arrow diagram (Fig. 7.26) will only show the relationship between each activity.

ACTIVITY LISTING				
Activity no.	Activity	What precedes?	What is concurrent?	What succeeds?
1	Cut and bend rebar	0	2, 3	4
2	Cast kicker	0	1, 3	4
3	Make formwork	0	1, 2	4
4	Position steel	1	2, 3	5
5	Fix formwork	3	–	6
6	Blown out column	5	–	7
7	Concrete column	6	–	8
8	Strike formwork	7	–	–

Figure 7.25

The arrow diagram is now the workload, based on the method statement (Fig. 7.27), and the planning logic is redrawn showing event nodes (Fig. 7.28).

The critical path analysis now has to be presented to the site management.

Programming

The calculation of the earliest start time is based on the **forward pass**. Other activities are also calculated, such as the **latest finish time** and the **earliest finish time**, and these dates will show the **float time**, if any, on each activity (Fig. 7.29).

The total time for the critical path analysis (CPA) is 93 days. This represents the quickest time for completion of the project. One of the advantages of a CPA was the identification of **critical activities**, i.e. those activities that must be finished on time or the project would overrun the completion date. Some activities will be **non-critical**. The latest start time is now calculated using the **backward pass** method. The activity durations are *deducted* from the total time to complete the project (Fig. 7.30).

Some activities will show different numbers for the earliest start time (EST) and latest start time (LST).

The difference between the EST and the LST is called the **float** and the activity is non-critical. So the activity 'making formwork' is a non-critical activity and has a float time of

LST	33 days
EST	18 days
Float	15 days

The site agent could delay making the formwork for 15 days if this was necessary and still achieve on-time completion. The activity 'fix formwork' has no float time, as can be seen in Fig. 7.30.

This activity must start and finish on time, otherwise the project will overrun. The critical activities would be marked in red, showing the critical path. The next type of planning technique builds on the advantages of critical path analysis.

Network diagram

Terms

A network diagram as illustrated is called a **precedence diagram**; the graphical conventions used in a precedence diagram are shown in Fig. 7.31.

The method of planning is the same as the CPA. The difference is in showing the relationships and the presentation of the planning strategies (Fig. 7.32).

There are other activity constraints, and multiple constraints can be introduced into the planning logic.

Method statement

The activity to be programmed is the external works; the road and paths to the estate road (Fig. 7.33).

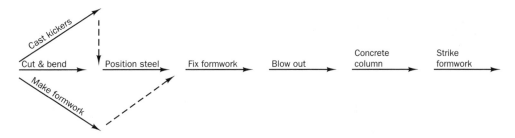

Figure 7.26 Arrow diagram

METHOD STATEMENT					
Activity	Quantity	Output	Gang size	Gang hours	Remarks
Cut and bend rebar	1 tonne	40 h/t	2	20	
Cast kicker	40 no.	0.5 h/no.	1	20	
Make formwork	4 no.	4.5 h/no.	1	18	
Position steel	1 t	25 h/t	2	12½	Say 13
Fix formwork	40 no.	3.0 h/no.	4	30	
Blown out column	40 no.	0.2 h/no.	2	4	
Concrete column	40 m³	2 h/m³	4	20	
Strike formwork	40 no.	0.8 h/no.	4	8	

Figure 7.27

The planning logic has to be prepared by asking the three questions used for CPA and, with precedence diagrams, adding some constraints:

- What precedes the activity?
- What activities are concurrent?
- What activities succeed?
- What activities can start immediately after another activity?
- What activities cannot finish until another activity is completed?
- What lag times have to be introduced?

Gantt chart

The Gantt chart is very similar to the bar chart. The contract programme is a long-term programme and is reviewed in detail by short-term planning. The **short-term planning** will be

- three monthly
- monthly
- weekly
- daily

The planner will try to achieve 95% of the activities planned, and the weekly planning meeting will discuss and finalise the labour plans for the following week.

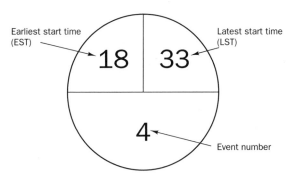

Figure 7.28 Event nodes

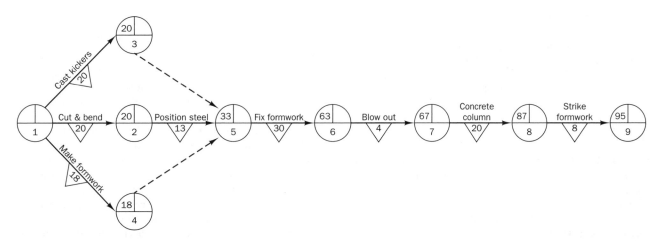

Figure 7.29 Critical path analysis: forward passes

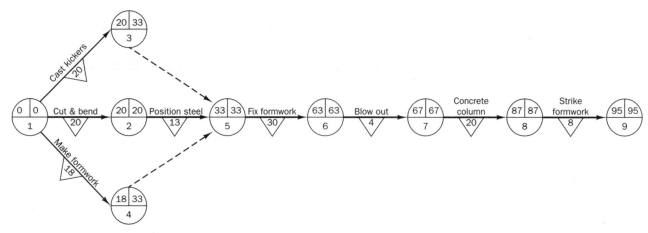

Figure 7.30 Critical path analysis: backward passes

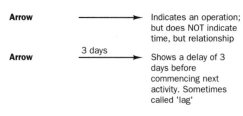

Arrow ⟶ Indicates an operation; but does NOT indicate time, but relationship

Arrow ——3 days——⟶ Shows a delay of 3 days before commencing next activity. Sometimes called 'lag'

Precedence box

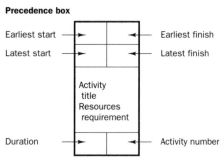

Earliest start — — Earliest finish

Latest start — — Latest finish

Activity title
Resources requirement

Duration — — Activity number

Figure 7.31 Graphical conventions of a precedence diagram

Terms

- **Anticipated actual hours.** The actual time taken by an operative to achieve a bonus target.
- **Bonus hour.** The output for an activity based on 60 standard minutes.
- **Bonus target.** The incentive target based on work measurement standard time.
- **Day balance.** Establishing sufficient work for the operative to achieve in one normal working day.
- **Gang/plant balance.** The number of operatives in a gang which will maximise the control plant's work.
- **Productivity index.** The individual operative's work rate expressed as a percentage of the bonus hours earned.

Techniques

The planner has to produce a weekly programme that the operatives can achieve, by balancing all the labour and plant resources and coordinating the individual operative or gang's activity to achieve 95% of the planned targets.

The planner uses the bonus targets to arrive at the **operative workload**. The bonus targets are based on the **qualified worker** working at **standard performance** under capable supervision. The individual does not necessarily match the definition of a **qualified worker**. The average needs to be tailored to suit the individual's rate of performance.

The previous week's bonus earnings are used to predict the performance index (Fig. 7.34).

What is the performance index of the operative?

$$\frac{\text{bonus hours}}{\text{actual hours}} \times 100 = \text{performance index (PI)}$$

i.e.

$$\frac{45}{39} \times 100 = 115 \text{ (PI)}$$

The next week this operative is to carry out this activity with a bonus value of 30 bonus hours (abbreviated to 'bh'). How long will it take the operative to complete this activity – that is, the anticipated actual hours (abbreviated to 'aah')?

$$\frac{\text{bonus hours planned}}{\text{performance index}} \times 100 = \text{anticipated actual hours}$$

i.e.

$$\frac{30}{115} \times 100 = 26 \text{ aah}$$

The normal working day (NWD) is 8 hours, so the operative is **predicted** to complete this work in

$$\frac{\text{anticipated actual hours}}{\text{normal working day (in hours)}} = \text{duration in days}$$

i.e.

$$\frac{26 \text{ aah}}{8 \text{ hours}} = 3 \text{ NWD and 2 hours}$$

If the normal working day started at 8.00, this operative should with some degree of certainty have completed the activity by 10.00 a.m. on the fourth day. Just in time for the tea break!

Since the workloading is calculated using bonus hours, the weekly planning should take into account the individual's performance index. For instance, the normal working week is 39 hours (NWW = normal working week), but during the summer period the site works a 45-hour week. The gang allocated to the concreting is a very efficient gang but it is the first time that the gang have worked on site, so an estimated performance index is selected for this 3-person gang.

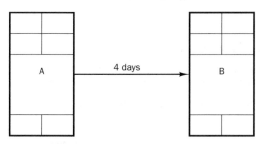

Activity B cannot START until activity A is COMPLETED

Activity B cannot START until 4 days after activity A is COMPLETED. For example, cement sand floor screed must be allowed to dry out before floor tiling.

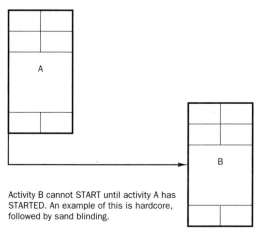

Activity B cannot START until activity A has STARTED. An example of this is hardcore, followed by sand blinding.

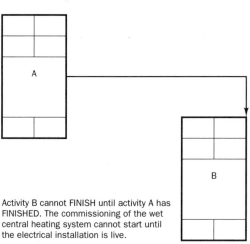

Activity B cannot FINISH until activity A has FINISHED. The commissioning of the wet central heating system cannot start until the electrical installation is live.

Figure 7.32 Planning strategies: activity constraints

The working day during the summer period is 9 hours (45/5 = 9 hour day). The gang comprises of 3 labourers or GBOs (general building operatives)

Actual gang hours per day = 3 × 9 = 27 hours.

METHOD STATEMENT					
Activity	Quantity	Output	Gang size	Gang hours	Remarks
Formation dig	300 m^3	0.10 /m^3	1	30	
Excavate and lay surface water drain	50 m^3	0.25 h/m	2	6.25	say 7
Sub-base	200 m^3	0.15 h/m^3	1	30	
Excavate service runs	50 m^3	0.20 h/m^3	1	10	
Lay services	100 m	0.10 h/m^3	1	10	
Road kerbs	100 m	0.20 h/m	2	10	
Road base	75 m^3	0.25 h/m^3	2	9.3	say 10
Wearing course	30 m^3	0.20 h/m^3	2	3	

Figure 7.33

BONUS CALCULATION SHEET										
Works no.	Name	Hours worked					Total hours	Bonus £	Quantity	Bonus target	Bonus hours
		M	T	W	T	F					
010	Brown	8	8	8	8	7	39	27.00	10 m^3	$4\frac{1}{2}$ h/m^3	45
	Bonus hours 45 Actual hours 39										
	Gain				6 at £4.50			27.00			

Figure 7.34

Assume a performance index of 125.
The predicted bonus hours is calculated using the formula:

$$\frac{\text{actual hours available} \times \text{performance index}}{100} = \text{bonus hours}$$

i.e.

$$\frac{27 \times 125}{100} = 33.75 \text{ bh per day}$$

The bonus target for placing concrete in foundations is 3 bh/m^3. How many cubic metres of concrete will the gang lay in one working day?

$$\text{quantity per day} = \frac{\text{bonus hours earned in day}}{\text{bonus target per cubic metre}}$$

i.e.

$$\frac{33.75 \text{ bh}}{3 \text{ h/m}^3} = 11 \text{ m}^3 \text{ of concrete}$$

The site checker can order 11 m^3 of concrete and with certainty knowing that the gang should place this amount within the working day.

This type of planning is vital in **gang balancing**, where the individual operatives are grouped and different tasks assigned, yet all the gang needs to be working for the normal working day. For example, the lorry manning could be illustrated using the Gantt chart techniques. First the planning logic and data needs calculating using the method statement (Fig. 7.35).

Since the spoil is to be taken off site, the number of lorries will have to be calculated. The control operation will be determined by the hire cost. Planning aims to maximise resources and minimise costs. The most expensive plant becomes the **control operation**. All the other activities are balanced around the control operation. The JCB excavator would cost, on internal hire, about £25.00 per hour while the

METHOD STATEMENT					
Activity	Quantity	Output	Gang size	Gang hours	Remarks
Excavate foundation Load to lorry	300 m³	0.1 h/m³	1 JCB 1 lab	30	

Figure 7.35

$6\,m^3$ tipper lorry would be charged to site at £15.00 per hour. The JCB has to be fully utilised, since it is the control operation.

The **struck capacity** of the lorry is $6\,m^3$, but that is bulked. When soils are excavated they bulk or expand in volume, but the **bulking factors** differ according to the soil type. In our example the bulking factor is 25% and the amount of excavated soil that will fill the lorry needs to be calculated.

$$\frac{\text{bulked capacity}}{\text{of lorry}} \times \frac{100}{100 + \text{bulking factor}} = \text{excavated soil}$$

i.e.
$$6\,m^3 \times \frac{100}{100 + 25} = 4.8\,m^3$$

So $4.8\,m^3$ of excavated soil will bulk by an additional 25% of its volume to fill a $6\,m^3$ lorry.

We must now calculate the time the excavator will take to load the lorry:

$$\text{quantity} \times \text{output} = \text{loading time}$$
$$4.8\,m^3 \times 0.1\,h/m^3 = 0.48\text{ hours}$$

and the loading time in minutes is:

$$0.48\,h \times 60\,min/h = 28.80\,min$$

That assumes that the plant operator will work at **standard performance**. The bonus performance should now be matched to the skill and efficiency of the plant operator. The **performance index** is anticipated to be 125.

$$\frac{\text{anticipated actual}}{\text{loading time}} = \frac{\text{bonus minutes per load}}{\text{performance index}} \times 100$$

$$\frac{28.80\text{ bonus minutes}}{125} \times 100 = 23.04\,min$$

The actual time to load a $6\,m^3$ lorry is 23 minutes. The lorry has to transport the spoil to a tip and return to be loaded again. That is called the **round trip time**. In our example it is 20 minutes. The Gantt chart now will depict the day's activity, balancing the lorries to the control operation and indicate the number of wagon loads taken away. That will help the site checker to monitor the performance. Any large variance should be reported to the site agent for action.

Self-assessment tasks

Prepare the weekly planning schedule for casting 40 reinforced concrete columns. Refer to Figs 7.25, 7.26, 7.27 and 7.30.

1. Produce a flow diagram illustrating the work sequence for casting one column.
2. Describe the various planning stages used to produce a critical path analysis programme. Start at the sequencing of activities and finish at the critical path analysis programme suitable for the site supervisor.
3. Describe the advantages and disadvantages of critical path analysis programming techniques compared to a bar chart programming technique. Base your comments on the column casting programme.

Project planning methods
Based on the column casting operation prepare the following data on a spreadsheet format.

1. Copy out the method statement shown in Fig. 7.27. Make sure that the calculation formulae are used in each cell describing 'gang hours'.
2. The labour availability has changed. Adjust the method statement to comply with these gang sizes:
   - steelfixing gang   6 operatives
   - formwork gang   3 operatives
   - concrete gang   5 operatives
3. Based on the revised method statement, produce a short-term bar chart programme with the daily labour requirement.
4. Produce a histogram showing the type and number of labour on a daily basis.

7.3 Selection of resources for a project

Topics covered in this section are:

- method statements
- planning techniques
- safety requirements

Method statements

The method statement is a key document in project planning, setting out the method and sequence of working. Initially the planner with the site agent will agree the work stages.

The builder has been awarded a small two-storey extension to a house. The extension is traditional masonry cavity wall with a solid ground floor. The project was obtained by open tender, with a profit of 10%. The contract sum was a lump sum fixed price amounting to £13 867.00. The sequence of work is often shown as a flow diagram (Fig. 7.36).

Having agreed the main stages of the work, quantities can then be **taken off** into these stages using the method statement sheets. Often the planner will take off quantities on to 'dimension paper' using the techniques of the quantity surveyor.

Obtaining the quantities

There is a set of contract drawings that have been recorded and a copy of these drawings should be used by the planner. The planner will record in the **drawing register** (Fig. 7.37) all the drawings that were issued.

Where the drawings have been amended, the previous drawing should be filed and clearly marked 'SUPERSEDED', with the date clearly indicated. Contractually the architect can issue further drawings, but the onus is still on the main contractor to complete on time. The **date of possession** and **date of completion** are fixed dates, so any overrun by the main contractor will result in loss of money. The employer can deduct from payments due to the main contractor a set amount per week called **liquidated and ascertained damages**. If there is a delay, the main contractor can request an **extension of time** for a **relevant event**. The delay in releasing architect's drawings is a relevant event, so note carefully the dates on which drawings are issued. If a claim is to be made under clause 25 of the contract the information in the drawings register would be most helpful to the quantity surveyor.

The brickwork up to the first floor needs to be taken off the method statement. The quantities can be recorded on **dimension paper** and used for

- method statement workloadings
- ordering materials
- bulk targeting for operatives

Remember that the quantities are net or **as fixed**. The drawings required are L02 (the ground floor plan), which will give outside dimensions and references to component drawings such as drawing 'C14, Openings', and drawing L12 (Section thro building A/A) which will give the datum heights

for first floor. The pre-ruled dimension paper is sometimes called quantity paper.

The drawings are checked for dimensioning accuracy by establishing control dimensions. The control dimensions are the overall length and width and are marked such on the plan.

Once satisfied that all the dimensions check, the taking off can commence. The sequence of taking off the brickwork to first floor is:

- measure the outer skin without deducting door and window openings
- measure forming the cavity without deducting door and window openings
- measure the cavity insulation without deducting door and window openings
- measure the inner skin blockwork without deducting door and window openings
- prepare a door and window schedule
- measure forming the door opening – jambs, head, and sill if necessary – and deduct the cavity wall area already measured (called adjustment of openings)
- measure forming the window opening – jambs, head, sill

After taking off, the dimensions are **squared** or extended and the net as-fixed quantities obtained for each element of work.

Where dimensions are not 'finished' but have to be calculated, the calculated dimensions are shown as **waste calculations** or **side casts** in the description column of the dimension paper (Fig. 7.38).

The use of the centre-line perimeter is particularly important in the measurement of brickwork areas, and quantities of concrete and excavation. The external perimeter of the wall is sometimes used, but this overmeasures at the corner. (See Figs 7.39 and 7.40.)

Once the take-off has been completed, the next step is to decide on the outputs.

Outputs

There are several methods of calculating **labour output**, each with varying degrees of accuracy. The estimator has an item bank of labour constants for use when compiling the estimate. The trades foreperson will have an idea of labour output for the trade from past experience. The craftsperson will have a shrewd idea of the time it will require to complete the operation. Often the operative will try to negotiate a better 'price' with the bonus surveyor. The craftsperson will list all the operations involved and claim that listening to instructions and setting out, plus inspection for quality, are all extra to the bonus price. The debate could be endless, and that is the reason that the use of **work measurement standard times** is so valuable. The operatives used as a sample for time study must have completed the work to the right quality standard.

The **standard time** to complete one unit of production required the operative to perform all the necessary safety precautions, receive instructions and carry out all the necessary quality checks. There can be no doubt that this type of output based on work study standard times is the most accurate, but is also the most expensive to obtain. Few building contractors will have a work study department

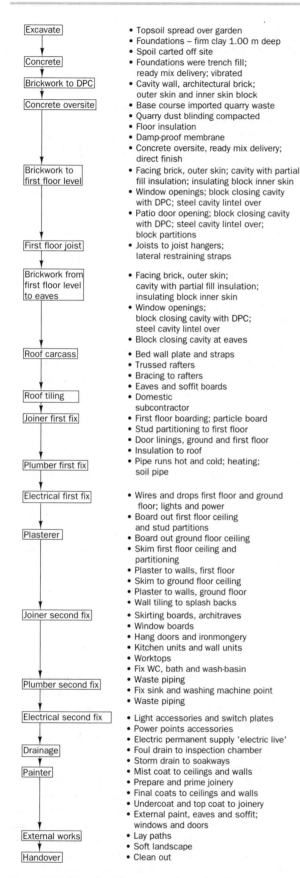

Excavate	• Topsoil spread over garden
↓	• Foundations – firm clay 1.00 m deep
Concrete	• Spoil carted off site
↓	• Foundations were trench fill;
Brickwork to DPC	ready mix delivery; vibrated
↓	• Cavity wall, architectural brick;
Concrete oversite	outer skin and inner skin block
	• Base course imported quarry waste
	• Quarry dust blinding compacted
	• Floor insulation
	• Damp-proof membrane
	• Concrete oversite, ready mix delivery;
	direct finish
Brickwork to	• Facing brick, outer skin; cavity with partial
first floor level	fill insulation; insulating block inner skin
	• Window openings; block closing cavity
	with DPC; steel cavity lintel over
	• Patio door opening; block closing cavity
	with DPC; steel cavity lintel over;
	block partitions
First floor joist	• Joists to joist hangers;
	lateral restraining straps
Brickwork from	• Facing brick, outer skin;
first floor level	cavity with partial fill insulation;
to eaves	insulating block inner skin
	• Window openings;
	block closing cavity with DPC;
	steel cavity lintel over
	• Block closing cavity at eaves
Roof carcass	• Bed wall plate and straps
	• Trussed rafters
	• Bracing to rafters
	• Eaves and soffit boards
Roof tiling	• Domestic
	subcontractor
Joiner first fix	• First floor boarding; particle board
	• Stud partitioning to first floor
	• Door linings, ground and first floor
	• Insulation to roof
Plumber first fix	• Pipe runs hot and cold; heating;
	soil pipe
Electrical first fix	• Wires and drops first floor and ground
	floor; lights and power
	• Board out first floor ceiling
	and stud partitions
Plasterer	• Board out ground floor ceiling
	• Skim first floor ceiling and
	partitioning
	• Plaster to walls, first floor
	• Skim to ground floor ceiling
	• Plaster to walls, ground floor
	• Wall tiling to splash backs
Joiner second fix	• Skirting boards, architraves
	• Window boards
	• Hang doors and ironmongery
	• Kitchen units and wall units
	• Worktops
	• Fix WC, bath and wash-basin
Plumber second fix	• Waste piping
	• Fix sink and washing machine point
	• Waste piping
Electrical second fix	• Light accessories and switch plates
	• Power points accessories
	• Electric permanent supply 'electric live'
Drainage	• Foul drain to inspection chamber
	• Storm drain to soakways
Painter	• Mist coat to ceilings and walls
	• Prepare and prime joinery
	• Final coats to ceilings and walls
	• Undercoat and top coat to joinery
	• External paint, eaves and soffit;
	windows and doors
External works	• Lay paths
	• Soft landscape
Handover	• Clean out

Figure 7.36 Flowchart from excavation to handover

DRAWING REGISTER								Job 1670
Drawing no.	Title	Date received	A	B	C	D	E	Remarks
L01	Block plan	4/8/94	✓					
L02	Ground floor plan	4/8/94	✓					
L03	First floor plan	4/8/94						
L04	Front elevation	4/8/94	✓					
L05	Rear elevation	4/8/94	✓					
L06	Side elevation	4/8/94						
L07	Foundation plan	5/8/94						
L08	First floor joist plan	5/8/94	✓	✓				
L09	Roof carcass plan	5/8/94						
L10	Services layout ground floor	5/8/94						
L11	Services layout first floor							
L12	Section through building A/A	4/8/94						
C13	Substructure section	5/8/94						
C14	Openings	4/8/94	✓					
C15	Stairs	4/8/94						
C16	Roof eaves verge	4/8/94	✓					
A17	Concrete sill	4/8/94	✓	✓				

Figure 7.37

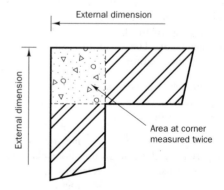

PD House

```
                                1.60
                            0.225 ddt
                                1.375

                                6.60
            2/.30               0.60
                         2) 7.20
                            3.6

roof slope   √(3.60 × 3.60) + (1.38 × 1.38)
                            3.85

                                8.60
            2/.10               0.20
                                8.80
   8.80
   3.85
```

Roof coverings 30 deg, 380 × 230 Redland interlocking tiles, 75 mm headlap, 38 mm × 25 mm battens and underlay

Figure 7.38 Calculating for waste

Figure 7.39 External dimension overmeasures at corners

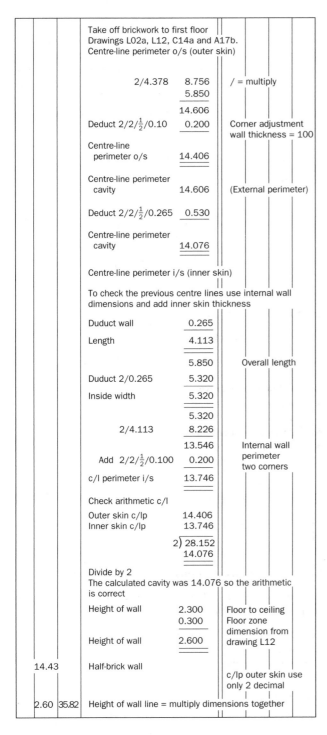

Figure 7.40 Measurements using the centre-line perimeter method: c/l = centre line; c/lp = centre-line perimeter

available to support line management in planning and bonus issues, so the estimator's feedout (Fig. 7.41) is used to calculate the bonus. Since the estimator's feedout is in monetary terms, the site planner cannot readily use it to assess the output in hours for works programming.

What activities has the estimator allowed for in the £0.73 per metre of joist? According to the rules of measurement (SMM7), in the labour constant the estimate was to include:

- labour and all cost in connection therewith
- assembling, fitting and fixing materials and goods in position

G20 Carpentry/Timber framing First fixing 6 Floor members 50 × 225	100	m	0.73	

Figure 7.41 Extract of estimator's feedout

- waste of materials
- square cutting

The joiner's rate, according to the estimate, allows for:

- selecting timber and checking quality
- measuring and cutting to length
- hoisting to required level
- offering into position
- adjustment of joist
- checking line and level
- fixing in position

The planner now needs to know the output in hours. The estimator, when preparing the bid, uses two payment rates: the basic pay for the operative as agreed by the **National Joint Council for The Construction Industry** and the **all-in hourly rate**. The all-in hourly rate includes an amount for additional payments by the employer (builder), such as National Insurance contributions, insurances and training levy to the Construction Industry Training Board (CITB). The estimator's feedout for the **labour constant** should be on the basic rate of pay, not the all-in hourly rate.

The output in hours would be obtained by:

$$\frac{\text{estimator's feedout in £/m}}{\text{basic hourly pay}} = \text{output in hours}$$

For example, the joiner will receive a basic weekly wage of £179.40. The normal working week is 39 hours, so the basic pay per hour is

$$\frac{\text{basic weekly wage}}{\text{normal working week}} = \frac{179.40}{39} = 4.60 \text{ per hour}$$

The estimator's feedout allowed £0.73 per metre length of floor joist. Converting the estimator's feedout to hours per metre:

$$\frac{\text{£0.73 per metre}}{\text{£4.60 per hour}} = \text{£0.158 h/m of joist}$$

Now the planner can use that output data for workloading the method statement.

The work-in-place item does not always correspond exactly with the bonus outputs, and a work study technique called **synthetics** and **analytical estimating** can be used to arrive at a reasonably accurate assessment of the labour output. The bonus output databank contains the information shown in Table 7.5, but, unfortunately our bill of quantities specifies 38 × 225, so what is the bonus target? If we identify the *constant* elements in the bonus rate, this will leave the *variable* elements.

Table 7.5 Joiner's bonus constants

Operation	Bonus target
Joists 38 × 200	0.16 h/m
38 × 250	0.18 h/m

From Table 7.5 we can see that for every additional 50 mm depth of joist add 0.02 h/m. The specified joist was 38 × 225, so the bonus output will be:

$$38 \times 200 = 0.16 \, \text{h/m}$$

$$\frac{25^*}{30} \times 0.02 = 0.01 \, \text{h/m}$$

i.e. bonus target = 0.17 h/m

*an additional 25 mm, given each 50 mm, is equivalent to 0.02 h/m

When the planner is preparing the works programme (sometimes called the contract programme or master programme) there is no adjustment for the **productivity index** on the bonus output. There is also an allowance built into the programme for holidays and inclement weather. The wage negotiating councils will agree on the holiday entitlement but usually the mid-winter holiday is a total closedown and the public holidays are added into the contract programme.

Bonus targets

It is preferable to issue **bulk targets** to operatives (Fig. 7.42). The bonus surveyor or planner must list all the work to be done by the operative or gang. Even large gangs, made up of

BULK TARGET SHEET

Job: Foul drainage to house type A in uPVC based on drawing L12 Drainage layout

Job no. 123

Bulk target 110

Operations	Quantity	Bonus target	Bonus hours	Remarks
Set out			———	Include in bonus target
Excavate	20 m³	3 h/m³	60.00	Firm soil, no timbering required
Excavate inspection chambers	2 m³	3.26 h/m³	6.52	
bed pea gravel	40 m	0.17 h/m	6.80	
Lay pipe runs	36 m	0.24 h/m	8.64	
junctions	4 no.	0.22 h/no.	0.88	
bends	5 no.	0.24 h/no.	1.20	
Lay branch runs	4 m	0.28 h/m	1.12	
bends	4 no.	0.24 h/no.	0.96	
gully	4 no.	0.88 h/no.	3.52	
conc. haunch	4 no.	0.33 h/no.	1.32	
rodding eye	4 no.	0.77 h/no.	3.08	
Shallow inspection chambers	3 no.	0.71 h/no.	2.13	
Testing drain run			———	Include in bonus target
Pea gravel haunch and surround	40 m	40.42 h/m	16.80	
Earth backfill	12 m	1.25 h/m³	15.00	wheel ne
Wheel to spoil heap surplus	8 m	2.10 h/m³	16.80	30 m
Cover and frame	3 no.	0.35 h/no.	1.05	
		Bulk target	145.82 bonus hours	
		Working week is 45 hours		
		2 operatives at 45 hours	90.00 actual hours	
		Savings on bonus hours	55.82 bonus hours	

Figure 7.42

various tradespersons, can be issued with a bulk target. A monetary incentive scheme is the motivation for the operative to achieve standard performance. Normally, issuing the bonus target in hours at the start of the operation only partly motivates the operatives. Beating the hours target is the object, but the real incentive is the take-home pay. The bonus paid is calculated *after* the operation, but as an **incentive** it would be better to express the target, in monetary terms, not in work content hours. To do this the bonus target must be issued as a bulk target, which involves the following tasks:

- identify the work content (usually not more than one week's work)
- establish the gang size
- calculate the 'target bonus' in monetary terms

The foul drainage in uPVC drainage goods is to be bulk targeted. The bonus scheme is a geared incentive 50/50 scheme.

Identify the work content

Jobs to be carried out:

- set out drain runs and inspection chambers
- excavate and tip aside trench
- bedding of pea gravel
- lay pipe run
- test drain
- haunch and surround in pea gravel
- earth backfill
- inspection cover and frames

Establish the gang size

Two operatives, both labourers. Their basic weekly pay is £136.50.

Calculate the target bonus in monetary terms

Since the scheme is a 50/50 geared incentive, the hours saved are paid at 50% of basic hourly pay.

Basic pay per week: £136.50
Basic week: 39 hours
Basic pay per hour: £3.50
Bonus potential earnings (see Fig. 7.42):

Individual bonus earning if the target work content is achieved will be:

$$\frac{\text{bonus for gang}}{\text{gang size}} = \frac{£97.69}{2} = £48.84$$

The bulk target would be issued with that incentive: if they achieve the work planned the operatives will earn £48.84 in bonus payment.

Part of the work carried out to establish the bonus target can be used as **workloading** for the weekly and monthly stage programmes.

Workloading

One of the important skills the contract planner must acquire is the ability to build the project on paper. The builder legally must ensure a safe working environment. The Control of Substances Hazardous to Health regulations require the builder to carry out risk assessment for using hazardous substances. Employees must be made aware of

- risks to health from any exposure to hazardous substances
- precautions to be taken to offset the risks.

Method study job sheets are very important in this area as they will outline

- methods of working
- plant and equipment
- safety precautions
- quality control procedures
- hazardous substances, risk assessment and precautions

Even with this array of information the planner will have to interpret data to suit the uniqueness of each project; for example, the plant balancing for concreting operations. The contract programme will detail the 'planned requirements'. For example, the contract requirement for concrete operations is $78\,\mathrm{m}^3$. What size mixer will be required to keep to programme?

The weekly concrete requirement is:

$$\frac{\text{total quantity}}{\text{bar duration}} = \text{planned weekly output}$$

i.e.
$$\frac{780\,\mathrm{m}^3}{2} = 390\,\mathrm{m}^3 \text{ per week}$$

The concrete cost comparison indicated that site-mixed concrete was cheaper than ready mix. Hence, the decision is made to mix the concrete on site but what size of mixer would be required?

The placing gang of three general operatives will use $390\,\mathrm{m}^3$ of mixed concrete in one week. The concrete will need to be transported and placed after mixing. To avoid extra payments (overtime) to the labourers placing the concrete, the mixing week is reduced by about 1 hour per day.

The mixer's week is $39 - 5 = 34$ hours. In that time the mixer must achieve the planned output. The concrete requirement per hour is:

$$\frac{\text{planned output}}{\text{mixing week in hours}} = \text{planned hourly output}$$

i.e.
$$\frac{390}{34} = 11.47\,\mathrm{m}^3 \text{ per hour}$$

The concrete batching plant must therefore achieve a rate of $11.47\,\mathrm{m}^3$ of concrete per hour to maintain the programme.

Concrete mixers have different batch times, depending on the methods of mixing. The mixing time for the reversible drum mixer is 2 minutes per batch. The minimum batch size required can then be calculated:

$$\frac{\text{planned output per hour}}{\text{batches mixed per hour}} = \text{minimum batch size (m}^3)$$

i.e.
$$\frac{11.47\,\mathrm{m}^3}{60 \div 2} = 0.382\,\mathrm{m}^3$$

The minimum batch mixed must be $0.382\,\mathrm{m}^3$ or the work will fall behind programme. Mixers are manufactured in standard sizes, so the reversible drum mixer would need to have a mixing capacity of $0.4\,\mathrm{m}^3$ or 400 litres.

Mixing the concrete on site presents a problem of storage space. The site layout was planned to maximise the space resource, and the space required for the washed gravel, sand or cement will depend on the programmed output and the

mixes of concrete. The concrete should be equivalent to C15P. BS 8110 gives mix weights per cubic metre for different mixes and should always be consulted when calculating batch weights.

The stock holding depends on the

- rate of usage
- reliability of the supplier

The **supplier evaluation** carried out by the buyer will indicate the supplier's performance on delivery dates. According to the contract programme, the volume of concrete placed must be $11.47\,\mathrm{m}^3$ per hour or the operation will fall behind programme. In an 8-hour working day, the amount of concrete placed will be:

concrete per day = concrete per hour × length of working day

$$= 11.47 \times 8$$
$$= 91.76\,\mathrm{m}^3$$

The specification in the bill of quantities will describe the batch weights for a cubic metre of mixed concrete. For instance, concrete mix proportions for every cubic metre of concrete allow 840 kg of coarse aggregate. The total weight of coarse aggregate stocked per day to maintain the programme is:

$$91.76\,\mathrm{m}^3 \text{ of concrete} \times \frac{840\,\mathrm{kg}}{1000} = 77.08 \text{ tonnes}$$

For the site layout decisions on storage areas, the stockpile should be measured in volume or area. To convert the day's requirement of coarse aggregate into volume, the bulk density is used:

$$\text{stockpile volume} = \frac{\text{day's requirement}}{\text{bulk density}}$$

$$= 77.08 \text{ tonnes} \times \frac{1000\,\mathrm{kg/tonne}}{1400\,\mathrm{kg/m}^3}$$

$$= 55\,\mathrm{m}^2$$

This gives the volume of the coarse aggregate stockpile. Using the techniques for site layout planning such as cutouts and string diagrams, the planner will arrive at the best location for the batching plant and storage areas. All this information is based on the contract programme.

Planning techniques

Bar chart

Bar chart programming is easily understood and the operation sequences are listed. The bar duration is graphical and operational overlaps are easily seen, although site progress must be monitored and recorded.

The **peak labour requirement** is also shown on the bar chart. This is used to calculate **welfare facilities** and the **site organisation** or 'set up'. Contracts management will use a series of staff/operative ratios to establish the site staff. The decision on the number of site staff will be taken by the contracts manager and the estimator will allow for the site staff in the **preliminary** section of the bill of quantities. Figure 7.43 shows the extract from the bill of quantities.

	A40 Contractors's general cost items				
	Management and staff				
a	Fixed charge	Item			
b	Time related	Item			

Figure 7.43

The person in charge of the site organisation is called the **site agent** (sometimes the site manager or project manager). The other line managers are:

- general foreperson
- trades forepersons
- chargehand craftsperson
- leading hand craftsperson

and, for the general labourers,

- walking ganger
- ganger

The above staff are **line management**, dealing directly with productive operations. Other specialist staff who would be used on site are described as **service management**, such as

- site quantity surveyor
- site cost and bonus surveyor
- site planner
- site cashier
- site checker

In addition to line and service management, there could be administrative and clerical staff, such as

- secretaries
- typists
- reception and filing clerks

The number of site staff and amount of organisation will vary with each building company. There are several common management structures that define the role of the staff responsibility, accountability and authority, and the different management hierarchies or levels are usually indicated on the site organisational framework.

Some of the management ratios deal with the span of control. A typical ratio would be six staff reporting directly to one superior (Fig. 7.44).

The **organisational framework** shows two levels or tiers of management. As the general foreperson reports directly to the site agent, this is known as a **direct** relationship. The general forepersons, planner and quantity surveyor are on the same level of management, and are described as having a **lateral relationship** as they all have the same status in the organisational framework. The line managers such as the general

foreperson and the service management – like the planner and quantity surveyor – all are responsible to the site agent. Yet to get the work completed they must all interact with each other but they cannot order compliance with their instructions, since they are in a lateral relationship.

Each member of staff will have a defined work load, which is established by **job analysis**. For instance, the following is a list of duties or tasks performed by the cost and bonus surveyor:

- physically measure operatives' previous week's work
- calculate individual operative's productive bonus pay
- submit operatives' bonus lists to the respective general foreperson for approval
- submit approved bonus list to the site cashier for wages
- prepare the weekly site costs
- record the week's actual costs and budgets in accordance with the contract bill
- submit the weekly and accumulative (to date) cost to the site agent
- assist the planner to prepare the weekly programmes and calculate target bonus earnings

It can be seen that the cost and bonus surveyor is responsible for calculating bonus payments, yet that person's authority is limited. According to the job description the cost and bonus surveyor should submit operatives' bonus lists to the respective general foreperson for approval. Although the cost and bonus surveyor's authority is limited, that person is accountable for the production of the bonus calculations. If the calculations are wrong, then the cost and bonus surveyor is accountable to a superior.

It can be seen from Fig. 7.45 that the cost and bonus surveyor has a direct relationship with the planner, but to perform the job function correctly the cost and bonus surveyor must also interact with the general foreperson. The management relationship is neither direct or lateral, since they are on different management levels. To accomplish the formal communication framework there must be a new relationship, known as a **functional relationship**, otherwise the organisation cannot work effectively. The cost and bonus surveyor produces the productive bonus list for approval by the general foreperson, and as they are on different management tiers, a 'functional relationship' exists.

What should happen if an operative finds a mistake in the bonus calculations? Officially the operative should approach his or her immediate supervisor, who will contact the planner and, in turn, the planner, who has direct responsibility for the work, will contact the cost and bonus surveyor. It may appear to be an unneccessarily lengthy process, but that is the formal organisational structure. Within that formal structure there may also exist an informal relationship and structure through general socialisation.

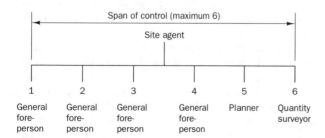

Figure 7.44 Direct relationship: 6 staff to 1 superior

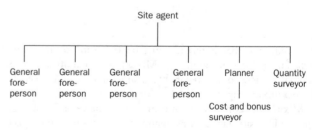

Figure 7.45 Direct relationship between cost and bonus surveyor and planner

The **job analysis** will identify tasks to be performed and indicate the direct, lateral and functional relationships that exist to achieve the work. It will also explain the responsibility, authority and accountability of each staff member. This information is not available from the bar chart programme, but an organisational chart should be displayed to ensure that all staff are aware of how they interact as a group and the lines of communication that are to be networked.

Information available to site

The bar chart programme will establish the order in which the operation will be carried out, detailing the planned resource requirement, especially labour and plant. The method of working is defined in the method statement. The bar chart will also show the bar duration, and start and completion dates for each operation. The site management team, however, will want additional information, particularly on short-term programmes such as the three-monthly, monthly and weekly programmes, which should show the target performance index and key control stages for monitoring progress.

Labour requirement

The **total labour force**, and particularly the **peak labour force** is used to establish the health, welfare and safety requirements. The labour requirement should be analysed by trades, which will allow the checker or the site cashier to monitor the actual against the planned workforce and alert the site agent to any deviation from planned labour requirements to enable remedial action to be taken with the minimum of delay.

Figure 7.46 shows that the peak labour force is required during weeks 3 and 4, where a total of nine operatives are employed on site. That is fine for the calculation of the **welfare facilities**, but what happens to the 4/2 bricklaying gang during week 5, as no work is planned for that group? If they go to another job or another builder they may not be available for week 6, thus delaying the project.

CONTRACT PROGRAMME										
										Job 123
Operations		Weeks								Remarks
		1	2	3	4	5	6	7	8	
Excavate		2	2							
Concrete			3	3						
Brick to DPC				4/2	4/2					
Concrete floor					3	3				
Brick to first floor						4/2	4/2			
Labour requirement: GBO Bricklayer		2	5	5 4	5 4	3	2 4	2 4		
Total workforce		2	5	9	9	9	6			

Figure 7.46

Concrete floor			3	3		
Brick to first floor				4/2	4/2	
Labour requirement: GBO Bricklayer	2	5	5 4	5 4	5 4	2 4
Total workforce	2	5	9	9	9	6

Figure 7.47 Avoiding idle time by commencing brickwork at week 5

Resource balancing or scheduling seeks to redress the peaks and troughs and aims to offer continuous employment on the site. Part of the planner's job is to ensure continuity of work for the labour and plant resources. Would it be possible to start the brickwork to first floor in week 5 (see Fig. 7.47), thereby overlapping the concrete floor operation? At least we have balanced the bricklaying gang.

The planner cannot make that decision in isolation and what are the repercussions of that resource balance on following operations? The whole of the resources used need to be balanced and a compromise reached where the resources are used to maximum effect and costs are kept to a minimum. The same is true of materials, which need to be delivered on time to achieve an on-time project completion.

Material requirement

The planner has to ensure that the materials are available at the **right time** and in the **right quantity**, and the buyer's job is to help to ensure that the delivered materials are to the **right quality**. The right time and quantity are determined by the master programme.

The concrete operation is to be ready mix. Over a bar duration of two weeks the concrete placed is $780\,\text{m}^3$. Obviously the ready mix delivery will be phased into the programmed output:

$$\frac{\text{total quantity of concrete}}{\text{bar duration in hours}} = \text{concrete requirement per day}$$

i.e. $$\frac{780\,\text{m}^3}{2 \times 39} = 11.47\,\text{m}^3/\text{h}$$

If the 39-hour normal working week is used, then the concreting gang will be paid non-productive overtime to place and finish the concrete. The concrete placing week is reduced to allow the concrete to be placed:

$$\frac{780\,\text{m}^3}{2 \times (39 - 5)} = 11.47\,\text{m}^3/\text{h}$$

To maintain the programme the concrete to be placed per day is:

$$\text{concrete requirement per day} = \frac{\text{total quantity of concrete}}{\text{bar duration in days}}$$

i.e. $$\frac{780}{2 \times 5} = 78\,\text{m}^3$$

The placement rate is $11.47\,\text{m}^3/\text{h}$ and the daily placed concrete requirement to maintain the programme is $78\,\text{m}^3$. A concrete placing histogram will help to monitor the operations and locate the delivery times for the ready mix trucks. The ready mix trucks are delivering 6 m^3 loads, so the number of 6 m^3 truck deliveries is:

$$\frac{\text{concrete placed per hour}}{\text{truck delivery capacity}} = \frac{11.47 \text{ m}^3/\text{h}}{6 \text{ m}^3 \text{ loads}} = 2 \text{ loads/h}$$

So delivery is planned for a 6 m^3 load every 30 minutes.

The delivery of bricks will also have to be in lorry loads or pallets. The extra cost incurred by part delivery is frowned upon by planners, who expect a maximum utilisation of resources at a minimum cost. The procedure is:

- calculate the planned daily requirement
- obtain delivery periods and lead times
- obtain delivery load in bricks or pallets
- prepare the brick material delivery graph

This information will be vital in monitoring actual performance against planned performance. The bar chart programme is useful but does not indicate the relationship of the activities or the critical activities.

Critical path analysis

The aim of the site management team is to achieve completion on time and within budget. The budget as set out in the estimator's feedout. All the operations and activities are monitored, but which of them affect the overall contract period? Let us assume for instance, that a labour shortage has occurred in the steelfixing gang. One steelfixer will be off work for two days due to an illness and the erection gang will possibly have to be rearranged. It would be of great assistance if the site agent was aware of a slack period in the programme, and critical path analysis (CPA) programmes would give that information.

CPA also allows the site agent to delay start dates knowing the **float time** on non-critical activities. The fact that critical operations are clearly indicated makes the monitoring of operations more effective and efficient. The arrow diagram shows the planning logic. This is very useful for briefing contract staff at the pre-contract meeting. The site management will still require the target (or planned) performance index and the planned resource requirement to measure the effectiveness of the site operations.

Information available to site

Take a look at the following short-term critical path analysis of the erection sequence for a cross-walled reinforced concrete housing scheme. The line of balance method could have been used to illustrate the planning strategies, since there is a lot of repetition. The subnetwork was based on the master critical path analysis. The financial involvement of the erection of the shells obviously dictates considerable pre-planning time.

The erection sequence involves multi-skill working; some of the formworkers will place the steel rebars, while the scaffolders will spray the formwork with releasing agent. The whole erection sequence should be discussed with the site federation steward and the respective site union officials (Fig. 7.48).

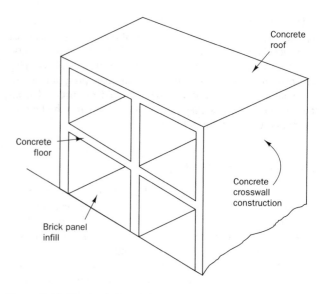

Figure 7.48 Diagram of a reinforced concrete structure

The main work activities are:

- shutter and cast wall kickers
- erect the inside wall formwork
- position wall rebars
- erect the outside of the wall formwork
- check plumb line and level
- concrete to cross-walls
- formwork to slab
- slab rebar
- concrete slab
- strike wall formwork
- strike slab formwork

The **arrow diagram** must be prepared first by asking these three questions:

- What activities precede?
- What activities are concurrent?
- What activities succeed?

Once the best sequence of activities has been resolved by the arrow diagram logic, the workloading of the network can commence.

The logic of the arrow diagram is tested by the workloading and resource requirements, which are planned and expected. The actual resources available can be quite different to the paper exercise, which is why the site management team should be actively involved in the preparation of the short-term programmes. The planning techniques are part of the site management's 'tools', and understanding the implications of float times can be very important to the success of the project.

'Erect first floor joist' has a float time, and therefore is a non-critical activity. What is the type of float? What options has the site manager been given by this programming technique?

- Option 1: Start activity at the earliest possible time (EST) (Fig. 7.49).
- Option 2: Start the activity at the latest possible time (LST) (Fig. 7.50).
- Option 3: Start the activity at the latest start time (LST) (Fig. 7.51).

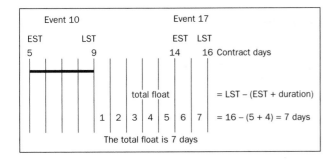

Figure 7.49 Option 1

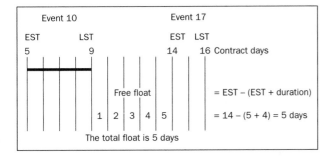

Figure 7.50 Option 2

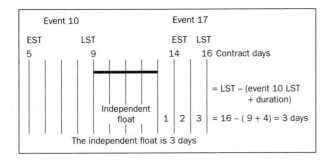

Figure 7.51 Option 3

Identifying the type of float will enable the site manager to maximise the limited resources available. Using the float times to the site manager's advantage will also allow on-time completion of the project. The site management team need to know the planned labour and plant resources. This is called the **resource requirement** (Fig. 7.52). Initially the planner will produce the resource requirements on a histogram and the labour and plant availability will be recorded.

Resource balancing

One of the tasks for site management is to ensure that the labour on site is of the **right quality**, of the **right type**, in the **right quantity** and at the **right time**.

The last objective, on labour at the right time, is given by the master network or critical path analysis. The type and quantity are usually depicted on the labour requirement histogram. The activities are all planned to commence at the earliest start times.

The **labour requirement histogram** (Fig. 7.53) shows the need for resource planning, or balancing. The overall mix of operatives is shown on the histogram, and an individual histogram would be prepared for each type of operative before the balancing of labour resources is attempted. The aim is to ensure continuity for each operative, but unfortunately there are always compromises, which means that the optimum is taken as the goal to achieve.

Key operations can also be identified by using a multiple activity chart and workloading the operations. The use of these charts focuses on the need for accurate planning data and work study standard times should be used. Once the operation has started the site agent and the planner can adjust the multiple activity chart with the individual operative's performance index.

Safety requirements

Safety on site: legislation

There are numerous pieces of legislation that affect and control activities in the construction industry. The main health and safety legislation is the **Health and Safety at Work, etc., Act 1974**. This act placed positive responsibilities on the building manager to ensure the safety of operatives and the general public. The specific aims of the act are:

- to secure the health, safety and welfare of workpeople
- to protect other persons against risks to their health and safety from the building operations
- to control the storage and use of dangerous substances
- to control the emissions of noxious or other offensive substances

Where the company employs more than **five operatives** the company must prepare and issue to all employees a **written safety policy**, which should include references to the following:

- health and safety are important issues
- it is the duty of management to take every reasonable precaution to prevent injuries

LABOUR RESOURCE REQUIREMENT																				
Operative type	Contract day number																			Remarks
	1	2	3	4	5	6	7	8	9	10	11	12	13	14	15	16	17	18	19	
Joiners	2	2	2	2	2	4	4	2	2	2			2					2	2	
Steelfixers				3	3	3				3	3	3	3							
Scaffolders				1																
Concretors											3	3		3	3	3	3			
Total labour force	2	2	2	6	5	7	4	2	2	5	6	6	5	3	3	3	3	2	2	

Figure 7.52

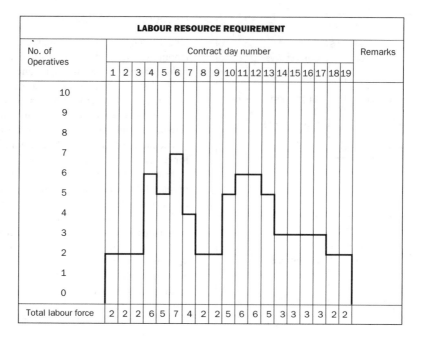

Figure 7.53

- employees have a duty to act responsibly and do everything possible to prevent injury to themselves and others
- a director with prime responsibility for safety must be identified
- the safety policy should be periodically reviewed and updated
- the person responsible for maintaining and updating the safety policy statement must be identified

The site manager's duties regarding health and safety of any operative or visitor on the site is:

- to ensure a safe working environment
- to ensure the safe use and maintenance of plant and equipment
- to ensure that working methods are safe to prevent personal injuries
- to provide the necessary safety training to site operatives
- to provide personal protective clothing where necessary
- to engender safe working practices and ensure that a safe environment is maintained by all the workforce

The enforcement of the Health and Safety at Work, etc., Act (HASAW) is the responsibility of the **Health and Safety Executive**, who are notified of building operations lasting more than **6 weeks**, using form **F10**.

Unfortunately accidents do occur on building sites; some fatal, others minor, and the Health and Safety Executive are notified of all **reportable accidents**. There are certain registers and placards that must be displayed on site. The Health and Safety Executive have the right to visit a site and, if necessary, be accompanied by the police. Where there is gross failure to comply with health and safety legislations the **Factory Inspector** can issue a **prohibition notice** on the building employer or the site agent who is the employer's representative on site. The prohibition notice takes effect immediately and the whole building activity is stopped. Prosecutions can be made against individuals who contravene HASAW, with a maximum penalty of two years'

imprisonment. Where the HASAW or other legislation is contravened the Factory Inspector can issue an **improvement notice** and a stipulated period of time is given to rectify the contravention.

Other pieces of legislation that affect the construction industry are:

- The Construction (Health, Safety and Welfare) Regulations 1996
- The Construction (Design and Management) Regulations 1994
- The Health and Safety (Safety Signs and Signals) Regulations 1996
- Abrasive Wheels Regulations 1970
- Construction (Head Protection) Regulations 1989, amended 1992
- Construction (Lifting Operations) Regulations 1961, amended 1992
- Controlled Waste (Registration of Carriers and Seizure of Vehicles) Regulations 1991
- Control of Substances Hazardous to Health Regulations 1988, amended 1993
- Electricity at Work Act 1989
- Environmental Protection (Applications, Appeals and Register) 1991–1994
- Environmental Protection (Prescribed Processes and Substances, etc.) Amendment Regulations 1994
- Factories Act 1961
- Fire Certificates (Special Premises) Regulations 1976
- Fire Precaution Regulations 1989
- Health and Safety at Work, etc., Act 1974
- Health and Safety (First Aid) Regulations 1981
- Management of Health and Safety at Work 1992
- Manual Handling Operations Regulations 1992
- Noise at Work Act 1989
- Offices, Shops and Railways Premises Act 1963
- Personal Protective Equipment at Work Regulations 1992
- Provision and Use of Work Equipment Regulations 1992
- Reporting of Injuries, Disease and Dangerous Occurrences (Amendment) Regulations 1995

- Safety Representative and Safety Committee Regulations 1977, amended 1992
- Safety Sign Regulations 1994
- Waste Management Licensing Regulations 1994
- Woodworking Machines Regulations 1974, amended 1989/90

The Acts listed above are just some of the legislation that governs construction activities. The construction industry can be a very dangerous place to work or visit and it is the responsibility of everyone to minimise the risks to themselves and others. Statistics published by the Health and Safety Executive indicate where common injuries occur, and some of these statistics are presented in Table 7.6.

Table 7.6 Accident analysis by activity

Activity	Percentage of reportable accidents
Transport	7%
Machinery	8%
Hand tools	8%
Struck by falling objects	9%
Striking against an object	12%
Handling	25%
Persons falling	26%

These statistics will help site management identify common hazards and carry out their **legal duty to assess the risks** involved, then, on the basis of the **risk assessment**, produce safety and health policies that limit the exposure of the workforce to known risks.

A **hazard** is defined as 'an activity with inherent potential to cause harm or injury', which means that nearly all building operations are hazardous. Risk assessment must be carried out and the likelihood of injury assessed on a rating scale, as shown in Table 7.7.

Table 7.7 Risk assessment

Effect of hazard		Likelihood of harm (risk)	
Category	Rating	Category	Rating
Major	3	High	3
Serious	2	Medium	2
Slight	1	Low	1

As the work of the safety committee increases, the safety policy and methods must be reviewed periodically. For example, the Control of Substances Hazardous to Health Regulations 1988 require that working methods that involve the use of hazardous materials should be reviewed every five years.

There should be a concerted effort by site management to reduce the risk of injury by:

- discontinuing the hazardous operation
- isolating the activity from other members of the workforce
- reducing the risk of exposure to the hazard
- limiting the period of exposure to the hazard
- providing personal protective clothing

This information should always be available to the operatives involved in the hazardous activities. While carrying out the risk assessment, the working methods could be reviewed by method study techniques. Once the best method of operation has been obtained, **work practice notes** can be issued. The work measurement is carried out on suitably trained operatives to establish the standard time and bonus targets.

Safety on site: placards and notices

Legislation requires that certain placards and posters be displayed on site. The Factories Act 1961 requires that the **prescribed abstract** of the Act be posted at the principal entrance. There are three prescribed abstracts:

- F1 for factories
- F2 for docks and warehouses
- F3 for work of building operations and works of engineering construction

The prescribed abstract F3 must include the following information:

- name of the medical attendant
- name of hospital and ambulance station
- name of safety supervisor

The Offices, Shops and Railways Premises Act 1963 could apply to site offices if there are more than 20 people employed and the duration is over six months. A copy of the **Abstracts of the Act** must be displayed or a booklet entitled *A guide to the 1963 OSRP Act* (HS(R)4). If the offices are stacked, then a **fire certificate** is required if more than 10 staff are employed. Other placards have to be displayed if applicable:

- **Form F2345** must be displayed if the site uses abrasive wheels. The Abrasive Wheels Regulations 1970 will apply.
- **Form F954** must be displayed where electricity is being used in accordance with the Electricity at Work Act 1989. **Treatment for electric shock** must also be displayed if form F954 is displayed.
- **Form F2470** must be displayed where the Woodworking Machines Regulations 1974 apply.
- A **fire certificate** must be displayed if applicable according to the Fire Certificate (Special Premises) Regulations 1976.
- A **Certificate of insurance** should also be displayed. Although this is not a placard, but a notice similar to the fire certificate, it must be displayed to comply with the Employer's Liability (Compulsory Insurance) Act 1969.
- The **company safety policy** should be displayed in a prominent position.

There are also various **booklets** that must be displayed in accordance with the construction regulations:

- Construction (General Provisions) Regulations 1961
- Construction (Health and Safety) Regulations 1966
- Construction (Lifting Operations) Regulations 1961
- Construction (Working Places) Regulations 1966

Registers

Certain legislation requires the use of **registers** to ensure compliance. These registers are either kept on site or at the head office, depending on the size of the project. Most of the registers must be kept available for inspection by the Factory Inspector or the Employment Medical Adviser for a period of two years from the date of the last entry.

General Register, F36

Part 1 shows the name and address of the employer and the nature of work to be carried out.

Part 2 deals with employment of young workers. The builder must notify the Health and Safety Executive of the employment of young people under the age of 18 using form F2404.

Part 3 has been superseded, but dealt with accidents or dangerous occurrences. This has been replaced by RIDOR under the Notification of Accidents and Dangerous Occurrences Regulations 1980.

Part 4 has also been superseded under the RIDOR regulations.

Prescribed Register F91

Part 1. Records of Weekly Inspections, Examinations and Special Tests.

- Section A: Scaffolding register. The weekly inspections are recorded in this section of all scaffolding above 2 metres high.
- Section B: Excavations. The weekly examination of the excavation faces and support work are recorded. This is in addition to the inspection of excavations and earth support work prior to each shift.
- Section C: Lifting appliances. The weekly inspection carried out by a competent person is recorded in this section.

Part 2. Records of reports of thorough examinations.

- Section D: Crane anchorage/ballast tests.
- Section E: Automatic safe load indicator test. Records weekly inspection by a competent person
- Section F: Hoists used for carrying passengers. This section records the date of installation and extension of the mast, together with the date of the test and the six-monthly thorough examination.
- Section G: Lifting appliances (except hoist). The identification of cranes, reports of the 14-monthly thorough examination and details of substantial repairs are recorded.
- Section H: Hoists. Materials hoists are given a six-monthly thorough examination and the results are recorded in this section.

Accident book, Form B1 510

This is required by the Social Securities Act 1975. All accidents must be reported in this book.

Accident report, Form F2508

This is used to notify the Health and Safety Executive of a

- fatal accident
- dangerous occurrence
- major injury/accident/condition
- accident causing incapacity for three or more days (a reportable accident)
- work-related disease

In the case of a **fatal accident** notify the local office of the Health and Safety Executive as soon as possible. Confirm the notification in writing within seven days on Form 2508. A **dangerous occurrence** is defined as a collapse such as the overturning of a hoist, crane or excavator.

A **major injury** is defined as

- a fracture of the skull, spine, pelvis, bone in the arm, wrist, leg or ankle
- amputation of the hand, finger, thumb
- loss of sight
- an injury requiring immediate medical attention
- loss of consciousness from electric shock

Notification is also required if the operative dies within one year from the injuries sustained by the accident.

The following records must be kept for a period of three years:

- date and time of accident
- name and occupation
- nature of injury
- location of accident
- names and addresses of witnesses
- brief description of the circumstances

In addition to keeping registers, the builder should also hold certain **test certificates**:

- Form F75: Test certificate for hoist
- Form F80: Test certificate for winches, crabs
- Form F87: Test certificate for wire ropes
- Form F96: Test certificate for cranes
- Form F97: Test certificate for chains and lifting gear

If all the above is not sufficient, the builder is required to notify the Health and Safety Executive under various pieces of legislation:

- Form F10: Notification of building operations or works of engineering construction. This only applies when the operations have a duration of more than six weeks.
- Form OSR 1: Notice of employment of persons in offices. This applies where more than 20 people are employed and where the site office is used for more than six months.
- Form F2404: Notice of taking into employment or transfer of a young person. This form is sent to the local careers office.
- Form F2508: Reportable accident, fatality or dangerous occurrence. A reportable accident is where the operative is unable to work for three or more days.
- Form F41: Notification in case of poisoning or disease. One copy is sent to the Employment Medical Adviser as well as the Health and Safety Executive.

Safety officer

Under the Health and Safety at Work, etc., Act 1974, the Safety Representatives and Safety Committees Regulations 1977 and the Construction (General Provisions) Regulations 1961, a **safety supervisor** must be appointed. The name of the safety supervisor is entered on the Abstract of the Factories Act, F3. The provision of a trained safety supervisor only applies where more than **20 operatives** are employed.

The safety committee should meet regularly and have trade union representatives, either site or shop stewards. The duties of the safety committee should include:

- advice on safety legislation
- advice on risk assessment
- organising safety training
- reviewing and editing the site safety policy
- updating the work standards on safety, health and welfare

Personal protective equipment

The safety supervisor should inspect the site and facilities to ensure compliance with the current health, safety and welfare legislation. Specific inspection should be given to the following areas of work:

- Excavations
  - barriers should be erected when trench depth exceeds 2 metres
  - safe access and egress should be provided
  - suitable personal protective equipment should be worn
  - sides of the excavation should be inspected before each shift
  - a weekly examination should be recorded in F91 register
- Bricklayer cutting bricks with abrasive wheels
  - safety helmets should be worn
  - eye goggles should be worn
  - Form F2346 should be displayed
  - exposure to dust should be limited
  - exposure to noise should be limited
- Working on scaffolding
  - guardrails and toeboards should be secure
  - ladder access should be tied
  - scaffold reveal and through ties should be secure
  - safety helmets should be worn
  - weekly inspection of scaffolding should be recorded in F91 register
- Crane lifting
  - banksman should be in attendance, using correct signs
  - slinging should be correct
  - automatic safe load indicator should be working
  - a weekly inspection should be recorded on F91 register
- Manual handling
  - the risk of injury due to lifting should be assessed under Manual Handling Operation Regulations 1992
  - appropriate action should be taken to reduce the risk of injury, safe lifting sequences should be complied with
- Using compressed air breakers
  - ears should be protected
  - industrial gloves should be worn
  - the site should be safe on completion
  - safety helmets should be worn
  - safety goggles should be worn
  - safety boots should be worn
- Cartridge-operated tools
  - a permit is required to use the equipment
  - industrial gloves should be worn
  - adopt a safe method of use
  - safety goggles should be worn
  - cartridge used should be of the correct strength
- Woodworking machinery
  - adopt safe method of working
  - guards should be correctly fitted
  - ear muffs should be worn
  - industrial gloves should be worn
  - safety boots should be worn
  - a mask should be worn, if necessary
  - placards should be displayed for the treatment of electric shock
  - there should be a clean working area
  - exposure to noise should be limited
- Painting
  - under Control of Substances Hazardous to Health, the materials being used should be known and safe handling procedures should be adopted.
  - risks and hazards should be identified
- materials and equipment should be used correctly
- personal protective equipment should be worn, such as masks, goggles, gloves, safety helmet and boots
- good housekeeping should be practised

Personal protection

As a guide the following personal protective equipment should be used:
- Eye protection:
  - power tools:
    - chipping
    - cutting
    - cropping
    - abrasive wheels
  - hand tools:
    - chipping
    - abrasing
- Ear protection
  - daily personal noise exposure, 85 dB
  - intermittent noise exceeding 85 dB
  - to limit noise:
    - reduce at source
    - isolate source
    - ear protection
    - reduce exposure time
- Head protection:
  - where risk of injury from:
    - falling objects
    - striking against objects
    - people working above
    - plant and equipment
- Hand protection:
  - where risk of injury from:
    - lifting goods
    - handling materials, especially chemicals
    - abrasion
    - contamination
- Foot protection:
  - where risk of injury from:
    - lifting goods
    - handling materials
    - inclement weather
    - contamination
    - plant and equipment

Welfare facilities

The temporary facilities, site accommodation and welfare arrangements are governed by the following legislation:

- Construction (Health, Safety and Welfare) Regulations 1996
- The Health and Safety (Safety Signs and Signals) Regulations 1996
- Offices, Shops and Railway Premises Act 1963
- Health and Safety at Work, etc., Act 1974

- Health and Safety (First Aid) Regulations 1981
- Fire Precautions (Factories, Offices, Shops and Railway Premises) Order 1989
- Health and Safety (Display Screen Equipment) Regulations 1992
- Fire Precautions (Special Premises) Regulations 1971

The amount of welfare facilities and office facilities depend on the peak labour force, which is calculated on the contract programme. Both nominated and domestic subcontractors can use the main contractor's welfare facilities as **shared facilities**. The main contractor completes **Form 3303** and issues each subcontractor with the certificate of shared welfare arrangements, **Form F2202**.

First aid boxes

At least one first aid box must be provided on site regardless of the number employed. The contents of the first aid boxes varies with the number of operatives on site (Table 7.8).

Table 7.8 Minimum content of first aid box

Dressings	Number of employees				
	>5	>10	>50	>100	>150
Guidance card	1	1	1	1	1
Sterile adhesive dressings	10	20	40	40	40
Sterile eye pads	1	2	4	6	8
Triangular bandages	1	2	4	6	8
Sterile coverings for serious wounds	1	2	4	6	8
Safety pins	6	6	12	12	12
Medium sterile unmedicated dressings	3	6	8	10	12
Large sterile unmedicated dressings	1	2	4	6	10
Extra large sterile unmedicated dressings	1	2	4	6	8
Sterile water in 300 ml containers if no running water	1	1	3	6	6

First aid personnel

A trained first aid person must be employed where 50 to 150 employees are on site. If there are over 150 employees then there must be 1 additional first aider for every 150 employees. A trained first aid person must possess a current first aid certificate issued by the St John's Ambulance Association, St Andrew's Ambulance Association or the British Red Cross Society. The certificate must not be over three years old.

Ambulance

The local ambulance authority should be notified within 24 hours when the peak workforce exceeds 25 operatives. A nominated person must be appointed to summon help from the ambulance authority. The nominated person's name should be entered on Form F3, and displayed.

First aid room

A first aid room is to be provided when more than 250 people are employed on the site. The names of occupational first aiders should be displayed and the room should be of sufficient size to be accessible for a stretcher. It should also be heated, bright, well ventilated, and regularly cleaned. The room should contain the following:

- sink with hot and cold water
- paper towels, soap and nail brush
- worktop, smooth and impervious
- drinking water
- clinical thermometer
- couch

Washing facilities

Where more than 20 but less than 100 operatives are on site, the following facilities must be available:

- hot and cold water
- soap and towels
- wash-hand basins at a ratio of 1 basin per 25 operatives

If the work last longer than 12 months and more than 100 operatives are employed, then the following wash-hand basins must be provided:

- 4 wash-hand basins for up to 100 operatives
- 1 additional wash-hand basin for every additional 35 operatives

Sanitary accommodation

Separate toilets must be provided for male and female operatives. The proportion of toilets provided must be

- 1 toilet per 25 operatives
- if over 100 operatives, then 1 additional toilet for every 35 additional operatives

Drying rooms

There should be adequate provision for personal clothing where more than five operatives are employed on site:

- provision for drying clothes
- accommodation for protective clothing

Messrooms

Where meals are to be available, then permission must be obtained form the Department of Health and Social Security. The canteen will be inspected by the Local Authority Environmental Health Officer for compliance with the food legislation.

Provision must be made for a messroom where more than 10 operatives are employed. The messroom should be cleaned regularly and provide:

- cooking facilities
- hygienic storage of foodstuff
- sink with hot and cold water
- drinking water
- tables and chairs or benches for peak labour force

Site security

The safety of the general public and site operatives must be considered by the site manager. All visitors to the site must report to the checker and be given protective clothing as appropriate. Directions and no-go areas must be pointed out to the visitors. Some site checkers require the visitors to sign the **Visitors' book** on entry and on leaving the site. Warning signs should be erected, alerting parents and children to the dangers of children playing on site. The site should always be left in a reasonably secure condition to prevent possible injury to children and unlawful visitors.

Compounds should be made available for the security of plant and equipment, fuel and other dangerous chemicals. Highly flammable liquids should be correctly stored in accordance with the Highly Flammable Liquids and Liquefied Petroleum Gases Regulations 1972. Small quantities of LPG (liquefied petroleum gas) up to 50 litres should be stored in fire-resistant cupboards; quantities over 50 litres should be stored with a retention sill (often called a bundwall) marked 'HIGHLY FLAMMABLE'. Welding cylinders should be stored in a secured area, fenced off and protected from inclement weather. A sign 'NO NAKED LIGHT' must be displayed.

Cartridge-operated tools and power tools must be securely locked in the equipment shed. Flammable substances are classified as:

- Class A: Free burning material, e.g. wood
- Class B: Burning liquids; oils, petrol
- Class C: Involving fire
- Class D: Involving metals

Sufficient fire-fighting equipment must be available and the various types of fire extinguisher are colour coded:

- red (water)
- cream (foam)
- black (CO_2)
- green (halon)
- blue (dry powder)

Temporary offices

The offices may have to comply with the Offices Shops and Railway Premises Act 1963. When more than 20 staff are employed a valid **fire certificate** must be obtained. Office space per person is defined:

- $3.7\,m^2$ per person and $11\,m^3$ of air space
- minimum $16\,°C$ temperature
- adequate ventilation
- cleaned at least once a week
- lighting should be sufficient for activity
- storage of personal protective clothing
- sufficient seating for all staff
- first aid box and trained first aid person

Separate sanitary and washing facilities must be provided for male and female staff (Table 7.9).

Table 7.9 Sanitary facilities for male and female staff

Number of staff	Toilet provision	Urinals	Wash-hand basins
1–15	1	–	1
16–30	2	1	2
31–50	3	2	3
51–75	4	2 (up to 60) 3 (over 61)	4
76–100	5	4	5
100 and over	1 per 25	1 per 25	1 per 25

Self-assessment tasks

Select **one** major stage of activity based on your design activity, e.g. substructure of the house, or first fix, second fix and commission of the mechanical services, or the erection of the structural frame of a building, or the estate road. The selection should reflect your chosen career path.

1. Prepare the flow diagram illustrating the sequences of operations. Be prepared to justify your sequence of operation.
2. Obtain the 'as fixed' quantities for each operation. Include in your evidence any methods used to check the accuracy of the quantities.
3. Produce the method statement for the work. There will be several alternative methods of operations. Select **one** best method and justify your selection. For each operation list the following:
   (a) plant and equipment requirement
   (b) personal protective equipment.
4. Produce a risk assessment, identifying hazards and safety precautions to be carried out for each operation.
5. Workload the method statement and obtain the bar duration for each operation. To obtain the plant and labour outputs consult a pricebook such as Laxtons or Wessex price books. This evidence could be used for the grading theme 'Information gathering and retrieval'. This workloading could then be prepared as a spreadsheet.
6. Produce a bar chart programme showing all the operations and daily labour requirement.
7. Produce a histogram showing the peak labour and the different types of operatives required to maintain the programme output.
8. Prepare a plant and equipment schedule based on the bar chart.
9. Match the material deliveries with the programmed output, allowing current lead times.
10. Produce a health and safety plan for the project.

7.4 Monitoring and controlling resources

Topics covered in this section are:

- labour control
- plant control
- material control
- waste control

Labour control

Requirement

The contract programme suggests the amount of labour required to achieve on-time completion. This is called the labour requirement and the basic data should be as accurate as possible. The labour output times should be based on work study data to ensure accurate predictions of bar durations and costs. The contract documents outline the end result, but the builder's estimator must also assess the reality against the probabilities. Risks are taken, not over safety, but risks relating to unknown details. These assumptions should be available to the site management team, who have the difficult task of achieving completion not only on time but also within the financial budget of the estimate.

The contract documents impose certain obligations on the builder or main contractor. For example, under Clause 8, 'Materials, goods and workmanship' to conform to description, testing and inspection the main contractor is to construct in such a manner that the 'workmanship shall so far as procurable be of ... standards described in the Contract bill'. This clause also gives the architect the contractual right to 'issue instructions requiring the exclusion from the works of any person employed thereon'. The **specification** section in the contract bill describes the 'acceptable' quality, which will often be based on a British Standard code of practice. The roof tiling may also be specified for a particular manufacturer (Fig. 7.54), who will publish fixing and laying details. The contract bill might use the manufacturer's workmanship specification and, by inclusion in the bill, it becomes the measure of acceptable workmanship (Fig. 7.55).

H60 Clay/concrete roof tiling 1. Roofing Tiles: BS 5534 Manufacturer:					

Figure 7.54 Specifying the tile type

	H60 Clay/concrete roof tiling H60.1.101 roof covering					
a	The roof tiles are Ludlow plus manufactured by Marley Tiles and laid in strict accordance to the manufacturer's instruction					

Figure 7.55 Specifying the tile manufacturer

There are now two specifications for workmanship: the BS code of practice and the manufacturer's workmanship specifications. The architect has the right to inspect the work and, if the workmanship is found to be substandard and unacceptable, can instruct it to be done again at the main contractor's expense. It is important therefore that the contractor has the right quality of operatives on site, and that the operatives know the standard of workmanship to be achieved.

The operatives will be qualified craftspersons or general building operatives, but they seldom read the BS code of practice and often use the expression **trade practice**. The estimator initially will highlight these possible areas of conflict. The report of these legally binding conditions must be sent to site management, and should be discussed during the pre-contract meeting to develop strategies to achieve the contract specification. The trades foreperson should be informed of these decisions and through quality control methods should ensure that the work conforms to the required standard.

The same applies to domestic subcontractors. Under Clause 19 of the JCT Standard Form of Building Contract, 1980 edition, the contractor can sublet part of the work with the agreement of the architect. The subcontractors must be selected from the **list** – that is, a list of the names of at least three subcontractors. The list may be amended by the builder, but only with the approval of the architect. If the main contractor has decided to sublet the roofing work, a subcontract will be agreed and signed by the two contracting parties. The main contractor (builder) will act as the acceptor and the consideration will be the roofing work completed as specified in the contract bill. The offeree will be the subcontractor and the consideration will be the subcontract sum. There are standard forms of *contract* available for domestic subcontracts, and the standard form of *subcontract* will mirror the main contract conditions. The procedure in selecting the subcontractor is:

- Select, from the list, at least three to quote for the subcontract work.
- Prepare the subcontract tender documents based on the main contract; copy the relevant bill of quantities sections, i.e. both specification sections and the measured work section.
- State the start and finish dates for the subcontract work based on the master or contract programme.
- Invite fixed price lump sum bids from the selected subcontract tenderers.
- Analyse the quotes and select the preferred subcontractor.
- Place the order and sign the subcontract; the BEC (Building Employers Confederation) Standard Form of Subcontract should be used.

The main contractor is still responsible for coordinating the work and finishing the work by the date of completion. Some of the conditions are put into the subcontract agreement, such as the subcontract date of commencement and completion, and the amount of liquidated and ascertained damages. Interim and final account payment details should be compatible with the main contract. The **information control** chart will coordinate the selection of the domestic subcontractor with the operation commencement date.

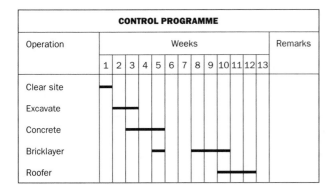

Figure 7.56

The control programme in Fig. 7.56 shows that the roofing subcontractor is programmed to start work on contract week 10. The programmed job duration is 3 weeks and the completion is by contract week 12. The site management, and especially the site planner, has to ensure that the subcontractor starts and finishes on time. Other staff need to be coordinated: the buyer will select and place the subcontract order, and the site planner must monitor the release of architect's details. The roofing samples must also be approved, and it is possible that the planning authority may have included as a planning condition that samples of the roof tiling are to be deposited with them for approval. Although that takes time, the main contractor must still achieve the contracted completion date. To ensure that the design and support functions are coordinated, the information control chart is used (Fig. 7.57).

Now that the subcontract has been placed, the site planner and site management must ensure that the subcontractor is available

- on time
- with the correct number of operatives

Availability

The roofing subcontractor is a **labour only** subcontractor, i.e. the main contractor will provide the materials and the subcontractor will provide the labour. The subcontract commencement date has been agreed and the main contractor will organise and monitor operations so that the subcontract can start on time.

INFORMATION CONTROL CHART														
Operation	Weeks													Remarks
	1	2	3	4	5	6	7	8	9	10	11	12	13	
Roofer		SA		ITQ		P	exp		exp	•	Operation starts			
								Expedite						
Subcontractor approval						Place subcontract								
			Invite to quote											

Figure 7.57

The contract programme determined the sequence of building operations, and the use of work study standard times and various allowances for inclement weather, holidays, etc., means that some 'slack time' has been built into the programme. The actual progress on site needs to be monitored and the programme must be updated as necessary. For example, if the bricklaying operation was delayed due to substandard workmanship and the architect's instruction ordered the removal and rebuilding of the wall to the contract specification, the resultant delay will have a 'knock on' effect for the following trades, including the roofing subcontractor. To allow for such a possibility, alternative strategies must be evaluated to minimise the time lost and cost.

One of the contract obligations accepted by the main contractor was to finish the project by the date of completion. Recruitment of additional operatives is a possibility, but there is a limit to the number of operatives on site, and there is also the risk of employing substandard labour. The offer of inflated earnings as an inducement may be a solution, but this will exceed the labour budgets. In addition, any 'new starters' will have a learning curve as it takes time to become familiar with the site layout, work patterns and quality standards. These risks are unacceptable and it is better to ask existing operatives to work extra hours. The **Working Rule Agreement** (WRA) for the building industry sets out the rules for payment, and the local union branch may insist on an **overtime permit**, the union officials expressing the view that full employment of its members is better than a small number of operatives working long hours. In our example, an overtime permit has been granted so the operatives can work 'overtime'. The normal working day is specified in the **national working rule**, but regional variations are negotiated for the normal start time. The normal start time is 8.00 a.m., with a mid-morning paid break of 10 minutes. The mid-day break of half an hour is taken at 12.30 p.m., and is a non-paid break. The normal working day is 8 hours, Monday to Thursday, and 7 hours on Friday, making a normal working week of 39 hours. The working day of eight hours will finish at 4.30 p.m.

Normal start time	8.00	
Mid-day break	12.30	
		4.5 hours
Half-hour lunch break		
Restart time	1.00	
Normal finish time	4.30	
		3.5 hours
Normal working day		8.0 hours

To make up the lost time the site agent is going to introduce a 44-hour working week, which will involve an additional 1 hour of **overtime working** each day. The negotiated wage structure allows for additional payments, sometimes known as **extra overtime payments**, for overtime working.

The WRA states: 'first hour overtime payment at time and a half'. The operative, for working 1 hour extra, is paid 1.5 hours

operative paid at overtime rates	1.5 hours
productive work	1.0 hour
so the **non-productive overtime** pay is	0.5 hour.

Over the week this extra overtime payment or non-productive overtime pay will accumulate, and its calculation is the responsibility of the site cashier. The cashier will 'make up' the wages and any additional payments to the operatives as part of their gross pay.

WAGE TARGET SHEET									
					Week ending			12/8/94	
					Tax week			22	
Works no.	Operative		Mon.	Tues.	Wed.	Thur	Fri.	Total	Remarks
120	Brayns	NW	8	8	8	8	7	39	hours
		OT	1	1	1	1	1	5	hours
		EOT	$\frac{1}{2}$	$\frac{1}{2}$	$\frac{1}{2}$	$\frac{1}{2}$	$\frac{1}{2}$	$2\frac{1}{2}$	hours
					Hours paid			$46\frac{1}{2}$	

Figure 7.58

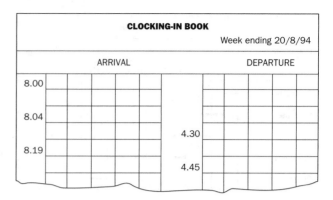

Figure 7.59

The operative 'Brayns' only worked for 44 hours (productive time) but will receive 461/2 hours pay for the 44 hours worked. The extra $2\frac{1}{2}$ hours paid is called 'extra overtime payment' or 'non-productive overtime' (Fig. 7.58).

It can be seen, therefore, that labour control is a vital activity in achieving on-time completion.

Monitoring labour

There are several documents in existence that will be used to monitor labour output. The cashier will need to know the hours worked by each operative, and their starting and finishing times will be recorded by the cashier or checker. Large sites often have clocking-in procedures, in which a 'clock card' is issued to each operative, who, on arrival, clocks in and, on leaving, clocks out. Abuse of the clocking system is dealt with by site disciplinary and nationally agreed procedures. 'Clocking in' for another operative could result in 'summary dismissal', as this is considered to be gross misconduct.

Lateness and absenteeism are covered by the industrial relations agreements, such as the Working Rule Agreement. The civil engineering contractors have a similar working rule agreement and BATJIC is an alternative union and employers' agreement. The Working Rule Agreement contains two parts:

- negotiation – dealing with rates of pay, hours worked, sick pay, etc.
- conciliation – detailing how individual disputes and collective disputes are to be resolved

Site industrial agreements can be introduced in conjunction with the national industrial relations framework. For instance, when considering the punctuality of an operative whose normal start time is 8.00 a.m., a 3-minute period is allowed before any deductions are incurred for lateness. The site cashier records the arrival of operatives in the 'Clocking-in book' (Fig. 7.59).

If an operative arrives at 8.05 a.m., then that person is **quartered** by the cashier for lateness. The operative will receive payment for the hours worked *less* a quarter of an hour for being late; hence the term 'quartered'. The same method is used with a clock-recording system using clocking-in cards. Some building companies require the operative to complete a time sheet.

Time sheets

The time sheet records the total time worked by the operative. After the cashier has checked the accuracy of the working times, the time sheet is sent to the cost and bonus surveyor. The time sheet may require the operative to record the hours worked on specific jobs. This will greatly assist the cost and bonus surveyor to establish the actual hours content for each operation. This sort of site feedback is ideal for the estimator as the labour constant data bank will reflect actual site performance.

The time sheet, which has total hours worked and a breakdown of hours spent on each job, is sometimes called a 'time and allocation sheet' (Fig. 7.60).

The time sheets should be verified by the walking ganger for general building operatives, or the trades foreperson for craftspersons. The site checker will make up the wages and pass the time sheets to the cost and bonus surveyor. After calculating the bonus and weekly cost the time sheets are sent to the quantity surveyor. The contractor's quantity surveyor will use the time sheets for any claims resulting from **variation orders** and **architect's instructions**. The trades foreperson will try to motivate and control the gangs to comply with the specified quality standard and required output as the estimate measures performance. Controlling labour means checking and maintaining the specified quality and coordinating activities. A site visit by the general or trade foreperson may not be carried out because it is sunny, but it should be remembered that there is a purpose for the site visit. One of the techniques used in work study indicated the utilisation of operatives, or plant, by random observations and the activity sampling method gave a general overview of whether operatives were working or idle. That is part of the reason for visiting the site. The site management team will be very busy managing, controlling operations and planning the work.

TIME AND ALLOCATION SHEET																	
												Week ending			20/8/94		
Works no.	Name	M	T	W	T	F	S	S	Operation	M	T	W	T	F	S	S	Remarks
208	Brown	9	9	9	9	8			Excavate	6	6	6	6	3			
209	Jones	9	8	9	8	7			Concrete	9	9	9	6	8			
									External paths	3	2	3	5	4			

Figure 7.60

Planning the work will maximise the resources available, but sometimes this is overlooked by the need to monitor site production.

Incentive scheme

Implementing an incentive scheme controls the labour output and releases valuable site management time for planning and organising. Minimising down time on resources will increase productivity. The introduction of an incentive payment scheme introduces a utility cost, i.e. the cost of the bonus surveyor and the stationery, which are part of the additional overhead cost. However, the returns far outweigh the cost, and accurate site data can be used to improve the estimator's labour constant databank through **site feedback**, allowing for more accurate planning and control of the site resources.

What type of incentive scheme should be used?

Work measurement specified the time taken for a qualified worker, working at standard performance and under capable supervision, to produce one unit of production. The accurate assessment of the work content is the basis of a satisfactory bonus incentive scheme. Whether a **geared** incentive scheme or a **direct** incentive scheme is used depends on the mix and quality of the workforce. In both these schemes the bonus allowance is adjusted to suit the type of incentive, whereas the standard time remains constant. The issue of bulk targets with a predicted bonus earning is probably the best type of bonus scheme. The incentive is more effective on an individual basis, but much of the work on a construction site is performed by a gang, thus making gang bonus schemes preferable in the building industry. The cost and bonus surveyor will calculate the bonus and prepare the site costs. Another name given to this service management function is **production control**, and the site planning, cost and bonus functions are carried out by the production control department.

Accurately completed time and allocation sheets are necessary if full benefit is to be gained from an incentive scheme. The bricklaying gang is a 2/1 gang: two bricklayers served by a bricklayer's labourer. The bonus targets are for the bricklayers only and the labourer is credited with half of the bonus hours earned by the tradespersons. The control of labour against the work measurement standard times is one method of comparing site performance. Most builders will also compare the labour and plant site costs against the estimator's feedout.

Plant control

Requirement

The strategies are laid out in the method statement and the **plant resource requirement** in the contract programme. During the method statement alternative construction methods will be considered and discarded. The method outlined in the method statement is the best method, based on information available at that time. Site or ready mix concrete decision will be subject to a cost comparison. Different methods of transporting and placing concrete will have been analysed. Static plant locations will have been scrutinised and the site layout will have been positioned to maximise resources. Labour to plant will have been looked at through the **multiple activity chart** and the gang balanced. Now the planner can schedule the crane's daily programmes throughout the erection period. The tower crane will be the most expensive plant item in the erection sequence. This is the control activity; all the site agent has to do when monitoring the performance of the erection gang is to observe the tower crane. If the crane is working, then so will the other members of the gang. The craneage programme demonstrates the principle of plant utilisation and labour plant balance. Using work study standard times the programme will develop a 'cycle time' which will repeat throughout the working day. The cycle time will include:

- banking and slinging for craneage
- lifting
- slewing
- receiving and unloading
- slewing
- dropping to the slinging point

The craneage programme shown in Fig. 7.61 is calculated in hours but in real life it is calculated in minutes.

The planned plant utilisation is

$$\text{utilisation percentage} = \frac{\text{hours worked}}{\text{total hours}} \times 100$$

i.e. $\dfrac{4\frac{1}{2} \text{ hours}}{4\frac{1}{2} \text{ hours}} \times 100 = 100\%$

whereas the concrete placing gang have only a utilisation percentage of

$$\frac{2 \text{ hours}}{4\frac{1}{2} \text{ hours}} \times 100 = 44\%$$

Where the **utilisation factor** or percentage drops below 60%, it should be reappraised. Having established the best plant type and the optium labour/plant balance, the site agent and planner now must control the activities by recording deviations and updating the construction methods file.

CRANEAGE DAILY PROGRAMME					
					Erection gang
Time	Tower crane	Joiner	Steel fixer	Concrete mixing	Concrete placing
8.00 / 9.00	Lift forms	Position forms			
	Hoist steel		Receive steel		
10.00	Lift wallform	stop end	Fix steel		
11.00	Lift conc.	Erect wallforms		Mix conc. Mix conc. Mix conc.	Prepare place conc.
12.00	Lift conc.	Ditto	Steel wall	Ditto	Ditto
Hours worked	4.0	3.0	2.5	2.0	2.0

Figure 7.61

Plant sheets

Apart from a full-scale method study and work measurement on plant, the basic control document is the plant time sheet. Some elementary utilisation factors can be achieved by activity sampling. Provided the sample is statistically determined and the observations are made at random times, there is a degree of accuracy. The **plant sheets** are prepared by the plant operator and one area of site control must be **earthworks**. In the civil engineering and building standard methods of measurement the earthworks are provisional and subject to site measurement. On a civil engineering contract the clerk of works is replaced by the **resident engineer** who acts for the client (in the contract called the employer). A typical work-in-place item is given in Fig. 7.62. The method statement for this work-in-place item will include some assumptions:

- bulking factor – the conversion of the bank cubic metres (as excavated) to loose cubic metres
- ground conditions – the nature of the soil and the topography, based on the site investigation report
- quantities to be excavated – taken from the bill of quantities

Certain constraints are added: some are contractual, such as the 'specification', which would identify the quality of the work, while others state restrictions on the working day. The estimator will limit the project time available to secure the bid and the plant availability will also limit the plant selection. As these assumptions need to be checked, the time sheet becomes an important record. Some significant information will be available from the plant operator's time sheet (Fig. 7.63).

The planned utilisation is 70%; anything in excess of that figure is a benefit to the site.

$$\text{plant utilisation} = \frac{\text{hours worked}}{\text{total hours}} \times 100$$

i.e.

$$\frac{33}{43} \times 100 = 76\%$$

The ganger in charge of the excavating section will want to highlight the **plant downtime** on weather caused by rain. Part of the contract conditions allows the main contractor to claim extra time for certain delays. The relevant events are outlined in clause 25 'Extension of time' under the JCT Standard Form of Building Contract. One of the 'relevant events' is **exceptionally adverse weather conditions**. The contractor's quantity surveyor will compile the **builder's claim** from this documentary evidence and the site diary.

The **plant breakdown time** only shows the effect on the excavator, but there is also a 'knock on' effect for the daywork lorries, the general operatives and the ensuing operations. In total, the downtime costs could be more considerable than just 6 hours. It should be noted that **plant efficiency** is different from **plant utilisation**: plant utilisation is a measure of the *availability* of the plant, but plant efficiency is a measure of its *productiveness*. The tracked loader relies on the track propulsion to dig. The rope-operated excavator relies on the bucket weight and the rope pull for its digging force and this type of hydraulically operated excavator is much more powerful. The bucket penetration is a combination of the bucket curling force and the stick force. The plant will have a typical **digging rate** but due to various factors the output will be **derated**. The derating factors are:

- soil digging resistance, such as hardness, coarseness, friction, adhesion and density
- ground conditions – often called the 'coefficient of traction factor'
- depth of dig
- slew angle for tipping
- target type, e.g. tip at side of trench or load to lorry

The **derating factors** can reduce the digging rate by as much as 33%, so a machine output rating of $60\,\text{m}^3/\text{h}$ 'banked' could be derated to:

$$\begin{aligned}
\text{production output} &= \text{machine output banked} \times \\
&\quad (100 \text{ per cent} - \text{derated percentage}) \\
&= 60\ \text{m}^3/\text{h} \times 75\% \\
&= 40\ \text{m}^3/\text{h}
\end{aligned}$$

Maintenance

The output of any machine is greatly increased by proper maintenance. **Heavy plant** such as scapers and static plant such as concrete mixers, cranes and hoists all need proper maintenance to ensure maximum utilisation. Plant operators should be trained and qualified to operate the plant safely. Training schemes operated by the Construction Industry Training Board (CITB) are available. The CITB Scheme for the Certification of Training Achievement of Construction Plant Operators covers the following plant:

- Excavating plant
  - crawler tractors
  - draglines
  - excavators over 5 tonnes
  - excavators below 5 tonnes
  - graders
  - loading shovels
  - motorised scrapers
  - soil compactors
  - trenchers
  - tractor/crawler
  - road rollers

a	D GROUNDWORK
	D20 Excavating and filling
	   .2 Excavating
	      .2 to reduced levels
	         .2 Maximum depth <1.00 m
						905	m³		

Figure 7.62

PLANT TIME SHEET

Plant number: 123   Week ending 28/8/94
Plant type: Tracked loader, 1 m³ bucket

Work no.	Plant operator	Operation	M	T	W	T	F	S	S	Total hours
109	J.C. Bee	Excavate to reduced level	7	6	8	7	5			33
		Plant break-down	2			2	2			6
		Weather hold-up, rain		3						3
		Change bucket			1					1
										43

Figure 7.63

- Concreting plant
  - concrete pumps
- Movement plant
  - cranes (wheeled and crawler)
  - tower cranes
  - truck-mounted cranes
  - dumpers below 10 tonnes
  - dumpers over 10 tonnes
  - site materials handler
  - hoists
  - lorry loaders

The plant operators will carry out the following maintenance;

- daily servicing – cleaning down, oil, fuel and water checks
- weekly maintenance – greasing for heavy plant and equipment

The plant operator is entitled to a maintenance bonus for completing the **daily** and **weekly maintenance**. A plant maintenance sheet is completed by the operator and verified by the site fitter. The maintenance bonus will then be paid in addition to any productive bonus earned by the plant operator.

The Working Rule Agreement (WRA) allows **extra payments** for responsibility and extra skill for general building operatives who are qualified to operate certain plant. The craftsperson is expected to provide certain tools – for example, the bricklayer has to provide a trowel – and to maintain the craftsperson's tools the WRA allows for the payment of **tool money** to those skilled operatives who provide and maintain their own tools.

The payment of maintenance time is also negotiated through the WRA. The plant operator on the concrete batching plant is allowed 30 minutes prior to normal start time to get a mix ready for normal start time. The plant operator receives **daily maintenance time** (DMT) at basic or flat rate. The **weekly maintenance time** (WMT) given to plant operators, such as 'drott drivers', is only paid at the flat rate and is not inflated like overtime payments.

Legislation

The **Health and Safety at Work, etc., Act 1974** places on the site agent the legal responsibility to

- secure health and safety of persons at work
- protect other persons against risks to health and/or safety

Statistics identify that 15% of the accidents occur when using plant and equipment.

The **Construction (Lifting Operations) Regulations** place a statutory duty on the crane user to carry out a thorough examination every 14 months. The **Certificate of Test and Thorough Examination of Crane, F96**, must be available for inspection by the Health and Safety Executive. The law also provides for weekly inspections to be carried out by a 'competent person', recording the results in one of the construction registers (Fig. 7.64).

The planner will try to reduce plant breakdowns to a minimum. Since plant is a large capital expenditure, the building company will have its own plant yard, holding certain common plant and hiring in other plant on an 'as needs' basis. The plant yard will be managed by the plant

STATUTORY INSPECTIONS, EXAMINATIONS AND TESTS			
Type of plant	Inspection	Examination	Testing
Cranes	Weekly record F91 (Part II)	At least every 14 months Form F91	Once every 4 years Form 96
Chains, ropes	Form F91 or Form F1946	Every 6 months Form F91	Before first use Form 97
Hoists		Every 6 months Form F91, section H	Before first use

Figure 7.64

manager with fitters (plant mechanics) available for site breakdowns and regular **preventative maintenance**. The return of plant to the yard is not acceptable to the site management, so **site fitters** will carry out preventative maintenance at suitable times. The plant manager and the site manager may be on the same management level, and there will therefore be a lateral relationship between them, but the site fitter will have a functional relationship when dealing with the site agent.

The preventative maintenance is in addition to the weekly and daily maintenance carried out by the plant operator. This routine maintenance will involve changing air filters on excavating plant, oil changes, plugs or injectors, belts and chains, safe load indicators and overload cutouts if the excavating plant is used for lifting. This is in addition to the legal inspection and recording necessary under Construction Regulations. The excavator bucket teeth are replaced at regular intervals, and ropes and wire are also replaced, with the aim of keeping plant downtime to a minimum.

Major repairs or overhauls are carried out in the plant yard, unless the site has its own fleet of machines. The major overhauls are part of the **planned maintenance**. The plant department records will show the working time for each major plant item; for example, after 5000 hours the injectors will be replaced. The computer-held record will indicate the necessary planned maintenance activity, which occurs even where the part is still functioning. The part is said to be 'life expired' and must be replaced.

Hire or buy?

The plant holding can be a large financial commitment to the building company, so the decision to hire or buy can 'tie up capital'.

The cash available to the builder is a resource that needs to be closely monitored. In the organisational framework the accountant, who is sometimes called the 'financial director', will be responsible for the efficient use of the company's money. This service manager will liaise with the line manager, such as the 'contracts director', on what type of plant and equipment to hold. The balance of plant requirement will then be subject to external hire arrangements.

Plant and equipment will be either **non-mechanical** or **mechanical**, with a further subdivision into small, heavy or large. Non-mechanical plant are defined as

- Small plant:
  - spades, picks, rakes, hocks
  - tampers, hammers, crowbars, bolt cutters
  - ladders, trestles, steps
  - barrows, buckets
  - ropes, slings, straps, lifting beams
  - trench sheeting
- Large plant:
  - scaffolding
  - shoring, gantries
  - formwork
  - sheet piling
  - trench boxes, drag boxes

The decision to hire or buy often depends on the cash flow position of the company and the demand for a particular type of plant. The use of the breakeven chart will highlight the minimum usage required to make the outright purchase of plant financially viable (Fig. 7.65).

The management must now evaluate the plant usage to decide whether to purchase this plant costing £10 000, with a maintenance and repair bill of £1670 per 1000 hours. The decision to invest in the plant purchase has not involved depreciation of the plant, cash flow predictions or any financial or fiscal benefits. Once the **usage breakeven point** has been established the financial director, with the plant manager, will prepare another breakeven chart comparing the internal hire rate with the anticipated external hire rate. Now that the right type of plant is available the materials will need to be scheduled to maximise the resources.

Material control

Requirement

The contract programme determines the material consumption rates. The buyer has the task of purchasing the materials

- at the right price
- of the right quality
- in the right quantity

- from the right supplier
- at the right time

The last task will involve the site planner and checker in ensuring that deliveries are made on time. The monitoring of suppliers by site staff is called **supplier evaluation**. Part of buying proficiency is the purchase of materials below the estimator's material constant, so all the contracting team's performance is measured by the one yardstick, the estimate.

The buyer will **take off** quantities from the contract drawings and use the bill of quantities 'as-fixed' quantities as a check. Since the quantities are measured net, the buyer must make allowances for waste. Material waste can occur in three areas:

- design waste
- purchase waste
- construction waste

Design waste may occur because of the architect's lack of building plant standardisation. The foundation spread is calculated from the formula

$$\text{foundation spread} = \frac{\text{building load, kN/m}}{\text{safe bearing capacity of soil, kN/m}^2}$$

$$\frac{50 \text{ kN/m}}{90 \text{ kN/m}^2} = 555 \text{ mm}$$

The architect's assembly drawing will show the foundations as being 575 mm wide. Unfortunately the standard bucket width for the excavator is 600 mm. The waste allowance that the buyer must make for the additional concrete is:

$$\frac{\text{design waste}}{\text{percentage}} = \frac{\text{width as built} - \text{width as detailed}}{\text{width as detailed}} \times 100$$

$$\frac{600 - 575}{575} \times 100 = \frac{25}{575} \times 100 = 4.35\%$$

The **ordered quantity** is calculated from the as-fixed quantity plus the waste percentage. Further waste allowances must be made for **purchase waste**. The supplier will only deliver in **full loads** or there will be a surcharge. Brick deliveries will be palletised for lorry crane offloading. The as-fixed quantity is calculated and converted into **purchase units of measurement**, in this case bricks rather than square metres of walling. If the foundations are 10 m by 5 m, the **take off** for the facing brick as-fixed quantity will be as shown in Fig 7.66. The buyer now has to convert the **as-fixed quantity** into purchasing units and obtain the **ordered quantity**:

$$
\begin{aligned}
\text{ordered quantity} &= \text{as-fixed quantity} + \text{waste} \\
&= 148 \text{ m}^2 \times 60 \text{ bricks/m}^2 \\
&\quad + 5\% \text{ (design and construction waste)} \\
&= 9324 \text{ bricks}
\end{aligned}
$$

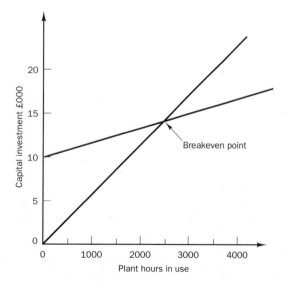

Figure 7.65 Hire or buy decision

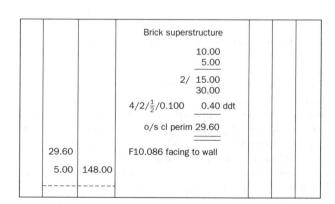

Figure 7.66

The supplier will only deliver in pallets containing 480 bricks, so this will make an extra material waste called a **purchase waste**.

$$\text{number of pallets} = \frac{\text{ordered quantity}}{\text{number of bricks per pallet}}$$

i.e. $\frac{9324}{480} = 19.425$

The supplier will not split the pallet, so the builder has to buy 20 pallets, not 19.425 pallets as required. This is also a purchase waste. Both the design waste and the purchase waste are outside the control of site management. At least the materials are available, but are the materials delivered at the right time?

Material availability

One of the contract conditions was to obtain the specified materials. The Standard Form of Building Contract, 1980, Private edition, makes this very clear. In the contract conditions, clause 8, 'Materials, goods and workmanship to conform the description, testing and inspection' states: 'all materials, goods and workmanship shall so far as procurable be of the respective kinds and standards described in the Contract bills'. The specification in the contract bill will describe the material and minimum quality.

Part of the buyer's intelligence is to know the **lead times** for materials. The delivery period is 14 weeks, so the information control chart will include that information. The weekly action list will be processed and coordinated by the site planner. The buyer's activity is monitored to ensure that the order is placed in time to allow for the on-time delivery of materials, since non-availability of materials could lead to an **extension of time** under clause 25.4 of the JCT Standard Form of Contract. The **relevant event** is described as '25.4.10.2 The contractor's inability for reasons beyond his control and which he could not reasonably have foreseen at the date of tender to secure such goods or materials as are essential to the proper carrying out of the Works.' With such a long lead time it is important that the buyer expedites the deliveries. All key and long lead time materials are monitored through the site planner to ensure that the deliveries match the programme work schedules. Some materials may even be delivered in specific quantities to match the contract programme.

Delivery schedules

The availability of site storage areas will determine the amount of materials delivered. The rate of consumption and the reliability of the supplier are also factors to consider when using delivery schedules. One example of the use of delivery schedules is the estate road construction. The tarmac spreader is the key operation and the delivery of lorry loads is matched to the spreader's work output. The plant/labour balance is calculated using a **multiple activity chart** and the supply of roadbase is delivered as full loads at predetermined times. Another example, showing the use of delivery schedules, involves a housing scheme. The **line of balance** planning technique is ideal for repetitive work and instead of delivering the total ordered quantity the materials are delivered in **house lots**. The following materials and goods are suitable for delivery in house lots:

- windows
- door frames and linings
- roof trussed rafters including ironmongery
- floor joists and joist hangers, straps, etc.
- door ironmongery
- second fix joinery, architraves, skirtings
- kitchen units

An added benefit of this type of delivery is material control. The checker will issue the material in house lots, recording the house number in a record book. The loading out of the materials by the general operatives is simpler and the skilled operatives should have all the materials available at final location to complete the operation. The bonus surveyor can use the delivery schedule to produce the bulk bonus target for issuing to the operatives. The general operatives doing the site clean should have minimum material waste to dispose. However, the production controller will have to be careful when producing the delivery schedules to ensure that all the materials and fixing materials are ordered (Fig. 7.67).

The delivery schedule can also be used as the checklist record for the checker when issuing materials. The checker will also process the supplier documentation.

Documents

The buyer will send a **copy order** to site, and the checker will prepare a file for **bulk basic materials** and **goods**. Bulk basic materials are also called **heavyside building materials**, such as

- concrete
- bricks and blocks
- carcassing timbers
- finishing timber
- roof tiles

On delivery, the supplier will give the checker a **delivery ticket**, outlining the materials and quantity. Once the delivery has been checked for quantity and quality the delivery ticket can be signed by the checker (Fig. 7.68).

Sometimes the supplier will use a transporting company to deliver the materials. This third-party haulier will use a **consignment note** as part of the delivery documentation. Where the delivery requires to be offloaded by crane such as steel reinforcement bars, the supplier will notify the builder of delivery using an **advice note**. The advice note usually allows three days to arrange for offloading facilities.

DELIVERY SCHEDULE: WINDOWS

Prepared by K.C.
Date: 29/8/94

Job no. 1256

Delivery dates	House no.	Window types					Total	Remarks
		C10V	C210V	310V	C212V	C312V		
6 August	1	2	3		2	2	9	
13 August	2	1		3	2	2	8	
20 August	3	2	2		1	3	8	
	Totals	5	5	3	5	7	25	

Figure 7.67

```
                    DELIVERY TICKET
To:    GNVQ Builders Ltd                    Date 12/8/94
       Any College                          Order no. 2324
Deliver to: Housing project
─────────────────────────────────────────────────────────
Description of goods                        Quantity
─────────────────────────────────────────────────────────
LBC Commons                                 2500
Hyload DPC 100 mm wide                      6 rolls
100 mm thermalite shield blocks             450 no.
LBC rustic facings                          9 pallets
─────────────────────────────────────────────────────────
Signed. . . . . . . . . . .
```

Figure 7.68

The checker will enter the delivery note details into a **Goods Received Book**. All the delivery tickets are entered and attached to the **Goods Received Note (GRN)**. At the end of the month the checker will forward the delivery tickets, consignment notes and advice notes to the accountant for payment. Where there is a shortage of delivery a **Credit Note** is raised to correct the error. The credit note is also used to adjust for substandard materials returned to the supplier. Details of the credit note are written on the GRN like a delivery ticket and sent to the accountant with the monthly returns. All the paperwork is in place to carry out the materials control and check on-site waste.

Waste control

The estimator in the unit rate has probably allowed for waste, but this is only an assumption and needs to be checked. Usually the bulk basic materials are monitored each month along with the monthly cost report, and this information is already available for this material waste control. The budget is the estimator's waste percentage in the material constant. The **as-fixed quantity** is used as the basis for the calculations. Stock needs to be physically counted and adjustments made for opening stock and closing stock. The estimator has allowed 2% waste on the ready mix concrete used for the concrete oversite.

as-fixed quantity $6.30\,\text{m}^3$
delivery ticket 01223 $7.00\,\text{m}^3$

The percentage waste is:

$$\frac{\text{delivered quantity} - \text{as-fixed quantity}}{\text{as-fixed quantity}} \times 100$$

$$= \frac{7.00 - 6.30}{6.30} \times 100 = 11.11\%$$

The production controller should alert the site agent to this excess waste. The budgeted waste for facing bricks was 7.5%, but the site agent needs to know the amount of waste actually occurring on site. The monthly report will use the as-fixed quantity in the bulk targets and the delivered quantity will come from the Goods Received Notes. The stock at the end of the month, called the **closing stock**, will be physically measured and the actual site waste will be calculated as:

As-fixed quantity:

as-fixed quantity $\times$ conversion factor
$296\,\text{m}^2$ $\times$ 60 bricks/per m^2 $= 17\,760$ bricks

Delivered quantity:

goods received note total for month   20 000
add opening stock   500
                                       ──────
                                        20 500
deduct closing stock   1500
                                       ──────
delivered quantity used in month   19 000 bricks

$$\frac{\text{percentage}}{\text{waste}} = \frac{19\,000 - 17\,760}{17\,760} \times 100 = 6.98\%$$

The figure of 6.98% is within the budgeted waste.

The monthly data will be accumulated to make a **to date waste** percentage and will form some of the data returned to the estimator as site **feedback**.

Updating the programme

Site meetings

One of the contractual obligations placed on the main contractor, according to the JCT Standard Form of Building Contract, is to 'provide the architect with two copies of his master programme'. Available on site for the architect or the clerk of works must be 'one copy of the contract drawings, an unpriced bill of quantities and the master programme'. The architect will monitor the progress of work and must be notifed as soon as practical of any delay to the work.

The **architect's site meeting** will be an important coordination and monitoring meeting. The design team will be represented and the meeting will be chaired by the project architect. The main contractor and nominated subcontractors will also be present, as will be, in special cases, the domestic subcontractors. The architect's site meeting agenda would be structured as follows:

- Apologies for absence
- Minutes of last meeting
- Matters arising and action taken
- Weather report since last meeting
- Contractor's report
  - labour force
  - general progress
  - reasons for delays
  - claims arising from delays
  - information received from last meeting
  - information outstanding from last meeting
  - information required
  - architect's instructions and variations
  - nominated subcontractor's work
  - nominated supplier's information and progress
- Dayworks
- Clerk of works' report
- Quantity surveyor's report
- Structural engineer's report
- Building service engineer's report
- Completion date
- Date of next meeting

The clerk of works (COW) acts as an inspector for the architect. On civil engineering projects this job would be done by the resident engineer. Clause 12, 'Clerk of Works' in the JCT Standard Form of Building Contract outlines the role of the COW. Any directive from the COW must be confirmed by the architect within two working days. The COW will also keep a site diary and report to the architect every week on progress. The record will include:

- number of main contractor's operatives on site each day, classified by their trade or skill
- number of nominated subcontractor's operatives on site
- weather conditions each day; amount of inclement weather each day
- material deliveries
- drawings received
- discrepancies in contract documents
- directives issued
- work stages inspected
- visitors to site

The builder may convene **daily** or **weekly** site coordination meetings with key staff. The weekly site meeting will be chaired by the site agent. The agenda will be based on the weekly programme sheets and the meeting will discuss

- progress to date
- reasons for delays
- briefing
  - architect's instructions
  - programmes for next week
- coordination of activities
- problems on
  - delivery of materials
  - subcontractors
  - labour requirements and availability
  - plant requirements and availability

The site agent will meet with the individual site forepersons to discuss the **weekly cost statement**. The cost and bonus surveyor will produce the data for this meeting, which is not proactive but retrospective. The costs are at least one week old and any remedial activity to redress adverse trends will take time to implement. The cost data will be produced as the work sections in the bill of quantities. Where there are considerable losses against the estimator's feedout, further investigation must be carried out by the cost and bonus surveyor. Individual gangs may need to be scrutinised about substandard performance against the bonus targets, reasons identified and remedial action taken. Formal minutes are not taken at this meeting but the weekly costs act as agenda items.

Site diary

The site agent will record the following information in the site dairy:

- weather report
- planned labour requirement/actual labour available
- industrial disputes and their outcome
- meetings with safety supervisor
- meetings with union representatives, shop stewards and site stewards
- telephone calls
- visitors to site (unless a visitors book is used)
- confirmation of architect's oral instructions and COW directives

Other vital information is recorded elsewhere for the contractor's quantity surveyor to use in claims preparation, such as

- ground levels, spot levels and trench bottom levels recorded by the site engineer on the location plan
- daywork hours recorded by the general foreperson or trades foreperson on the time sheets
- material deliveries and shortages recorded by the site checker
- plant breakdown time recorded by the cost and bonus surveyor from the plant time sheet
- concrete compression test results recorded by the site engineer
- air temperature recorded by the site engineer

This paperwork is absolutely essential if the main contractor is to secure an adequate return on investment. Part of that administrative procedure will be the weekly programme.

Weekly programme

Based on the works programme, short-term programmes will be prepared by the site planner with the respective trade and general forepersons. The weekly programme target is to achieve 95% of the planned work. Bulk targets ease the planner's work in workloading the gangs to ensure that a full week is planned. The trades foreperson and the general foreperson will monitor and coordinate other activities. Sufficient information must be given to the gang to complete the work. Service gangs need to load out materials in time for the skilled operatives and the general operative service gangs will perform the following duties:

- loading out for skilled operatives
- cleaning up after the skilled operatives
- cleaning up after the nominated subcontractors
- unloading material deliveries

Other operations may be performed by general operatives once specific training has been given. **Builder's work** in connection with the mechanical and electrical contractors is often assigned to the labourer or general operative gangs. The builder's work will include:

- cutting chases for cable drops and light switch boxes – protective equipment must be provided by the builder such as goggles, safety helmet, gloves and masks
- drilling holes through masonry walls – training must be provided in the use of electrical power drills and protective equipment must be provided

Further builder's work will be carried out by skilled operatives. For instance;

- the joiner will drill and notch holes in floor joists, and will provide fire stops at compartment walls and floors
- the bricklayer will make good around pipe penetrations to the masonry work
- the plasterer will make good the plaster around holes and chases

This detail is required at the weekly planning stage to achieve maximum utilisation of resources. The external works gangs are often semi-skilled or trained general operatives. When the work requires skilled operatives such as bricklayers for hard landscaping, the planner will coordinate this activity on the weekly programme (Fig. 7.69).

WEEKLY PROGRAMME

Week ending 20/8/94

Gang: External works T.A.R. + 3 = 4 operatives in gang

Monday	Tuesday	Wednesday	Thursday	Friday
Excavate kerb race and reduce level.	Complete excavation Concrete kerb race	Base course	Complete base Tarmac base	Tarmac base and dressing Clean up
40 bh	40 bh	38 bh	39 bh	40 bh

Total bonus hours = 197bh (bulk target)
Actual hours = 160h

Bonus hours 37bh at £4.00 = £148.00
Anticipated bonus shares = £37.00

Figure 7.69

The **walking ganger** will monitor the performance of this external works gang. The monitoring data should not be in bonus hours but in measured lengths of the path. For example, to maintain the programmed output, the walking ganger will want to know the proportion of the base course that should be completed by the end of Wednesday. The bulk target for the base course was 62 bonus hours, therefore, according to the weekly programme, the proportion to be completed by Wednesday amounts to 38 bonus hours (bh); that is,

$$\text{days output} = \frac{\text{days workload in bh}}{\text{total bonus target}} = \frac{38}{62} = 61\%$$

The total length of path was 120 m. The length of path base course that should be completed by Wednesday normal finish time is:

$$120\,\text{m} \times 61\% = 73\,\text{m}$$

One of the **production controller's** (or planner's) jobs is to assist the site management team to monitor progress. The weekly or short-term programmes are based on the monthly programmes.

Monthly programme

The contract programme is scrutinised to prepare the **monthly programme**. On large contracts there may also be **three-monthly programmes** developed by the site planning team. The method statements are divided into stages of work, and carefully workloaded to achieve maximum use of resources.

The operation 'brickwork' will include more than just laying bricks. The works programme will consider the main operations and the short-term programmes need to consider more detail. The brickwork operation will include:

- facing bricks to outer skin
- cavity with insulation
- block inner skin
- forming openings
  - block and DPC closing cavity at the sill
  - position window frame/door frame
  - reveal block and vertical DPC at jambs
  - lintel over and horizontal DPC
- soldier arch over opening
- block closing cavity at eaves
- bedding wall plate

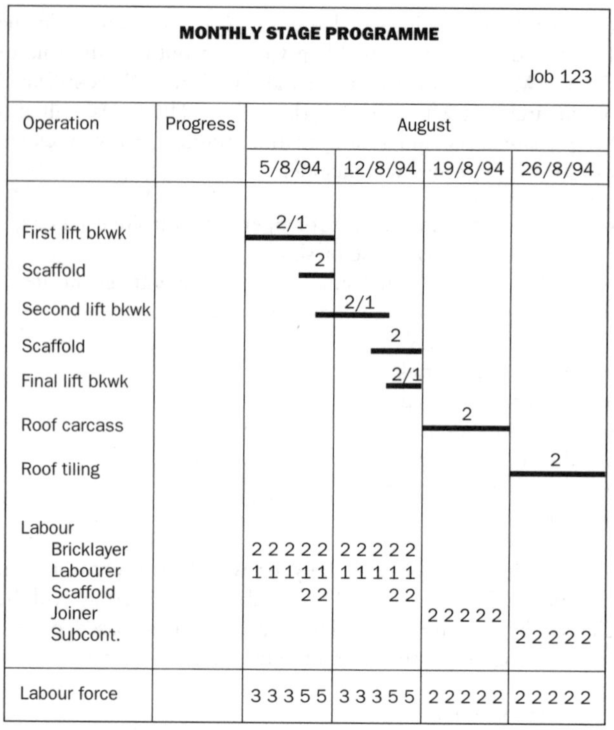

MONTHLY STAGE PROGRAMME

Job 123

Operation	Progress	August			
		5/8/94	12/8/94	19/8/94	26/8/94
First lift bkwk		2/1			
Scaffold		2			
Second lift bkwk			2/1		
Scaffold			2		
Final lift bkwk				2/1	
Roof carcass				2	
Roof tiling					2
Labour Bricklayer Labourer Scaffold Joiner Subcont.		2 2 2 2 2 1 1 1 1 1 2 2	2 2 2 2 2 1 1 1 1 1 2 2	2 2 2 2 2	2 2 2 2 2
Labour force		3 3 3 5 5	3 3 3 5 5	2 2 2 2 2	2 2 2 2 2

Figure 7.70

If resource planning is to succeed, then that is the sort of detail that must be considered by the planner. This will allow overlapping of activities and avoid outpacing previous operations (Fig. 7.70).

The planned performance index would be used for the workloading and the weekly programme would indicate the potential bonus earnings for achieving the planned output. Problems and difficulties are bound to occur, but good planning will reduce the disruption to an acceptable minimum. The planner will review the bonus earnings and monitor actual performance against planned performance. A weekly planning report is prepared and a status report compiled.

Monitoring progress

A contractual obligation placed on the contractor is: 'if and whenever it becomes reasonably apparent that the progress of the works is being or is likely to be delayed, the contractor shall forthwith give written notice to the architect of the material circumstances including the cause or causes of the delay and identify in such notice any event which in his opinion is a relevant event' (clause 25.2.1, JCT 1980). Not only is it good management to monitor progress but the success of the project both contractually and financially depends on conformity with the planning strategies. The initial planning strategies were devised from a set of assumptions based on the contract documents. There may be some divergence from these assumptions – for example, the building control officer has the right to instruct extra depth to the foundations at the inspection stage – and the main contractor has to comply with that instruction. However, the building control officer's instruction must be confirmed by the issue of an architect's instruction. There may also be longer periods of inclement weather than was considered at the planning stage of the contract, and for this and other reasons, it is essential to monitor and update the programme.

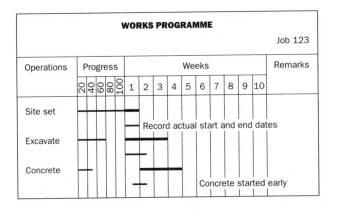

Figure 7.71

Recording of the progress on the works programme is achieved in two ways: firstly, as a percentage and, secondly, by recording the start and end dates of the operations (Fig. 7.71).

Indicating progress on the bar chart programme and completing the percentage progress is easily done, but is the contract actually running to programme? What is the planning status on site? The site management and contracts director will need to know, within a reasonable degree of accuracy, the planning status:

- the release of workforce from other projects
- plant delivery dates, which are crucial to the success of the project
- the signing of subcontracts, stipulating start and finish dates

Other resources are interrelated with this project and a delay in completing the brickwork may delay a new project, that has a **liquidated and ascertained damages** of £1000 per week.

The planning status for a project is calculated in this way. The information that is known and accurate is

- workloading of each operation in bonus hours
- actual performance of the operatives against work study standard times

As an example, we shall establish the planning status for the external works as indicated on the weekly programme. The monitoring period is the normal finish on Monday. The cost and bonus surveyor physically measures the work done (Fig. 7.72).

WEEKLY PROGRAMME

Week ending 20/8/94

Gang: External works T.A.R. + 3 = 4 operatives in gang

	Monday	Tuesday	Wednesday
	Excavate kerb race and reduce level.	Complete excavation Concrete kerb race	Base course
Planned bonus hours	40 bh	40 bh	38 bh
Actual bonus hours achieved	31 bh		

Figure 7.72

The programme in Fig. 7.72 shows a shortfall of 9 bonus hours (bh), but how long will it take for the operatives to complete that shortfall?

The gang has achieved 31 bonus hours in the normal 8-hour day, so the **performance index** can be calculated:

$$\text{performance index} = \frac{\text{bonus hours}}{\text{actual hours}} \times 100$$

i.e. $\dfrac{31}{32 \ (4 \ \text{operatives} \times 8 \ \text{h})} \times 100 = 97\%$

The planned performance index was:

$$\text{planned performance index} = \frac{\text{planned bonus hours}}{\text{actual hours}}$$

i.e. $\dfrac{40 \, \text{bh}}{32 \, \text{h}} = 125\%$

What will happen if the operatives continue to perform at the same performance index?

$$\text{bulk target} = 197 \, \text{bh}$$
$$\textit{deduct} \ \text{bonus hours achieved} = \underline{\ 31 \, \text{bh}}$$
$$\text{work left to do} = 166 \, \text{bh}$$

How long will it take to complete the remainder of the work? If the gang continue at the same performance index the anticipated actual time will be:

$$\text{bonus hours} \times \frac{\text{standard performance}}{\text{performance index}} = \frac{\text{anticipated actual}}{\text{hours (aah)}}$$

i.e. $166 \, \text{bh} \times \dfrac{100}{97} = 171 \, \text{aah}$

With the same gang loading of four operatives, the operation duration will be

$$\frac{\text{anticipated actual hours}}{\text{resources allocated}} = \frac{171}{4} = 42.75 \, \text{gang hours}$$

Taking the working day as 8 hours, the number of days overrun for this one operation will be

$$\frac{42.75}{8} = 5.34 \, \text{days}$$

$$5 \, \text{days} - 1 \, \text{day already taken} = \underline{4.00 \, \text{days}}$$
$$\text{operation overrun} = \underline{1.34 \, \text{days}}$$

The site agent must now decide what to do with the overrun. If the planner had illustrated the planning strategies by critical path analysis, the decision would have been much simpler. If the operation is critical then it must be completed on time. The site agent may ask the gang to work overtime to reduce the projected overrun. Another alternative is to introduce another member into the gang. Both alternatives will incur cost penalties. Overtime working is paid at a premium and, in accordance with the Working Rule Agreement, non-productive overtime payments will be made. Introducing another member into the gang will change work patterns and a diminished return on performance.

Critical path analysis allows the site agent some flexibility over activities and non-critical activities can use the float time to good effect.

The paths are a non-critical activity with a float time of 2 days, so the anticipated overrun of 1.34 days can be absorbed. If production drops further or if there are other delays, this activity might well become critical.

The selection of the planning technique is vital to the success of the project and the contractual obligation on the main contractor is to notify the architect of the impending delay.

Effect on contractual obligations

There are two key dates in the contract signed by the 'employer' (client) and the 'builder'

- date of possession
- date of completion

To reinforce the date of completion the employer may insist on **liquidated and ascertained damages** forming part of the tender and contract conditions. The builder has to complete on time unless there are **relevant events** which legitimately cause the builder to overrun the date of completion. Meticulous care should be taken on requests for architect's details to record the effect of variations on the planned work schedules.

Clause 25, 'Extension of time' in the JCT Standard Form of Building Contract 1980, outlines these relevant events:

- *force majeure* (often described as 'outside the control of the contractor' or 'an act of god')
- exceptionally adverse weather conditions
- loss or damage under clause 22, 'Perils (insurances)'
- civil commotion, strikes or lock-out
- compliance with architect's instructions
- non-receipt of requested design information
- delay on the part of a nominated subcontractor or supplier
- government legislation
- contractor's inability to foresee difficulties at the tender date
- delays by local authorities carrying out statutory obligations
- non-availability of site by date of possession

Even with this list of relevant events the main contractor must 'use constantly his best endeavours to prevent delay in the progress of the work ...' (clause 25.3.4.1, JCT 1980). Hence the use of the information control chart which coordinates the release of

- architect's information
- consultant's drawings, such as services layouts, specifications and nominations

The information received and not available is recorded in the architect's site minutes.

The information control chart also coordinates the main contractor's staff, such as the buyer. Weekly activity sheets are sent out to coordinate the on-time delivery of materials and domestic subcontractors and specific instructions are given on the timing of

- placing orders
- obtaining architect's approval
- delivery dates
- expediting when there are long lead times on material deliveries
- inviting quotes for subcontract work
- placement of domestic subcontracts

All this activity is intended to secure on-time completion of the project by the date of completion.

The contractor's quantity surveyor will be interested in the effects of **variations** to the contract documents. Under clause 13 of the JCT Standard Form of Building Contract the architect is empowered to vary the contract documents. Variation orders may arise through the alteration or modification of the design, quality or quantity of the works as shown in the contract documents, especially

- addition, omission or substitution of any work
- alteration to the kind or standard of materials
- restriction imposed by the employer, such as
  - access to the site or parts of the site
  - limitations of working space
  - limitations of working hours
  - specific order of work

The main contractor is obliged to complete the project by the date of completion and to reduce the impact of variation orders.

If, for example, the building control officer inspects the open foundation trenches and instructs additional digging to sound founding strata, the builder has to comply with this instruction, but requests an **architect's instruction** as contract confirmation (Fig. 7.73).

Now the contractor can complete the excavations and claim **extra payment** for the **variation order**. Clause 13 outlines the method of payment for variation orders:

- as bill rates
- pro rata bill rates
- fair valuation
- daywork rates

The main contractor has been involved in extra work yet must try to minimise the delay. The architect can substitute work and involve the contractor in additional expense. For example, the architect has issued a variation order, as shown in Fig. 7.74, substituting a standard skirting moulding for the special moulding described in drawing A02/123. What stage had the main contractor reached when this instruction was issued? The information control chart had previously highlighted this as a long **lead time** and the production of the special skirting had already commenced. Although no additional work has been added to the contract programme, the main contractor has incurred additional expense due to cancellation of the special order. Clause 25, 'Extension of time' does not reimburse the main contractor, although it recognises that the contract programme has been interfered with by the issue of variation orders. Clause 25 only stipulates

---

ARCHITECT'S INSTRUCTION

Issued by: Ace Designs
Address _ _ _ _ _ _ _ _ _ _ _ _ _ _ _ _ _ _ _
_ _ _ _ _ _ _ _ _ _ _ _ _ _ _ _ _ _ _

Employer: I. Pay
Address _ _ _ _ _ _ _ _ _ _ _ _ _ _ _ _ _ _
_ _ _ _ _ _ _ _ _ _ _ _ _ _ _ _ _ _

Contractor: I. Build
Address _ _ _ _ _ _ _ _ _ _ _ _ _ _ _ _   Serial no. 1
_ _ _ _ _ _ _ _ _ _ _ _ _ _ _ _   Job reference 123
Works: New Street   Issue date: 20/8/94
Address _ _ _ _ _ _ _ _ _ _ _ _ _ _ _   Contract date: 1/8/94
_ _ _ _ _ _ _ _ _ _ _ _ _ _ _

Under the terms of the above contract, I/we issue the following instructions

	OMIT	ADD
Confirmation of BCO dated 15/8/94 extra depth of dig to foundation approximately 500 mm. The depths to be confirmed by the COW		

Signed: Ace Designs

Figure 7.73

ARCHITECT'S INSTRUCTION

Issued by: Ace Designs

Address _ _ _ _ _ _ _ _ _ _ _ _ _ _ _ _ _ _

_ _ _ _ _ _ _ _ _ _ _ _ _ _ _ _ _ _

Employer: I. Pay

Address _ _ _ _ _ _ _ _ _ _ _ _ _ _ _ _ _

_ _ _ _ _ _ _ _ _ _ _ _ _ _ _ _ _

Contractor: I. Build   Serial no. 2

Address _ _ _ _ _ _ _ _ _ _ _ _ _ _ _ _   Job reference 123

_ _ _ _ _ _ _ _ _ _ _ _ _ _ _ _   Issue date: 30/8/94

Works: New Street   Contract date: 1/8/94

Address _ _ _ _ _ _ _ _ _ _ _ _ _ _ _ _

_ _ _ _ _ _ _ _ _ _ _ _ _ _ _ _

Under the terms of the above contract, I/we issue the following instructions

	OMIT	ADD

Omit
 Bill item, page 123, item a
     25 × 125 skirtings as assembly
     drawing A02/56
 	
 Add
     25 × 125 ogee softwood skirting
 	
 Signed: Ace Designs		

Figure 7.74

that extra time can be given. Clause 26 in the JCT Standard Form of Building Contract 1980 is entilted 'Loss and expense caused by matters materially affecting regular progress of the works'. This is the clause 26 through which the main contractor can claim **additional expenses** caused by a **relevant event** – that is, the contract procedure dealing with expense incurred by complying with a variation order.

After all these contractual procedures the main contractor must still complete the project by the date of completion, if at all possible. Certainly good planning, organising and monitoring progress will help to achieve a successful project, which is a project completed on time and within budget.

Self-assessment tasks

1. Prepare a written report describing how the following operations are monitored on site based on the bar chart programme you produced at the end of Section 7.3. Write a report under each of these headings, describing the one method under each heading to describe site monitoring operations:
   (a) labour
   (b) plant and equipment
   (c) materials

2. According to your chosen career path, obtain a copy of the standard contract conditions (or the dominant standard form of contract available). Using the table of contents or textbooks explaining the standard form of contract:
   (a) make notes on the contract clauses which allow changes in:
      (i) design and or specification
      (ii) necessitated by non-availability of materials
   (b) extension of time claims available to the contractor due to:
      (i)   delay in design information
      (ii) adverse weather conditions
      (iii) access onto the site caused by the client or design team

3. Based on your bar chart and the information on contractural changes and delays:
   (a) record on the bar chart the effects on the programme for the following contractural delays:
      (i) adverse weather conditions over a period of 4 days which has seriously delayed progress on a key operation
      (ii) non-availability of materials which has delayed the start of a key operation for 5 days
   (b) prepare a written report for
      (i) the contractor outlining methods available to reduce and accommodate changes in the contract during the contract period
      (ii) the design team on the causes of changes to project planning due to
         – non-availability of materials
         – changes to fundamental design details.

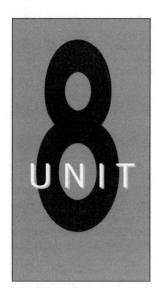

Financing the Built Environment

John Hassall

This unit is concerned with finance and cost control in the construction industry. The areas covered in this unit are:

- finance itself
- contractual arrangements
- finance and cost management

Finance

You should be familiar with the following different types of finance available and understand where each may be used:

- short term, e.g. focusing on overdrafts, bank loans and factoring
- medium, e.g. hire purchase, leasing and bank loans
- long term, e.g. mortgages, bank loans, debentures, share issue, venture capital and grants

You need to be aware of the common sources of finance available and where you can obtain them from:

- financial institutions, e.g. banks, merchant banks, building societies and finance houses
- local authorities, e.g. development funds and enterprise agencies
- central government, e.g. development funds, grants and tax incentives
- others, concentrating on trade credit and share issues

You should understand the reasons for investing in built environment projects. These include the following:

- security of investment
- financial return on investment; maximisation of profit
- meeting social needs' hospitals, roads, schools
- economic planning; infrastructure, area regeneration, employment

Finance usually comes with constraints such as conditions and penalties. You should be aware of the following and their effect on the financing of projects.

- repayment time; limiting your studies to single repayment and repayment over time
- cost of finance; limiting your studies to set-up charges and interest payment
- use of finance; limiting your studies to how the finance can be used
- eventual ownership: concentrating on who owns the development when completed and shared ownership
- penalties for defaulting on payment; limiting your studies to overdraft charges, confiscation of materials and plant, foreclosure of mortgage and repossession and company liquidation
- information about borrower' limited to identification of information a borrower may have to supply to the lender, for example, company history, company plans, financial accounts, cash-flow forecast, schedule of borrowings, relevant personal details for personal loans and mortgages

Contractual arrangements

You should understand why the following are esssential to a valid contract:

- offer
- acceptance
- consideration
- capacity
- validity

You do not need to be able to quote case law.

You should be aware of the documentation, which will accompany contracts for build environment projects concentrating on the following:

- Contract; an appreciation of the current Joint Contract Tribunal Standard Form of Building Contract and the I.C.E. Conditions of Contract
- Contract drawings
- Bills of quantities
- Specifications

You only need to be aware of the general areas, which each contract covers.

You should understand the common procurement methods for projects and how to evaluate them with respect to time, cost and quality.

The major methods are as follows;

- Competitive tendering where design and contract information is produced as a basis for the contractor's bid–
  1. Open tendering
  2. Selective tendering
- Management contracts, where an external organisation manages the project but does not undertake design or direct construction work
- Design and Build contracts, where a single organisation carries out both design and build under one contract
- Partnering contracts where a client selects a contractor on the basis of experience or reputation. Both partners work together on decisions which affect
  1. time
  2. quality
  3. costs of the project
- Negotiated tendering (sometimes subsequent to competition).

Finance and cost maintenance

You must understand the management processes associated with the control of finance during a project concentrating on

- cash-flow
- budgeting
- cost-value comparisons

You do not need to be able to produce cash-flows or budgets of cost-value comparisons but you should be capable of working through them and understanding their implications.

You should be aware of the advantages and disadvantages of using the following different methods of estimating cost at different stages ina project's life

- unit costs
- elemental costs
- measured costs

You should be able to calculate unit and elemental cost elements for projects but you do not need to produce measured costs.

8.1 Project finance

Topics covered in this section are:

- the need for finance
- terms and sources of finance
- types of finance
- liquidity and profitability
- motives for investment
- the conditions associated with the provision of finance

The need for finance

Buildings are expensive items. While this is obvious, many people unconnected with the construction industry have little idea just how expensive. In 1993, one of the major price books used within the construction industry quoted a figure of just over £1.4 million as the average cost of a building project in the United Kingdom. Obviously there are many smaller projects costing a great deal less but equally there are many projects which cost a great deal more: sometimes hundreds of millions of pounds.

The money for the projects comes from many sources. These sources are examined a little later, but let us first look at the different reasons for needing finance:

- The client simply does not have sufficient finance readily available.
- The client has sufficient finance but prefers to use someone else's money and does not want to deplete his own resources.
- It is less expensive to borrow money and pay the interest than to lose the interest that may be accruing from investments.

The client has insufficient funds

It is important to appreciate that, at present, clients fall into two main categories:

- those who require a building for their own use
- those who are having a building constructed in order to sell or lease it on completion to someone else

In both instances, the building may be required quickly and it is impossible for the client to produce the necessary finance in the timescale available. For example, a company may require an expansion of their premises in order to increase production rapidly to meet a sudden increase in demand. In such an instance, providers of finance may be more than happy to lend the necessary finance in the short term because they are satisfied that the increased income resulting from the new production will be more than adequate to meet any loan repayments involved. It must be remembered that construction companies require payment as the building is being built and, therefore, it is dangerous for the client to anticipate being able to make payments to the contractor from his normal income.

The client has sufficient funds

In many instances, the client may have more than enough finance to enable construction of the project to be completed without the need to seek outside financial support. However, if that finance is in the form of:

- investments that would have to be terminated with the resultant loss of interest
- cash that has been earmarked for other purposes, again quite possibly exceptional investment opportunities
- fixed assets that would have to be sold, which may be detrimental to the company's future production

then it may be more attractive to make use of outside finance even though there may be a considerable cost involved.

In many cases, the clients may use some of their own finance and obtain the balance from elsewhere. Indeed, many finance houses insist that the client provides some of the money required before agreeing to provide any loan at all.

The timing of the transaction is often of major importance in determining whether a client uses his own finance or seeks outside money.

It may be less expensive to borrow money

If interest rates are low and the client can borrow money cheaply, and therefore avoid having to terminate investments that may be ready to mature in a few months' time, outside finance is going to be less expensive than using the client's own financial resources.

It is generally accepted that it makes good business sense to be reasonably highly 'geared', i.e. to make use of other people's money rather than one's own, even though it is obviously expensive to do so. Let us now look at both types and sources of external finance available.

Terms and sources of finance

Terms of finance can be broadly divided into two categories: (a) short and medium term; and (b) long term. Short term is considered to be up to one year, medium term, one to five years and long term anything beyond five years. Short-term finance is normally obtained to assist a company with its cash flow and working capital requirements; long-term finance is generally used for investment purposes; and medium-term finance can be either.

Short/medium-term sources

- internal: transfers; profits
- bank loans: overdrafts; other types of loans
- loans: finance houses; hire purchase; merchant banks
- factoring credit: deferred payments to suppliers, subcontractors, etc.; miscellaneous deferred payments; deferred taxation, etc.

Long-term sources

- internal; profits; depreciation
- bank loans; from clearing banks; from other banks, etc.
- share issues; ordinary share issues; preference share issues
- non-bank loans; mortgages; debentures
- grants both from central and local government; government loans
- international; foreign company; foreign consortia; EU grants

Self finance

Although the need for external finance has been explained, it is worth while elaborating on the advantages and disadvantages of using one's own finance as compared with using alternative sources.

- There is no loss of control as far as the running of the company is concerned.
- There is no requirement for any accountability to external bodies resulting from the injection of new moneys.
- The affairs of the company are kept private. This is particularly important when considering larger companies.
- There is no direct cost involved. Costs may be of an indirect nature as mentioned earlier, i.e. loss of interest on existing and/or potential investments.

For the above reasons many clients would never consider using anything other than their own money to finance a new building. Having briefly looked at self finance, let us now turn to the other types and sources of finance. Because the concept of credit is fundamental to the whole area of external finance, it is worth while spending some time considering this topic.

Credit

Credit can be described as the use of time to pay for something, the amount of time provided being more or less proportional to the amount of money charged for the provision of the time involved. Common sense indicates that the longer a party has to pay off a loan, the more he will be charged in interest.

Figure 8.1 illustrates how credit works. As can be seen, credit can only operate successfully if the people who provide money are willing to wait for repayment. If suddenly everyone required repayment at the same time the credit system would collapse.

Only the cash transactions in Fig. 8.1 have to be in a 'balanced' situation. Provided that cash from the bank (in this case £9000) does not exceed cash held at the bank (£10 000), it

does not matter that cheques do not necessarily stay in 'credit'.

The above illustrates that 'cash' within a bank is the key and that obviously it cannot provide more cash than it has at hand. However, non-cash transactions are not constrained in the same way. The time taken for cheques to pass through the banking system is always a number of days, whereas cash is an instant requirement. Since it is highly unlikely that all the bank's customers will want the balance of their accounts in cash at the same time, the bank is able to use that money to create credit in the intervening period. In Fig. 8.1, the bank can invest £9000 of the £10 000 cash, thereby earning itself interest, only some of which will be passed back to customer A, while cheques provided by customer D by the bank, and subsequently to B and C by D, do not involve the use of cash at all, in effect merely being entries on bank statements and accounts.

Trade credit

This is essentially where suppliers provide customers who are part of the industry itself, i.e. contractors or subcontractors, with advantageous trading terms.

Thus a building contractor who has used a particular supplier for many years may be allowed extra time to pay bills.

Customers, such as D.I.Y. enthusiasts for example, would not enjoy such benefits.

Contractors who are not known to the supplier might only receive a shorter period in which to pay bills.

Trade Credit is now a fundamental part of the construction industry's operating processes and contractors are well advised to 'shop around' in order to obtain the best possible trade credit terms.

List of possible trade credit terms;

- extended payment periods – one month
-        – two months
-        – three months
-        – (usual)
- discounts, normally $2\frac{1}{2}\%$ but greater amounts may be negotiated
- early notificatin of special offers
- advantageous bulk-buying arrangements including deferred payment terms

Operation of trade credit

Materials do not have to be paid for when ordered or even when delivered. With trade credit in a period of, at least one month after the submission of the invoice is allowed before payment is required.

As stated above this period may be considerably longer than one month in the case of customers of long standing.

Should payment be made early extra discounts will normally be deducted from the invoice.

Risk

Clearly, lending money is a risky business and that risk is reflected in the amount of interest which borrowers have to pay for the privilege of borrowing the money. Equally, obviously the longer the timescale involved and the larger the loans, the higher the costs.

Additional costs will also be incurred if there is any doubt in the mind of the lender that there is additional risk involved.

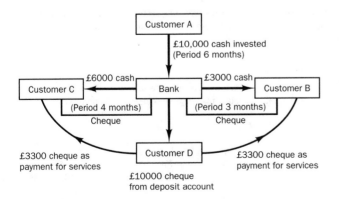

Figure 8.1 How credit is created

Types of finance

Dealing with each type of finance and its source in turn, let us begin with loans.

Bank loans

Overdrafts

This is the simplest form of short-term finance and is an arrangement whereby the borrower is allowed to spend some of the bank's money, usually up to a limit, with constraints imposed in some cases. The cost of the overdraft is usually a percentage charged on the amount of the overdraft at the end of each month or other agreed period. Where there is an established relationship between the customer and the bank, an overdraft facility can be arranged by simply making a phone call. It is very common for building contractors to have an overdraft facility, often of considerable size.

Other loans

Loans for fixed periods of time may be provided by the high street banks, merchant banks, building societies and other types of finance houses. In general terms, the more 'run of the mill' the organisation, the lower the rates of interest, but the lower the ceiling on the loans themselves. It is also the case that the high street banks are unwilling to become involved in very long term loans. Merchant banks

may, in addition to providing the finance, require some involvement in the project after its completion. Loans can be obtained from several different sources, one of the most common being mortgages through building societies and banks.

Share issues

The attraction with this form of raising finance is that there is relatively little direct cost involved. The organisation and implementation of a share issue does cost money, especially with major companies, and in these instances the company in question will employ an external organisation skilled in the arrangement of share issues to carry out the task. However, thereafter there are no direct costs. The drawbacks are, of course, that, firstly, this facility is only available to public companies and, secondly, that, inevitably, there is a reduction in control of the company as soon as external shareholders become involved. The type of share does affect this aspect, as can be seen when looking at Table 8.1.

Nevertheless, the obtaining of finance for major schemes by issuing shares is common. However, such a method of raising finance would not be used for anything other than very large sums of money.

Factoring

Factoring is a means of raising finance in the very short term, when difficulty is being experienced in obtaining it from the

Table 8.1 Comparison of different types of share, etc.

Type of share	Likely profitability	Likely risk	Potential purchasers	Issued by
Ordinary shares	Equal share of profits, also called 'Equity shares'	Along with deferred shares, these are the most risky of shares	1. Rich investors who want big returns 2. Corporate investors, for a balanced portfolio 3. Investors interested in capital gains, rather than revenue profits	Private and public companies
Deferred ordinary shares	Share of profits after ordinary shares have had a proportion of profit; rate will vary depending on profit, etc.	Along with ordinary shares, these are the most risky of shares	They are taken by the vendor of a business when he sells it to a company, as goodwill	General public companies but also private companies
Preference shares	Fixed rate of dividend (say 7%), but only if profits are made	Less than ordinary shares as they *usually* have a prior rate of repayment	Investors preferring security rather than large dividends	Public and private companies
Cumulative preference shares	As above, but if profits are not earned in one year the dividend accumulates and is paid when profits later improve	Less than ordinary shares as they *usually* have a prior rate of repayment	Investors preferring security rather than large dividends	Public and private companies
Participating preference shares	After taking the fixed rate (say 7%), these shares earn extra dividend if the ordinary shares exceed 7%	Less than ordinary shares as they *usually* have a prior rate of repayment	Investors preferring security rather than large dividends	Public and private companies
Debentures (loans to companies)*	Fixed rate of interest (say 6%), payable whether profits are made or not	Minimal	People wanting a secure investment with small return	Public and private companies, if permitted by their articles

*Debentures are not really shares but often considered within the shares area.

more normal channels. Factors lend money to cover temporary short falls, etc., usually at high interest rates for short periods of time.

Factoring is useful if money has to be obtained too quickly to be accommodated by banks or where there are doubts about the stability of the borrower. If the latter is the case, costs will be high because of the greater risk involved.

Grants and loans from government

It is probably better to describe government finance as financial assistance. Help is provided through various aspects of the tax system. Government-aided finance is frequently associated with regional development programmes and grants are made available for investment projects in certain identified industries. To some extent there is an element of 'flavour of the month' concerning the latter, but the steel industry is one to which such grants have applied. Local authorities may also provide financial assistance with such things as sheltered housing schemes.

The Industrial and Commercial Finance Corporation (ICFC) was set up just after World War Two to provide financial assistance for small and medium-sized companies in all industries, and this is still in operation. The ICFC is operated by the major banks and the Bank of England and continues to provide valuable assistance to smaller companies.

The following are some of the types of grant commonly available:

- renovation grants
- minor works grants
- housing and multiple occupation grants (normally referred to as HMO grants)
- disabled facilities grants
- development grants

All of these are available from local authorities. Some grants, such as those required for the provision of basic amenities, e.g. sanitary installations, the provision of hot and cold water, have to be given by the local authority; others are discretionary. Occasionally 100% of the cost of works can be granted; more normally up to 75% of the cost will be given as a grant.

Grants are also available from Housing Associations.

Bodies such as English Heritage also provide grants for work in connection with listed buildings and conservation area work.

Tideswell Church, in the Peak District, received a grant of almost £200 000 for, among other things, a complete re-roofing, while the Crescent at Buxton, in Derbyshire, a Grade One listed building, received a grant of over £1 million also from English Heritage.

Liquidity and profitability

The scale of profitability/risk involved and likely costs of each of the types of finance described above can be graphically illustrated, as shown in Table 8.2. It is not just the degree of risk that is involved but liquidity. Liquidity is simply the degree to which money is easily available. Banks have always been reluctant to make large advances as loans are called over a long period of time and because historically they are seen as the major provider of short-term finance for large numbers of customers.

Table 8.2

Liquidity	Type of advance	Period of loan	Approx. yield (MLR = 10%)	Profit-ability
Increasing ↑	Overdraft	Varies	10–11%	Increasing
	Money at short notice	1–28 days	9–10%	
	Discounted bills	2–months	9–10%	
	Loans to Industry,	12 months	11–12%	
	private to	2–5 years	12–13%	
	government	5 + years	12–15%	
	Special deposits to government	Until repaid	?	↓

As Table 8.2 shows, with overdrafts, profitability to the lender is low, but this is made up for by high liquidity and low risk, liquidity in deposits to governments is very poor at its worst, but has a very high profitability element and virtually no risk (that is, in the UK).

1. **Timescale.** Table 8.2 shows, therefore, that from the borrower's point of view, an overdraft is the most attractive method because of its relatively low cost and high availability. It has the drawback that it is only usually available on a short-term basis. Major finance, available over a much longer term is, unfortunately, only generally available from merchant banks and is both expensive and difficult to arrange because of the high standards of reliability and stability required of the lender by the borrower.

    For several reasons, therefore, the shorter the timescale of the loan in question, the better. This is, of course, why, in many instances, contract periods are kept as short as possible. While this is not always in the client's best interests, haste sometimes produces poorer quality work than is advisable. It is understandable that clients require very short contract programmes.

2. **Amount of finance.** As with timescale from the borrower's point of view, small is beautiful. Small loans are easily arranged, carry smaller interest rates, are more generally available and require the provision of less collateral (if any).

    As mentioned earlier, in order to avoid the problems posed by the obtaining of large loans, etc., one expedient is to spread the borrowing requirements among several sources of finance. Care is needed to ensure that the various providers of the finance are not upset by this method.

3. **The nature of the project.** Because some projects are much more prestigious than others, these are usually more easily financed. In other cases, the potential money-making nature of certain projects makes them also very easy to arrange finance for. It can be advantageous for the providers of finance to have their names associated with high profile projects. It is also not uncommon for say a number of rooms or suites in a newly built hotel to be retained by the financiers for their own use post completion.

4. **The client.** It is to some extent stating the obvious, but some clients experience much more difficulty in obtaining finance for projects than do others. The reasons for this include past performances, how reliable they are considered to be in the future, how likely it is that the project in question will be successful, the possibility of trouble during construction and, by no means least important, the client's representatives. If the financiers do not 'take to' the client, and if there are reservations in other respects, the loan could be turned down. It is

unlikely that an otherwise sound proposal would be rejected because of a personality clash; this would be very poor business, but personalities are certainly important and the borrowers should take great care in the selection of their representatives when attempting to obtain finance.

5. **Involvement of the finance provider.** As referred to earlier, there may be an involvement of the financiers in a simple manner, e.g. by retaining part of the project for their own use. There are situations, however, where their involvement is much greater. It is not unknown for the finance provider to require an input into site meetings during the construction process, a share of profits in the case of developments which are designed from the outset to be money-making, e.g. marinas, leisure complexes, etc., and even in the management of such developments. In such cases, while the major developer will be relinquishing some control, this may be the price that has to be paid to obtain the necessary finance. From the financiers' point of view it is merely a question of protecting their investment.

Lest it be thought that this is very commonplace, it should be realised that the type of situation described above is relatively rare and will only apply in major, wholly commercial, ventures.

Types of client and range of projects requiring finance

While certain types of construction tend to be built using internal finance, there are clients among all types who will require some if not all of their money from an external source. It is true that historically certain types of client have almost exclusively made use of one type of finance, while others have used all types. Table 8.3 lists the most common client types, the buildings normally commissioned by them, and the type(s) of finance most likely to be used.

Table 8.3 Types of client, project and finance

Type of client	Type of project	Finance type
Private individual	House, shop, small workshop, extension etc.	Mortgage, bank loan
Private company	Housing, offices, factories, shops	Mortgage, bank loan, factors
Local authority	Housing, schools, roads, shops, leisure centres	Investments, loans
Central government	Public buildings, defence establishments, roads, etc.	Deposits, investments, IMF loans, etc.
Public corporation/ company	Offices, factories, housing, plants	Loans, share issues
Public utility	Offices, factories, civil engineering projects	Loans, deposits
Consortium	Shopping complexes, city centre redevelopments	Share issues

Other types of client, while not falling exactly into any of the categories listed in Table 8.3 – e.g. health authorities – are not sufficiently dissimilar to warrant separate consideration. Similarly, the sources of finance shown are not exhaustive merely representative. At this point, it is worth giving some indication of how the credit of a typical bank is distributed (see Fig. 8.2).

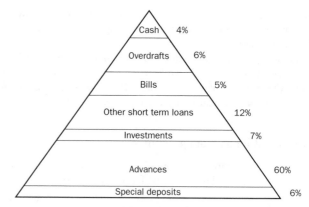

Figure 8.2 Distribution of a typical bank's credit allocation

Motives for investment

If borrowing money is so expensive, difficult to arrange and fraught with problems, why is it done at all, especially when a client has funds of his own? The reasons could be summarised as follows:

- financial return
- securing an existing investment
- meeting social needs (central and local government)
- political reasons (central and local government)
- economic planning reasons

Financial return

Within the commercial and industrial sections of the construction market, buildings will be erected as a means of making money.

As explained briefly at the beginning of this chapter, buildings will be constructed by someone in order to sell off the whole or parts of the building to a secondary client or clients at a profit. These property developers will have very little interest in the project itself, except as a means of producing a profit. The eventual sale of the building, or the revenue realised through lettings, must obviously exceed, by a significant amount, the total sum of the construction, which usually includes the land purchase and the cost of the finance obtained. In recent years many buildings in the commercial and industrial sectors have been procured by property developers who have been unable to sell them and have consequently run into financial difficulties due to lack of income from the unoccupied buildings.

In addition to the above, clients may require premises to be built in order to cope with their own expansion. More buildings equal higher production, equal more profit, is the philosophy in this instance. Before large loans are obtained for such purposes, however, the client will have had to ensure great profits (which is not always the case) and that these profits would more than match the cost of the finance. It must be appreciated, however, that there may be situations where expansion must take place even though profits may not be forthcoming for some time, just to ensure that the company's position in the marketplace can be maintained. In such cases, very-long-term finance may be needed, as well as an understanding and patient finance house. In such a situation, as mentioned earlier, the cost of the finance involved is likely to be high.

Securing an existing investment

It is sometimes the case that after a project has been constructed it then becomes obvious that, in order for that building to realise its money-making potential, other similar buildings need to be provided. Companies are often reluctant to move in isolation. Construction of further buildings – in the domestic field more houses, a shopping precinct, a pub – may be required in order to attract buyers. Without this additional investment, it may be that the original housing phase or office block, factory, etc., may never be sold. While this would indicate that the original market research was faulty, there is little point in crying over spilt milk, and the only solution may be to make another investment in the locality.

Meeting social needs

Within governments, particularly local governments, it is often necessary for projects to be constructed in order that urgent social needs are met. In the past, this has applied particularly to schools, nowadays the emphasis has moved somewhat towards homes for aged persons and sheltered housing for the elderly.

While finance for such schemes will ideally come from income through taxation, etc., the timing of the project may be short term, so that external finance can be obtained. Before this is approved it will have been necessary for a cost/benefit analysis to have been carried out. This will be explained later.

Political reasons

Leaving aside actual needs of a community, it is not unknown for governments to build for political reasons. Many people would argue that the Channel Tunnel is such an example. Many bypasses are constructed because of political pressure. As with the situation described above, the whole of the finance for the project in question may not be available when required and assistance is sought externally. Again the Channel Tunnel is a good example. Here, finance was obtained from many different sources and although very much a governmentally inspired project, there is a great deal of private finance involved.

In such situations, public accountability has to be borne in mind at all stages. It is very unfortunate that in a good many cases initial cost estimates (see later) are greatly exceeded. The Barbican, Sydney Opera House, the British Museum Library and, of course, the Channel Tunnel have all exceeded original estimates enormously. In these cases, doubling of the cost was the smallest increase, 500% not being unusual.

Economic planning reasons

Tied in with the above, in both public and private sectors, it may be necessary for certain construction projects to be completed, which may be non-profit making, before other projects can be completed or even commenced, which will bring prosperity to a company (private) or to an area/town (public). An example of such a project would be the provision of a road system to a housing estate, or an out-of-town shopping area. The local planning authority may have decided that for the economic growth of the town in question, it is necessary for traffic-free shopping areas to be created. Before this can be achieved new road systems may well be necessary, often costing millions of pounds. In such instances, the money may well have to be provided quickly and external finance may be the only answer.

Conditions associated with the provision of finance

Repayment

Different forms of finance are repaid in a variety of ways. Most forms of loan are repaid on a simple periodic repayment basis, monthly, bimonthly, quarterly, etc., the interest involved being included within the repayments. While it is normal for there to be a fixed number of equal repayments, commencing one month after the loan is provided, there are many variations on this theme. The first payment may be deferred (this will normally increase the ultimate total cost of the loan of course), and it is the case with some loans that unequal repayments are made, lower initial sums being gradually increased during the term of the loan.

Mortgages are repaid in a not dissimilar way. Major differences include: the much longer timescale involved, up to thirty years; the fact that the repayments will, usually, be liable to change due to the prevailing bank rate of interest at the time; and the different arrangements that would apply should repayments not be maintained satisfactorily. Some mortgages have fixed repayments but this is now less popular than in the past (whereas initial repayments gradually increasing is gaining in popularity). As far as repayment of an overdraft is concerned, this is often a fairly informal affair, the bank simply asking that the client in question pays off, or at least reduces, the overdraft. The borrower will then make every effort to accede to the banks demands.

The repayment of a factor's loan is straightforward and is required to be by a specified date, together with the fee involved. In addition to providing the finance, the factor will collect debts owed to the company for whom they provide the temporary finance, as well as assisting in the general financial management of the company.

The other forms of financial assistance do not involve repayments in the accepted sense of the term, but special arrangements agreeable to both lender and borrower may be incorporated into loan/advance arrangements.

Eventual ownership

It should be borne in mind that failure to repay loans and advances will result in very serious repercussions. The foreclosure of a mortgage will result in the building in question becoming, to all intents and purposes, the property of the financiers, who may then dispose of it as they see fit. In hire-purchase type agreements, it is not possible for the lender to obtain possession of the item in question, after a percentage of the amount borrowed has been repaid. However, failure to repay would result in litigation for the recovery of the sums involved.

Taxation

This matter has already been referred to briefly, but to conclude this section it is worthwhile looking a little more carefully at the range and impact of taxation, particularly on small businesses.

The various governments since 1970 have introduced measures designed to encourage investment in and consequent growth of small businesses. The fact that there has always been a large number of very small companies in construction has meant that these measures have always been important to the built environment.

Tax relief, in one form or another, and lower rates of corporation tax, for example, have been the main methods employed to help small firms. In the past, raising the bottom limit for VAT payments has also helped and the government has, through its Loan Guarantee Scheme, encouraged banks to finance small firms by guaranteeing most of the loan in question.

For all companies, the prevailing philosophy that property appreciation will attract lower taxes than straightforward income has historically made investment in property attractive. The lowering of property values result in negative equity (the market value of the building being less than it cost its owner), but in a sense this makes the previous statement even more applicable. Since it is still generally accepted that when the economy recovers more or less fully, the property values will rise, so the current investment potential of property is still a major factor.

Taxation needs to be considered when deciding whether to raise capital by share issues or by means of fixed interest loans. The cost in the latter case is substantially reduced when these costs are offset against profits. Obviously, this is not of much worth to a company that is not earning any taxable profits, but it should be borne in mind by companies that are producing substantial profits. It would not be an exaggeration to say that investment in property by means of borrowing of money is used as a deliberate means of reducing tax payments.

Penalties for defaulting on payment

While this has been touched upon above under 'Eventual ownership' there are other penalties which may be applied should the borrower fail to satisfactorily repay a loan.

With an overdraft charges may be levied or, if charges are already being added, these may be increased.

Another temporary penalty may be the acquisition by the lender of possessions, usually materials and/or equipment of the borrower. These possessions would be returned after the repayment situation becomes satisfactory again. Some additional charge would almost certainly be made, however, before the materials and/or equipment could be recovered.

In addition to foreclosure and repossession of a property already mentioned, failure to repay a large loan can result, and has resulted, in the liquidation of the company.

Ultimately, it may be the case that the inability of a company to repay loans, etc., results in the liquidation or bankruptcy of the company. This is often the case when a negative cash-flow situation, referred to later, occurs.

Information about borrowers

While we have already seen that it will be easier for some companies and people to obtain finance than others, it is necessary at this point to indicate what information will be required by the potential borrower. The following should be seen as being minimal, some providers of finance may require additional information

- current assets and liabilities
- potential future development and plans
- the past history of the company
- references
- cash flow information
- ratio analysis information

In the case of personal loans and mortgages, those personal details relevant to the borrower's ability to repay the loan, e.g. current earning capacity, existing financial commitments, job security, etc.

In the case of large long-term loans, it is very likely that company accounts for several years will be required.

Such information as is required will have to be verified.

Self-assessment tasks

1. Examine ordinary, deferred ordinary and preference shares and list the advantages and disadvantages of each to potential investors.
2. Undertake an investigation into the share situation of a number of major construction companies, using newspapers such as the *Financial Times, The Times, The Daily Telegraph* and *The Guardian*. You should compare current share prices and how these have risen and/or fallen over a period of, say, one month. Use a graph to show the variations.
3. Investigate the following and produce a report explaining their meaning, usage and scope;
   (a) debentures
   (b) gearing
   (c) negative equity
   (d) long-term finance
   (e) factoring.
4. Make an examination of various types of government grants, both central and local, to establish the uses which could be made of these within the construction industry. Your report should include values, timescales and the types of users most likely to be involved.
5. Prepare a study of the situations which may result in the foreclosure of a mortgage and/or repossession of a property. This study should include the methods available to the borrower to avoid the occurrence of these situations.
6. Produce reports investigating the financing of:
   (a) a single domestic construction project
   (b) a single commercial/industrial project.
   Each report should include descriptions of the type(s) and source(s) of finance used, the motives for investment and conditions and penalties involved in the finance provision.
7. The British Government (irrespective of party) has always used the Construction Industry as one of its principal economic regulators. Explain how this is carried out.
8. (a) Explain how the formation of a consortium can simplify the process of obtaining finance for a major building project
   (b) Describe the problems associated with this process.
9. Produce a matrix of various forms of project finance and score these forms in terms of cost, ease of repayment, convenience and as many other factors as you can think of. The matrix should be similar in format to Table 8.5.
10. Describe the advantages and disadvantages of using a Share Issue to raise capital.

These tasks all provide opportunities to demonstrate communication key skills. You can also demonstrate Information technology key skills by word-processing your reports and using a spreadsheet to handle the data collected in Task 2.

8.2 Contractual arrangements

Topics covered in this section are:

- the essentials of a valid contract
- the documentation accompanying contracts for construction projects
- the methods of procurement for projects
- the evaluation of the procurements methods described

Contracts

For any contract to be legally valid there are a number of essentials which have to be in existence. These are:

- an offer
- an acceptance
- consideration

In addition, validity itself and capacity have to exist.

Offer

Obviously this is the first requirement for any contract to exist. The offer in its most simple terms can be illustrated by the following example. A person goes into a shop and makes an offer, by, in effect, offering to pay the shopkeeper 27p for a particular bar of chocolate. If the shopkeeper accepts the normally unspoken offer, a contract has been formed. It must be noted that it is not the shopkeeper who is making the offer by putting a price on the item. The putting of a price on an item is called an 'Invitation to Treat'.

In the construction industry the offer is made by the tendering contractor.

Acceptance

By agreeing to receive the 27p for the bar of chocolate the shopkeeper is making an acceptance. Similarly, in construction the employer/client is making an acceptance by agreeing that W. E. Bodgit & Co., will build the project in question for £x million.

Consideration

In the vast majority of cases consideration is money. In the shop example, the consideration is the 27p; in the building example, the £x million. However, there are instances where consideration may be anything which has value to the recipient. Service of some form is a common example of such consideration. One party to the contract may agree to provide goods if the other party provides consideration in the form of digging the first party's garden and mowing his lawn every week.

Capacity

A contract would not be valid in law if either of the parties obviously did not have the capacity to fulfil the requirements of the contract.

Validity

In addition, for the validity of the contract to be adequate in law, the forming of the contract and such things as the quality of the consideration, e.g. whether it actually existed, would have to be clearly established.

Documentation

Although in law it is quite possible to have a contract without any documentation whatsoever, this is not be recommended and even the most minor of construction projects will require a considerable number of documents to be used. Projects differ in the numbers and types of document used, but the following list contains all of those documents used in the construction industry in this country.

- Form of Contract
- Invitation to Tender
- Form of Tender
- Various forms of subcontract
- Bill of quantities

Not all of these will be used and other documents such as letters of intent, specifications may be used as well as or in place of some of these forms. It must be emphasised that the details given below form a very simplistic explanation of the documentation which is likely to be used on construction projects. It must also be emphasised that many projects will have specific requirements of their own, necessitating additional documentation.

Form of Contract

Because of the wide variety of types of client and project, a fairly large number of forms of Contract are commonly used. The following list includes those forms most popularly used and the types of project which would use them.

- Joint Contracts Tribunal (JCT) 80/98 – all types of project
- JCT – Intermediate Form of Contract 84 – projects of a relatively straightforward nature but of almost any value
- JCT Minor Works Contract – for small projects which are also very simple in nature
- GC/WORKS 1 – used for government projects
- JCT Form of Contract with Contractors – Design 81 – the so-called design and build contract for use on projects where both the design of a project and its construction are carried out by the same company
- NEC Family (New Engineering Contract) – recently introduced. Designed to counter criticisms of the existing forms of Contract, which are considered by many to be too complex, especially for small contractors and clients who know very little about both Law of Contract and the construction industry

Table 8.4 Uses of different types of contract

Value of job	No. of jobs for each form of contract								
	JCT 80	Minor works	Intermediate	Fixed fee	Contractor's design	Non JCT mang't CNTs	BPF/GC/ wks 1	JCT 63	Other
Over £10 million	2ᵃ	–	–	–	–	11	–	2	4
	4	–	–	–	–	–	–	0	–
£5–10 million	3	–	–	1	1	5	3	27	–
	1	–	–	–	–	2	–	2	4
£1–5 million	11	–	2	3	9	21	2	10	1
	96	3	8	–	10	0	4	27	5
£250 000–£1 million	12	1	4	–	–	2	1	4	–
	326	22	82	5	21	1	3	43	12
£75 000–£250 000	20	63	42	1	1	–	5	–	–
	335	202	140	–	20	–	4	63	48
Totals	810	291	278	10	62	42	22	178	74

ᵃ Upper figures = private sector jobs.

- Institution of Civil Engineers (ICE) Conditions of Contract – most civil engineering work.

The student is advised to refer to the many books on Contract usage, widely available, for a more detailed explanation of Forms of Contract.

Within building the most commonly used form is the JCT 80, recently updated as JCT 98. Approximately half of all contracts use this form. Within civil engineering the dominance of the ICE Conditions is even more marked. Table 8.4 illustrates the use of the most commonly used forms of contract.

These figures were obtained from a questionnaire carried out by *Building* magazine in 1997, but the distribution of contracts has remained similar to this pattern for much of the past ten years.

Invitation to tender

This is a document, in effect a letter, sent to all tenderers, together with tender drawings, etc., inviting the contractor to submit a bid for the work in question.

Form of Tender

This is the document returned by the tendering contractor to the employer/client or his representative, indicating the sum required by the contractor to carry out the works in question. This is in effect the offer in normal circumstances. The acceptance would be in the Form of Contract or, in some cases by a Letter of Intent.

Various forms of subcontract

These are the agreements between the main contractor and the various subcontractors covering only the works to be carried out by each subcontractor.

Bill of quantities

Usually a substantial document itemising in considerable detail all the works contained in the project in question. This document is priced by the tendering contractors' estimators and this formally forms the basis of the tender figure.

Procurement

There are different interpretations of this term, but a simple definition is the process of obtaining a building. More commonly, procurement is used to mean the process of obtaining a contractor to construct the building.

Again, simplifying things as much as possible, procurement can be by means of one or two methods.

Traditional. The client employs an architect and other consultants for all professional services, a contractor then being employed under a straightforward competitive tendering basis, or:

Design and build. The client employs only one organisation, this organisation carrying out design and all the other professional services as well as actually carrying out the construction work.

There are many variations of both methods. When commissioning, the client must very carefully weigh up the advantages and disadvantages, firstly, of the two main methods and then select the options within that method that are likely to be most advantageous to him.

Let us briefly look at the various possibilities.

- Traditional (competitive)
  - open tendering
  - selective tendering
  - two-stage tendering
  - serial tendering
  - continuation tendering
  - schedules of rates
- Alternative methods (sometimes competitive)
  - design and build
  - package deals
  - negotiated contracts
  - cost plus contracts
  - target tendering
  - management contracting
  - construction management
  - turn-key contracts
  - partnering

Table 8.5 Strengths and weaknesses of procurement options (1 = good; 5 = poor)

Option	Cost	Quality	Speed	Early start	Client involvement	Facility for change	Increase between tender sum and final account
Open tendering	1	5	4	5	4	3	2/3
Selective tendering	2	3/4	4	5	4	3	2/3
Design and Build	4	2/3	2/3	3/4	1/2	1/2	1/2
Negotiated	5	2/3	2/3	3	1/2	3	2
Target tendering	3	2	2/3	2/3	2	4/5	1/2
Two-stage tendering	3	2/3	1	1	3	2/3	2/3
Management contracting	4	1	3	4	2	3	2/3
Construction management	4	1	3	4	2	3	2/3
Continuity/serial tendering	3	2–4	1–3	1–3	3	1–5	1–2
Partnering	3–4	2	3	2	1	1	2

It is important to note that whereas traditional methods tend to involve only the tendering process, alternative methods frequently include the complete contractual arrangements. It is also worth noting that while professional practices may be involved in some of the alternative procurement methods, that involvement is much smaller and less influential. The choice of traditional or alternative may well be influenced by both the source and availability of finance.

All the various procurement methods have advantages and disadvantages and the providers of finance may well have their priorities which lead to the selection of a particular , procurement path. The main tendering/procurement options and their strengths and weaknesses are shown in Table 8.5.

Procurement methods

Table 8.5 presents the most common methods of procurement. Each method is scored on a 1–5 scale for each of the headings listed. For example, the lowest tender sums are normally produced by open tendering. Under 'cost', open tendering scores 1. However, as quality tends to be poor with open tendering, under 'quality' a score of 5 is applied.

There are two things to note with regard to this matrix. Firstly, there is some subjectivity involved and the scores entered have been decided on the basis of the author's experience. Secondly, the table is not exhaustive. It is the author's belief that although there may be some minor differences of opinion concerning the relative merits of the methods, a reasonably accurate picture is shown.

The type of organisation commissioning the building will have their priorities and the source(s) of finance will determine ultimate choice. A few simple examples should illustrate this point.

1. Local authorities must consider public accountability, therefore open tendering, considered to bring about the cheapest tenders, will frequently be the chosen method.
2. A highly profiled public company will be looking for a high-quality building and will be less interested in cost. They may also require some input into design. In such an instance, design and build may be the most advantageous choice.
3. A chain of quick food restaurants will be seeking rapid completion, but also with economy. Two-stage tendering should bring about both of these objectives.

Forms of tendering

We have already looked very briefly at forms of tendering within the procurement process, but it is now necessary to describe these forms in more detail.

Open tendering

An advertisement is placed in various publications inviting contractors who would be interested in competing for the project in question to apply for the tender documents. All contractors who apply can then submit their tender by a specified date and time to the architect's or quantity surveyor's offices. In most cases, the company submitting the lowest tender will be awarded the contract.

This is considered to be the method of tendering most likely to produce the lowest tender figure. It is therefore popular with local authorities and other bodies who have to consider public accountability. Unfortunately, because any contractor may submit a tender, a poor-quality building may be produced, due to the low level of building expertise of the contractor and the low level of price. Another drawback of open tendering is that the actual tendering costs may be high.

Selective tendering

This method is essentially the same as open tendering, with one major exception. As the name implies, the contractors are 'selected', usually by the architect before tendering begins. This ensures that only reputable and competent contractors will be used. This also lessens the cost of tendering and eliminates the waiting period necessary with the advertising aspect of open tendering.

Most architectural practices and property development organisations will maintain a list of approved contractors, which is continually updated. Poor performance on a project will probably result in that contractor's name being removed from the list. Figure 8.3 illustrates the process by which the preselection list is produced.

Two-stage tendering

One of the criticisms of both open and selective tendering is that they are very time consuming. In addition, it is necessary

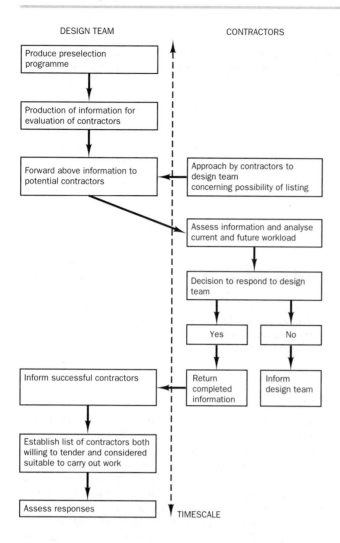

DESIGN TEAM   CONTRACTORS

Figure 8.3 The production of approved lists of contractors (preselection)

for the design of the project to be complete, or virtually so, before the tendering process can begin; to short-circuit this two-stage was introduced. Briefly, it operates as follows: contractors are invited to submit a first-stage tender on the basis of a very simplified bill of quantities or schedule of rates and a set of drawings which are fairly basic. Such a bill of quantities and drawings can be produced long before the design work has been completed.

One contractor, usually the lowest tenderer, is selected on the basis of the first-stage tender.

During further design work, the chosen contractor is able to get to know the design team and the design process. When the design work is complete, a complete bill of quantities can be produced and the contractor will price this in order for a contract sum to be established. The rates used in the original bill are now used in the complete bill so that levels remain constant and the pricing process is completed very quickly, thereby enabling contract signature and commencement on site to occur very quickly.

Serial tendering

During the 1960s, a number of local authorities formed a consortium called the Consortium of Local Authorities Special Programme (CLASP). The objective was to produce a

universal design for schools throughout all the counties represented. Commonality brought with it economy, speed of construction, simplified maintenance and many other advantages. Not only did the actual construction introduce new ideas, but the procurement programme did likewise and contractors were invited to tender for several of the schools as part of one contract, even though the schools were in different locations or different counties. Thus was born serial tendering.

The student can be forgiven for feeling a little confused by the terms 'serial tendering' and 'serial contracting'. In essence, however, they mean the same thing. One refers to the tendering process, the other to the construction process. Both are used to describe the situation whereby a number of contracts are tendered for and constructed by the same contractor.

With the CLASP system, the schools were made up of various combinations of different basic units – for example, there were basic classroom units, an assembly hall unit, a gymnasium unit and so forth. The same tender price for each unit was used for all the projects and negotiation being necessary for all the unique aspects of each school, for example, the playing fields and external works generally.

Today, serial tendering could be used for the construction of a chain of roadside restaurants of the Little Chef, Happy Eater type, or the refurbishment of McDonald type restaurant chains which take place quite frequently.

There are additional problems for tendering contractors posed by serial tendering, when compared to other forms, but we shall look at these later.

Continuity tendering

Again, there is some confusion over the use of the terms 'continuity tendering' and 'continuation tendering' (and 'continuity contracts' and 'continuation contracts').

Continuation tendering is used by some to refer to all forms of tendering that have a 'follow-on' element, for example, the number of different contracts with a serial tender. Another form of continuation tender/contract is the continuity tender. Here one large project is subdivided into a number of phases. Competing contractors then tender on the basis that the winner will carry out the first phase, and if the client is satisfied with the quality of work and progress, etc., the other phases are then awarded to that contractor using the same rates as used on the first phase.

However, some contractors and textbook authors turn the terms continuation and continuity around. Similar problems exist with continuity tendering as do with tendering for a serial contract as far as contractors are concerned.

Term contracts

The third type of 'follow-on' contract is the term contract. This is used primarily for maintenance work. Tendering contractors, usually on a selective basis, are issued with a schedule of works items and price each unit having at best an approximate idea of the probable number of items in question. Such an item might be the replacement of a window or door. The 'term' in the title refers to the period of time involved. With term contracts, therefore, it is known at the outset that the work will end at a certain date.

Target tendering

Target tendering requires elements of a number of other tendering processes to be involved first. Initially, a selected list will be drawn up and the selected contractors invited to tender using a simplified bill of quantities. This is virtually the same as the first stage of two-stage tendering. The lowest tendering contractor will then be issued with more detailed information and a target price will be calculated using this new information and the original rates from the stage where applicable. At this point, the client's quantity surveyor may become involved with the contractor's quantity surveyor, to further negotiate the target sum. This negotiation does not always occur, the target being arrived at by the contractor independently.

From this point onwards, the project operates in a similar manner to a 'cost-plus' contract. All the contractor's costs are recorded and monitored by the client's quantity surveyor. It may be the case that the quantity surveyor is unhappy about some of the recorded costs being included and requires them to be removed from the total. This will normally be because it is the quantity surveyor's opinion that the cost in question has been incurred due to bad management or a mistake by the contractor.

Eventually, a total cost will be agreed. If that cost is higher than the target figure, the contractor will only receive the target figure. If, however, the cost is lower than the target, the contractor will receive a sum normally halfway between the cost and the target. In this way, both client and contractor benefit from the 'good house-keeping'. The client is also confident that the target is the maximum figure that will have to be paid.

It is worth while reiterating that, as with several procurement paths, a number of tendering methods are often employed. Examples of a 'target' calculation are shown below.

Examples

1. Original target cost = £3 470 000
   Actual agreed cost = £3 525 000
   Saving = minus £55 000
   ∴ Amount paid to contractor = £3 470 000
2. Original target cost = £3 470 000
   Actual agreed cost = £3 110 000
   Saving = plus £360 000
   ∴ Amount paid to contractor is:
   $3 110 000 + \frac{1}{2} (360 000)$ = £3 290 000

Tendering for 'cost plus' contracts

'Cost plus' contracts are those in which all the contractor's relevant and reasonable costs expended on the contract in question are reimbursed after careful scrutiny by the client's quantity surveyor. To this cost is added an amount to cover overheads and profit. This 'on cost' is the aspect of the project with which the tender would be primarily concerned. The competing contractors would submit tenders which would concentrate on the size and/or nature of the 'plus'. Some tenders are of a fixed fee basis and, in such a case, the lowest lump sum fixed fee tender would win. Other contracts may be on percentage fee basis. If, therefore, one contractor's tender was 'cost plus 2.5%', this would be preferred to one adding 3.0% and so on. 'Cost plus fluctuating fee' is another method and, in such an instance, the tender may state, 'cost plus 3.0% on the first 50% of the cost, 25% of the next 25% of the cost and 2.0% on the remainder'.

It is important to appreciate that many different types of 'plus' may be introduced into the tendering situation.

Tendering for design and build projects

While it is still the case that between 60 and 65% of projects are built using traditional procurement methods, design and build contracting is steadily increasing its share of the market. With this method of procurement, the client does not employ a design team in the normal way. The main contractor is made responsible for design as well as the construction of the project. This eliminates much of the difficulty experienced with traditionally procured contracts as far as communication is concerned, as there is only one body with whom the client has to communicate.

However, the client may still invite several trusted contractors to tender for the project. In such circumstances, the client will have a number of different aspects to consider. The major ones are:

- *Design* It is highly likely that the various designs may differ considerably. They will certainly differ a little at least.
- *Cost* Similarly, the total costs will vary.
- *Timescale* Unless stipulated by the client, commencement dates, programme periods as well as completion dates will vary.
- *Quality* The standards of workmanship and materials will vary.
- *Payment terms* More and more frequently, different payment terms are being introduced to attract clients.

There are other considerations, but it is obvious that it is no easy task to compare widely differing projects with so many varying factors and it must be uppermost in the tendering contractor's mind that the tender should be attractive in all of the areas listed above.

Tendering for management contracts and similar forms of procurement

During the past decade, management contracting, construction management and project management have gradually assumed considerable importance within the UK construction industry and now account for approximately 15% of the value of work. Because of the large size of the projects constructed using these methods of procurement, it is important to appreciate that, as a percentage of the number of projects built, the figure is much smaller.

With these methods of procurement, it is generally true to say that as far as the client is concerned, it is the management only which is tendered for initially. The tendering organisations submit their tender for managing the contract, all the constructional work being let out to what amount to subcontractors. The management contractor is there to organise, coordinate, plan, arrange payments and generally administer the contract.

The tender may be on a percentage fee basis, e.g. 3% of the eventual contract sum (not unlike a cost plus project), or it may incorporate special features which increase the attractiveness of the tender.

On one project, in the author's experience, the successful management contractor included within their bid, the free construction of a permanent office block for the management and administration of the project. On completion of the project the office block was offered for sale on the open market. The sale price agreed was substantially higher than the construction costs and this profit (anticipated at the tender stage) had enabled the contractor to submit a much lower tender figure than the other contractors. Obviously, there were risks involved. If the office block had not been sold, or had to be sold at a much lower price, a large loss would have been incurred. It is this kind of inventiveness, however, that can often make a tender successful.

Partnering

A relatively recent introduction in the construction industry, partnering concentrates on cooperation and the avoidance of confrontation. The client selects a contractor on the basis of reputation and, probably, past experience, this experience being very positive. While it is necessary for a formal contract to be entered into, decisions, both of major and minor natures, are taken by both 'partners' together. This is particularly so with issues such as timescale, standards and, of course, costs. In this way there is the avoidance of 'blame' should things not work as smoothly as was hoped. As both parties agree to the decisions made there is no point arguing as to what should have been done and both parties concentrate on finding solutions to the problems encountered. As there is a great deal of discussion and working together fewer problems should occur anyway.

As far as the client's selection of his partner is concerned, there may be the requirement for interested contractors to make a presentation to the client. However, there is no competition in the normal sense of competitive tendering.

Self-assessment tasks

1. Describe the process of setting up a contract within the construction industry and give examples where applicable.
2. Investigate:
   (a) open tendering and
   (b) two-stage selective tendering
   and explain where each would be suitable.
3. Define 'public accountability' and explain how this can be ensured by the use of open tendering rather than any other method of procurement.

---

4. Select a method of procurement for each of the following projects, justifying the choice in each case:
   (a) An aged persons' home for the South Beds District Council, valued at approximately £860 000 to be completed in two years' time.
   (b) A housing development of 40 dwellings for Milton Keynes Development Corporation, value approximately £1.8 million, to be completed in three years' time.
   (c) The conversion of an existing office block in north London into a recording studio for a private client, to be completed in eight months' time.
   (d) A factory for a private food-manufacturing company in Manchester, total value £3.25 million; total time available from the client approaching the architect with the brief to occupation, 15 months.
5. In recent years new procurement methods have been introduced and the use of these methods continues to increase steadily. Explain why this is, and provide examples of clients and projects most likely to be procured by non-traditional means.
6. Explain how partnering differs from one of the following methods of procurement:
   (a) management contracting
   (b) turn-key contracts
   (c) design and build
7. Compare any two of the following forms of contract and suggest types of project where each of the contract forms would be the most suitable:
   (a) JCT 84 Intermediate Form of Contract
   (b) JCT Minor Works Contract 1980
   (c) JCT 98 Standard Form of Building Contract
   (d) ICE Conditions of Contract.
8. Describe the main advantages and disadvantages of two-stage tendering to:
   (a) the client, and
   (b) the contractor.
9. Give at least four different forms of 'consideration' which would be acceptable as a valid essential of a contract
10. Explain the circumstances in which a contract, using drawings and specification, would be preferable to the use of a full bill of quantities to
    (a) the client, and
    (b) the contractor

8.3 Financial and cost management

Topics covered in this section are:

- the management processes for the control of finance during construction projects
- the methods available for the determining of estimated costs of construction projects
- the appropriateness of the different methods of cost estimating to the different stages of construction projects
- the calculation of project unit and elemental cost estimates

Included within these topics are the following:

- cash flow
- budgeting
- cost centres

Management processes

These will differ for different types of organisations. With public organisations – for example local authorities – public accountability will be of major importance, but will be of no importance whatsoever for totally private organisations.

Organisations in the middle, e.g. public companies, will have to provide sufficient accountability to satisfy their shareholders, and trusts are in almost the same situation as local authorities. Let us first categorise organisations into:

- purely private organisations
- totally public institutions
- 'in-between' organisations

It is important to appreciate that the different types of organisations being considered will have widely differing objectives. While making a profit is probably the major objective of private and public companies, profit itself will be of very little importance to many other organisations. It is true that they too will have to avoid making a loss in most instances, but that is by no means the same thing. What is important to all types of organisations, however, is cash flow.

Cash flow

If an organisation does not consider cash flow as the most important factor in its operations, then financial control is not being exercised, and unless extraordinarily good fortune attends that organisation, it will fail.

It is very possible – and indeed happens quite frequently, especially during a recession – for a company to be operating profitably, i.e. making more money than it is spending, and yet go bankrupt. If income to which the company is due is not received in sufficient quantities at the right time, to at least match the expenditure that organisation has to pay, then that company will fail even though each of its operations may have made a profit. Profits on paper are worthless if they cannot be obtained. It is just as important, therefore, for a company, its contracts and its overall operation for that matter, to operate with a positive rather than a negative cash flow as it is for that company and those contracts to make a profit. Surplus cash resulting from positive cash flow can be used for investments and therefore make profits indirectly. These profits can often exceed losses made in contracting and general operating.

Obtaining positive cash flow

Positive cash flow is where money coming in exceeds money going out, and this situation is unlikely to be established by accident. Estimators and surveyors within contracting organisations can do a great deal to improve cash flow, and ways in which this is achieved can be summarised as follows.

- making adjustments to various parts of the tender, including loading the rates (estimator)
- maximising income and minimising expenditure on contracts (surveyor).

In addition, management working in conjunction with the buying department and the surveyor can improve cash flow by means of a careful use of time.

Estimator's role

Let us first consider the role of the estimator in the cash flow discussion. By making adjustments within the bill of quantities to unit rates, preliminary sums and profit allocations, the estimator is able to ensure that early money is generated for the contractor. This is illustrated below.

Obviously, at the end of the contract there will be less money coming in than was originally intended, but then it is hoped that the early additional positive cash flow will have brought in a sufficient return on investment to more than make up for the reduced income at the end of the project.

Similarly, adjustments made to the preliminary sums, e.g. increasing the value of the setting-up site items and reducing the amount for the cleaning of the project will have the same effect. Finally, disproportionately allocating the overhead and profit percentages can also improve early cash flow.

It is important to emphasise, however, that such processes carry a considerable element of risk and should not be carried out without the approval of senior staff within the contracting organisation.

Example

In a typical contract, let us say that there are 12 000 cubic metres of excavation. The estimator has calculated a rate of (say) £5.50 per cubic metre as being necessary in order for the contractor to make a profit of 50p per cubic metre. In theory, therefore, the excavation will produce a total profit of:

$$12\,000 \times 50p = £6000.$$

Similarly, at the end of the job there is an item of emulsion painting to plastered walls. The total area in question is 18 000 square metres and the rate the estimator has calculated is £3.75 per square metre, again to produce a profit of 50p per square metre.

The potential profit is therefore:

$$18\,000 = 50p = £9000.$$

Now to bring in early money, thereby improving the cash flow, some or all of the profit on the painting could be taken from the finishing section of the bill of quantities and added to the excavation section.

$$\text{rate} = \frac{£9000}{12\,000\,\text{m}^3} = 75\text{p/m}^3$$

$$£5.50/\text{m}^3 \text{ (original rate)} + 75\text{p/m}^3 \text{ (painting)}$$
$$= £6.25/\text{m}^3 \text{ for excavation.}$$

This will have the effect of bringing in an extra £9000 very soon after the job has commenced without increasing the tender figure. It also has the added bonus that if the quantity of excavation should increase (which is not unusual), an extra 75p will be recovered for every extra cubic metre excavated.

Surveyor's role

As the importance of cash flow has been increasingly appreciated during the last two decades, so the pressure on contractor's surveyors to maximise incoming finance and minimise outlay has also increased. The major area of income is through interim valuations while expense is incurred primarily through payments to subcontractors and to suppliers of materials.

In order to make cash flow as positive as possible, it is necessary for the contractor's surveyor to persuade the client's quantity surveyor to include in the valuation every penny to which the contractor is entitled. The full value of variation works (required by architect's instructions, etc.), materials on site and materials off-site which have been identified as being specifically for the project in question, must be included in the valuation.

In point of fact, the majority of contractors' surveyors will endeavour to exaggerate such values but that is beyond the scope of this chapter, and not completely honest!

On the other hand, the surveyor must ensure that subcontractors are only paid the minimum. This means that their applications for payment will have to be very carefully checked as it is by no means unknown for subcontractors to inflate their applications too! The main contractor's surveyors will do their utmost to hold onto payments to their own subcontractors for as long as possible.

With the frequency of bankruptcies in the construction industry, it is important for contractors to be careful that they do not overdo the late payment of subcontractors and suppliers. Reluctance to pay is one indication that a company is in financial difficulties. If this is suspected, a contractor may find the client making excuses for holding onto payments, credit is suddenly difficult to obtain and before long the company is in genuine financial difficulty.

Cash flow forecasting

In the same way that paper profits which cannot be obtained are of no use, so a sudden positive cash balance which arrives unexpectedly cannot be utilised as effectively as if it was known about in advance. It is very important, therefore that the cash flow on a contract both for client and contractor can be predicted as accurately as possible. Only in this way can proper use be made, as far as investments are concerned, of 'spare' cash.

While forecasting anything within the world of finance is notoriously difficult, the cash flow on most projects follows a fairly predictable profile. This profile has come to be referred to as the *S* curve, simply because it is a lazy *S* in shape, as illustrated in Fig. 8.4.

Clearly, the five months from the fifth month onwards are much more productive than the previous five months. The client would therefore need to ensure that he has much more finance available during this period than before it.

Equally obviously, the contractor can expect to receive larger payments during this period and this would be the time that he may be able to anticipate some investment possibilities of his own.

It is important to realise that whereas the client cash flow on a contract is always negative, that of the contractor is both negative and positive. One of the clearest ways of depicting a contractor's cash flow on a project is by means of a 'saw-tooth' diagram, as shown in Fig. 8.5. Unfortunately for the contractor, although a valuation is usually carried out at the end of each month, the client is normally allowed 14 days to pay after the interim payment certificate is issued. Since this process takes several days, it will normally be about three weeks after the end of the month before payment is received. Income is shown at weeks 7, 11, 15, etc., on Fig. 8.5.

Expenditure on a contract is more or less continuous, as shown by sloping lines, whereas payments are in single lump sums, as shown as instant vertical lines.

It is now time to turn to another very important financial management process; budgeting.

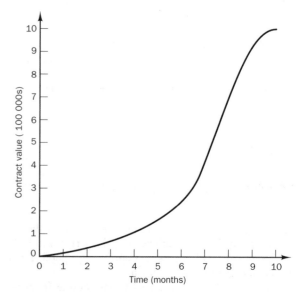

Figure 8.4 Cash flow profile: the S curve

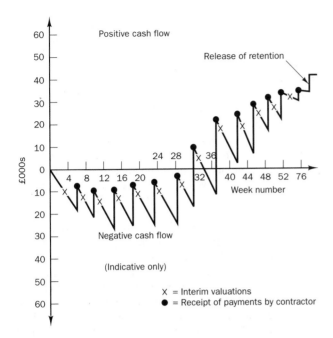

Figure 8.5 Saw-tooth diagram

Budgeting

This can be defined as the **forecasting** and **monitoring** of both **income** and **expenditure**.

It is important to note particularly all four emboldened words. For many people, budgeting is seen merely as the allocation of anticipated income, the 'let's see how we can spend our money' approach. No attempt is made to make adjustments to the budget if income is different to that expected, either greater or smaller, or to relate the actual expenditure to income. It may seem obvious that all aspects above are considered, but it is by no means universal practice for the above definition to be applied.

The size and complexity of a company's financial operations will obviously affect the budgeting process and many small firms have need of only relatively simple budgeting, but budgeting needs of large organisations are enormous.

Space does not permit more than a passing glance at types and uses of key budgets, but these can be listed as:

- sales/revenue budget
- production budget
- buffer budget
- departmental budgets

The sales/revenue budget is the major controlling budget and the other budgets listed are produced so that the sales/revenue budget, which could be called the master budget, is as accurate as possible.

Each departmental budget could include: selling, marketing, administration, research and development, distribution, finance costs, plus areas specific to their department.

Budgeting carries with it many problems and in this brief overview of the subject, we should include a list of the major problems.

- the unpredictability of most aspects
- the fact that the more complex the process the less accurate it is likely to be

- the general perception of budgeting – the 'is it worth the trouble?' approach
- the whole area of credit and its problems
- the actual cost of the preparation of budgets
- the timescale and the obsolescence of the information
- market changes

In association with budgeting there is another important aspect of cost control: that of cost centres.

Cost centres

We have seen that it is very important to be able to compare how we spend money with how we anticipated spending it. To enable us to do this more easily, it has been found to be worth while introducing a system of cost centres. In essence, this is simply a system whereby all a company's financial expenditure and income is allocated to specific categories or centres. Usually, each centre is given a number and in the case of larger organisations each cost centre is subdivided if it is felt that the centre is too wide to be controlled accurately. The subdivisions may themselves be further subdivided if it is considered that the subdivision is still too wide. Table 8.6 is a very simple example of a cost centre system.

In addition to the general cost centres listed in Table 8.6, it is almost universally the case now that contractors allocate a cost centre to each contract, this then being subdivided in accordance with the general cost centres operating throughout the company. Contract numbers may well be in the form of a prefix. Cost centre 3033 would therefore indicate that the cost in question is a payment to a nominated subcontractor on contract number 3.

In terms of controlling costs, it is a relatively simple matter for someone to check, for example, the expenditure on fees to consultants without spending time sorting these payments from many other unconnected transactions. Obviously, such systems lend themselves to computerisation and most systems can indicate in seconds the information required.

Table 8.6 Cost centres and typical subdivisions

Number	Description
01	Materials for general use
02	Salaries
03	Subcontractors' payments
04	Plant
05	Maintenance
06	Company investments
07	Assets
08	Staff expenses
09	Training
010	Research and development

		Subdivisions
02	Salaries	021 Head office staff salaries
		022 Hourly paid workers' wages
		023 Directors' salaries
		024 Fees to consultants etc.
03	Sub-contractors payments	031 Domestic subcontractors
		032 Labour on subcontractors
		033 Nominated subcontractors
		034 Contra-charges domestic etc.

While many major organisations operate other techniques for controlling costs – for example, ratio analysis – we must move on to consider the methods by which finance enables design and construction to evolve.

Finance and design

The fact that many clients have relatively little clear idea of what they require in their new building makes the designer's job even more difficult. It is vitally important, therefore, that clients are made aware at the outset that the design process is often long and expensive.

Since it is highly likely that the professional fees on a building contract will exceed 10 per cent of the eventual contract sum, it will be necessary for a client anticipating building costs of £10 million to obtain at least £11 million.

In order for the architect/design team to fulfil their obligations satisfactorily, they need to know that the client will appreciate the necessity for there to be changes in design long before the project is finalised. It is often the case that many such changes occur during the early stages in design as the architect and quantity surveyor attempt to match the client's requirements with his available budget. There are many techniques which are available for the **approximate estimating and cost planning** stages of a contract and although we shall be looking at them in a little more depth later in the chapter a list of the more common estimating methods used is given below.

- square metre cost
- user unit cost
- cubic metre cost
- cost models
- elemental cost planning (not really estimating)

Other less common methods include the storey enclosure method and parametric cost analysis.

It is certainly the case that in the first instance the original design may be too expensive for the client when the initial approximate estimate is calculated. This will result in one of two things:

- the client will like the design so much that he will agree to the anticipated higher ultimate cost, or
- the client will be unwilling to raise further finance and the architect must then redesign the scheme in order to lower its cost

It is possible that the architect will produce several designs before obtaining the client's approval of one. The above process could still result in a cost beyond the client's budget, so further redesign may be necessary.

Contractor's costing

It is important at this point to refer to the contractor's costing process. While it is obviously very important for the client to be kept fully informed of the actual and likely costs of the project at all times, it could be argued that it is even more important for the contractor to be aware at all times of exactly how much he needs to be paid in order not to lose money on the contract. Without accurate costs from subcontractors, for example, he will be unsure of how much

to charge the client for any extra works carried out by either subcontractors or his own workforce. It is also essential that the contractor knows how much a contract is worth to him at any time, i.e. the actual value of the project.

For various reasons, the amounts paid to the contractor through the valuations may not be the amount the contractor is entitled to. Under-, or more likely, over-valuing may have occurred and if this is the case it will be necessary for a document called a **cost/value reconciliation** (CVR) to be produced. This is in a sense the equivalent of the client's cost report, but it concentrates on comparing the actual cost of a project with its actual value. For this to be of any real use, both value and cost must be accurately calculated. In addition, they must be compared at exactly the same time, i.e. on a given day. Obviously, to compare the costs of a project up to and including, say, 20 August, with the value at 25 August will produce an artificially optimistic figure.

A number of problems exist with CVRs. As mentioned earlier, most contractors' surveyors are well aware that they will be expected to 'maximise' the monthly valuations. This may well lead to over-valuing. In the case of a contract which is not particularly profitable, to reduce the valuation figure to the true by deducting the amount of the over-valuing will show the contract in an even worse light financially. There is considerable temptation in such a case to lessen the deduction for the over-value in the hope that things may improve in the future. In truth things rarely do improve; indeed they often worsen and this makes the situation much worse.

Cost estimates and specifications

The ultimate cost, that is to say how much the eventual cost to the client of the completed project varies from the original estimate, will depend on a number of factors, the most significant of which is the specification. The specification will influence the cost estimate in two major ways. Firstly, the level of specification and, secondly, its depth.

Example A

Joe Soap is going to buy a new car. He decides that he wants a car with a top speed of 140 mph, a 0–60 mph acceleration time of 6 seconds and every conceivable accessory, air conditioning, ABS brakes, CD player, etc. He has £10 000 to spend. Joe is going to be disappointed. He will not get a new car of that specification for that amount of money.

Example B

Frank Plank and his wife decide that they want to move house. They tell the estate agent that they want a three-bedroomed detached bungalow. How much will they have to pay? In addition to knowing that the desired property has to have three bedrooms, be detached and have one storey, the estate agent will need rather more information if he is to provide Mr and Mrs Plank with a reasonably narrow band. From the information so far provided, the estate agent will find it difficult to be more specific than saying that the cost will be between £70 000 and £150 000. That will be of very little use to Mr and Mrs Plank. The location, size of bedrooms, number of bathrooms, form of heating, whether or not double-glazed, quality of fittings, whether or not there is a garage, etc., is secondary information, but is clearly necessary.

Level of specification

The level of the specification will set the standard of the project and hence its cost. Let us use simple examples to illustrate this.

In example A, the detailed information provided by Joe was sufficient for him to be told that no such new car existed. In example B, the amount of secondary information provided enables a more accurate figure to be quoted.

In the same way, the more comprehensive the client's brief to the architect, and subsequently the more detailed the specification used by the architect in his design, the more accurate will be the quantity surveyor's cost estimate, and, incidentally, the easier the task. In a major UK project completed some ten years ago, the quantity surveyors produced a cost estimate for the services package (the project was under a management contract) using minimal information, of just under £20 million. The successful tender figure for the package was slightly over £11 million! It was fortunate for all concerned that the inaccuracy was the 'right way round'!

The client would not have been amused if an additional £9 million had been required! The cause of the inaccuracy was solely the scarcity of accurate information.

Depth of specification

In the above examples the information, though relatively brief, was sufficient to provide reasonable upper and lower cost limits. In much the same way, the information provided by the client to the architect in his brief – overall size of building, number of offices required, the location, time constraints, etc., and probably some indication of the quality level – will help the architect and quantity surveyor to produce initial cost estimates sufficiently accurate to indicate whether the client's budget is more or less sufficient or hopelessly inadequate. It will now be up to the architect to choose a specification that will much more accurately fix cost: the types of facing bricks, roofing tiles, floor wall and ceiling finishes will be chosen, method of heating and ventilating, degree of sophistication in the sanitary provisions and standard of landscaping for approval by the client.

Again the use of examples will help to illustrate this. Facing-bricks vary in cost from about £250 per thousand (although there are some cheaper), to more than twice that figure. This difference could make a 30–40% difference in the cost of the external walls. Turning to the floor finish, the cheapest floor finishes, e.g., thermoplastic tiling, will cost less than £10.00 per square metre, whereas marble flooring will be up to 10 times that figure in some cases. Emulsion-painted plaster to walls is approximately £8.00 per square metre and, at the other end of the scale, individually designed ceramic tile schemes can cost up to £200.00 per square metre.

Leaving aside such dramatic examples as these, a specification which details the type of mortar to be used, all the tolerances to be achieved and standards of workmanship necessary in all areas will leave very little room for possible disputes later which could, in the case of a poorly detailed specification, lead to extra costs being borne by the client.

As the project progresses, it becomes easier to predict costs because more and more of the design becomes 'frozen' as it is called, i.e. fixed and unlikely to be changed.

It is true that the construction industry is plagued with changes in projects, but the more detailed the specification, the less likely that large numbers of changes occur (which almost always leads to the client paying more). Delays in completion are also likely, which may also add even more cost!

Methods of calculating the approximate cost of the project

Although there are many methods of approximate estimating, a number of them are so seldom used nowadays, as to be only of historical interest, while others can only be usefully used in relatively few situations. The main methods are:

- superficial floor area: cost per square metre
- volume: cost per cubic metre
- user/unit method
- parametric cost analysis
- storey enclosure method
- cost models

Cost per square metre

This is by far the most popular method of estimating the cost of a building. As costs of construction per square metre of floor area are generally available for all types of buildings, it is a simple matter to find similar buildings to the project being designed and ascertain the costs per square metre of these buildings. A likely cost for the new building is assessed from the information available and this figure is multiplied by the number of square metres of floor area in the proposed building.

Example

Floor area of proposed building $= 1250\,m^2$
Cost/m^2 of similar buildings very recently having been built
$\quad = £620, £645, £595, £617$
Average cost $= £619.25$
Estimated cost of proposed project $= £619.25 \times 1250$
$\qquad\qquad\qquad\qquad\qquad\qquad = £774\,062.50.$

To this figure, would need to be added any allowances for inflation, different locality, different standard of finishes, etc.
In some cases, of course a deduction may apply.

Cost per cubic metre

The procedure with this method is virtually identical to the superficial area method, except that the heights of storeys, etc., may be accurately known. Otherwise the calculations including the necessary adjustments are the same.

User/unit method

This method takes the anticipated number of users (e.g. school pupils) or units (hospital beds) and multiplies this number by the cost of providing 'a school place' or a 'hospital bed', calculated for other similar projects.

Example

Project: 800 place upper school construction costs for other recently completed similar sized school (per pupil) = £8950, £9000, £8770, £9550.
   Average £9092.50
   Total cost = 800 × £9092.50 = £7 274 000.00

Again the above adjustments would need to be added. In the case of schools, the cost of specialist equipment, laboratories, computing suites, gymnasiums, etc., would also have to be added as these vary greatly from school to school.

Parametric cost analysis

As the name implies, the number of parameters are established and buildings of similar size and nature are selected. Their costs are analysed and the costs applying particularly to the parameters being used are applied to the proposed building. As with other methods, the timescale needs to be adjusted, but since the parameters chosen will reflect similarity, there is less need for adjustments in other directions than with the above-mentioned methods.

Storey enclosure method

In this method, the number of storey enclosure units (SEUs) is calculated and the corresponding number of SEUs calculated for the buildings being used as guides. Their costs per SEU are then obtained on average cost per SEU arrived at, and this figure is multiplied by the number of SEUs in the proposed building.

Cost models

With this method (a much more recent innovation than the methods described above), careful research is carried out to find buildings that are so similar to the one being proposed that they can be used as models for the costs of the new building. Clearly, no two buildings are identical and the quantity surveyors will identify minor differences between the two buildings and make any necessary adjustments.

RIBA Plan of Work

When producing the various cost estimates for a project, each one being more accurate than its predecessor as more information becomes available, it is useful to link the various estimates with the different stages of the Royal Institute of British Architects Plan of Work.

Thus, at Stage 1, all that will be known is likely to be the probable floor area and some idea of the standard of the building. An initial cost estimate based on a simple building cost per square metre of floor area is all that will be possible.

Later, when, say, a sketch scheme has been approved, more accurate methods can be employed. Obviously there is no point using a cost estmating method which is complex and which requires a great deal of information if that information is not available.

Costing categories

It will be worth while at this point to categorise the various methods of costing. These are:

- unit costing
- elemental costing
- measured costing

Unit costing

This is where the units of work as found in a bill of quantities are costed individually. These are referred to as unit rates. In normal circumstances, each unit rate will have a number of constituent parts, e.g. labour, material, plant, sundries. Examples of these are: brickwork and carpentry items. Others may have only a labour constituent, for example, excavation by hand items. There are also some items that have only a plant constituent, e.g. removal of excavated material to spoil heaps.

Normally the unit rates in question are analysed and each part priced in accordance with statistics from other projects or from the personal experience of the person doing the costing, or, more often than not, a combination of the two. A number of price books are published and revised annually, which are useful for this process. They should be used with care, however, as they tend to be rather general in their approach. Examples of a unit rate being analysed and costed are shown in Table 8.7.

In the table, very accurate figures have been used and such examples would be found in a contractor's estimate. For approximate estimating purposes, unit costs of probably £70.00 or £80.00 would be used for the concrete item and probably £20.00 for the brickwork item. Also, whereas the items in a bill of quantities which differ slightly from each other would be priced differently by the contractors to reflect

Table 8.7 Costing and analysis of a unit rate (per m³)

Item	Labour	Material	Plant	Sundries	Total
Reinforced concrete grade 25 N/mm² filled into formwork in walls not exceeding 100 mm thick	4.30 h @ £6.80 = £29.24	£45.50	£1.25	–	£75.99
Common bricks BS 3921 @ prime cost sum of £130 per 1000 in (1 : 2 : 9) mortar in skins of hollow walls 102.5 mm thick	1.30 h @ £7.20 = £9.36	£8.45 –	–	£1.10 –	£18.91 –

those differences, the items in the approximate estimate would be priced at the same rate (see Table 8.8).

Table 8.8 Comparison of unit rates and an approximate estimate (per m³)

Item	Contractor's unit rates	Unit rates in approximates estimate
Reinforced concrete in-situ lightweight concrete: 20.5 N/mm²; vibrated in walls exceeding 450 mm thick	£83.94	£86.00
Reinforced concrete in-situ lightweight concrete: 20.5 N/mm²; vibrated in walls exceeding 150–450 mm thick	£85.25	£86.00
Reinforced concrete in-situ lightweight concrete: 20.5 N/mm²; vibrated in walls not exceeding 150 mm thick	£87.59	£86.00

Clearly, for any but the smallest projects, producing an approximate cost by means of unit costing is fairly time consuming and therefore an expensive process. One method of reducing both is to use elemental costing.

Elemental costing

With elemental costing, the project is divided into a number of elements. Typically, these elements might be as follows (note that the starred items may be further divided):

- *Substructure*
  - foundations

- *Superstructure*
  - external walls
  - roof
  - floors and frame*
  - internal walls
  - staircases
  - doors and windows*
  - wall finishes
  - floor finishes
  - ceiling finishes

- *External works*
  - drainage
  - car-parking
  - landscaping

- *Commissioning*
  - fittings
  - furnishings
  - specialist equipment
  - furniture

The list of elements will vary from project to project: a single-storey building will have no floor element, no staircase and so on. In a highly technologically advanced building, there may be many more subdivisions than shown in the above list.

As far as costing is concerned, each of the elements is then costed either on a lump sum basis or on a cost per square metre floor area basis, or both, and use will be made of as

many sources of relevant information as possible. *Architects' Journal* and *Building Magazine* are just two widely available publications which frequently include an elemental breakdown of the costs of projects.

Table 8.9 shows such an example. Great skill and experience are required to ensure that the information being used as a guide is interpreted accurately. (Note that the example given by the table is very simplified.)

Table 8.9 Elemental cost plan (approx. gross floor area: 950 m²)

Element	Cost (£/m² floor area)	Total cost
Substructure	70	**66 500.00**
Superstructure:		
Frame	86	81 700.00
External Walls	48	45 600.00
Floors	28	26 600.00
Roof	65	61 750.00
Internal walls/doors	39	37 050.00
Windows and external doors	29	27 550.00
	295	280 250.00
Finishes		
Walls	26	24 700.00
Floors	46	43 700.00
Ceilings	19	18 050.00
	91	86 450.00
Fittings/furnishings	35	33 250.00
Services		
Sanitary/services	62	58 900.00
Electrical work	82	77 900.00
Other services	50	47 500.00
	194	184 300.00
External works	95	90 250.00
Sub-total		**654 550.00**
Preliminaries (say 12%)		78 546.00
Contingency		20 000.00
Total anticipated cost		**£753 096.00**

Total cost/m² = £792.73

Measured costing

As the term implies, measured costing is the exercise of costing accurately measured items and quantities; as such, it is likely to be much more accurate than other methods of estimating the eventual cost of a project. By the same token, however, it is also a much more time consuming and therefore expensive process. It is necessary for there to be a complete bill of quantities (BOQ) or similar document, and as the preparation of a BOQ takes a considerable amount of time, this is not a method that can be employed at an early stage in the project.

Costing progress and cost reports

From the descriptions of the various methods of costing, it should be clear that there is a time when each comes into its own. The more information obtained, the more accurate the process becomes. This progression is continued all the way through the construction phase as well as during the design stages, and each month the quantity surveyor will forward to the client and architect a cost report which will indicate the financial health or otherwise of the project. This report will indicate the anticipated ultimate cost of the project as well as its cost to date. There will also be indications of areas of potential extras and/or reductions in cost, possible delays and other problems that may occur.

Post-contract financial processes

The financial processes that occur after the contract has begun are known generally as post-contract processes, and can be summarised as:

- interim valuations
- final accounts
- claims for reimbursement of loss and/or expense

Interim valuations

Since construction contracts are very expensive items, paying for them is a complex business. Fairly obviously the client would be unwilling, to say the least, to pay the total cost of the project before the contractors even began work, and the contractor would be equally unwilling to wait until the work was completed before receiving payment. What has evolved over a long period of time, therefore, is a system of interim payments during the construction period.

There are two main types of interim valuations, known as:

- monthly (periodic) valuations
- stage payments

A combination of the two may also be used.

Monthly (periodic) valuations

At the end of each month, the value of the work carried out so far is valued and a certificate to that effect is issued by the architect. According to the contract the client will then have to make a payment to the contractor as stated on the certificate within a fixed number of days, usually 14.

Again, according to the contract, it is the responsibility of the client's representatives (architect and quantity surveyor) to value the work. In practice, however, it is the quantity surveyors of both client and contractors who meet, usually on site, to agree the monthly valuation figures. The client's quantity surveyor then prepares a recommendation for the agreed figure and this is presented to the architect as quickly as possible after the valuation meeting. The flow chart shown in Fig. 8.6 illustrates how a monthly interim valuation is produced.

As can be seen from Fig. 8.6, the delay in receipt of payment is considerable. When it is realised that included within the total will be the value of work carried out in the first few days of the preceding month, it means that the main and subcontractors may have been waiting almost eight weeks for payment. It is hardly surprising that cash flow within the industry is a major problem.

A periodic valuation will normally be made up of some or all of the following:

- a proportion of the preliminaries
- value of the measured work completed

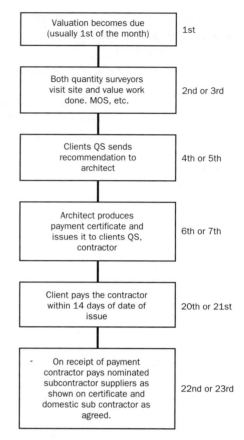

Figure 8.6 Flow chart of interim valuations

- value of the work covered by prime cost and provisional sums
- value of the work carried out in variation works (i.e. in accordance with architect's instructions). This may include work valued on a daywork basis
- value of the unfixed materials on site
- value of the materials held off site at suppliers' works. (these must be ready for incorporation into the works and permanently identified as being for the specific contract in question)
- value of fluctuations if allowable

From the total of the above will be deducted a percentage usually 3 or 5%, depending on the size of the contract. This is called the retention percentage and is held by the client as a form of protection, in case some of the work requires repair, etc.

From the ensuing total is deducted the total amount paid to the contractor through previous valuations. Figure 8.7 shows a typical monthly valuation summary.

Note that the summary in Fig. 8.7 is presumed to relate to firm price contract; that is to say, no sums for increases in the costs of labour and/or materials will be paid to the contractor.

If the contract is a fixed price, any increases in costs for labour and/or materials (normally called fluctuations) are paid to the contractor, normally using one of the several index methods available, the most common of these being the NEDO index. This index, published monthly by the National Economic Development Organisation, states how much various categories of work have increased or decreased on a monthly basis.

```
Never-Never Town Hospital interim Valuation No. 7 (31 May)

The figures in brackets are the totals for each section in the bill
of quantities.


Summary

Preliminaries (£120 021)                              71 517.00
Measured Work (£650 560)                             369 963.00
and provisional sums (£314 413)                      167 761.00
Variation works (contingency; £50 000)                27 270.00
Dayworks                                               7 427.00
Materials on site                                     61 116.00
Materials off site                                    16 661.00

                                                     721 715.00
Less Retention (3%)                                   21 651.00
Less Total valuations 1–6                            583 687.35

Total due in valuation 7                            £116 349.20
```

Figure 8.7 Interim valuation summary

Stage payments

The alternative to periodic valuations is payment by stages. As certain predetermined stages in construction are completed, set amounts of money are released to the contractor. The values of the various stages are also agreed between the two quantity surveyors at the beginning of the construction work. The work included within the various stages differs from project to project, but Table 8.10 shows a representative example of the typical stages.

Table 8.10 Typical stages in a stage payment agreement

Stage number	Work included
1	Set up site
2	Foundation excavation
3	Completion of substructure
4	Work to first-floor level
5	Work eaves level
6	Roof completion
7	Internal walls
8	Services installation
9	Finishes
10	Glazing
11	External works

In some cases, some of the stages listed in Table 8.10 might be combined, e.g. the first stage might be the completion of the substructure as an entity. In others, some of the stages would be subdivided, e.g. the services installation into first and second fixing. There may also be a section for joinery, and so on.

Uses of the various methods of payment

Monthly (periodic) valuations

This is easily the most common form of valuation and is suitable for all types of project. Obviously, the larger the project the more complex the valuation process. Although it is important for both client and contractor that the valuations are fair representations of the value of the work carried out, it is worth remembering that it is accepted that they can never be completely accurate. As there is the time delay involved in receipt of payment, referred to earlier, it is not a major problem if a slight over-valuing occurs.

On major projects it is normally the contractor's surveyors who also produce the supporting information for a valuation, the client's quantity surveyors then checking this information. The most time consuming aspect is the valuing of the measured work. This involves the measuring of all the work completed and then pricing that work using the rates in the bill of quantities. It may take several surveyors a number of days to produce all the information required for the valuation.

Alternatively, to speed up the process, an approximation of the work completed can be made, item by item. For example, instead of physically measuring how many cubic metres of concrete in floor slabs have been laid, the surveyors agree that, for example, 35% of the total slabs are complete. If, in the total bill of quantities, items for concrete on floor slabs (there may be several different classifications) is £65 000, then the sum to be included in the valuation would be 35% of £65 000 = £22 750.

Stage payments

While much less popular than monthly variations, stage payments are particularly useful in two sets of circumstances:

● multiple units
● early completion

Multiple units. On a contract where many similar buildings are being constructed, e.g. a housing site, valuing by counting stages is much quicker and more efficient than on a periodic basis. It is sometimes the case that a combination of periodic valuations and stage payments is used. In such an instance, at each period end, the number of houses at each stage are counted and these numbers multiplied by the value of the stages in question. This is illustrated by Table 8.11

Table 8.11 Stage payments

Stage number	Number of houses at stage	Value at stage (£)	Total (£)
1	16	500	8 000.00
2	16	750	12 000.00
3	12	1950	23 400.00
4	8	3610	28 880.00
5	6	2910	17 460.00
6	6	2690	16 140.00
7	4	1410	5 640.00
8	2	5750	11 500.00
9	2	2940	5 880.00
10	2	700	1 400.00
11	–	890	–
Total			130 300.00

Note it is important to appreciate that, with the stage payment system, once the total has been calculated the procedure concerning retention and previous payments is exactly as shown with monthly valuations.

Within the value of the stages would be incorporated the value of the preliminaries.

Early completion. As payment for a stage becomes due as soon as that stage is completed, a contractor who advances the contract well ahead of programme can benefit by receiving several payments in one 'normal' period. It will also help the client to obtain early occupation of the building. As the actual valuation process is much simpler than with monthly valuations, it is an easy matter for payments to be made close together.

From the client's point of view, delay in the contract which results in the non-completion of any stages within say a two-month period would result in no payment whatsoever having to be made.

Valuing the preliminaries

The valuing of the preliminaries is normally carried out using one of the following methods:

- equal monthly amounts
- a percentage basis
- a preliminaries schedule

Equal monthly amounts

This is the simplest method and, not surprisingly, the least accurate. The total value of the preliminaries element is divided by the number of months in the programme. This is the amount included in the valuation. Obviously, if a contract has been held up for whatever reason, the contractor is going to receive the same amount for preliminaries as if he had worked extremely well and moved ahead of programme. It is therefore a good method for the contractor and a bad one for the client if the contract is behind programme, and vice versa if it is ahead of schedule.

A percentage basis

The simplest way of illustrating this method is by example. Let us assume that the value of the measured work is £914 000 and the value of the preliminaries section is £355 000. If the value of the completed measured work is £311 000, the value to be included for the preliminaries is:

$$\frac{£311\,000}{£914\,000} \times £355\,000 = £120\,793$$

With this method, a more accurate result is achieved than with the first method illustrated. However, if the contractor is delayed due for any reason, thereby limiting production, this method will not be helpful as he will still be incurring such preliminary costs as site supervision, site accommodation, site security, etc.

A preliminaries schedule

The third method, using a preliminaries schedule, is now used on the majority of projects because as it is seen to be the fairest method. A typical schedule is illustrated in Fig. 8.8, with the sums adjusted where necessary to take account of the fact that the project is running a little behind programme. As you can see, each preliminary item is spread across the duration of the contract, in the way that the item is expected to be utilised. With site supervision, for example, we can see that the sum allowed increases after the first few months as more supervisory staff are brought on site. Towards the end of the contract, the monthly amount reduces, as less staff are needed.

The schedule is drawn up and agreed between the two quantity surveyors at the beginning of the contract. This may take a little time as there is usually a certain amount of difference of opinion involved. It is in the interests of the contractor to put as many items as possible in the early parts of the schedule. The client's quantity surveyor will be anxious, however, to keep as much of the preliminary item money in hand for as long as possible.

Valuing the other elements of the valuation – the variations, dayworks and materials on site – is more straightforward. In these cases, it is essentially a matter of totalling the amounts agreed for the variations, etc.

It is, nevertheless, essential that the contractor recovers as much money as possible for these items and his surveyor must make every effort to value the variations, etc., as soon as the work involved has been completed.

Item	Total	1	2	3	4	5	6	7	8	9	10	11	12	13	14	15	16	17	18
Supervision	25000	1000	1000	1000	1500	1500	1500	1500	1500	1500	1500	1500	1500	2000	2000	2000	1000	1000	500
Cabins	4000	200	200	200	300	300	300	300	300	300	200	200	200	200	200	200	200	200	100
Clerk of Works office	680	200	–	–	–	100	–	–	–	100	–	–	–	100	–	–	180	–	–
Telephone	1500	–	–	400	–	–	300	–	–	300	–	–	200	–	–	200	–	–	100
Welfare facilities	3600	400	200	200	200	200	200	200	200	200	200	200	200	200	200	200	200	100	100
Engineers	5000	–	1000	1000	1000	500	500	500	500	–	–	–	–	–	–	–	–	–	–
Scaffolding	21000	–	–	–	–	–	3000	2000	1500	1500	2500	2500	2500	2500	1500	1500	–	–	–
Small tools	2400	–	–	200	200	200	200	200	200	200	200	200	200	200	200	–	–	–	–
Cranes	10000	–	–	–	4000	2000	2000	2000	–	–	–	–	–	–	–	–	–	–	–
Power	3175	100	230	230	230	250	250	150	150	130	130	150	150	150	250	250	150	75	70
Temporary roads	1000	500	50	50	50	50	50	50	150	–	–	–	–	–	–	–	–	–	–
Security	6300	350	350	350	350	350	350	350	350	350	350	350	350	350	350	350	350	350	350
Test cubes	500	–	100	100	100	50	50	50	50	–	–	–	–	–	–	–	–	–	–
Drying out	1500	–	–	–	–	–	–	–	–	–	–	–	–	–	–	400	300	300	500
TOTALS	85635																		

Figure 8.8 Preliminaries schedule

Final accounts

As explained earlier, valuations are approximations of the value of the work completed at various times. Ultimately, however, it is necessary to calculate the exact amount due to the contractor for the construction of the whole project. The document thus produced is called the final account.

While the process is complicated it is obviously important for the contractor that the final account is agreed as quickly as possible after completion of the contract. In theory this should be within six months of the completion date, but in practice it is quite common for the process to take much longer. Some final accounts takes years to conclude and, in one instance within the author's experience, he was handed a final account to 'sort out' and agree seven years after the contract had been completed! On that particular contract the eventual agreement resulted in £17 000 being paid to the contractor. Seven years of compound interest on £17 000 would have amounted to a large sum! The problem with that contract, and generally with all contracts whose final accounts take a long time to resolve, is the inadequacy of information. It is of vital importance that accurate on-site measurements of all provisionally measured work, i.e. substructure, drainage, etc., are taken and agreed by both surveyors as the work is carried out.

Similarly, the work involved in variations should be measured, valued and agreed immediately. This is particularly the case with work that has to be valued on a daywork basis.

Final account preparation

The basic process uses the bill of quantities as a basis. Each section of the bill is then revalued in much the same way as in the preparation of interim valuations. In this case, however, there is no approximation involved.

The 'add and omit' technique

The use of 'adding and omitting' is widespread in final accounts (as it is on other situations), and is a very simple process. In essence, if one part of the project has changed, then the value of the original work as found in the bill of quantities is completely omitted from the final account and the total value of the changed work is added in its place.

As an example, let us take substructure work. In most contracts, the substructure is measured 'provisionally'. This means that because it is not known before commencement how deep the foundations will be, a 'best estimate' of the quantities involved is made, and when the work is carried out it is then measured exactly.

In a simplified example, let us look at a few of the major items in a typical substructure. These items are listed in Table 8.12 (note that the descriptions are very brief and are not in accordance with the SMM7).

Table 8.12 Remeasured quantities in a typical substructure

Item	BOQ quantity	Rate	Remeasured quantity
Remove topsoil	3500 m^2	1.35	3600 m^2
Reduced level excavation	4110 m^3	14.30	4425 m^3
Trench excavation	560 m^3	15.60	720 m^3
Concrete foundations	250 m^3	61.20	300 m^3
Concrete in beds	210 m^3	64.50	240 m^3

It would be possible for the original quantities to be subtracted from the remeasured ones and the extra quantities multiplied by the BOQ rates. However, there are two reasons for not doing this:

- it involves further calculations and, therefore, more possibilities for error
- it is a longer process

In the example above (which lists only a very small number of items) compared with a real-life situation) the total value (easily extracted from the bill of quantities) is £99 394.00. In adding and omitting, this sum is omitted from the final account (see below). The total value of the actual work is £112 105.00.

As can be seen in the example, adding and omitting will normally be used in most of the elements of the final account. The alternative method of adjusting for the difference between the actual substructure work and the provisionally measured work in the bill of quantities involves many calculations, e.g.

Topsoil	$3600 - 3500 = 100 \times 1.35 = 135.00$
Reduced level	$4425 - 4110 = 325 \times 14.30 = 4647.50$
Trench	$720 - 560 = 160 \times 15.60 = 2496.00$
Concrete foundations	$300 - 250 = 50 \times 61.20 = 3060.00$
Concrete in beds	$240 - 210 = 30 \times 64.50 = 1935.00$
	Total extra $= 12 273.50$

As stated earlier, in a real-life situation the substructure bill of quantities could number several hundred items. It is much easier and, more importantly, safer to add and omit in entirety. A summary of typical final account is shown in Fig. 8.9.

Just to reinforce the point again, all the OMIT sums come straight from the bill of quantities while the ADDS are calculated from such things as remeasured foundation dimensions, daywork sheets and surveyor's calculations of the value of variations.

As far as the measured work which is not provisionally measured is concerned (marked *) as this does not change, the value can either be left alone or shown on the final account, on both adds or omits.

If the contract in question is subject to fluctuations, these would be added or subtracted from the total above.

It is worth while noting the contingency sum. This is a sum of money included in the original bill of quantities to cover alterations which add to the ultimate cost of the project at the final account stage; the whole of the contingency sum is

---

FINAL ACCOUNT FOR CONTRACT No. 1234

TENDER SUM   £2 115 605.00

	Add	Omit
Substructure	112 105	99 394
Measured work*	–	–
Drainage	61 215	49 395
External works	39 416	35 499
Prime cost and provisional sums	1 261 410	1 193 216
Contingency	–	100 000
Variations	164 311	–
Dayworks	61 214	25 000
	1 699 671	1 502 504
	1 502 504	
TOTAL TO ADD	197 167	

TOTAL OF FINAL ACCOUNT £2 312 772.00

* Not subject to remeasurement.

Figure 8.9 Summary of a typical final account

omitted and in its place is found the total for the actual cost of variations. In the majority of instances, the contingency sum is less than the cost of variations, sometimes by a considerable amount.

Roles of contractor's and client's quantity surveyors at final account stage

In many instances, due to the fact that the amount of fee available to the client's quantity surveyor (for his work in the preparation of the final account) is very small, the bulk of the work is done by the contractor's quantity surveyors. Almost all of the information and the clerical work involved in the calculations necessary is completed by the contractor who then passes this information to the client's quantity surveyor for checking/verification.

Unfortunately, even the checking can take a very long time if the client's quantity surveyor is busy with work on new contracts. As can be appreciated, as the contract is now complete, there is much less pressure and the only organization likely to benefit from the agreement of the final account is the contractor. Even his quantity surveyors will almost certainly be busy working on new contracts and putting off the final account will often make life easier. The student will now be able to at least begin to see why final account agreement can take such a long time. It is true that there are contractual stipulations involved in the finalisation of the account, but unfortunately these are often ignored as the contractor is usually unwilling to upset both the client and the quantity surveyor as this may jeopardise his chances of obtaining further work from this client and may adversely affect his relationship with the quantity surveyor.

Claims for reimbursement of loss and/or expense

Many books have been written concerning this area of finance and only a brief mention is made here, even though the subject is extremely important and interesting.

On many contracts, the main and subcontractors become involved in situations which cause them to suffer loss and/or expense for which they should obtain reimbursement according to the form of contract. Claims for reimbursement are quite commonplace and can amount to huge sums of money. In the author's own experience, claims for well over £600 000 on a contract valued at tender stage at £4.2 million, and for £48 000 on a contract sum of £260 000 illustrate the importance of such claims.

The preparation of these claims is normally the province of the contractor's quantity surveyor, usually assisted by management staff. In some instances, the roles may be reversed.

The preparation of such claims, and the processes leading up to their preparation, are too complex to be discussed here, but the student's attention should be drawn to the fact that in many cases the failure to obtain rightful reimbursement results in large losses on contracts and it is vitally important, therefore, that all contractor's staff are alive to the importance of claims.

It should also be stressed that the tendency during the past decades for unscrupulous contractors to 'rescue' contracts that were making losses by inventing spurious claims is a practice that should be abhorred and has tarnished many contractors' reputations.

Example

Approximate estimates

(a) *Office block*
  (i) Likely usable floor area of proposed project: 1250 m^2
  (ii) From a reliable used reference source, e.g. BCIS Index, or one of the well-known frequently used price books, e.g. *Spon's Architects and Builders Price Book*, the cost per m^2 of the type of building in question is obtained as £675–850.
  (iii) The area is multiplied either by both cost figures to provide a range;

$$1250 \times £675 = £843\,750$$
$$1250 \times £850 = £1\,062\,500$$

or by a figure within that chosen range:

$$1250 \times £780 - £975\,000$$

If the quality of the proposed building was thought to be high, obviously a figure near the top end would be chosen.

At this point the client would be advised that the project would probably cost between £900 000 and £1.2 million.

(b) *Hotel*
3500 m^2 floor area. Fairly high specification. Range:

£1175–1450/m^2

Range therefore

$$3500 \times 1175 = £4\,112\,500$$
$$3500 \times 1450 = £5\,075\,000$$

Average say:

$$3500 \times 1330 = £4\,655\,000$$

Allowances would need to be made in examples (a) and (b) for geographical location and the currency of the source.

Self-assessment tasks

1. Investigate one particular local construction project and produce a report of the investigation. Your report should include:
   (a) a description of the financial control processes used in the project
   (b) a note on the relationship between the accuracy of cost estimates and the level of specification at different stages of the project.
2. Explain how the depth of a specification may affect both the cost of a building and the time taken to construct that building.
3. Investigate the cost per square metre method of approximate estimating in order to establish how popular it is and why it is used.
4. Similarly, investigate the user/unit method of approximate estimating in order to establish the advantages and disadvantages of this method when compared to the square metre method.
5. Examine why the use of a preliminaries schedule is the most suitable method for valuing the preliminaries element in interim valuations.
6. Investigate over-valuing of interim payments. Why does this occur? is the practice of long-term benefit to anyone? What measures can be taken to avoid it?
7. List the headings under which value would be included in a valuation and explain how the valuing of each would be achieved.

8. Examine the cost/value reconciliation process and explain why it is so important in the financial control of a project.
9. Explain the terms positive and negative cash flow and why cash flow is of major importance to contractors.
10. Explain why it is just as important to include income as well as expenditure in budgets.
11. 'Positive cash flow is more important than profit.' Comment on this statement.
12. Explain why the adjudication of a tender by a contractor prior to its submission may be more important than all other aspects of the tender preparation.

Further reading

It is strongly recommended that you read as many of the following publications as possible. In each section the first book referred is *probably* going to be of most use and well worth buying, but all the books should be perused if possible.

Finance

Lavender S D 1992 *Economics for Builders and Surveyors* Longman
Gruneberg S L 1997 *Construction Economics: An Introduction* Longman
Seeley I H 1996 *Building Economics* (4th edition) Macmillan
Briscoe G 1992 *The Economics of the Construction Industry* Batsford/CIOB

Contractual arrangements

Ashworth A 1996 *Pre-contract Studies* Longman
Ashworth A 1996 *Contractual Procedures in the Construction Industry* (3rd edition) Longman
Turner D 1994 *Building Contracts: A Practical Guide* (5th edition) Longman
Turner D 1995 *Design and Build Contract Practice* (2nd edition) Longman
Chappel D 1991 *Which Form of Building Contract?* ADT Press
Chappel D 1993 *Understanding JCT Standard Building Contracts* (3rd edition) E & F N Spon

Financial and cost management

Ashworth A 1996 *Cost Studies of Buildings* (3rd edition) Longman
Smith R C *Estimating and Tendering for Building Work* Longman
Briscoe G 1992 *The Economics of the Construction Industry* Batsford CIOB
Seeley I 1996 *Building Economics* (4th edition) Macmillan

In addition you are strongly advised to make frequent reference to journals and magazines, in particular *Building*, *Construction News*, and *Architects Journal*. Newspapers such as the *The Times*, *The Daily Telegraph*, *The Guardian*, *The Financial Times* and *The Independent* also have articles relating to important financial and construction issues in them.

Answers to selected self-assessment tasks

3.2 1000 W

3.4 Instead of $R_{cavity} = 0.18 \text{ m}^2 \text{ K/W}$, we now have $R_{foam} = 0.05 \div 0.024 = 2.083 \text{ m}^2 \text{ K/W}$. Including this in the calculation gives $R_{total} = 2.881 \text{ m}^2 \text{ K/W}$. So, $U = 1 \div 2.881 = 0.35 \text{ W/m}^2 \text{ K}$
Comment: This is less than the maximum permitted value for the *U*-value of walls for new dwellings (see Table 3.3).

3.7 1. 100%
2. 68%

3.9 D

3.10 69.5 dB

3.11 2. For hospital kitchens, Table 3.6 gives NC = 40. Comparing the NC40 curve in Fig. 3.7 with the results plotted shows that at no frequency is the background noise greater than the NC40 criterion.

3.12 16 lx

3.13 2. Summer
3. Yes
4. 47 dB (approx.)
5. Probably a class of students
6. Quite a lot of noise for a very short time at around $t = 19$ hours – this may have been a person using a vacuum cleaner!
7. 19 to 24 °C (approx.)

3.15 1. 20 mm (approx.)

3.19 1. (a) 0.0015; (b) 6.37 N/mm^2
2. 2000 N

3.20 4244 N/mm^2

3.21 Forces: 11 kN and 8 kN; stresses 690 N/mm^2 and 500 N/mm^2 resp. (to two sig. figures)

3.23 29.4 N/mm^2; 29.4 MN/m^2

3.25 1. (a) very low resistivity is needed
(b) very high resistivity is essential
2. (a) reduces the resistance
(b) increased danger of electric shock

3.28 Using Table 3.10 and estimating the initial and maximum temperatures to be 20 °C and 600 °C (say), the expansion will be around 70 mm; the steel will severely buckle.

3.29 2. D

3.34 3. B

3.36 1. A
2. C

3.38 128 W; the cable produces heat

3.39 2. 1092 kWh; £76.44
5. A

3.40 2. Most definitely, yes. Electromagnetic induction occurs provided that the magnetic field through the coil is changing. It does not matter whether it is the magnet that is moving or the coil. (Note, however, that there is no induction if both the magnet and the coil move in the same direction.)

3.42 1. 6 V
2. 4.24 V
3. 20 ms or 0.02 s

3.43 2. The output voltage is directly proportional to the number of turns on the secondary, as expected.
3. No. The output voltage is a little lower than expected from theory. This is because the transformer is not 100% efficient

3.44 1. Zero; transformers only work with a.c. supplies.
2. 30 V (r.m.s.); it has been assumed that the transformer is 100% efficient.

3.45 While aluminium is a very good conductor of electricity, steel is very strong.

3.46 2. (a) 20 MW; (b) 5 kW; (c) heat is produced in the cable

3.47 D

3.49 2. (a) very slightly alkaline
(b) yes, sulphate of calcium, etc.
(c) milligram per litre (this is similar to *parts per million*, as 1 litre of water has a mass of approx. 1 kg)

Index

LEEDS COLLEGE OF BUILDING
LIBRARY
NORTH STREET
LEEDS LS2 7QT
TEL: (0113) 222 6097 and 6098

17 AUG 2004